The I-Series

Microsoft® PowerPoint 2002

Introductory

Stephen Haag
University of Denver

James T. Perry
University of San Diego

Merrill Wells
University of Denver

Boston   Burr Ridge, IL   Dubuque, IA   Madison, WI   New York   San Francisco   St. Louis
Bangkok   Bogotá   Caracas   Kuala Lumpur   Lisbon   London   Madrid   Mexico City
Milan   Montreal   New Delhi   Santiago   Seoul   Singapore   Sydney   Taipei   Toronto

McGraw-Hill Higher Education

A Division of The **McGraw-Hill** Companies

The I-Series: Microsoft PowerPoint 2002, Introductory

Published by McGraw-Hill/Irwin, an imprint of The McGraw-Hill Companies, Inc. 1221 Avenue of the Americas, New York, NY 10020. Copyright © 2002 by The McGraw-Hill Companies, Inc. All rights reserved. No part of this publication may be reproduced or distributed in any form or by any means, or stored in a database or retrieval system, without the prior written consent of The McGraw-Hill Companies, Inc., including, but not limited to, in any network or other electronic storage or transmission, or broadcast for distance learning.

Some ancillaries, including electronic and print components, may not be available to customers outside the United States.

This book is printed on acid-free paper.

2 3 4 5 6 7 8 9 0 WEB/WEB 0 9 8 7 6 5 4 3 2

ISBN 0-07-247036-4

Publisher: *George Werthman*
Sponsoring editor: *Dan Silverburg*
Developmental editor: *Melissa Forte*
Manager, Marketing and Sales: *Paul Murphy*
Senior project manager: *Jean Hamilton*
Production supervisor: *Rose Hepburn*
Coordinator freelance design: *Mary L. Christianson and Jennifer McQueen*
Lead supplement producer: *Marc Mattson*
Senior producer, Media technology: *David Barrick*
Interior freelance design: *Asylum Studios*
Cover freelance design/illustration: *Asylum Studios*
Compositor: *GAC Indianapolis*
Typeface: *10/12 New Aster*
Printer: *Webcrafters, Inc.*

Library of Congress Control Number: 2001099817

http://www.mhhe.com

about McGraw-Hill/Irwin

INFORMATION TECHNOLOGY AT MCGRAW-HILL/IRWIN

At McGraw-Hill Higher Education, we publish instructional materials targeted at the higher education market. In an effort to expand the tools of higher learning, we publish texts, lab manuals, study guides, testing materials, software, and multimedia products.

At McGraw-Hill/Irwin (a division of McGraw-Hill Higher Education), we realize that technology has created and will continue to create new mediums for professors and students to use in managing resources and communicating information to one another. We strive to provide the most flexible and complete teaching and learning tools available as well as offer solutions to the changing world of teaching and learning.

McGraw-Hill/Irwin is dedicated to providing the tools for today's instructors and students to successfully navigate the world of Information Technology.

- **SEMINAR SERIES**—McGraw-Hill/Irwin's Technology Connection seminar series offered across the country every year demonstrates the latest technology products and encourages collaboration among teaching professionals.

- **MCGRAW-HILL/OSBORNE**—This division of The McGraw-Hill Companies is known for its best-selling Internet titles, *Internet & Web Yellow Pages* and the *Internet Complete Reference*. For more information, visit Osborne at www.osborne.com.

- **DIGITAL SOLUTIONS**—McGraw-Hill/Irwin is committed to publishing digital solutions. Taking your course online doesn't have to be a solitary adventure, nor does it have to be a difficult one. We offer several solutions that will allow you to enjoy all the benefits of having your course material online.

- **PACKAGING OPTIONS**—For more information about our discount options, contact your McGraw-Hill/Irwin sales representative at 1-800-338-3987 or visit our Web site at www.mhhe.com/it.

about the i-series

THE I-SERIES PAGE

By using the I-Series, students will be able to learn and master applications skills by being actively engaged—by *doing*. The "I" in I-Series demonstrates Insightful tasks that will not only Inform students, but also Involve them while learning the applications.

How will The I-Series accomplish this for you?

- Through relevant, real-world chapter opening cases.
- Through tasks throughout each chapter that incorporate steps and tips for easy reference.
- Through alternative methods and styles of learning to keep the student involved.
- Through rich, end-of-chapter materials that support what the student has learned.

I-Series titles include:

- Microsoft Office XP, Volume I
- Microsoft Office XP, Volume I Expanded
- Microsoft Office XP, Volume II
- Microsoft Word 2002 (Brief, Introductory, Complete Versions) 12 Chapters
- Microsoft Excel 2002 (Brief, Introductory, Complete Versions) 12 Chapters
- Microsoft Access 2002 (Brief, Introductory, Complete Versions) 12 Chapters
- Microsoft PowerPoint 2002 (Brief, Introductory Versions) 8 Chapters
- Microsoft Windows 2000 (Brief, Introductory, Complete Versions) 12 Chapters
- Microsoft Windows XP and Bonus Books to come!

To accompany the series:
The I-Series Computing Concepts text (Introductory, Complete Versions)

For additional resources, visit the I-Series Online Learning Center at www.mhhe.com/i-series/

about the i-series—Preface

GOALS/PHILOSOPHY

The I-Series applications textbooks strongly emphasize that students learn and master applications skills by being actively engaged—by *doing*. We made the decision that teaching how to accomplish tasks is not enough for complete understanding and mastery. Students must understand the importance of each of the tasks that lead to a finished product at the end of each chapter.

Approach

The I-Series chapters are subdivided into sessions that contain related groups of tasks with active, hands-on components. The session tasks containing numbered steps collectively result in a completed project at the end of each session. Prior to introducing numbered steps that show how to accomplish a particular task, we discuss why the steps are important. We discuss the role that the collective steps play in the overall plan for creating or modifying a document or object, answering students' often-heard questions, "Why are we doing these steps? Why are these steps important?" Without an explanation of why an activity is important and what it accomplishes, students can easily find themselves following the steps but not registering the big picture of what the steps accomplish and why they are executing them.

I-Series Applications for 2002

The I-Series offers three levels of instruction. Each level builds upon knowledge from the previous level. With the exception of the running project that is the last exercise of every chapter, chapter cases and end-of-chapter exercises are independent from one chapter to the next, with the exception of Access. The three levels available are

Brief Covers the basics of the Microsoft application and contains Chapters 1 through 4. The Brief textbooks are typically 200 pages long.

Introductory Includes chapters in the Brief textbook plus Chapters 5 through 8. Introductory textbooks typically are 400 pages long and prepare students for the Microsoft Office User Specialist (MOUS) Core Exam.

Complete Includes the Introductory textbook plus Chapters 9 through 12. The four additional chapters cover advanced level content and are typically 600 pages long. Complete textbooks prepare students for the Microsoft Office User Specialist (MOUS) Expert Exam. The Microsoft Office User Specialist program is recognized around the world as the standard for demonstrating proficiency using Microsoft Office applications.

In addition, there are two compilation volumes available.

Office I Includes introductory chapters on Windows and Computing Concepts followed by Chapters 1 through 4 (Brief textbook) of Word, Excel, Access, and PowerPoint. In addition, material from the companion Computing Concepts book is integrated into the first few chapters to provide students an understanding of the relationship between Microsoft Office applications and computer information systems.

Office II Includes introductory chapters on Windows and Computing Concepts followed by Chapters 5 through 8 from each of the Introductory-level textbooks including Word, Excel, Access, and PowerPoint. In addition, material from the companion Computing Concepts book is integrated into the introductory chapters to provide students a deeper understanding of the relationship between Microsoft Office applications and computer information systems. An introduction to Visual Basic for Applications (VBA) completes the Office II textbook.

Approved Microsoft Courseware

Use of the Microsoft Office User Specialist Approved Courseware logo on this product signifies that it has been independently reviewed and approved to comply with the following standards: Acceptable coverage of all content related to the Microsoft Office Exams entitled Microsoft Access 2002, Microsoft Excel 2002, Microsoft PowerPoint 2002, and Microsoft Word 2002, and sufficient performance-based exercises that relate closely to all required content, based on sampling of the textbooks. For further information on Microsoft's MOUS certification program, please visit Microsoft's Web site at www.microsoft.com.

about the authors

STEPHEN HAAG

Stephen Haag is a professor and Chair of Information Technology and Electronic Commerce and the Director of Technology in the University of Denver's Daniels College of Business. Stephen holds a B.B.A. and an M.B.A. from West Texas State University and a Ph.D. from the University of Texas at Arlington. Stephen has published numerous articles appearing in such journals as *Communications of the ACM*, *The International Journal of Systems Science*, *Applied Economics*, *Managerial and Decision Economics*, *Socio-Economic Planning Sciences*, and the *Australian Journal of Management*.

Stephen is also the author of 13 other books including *Interactions: Teaching English as a Second Language* (with his mother and father), *Case Studies in Information Technology, Information Technology: Tomorrow's Advantage Today* (with Peter Keen), and *Excelling in Finance*. Stephen is also the lead author of the accompanying *I-Series: Computing Concepts* text, released in both an Introductory and Complete version. Stephen lives with his wife, Pam, and their four sons, Indiana, Darian, Trevor, and Elvis, in Highlands Ranch, Colorado.

JAMES PERRY

James Perry is a professor of Management Information Systems at the University of San Diego's School of Business. Jim is an active instructor who teaches both undergraduate and graduate courses. He holds a B.S. in mathematics from Purdue University and a Ph.D. in computer science from The Pennsylvania State University. He has published several journal and conference papers. He is the co-author of 56 textbooks and trade books such as *Using Access with Accounting Systems*, *Building Accounting Systems*, *Understanding Oracle*, *The Internet*, and *Electronic Commerce*. His books have been translated into Dutch, French, and Chinese. Jim worked as a computer security consultant to various private and governmental organizations including the Jet Propulsion Laboratory. He was a consultant on the Strategic Defense Initiative ("Star Wars") project and served as a member of the computer security oversight committee.

RICK PARKER

Rick Parker received his bachelor's degree from Brigham Young University. He received his Ph.D. in animal physiology at Iowa State University. After completing his Ph.D., he and his wife, Marilyn, and their children moved to Edmonton, Alberta, Canada, where he completed a post-doctorate at the University of Alberta. He accepted a position as a research and teaching associate at the University of Wyoming, Laramie, Wyoming.

Rick developed a love for the power and creativity unleashed by computers and software. After arriving at the College of Southern Idaho, Twin Falls, in 1984, he guided the creation and development of numerous college software courses and software training programs for business and industry. He also led the conversion of an old office occupations technical program into a business computer applications program, which evolved into an information technology program. During the early adoption of computers and software by the college, Rick wrote in-house training manuals and taught computer/software courses.

Rick currently works as a professional-technical division director at the College of Southern Idaho. As director, he supervises faculty in agriculture, information technology and drafting, and electronics programs. He is the author of four other textbooks.

MERRILL WELLS

The caption next to **Merrill Wells'** eighth grade yearbook picture noted that her career goal was to teach college and write books. She completed an MBA at Indiana University and began a career as a programmer. After several years of progressive positions in business and industry, she returned to academia, spending 10 years as a computer technology faculty member at Red Rocks Community College and then becoming an information technology professor at the University of Denver, Daniels College of Business. She completed her first published book in 1993 and began presenting at educational seminars in 1997. Other publications include *An Introduction to Computers*, *Introduction to Visual Basic*, and *Programming Logic and Design*.

about the i-series—key features

Each textbook features the following:

Did You Know Each chapter has six or seven interesting facts—both about high tech and other topics.

Sessions Each chapter is divided into two or three sessions.

Chapter Outline Provides students with a quick map of the major headings in the chapter.

Chapter and MOUS Objectives At the beginning of each chapter is a list of 5 to 10 action-oriented objectives. Any chapter objectives that are also MOUS objectives indicate the MOUS objective number also.

Chapter Opening Case Each chapter begins with a case. Cases describe a mixture of fictitious and real people and companies and the needs of the people and companies. Throughout the chapter, the student gains the skills and knowledge to solve the problem stated in the case.

Introduction The chapter introduction establishes the overview of the chapter's activities in the context of the case problem.

Another Way and Another Word Another Way is a highlighted feature providing a bulleted list of steps to accomplish a task, or best practices—that is, a better or faster way to accomplish a task such as pasting a format onto an Excel cell. Another Word, another highlighted box, briefly explains more about a topic or highlights a potential pitfall.

Step-by-Step Instructions Numbered step-by-step instructions for all hands-on activities appear in a *distinctive color.* Keyboard characters and menu selections appear in a **special format** to emphasize what the user should press or type. Steps make clear to the student the exact sequence of keystrokes and mouse clicks needed to complete a task such as formatting a Word paragraph.

Tips Tips appear within a numbered sequence of steps and warn the student of possible missteps or provide alternatives to the step that precedes the tip.

Task Reference and Task Reference Round-Up Task References appear throughout the textbook. Set in a distinctive design, each Task Reference contains a bulleted list of steps showing a generic way to accomplish activities that are especially important or significant. A Task Reference Round-Up at the end of each chapter summarizes a chapter's Task References.

MOUS Objectives Summary A list of MOUS objectives covered in a chapter appears in the chapter objectives and the chapter summary.

Making the Grade Short answer questions appear at the end of each chapter's sessions. They test a student's grasp of each session's contents, and Making the Grade answers appear at the end of each book so students can check their answers.

Rich End-of-Chapter Materials End-of-chapter materials incorporating a three-level approach reinforce learning and help students take ownership of the chapter. Level One, review of terminology, contains a fun crossword puzzle that enforces review of a chapter's key terms. Level Two, review of concepts, contains fill-in-the blank questions, review questions, and a Jeopardy-style create-a-question exercise. Level Three is Hands-on Projects.

Hands-on Projects Extensive hands-on projects engage the student in a problem-solving exercise from start to finish. There are six clearly labeled categories that each contain one or two questions. Categories are Practice, Challenge!, On the Web, E-Business, Around the World, and a Running Project that carries throughout all the chapters.

Teaching and Learning resources/overview

We understand that, in today's teaching environment, offering a textbook alone is not sufficient to meet the needs of the many instructors who use our books. To teach effectively, instructors must have a full complement of supplemental resources to assist them in every facet of teaching, from preparing for class to conducting a lecture to assessing students' comprehension. The **I-Series** offers a complete supplements package and Web site that is briefly described below.

INSTRUCTOR'S RESOURCE KIT

The Instructor's Resource Kit is a CD-ROM containing the Instructor's Manual in both MS Word and .pdf formats, PowerPoint Slides with Presentation Software, Brownstone test-generating software, and accompanying test item files in both MS Word and .pdf formats for each chapter. The CD also contains figure files from the text, student data files, and solutions files. The features of each of the three main components of the Instructor's Resource Kit are highlighted below.

Instructor's Manual Featuring:

- Chapter learning objectives per chapter
- Chapter outline with teaching tips
- Annotated Solutions Diagram to provide Troubleshooting Tips, Tricks, and Traps
- Lecture Notes, illustrating key concepts and ideas
- Annotated Syllabus, depicting a time table and schedule for covering chapter content
- Additional end-of-chapter projects
- Answers to all Making the Grade and end-of-chapter questions

PowerPoint Presentation

The PowerPoint presentation is designed to provide instructors with comprehensive lecture and teaching resources that will include

- Chapter learning objectives followed by source content that illustrates key terms and key facts per chapter

- FAQ (frequently asked questions) to show key concepts throughout the chapter; also, lecture notes, to illustrate these key concepts and ideas
- End-of-chapter exercises and activities per chapter, as taken from the end-of-chapter materials in the text
- Speaker's Notes, to be incorporated throughout the slides per chapter
- Figures/screen shots, to be incorporated throughout the slides per chapter

PowerPoint includes presentation software for instructors to design their own presentation for their course.

Test Bank

The I-Series Test Bank, using Diploma Network Testing Software by Brownstone, contains over 3,000 questions (both objective and interactive) categorized by topic, page reference to the text, and difficulty level of learning. Each question is assigned a learning category:

- Level 1: Key Terms and Facts
- Level 2: Key Concepts
- Level 3: Application and Problem-Solving

The types of questions consist of 40 percent Identifying/Interactive Lab Questions, 20 percent Multiple Choice, 20 percent True/False, and 20 percent Fill-in/Short Answer Questions.

ONLINE LEARNING CENTER/ WEB SITE

The Online Learning Center that accompanies the I-Series is accessible through our Information Technology Supersite at http://www.mhhe.com/catalogs/irwin/it/. This site provides additional review and learning tools developed using the same three-level approach found in the text and supplements. To locate the I-Series OLC/Web site directly, go to www.mhhe.com/i-series. The site is divided into three key areas:

- **Information Center** Contains core information about the text, the authors, and a guide to our additional features and benefits of the series, including the supplements.

- **Instructor Center** Offers instructional materials, downloads, additional activities and answers to additional projects, answers to chapter troubleshooting exercises, answers to chapter preparation/post exercises posed to students, relevant links for professors, and more.
- **Student Center** Contains chapter objectives and outlines, self-quizzes, chapter troubleshooting exercises, chapter preparation/post exercises, additional projects, simulations, student data files and solutions files, Web links, and more.

RESOURCES FOR STUDENTS

Interactive Companion CD This student CD-ROM can be packaged with this text. It is designed for use in class, in the lab, or at home by students and professors and combines video, interactive exercises, and animation to cover the most difficult and popular topics in Computing Concepts. By combining video, interactive exercises, animation, additional content, and actual "lab" tutorials, we expand the reach and scope of the textbook.

SimNet XPert SimNet XPert is a simulated assessment and learning tool. It allows students to study MS Office XP skills and computer concepts, and professors to test and evaluate students' proficiency within MS Office XP applications and concepts. Students can practice and study their skills at home or in the school lab using SimNet XPert, which does not require the purchase of Office XP software. SimNet XPert will contain new features and enhancements for Office XP, including:

NEW! **Live Assessments!** SimNet *XP*ert now includes live-in-the-application assessments! One for each skill set for Core MOUS objectives in Word 2002, Excel 2002, Access 2002, and PowerPoint 2002 (total of 29 Live-in-the-Application Assessments). Multiple tasks are required to complete each live assessment (about 100 tasks covered).

NEW! **Computer Concepts Coverage!** SimNet *XP*ert now includes coverage of computer concepts in both the Learning and the Assessment sides.

NEW! **Practice or Pretest Questions!** SimNet *XP*ert has a separate pool of 600 questions for practice tests or pretests.

NEW! **Comprehensive Exercises!** SimNet *XP*ert offers comprehensive exercises for each application. These exercises require the student to use multiple skills to solve one exercise in the simulated environment.

ENHANCED! **More Assessment Questions!** SimNet *XP*ert includes over 1,400 assessment questions.

ENHANCED! **Simulated Interface!** The simulated environment in **SimNet XPert** has been substantially deepened to more realistically simulate the real applications. Now students are not graded incorrect just because they chose the wrong sub-menu or dialog box. The student is not graded until he or she does something that immediately invokes an action.

DIGITAL SOLUTIONS FOR INSTRUCTORS AND STUDENTS

PageOut PageOut is our Course Web Site Development Center that offers a syllabus page, URL, McGraw-Hill Online Learning Center content, online exercises and quizzes, gradebook, discussion board, and an area for student Web pages. For more information, visit the PageOut Web site at www.pageout.net.

Online Courses Available OLCs are your perfect solutions for Internet-based content. Simply put, these Centers are "digital cartridges" that contain a book's pedagogy and supplements. As students read the book, they can go online and take self-grading quizzes or work through interactive exercises.

Online Learning Centers can be delivered through any of these platforms:

McGraw-Hill Learning Architecture (TopClass)

Blackboard.com

College.com (formerly Real Education)

WebCT (a product of Universal Learning Technology)

your guide to the i-series

Did You Know?

A unique presentation of text and graphics introduce interesting and little-known facts.

Chapter Objectives

Each chapter begins with a list of competencies covered in the chapter.

Task Reference

Provides steps to accomplish an especially important task.

Making the Grade

Short-answer questions appear at the end of each session and answers appear at the end of the book.

x

your guide to the i-series

Step-by-Step Instruction

Numbered steps guide you through the exact sequence of keystrokes to accomplish the task.

Tips

Tips appear within steps and either indicate possible missteps or provide alternatives to a step.

Screen Shots

Screen shots show you what to expect at critical points.

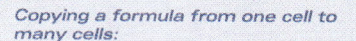

End-of-Chapter Hands-on Projects

A rich variety of projects introduced by a case lets you put into practice what you have learned. Categories include Practice, Challenge, On the Web, E-Business, Around the World, and a running case project.

Another Way/ Another Word

Another Way highlights an alternative way to accomplish a task; Another Word explains more about a topic.

Task Reference RoundUp

Provides a quick reference and summary of a chapter's task references.

xi

APPROVED COURSEWARE

What does this logo mean?

It means this courseware has been approved by the Microsoft® Office User Specialist Program to be among the finest available for learning *Microsoft Word 2002, Microsoft Excel 2002, Microsoft Access 2002, and Microsoft PowerPoint 2002*. It also means that upon completion of this courseware, you may be prepared to become a Microsoft Office User Specialist. The I-Series Microsoft Office XP books are available in three levels of coverage: Brief level, Intro level, and the Complete level. The I-Series Introductory books are approved courseware to prepare you for the MOUS level 1 exam. The I-Series Complete books will prepare you for the expert level exam.

What is a Microsoft Office User Specialist?

A Microsoft Office User Specialist is an individual who has certified his or her skills in one or more of the Microsoft Office desktop applications of Microsoft Word, Microsoft Excel, Microsoft PowerPoint®, Microsoft Outlook® or Microsoft Access, or in Microsoft Project. The Microsoft Office User Specialist Program typically offers certification exams at the "Core" and "Expert" skill levels.* The Microsoft Office User Specialist Program is the only Microsoft approved program in the world for certifying proficiency in Microsoft Office desktop applications and Microsoft Project. This certification can be a valuable asset in any job search or career advancement.

More Information:

To learn more about becoming a Microsoft Office User Specialist, visit www.mous.net

To purchase a Microsoft Office User Specialist certification exam, visit www.DesktopIQ.co

To learn about other Microsoft Office User Specialist approved courseware from McGraw-Hill/Irwin, visit http://www.mhhe.com/catalogs/irwin/cit/mous/index.mhtml

---

* The availability of Microsoft Office User Specialist certification exams varies by application, application version and language. Visit www.mous.net for exam availability.

Microsoft, the Microsoft Office User Specialist Logo, PowerPoint and Outlook are either registered trademarks or trademarks of Microsoft Corporation in the United States and/or other countries.

acknowledgments

The authors want to acknowledge the work and support of the seasoned professionals at McGraw-Hill. Thank you to George Werthman, publisher, for his strong leadership and a management style that fosters innovation and creativity. Thank you to Dan Silverburg, sponsoring editor, who is an experienced editor and recent recruit to the I-Series. Dan quickly absorbed a month's worth of information in days and guided the authors through the sometimes-difficult publishing maze. Our special thanks go to Melissa Forte, developmental editor, who served, unofficially, as a cheerleader for the authors. The hub of our editorial "wheel," Melissa shouldered more than her share of work in the many months from prelaunch boot camp to bound book date. We are grateful to Gina Huck, developmental editor, for her dedication to this project. From the project's inception, Gina has guided us and kept us on track. Sarah Wood, developmental editor, paid attention to all the details that required her special care.

Thank you to Valerie Bolch, a University of San Diego graduate student, who did a wonderful job of creating some of the end-of-chapter exercises and tech editing the Excel manuscript. Ron Tariga helped categorize and display several Office XP toolbar buttons. Thank you to Stirling Perry, who took screen shots of all of the Office XP toolbar buttons and organized them into logical groups. Wendi Whitmore, who provided screen shots of Office 2000 toolbars, prior to the release of Office XP. Many thanks to Linda Dillon, who provided creative input and feedback for the PowerPoint end-of-chapter materials. Also, the labor of Carolla McCammack in tech editing many of the Access chapters has been invaluable.

Thank you to Marilyn Parker, Rick's partner for 32 years, for her help, support, and tolerance. She helped with some of the manuscript details, supported Rick's need for time, and tolerated his emotional absence. Rick's sons, Cole, Morgan, Spence, and Sam, were patient and helpful during the time required for all the steps in the production of this book. All of them filled in and did "his" chores at times as they tolerated his distractions. Also, thanks to Mali Jones for her excellent technical editing.

We all wish to thank all of our schools for providing support, including time off to dedicate to writing: University of San Diego, University of Denver, and the College of Southern Idaho.

If you would like to contact us about any of the books in the I-Series, we would enjoy hearing from you. We welcome comments and suggestions that we might incorporate into future editions of the books. You can e-mail book-related messages to us at i-series@mcgraw-hill.com. For the latest information about the I-Series textbooks and related resources, please visit our Web site at www.mhhe.com/i-series.

dedication

TO my wonderful family:

Rick, Daniel, Dusty, Tori, Evan, Connor, and Gage

for all that they do to support me when writing isn't easy and to celebrate the times when it goes well.

M.W.

brief contents

ABOUT THE I-SERIES — iv
YOUR GUIDE TO THE I-SERIES — x
COMMON MICROSOFT OFFICE XP FEATURES — OFF 1.1

CHAPTER 1
PRESENTATION BASICS — PP 1.1
SESSION 1.1 Introduction to Presentation Graphics • **SESSION 1.2** Creating a New Presentation

CHAPTER 2
ORGANIZING YOUR PRESENTATION — PP 2.1
SESSION 2.1 Printing • **SESSION 2.2** Outlining Ideas

CHAPTER 3
REFINING YOUR PRESENTATION — PP 3.1
SESSION 3.1 Adding and Modifying Objects • **SESSION 3.2** Standardizing Presentations

CHAPTER 4
ENHANCING YOUR PRESENTATION WITH GRAPHICS — PP 4.1
SESSION 4.1 Effectively Using Art • **SESSION 4.2** Adding Other Graphic Elements

CHAPTER 5
CREATING A MULTIMEDIA PRESENTATION — EX 5.1
SESSION 5.1 Using Animations • **SESSION 5.2** Using Other Audio Multimedia Components

CHAPTER 6
COLOR SCHEMES AND DRAWING — EX 6.1
SESSION 6.1 Choosing a Color Scheme • **SESSION 6.2** Creating Custom Art

CHAPTER 7
INTERNET/INTRANET PRESENTATIONS — EX 7.1
SESSION 7.1 Interactive Presentations • **SESSION 7.2** Using PowerPoint to Publish Web Pages

CHAPTER 8
POWERPOINT POWER FEATURES — EX 8.1
SESSION 8.1 PowerPoint User Features • **SESSION 8.2** Sharing Presentations

END-OF-BOOK
REFERENCES — REF 1.1
GLOSSARY — EOB 1.1
GLOSSARY FOR COMMON MICROSOFT OFFICE XP FEATURES — EOB 2.1
INDEX — EOB 3.1

table of contents

ABOUT THE I-SERIES	iv
YOUR GUIDE TO THE I-SERIES	x
COMMON MICROSOFT OFFICE XP FEATURES	OFF 1.1
INTRODUCTION	OFF 1.2

SESSION 1.1
Introducing Microsoft Office XP	OFF 1.2
Making the Grade	OFF 1.10
SUMMARY	OFF 1.10
TASK REFERENCE ROUNDUP	OFF 1.11
LEVEL ONE: REVIEW OF TERMINOLOGY	OFF 1.12
LEVEL TWO: REVIEW OF CONCEPTS	OFF 1.13

CHAPTER 1
PRESENTATION BASICS — PP 1.1

CHAPTER CASE
TEACHING STUDENTS TO USE PRESENTATION GRAPHICS	PP 1.2

SESSION 1.1
INTRODUCTION TO PRESENTATION GRAPHICS	PP 1.3
Getting Started with PowerPoint	PP 1.3
Understanding the Presentation Window	PP 1.7
Navigating a Presentation	PP 1.9
Updating and Saving a Presentation	PP 1.13
Making the Grade	PP 1.18

SESSION 1.2
CREATING A PRESENTATION	PP 1.19
Creating a Blank Presentation	PP 1.19
AutoContent Wizard	PP 1.25
Using a Design Template	PP 1.29
The Notes Pane	PP 1.34
Getting Help	PP 1.36
Exiting PowerPoint	PP 1.37
Making the Grade	PP 1.37

SESSION 1.3
SUMMARY	PP 1.38
TASK REFERENCE ROUNDUP	PP 1.39
LEVEL ONE: REVIEW OF TERMINOLOGY	PP 1.41
LEVEL TWO: REVIEW OF CONCEPTS	PP 1.42
LEVEL THREE: HANDS-ON PROJECTS	PP 1.43
RUNNING PROJECT	PP 1.48

CHAPTER 2
ORGANIZING YOUR PRESENTATION — PP 2.1

CHAPTER CASE
TEACHING PRESENTATION GRAPHICS USING PRESENTATION GRAPHICS	PP 2.2

SESSION 2.1
PRINTING	PP 2.3
Print Preview	PP 2.3
Creating Headers and Footers	PP 2.4
Understanding Page Setup	PP 2.11
Exploring the Print Dialog Box	PP 2.12
Making the Grade	PP 2.18

SESSION 2.2
OUTLINING IDEAS	PP 2.18
Using PowerPoint's Outline View	PP 2.18
Integrating with Microsoft Word	PP 2.23
Making the Grade	PP 2.29

SESSION 2.3
SUMMARY	PP 2.29
TASK REFERENCE ROUNDUP	PP 2.30
LEVEL ONE: REVIEW OF TERMINOLOGY	PP 2.31

xvi

LEVEL TWO: REVIEW OF CONCEPTS	PP 2.32
LEVEL THREE: HANDS-ON PROJECTS	PP 2.33
RUNNING PROJECT	PP 2.38

CHAPTER 3
REFINING YOUR PRESENTATION PP 3.1

CHAPTER CASE
STAFFING PRESENTATION WITH POWERPOINT   PP 3.2

SESSION 3.1
ADDING AND MODIFYING OBJECTS   PP 3.3
Understanding PowerPoint Objects   PP 3.3
Formatting Objects   PP 3.7
Using Proofing Tools   PP 3.20
Making the Grade   PP 3.27

SESSION 3.2
STANDARDIZING PRESENTATIONS   PP 3.27
Creating a Summary Slide   PP 3.27
Understanding Templates   PP 3.29
Modifying PowerPoint Masters   PP 3.33
Using Animation Schemes   PP 3.40
Using Presentation Tools   PP 3.42
Making the Grade   PP 3.45

SESSION 3.3
SUMMARY   PP 3.45
TASK REFERENCE ROUNDUP   PP 3.46
LEVEL ONE: REVIEW OF TERMINOLOGY   PP 3.49
LEVEL TWO: REVIEW OF CONCEPTS   PP 3.50
LEVEL THREE: HANDS-ON PROJECTS   PP 3.51
RUNNING PROJECT   PP 3.56

CHAPTER 4
ENHANCING YOUR PRESENTATION WITH GRAPHICS   PP 4.1

CHAPTER CASE
PHONE MINDER SALES PRESENTATION WITH POWERPOINT   PP 4.2

SESSION 4.1
EFFECTIVELY USING ART   PP 4.3
Understanding Picture Types   PP 4.3
Inserting Clip Art   PP 4.4
Opening File Art   PP 4.12
Creating Word Art   PP 4.15
Saving Art Objects   PP 4.18
Making the Grade   PP 4.22

SESSION 4.2
ADDING OTHER GRAPHIC ELEMENTS   PP 4.22
Building Tables   PP 4.22
Graphing   PP 4.27
Defining Other Types of Charts   PP 4.35
MAKING THE GRADE   PP 4.41

SESSION 4.3
SUMMARY   PP 4.41
TASK REFERENCE ROUNDUP   PP 4.42
LEVEL ONE: REVIEW OF TERMINOLOGY   PP 4.45
LEVEL TWO: REVIEW OF CONCEPTS   PP 4.46
LEVEL THREE: HANDS-ON PROJECTS   PP 4.47
RUNNING PROJECT   PP 4.52

CHAPTER 5
CREATING A MULTIMEDIA PRESENTATION   PP 5.1

CHAPTER CASE
TEACHING VITAL STATISTICS WITH POWERPOINT   PP 5.2

SESSION 5.1
USING ANIMATIONS   PP 5.3
Animating Slide Objects   PP 5.3
Making the Grade   PP 5.19

SESSION 5.2
USING OTHER AUDIO MULTIMEDIA COMPONENTS   PP 5.19
Identifying Sources for Media   PP 5.27
Making the Grade   PP 5.31

SESSION 5.3
SUMMARY   PP 5.31

xvii

TASK REFERENCE ROUNDUP	PP 5.32
LEVEL ONE: REVIEW OF TERMINOLOGY	PP 5.35
LEVEL TWO: REVIEW OF CONCEPTS	PP 5.36
LEVEL THREE: HANDS-ON PROJECTS	PP 5.37
RUNNING PROJECT	PP 5.42

CHAPTER 6
COLOR SCHEMES AND DRAWING   PP 6.1

CHAPTER CASE
USING POWERPOINT TO REPORT PROGRESS   PP 6.2

SESSION 6.1
CHOOSING A COLOR SCHEME	PP 6.3
Using Color Schemes	PP 6.3
Customizing the Color Menus	PP 6.11
Customizing Slide Backgrounds	PP 6.12
Making the Grade	PP 6.19

SESSION 6.2
CREATING CUSTOM ART	PP 6.18
Creating and Modifying Drawing Objects	PP 6.19
Editing Objects	PP 6.28
Stacking and Grouping Objects	PP 6.35
Making the Grade	PP 6.39

SESSION 6.3
SUMMARY	PP 6.39
TASK REFERENCE ROUNDUP	PP 6.40
LEVEL ONE: REVIEW OF TERMINOLOGY	PP 6.43
LEVEL TWO: REVIEW OF CONCEPTS	PP 6.44
LEVEL THREE: HANDS-ON PROJECTS	PP 6.45
RUNNING PROJECT	PP 6.50

CHAPTER 7
INTERNET/INTRANET PRESENTATIONS DRAWING   PP 7.1

CHAPTER CASE
USING POWERPOINT TO BUILD A DONOR INFORMATION KIOSK   PP 7.2

SESSION 7.1
INTERACTIVE PRESENTATIONS	PP 7.3
Adding Navigation to Your Presentation	PP 7.3
Hyperlinking Other Objects	PP 7.11
Making the Grade	PP 7.17

SESSION 7.2
USING POWERPOINT TO PUBLISH WEB PAGES	PP 7.17
Preparing for Web Publishing	PP 7.17
Creating a Personal Web Page	PP 7.18
Saving Existing Presentations as Web Pages	PP 7.22
Web Access from PowerPoint	PP 7.25
Getting Help on the Web	PP 7.26
Making the Grade	PP 7.27

SESSION 7.3
SUMMARY	PP 7.27
TASK REFERENCE ROUNDUP	PP 7.28
LEVEL ONE: REVIEW OF TERMINOLOGY	PP 7.31
LEVEL TWO: REVIEW OF CONCEPTS	PP 7.32
LEVEL THREE: HANDS-ON PROJECTS	PP 7.33
RUNNING PROJECT	PP 7.38

CHAPTER 8
POWERPOINT POWER FEATURES   PP 8.1

CHAPTER CASE
COLLABORATING AND SHARING THE PHONEPERFORMANCE PRESENTATION   PP 8.2

SESSION 8.1

POWERPOINT POWER USER FEATURES	PP 8.3
Taking Your Show on the Road	PP 8.3
Creating and Managing Playlists	PP 8.7
Automating Tasks with Macros	PP 8.9
Modifying Menus and Toolbars	PP 8.11
Revising PowerPoint Settings	PP 8.16
Enhancing PowerPoint with Add-Ins	PP 8.17
Making the Grade	PP 8.19

SESSION 8.2

SHARING PRESENTATIONS	PP 8.19
Understanding Online Collaboration Tools	PP 8.19
Web Broadcasting	PP 8.28
Making Online Meetings Work For You	PP 8.33
Making the Grade	PP 8.36

SESSION 8.3

SUMMARY	PP 8.36
TASK REFERENCE ROUNDUP	PP 8.37
LEVEL ONE: REVIEW OF TERMINOLOGY	PP 8.43
LEVEL TWO: REVIEW OF CONCEPTS	PP 8.44
LEVEL THREE: HANDS-ON PROJECTS	PP 8.45
RUNNING PROJECT	PP 8.50

END-OF-BOOK

REFERENCE 1: POWERPOINT FILE FINDER	REF 1.1
REFERENCE 2: MOUS CERTIFICATION GUIDE	REF 2.1
REFERENCE 3: TASK REFERENCE ROUNDUP	REF 3.1
REFERENCE 4: MAKING THE GRADE ANSWERS	REF 4.1
GLOSSARY	EOB 1.1
GLOSSARY FOR COMMON MICROSOFT OFFICE FEATURES	EOB 2.1
INDEX	EOB 3.1

xix

Common Microsoft Office XP Features

did you know?

the *"XP" in Microsoft Office XP stands for "experience"—specifically, an exciting new set of experiences enabled by this new release?*

Microsoft *was created by Paul Allen and Bill Gates in 1975 in Albuquerque, New Mexico, long before they moved their offices to Redmond, Washington?*

Allen *and Gates developed a version of the BASIC computer language for the first personal computer, known as the Altair 8800?*

the *inventor of the Altair 8800, Dr. Ed Roberts, is now a family physician in Cochran, Georgia?*

Dr. *Roberts coined the phrase "personal computer" since it was the first computer designed for personal use?*

what *was the basic configuration of the Altair 8800? (see www.mhhe.com/i-series for the answer)*

Chapter Objectives

In this chapter you will:

- Be introduced to the Office XP suite
- Find out what new features exist in Office XP
- Become familiar with the different versions of Office XP and which four applications are included in all versions
- Learn about the common screen elements such as the title bar, menu bar, and toolbars
- Learn how to switch between two or more open applications
- Learn how to use Office XP's newest features: the task pane and smart tags
- Become familiar with how to get help in an application
- Learn how to customize your Office Assistant
- Learn about the newest Help features: Answer Wizard and Ask a Question

OFF 1.1

OFF 1.2   COMMON OFFICE FEATURES

CHAPTER OUTLINE:

1.1 Introducing Microsoft Office XP

INTRODUCTION

Office XP is the newest version of the popular Microsoft integrated application suite series that has helped personal computer users around the world to be productive and creative. Specifically, an ***application*** is a program that is designed to help you accomplish a particular task, such as creating a slide-show presentation using PowerPoint. An ***integrated application suite***, like Office XP, is a collection of application programs bundled together and designed to allow the user to effortlessly share information from one application to the next.

SESSION 1.1 INTRODUCING MICROSOFT OFFICE XP

There are several versions of Office XP available to users with a diversity of personal and business needs. They include the Standard edition, the Professional edition, the Professional Special edition, and the Developer edition. Each edition comes with a collection of different programs, but all include the basic applications of Word, Excel, Outlook, and PowerPoint, which is the collection known as the ***Standard edition***. The ***Professional edition*** adds Access to the collection, whereas the ***Professional Special edition*** includes Access, FrontPage, and Publisher. A summary of some of the more popular applications available in Office XP is listed in Figure 1.1.

FIGURE 1.1

Application programs available in Microsoft Office XP

Office XP Application	Summary of What the Program Does
Word 2002	Word is a general-purpose word-processing tool that allows users to create primarily text-based documents, such as letters, résumés, research papers, and even Web pages.
Excel 2002	Excel is an electronic spreadsheet tool that can be used to input, organize, calculate, analyze, and display business data.
PowerPoint 2002	PowerPoint is a popular presentation tool that allows users to create overhead transparencies and powerful multimedia slide shows.
Access 2002	Access is a relational database tool that can be used to collect, organize, and retrieve large amounts of data. With a database you can manipulate the data into useful information using tables, forms, queries, and reports.
Outlook 2002	Outlook is a desktop information management tool that allows you to send and receive e-mail, maintain a personal calendar of appointments, schedule meetings with co-workers, create to-do lists, and store address information about business/personal contacts.
FrontPage 2002	FrontPage is a powerful Web publishing tool that provides everything needed to create, edit, and manage a personal or corporate Web site, without having to learn HTML.
Publisher 2002	Publisher is a desktop publishing tool that provides individual users the capability to create professional-looking flyers, brochures, and newsletters.

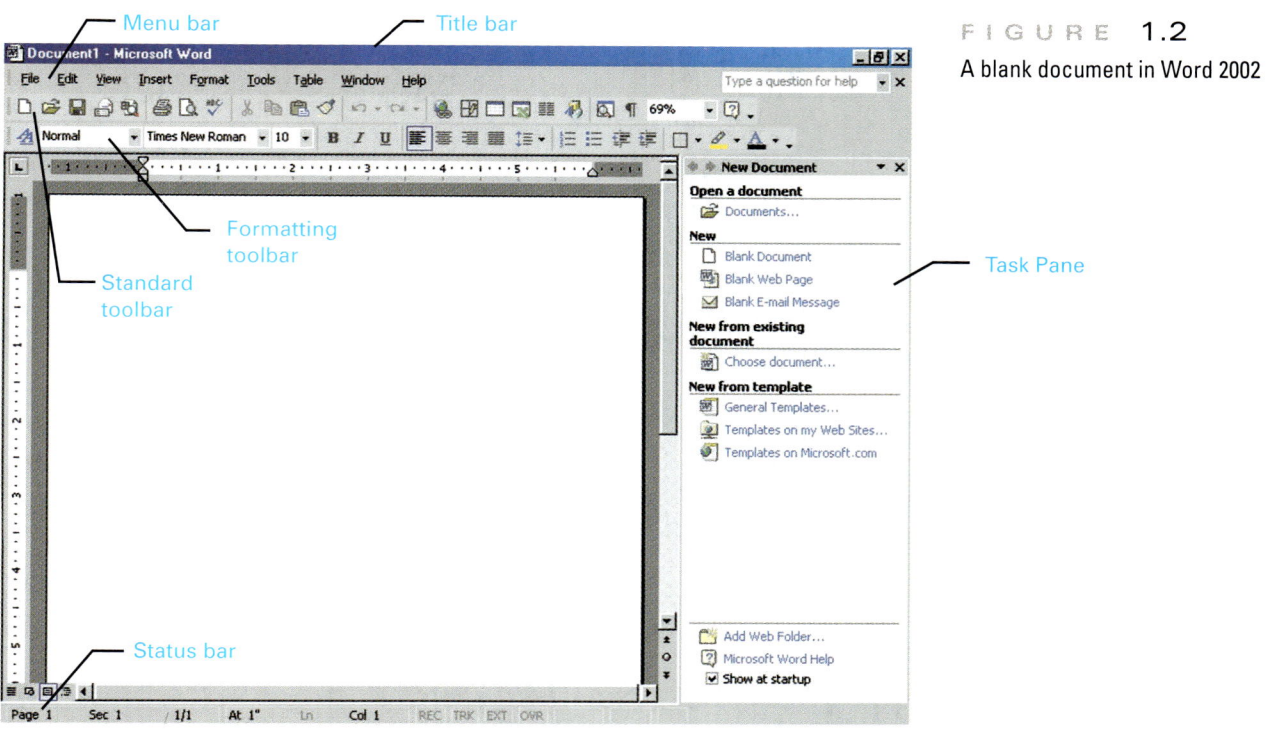

FIGURE 1.2

A blank document in Word 2002

Identifying Common Screen Elements

When you open two or more of the Microsoft applications, you will notice the similarities in the programs. This design is done intentionally so that as you learn to use one application, you will be able to quickly navigate through the remaining Office XP programs. When you first open Word, you will find a blank document as seen in Figure 1.2. In this exercise you will get to preview a blank document in Word and a blank workbook in Excel. Notice the common features of the two programs as you work with them. These features will be explained over the next few pages.

anotherword

. . . on the Office XP Suite

Collectively, the programs are officially referred to as **Microsoft Office XP,** but individually each application is referred to as version 2002.

Opening multiple applications in Office XP:

1. Click the **Start** ![Start] button on the taskbar to display the pop-up menu

2. Move your cursor up the menu and stop on **Programs.** Another menu will appear listing all the programs available on your computer

3. Locate **Microsoft Word** in the program list and click it. After a few seconds you should see a blank document as previously seen in Figure 1.2. Now compare the screen layout with that found in Excel

4. Click the **Start** button, then point to **Programs,** once again

OFFICE

FIGURE 1.3

A blank workbook in Microsoft Excel

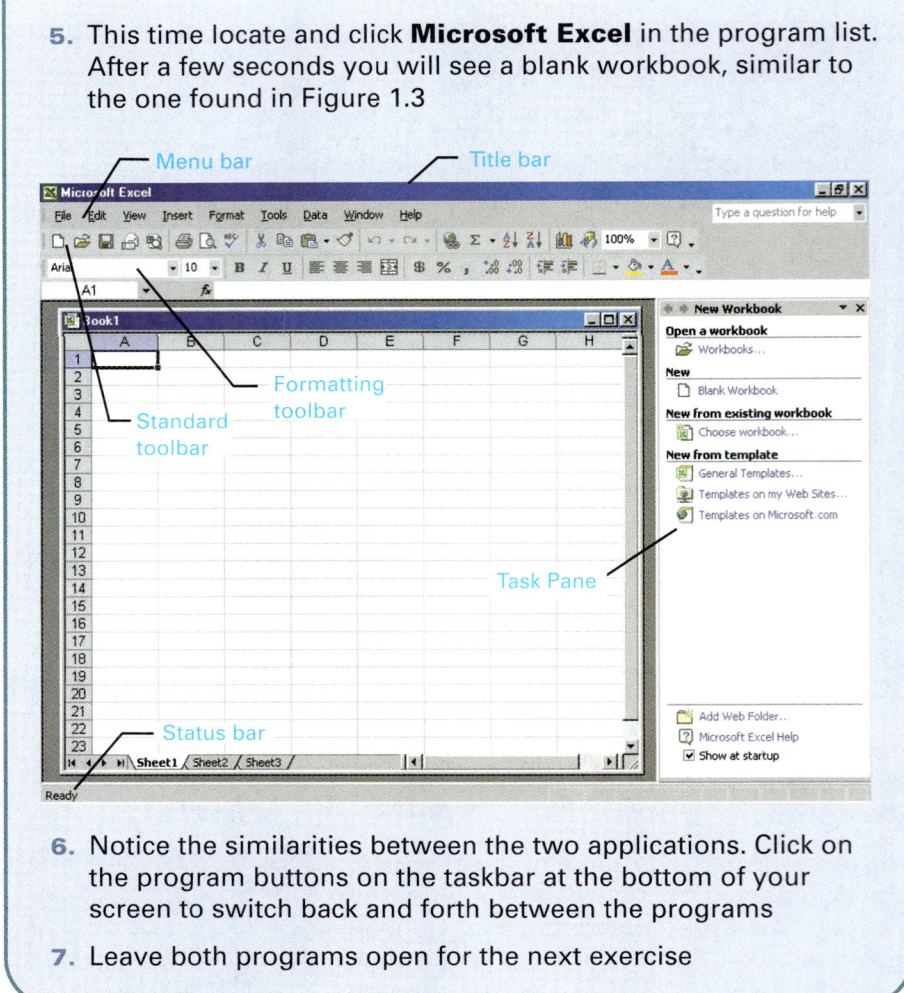

5. This time locate and click **Microsoft Excel** in the program list. After a few seconds you will see a blank workbook, similar to the one found in Figure 1.3

6. Notice the similarities between the two applications. Click on the program buttons on the taskbar at the bottom of your screen to switch back and forth between the programs

7. Leave both programs open for the next exercise

Title Bar, Menu Bar, and Toolbars

As you examine the Word and Excel programs, you will notice that each application contains similar elements such as a title bar, a menu bar, a toolbar, and a status bar. The *title bar* at the top of each screen displays the application's icon, the title of the document you are working on, and the name of the application program you are using.

The *menu bar* displays a list of key menu options available to you for that particular program. In addition to a few program-specific menu items, all of the Office XP applications generally will contain the identical menu options of File, Edit, View, Insert, Tools, Window, and Help. To use these menus, you simply click one time on the desired menu, and a submenu will then appear with additional options.

On the third row of each application is the *toolbar,* which is a collection of commonly used shortcut buttons. A single click on a toolbar button activates a program feature that also can be found in one of the menu options. Most office applications will display the **Standard toolbar,** which contains the popular icons such as Cut, Copy, and Paste. The table displayed in Figure 1.4 shows a list of these common buttons and their functions.

Another popular toolbar found in Office XP applications is the **Formatting toolbar,** which allows you to change the appearance of text,

---

anotherway

. . . . to switch between applications

You also can switch between applications by using what is known as the Alt+Tab sequence. Press and hold the **Alt** key, then press **Tab** one time. Let go of both keys when you see the gray box in the middle of your screen displaying program icons. This will allow you to quickly cycle back and forth through any open programs.

FIGURE 1.4

Standard toolbar buttons and their function

New	Opens a new blank document, workbook, presentation, or database.
Open	Opens a previously created document, workbook, presentation, or database.
Save	Allows you to quickly save your work. The first time you save, you will be prompted for a file name and location.
E-mail	New to Office XP, this button lets you quickly send the existing document as an email message.
Print	Prints a document.
Cut	Removes selected information from your document and temporarily places it on the Clipboard.
Copy	Duplicates selected information and places it on the Clipboard.
Paste	Copies information on the Clipboard to the current document.
Undo Typing	Reverses the last action or keystroke taken. This is a great safety net for those uh-oh type mistakes!

such as bold, italicize, or underline. There are many toolbars available to display and some will appear as you use certain features in Office applications.

Task Panes, Clipboard, and Smart Tags

Most of the Office XP applications include a new feature known as the **Task Pane** as shown in Figure 1.5. This window allows you to access important tasks from a single, convenient location, while still working on your document. With the Task Pane window you can open files, view your clipboard, perform searches, and much more. By default, when you open an Office XP application, the Task Pane window is displayed to allow the user to open a file. As you select various functions of the application, the contents of the task pane will automatically change. You can close the task pane at any time by clicking on the close button, and redisplay the window by selecting it from the View menu.

One of the options available on the task pane is the **Clipboard,** which is a temporary storage location for selected text. In Office XP, you can actually view the contents of up to 24 items that have been cut or copied to the clipboard. This is a very powerful tool that will allow you to collect 24 sets of data and then let you quickly paste those data to a new location or document. When you paste any of the clipboard contents to your document, a Smart Tag button will appear next to the text. This smart tag, known as the **Paste Options button,** will prompt the user (when clicked) with additional features such as allowing you to paste with or without the original text formatting. There are additional **smart tag buttons** that appear as needed to provide options for completing a task quickly. In this next exercise you will get to practice using the Task Pane, Clipboard, and Paste Options smart tag button.

---

anotherway

. . . to activate a menu option

You also can activate a menu option by using shortcut key strokes. In the menu you will notice that one letter of each option is underlined. These designated letters can be used in conjunction with the Alt key to quickly access a menu task. For example, you can press **Alt+F+S** to save your file.

---

anotherword

. . . on the Clipboard

It is important to note that the Clipboard contents are available to all applications and not just the original application from where it was extracted.

FIGURE 1.5

Task Pane in Microsoft Word

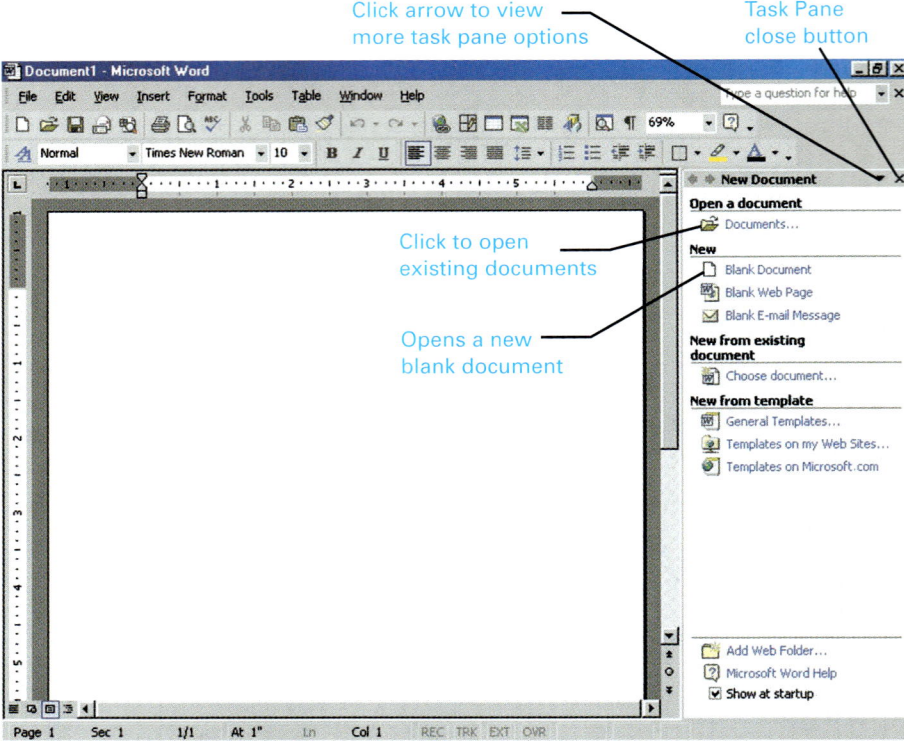

Working with the Task Pane

1. In the Excel application, type **Hello Office XP!** in cell A1 and press **Enter**

2. Click cell A1 and then change the font size of the text to size **22.** Click the **Italic** button on the Formatting toolbar to italicize your text as shown in Figure 1.6

3. Click the **Copy** button on the Standard toolbar. This will copy the contents of cell A1 to the clipboard

4. Press **Alt+Tab** to switch back to the Word program

5. Click the **Paste** button and press **Enter.** The text should appear in the blank document exactly as it was typed and italicized

6. At the top of the Task Pane window, click the **drop-down menu arrow** and select **Clipboard** from the drop-down list. You can now view the Clipboard task pane and the text that was copied to it

7. In the Clipboard Contents task pane, click on the **Hello Office XP!** item as indicated in Figure 1.7. This will paste the text a second time into your document

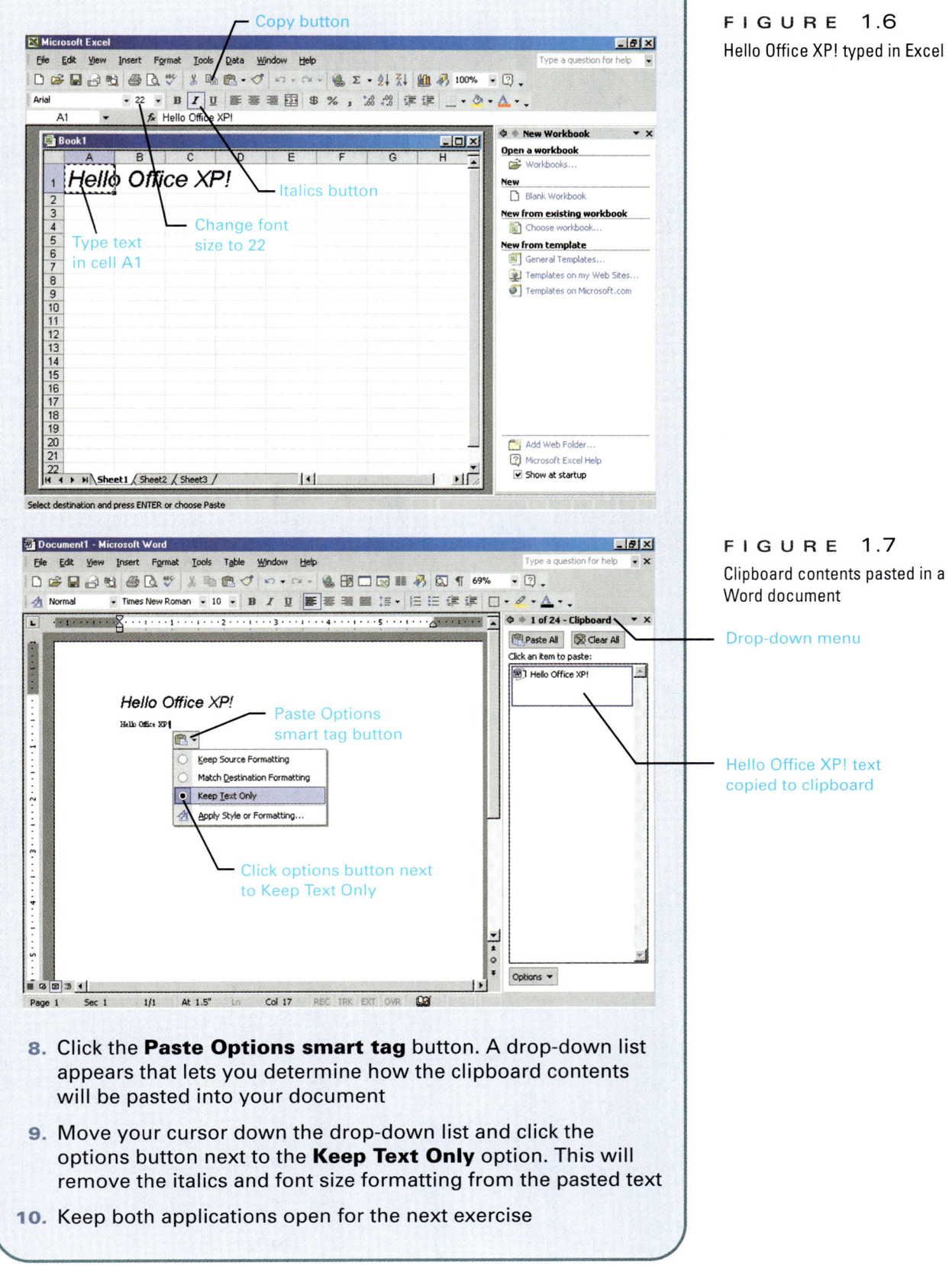

FIGURE 1.6
Hello Office XP! typed in Excel

FIGURE 1.7
Clipboard contents pasted in a Word document

8. Click the **Paste Options smart tag** button. A drop-down list appears that lets you determine how the clipboard contents will be pasted into your document

9. Move your cursor down the drop-down list and click the options button next to the **Keep Text Only** option. This will remove the italics and font size formatting from the pasted text

10. Keep both applications open for the next exercise

Getting Help

When you use any of the Office XP applications, you may find yourself in need of some assistance. There are several ways to obtain help, and fortunately for the user, they are once again consistent across the applications. To get help, the user can use the Help menu option, press F1, or use the Office Assistant, Answer Wizard, or Ask a Question text box.

The most common way of getting help is to use the Help menu option or press the F1 function key. If you do ask for help, an ***Office Assistant*** will appear ready to help you with your question as shown in Figure 1.8. In Office XP applications, the Office Assistant is hidden by default and only appears when Help is activated. One of the fun aspects about the Office Assistant is that you can select your favorite character to help you. The standard assistant is known as ***Clippit*** (the paper clip), but you also can choose ***F1*** (the robot), ***Links*** (the cat), or ***Rocky*** (the dog), among others.

Regardless of which one you use, once you request help and your assistant appears, you must then type in your help question in the Office Assistant balloon and click on the Search button. The results of your search will be displayed in a Help window for you to review or print. For those users who prefer not to use an Office Assistant, you can right-click on the character and choose the option to hide the assistant.

The ***Answer Wizard,*** located in the Microsoft Help dialog box, is another means of requesting help through your application. In order to use the Answer Wizard, you must first hide the Office Assistant and then click on Help menu. Once the Help dialog box is displayed, simply click on the Answer Wizard tab and type in your question in the text box. Another way to get help without using the Office Assistant is to use the new feature called ***Ask a Question.*** Located in the top-right corner of your window, this is perhaps the most convenient method for getting help because the user simply has to key in a search topic in the text box and press enter, without having to launch the Answer Wizard or Office Assistant. You will get to practice requesting help in the next exercise.

FIGURE 1.8

The Office Assistant appears when you ask for help

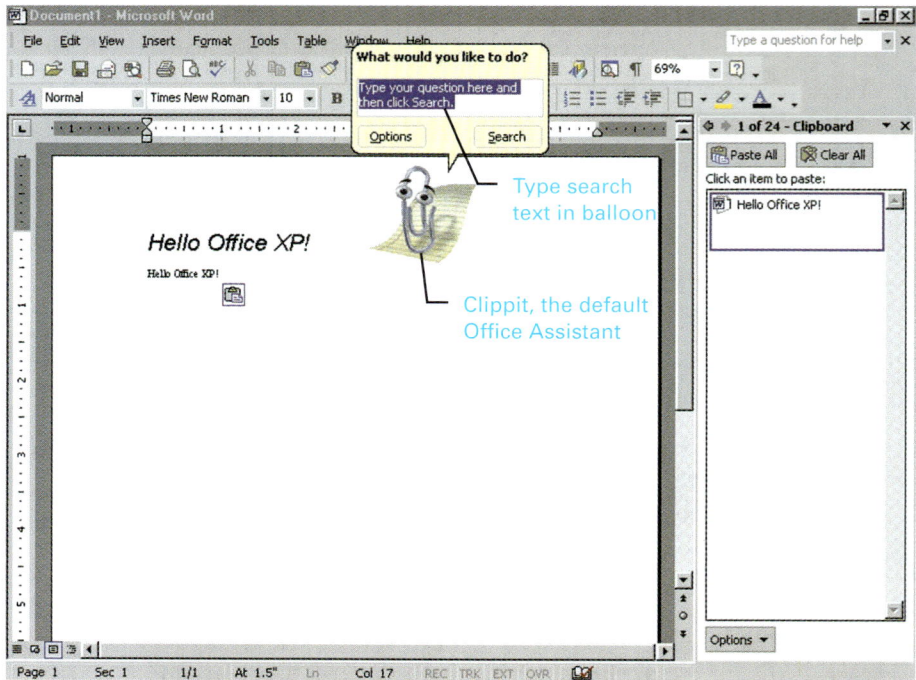

www.mhhe.com/i-series   OFF 1.9

To get help:

1. In your Word document or Excel workbook, press the **F1** function key. This should activate your Office Assistant to the screen

   tip: *If the office assistant does not appear, click on the* **Help** *menu and select* **Show the Office Assistant**

2. In the Office Assistant balloon, type **Speech Recognition,** then click the **Search button**

3. In the next balloon that appears, click the **About Speech Recognition** bullet. This will open up the Microsoft Help window with the speech recognition search results as shown in Figure 1.9. Press the **ESC** key on your keyboard to remove the Office Assistant balloon

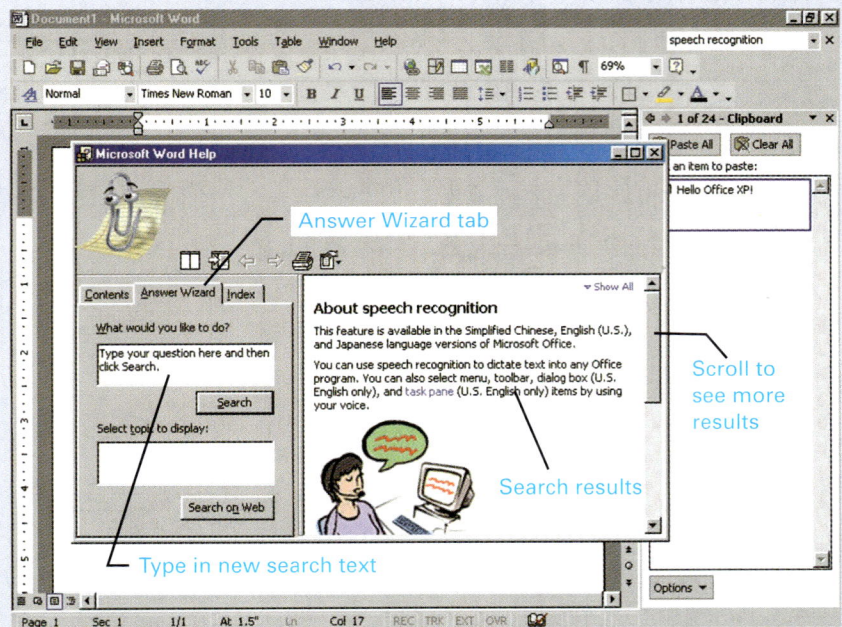

FIGURE 1.9

Results of search displayed in Microsoft help window

4. After looking over your search results, click the **Close** button of the Help window

5. Right-click the **Office Assistant** and, in the menu that pops up, select **Choose Assistant**

6. Click either the **Back** or **Next** button in the Office Assistant dialog box as shown in Figure 1.10 until you find an assistant that you like, and then click **OK**

7. Right-click the **Office Assistant** again, and this time select **Hide.** This will hide the Office Assistant until you request help again

8. **Close** any open documents and programs

OFFICE

OFF 1.10   COMMON OFFICE FEATURES

FIGURE 1.10
Office Assistant dialog box

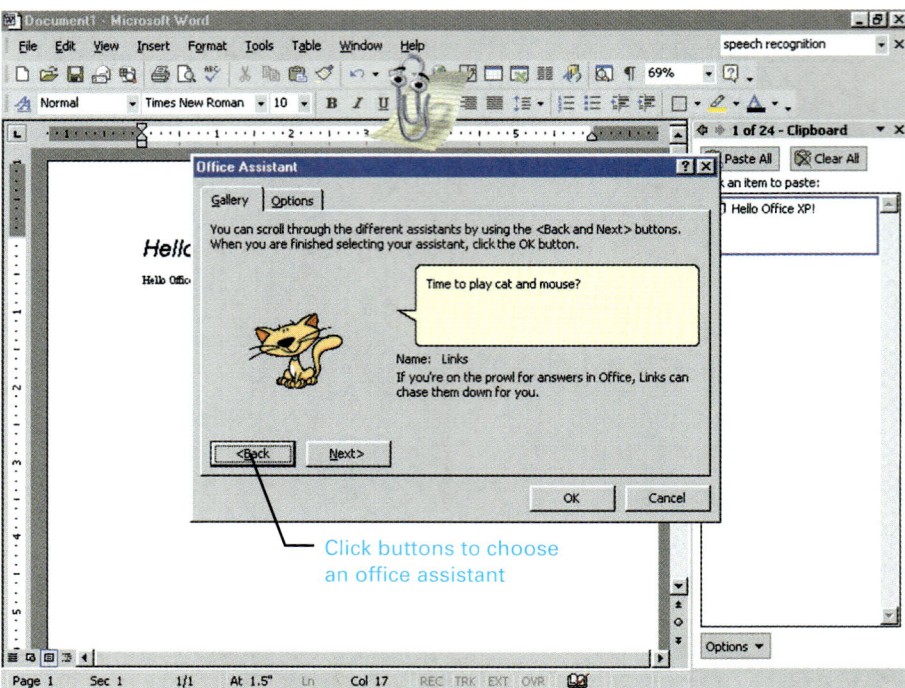

SESSION 1.1

making the grade

1. What four application programs are available in all versions of Office XP?
2. What is the default Office Assistant character?
3. How many items can be posted to the clipboard contents?
4. Which two toolbars are the most frequently used in all applications?
5. What is the quickest and most convenient method for getting help in any of the Office XP applications?

SUMMARY

In this chapter you have been introduced to the common elements of Microsoft's newest integrated application suite, known as Office XP. Regardless of which version of the program you are using, you always will have access to the Word, Excel, PowerPoint, and Outlook applications. As you learn to navigate through these applications, you will notice many similarities that allow the user to easily adapt from one application to the next. These common features include the title bar, the menu bar, and toolbars. You learned that the standard and formatting toolbars are the most commonly used toolbars in Office XP, but that there also are many toolbars available for users to select from or that automatically appear when completing a task.

Through the exercises in this chapter, you learned how to use one of Office XP's newest features, the task pane. This window allows the user quick access to various task sequences such as opening a file, viewing the Clipboard contents, performing a search, and inserting clip art. While the

Clipboard is not new to Microsoft products, it is more powerful in this version because it allows the user to post up to 24 different items in its contents. Finally, when in desperate need of answers, the user can always turn to the many help modes of Office XP. You can use one of the customized Office Assistants such as Clippit, use the Answer Wizard in the Help dialog box, or use the Ask a Question text box to find a quick solution to a problem.

task reference roundup

Task	Page #	Preferred Method
Switch between applications	OFF 1.3	• Press **Alt+Tab**
Copy and Paste using Clipboard task pane	OFF 1.5	• Highlight/select text to be copied
		• Click the **Copy** button on the toolbar
		• Place cursor in desired paste location
		• Click on item in Clipboard task pane to paste
Obtaining Help	OFF 1.8	• Press **F1** or click **Office Assistant**

review of terminology

CROSSWORD PUZZLE

Across

2. The dog Office Assistant
6. Office XP version that consists of Word, Excel, PowerPoint, and Outlook
7. Relational database tool that can be used to collect, organize, and retrieve large amounts of data
8. Is located in the Help dialog box and provides another means of requesting help
10. A popular presentation tool that allows users to create multimedia slide shows
11. Temporary storage location for up to 24 items of selected text that has been cut or copied
13. This window allows you to view clipboard contents in addition to other important tasks
14. A collection of commonly used shortcut buttons

Down

1. Toolbar that allows you to change the appearance of your text
3. The cat office assistant
4. Button that appears when you paste into your document
5. Buttons that appear as needed to provide options for completing a task quickly
9. The paper clip Office Assistant
12. Displays a list of key menu options available to you for that particular program

OFF 1.12

review of concepts

LEVEL TWO

FILL-IN THE BLANKS

1. _____ is the newest version of the popular Microsoft integrated application suite series.
2. An _____ is a program that is designed to help you accomplish a particular task, such as creating a slide-show presentation.
3. By default, when you open an Office XP application, the _____ window is displayed to allow the user to open a file.
4. The standard Office Assistant is known as _____ (the paper clip), but you can also choose _____ (the robot), _____ (the Cat), or _____ (the dog).
5. In Office XP, you can actually view the contents of up to _____ items that have been cut or copied to the clipboard.
6. A single click on a toolbar button activates a program feature that also can be found in one of the _____ options.
7. Most office applications will display the _____ toolbar, which contains the popular icons such as Cut, Copy, and Paste.

REVIEW QUESTIONS

1. What are some of the common features found in all Office XP applications?
2. What tools can you use to get help or search for additional information?
3. What is the Task Pane window used for?
4. What are smart tag buttons and when do you have access to them? Give an example of one.
5. What are the four basic applications that are included as part of all versions of Office XP?

MATCHING

Match the term with the related definition.

1. _____ Access 2002
2. _____ Clipboard
3. _____ Excel 2002
4. _____ Formatting toolbar
5. _____ PowerPoint 2002
6. _____ Standard toolbar
7. _____ Task pane
8. _____ Word 2002

a. A temporary storage location for up to 24 items of selected text that has been cut or copied.
b. Collection of buttons that allows you to change the appearance of text, such as bold, italicize, or underline.
c. Collection of buttons that contains the popular icons such as Cut, Copy, and Paste.
d. Electronic spreadsheet tool that can be used to input, organize, calculate, analyze, and display business data.
e. General-purpose word-processing tool that allows users to create primarily text-based documents.
f. A popular presentation tool that allows users to create overhead transparencies and powerful multimedia slide shows.
g. Relational database tool that can be used to collect, organize, and retrieve large amounts of data.
h. This window allows you to access important tasks from a single, convenient location, while still working on your document.

www.mhhe.com/i-series

OFF 1.13

OFFICE

NOTES

www.mhhe.com/i-series

NOTES

www.mhhe.com/i-series

OFFICE

NOTES

NOTES

www.mhhe.com/i-series

OFFICE

NOTES

www.mhhe.com/i-series

did you know?

between the years of 1999 and 2001 computer crime quadrupled according to a survey by the FBI and San Francisco's Computer Security Institute.

more than 1,200 computer viruses are in circulation.

the first automobile to cross the United States took 52 days in 1903 to travel from San Francisco to New York.

there are more than 200 satellites orbiting earth solely for the purpose of private communications services, including pagers, telephones, and computers.

penicillin causes about 300 deaths in the United States every year.

POTUS is an acronym for _____ .

Chapter Objectives

- Open an existing presentation
- Update and save an existing presentation—PPT2002-1-2
- Create and save a new presentation—PPT2002-1-1
- Use the AutoContent wizard—PPT2002-1-1
- Reorganize a presentation—PPT2002-1-2 and PPT2002-4-8
- Use a Design template to create a new presentation and update an existing presentation—PPT2002-1-1
- Add and format slide text—PPT2002-2-2

CHAPTER

1

one

Presentation Basics

chapter case

Teaching Speech Students to Use Presentation Graphics

Victoria Faust has been an Information Technology (IT) instructor at Merrillville College for the past 10 years. Since Merrillville is a small school, Victoria is the only full-time faculty member teaching programming languages. She also holds seminars each semester for faculty who want to learn to use technology in their classrooms. Common topics include how to build Web sites to support instruction, using spreadsheets, and presentation graphics.

The college's Speech instructor, Carol Hough, attended one of the seminars on using PowerPoint in the classroom and decided that not only should she use PowerPoint when presenting to her students, but that her students should use PowerPoint in at least one of their speeches. Since Carol was not comfortable teaching technology, she asked Victoria to provide PowerPoint instruction to 200 Speech 101 students.

After meeting again, Victoria and Carol want to start small with three sections of Speech 101 students learning to use PowerPoint in only one speech. Carol needs the time to develop her PowerPoint skills and get comfortable with grading speeches that use technology. Victoria can't possibly meet with all eight sections of Speech 101 to provide PowerPoint instruction and still meet the demands of her own teaching load.

Victoria believes that the students will need two 30-minute presentations. The first presenta-

FIGURE 1.1
Features of PowerPoint

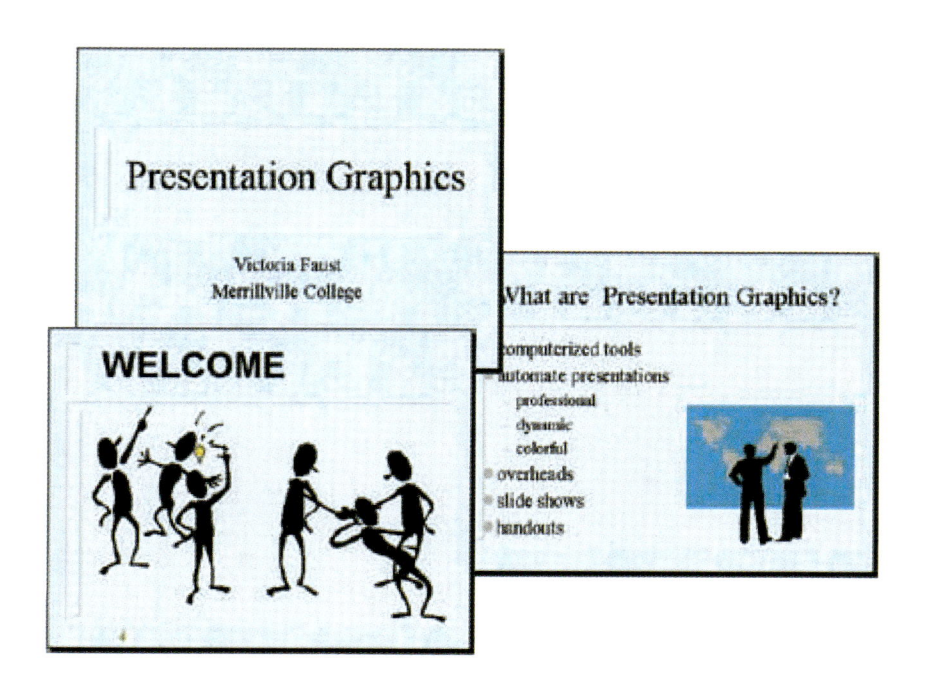

tion will outline the capabilities of PowerPoint and how to effectively use it when presenting. The second will provide instruction on how to build simple PowerPoint presentations. The first presentation should take place when the speech is assigned and the second about a week before students will be required to present.

Victoria's first presentation can use an adaptation of a PowerPoint slide show that she created for the instructional technology seminars. She believes that the second presentation should be developed from scratch, since her current materials are not geared toward a student audience.

You are Victoria's teaching assistant and have been asked to review and update the existing PowerPoint slide show.

SESSION 1.1 INTRODUCTION TO PRESENTATION GRAPHICS

PowerPoint is a full-featured presentation graphics application capable of creating dynamic slide shows. Slide shows can contain audio, video, graphics, and be fully interactive. The screens can be projected, printed, converted into overheads, or published on the Web. Presentations can be delivered by a speaker, displayed in a self-running kiosk, or published as Web pages with threaded discussions.

Ancillary PowerPoint output includes Web pages, online meetings, audience handouts, meeting notes, presentation outlines, and speaker's notes. Using presentation graphics greatly enhances the professionalism and delivery of most presentation content. PowerPoint can be used to sell a product or idea, present financial or other information, document a meeting, report project status, or educate.

GETTING STARTED WITH POWERPOINT

Like all Office products PowerPoint can be opened from the Start menu, or by opening a PowerPoint document directly. When a PowerPoint document is double-clicked in Windows Explorer, PowerPoint is launched and then the file is loaded with no further user action.

CHAPTER OUTLINE

1.1 Introduction to Presentation Graphics

1.2 Creating a New Presentation

Starting PowerPoint:

1. Verify that Windows has loaded and is ready to launch programs
2. Click the **Start** button on the taskbar, point to **Programs,** and then select **Microsoft PowerPoint** from the Programs menu

PP 1.4   CHAPTER 1 **POWERPOINT**   1.1 Introduction To Presentation Graphics

FIGURE 1.2
Launching PowerPoint from the Start Menu

tip: *Your screen may appear slightly different from what is depicted due to the operating system and software installed*

If Microsoft PowerPoint is not listed in your Programs menu, you will need to either install PowerPoint or seek technical assistance

3. After a short pause, the Microsoft PowerPoint copyright information is displayed on the screen and then the Microsoft PowerPoint window displays

FIGURE 1.3
The Microsoft PowerPoint Window

tip: *The specific files listed in the Open a presentation list will reflect presentation files loaded on your system*

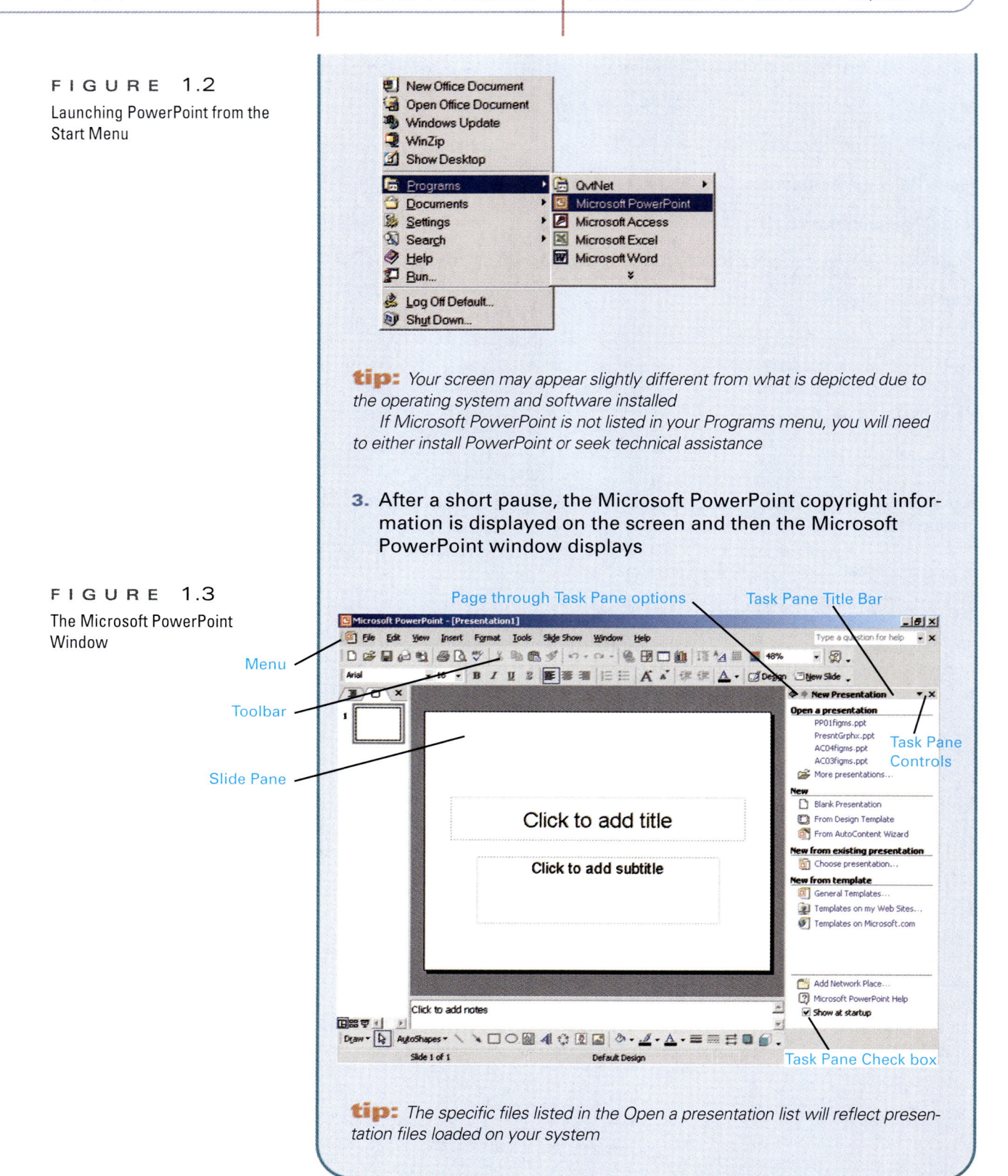

Like all Microsoft Office 2002 applications the PowerPoint opening page contains a menu, a toolbar, an edit area (called the Slide Pane), and a Task Pane. The most commonly used operations are listed in the **Task Pane** on the right hand side of the screen. The initial Task pane options for opening a presentation include opening an existing file, creating a new blank presentation file, using an existing presentation file as the foundation of a new presentation, or using one of Microsoft's templates. The last option in the Task Pane is a check box that will set the Task Pane so that it does not show each time PowerPoint loads. When the Task Pane is not helpful, it can be closed using the close button in its title bar. A closed Task pane will reopen when any menu option requiring it for completion is selected. For example, clicking the File menu and selecting Open will display the Task pane allowing the user to select how to open the new file. Clicking the New button on the toolbar will also open the Task pane.

Opening an Existing Presentation

You have met with Victoria and discussed some changes that need to be made to repurpose the existing presentation. You will begin your review of Victoria's existing presentation by opening it in PowerPoint.

---

task reference

Opening a PowerPoint Presentation:

- If the presentation you would like to open is listed in the Open a presentation list of the Task pane, click it

  or

- If your presentation is not listed, click **More presentations** in the Open a presentation list of the Task pane

  - Navigate to the drive and folder containing your presentation
  - Select the presentation and click **Open**

Opening the PresntGrphx.ppt presentation:

1. Make sure that you have placed your copy of the data disk for this course in the proper drive and that PowerPoint is already open. Instructions for creating the data disk can be found at www.mhhe.com/i-series

2. The presentation files displayed in the Open a new presentation list of the PowerPoint Task Pane are those that have been accessed on your computer most recently

3. If the **PP01PresntGrphx.ppt** presentation does not display, click the More presentations option in the Task Pane to display a standard Open file dialog box

   tip: *The file extension (.ppt) may not display on your computer. The display of file extensions is controlled by your Windows setup*

4. Click the Look in drop-down arrow and select the drive containing your data disk. Find the materials for PowerPoint Chapter 1 and select the **PP01PresntGrphx.ppt** file

FIGURE 1.4

Microsoft PowerPoint Open Dialog Box

- Select the drive
- Controls how the files display
- A preview displays if the Preview view is selected

tip: The Open dialog box will display the files from My Documents on your computer so the files and folders displayed will be different on each computer

FIGURE 1.5

PP01PresntGrphx.ppt opened in PowerPoint

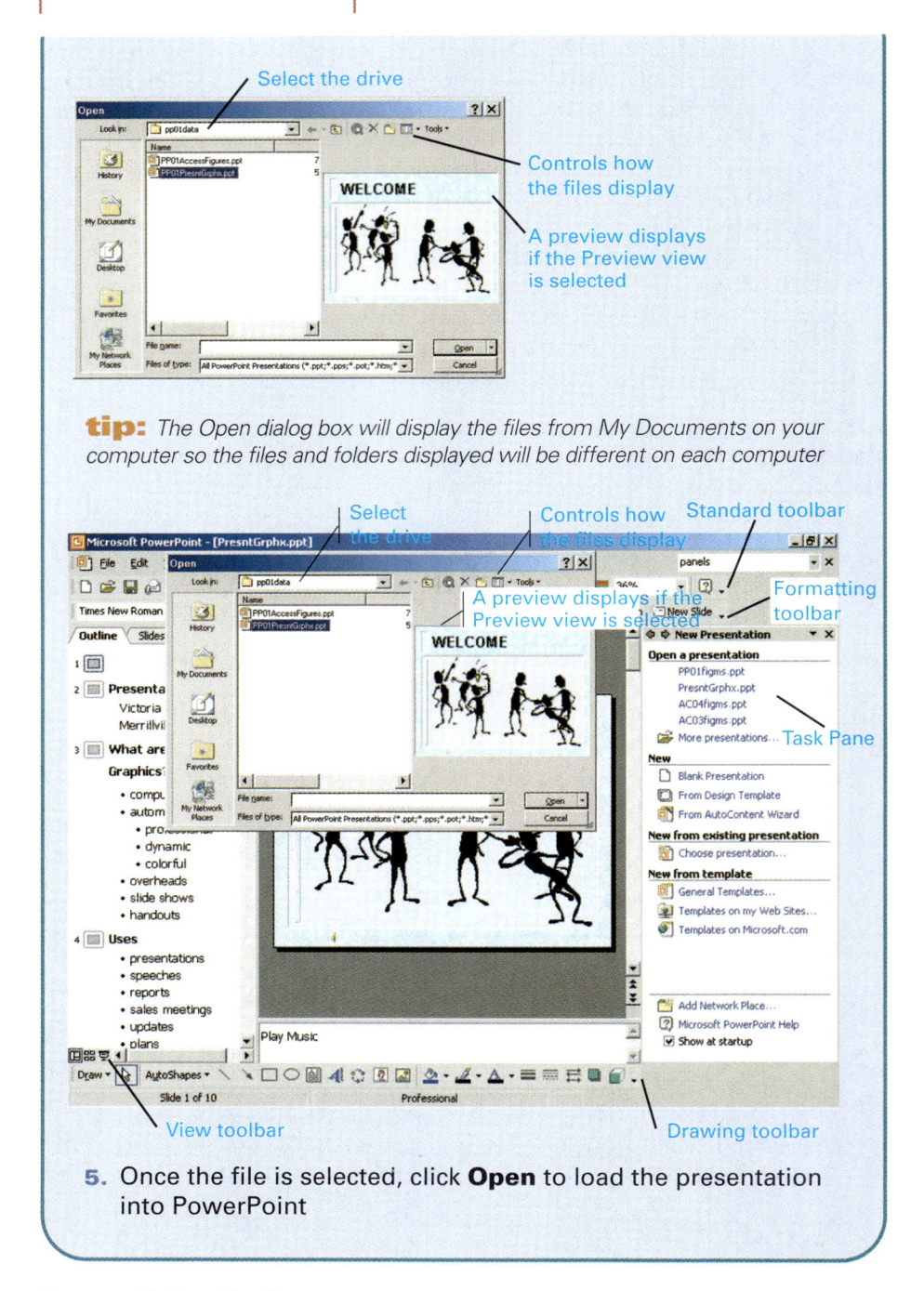

- Select the drive
- Controls how the files display
- Standard toolbar
- A preview displays if the Preview view is selected
- Formatting toolbar
- Task Pane
- View toolbar
- Drawing toolbar

5. Once the file is selected, click **Open** to load the presentation into PowerPoint

PowerPoint Toolbars

PowerPoint opens with several toolbars available as shown in Figure 1.5. A *toolbar* is a horizontal or vertical ribbon of icons that provides shortcuts. Pausing the mouse pointer over a toolbar icon will darken the button and display a Screen Tip. *Screen Tips* show information about the screen element that is being pointed to.

Many of the toolbar options are the same across all Windows applications. For example, most of the options of the Standard toolbar (New, Open, Save, e-mail, Search, Print, Print Preview, Spell check, Cut, Copy, Paste, Undo, and Redo) are seen in all standard Windows products. There are also options that are specific to PowerPoint like the New Slide button on the Formatting Toolbar.

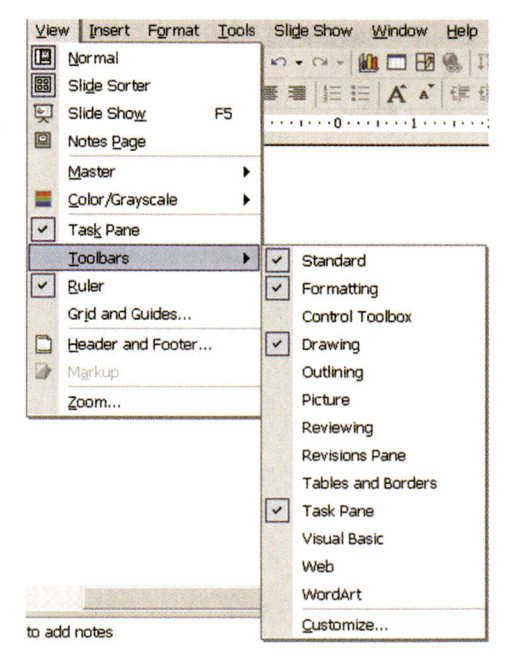

The names of the toolbars describe what they do. The ***Standard toolbar*** has options that are used across all Windows applications like Save. The ***Formatting toolbar*** is used to format text and slides. It contains options for font and point sizes, character formats, text alignment, slide design, and so on. The ***Drawing toolbar*** provides tools for adding artwork to a presentation using text, shapes, WordArt, pictures, and more. The ***View toolbar*** allows you to easily move between PowerPoint views (views are covered later).

Use the Toolbars option of the View menu to control what toolbars display. Notice in Figure 1.6 that the Task Pane is controlled from the Toolbars menu also. Toolbars can either float or anchor. A floating toolbar appears in its own window and "floats" above your work. You can move it by dragging its title bar. An anchored toolbar is "fastened" to one of the edges of a window. Floating toolbars can be anchored by dragging them to an edge of the window. Anchored toolbars (like Standard and Formatting) can be made to float by clicking and dragging on a button divider (the vertical line that separates groups of buttons). Although PowerPoint has a standard look when it is first loaded on a machine, the interface can be customized to suit the user without impacting the overall functionality of the application.

Now that you have a presentation open and an understanding of the toolbars, you can explore the PowerPoint window and understand how the various panes function.

FIGURE 1.6
The Toolbars Option of the View Menu

UNDERSTANDING THE PRESENTATION WINDOW

The PowerPoint Window is made up of a series of panes. Each ***pane*** is a window within PowerPoint that supports a common user operation. The pane(s) that display are controlled by user preferences and the active ***View***.

Exploring Normal View Panes

Unless PowerPoint has been customized, ***Normal view*** is the startup view. Normal view is the main editing view used to develop presentations and contains four panes. Take a look at Figure 1.7 to see the Normal view containing the Outline pane, Slide pane, Notes pane, and the Task pane.

The ***Outline pane*** contains two tabs, the ***Outline tab*** and the ***Slides tab.*** The Outline tab displays an outline of the current presentation consisting of the titles and text from each slide. Besides displaying the flow of a presentation, the Outline tab can be used to make corrections to text, add new text, and rearrange existing text. The Slides tab displays the slides of the slide show as thumbnail-sized images. Thumbnails make it easier to navigate through a presentation and to evaluate the effects of design changes. Using thumbnails, slides can be rearranged, added, or deleted. When the pane is narrowed, the tab names become icons and the thumb-

FIGURE 1.7
PowerPoint Normal View

Outline and Slides tabs of the Outline pane

Splitter bar—drag to adjust pane size

Notes pane for speaker's notes

Slide pane for editing graphics and text

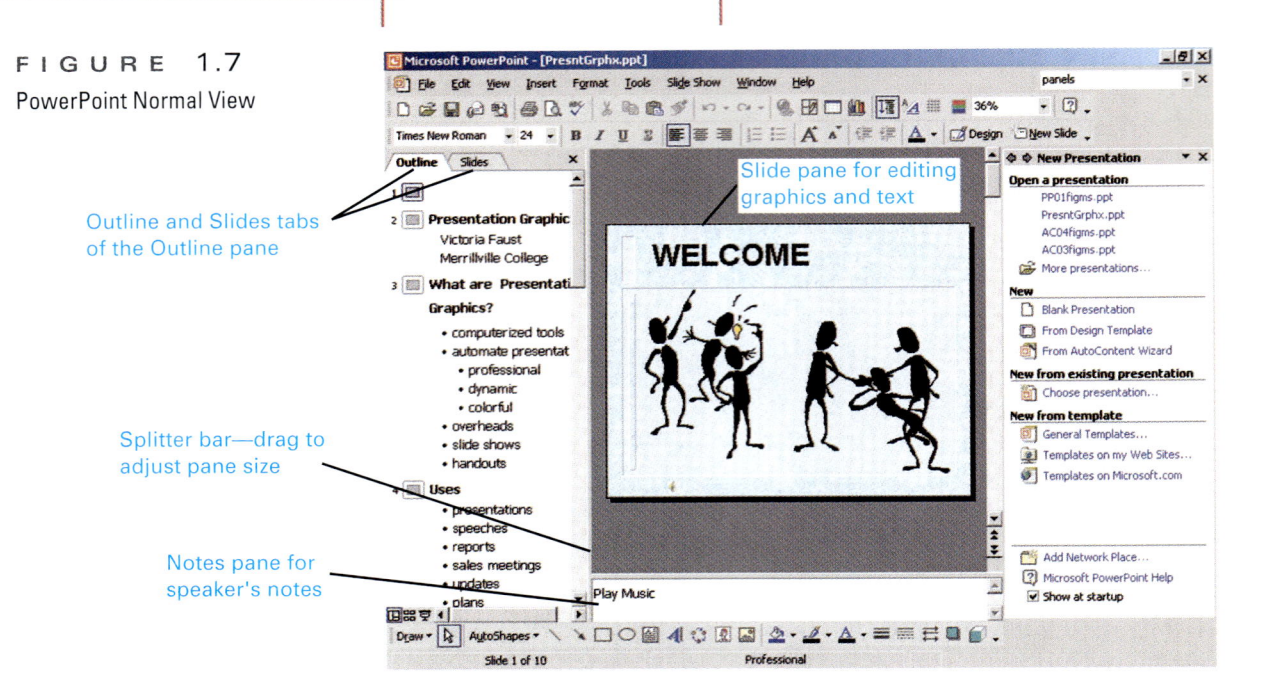

nails reduce in size. Conversely, widening the panes brings back the tab names and increases the size of the thumbnails. Since the Outline pane is a window, it can be closed using the button at the top right.

The **Slide pane** displays one slide as it will appear during the slide show. All text and graphics display and can be edited. As was just mentioned, text can also be edited in the Outline pane. The Slide pane is the only place to add, edit, and customize graphic and media elements of a presentation. Graphic and media elements that can be placed on a slide include tables, charts, drawing objects, text boxes, movies, sounds, hyperlinks, and animations.

The **Notes pane** allows the entry of text that will not display as part of the presentation. This facility is normally used to record speaker's notes but can hold any type of notation. For example, Figure 1.7 shows "Play Music" in the speaker's notes because the slide contains an audio element that the speaker needs to initiate before speaking about the slide content. Notes can be printed for the speaker, used as audience notes, or placed on a Web page.

The size of each pane can be adjusted by dragging the pane borders. Other views are available with different panes, but the same concepts apply.

PowerPoint 2002 Task Panels

Microsoft Office 2002 uses a Task pane window to present options to the user. The PowerPoint Task pane includes multiple Task panels. The display of the Task panel will vary in response to user activity. Separate Task panel panes are designed to help users create a new presentation, select a slide layout, choose a design template, pick animation elements of a presentation, control how slides move on and off the screen, search for files, and copy multiple items at once.

The displayed Task panel changes as the user selects menu options or toolbar buttons. The down arrow in the Task pane title bar allows a knowledgeable user to navigate directly to the appropriate Task pane panel. The left and right arrow buttons in the title bar of the Task pane will move between the most recently used task panes. The down arrow will open a menu used to select the appropriate Task pane panel. The close button will remove the Task pane until it is needed to complete a user request or it is specifically opened from the View menu.

The operations contained in each Task pane panel will be covered as you modify and build presentations.

Exploring Views

Microsoft PowerPoint has three main views used during presentation development. The View used is determined by the task at hand and personal preferences. Normal view, the default opening view consisting of the Outline, Slides, and Notes panes, has already been explored. Normal view panes are designed for writing and editing a presentation. The Task pane displays with *all* PowerPoint views.

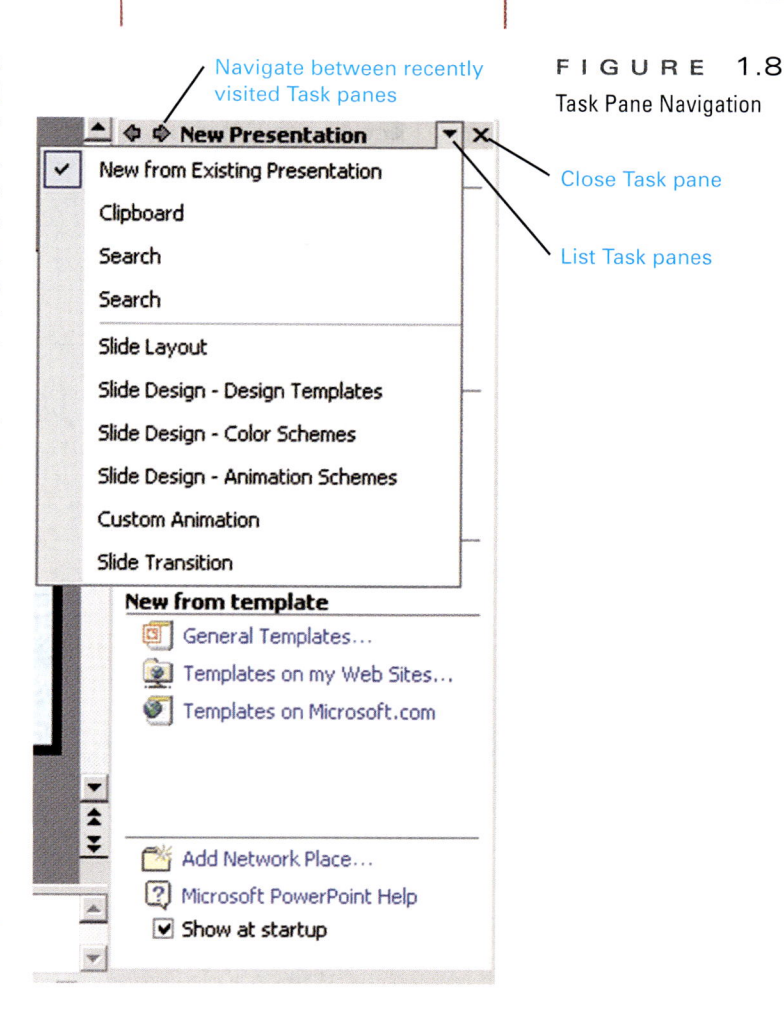

FIGURE 1.8
Task Pane Navigation

As its name implies, **Slide sorter view** is designed to simplify the reorganization of an existing presentation. The view consists of thumbnails of each presentation slide. Using drag and drop, the slides of a presentation are placed in a new order. Slide sorter view can also be used to preview transition and animation effects, but is not effective for editing presentation text and graphic content.

Slide show view is used to preview the presentation. Each slide fills the presentation screen so that developer can see the presentation the way the audience will—including animations and transitions. No editing is possible in this view.

NAVIGATING A PRESENTATION

Regardless of the view being used, slide navigation is critical. In Normal view, navigation can be applied to move between slides or from object to object on a single slide to allow content edits. When previewing a presentation in Slide show view navigation is more restricted, providing movement forward one slide, backward one slide, and to a specific slide in the slide show, but not to a slide object such as title text.

Normal View Navigation

When creating and editing a presentation, Normal view will be used to move between slides and from object to object within a slide.

PP 1.10 | CHAPTER 1 **POWERPOINT** | **1.1** Introduction To Presentation Graphics

FIGURE 1.9
Slide Sorter View

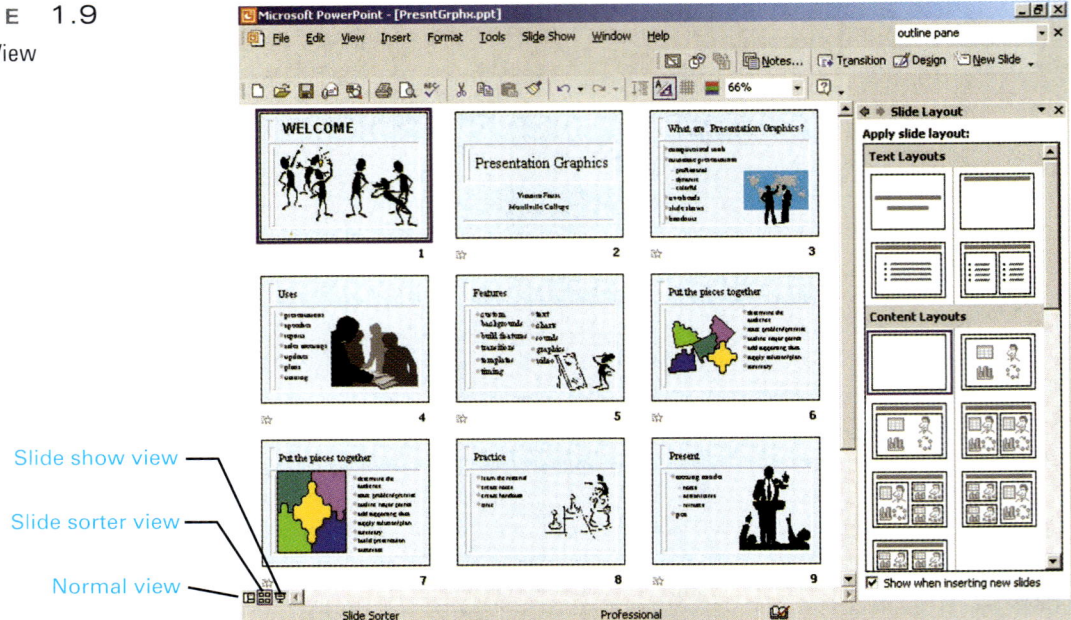

Slide show view
Slide sorter view
Normal view

task reference
Navigating in Normal View:
- Go to next slide—Using the Outline pane, click in the next slide's outline or icon
- Go to a specific slide—Using the Slides pane, drag the scrollbox until the Screen Tips show the desired slide
- Move one slide at a time—Use the Next and Previous buttons at the bottom of the Slides pane scrollbar

Moving around in PresntGrphx.ppt presentation:

1. Verify that PowerPoint is running and that the **PP01PresntGrphx.ppt** presentation is open

2. Verify that the presentation is in **Normal** view

   tip: *If you are not sure that the presentation is in Normal view, click the Normal view button on the View toolbar (see Figure 1.9)*

3. Use the Slides pane scrollbox to move to slide **9** (see Figure 1.10)

4. Click in the Slides pane scrollbar (between the scrollbox and arrows) to move one screen at a time to slide **6**

5. Click the **Slides** tab of the Outline pane. Use the Slides tab of the Outline pane to move to Slide **1**

6. In the Outline pane, click on the **Outline** tab. Drag the right border of the Outline pane to widen it

www.mhhe.com/i-series   PP 1.11

FIGURE 1.10

Normal View Navigation

Click to move up one slide

Drag scrollbox, Screen tip displays slide number and title

Click to move down one slide

Previous slide

Next slide

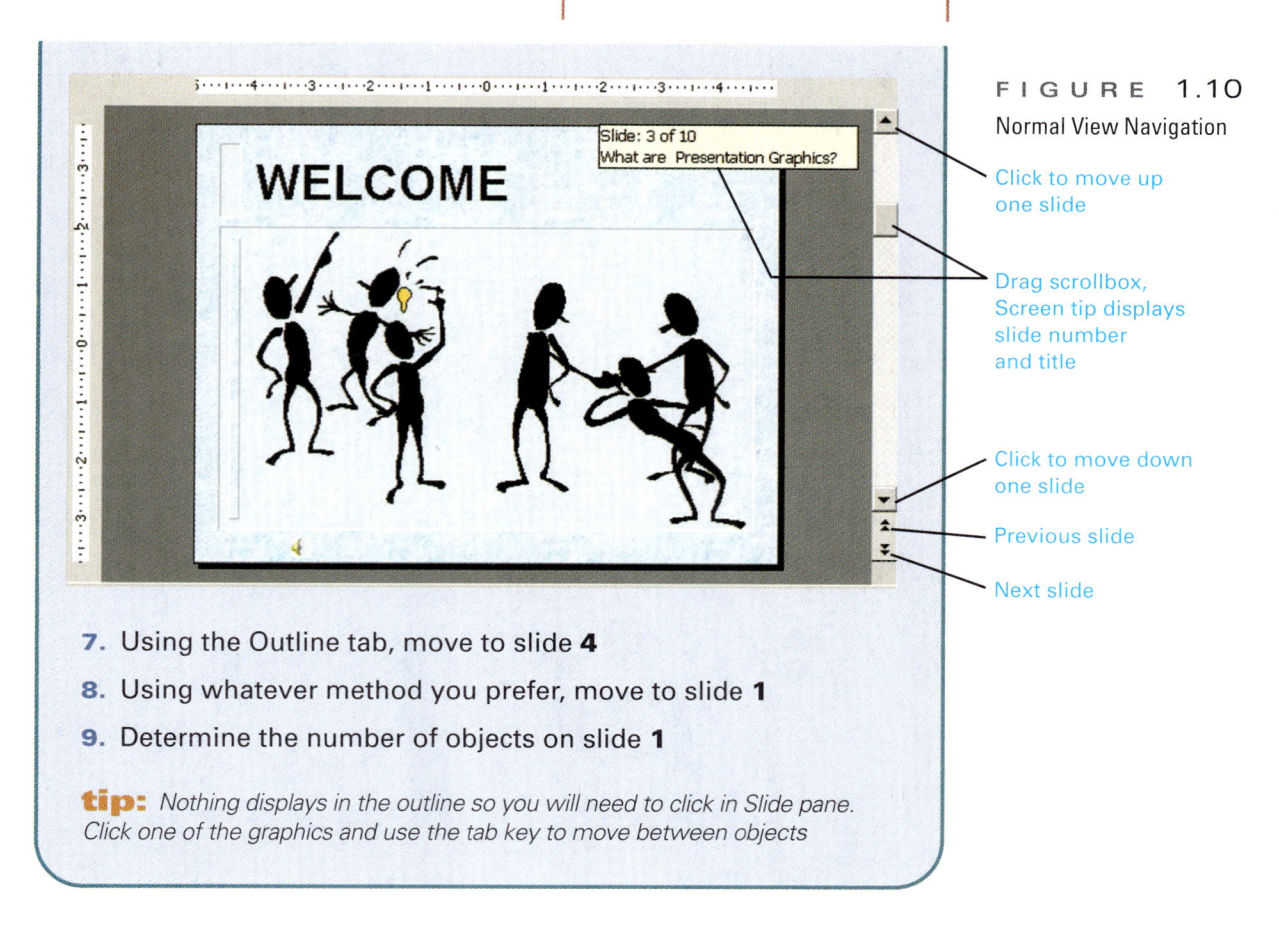

7. Using the Outline tab, move to slide **4**
8. Using whatever method you prefer, move to slide **1**
9. Determine the number of objects on slide **1**

tip: *Nothing displays in the outline so you will need to click in Slide pane. Click one of the graphics and use the tab key to move between objects*

Step 9 was intended to introduce the objects used to create slide content. Each text element is an object as is each graphic and media element. Slide 1 of PP01PresntGrphx.ppt contains seven objects. The Welcome text is one object, the audio indicator (the stereo speaker at the bottom) is another object, and there are five beanie objects. The left group of beanies is actually three separate graphics, and the right grouping is two different graphics. Did you find them all?

Slide Show View Navigation

Slide show view is a full-screen preview of a presentation with no Task pane or Windows Taskbar available. Keyboard shortcuts like Alt+Tab can still be used to move between application windows. The active slide (not the first presentation slide) will be the first to display when Slide show view initiates. Navigation from slide to slide is most commonly accomplished using the mouse, but the keyboard, shortcut menus, and the slide navigation button can also be used.

task reference

Navigating in Slide Show View:

- Go to next slide—click the mouse
- Go to the previous slide—Press **Backspace**
- Go to a specific slide—Type the slide number and press **Enter**
- End the slide show—**Esc**

POWERPOINT

PP 1.12   CHAPTER 1 **POWERPOINT**   **1.1** Introduction To Presentation Graphics

FIGURE 1.11
Opening PP01PresntGrphx.ppt Slide

Using Slide show view with the PresntGrphx.ppt presentation:

1. Verify that PowerPoint is running and that the **PP01PresntGrphx.ppt** presentation is open
2. Make the first presentation slide the active slide, if it is not already
3. Click the **Slide show view** button in the View toolbar below the Outline pane

Audio
Navigation button

4. Click the speaker icon to hear the audio
5. Click the mouse to move to the next slide
6. Continue clicking until you are on the Uses slide

tip: *The way that each slide appears on the screen is a transition. The way that text appears on the screen is an animation*

7. Use the **backspace** key to move to the previous slide
8. Continue clicking through to The End slide
9. Type **3** and press **Enter** to move to slide 3
10. Click the **Navigation** icon at the bottom left of the slide (you can also right-click the slide) to open the shortcut menu. Test the **Next, Previous,** and **Go** options
11. Press **Esc** to end the slide show

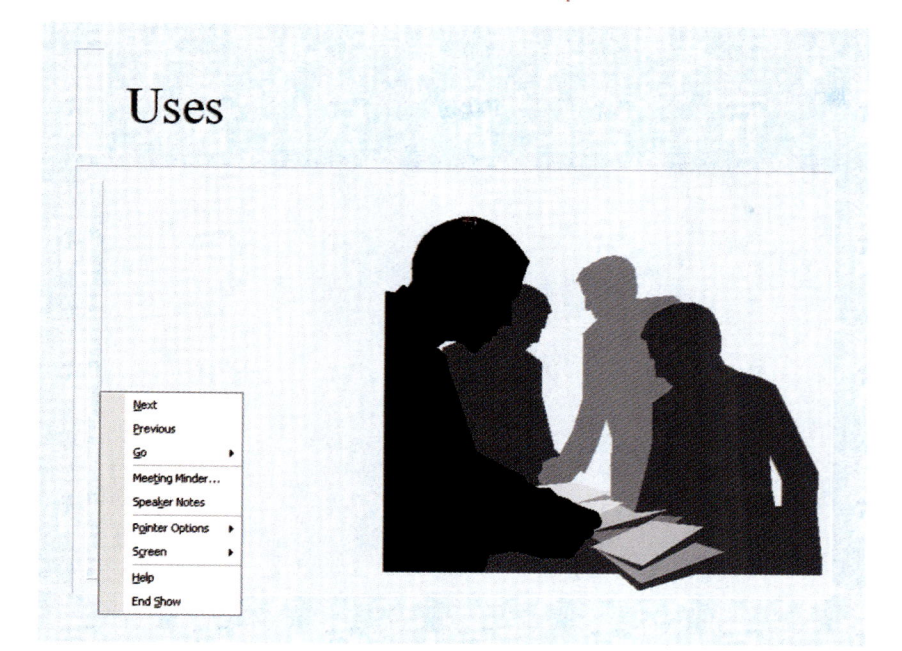

FIGURE 1.12
The Shortcut Menu

Most slides consist of a title, bulleted topics, and graphics. Bulleted lists help the speaker and the audience stay on track. Transitions are the way the slides enter and leave the screen, and animations control how text is introduced. These elements constitute the most common PowerPoint features.

UPDATING AND SAVING A PRESENTATION

Now that you have reviewed Victoria's presentation, it is time to make some modifications so it will better fit its new purpose. Remember that the Outline pane is most effective for making changes to presentation text, and the Slide pane can be used to update any slide element.

Using the Outline Pane

It is common to need to rearrange and delete slides in your presentation. Extra slides can be the result of using a wizard, repurposing a presentation, or changes in the design. The Outline pane is ideal for reorganizing slides.

Modifying the PresntGrphx.ppt presentation using the Outline pane:

1. Verify that PowerPoint is running and that the **PP01PresntGrphx.ppt** presentation is open
2. Verify that the presentation is in Normal view
3. Make slide 10 the active slide
4. In the Outline pane click and drag the icon for slide 10 until the position indicator line is before slide 9

FIGURE 1.13

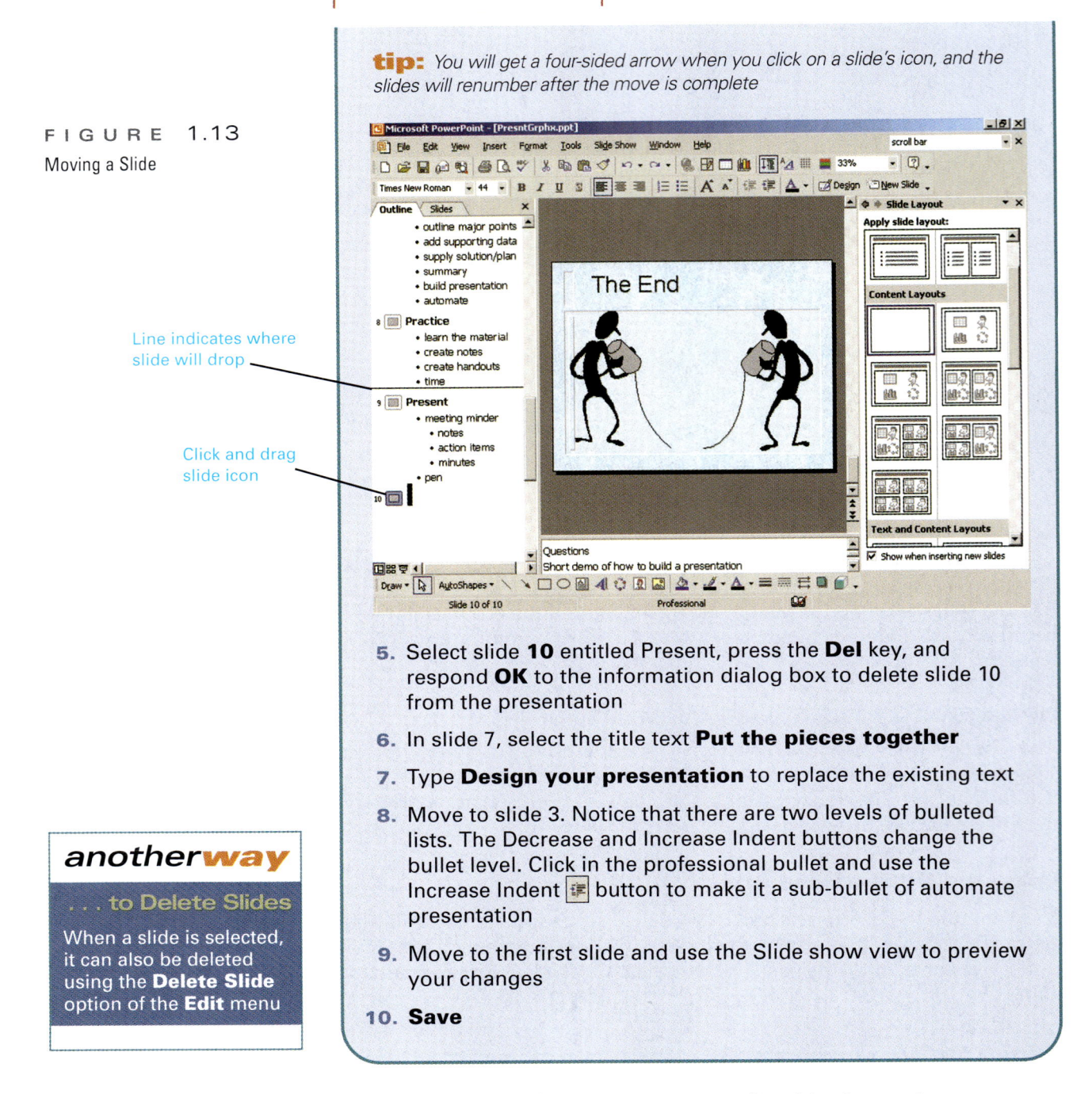

Moving a Slide

Line indicates where slide will drop

Click and drag slide icon

tip: *You will get a four-sided arrow when you click on a slide's icon, and the slides will renumber after the move is complete*

5. Select slide **10** entitled Present, press the **Del** key, and respond **OK** to the information dialog box to delete slide 10 from the presentation

6. In slide 7, select the title text **Put the pieces together**

7. Type **Design your presentation** to replace the existing text

8. Move to slide 3. Notice that there are two levels of bulleted lists. The Decrease and Increase Indent buttons change the bullet level. Click in the professional bullet and use the Increase Indent button to make it a sub-bullet of automate presentation

9. Move to the first slide and use the Slide show view to preview your changes

10. **Save**

another way

. . . to Delete Slides

When a slide is selected, it can also be deleted using the **Delete Slide** option of the **Edit** menu

To accomplish the reorganization outlined in the previous steps, you could also have simply deleted the extra slide.

Using the Slide Pane

The Slide pane can also be used to edit and delete slides, but not to change the order of slides in a presentation. To delete a slide all you need to do is make the slide your active slide and then press the Del key. To edit slide text, select it and overtype with the new text. The clipboard can be used to cut, copy, and paste text between slides.

Modifying the PresntGrphx.ppt presentation using the Slide pane:

1. Verify that PowerPoint is running and that the **PP01PresntGrphx.ppt** presentation is open
2. Verify that the presentation is in Normal view
3. In slide **9,** click on The End to open that text box
4. Click and drag to select **The End**
5. Type **Questions?** to replace the existing text
6. Move to slide 6
7. Select the title text, Put the pieces together, and overtype it with **Design your presentation**
8. Make slide 8 the active slide

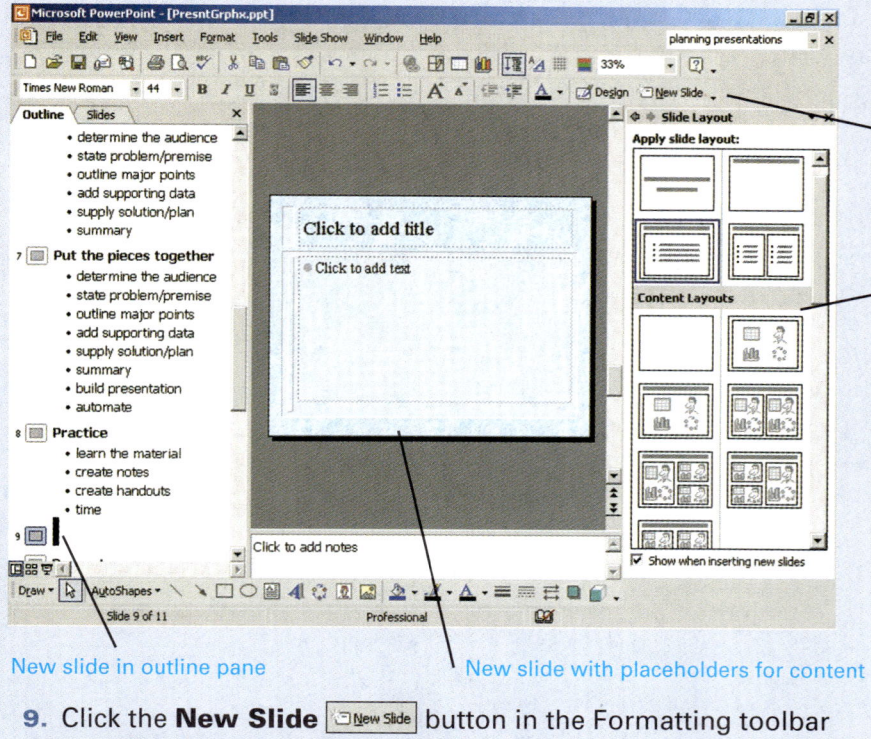

FIGURE 1.14
Inserting a New Slide

New slide in outline pane

New slide with placeholders for content

Insert new slide

Slide layout options

9. Click the **New Slide** button in the Formatting toolbar to add a new blank slide
10. Click in the title placeholder and type **Presentation Guidelines**
11. Click into the bulleted list placeholder and enter the following list

    • One topic/idea per screen

    —Less than 30 words/screen

    —6 words X 7 bullets

    • About 3 min./slide

    • Guide speaker and audience

> **tip:** Use the Increase Indent and Decrease Indent buttons on the toolbar to change the level of bullet indention. The bullets need not match those shown here; you will learn to set custom bullets later
>
> 12. Move to the first slide and use the Slide show view, preview your changes, and **Save** your work

The **Undo** button of the Standard toolbar can be used to correct many mistakes made while editing. The **Redo** button will repeat an undone action. Up to 20 actions listed from the most recent to the least recent are listed in the Undo drop-down list. When an action from the drop-down list is selected, that action and the actions above it on the list will be undone. That means that the fourth action in the list cannot be undone without also undoing the first, second, and third actions.

> ### Using Undo and Redo in the Slide pane:
>
> 1. Verify that PowerPoint is running and that the **PP01PresntGrphx.ppt** presentation is open
> 2. Verify that the presentation is in Normal view
> 3. In slide 3, select and delete the overheads bullet
> 4. In slide 2, add the text **Edited by <yourname>** on a new line after Merrillville College

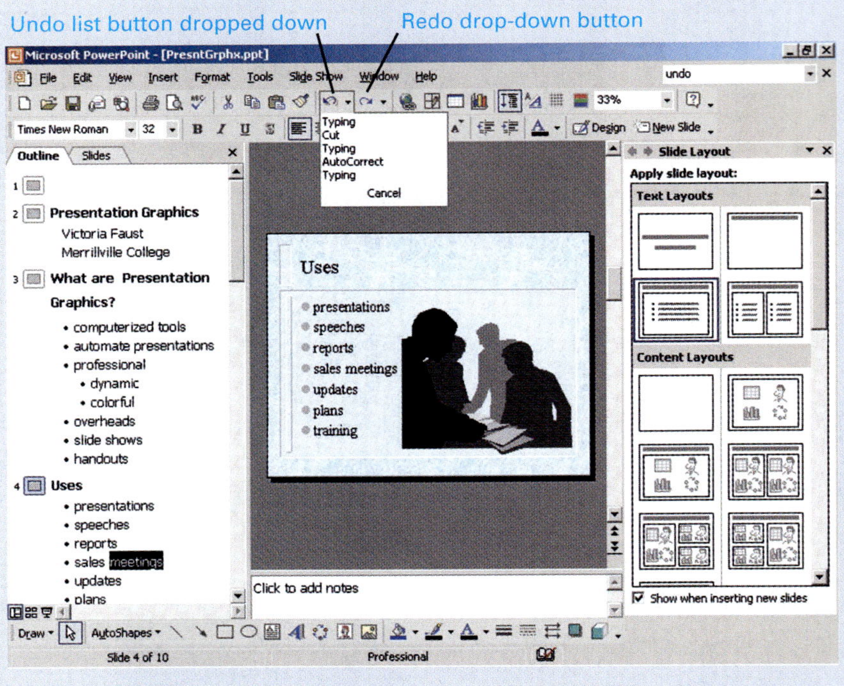

FIGURE 1.15
Undo and Redo Buttons

> 5. Move to slide 6; select and delete the summary bullet

6. Choose the Undo option that will undo all of the changes you have made in this series of steps

tip: *Your undo list will reflect the last 20 edits that you have made during your current session*

7. Verify that the undo was successful
8. Use the Redo button to reinstate all of your changes
9. Verify that the redo was successful

Although Undo and Redo were demonstrated from the Slide pane, it also is effective on changes made in the Outline pane and the Notes pane. Reorganizations applied to slides in Slide Sorter view can also be undone.

Understanding File Management

When an existing PowerPoint file is opened, a copy of that file is created in the computer's memory. Changes made to the presentation are stored in the computer's memory. A new PowerPoint presentation exists only in the computer's memory until it is saved to an auxiliary storage medium like a hard drive or diskette.

Using the Save command of the File menu with a previously existing presentation will store any changes over the original file. This is equivalent to clicking the Save button on the Standard toolbar. Using the Save command of the File menu with a new presentation will initiate the Save As command, since PowerPoint does not have a filename and location for the save operation. Using the Save As option of the File menu will allow the name and/or location of the file to be changed without updating the original file.

To effectively find and use PowerPoint presentations, files must be organized into folders. Windows folders can be created before a presentation is saved or as part of the save process. All files needed to run a presentation should be stored in the same folder. For example, large sound files are not stored as part of the presentation, but should be placed into the presentation folder for organization, since they are needed for the presentation to run.

Saving your changes:

1. Verify that PowerPoint is running and that the **PP01PresntGrphx.ppt** presentation is open
2. Verify that the presentation is in Normal view
3. Select the **Save As** option of the **File** menu so that you can save the file with a new name
4. Choose the drive and folder for your file
5. Click the **Create New Folder** button, name the new folder **pp01**, and click **OK**

FIGURE 1.16

Save As Dialog Box

- Select the drive and folder where the file will be stored
- List of files in the current folder
- Format for the file to be saved
- Create New Folder
- The name of the file to be saved

6. Change the filename to **<yourname>PP01PresntGrphx.ppt** and click the **Save** button

tip: The files listed in your Save As dialog box will reflect the drives, folders, and files on your computer

7. Now clicking the **Save** on the toolbar will save your changes to this file

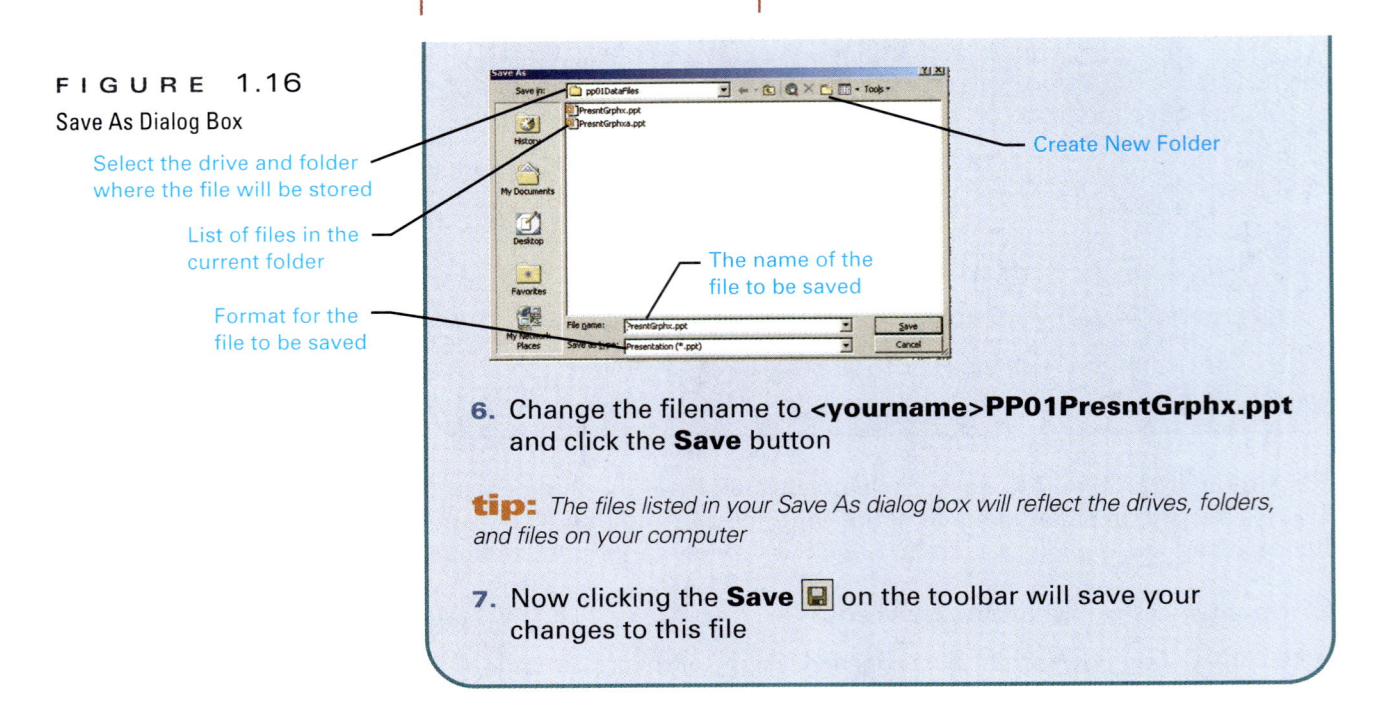

anotherword
...on Saving Files

PowerPoint automatically saves presentations for recovery in case the program locks up. The AutoRecover settings determine the frequency and location of these backups. You can adjust these settings from the **Save** tab of the **Tools/Options** menu. When PowerPoint is not shut down properly, any AutoRecover files will be displayed in the Task pane the next time PowerPoint is opened.

The Save as type list of the Save As dialog box will allow a presentation to be saved in the format of previous PowerPoint versions and in other formats like Web pages. Just as PowerPoint presentations can be saved in different formats, files from other Office applications can also be opened in PowerPoint. PowerPoint uses converters to change the files into a presentation.

Windows file management options like copying, renaming, and deleting files can be accomplished in either the Open or Save dialog boxes. In either dialog box, right-clicking on a file will display a pop-up menu of available operations. The restriction is that an open file cannot be deleted or renamed.

SESSION 1.1 making the grade

1. Describe how PowerPoint is useful.
2. How do you run a PowerPoint presentation?
3. Describe the use of the Undo and Redo buttons.
4. How are the Outline and Slide panes of Normal view used?

SESSION 1.2 CREATING A NEW PRESENTATION

Now it's time to get started on Victoria's second presentation. This is to be a 30-minute presentation on how to use PowerPoint that will be planned and created from scratch.

CREATING A BLANK PRESENTATION

When creating a new presentation in Microsoft PowerPoint, it is important to have a basic design in mind. Presentations are most effective when the audience and purpose are carefully considered.

Select backgrounds and colors suited to the audience, message, and presentation method. In general, use a consistent color scheme and slide layout. Each slide should contain 30 or fewer words. Use at most seven bullets per slide with each bullet containing between one and six words. Plan to create one slide for every two to three minutes of the presentation. When laying out a presentation consider the following:

- Purpose
  - Inform?
  - Educate?
  - Stimulate discussion?
- Who is the audience?
  - What is the size of the audience?
  - What color and layout preferences do they have?
  - What styles of graphics are appropriate?
- Where will the presentation take place?
  - Small room?
  - Large room?
  - With overheads? projector? handouts?
- What is the presentation format?
  - Speaker presentation?
  - Self-running slide show or kiosk?
  - Web pages?
- Are there any special needs to effectively communicate the content of the presentation?

A new presentation can be created using the AutoContent wizard, a design template, or by opening a blank presentation. The **AutoContent wizard** contains a group of templates with suggested presentation content and can be the fastest way to develop new presentations. **Design templates** contain background, color, and animation templates that can be applied to your presentation. A **blank presentation** opens with a slide containing layout designs with no color, backgrounds, or animations.

Let's start by taking a look at a blank presentation to make the features of the other options more apparent. The Task pane is an ideal place to open a new presentation.

Opening a blank presentation:

1. Start PowerPoint if it is not already running

2. Use the **Task Pane** option of the **View** menu to activate the Task pane if it is not displaying

3. If the New Presentation Task pane is not displaying, activate it by selecting **New Presentation** in the Task pane drop-down list

FIGURE 1.17
Task Pane Drop-Down List

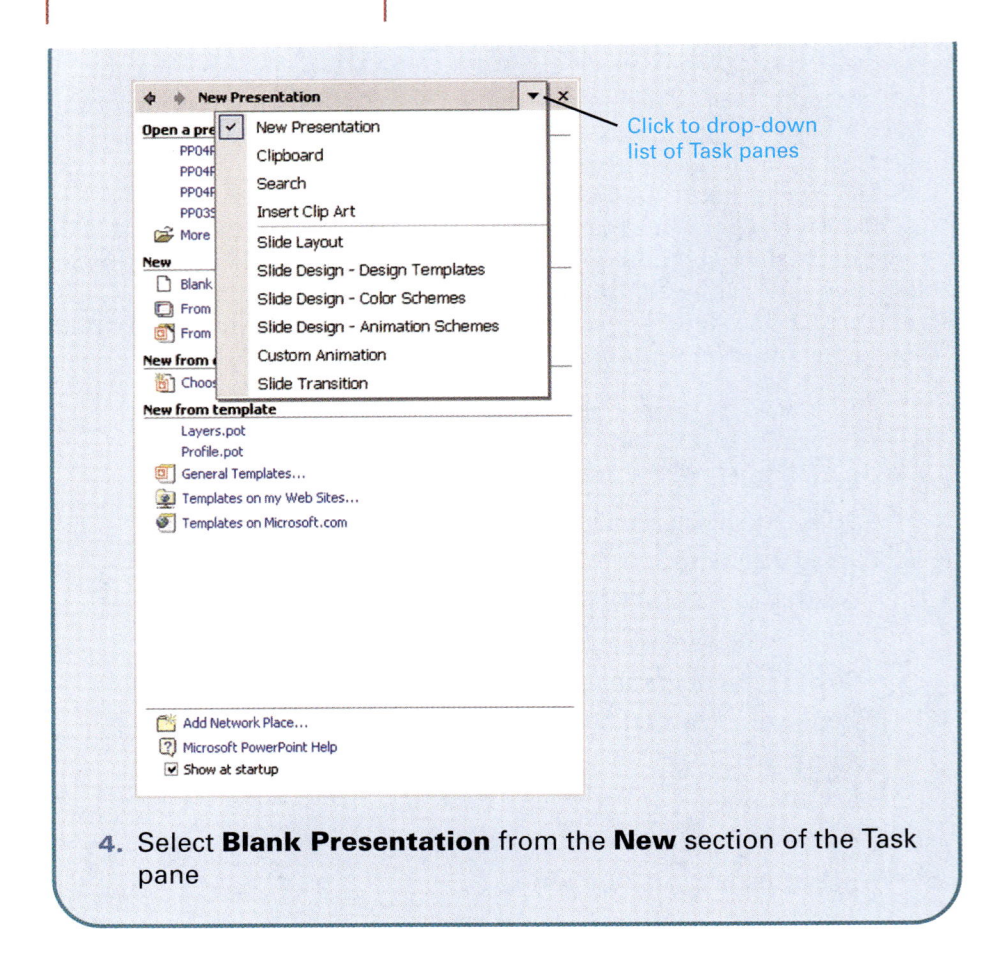

Click to drop-down list of Task panes

4. Select **Blank Presentation** from the **New** section of the Task pane

As you can see, a blank presentation is truly starting from scratch. You will need to select the slide layout and add content to build the presentation.

Selecting Slide Layout

The ***slide layout*** sets the format of the text and graphic content of a slide. When a blank presentation is opened or a new page added to an existing presentation, the Slide Layout Task pane displays. The Slide Layout Task pane shows standard presentation page layouts containing various combinations of text and graphics.

Setting slide layout:

1. If a new presentation is not active from the previous steps, click the **New** button on the toolbar to create a new presentation

2. Use the **Task pane** option of the **View** menu to activate the Task pane if it is not displaying

3. If the Slide Layout Task pane is not displaying, activate it by selecting **Slide Layout** in the Task pane drop-down list

PP 1.21

FIGURE 1.18
Slide Layout Task Pane

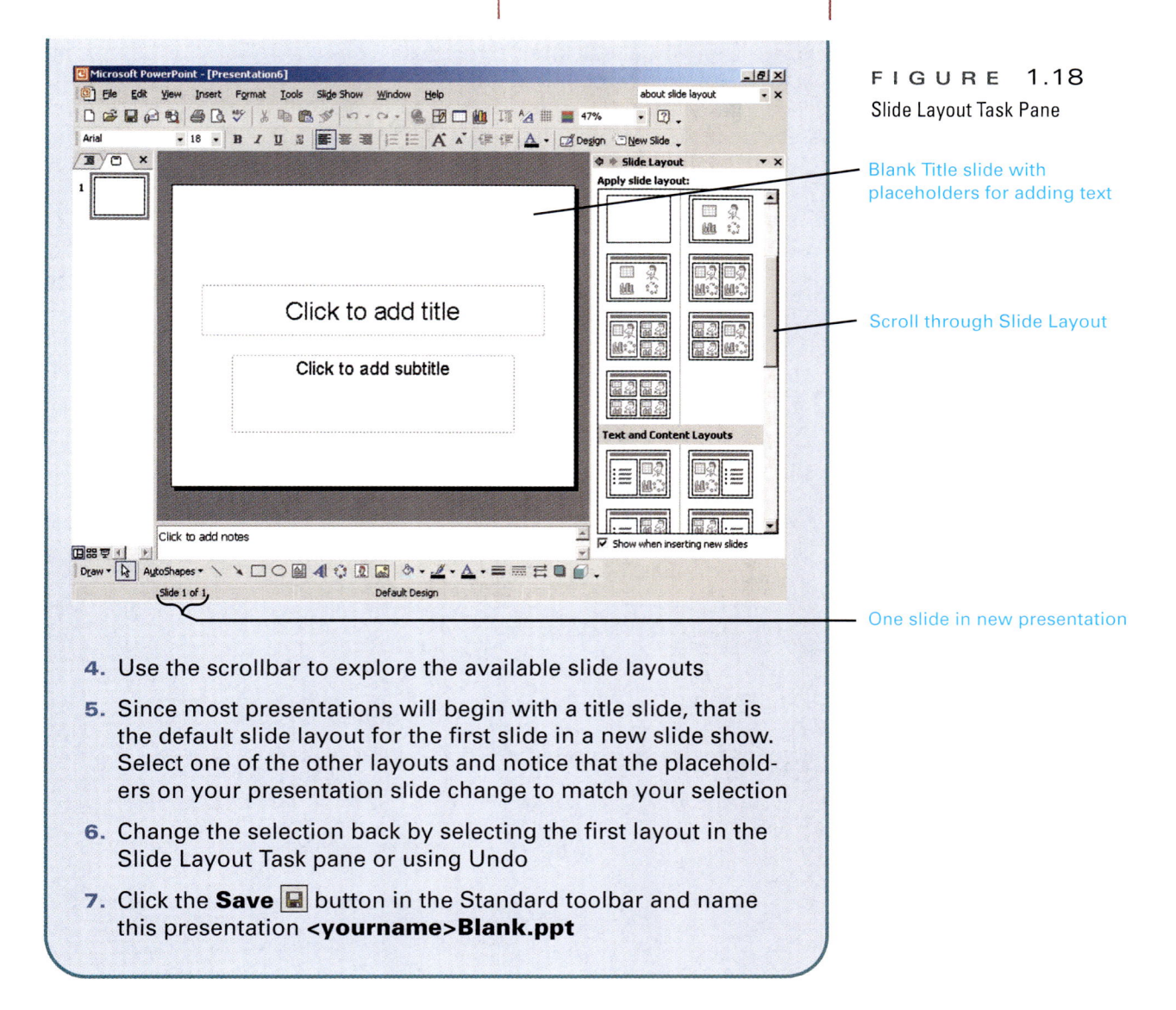

Blank Title slide with placeholders for adding text

Scroll through Slide Layout

One slide in new presentation

4. Use the scrollbar to explore the available slide layouts

5. Since most presentations will begin with a title slide, that is the default slide layout for the first slide in a new slide show. Select one of the other layouts and notice that the placeholders on your presentation slide change to match your selection

6. Change the selection back by selecting the first layout in the Slide Layout Task pane or using Undo

7. Click the **Save** button in the Standard toolbar and name this presentation **<yourname>Blank.ppt**

The Slide Layout Task pane is divided into three types of layouts, Text Layouts, Contents Layouts (graphics), and Other Layouts that combine text with other media. Pausing the mouse over a Task pane layout will display the name of that layout. The layout chosen is governed by the content to be placed on the page.

Using Slide Placeholders

Microsoft PowerPoint uses **Slide Placeholders** to indicate the Slide Layout of a new slide. Each placeholder is designed to contain text, graphics, or other media. Default formatting is applied to each placeholder. For example, the title placeholder in the layout selected has Arial 44-point format, while the subtitle placeholder has Arial 32-point format (you can determine this by clicking in each and viewing the settings on the Formatting toolbar). The benefit of predefined formatting is consistency throughout your presentation and across presentations that will be used for the same audience.

The size of a placeholder can be adjusted using the sizing handles. Sizing handles are the circles that appear in the border of a placeholder when it is clicked. When the cursor pauses over a sizing handle, it will

POWERPOINT

change to arrows indicating the resizing direction that can be accomplished with that particular handle.

At first glance, the point sizes used by default in placeholders seem large, but remember that the audience needs to be able to see slide content projected and from a distance. Unless you are creating a kiosk that will be viewed by one user at a time on a computer monitor, stick with the large font sizes.

FIGURE 1.19

Adding Text to Slide Placeholders

Adding text to a slide placeholder:

1. Verify that PowerPoint is running and that you have a new slide using Title Slide Layout as your active slide (from the previous steps)

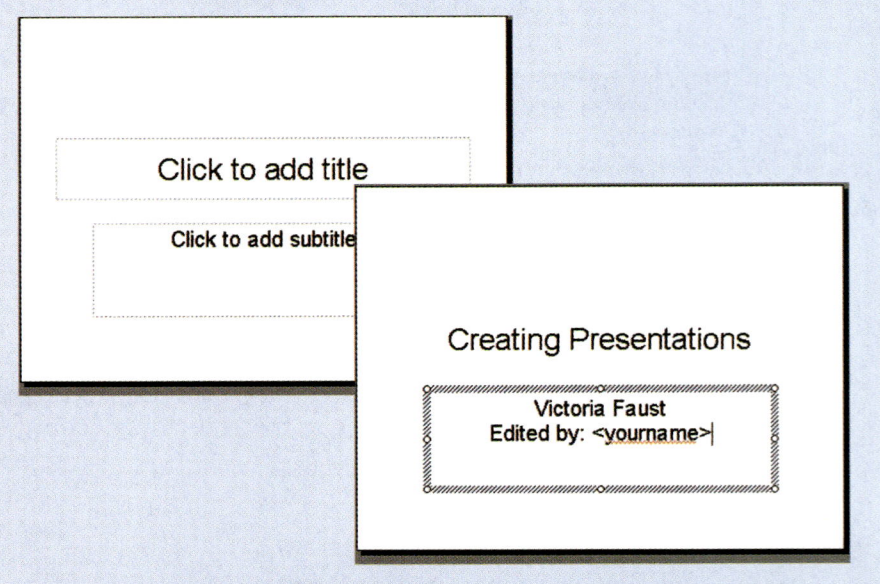

2. Click in the title placeholder and type **Creating Presentations**

   tip: *The title placeholder says Click to add title*

3. Click in the subtitle placeholder and type **Victoria Faust,** press **Enter,** and then **Edited by: <yourname>**

   tip: *The subtitle placeholder says Click to add subtitle*

4. Click the **New Slide** button on the Formatting toolbar to add a new slide to your presentation (notice that the default format is different since this is not the first slide in the presentation)

5. Set the Slide Layout to **Title and 2-column text** (the fourth layout)

6. Add the content shown in the next figure

7. Make slide 1 your active slide and run your slide show by clicking the **Slide Show** button of the View toolbar

8. **Save**

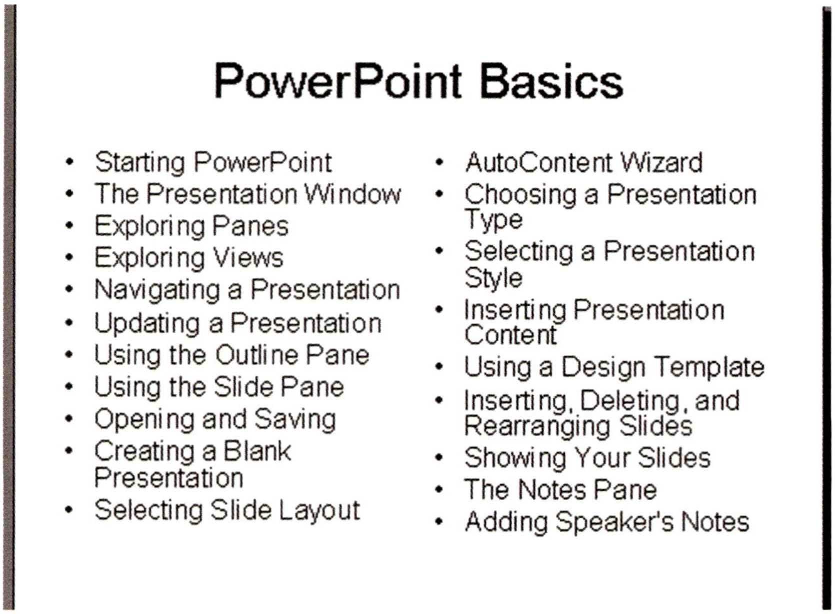

FIGURE 1.20

Title and 2-Column Text Slide Layout

PowerPoint Basics

- Starting PowerPoint
- The Presentation Window
- Exploring Panes
- Exploring Views
- Navigating a Presentation
- Updating a Presentation
- Using the Outline Pane
- Using the Slide Pane
- Opening and Saving
- Creating a Blank Presentation
- Selecting Slide Layout

- AutoContent Wizard
- Choosing a Presentation Type
- Selecting a Presentation Style
- Inserting Presentation Content
- Using a Design Template
- Inserting, Deleting, and Rearranging Slides
- Showing Your Slides
- The Notes Pane
- Adding Speaker's Notes

At this point the presentation is pretty bland, but that can be remedied by adding formatting, backgrounds, graphics, transitions, and animations. It was important to understand what an unornamented presentation looks like to see the value of other presentation elements.

Slide placeholders can be resized, repositioned, and reformatted. For example, a text placeholder can be formatted with borders and background colors. Did you notice that as you entered text in the previous steps, the font size was reduced? When you enter text, PowerPoint uses the Text AutoFit feature to resize it to fit into the placeholder (the minimum font is 8 point). Adjusting the size of a placeholder will also resize the text it holds.

As slide text is typed, PowerPoint's Spell Checker places wavy red lines under words that may be misspelled. Words that are not contained in the Spell Checker dictionary will be marked for review. Misspellings can be corrected like any typographic error or by right-clicking on the word with the wavy line to display a list of suggested spellings. A correct spelling can be selected from the list of suggestions, PowerPoint can be told to ignore the spelling, or it can be told to add this spelling to the dictionary.

Using the Increase Indent and Decrease Indent buttons on the formatting toolbar adjusts the indention level of bulleted text on the slide. The 2-column list that you entered needs to have some of the items indented.

Adjusting the indention of slide bullets:

1. Verify that PowerPoint is running and that you have the presentation created in the previous steps open
2. Make the second slide your active slide
3. Use the **Increase Indent** button to adjust the bulleted list as shown in the next figure

FIGURE 1.21
Adjusted Bullet Indention

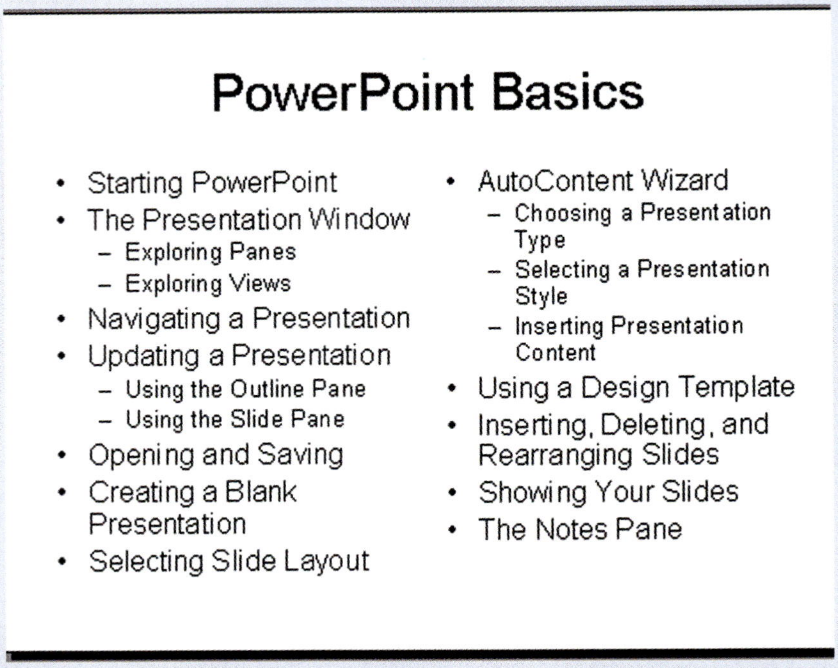

PowerPoint Basics

- Starting PowerPoint
- The Presentation Window
  - Exploring Panes
  - Exploring Views
- Navigating a Presentation
- Updating a Presentation
  - Using the Outline Pane
  - Using the Slide Pane
- Opening and Saving
- Creating a Blank Presentation
- Selecting Slide Layout
- AutoContent Wizard
  - Choosing a Presentation Type
  - Selecting a Presentation Style
  - Inserting Presentation Content
- Using a Design Template
- Inserting, Deleting, and Rearranging Slides
- Showing Your Slides
- The Notes Pane

4. Make slide 1 your active slide and run your slide show by clicking the **Slide Show** button of the View toolbar
5. **Save**

*another*way

. . . to Adjust Bullet Indention

Changing the indention level of bullets in a bulleted list is also called promoting (Decrease indent) and demoting (Increase indent) list items. The indent of a list item can also be increased using the Tab key before typing the list text or at the beginning of existing list text. Conversely, Shift+Tab will decrease the indent level.

After viewing the presentation, you decide that the second slide is just too busy. You want to make the second column of slide 2 a new slide. This can be accomplished by decreasing the indention level of the first item in the second column.

Splitting a bulleted list into two slides:

1. Verify that PowerPoint is running and that you have the presentation created in the previous steps open
2. Make the second slide your active slide
3. In the Outline pane, position the cursor at the beginning of the first bulleted item in the second column
4. Click the **Decrease Indent** button
5. Decrease the indent of the three items that were indented under AutoContent wizard

tip: *You can select all three lines and simultaneously decrease all of their indention levels*

6. Make slide **1** the active slide and run your slide show by clicking the **Slide Show** button of the View toolbar
7. **Save**

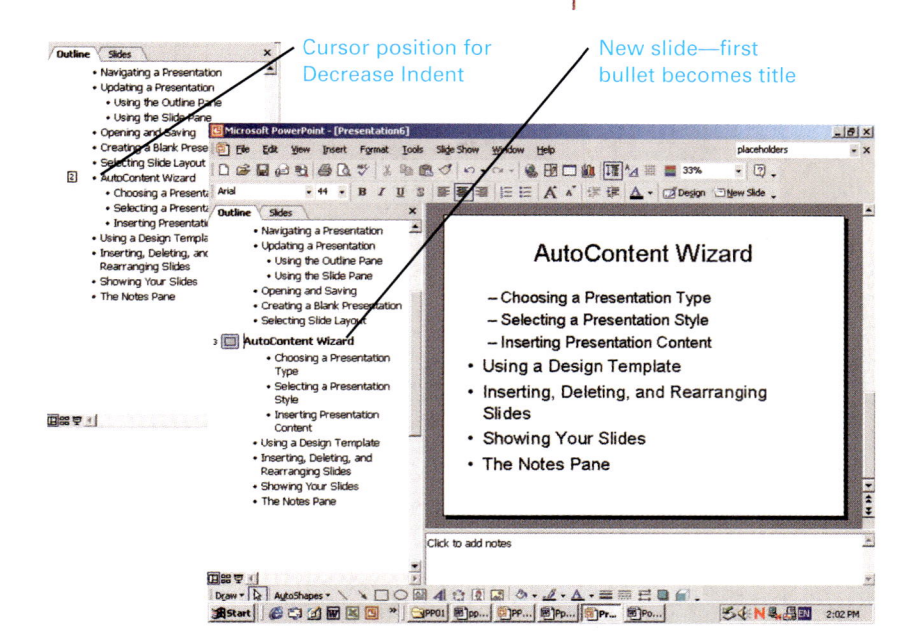

FIGURE 1.22

Slide 2 Split into Two Slides

When it comes to building speaker-led presentations, less text is usually better. The bullets are to guide the speaker and the audience while the speaker presents the important facts of the presentation. The audience can become lost when too much information is presented on a slide or uninterested when the speaker is simply repeating what they can read for themselves.

AUTOCONTENT WIZARD

Wizards are helpful tools in Office that walk users through complex tasks. The AutoContent wizard is the fastest way to create a professional-looking presentation. The wizard will ask a series of questions, then create a presentation based on your answers. The wizard uses a Design template to provide slide backgrounds and a content template to suggest subject matter for the presentation.

task reference
Activating the AutoContent Wizard:

- With PowerPoint running select **New** from the **File** menu to activate the New Presentation Task pane

- From the New option of the Task pane select **From AutoContent Wizard**

Using the AutoContent wizard:

1. Verify that PowerPoint is running

2. If the New Presentation Task pane is not displayed, select **New** from the **File** menu to activate it

FIGURE 1.23
AutoContent Wizard

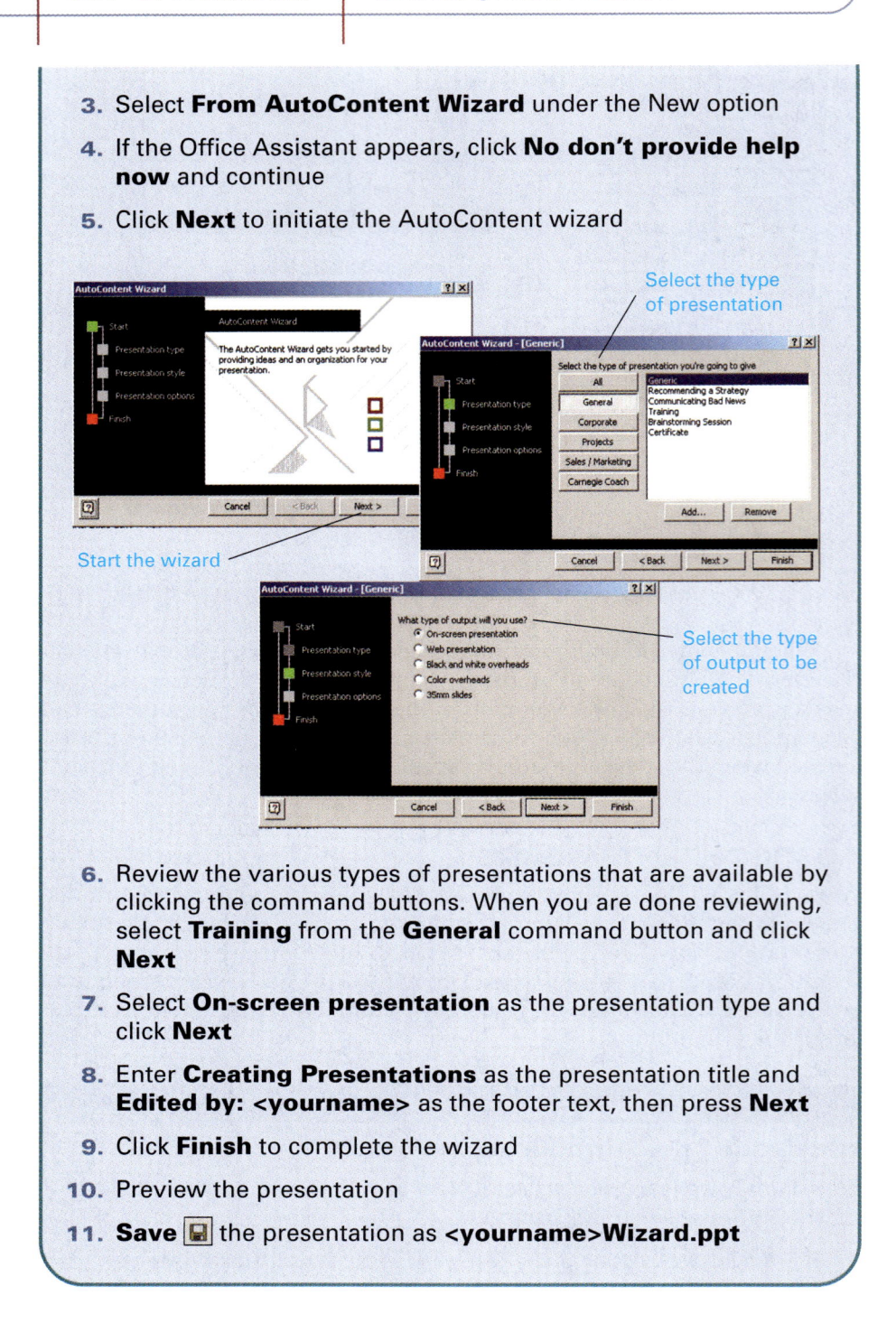

3. Select **From AutoContent Wizard** under the New option
4. If the Office Assistant appears, click **No don't provide help now** and continue
5. Click **Next** to initiate the AutoContent wizard

6. Review the various types of presentations that are available by clicking the command buttons. When you are done reviewing, select **Training** from the **General** command button and click **Next**
7. Select **On-screen presentation** as the presentation type and click **Next**
8. Enter **Creating Presentations** as the presentation title and **Edited by: <yourname>** as the footer text, then press **Next**
9. Click **Finish** to complete the wizard
10. Preview the presentation
11. **Save** the presentation as **<yourname>Wizard.ppt**

The Wizard has created nine slides with suggested content that are now ready to be modified. Modifications can include editing text, changing slide layout, selecting a design template, adding new slides, or deleting unneeded slides just as you would in any other presentation.

Choosing a Presentation Type and Style

At the beginning of the AutoContent Wizard, you were prompted to select a presentation type. The presentation type determines which design and content templates PowerPoint uses to build a presentation. Choose the presentation type based on the content to be presented, since the Design

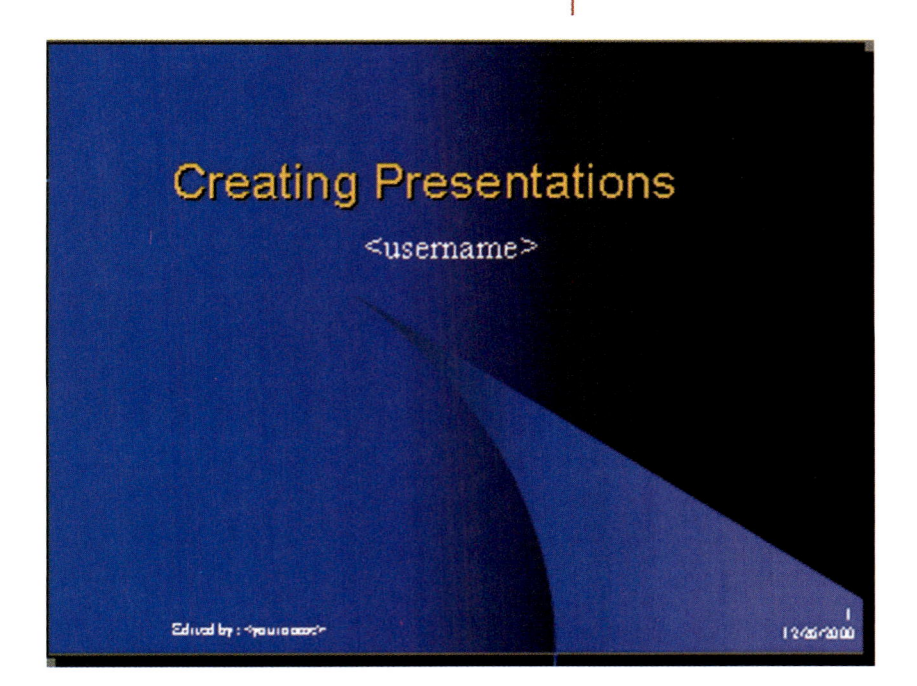

FIGURE 1.24

Creating Presentations Generated by AutoContent Wizard

template backgrounds, transitions, and colors can all be changed after the presentation is built.

The Wizard Style selection allows PowerPoint to optimize the presentation settings for a specific delivery environment. For example, Web presentations have different color and background settings than projected presentations. All of these options can be customized, but there is no one place to change style settings.

Inserting Presentation Content

Editing the presentation created by the AutoContent wizard is just like making changes to user developed content. Changes are most often made in Normal view using either the Outline or the Slides pane. The content for Victoria's presentation needs to replace what was generated by the AutoContent wizard.

The first AutoContent slide contains the presentation title provided to the AutoContent wizard and a user name. The user name is created when Office is installed. If you are working on a computer and you installed the software, it should be a name that you provided. If you are working on someone else's computer or one that came preinstalled, the user name will not be meaningful. Seeing something like "Valued Gateway customer" is not uncommon. Whatever the text, you will need to change it to Victoria's name since she is the presenter.

Editing AutoContent wizard text:

1. Verify that PowerPoint is running and that the AutoContent wizard presentation created in the previous steps is open

2. In the Outline pane click and drag to select the current user name and type **Victoria Faust**

3. In slide 2 select Define the subject matter and type **Using PowerPoint to enhance presentations**
4. Select State what the audience will learn in this session and type **Presentations with pizzazz** and press **Enter**
5. Press tab to increase the bullet indent, type **Content,** and press **Enter**
6. Type **Backgrounds** and press **Enter**
7. Type **Animations** and press **Enter**
8. Select Find out any relevant background and interest of the audience and type **Special presentation needs?**

FIGURE 1.25
AutoContent Wizard Updates

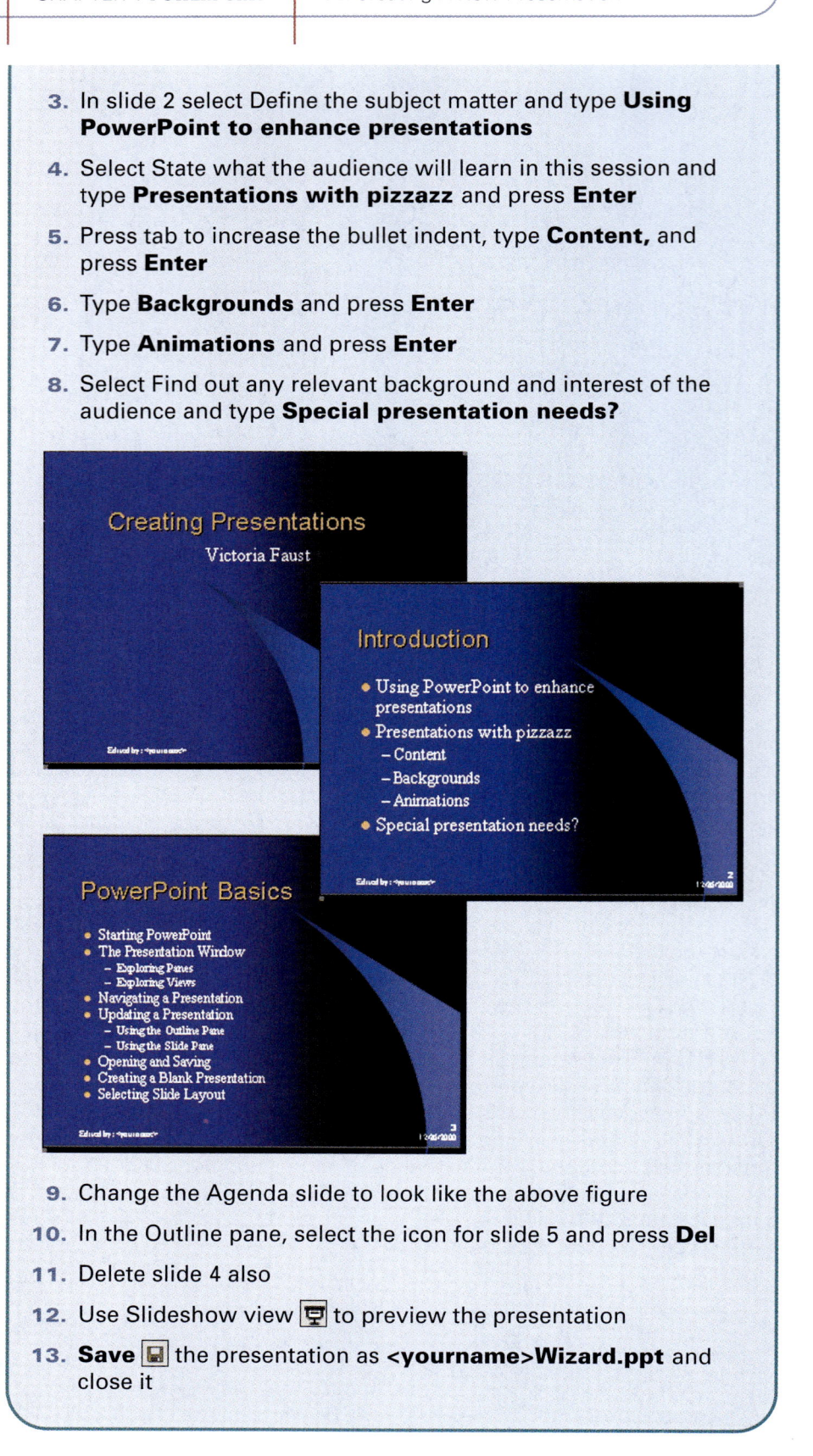

9. Change the Agenda slide to look like the above figure
10. In the Outline pane, select the icon for slide 5 and press **Del**
11. Delete slide 4 also
12. Use Slideshow view to preview the presentation
13. **Save** the presentation as **<yourname>Wizard.ppt** and close it

Although we did not completely build the presentation, hopefully this has been enough of an introduction for you to determine whether or not you will find the AutoContent Wizard useful. It would probably be helpful for you to revisit the AutoContent Wizard and review the types of presentations it can generate. Although the generated content must be modified, the wizard can help put together well-organized presentations.

USING A DESIGN TEMPLATE

So far we have explored two of the three New options in the New Presentation pane. The final option, From Design Template, is a selection stylistically between using a Blank presentation and using the AutoContent wizard. A Design Template contains slide backgrounds, placeholder formats, transitions, and animations without any suggested content. Besides starting a presentation with a Design template, a template can be added to an existing presentation using the Slide Design panel of the Task pane.

Choosing a Template

Choosing a good template is a matter of understanding your audience, the content of the presentation, and the personality of the speaker. How the presentation will be delivered is also important. For example, blue tones tend to project well while browns and reds can be difficult on the eyes when projected. When projecting a presentation, it is always best to test the projection system that will be used. Each projection system has color biases that can be significant enough to require changing the template.

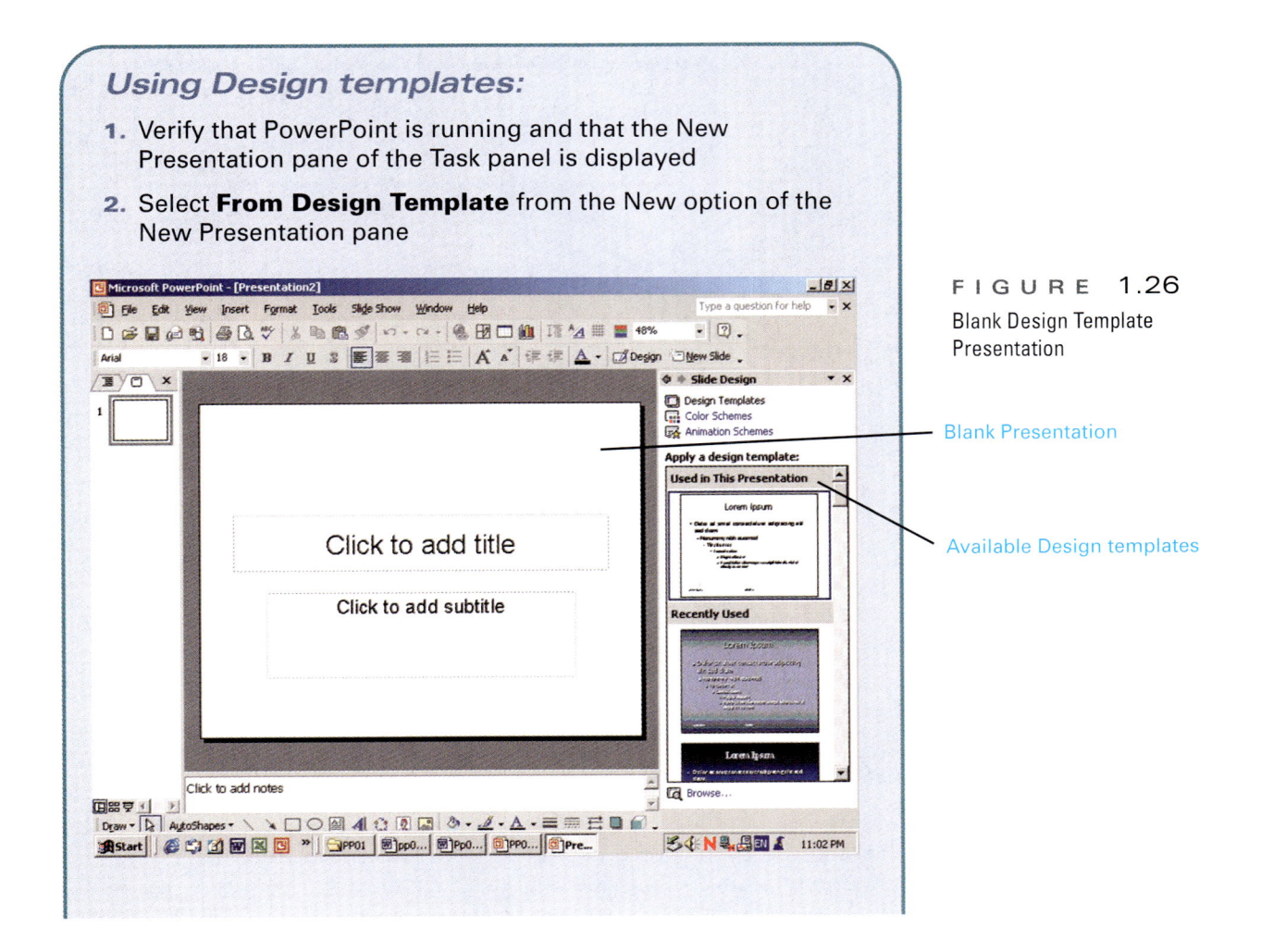

Using Design templates:

1. Verify that PowerPoint is running and that the New Presentation pane of the Task panel is displayed

2. Select **From Design Template** from the New option of the New Presentation pane

FIGURE 1.26

Blank Design Template Presentation

3. Scroll through the available Design templates, selecting each to see how it will appear in your presentation. A blank presentation is now open and ready for you to add content
4. Use the **Open** button to reopen **<yourname>Blank.ppt**
5. Ensure that the Slide Design panel of the Task pane is visible by choosing **Slide Design—Design Template** from the Task pane drop-down menu or click the **Slide Design** on the Formatting toolbar
6. Choose the **Proposal Design template** to add this template to your existing presentation

tip: *The name of a design is listed in the screen tip that appears when you pause the mouse over a template*

FIGURE 1.27
Proposal Design Template

7. Make slide 1 your active slide and run your slide show by clicking the **Slide Show** button of the View toolbar
8. Use the **Save As** option of the **File** menu to save the presentation as **<yourname>DesignTemplate.ppt**

The Design template panel is divided into three sections, Used in This Presentation, Recently Used, and Available for Use. New templates can be added to the collection by customizing an existing template or retrieving additional templates from the Web.

Adding and Editing Slide Content

Adding text content to any slide is as simple as navigating to that slide, clicking where you would like the new text to appear, and then typing the new content. Controlling how that text will appear in your presentation is a little more difficult.

As you have experienced, text can be added in either the Outline or Slide pane of Normal view. In the Outline pane, the first line of slide text entered is treated as the slide title. Pressing Enter after the title text will create a new slide, and any text entered will be treated as the title for the new slide. The Increase Indent button on the toolbar is used to control text indention causing title text to be converted to bulleted text. Pressing Enter in a bulleted list will add a new bullet to continue the list. A new slide is added to the presentation using the New Slide button on the toolbar, or the Decrease Indent button will cause bulleted text to be at the slide title level. These actions are demonstrated in the next series of steps.

F I G U R E   1.28

Slide Layout Task Panel

Editing in the Outline pane:

1. Verify that PowerPoint is running and that the New Presentation pane of the Task panel is displayed
2. Select **Blank presentation** from the New option of the New Presentation pane
3. Select **Title and Text,** the first bulleted list layout from the Task pane
4. Click the **Outline** tab of the Outline pane if necessary
5. Type **Slide 1 Title** and press **Enter**
6. Type **Slide 1 Bullet 1.** Notice that this text appears as the title on a second slide when a Bullet on the first slide is wanted
7. Use the **Increase Indent** button to make this a bulleted item of the first slide
8. Move to the end of the Slide 1 Bullet 1 text and press **Enter.** Notice that the new line is a bullet
9. Type **Slide 1 Bullet 2** and press **Enter.** Notice that another bullet is added
10. Use the **Decrease Indent** button to make this a new slide and type **Slide 2 Title** and press **Enter**
11. Type **Slide 2 Bullet 1** and Press **Enter**
12. Use what you have learned to complete the presentation shown in Figure 1.29
13. **Save** the presentation as **<yourname>EditExercise.ppt**

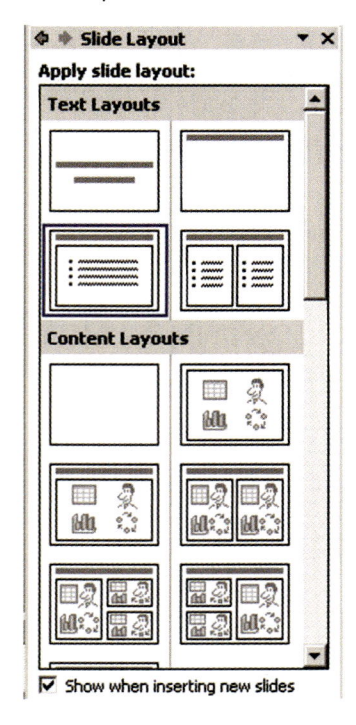

F I G U R E   1.29

Completed Presentation

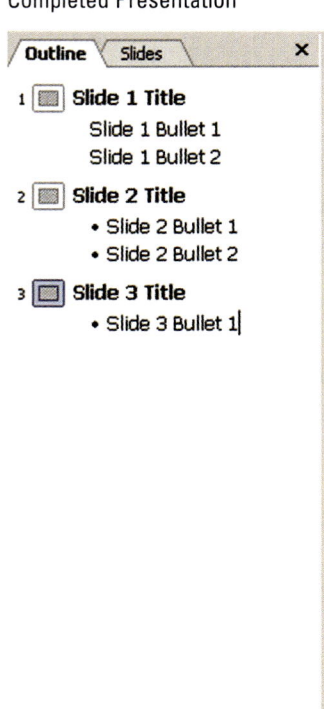

The Slide pane controls text indention a little differently. In the Slide pane, text placeholders indicate where text can be added to a slide. In the slide title placeholder, the Increase Indent and Decrease Indent buttons are disabled—so the current slide title cannot be converted to a bullet item for the previous slide. The bulleted list placeholder is used to add bulleted text, so each time Enter is pressed, a new bullet item is created. The Increase and Decrease Indent buttons are used to create different levels of bullets, but not to make one of the bullets a title on a new slide as was possible in Outline view.

another way

. . . to Change Indention Level

Remember that Tab and Shift+Tab can be used to increase and decrease the indention level of a bullet without removing your hands from the keyboard.

To correct errors in either view, use the **Backspace key** to move backwards deleting one character at a time. The Backspace key is a repeating key on most keyboards so holding it down continues the deletion. The **Del** key deletes the character in front of the cursor. Again this is a repeating key that will continue to delete as long as it is depressed. The arrow keys work to move the cursor without impacting text so they can be used to position the cursor for edits. The mouse can also be used to position the cursor and select text for editing.

In general, users prefer the Outline pane for entering and maintaining presentation text. The Slides pane is most effective to add and maintain media elements of a presentation.

Inserting, Deleting, and Rearranging Slides

Reorganizing the slides in an existing slide show is easily accomplished when using the correct view for the task. Both the Outline view and the Slide Sorter view can be used to insert, delete, and reorganize a slide show. The Slide Sorter view is specifically designed for reordering slide shows. All slides are displayed as thumbnails that can be operated on. To delete a slide, simply select it and press the Del key. To move a slide, select it and then drag it to the desired location.

Using Slide Sorter view:

1. Verify that PowerPoint is running
2. Use the **Open** button to open **PP01AccessFigures.ppt**
3. Review the 31 slides in this presentation to become familiar with them
4. Click the **Slide Sorter** view button on the View toolbar
5. Use the Zoom control to reduce the size of the thumbnails until you can see all of the slides on one screen
6. Select slide **26** and drag it until the line is before slide 23
7. Select slide **21** and press **Del**
8. Select slide **30** and choose **New Slide** from the toolbar
9. Return to **Normal** view and use the Zoom control to adjust the slides to a workable size for you
10. Use the Slide or Outline pane to renumber the Figures so that the figure number matches the slide number

tip: *The first part of the number is the Chapter and the second part is the figure number. Slide 20 is Figure 4.20 and Slide 23 is Figure 4.23*

11. Save the file as **<yourname>PP01AccessFigures.ppt**

Adding Slides from Another Presentation

Using a similar presentation as the foundation for a new slide show can considerably reduce development time. All or part of an existing presenta-

www.mhhe.com/i-series   PP 1.33

FIGURE 1.30
Slide Sorter View

Zoom control

View toolbar

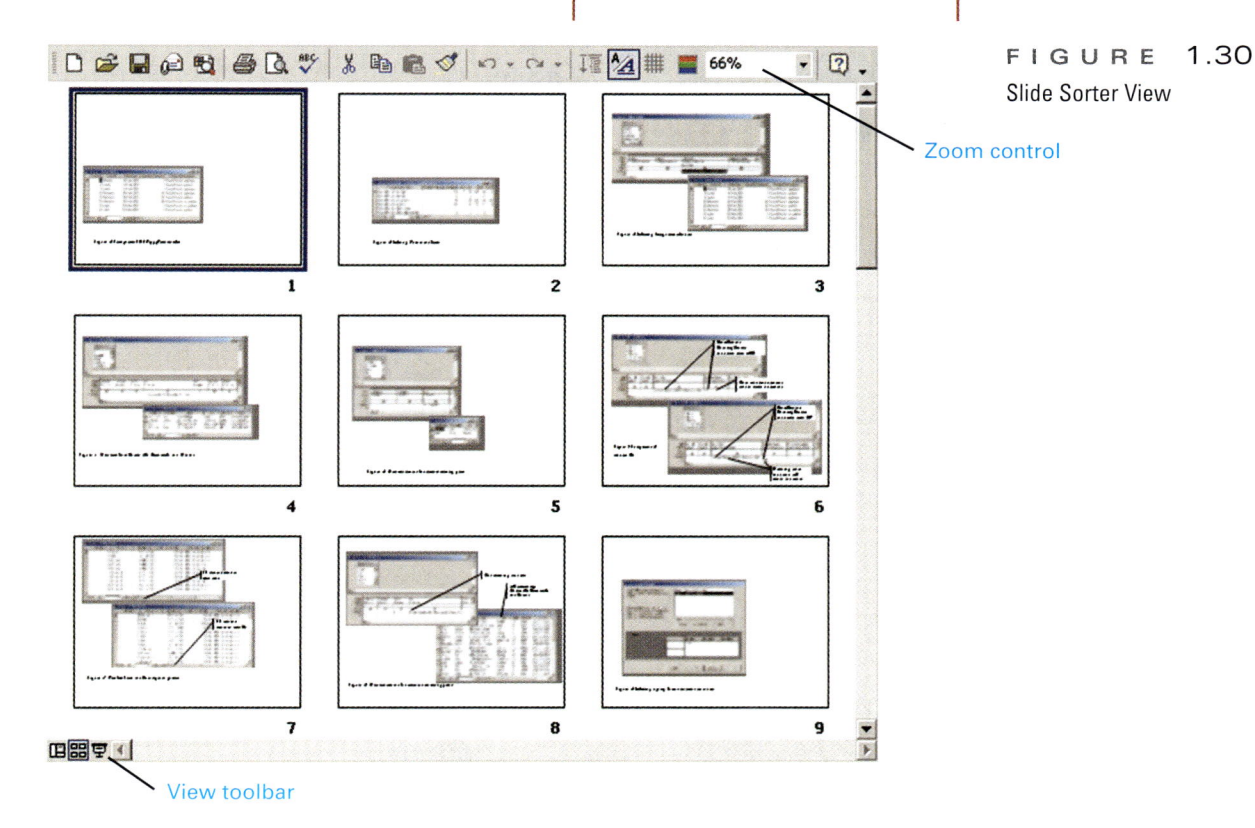

tion can be selected and inserted into a new presentation. Inserted slides from another presentation maintain all text and graphics, but the color and design from the current presentation are applied.

Suppose that you wanted Victoria's second presentation to use the same opening and closing slides as the first presentation. You could try to rebuild them, or simply insert them from the other presentation.

Inserting slides from another presentation:

1. Verify that PowerPoint is running
2. Close any open presentations
3. Use the **Open** button to open **<yourname>DesignTemplate.ppt**
4. Move to the first slide of the DesignTemplate presentation
5. Click **Slides From Files** in the **Insert** menu
6. Click the **Browse** button and navigate to **PP01PresntGrphx.ppt**
7. Select the first and last slides of PP01PresntGrphx and click **Insert**

tip: *Slides are unselected by clicking them again*

8. **Close** the Slide Finder dialog box

POWERPOINT

FIGURE 1.31
Slide Finder Dialog Box

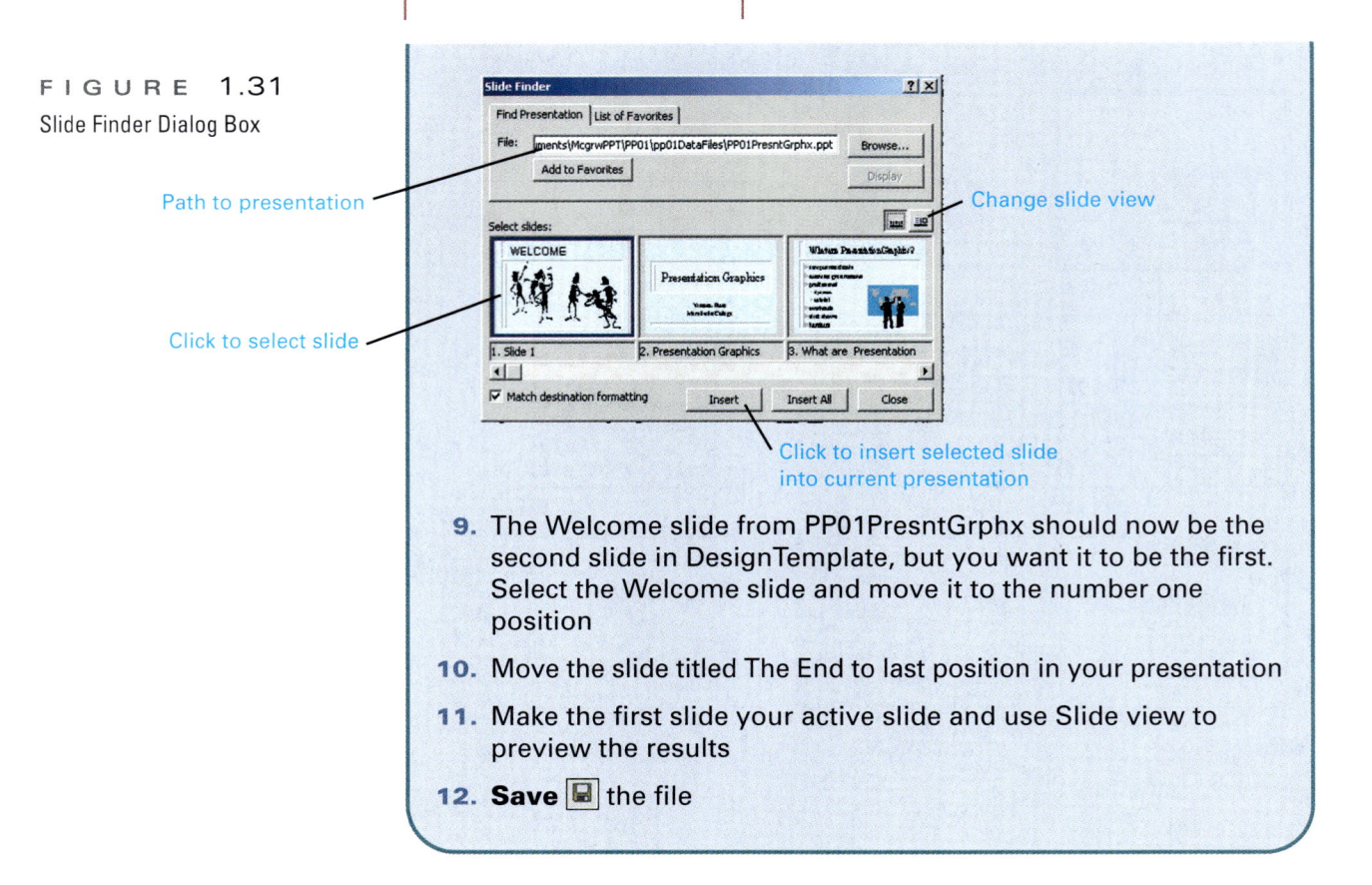

Path to presentation

Click to select slide

Change slide view

Click to insert selected slide into current presentation

9. The Welcome slide from PP01PresntGrphx should now be the second slide in DesignTemplate, but you want it to be the first. Select the Welcome slide and move it to the number one position

10. Move the slide titled The End to last position in your presentation

11. Make the first slide your active slide and use Slide view to preview the results

12. **Save** the file

Inserted slides typically need to be moved and edited to effectively fit the new presentation, but can save significant development effort.

THE NOTES PANE

Each slide of a presentation has an associated Notes pane that can be used to add speaker's notes, development notes, or any other information to be stored with a slide. The Notes pane can contain text and graphics, but cannot exceed one page per slide.

Entering and changing text in the Notes pane works just like entering text in the other panes of the Normal view. PowerPoint also has a Notes Page view so that you can view and edit the entire page.

Inserting notes:

1. Verify that PowerPoint is running

2. Close any open presentations

3. Use the **Open** button to open **<yourname>DesignTemplate.ppt**

4. Move to the first slide of the DesignTemplate presentation

5. Notice that there are already notes in the Notes pane for this slide since it was copied from another presentation

6. Move to the last slide and review the notes there

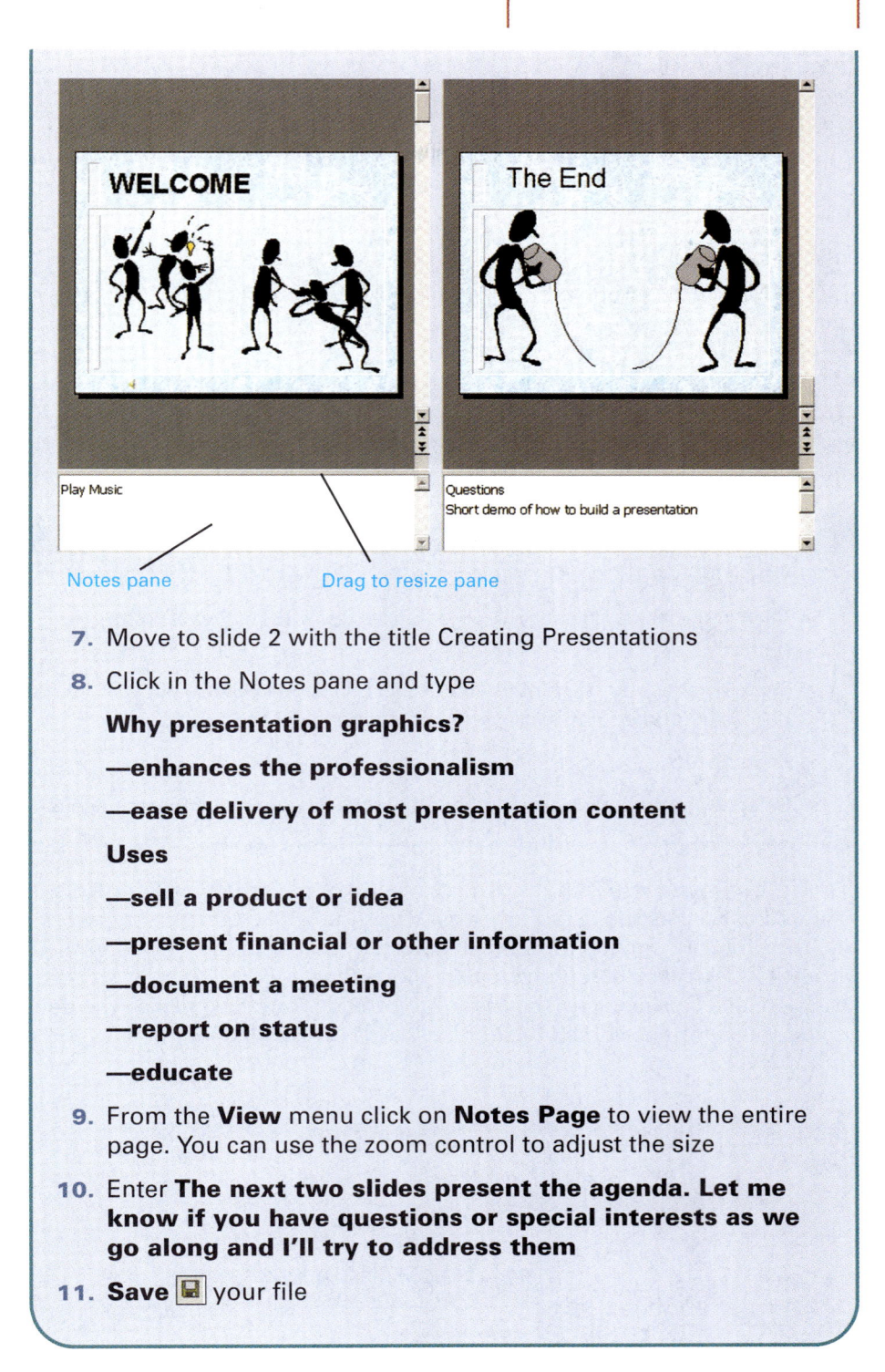

FIGURE 1.32
Existing Notes in Notes Pane

7. Move to slide 2 with the title Creating Presentations
8. Click in the Notes pane and type
   Why presentation graphics?
   —**enhances the professionalism**
   —**ease delivery of most presentation content**
   Uses
   —**sell a product or idea**
   —**present financial or other information**
   —**document a meeting**
   —**report on status**
   —**educate**
9. From the **View** menu click on **Notes Page** to view the entire page. You can use the zoom control to adjust the size
10. Enter **The next two slides present the agenda. Let me know if you have questions or special interests as we go along and I'll try to address them**
11. **Save** your file

After notes are entered, they can be printed as notes pages to be used by the speaker or as handouts for the audience. In the Notes view the slide and/or the Notes placeholder can be selected for modification. Drag the sizing handles to adjust the placeholder size or move the placeholder by dragging it. Sizing handles are the circles that appear in the border of a placeholder when it is selected. Pausing over a sizing handle will change the cursor to arrows indicating the resize direction of that particular handle.

POWERPOINT

GETTING HELP

Even people who regularly use PowerPoint need direction on how to accomplish new tasks or those that are not frequently performed. PowerPoint supports several methods of obtaining help. The chosen technique for getting help depends on work style preferences and the question type.

Ask a Question

Like other Office applications the PowerPoint Menu has the Ask A Question drop-down list box. This is an effective way to request help on a specific topic. Type in a question and press enter. A list of related topics will display as shown in the next figure. Selecting a topic will open Microsoft PowerPoint Help with more selections, which can be clicked to bring up instructions. The instructions can display on your screen as you work through them in PowerPoint.

---

task reference

Getting Help:

- Click in the Ask A Question drop-down text box in the PowerPoint menu.
- Type in keywords relevant to your topic. Full sentences are not necessary and do not improve the performance of the search.
- Press **Enter**.
- Select from the topics provided or adjust the keywords and search again.

The *Contents* or *Index* tabs display when Microsoft PowerPoint Help is initiated as well as the default *Answer Wizard* tab. The *Contents* tab works like the table of contents for a book. Selected topics can be viewed in their entirety, which can be helpful when more than just a series of steps to complete a task is needed. The *Index* tab provides a way to search the document index for keywords. A list of keywords is provided, or you can enter your own.

FIGURE 1.33
Getting Help

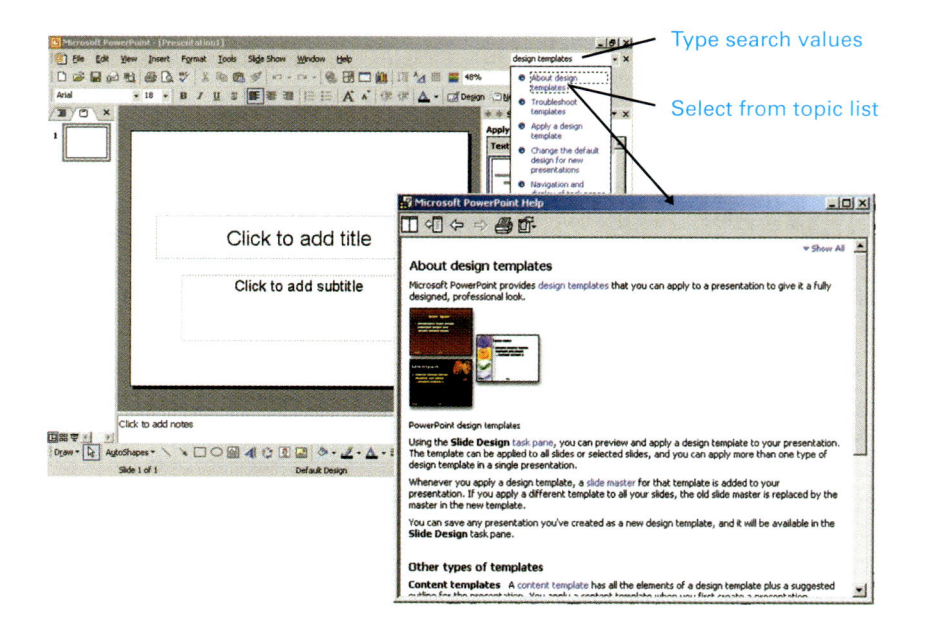

The Office Assistant

Dropping down the Help menu in the PowerPoint window displays a complete list of help options. The menu options are to start help, initiate the Office Assistant, access help on the Web, or use the What's This tool.

The What's This tool changes the pointer to an arrow and a question mark. With this tool active, point and click on any interface component and receive a brief description of its function and operation. What's This closes after one interface item is described.

The Office Assistant is the animated interface to Office Help and can be initiated by pressing F1, choosing Microsoft PowerPoint Help from the Help menu, or selecting Show the Office Assistant from the Help menu. The default Office Assistant is a paperclip named Clippit, but custom assistants can be chosen. Regardless of how the assistant is initiated, typing a question in the text box and clicking Search will open Microsoft PowerPoint Help (shown in the previous figure) with topics related to your search.

Right-clicking the Office Assistant presents a pop-up menu used to control how the assistant works. Available visual presentations include Merlin the magician, a robot, a cat, and a dog. If he is left active and set to do so, the assistant will provide tips as you work. He can also be hidden or disabled.

EXITING POWERPOINT

Exiting PowerPoint is accomplished by choosing the close button (the X in the right of the title bar) of the main PowerPoint window. The Exit option of the File menu will also close PowerPoint. If there are unsaved changes in the presentation or notes, you will be prompted to save them before exiting PowerPoint. When all saves are complete, PowerPoint will close.

---

making the grade — SESSION 1.2

1. What is a Design template and why would you use one?
2. Describe how the AutoContent wizard is useful.
3. How can you change the indention level of a bullet?
4. How would you find out how to change the font size of text in a slide?

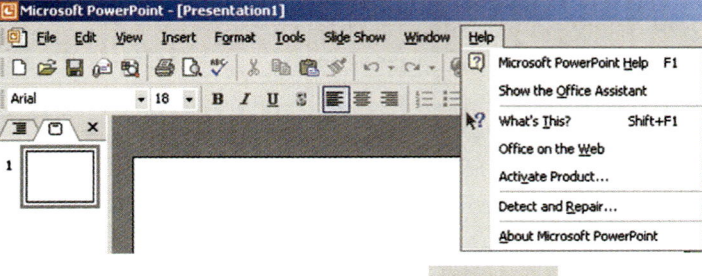

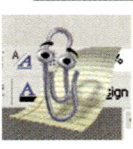

FIGURE 1.34

Help Menu and Office Assistant

SESSION 1.3 SUMMARY

PowerPoint is a full-featured presentation graphics application that supports projected presentations, overheads, handouts, and slides. In addition to creating presentations, PowerPoint is ideal for creating self-running kiosks and Web pages. Materials to support a presentation like audience handouts and speaker's notes are easily created.

The PowerPoint window layout is determined by the view that is being used. Each view has one or more panes for accomplishing specific tasks. In the Normal view, the Outline, Slide, and Notes panes are available. The Outline pane is useful for entering, formatting, and rearranging slide text. The Slide pane shows a miniature of the slide as it will be in the presentation. Text and media elements can be edited in the Slide pane. The Notes pane is used to add notes to a slide that will not be displayed during a normal presentation. The notes can be printed for the speaker or as audience handouts.

The Slide Sorter view displays each presentation slide as a thumbnail and is used to reorder, delete, and insert slides. The Slide Show view is an effective way to preview slides since each slide is shown as a full screen. You cannot edit the presentation in this mode.

Like other Office applications, PowerPoint uses a Task pane to present options. PowerPoint's Task pane has several panels that support specific operations. The New Project panel contains options for opening new projects starting with a blank presentation, using the AutoContent wizard, or using a Design template. A blank presentation contains no formatting, a Design template contains backgrounds and text formats, and the AutoContent wizard uses design templates and suggests presentation content. Other panels of the Task pane can be used to select and apply slide layouts and Design templates.

Using existing presentations is an effective way to reduce development time on a new project. One method is to open the existing project, use the File/Save As menu option to save it under a new name, and then edit it for its new use. The Insert/Slides From Files menu option is used to insert slides from existing presentations into the current presentation.

To obtain Help in PowerPoint the Ask A Question drop-down list box, the Office Assistant, F1, or What's This features can be accessed. All of the options except What's This provide roughly the same assistance, so it is largely a question of what interface is most comfortable.

MOUS OBJECTIVES SUMMARY

- Create presentations (manually and using automated tools)—PPT2002-1-1
- Add slides and delete slides from presentations—PPT2002-1-2
- Insert, format, and modify text—PPT2002-2-2
- Rearrange slides PPT2002-4-8

task reference roundup

Task	Page #	Preferred Method
Opening a PowerPoint Presentation	PP 1.5	• If the presentation you would like to open is listed in the Open a presentation list of the Task Pane, click it
		• If your presentation is not listed, click **More presentations** in the Open a presentation list of the Task pane
		• Navigate to the drive and folder containing your presentation
		• Select the presentation and click **Open**
Navigating in Normal View	PP 1.10	• Go to next slide—Using the Outline pane, click in the next slide's outline or icon
		• Go to a specific slide—Using the Slides pane, drag the scrollbox until the Screen Tips show the slide that you want
		• Move one slide at a time—Use the Next and Previous buttons at the bottom of the Slides pane scrollbar
Navigating in Slide Show View	PP 1.11	• Go to next slide—click the mouse
		• Go to the previous slide—Press **Backspace**
		• Go to a specific slide—Type the slide number and press **Enter**
		• End the slide show—**Esc**
Activating the AutoContent Wizard	PP 1.25	• With PowerPoint running select **New** from the **File** menu to activate the New Presentation Task pane
		• From the New option of the Task pane select **From AutoContent Wizard**
Getting Help	PP 1.36	• Click in the Ask A Question drop-down text box in the PowerPoint menu
		• Type in keywords relevant to your topic. Full sentences are not necessary and do not improve the performance of the search
		• Press **Enter**
		• Select from the topics provided or adjust the keywords and search again

chapter one

review of terminology

LEVEL ONE

CROSSWORD PUZZLE

Across

5. Indicate locations for text and graphic in the slide pane
6. A specialized area in a window
7. Able to reverse the last 20 actions
8. Helpful hints when you pause over a screen object
9. Wizard that suggests slide show content
12. Normal view pane used to add speaker's notes
13. Pane used only to enter and edit text
14. View used to reorganize a slide show
15. Pane with panels for common tasks

Down

1. Pattern used to create a presentation
2. Pane used to edit text and graphics
3. Task pane panel used to select the layout of a slide
4. Type of template that includes suggested bullets
10. Ribbon of buttons
11. Type of template that includes background graphics

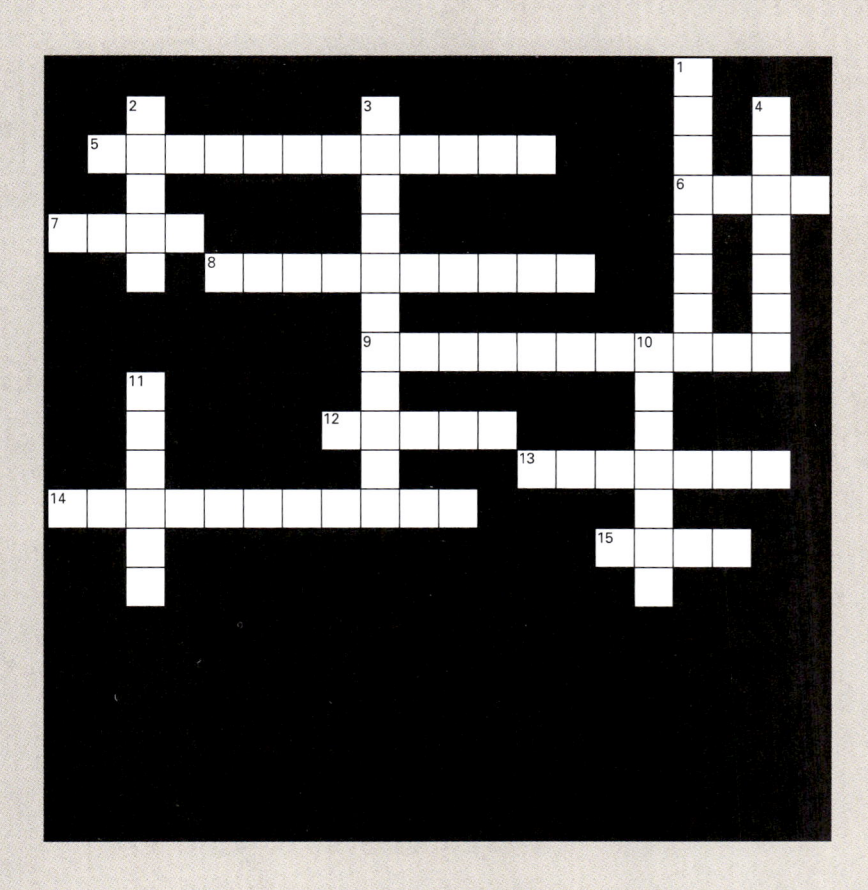

PP 1.41

POWERPOINT

review of concepts

chapter one

LEVEL TWO

FILL-IN

1. The _____ help facility changes the pointer to an arrow and a question mark.
2. Each slide can have _____ page(s) of notes.
3. Slides from another presentation can be inserted into the current presentation using the _____ option of the _____ menu.
4. The _____ view is specifically designed for reordering slides in a slide show.
5. The keyboard key that removes the character in front of the cursor is _____ .
6. When the Task pane is not displaying, it can be activated from the _____ menu.

REVIEW QUESTIONS

Each of the following topics should be addressed in one to three paragraphs.

1. Discuss what you would need to do and to consider when creating a presentation of the contents of this chapter.
2. Discuss the most effective way to add several slides worth of text to a presentation.
3. Describe how you would change the Design Template being used by the current presentation.
4. What are slide placeholders and how are they used?
5. Outline at least two ways to add a new slide to a presentation.
6. What causes the text to change size in a slide placeholder?

CREATE THE QUESTION

For each of the following answers, create the question.

ANSWER

1. Click the Down Arrow in the pane's Title bar.
2. Select Normal view, move to the correct slide, then click in the Notes pane, and type your slide notes.
3. Six words by seven bullets.
4. Click in the text box, select the text to be changed, and then type the replacement text.
5. A Screen Tip displays.

QUESTION

1. _____
2. _____
3. _____
4. _____
5. _____

FACT OR FICTION

For each of the following determine whether the statement is fact, fiction, or both and present your arguments for that conclusion.

1. Selecting a slide in the Slide Show view and pressing the Del key will remove the slide from the presentation.
2. The Standard toolbar has options that are used in most Windows applications like Open and Print.
3. The Outline tab of the Outline pane always displays the word Outline.
4. Speaker's notes always display when the slide show is run.
5. The size of any pane can be adjusted by dragging its border.

PP 1.42

chapter one hands-on projects

practice

1. Creating an Informative Presentation for Curbside Recycling

Curbside Recycling is a Muncie, Indiana, recycling organization that picks up recyclables from homeowners. Neighborhoods subscribe to the service so that pickup is cost-effective. Curbside provides special containers to subscribers for sorting recyclables: a blue container for paper products and a purple container for aluminum, plastic, and glass products.

Subscribers place their recycling containers on the curb for biweekly pickup. Each recycling container is weighed before being emptied. Curbside drivers carry handheld recording devices used to track each pickup. Subscribers receive quarterly profit-sharing checks based on their contributions. If Curbside does not make a profit, subscribers don't get paid for their recyclables. If Curbside makes a profit, subscribers share in that profit. Curbside has asked you to help develop a presentation that will effectively market their services to communities.

1. Use the Task pane to open a blank presentation
2. Save the presentation as **<yourname>Curbside.ppt**
3. The first slide is your title slide and should contain the company name as the title and your name as the subtitle
4. Use the **New Slide** button of the Formatting toolbar to add a second slide to your presentation
   a. Make the slide title **Benefits of Recycling**
   b. Add three to six bullets reflecting the community and environmental benefits of recycling
5. Use the **New Slide** button of the Formatting toolbar to add a third slide to your presentation
   a. Make the slide title **Our Services**
   b. Add three to six bullets reflecting Curbside's services as outlined in the scenario

FIGURE 1.35
Curbside Presentation

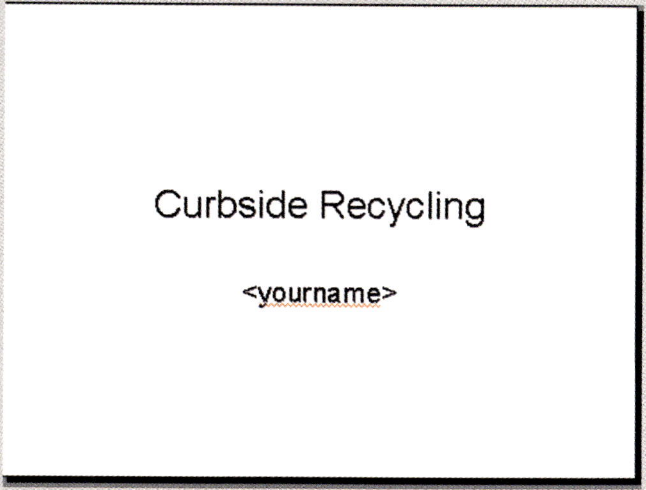

6. Use the **New Slide** button of the Formatting toolbar to add a fourth slide to your presentation
   a. Make the slide title **Customer Benefits**
   b. Add three to six bullets that reflect how the service benefits customers including how the customer is paid
7. In the Notes pane of slide 1 type

   Welcome the audience and thank them for their time

   Introduce yourself and your position with Curbside

8. Add relevant notes to each of the other slides
9. Save the presentation as **<yourname>Curbside.ppt** and exit PowerPoint if your work is complete

hands-on projects

chapter one

LEVEL THREE

challenge

1. Little White School House Meeting Presentation

Samuel Mink is the director of the Little White School House, a small private mountain community school. There are 142 students from preschool through grade 6. The staff consists of eight teachers, the director, a secretary, and community volunteers. Each semester students and their parents gather for a question and answer session with the school's staff. Parents considering putting their children in LWSH are also invited to get a feel for how the school operates. You are the chair of the PTA and will be running the meeting. You have decided to use PowerPoint with a projector since the meeting will be held in the cafeteria where keeping everyone's attention can be difficult.

1. Create a New From Design Template presentation
2. Save the presentation as **<yourname>LWSH.ppt**
3. Apply the Crayons Design template
4. In the title slide
   a. Enter **Little White School House** as the title and adjust its size and position until it appears like the next figure
   b. In the subtitle enter your name and the text **Parent Teacher Association President**
5. Add a new slide to the presentation
6. In the new slide
   a. Make the title **Parent Teacher Association Officers**
   b. Create the following bulleted list
      - **<yourname>**, President
      - Mark Bilker, Vice President
      - Randi Romer, Secretary/Treasurer
      - Heather Wells, Fund-Raising
7. Add a new slide to the presentation
8. In the new slide
   a. Make the title **Faculty and Staff**
   b. Create the following bulleted list
      - Inez Parker   Secretary
      - Samuel Mink   Director
      - Margaret Frost   Preschool Teacher
      - Rachael Dawson   1st Grade Teacher
      - Robert Gibbs   2nd Grade Teacher
      - Randi Evans   3rd Grade Teacher
      - Asayah Muhamad 4th Grade Teacher
      - David Mackall   5th Grade Teacher
      - Kasey Johnson   Music Teacher
      - Ennis Johnson   Art Teacher
9. Go to slide 1 and run your presentation
10. After reviewing the presentation, you decide that the Faculty and Staff slide is too busy. Divide it into three appropriately titled slides. The first slide is for Staff (secretary and director with the director listed first). The second slide is for classroom teachers, and the third is for Music and Arts teachers
11. Add another slide with the title **Agenda** but no content because the agenda has not yet been determined
12. Make the first and last slides from PP01PresntGrphx.ppt the first and last slides of this presentation. Edit the notes to be appropriate for this presentation
13. Save the presentation as **<yourname>LWSH.ppt** and exit PowerPoint if your work is complete

FIGURE 1.36
Little White School House Opening Slide

chapter one

hands-on projects

on the web

1. Wheeler Helping Hand Association Volunteer Training Presentation

The Wheeler Helping Hand Association (WHHA) is an alliance of missions, food banks, and service organizations supporting central Indiana. The goal of the group is to provide assistance to people who need food, shelter, clothing, job training, and counseling. The organization has two full-time staff to organize and coordinate hundreds of volunteers. Volunteers are the backbone of the organization doing everything from cooking to counseling.

All supplies are donated through charitable contributions. Most of the contributions are received through churches, but there is also an annual Thanksgiving phone drive and a new Internet contributions site. The Internet contributions site has two purposes. The first is to let people know what the current needs of the organization are by posting a list of the most needed food, clothing, and services. The second is to promote the Wheeler Helping Hand vision and accept monetary contributions.

You have been a volunteer for several years and are now in charge of training new volunteers. You have decided to create a PowerPoint presentation for this task. Besides using a projected presentation in the training sessions, it will be important for volunteers to have handouts that they can refer to while completing their work.

1. Use your favorite search engine to find organizations and services that could benefit the WHHA clientele. Record the information from at least six sites to be presented to the other volunteers
2. Open PowerPoint and create a new presentation using the AutoContent wizard
   a. Select **Training** for the type of presentation
   b. Select **On screen presentation** as the type of output
   c. Make the title **Wheeler Helping Hand Association**
   d. Include your name in the footer
3. On the first slide change the user name to **Volunteer Training Guide**
4. Edit the second slide to contain the following bullets
   - **WHHA Volunteer Training**
   - **Resources for clients**
   - **Volunteer background of trainees**
5. Delete slides 3 through 5
6. Make the title of the Topic 1 slide **Internet Resources** and add your sites as bullets
7. Save the presentation as **<yourname>WHHA.ppt** and exit PowerPoint if your work is complete

FIGURE 1.37
Wheeler Helping Hand Association Opening Slide

hands-on projects

e-business

1. Exotic Flora Kiosk

Exotic Flora is a consortium of small florists around the world providing unique fresh flower arrangements for every occasion. Each florist pays a membership fee and agrees to deliver ordered arrangements within 24 hours of payment verification. All arrangements are guaranteed to match the order and to last for at least 10 days.

The bulk of flower orders are generated through an e-storefront that accepts orders, verifies payment, and forwards the order to the appropriate florist. Forty-two percent of the profit for each order goes to the e-storefront management organization, ten percent goes to the Exotic Flora association, and the florist who delivers the flowers keeps the remainder.

The member florists have decided to add a series of mall kiosks to their marketing strategy. Each kiosk will use touch screen technology to allow the user to select arrangements, enter a message for the recipient, set a delivery date, and pay by credit card. The kiosk orders will be retrieved four times each day, verified, and routed using the same mechanism as the online orders. You have been asked to build the kiosk.

1. Open PowerPoint, create a new presentation using a Design Template, and name it **ExoticFlora.ppt**
2. Choose the Layers Design template
3. On the first page make the title **ExoticFlora** and the subtitle www.exoticflora.com
4. Insert a new slide
   a. Make the title **Our Guarantee**
   b. Make the body text
      - Unique flowers anywhere in the world in 24 hours
      - Fresh flowers that last at least 10 days
      - If it's not what you ordered, it's free
5. Insert a new slide for each of the following arrangements. Make the slide title the name of the arrangement. Make the body text the description of the arrangement with the price on a new line. We'll add the pictures in a later chapter
   a. Tropical Splash: 4 Ginger, 4 Heliconia, large and lush tropical foliage, 49.00
   b. Tropical Delight: 3 Anthurium, 3 Ginger, 2 Birds of Paradise, and tropical foliage, 65.95
   c. Hearts of Fire: one dozen traditional red Anthurium with lush tropical foliage, 49.50
   d. Kea Tropical Mix: 6 assorted Anthurium, 1 red Ginger, 1 pink Ginger, 2 Birds, 3 Dembrodium, foliage, 65.78
   e. Ohanu Tropical Mix: a seasonal mix of tropical flowers including Gingers, Birds, Heliconia, Psitcorums, Dendrobium, and foliage, 47.50
6. Save the presentation as **<yourname>ExoticFlora.ppt** and exit PowerPoint if your work is complete

FIGURE 1.38
ExoticFlora Opening Slide

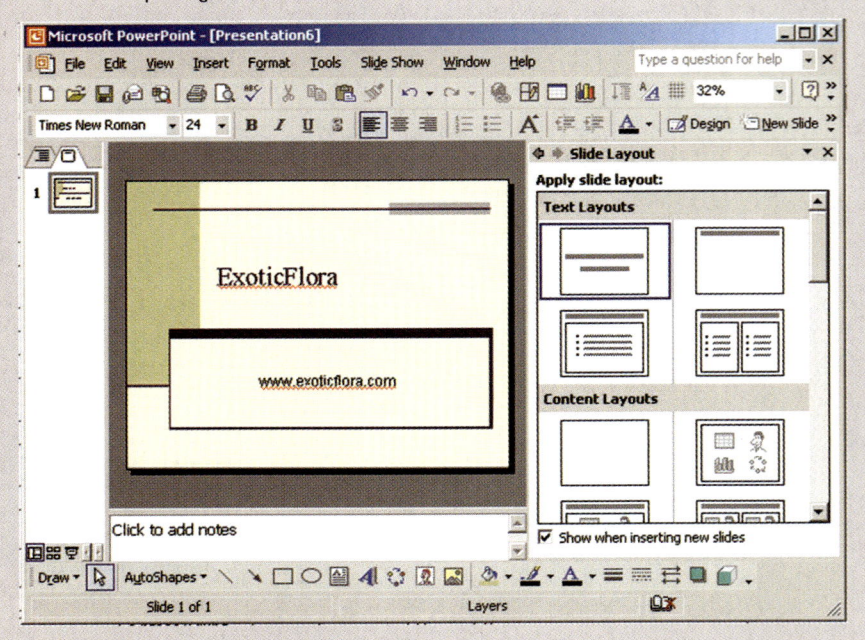

chapter one — hands-on projects

around the world

1. Tracking International Trade Consultants

The Alliance for Global Commerce (AGC) is an organization that tracks and rates businesses participating in international trade. The AGC vision was to create something like the Better Business Bureau on an international scale. Initially the three founders gathered data on trade incidents necessary to support their own trade activities and then published the data in a newsletter distributed to trade, retail, and wholesale organizations. After that, the newsletter recipients reported the trade incidents that were tracked and published in the newsletter. Incidents are any behavior of a trade organization that negatively impacts the viability of the trade pact. The most common incidents are failure to pay, shipping substitute products, and shipments over one week late.

You have been asked to prepare a presentation for an International Trade Seminar to be held in London next month. The presentation is to advertise AGC's services and set standards for trade.

1. Start PowerPoint and use the AutoContent Wizard to create a new presentation with the following attributes
   a. Use **Reporting Progress or Status** from the **Projects** CommandButton
   b. Choose **On-screen presentation** as the presentation type
   c. Make the title **Alliance for Global Commerce**
   d. Put your name in the footer
   e. Make the subtitle **Tracking Trade Relations**
2. Delete the slide titled Status Summary
3. Change the title of the Progress slide to **Status** and adjust the bullets to read
   - Over 3,050 businesses tracked
     - 16 countries represented
   - Thanks to participants
     - Setting standards
     - Reporting incidents
4. Change the next slide to
   a. Make the title **Sample Incident Statistics**
   b. Add these bulleted items
      - CO   0
      - IN   12
      - CA   4
      - MI   6
      - OH   0
5. Add your state if it is not already in the list with three incident reports
6. Add the last slide from **PP01PresntGrphx.ppt** to the end of your presentation
7. Look in your local phone book or on the Internet and find four international trade businesses. Enter each as a bulleted item on the Resources slide
8. Delete the Deliveries and Technology slides
9. Delete the bulleted items on the Costs and Schedule slide and put **TBD** (To be determined)
10. Save the presentation as **<yourname>AGC.ppt** and exit PowerPoint if your work is complete

FIGURE 1.39
AGC Opening Slide

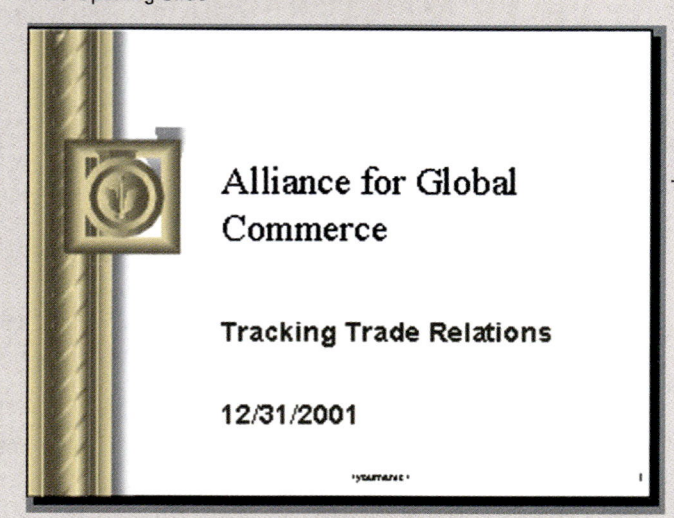

Alliance for Global Commerce

Tracking Trade Relations

12/31/2001

running project

Montgomery-Wellish Foods, Inc.: Welcoming New Employees

Daniel Wellish is the CEO of Montgomery-Wellish Foods, Inc. (MWF), a large international food distributor. MWF processes and packages food that can be found on every aisle of your local grocery store and has facilities in every contiguous state and five foreign countries. Each MWF brand has a brand manager, and each product has a product manager. These managers are responsible for the marketing, production, and distribution of their products and the development of new products.

Each year MWF hires the best and the brightest business graduates from across the United States and puts them through a rigorous training program. These trainees will spend a year or two assisting a product manager and then move on to manage their own product. There are 68 trainees in the current program.

The training program includes a welcome from Daniel, an orientation to the company, general financial and business training, and presentation skills. Presentation skills are critical to product managers since they have to prepare status reports for executive management, speak in public about their product, and conduct product team meetings.

You are on MWF's Information Technology staff and have been assigned to assist the CEO in the preparation of his presentation to the new recruits. Daniel has created an outline of the welcome and asked you to prepare a professional PowerPoint presentation.

1. Start PowerPoint and create a new presentation using the Digital Dots Design Template.
2. On the title slide:
    a. Set the title text to **Welcome!**
    b. Set the subtitle text to **Montgomery-Wellish Foods, Inc Daniel Wellish, CEO**
3. Create the four slides outlined below
    - **Montgomery-Wellish Foods, Inc**
        - **35-year history of excellence**
        - **Over 8,000 products**
        - **More than 600 brands**
        - **Covering 50 states and 8 countries**
    - **Company Profile**
        - **Fortune 100**
        - **Growth through acquisition**
        - **300 new products per year**
        - **One of the most profitable companies in the U.S.**
    - **Our Program**
        - **Hire the best and brightest**
        - **Provide extensive training**
        - **90% of promotions from within**
    - **Thank You**
4. Preview the presentation and make any necessary corrections
5. Save the presentation as **<yourname>MWF.ppt** and exit PowerPoint if your work is complete

FIGURE 1.40
Daniel Wellish's Opening Slide

> **Welcome!**
> Montgomery-Wellish Foods, Inc
> Daniel Wellish, CEO

did you know?

computer *viruses were first discovered in the late 1980s, and since that time, IBM's Thomas J. Watson Research Center has collected more than 10,000. It is estimated that six to nine new viruses are found daily.*

the *first commercial passenger airplane with a bathroom began flying in 1919.*

the *first parking meter was installed in Oklahoma City, Oklahoma, in 1935.*

nanotechnology *has produced a guitar no bigger than a blood cell. The guitar, 10 micrometers long, has six strummable strings.*

the *"save" icon on Microsoft Word shows a floppy disk, with the shutters on backwards.*

the *first portable computer introduced in 1983 by Compaq weighed _____ pounds.*

Chapter Objectives

- Add Header and Footer content to slides—PPT2002-1-3
- Add Header and Footer content to Notes and Handouts
- Print a Slide Show, Notes, and Handouts—PPT2002-5-1
- Print Help topics
- Use PowerPoint's outlining features and import Word content—PPT2002-2-1
- Import and export Word documents—PPT2002-2-1 and PPT2002-6-4

CHAPTER

2

two

Organizing Your Presentation

chapter case

Teaching Presentation Graphics Using Presentation Graphics

Randy Rae is the training director of a large government installation in the western United States. The facility hosts several thousand government employees with training needs that run from mundane bookkeeping to exotic technology. Short sessions can run for a few days, but two to ten-week sessions are more the norm. The facility is completely contained with guest accommodations and food services to support 300 simultaneous guests.

Randy's staff includes ten full-time trainers and a wide assortment of specialty trainers. Although the technology classrooms have contained computers for several years, all training has been accomplished using flipcharts, whiteboards, and overheads.

The training rooms are being overhauled and in two months' time will each have high-quality ceiling mount projection units. The electronic stages at the front of each room will include a projection wall that doubles as a whiteboard and a height-adjustable podium with built-in laptop computer bay. Full-time trainers will be provided with high-end laptops. Laptops will also be available to part-time trainers and trainees by checkout. The Microsoft Office suite has been selected as the standard software for training.

Randy recognizes that the new classrooms will be a big technological jump requiring proper training for his staff. An expected outcome of the high-tech classrooms is that all of the trainers will use

FIGURE 2.1
Features of PowerPoint

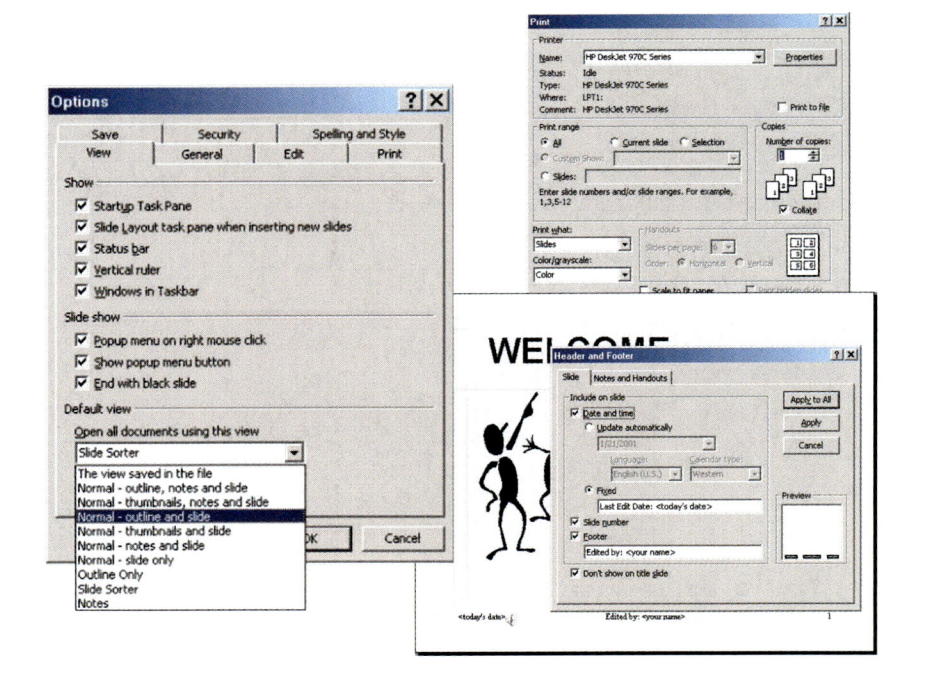

the technology to teach every subject. An integral component of this technology will be presenting with PowerPoint.

Between 60 and 100 trainers need to effectively learn PowerPoint and then have technical support while they convert their topics to slide shows. Most of the trainers have some computer experience and are comfortable with word processing, which was the standard for creating overheads in the past. Randy has hired five local college students as assistants who will be responsible for supporting the trainers during the curriculum conversion.

Randy has asked his friend Victoria Faust from Merrillville College to provide the PowerPoint training. Victoria believes that the trainers will need two 6-hour days with PowerPoint. The first day will concentrate on PowerPoint features, and the second day will get them started on their training content. Victoria plans to emphasize converting existing documents to PowerPoint outlines to help the trainers rapidly update their content. As Victoria's assistant, you have been asked to review her existing materials and create the opening presentation.

> **CHAPTER OUTLINE**
>
> **2.1** Printing
> **2.2** Outlining Ideas

SESSION 2.1 PRINTING

You have been updating presentations for Victoria to use in her regular classes, but are not familiar with much of the content that will be presented to the trainers. Victoria has asked you to familiarize yourself with PowerPoint's printing features, outline facilities, and ability to import documents created in other applications.

In any application, effective printing is critical to distributing usable output. With PowerPoint the most common output is a projected slide show, but printing is the most effective way to document a presentation, create audience handouts, and view speaker's notes. Sometimes a presentation is delivered using transparencies with an overhead projector. In such cases, the transparencies are generally printed using a printer that will accept transparencies in the paper tray.

PRINT PREVIEW

The **Print Preview** button on the standard toolbar presents a document as it will appear when printed. PowerPoint's Print Preview screen provides options for selecting what to print (slides, notes, handouts, or outline) and the ability to update a few of the printing options such as:

- Choosing landscape or portrait orientation for handouts, notes pages, and outlines
- Adding a frame around each slide for printout only
- Setting header and footer options
- Selecting color options

FIGURE 2.2
Print Preview

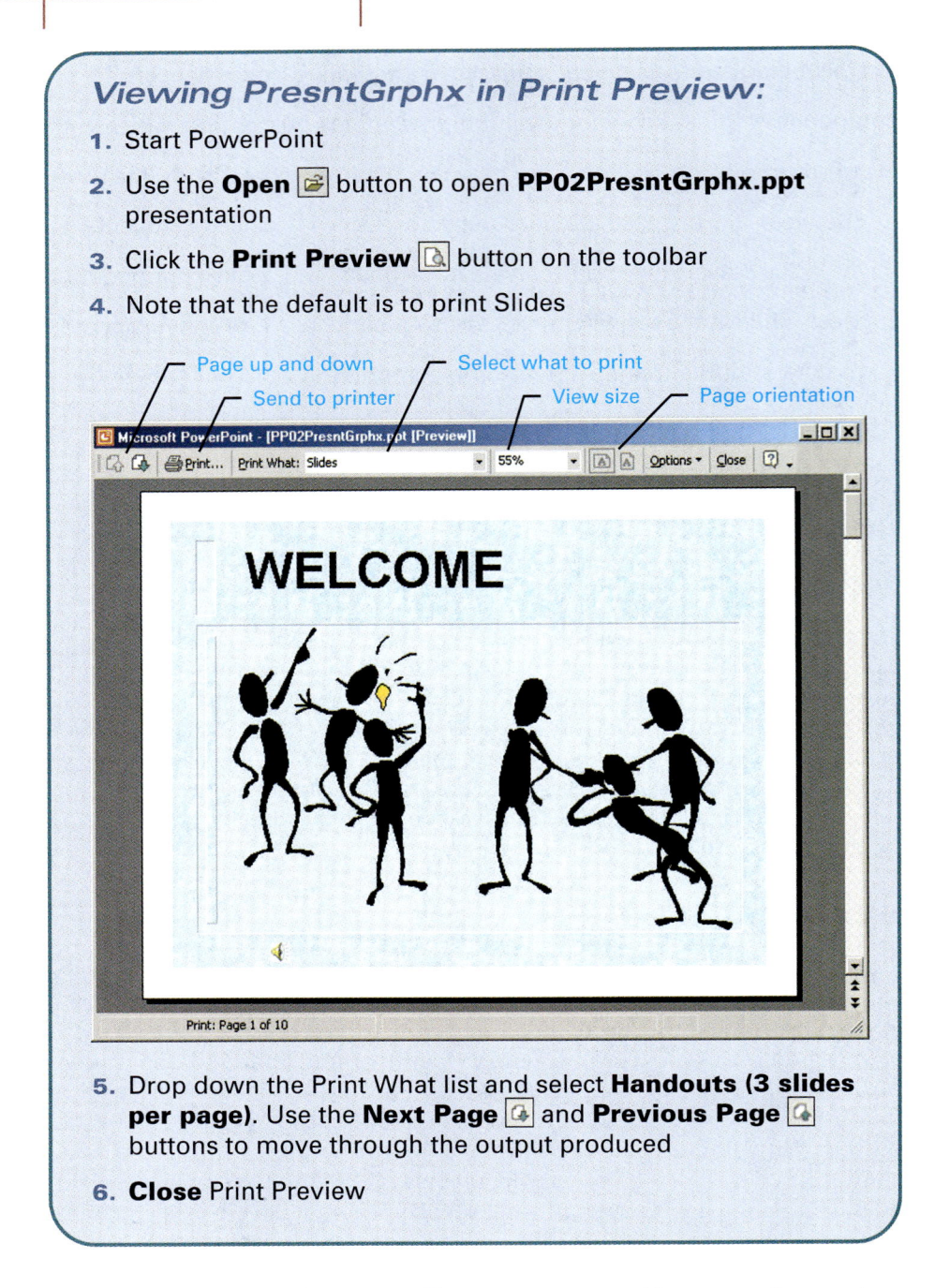

> **Viewing PresntGrphx in Print Preview:**
> 1. Start PowerPoint
> 2. Use the **Open** button to open **PP02PresntGrphx.ppt** presentation
> 3. Click the **Print Preview** button on the toolbar
> 4. Note that the default is to print Slides
>
> *Page up and down — Select what to print*
> *Send to printer — View size — Page orientation*
>
> 5. Drop down the Print What list and select **Handouts (3 slides per page)**. Use the **Next Page** and **Previous Page** buttons to move through the output produced
> 6. **Close** Print Preview

Print preview is the most effective way to verify output formatting. When the preview is satisfactory, the Print button will send the output directly to the printer. Minor adjustments to the output, as previously noted, can be applied from print preview. Significant changes to layout or printer options require using the Page Layout and Printer dialog boxes discussed in the other topics of this session.

CREATING HEADERS AND FOOTERS

A *header* is any text that prints in the top margin of a page or pages, and a *footer* is any content that prints in the bottom margin. Common header/footer content includes the date, page number, Company/presenter name, and document revision information such as "Draft" or "Confidential."

PowerPoint supports two different types of headers and footers. The slide header/footer belongs to each slide and will display on the screen in a slide show and print as part of the contents of each slide. The Notes and Handouts headers/footers will appear only when viewing or printing the Notes, Handouts, and Outline pages and are designed to be printed at the top and bottom of each Notes, Handouts, or Outline printed page. This is an important distinction, since multiple presentation slides can be printed on one physical page and this type of header/footer will only appear once per page. The positioning of the header/footer placeholders is controlled by Notes and Handouts masters whose customization will be covered in a later session.

Adding Headers and Footers to Slides

Headers and footers added to a slide will appear on the slide during a show and print with that slide in handouts and notes pages. The header/footer content can be set for one slide, a group of slides, or the entire presentation. To create a header or footer, type the text to be contained by each header/footer placeholder using the Header and Footer dialog box.

The Slide Master controls the positioning of the placeholders for header/footer data in a slide. The default layout positions all content as a footer across the bottom of a slide. While the master could be customized to display some or all of the data across the top of a slide as a header, this placement would disrupt the visual impact of the presentation and is rarely used. Customizing the Slide Master will be covered in a later session.

Slide headers and footers can be added and updated using the Header and Footer option of the View menu in either the Normal or Slide Sorter view. They can also be accessed from Print Preview. Set header and footer content in whatever view is active since there are no specific advantages to using one method of viewing over another.

Most presentation editing is accomplished using Normal view, so it is logical to add slide headers and footers from that view. The Outline pane can be used to select a slide or slides before activating the Header and

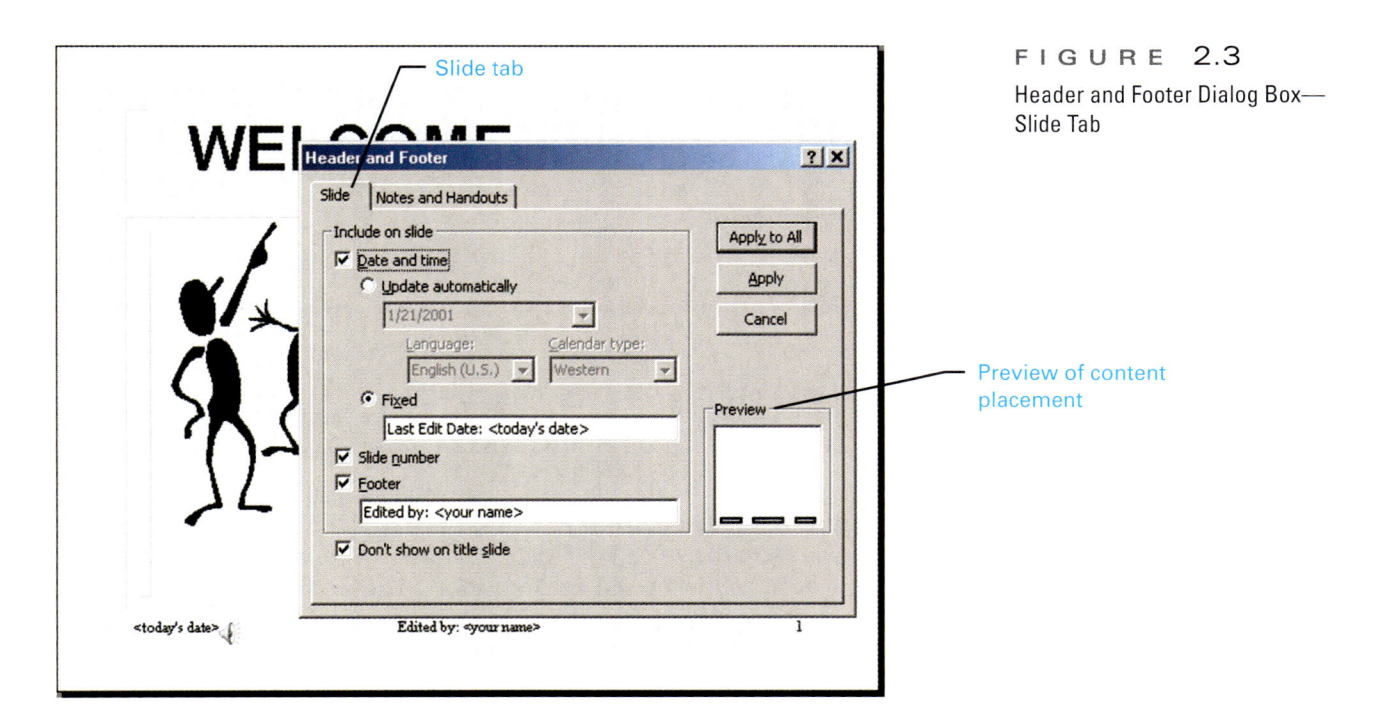

FIGURE 2.3

Header and Footer Dialog Box—Slide Tab

Footer dialog box. To select contiguous slides, click the first slide and then hold the Shift key while clicking the last slide. To select noncontiguous slides, click the first slide and then hold the Ctrl key while clicking the remaining selections.

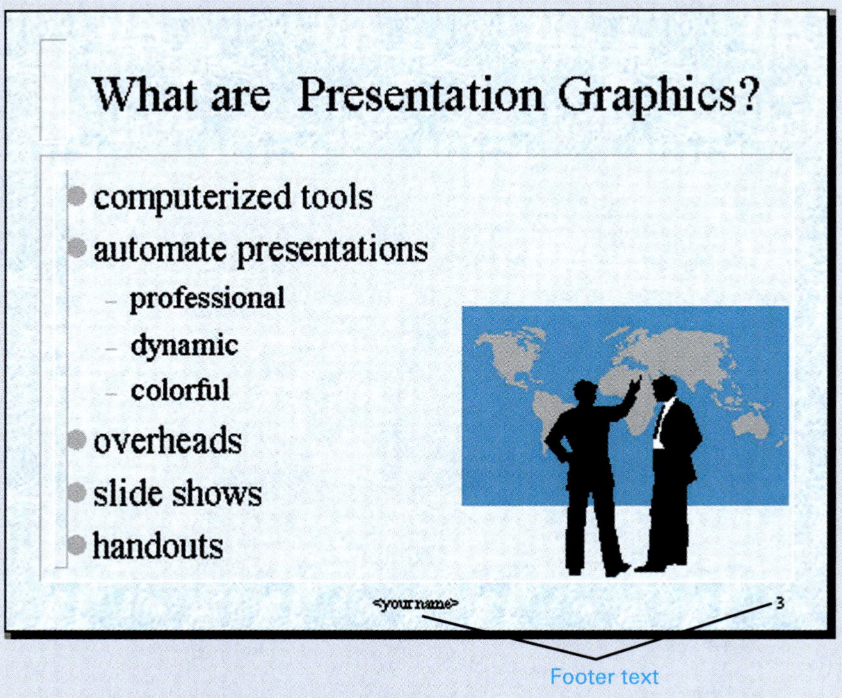

FIGURE 2.4
Footer on Slide 3

> ### Adding Footer content in Normal view:
> 1. Verify that PowerPoint is running with **PP02PresntGrphx.ppt** as the open presentation
> 2. In the Outline pane of Normal view, select slide **3** titled What Are Presentation Graphics?
> 3. From the **View** menu select **Header and Footer . . .**
> 4. Uncheck the **Date and Time** option. Notice the change in the preview
> 5. Check the **Slide number** option. Notice the change in the preview
> 6. Place your name in the Footer Text Box
> 7. Click **Apply** to update only the selected slide
>
> *What are Presentation Graphics?*
> - computerized tools
> - automate presentations
>   - professional
>   - dynamic
>   - colorful
> - overheads
> - slide shows
> - handouts
>
> <yourname>   3
>
> Footer text
>
> 8. Use the previous figure to verify your results

After setting the header/footer content, click the Apply button to place the defined text on the selected slide(s). Clicking Apply to All will place the content on every slide in the presentation. The position of the header/footer elements is defined in the Slide Master, which you will learn to customize in a later session.

Slide Sorter view is used to reorganize slides and is an easy place to modify the header/footer content of slides. As in Normal view, multiple slides can be selected using the Shift and Ctrl keys. Once the selections are made, the Header and Footer dialog box is accessed from the View menu.

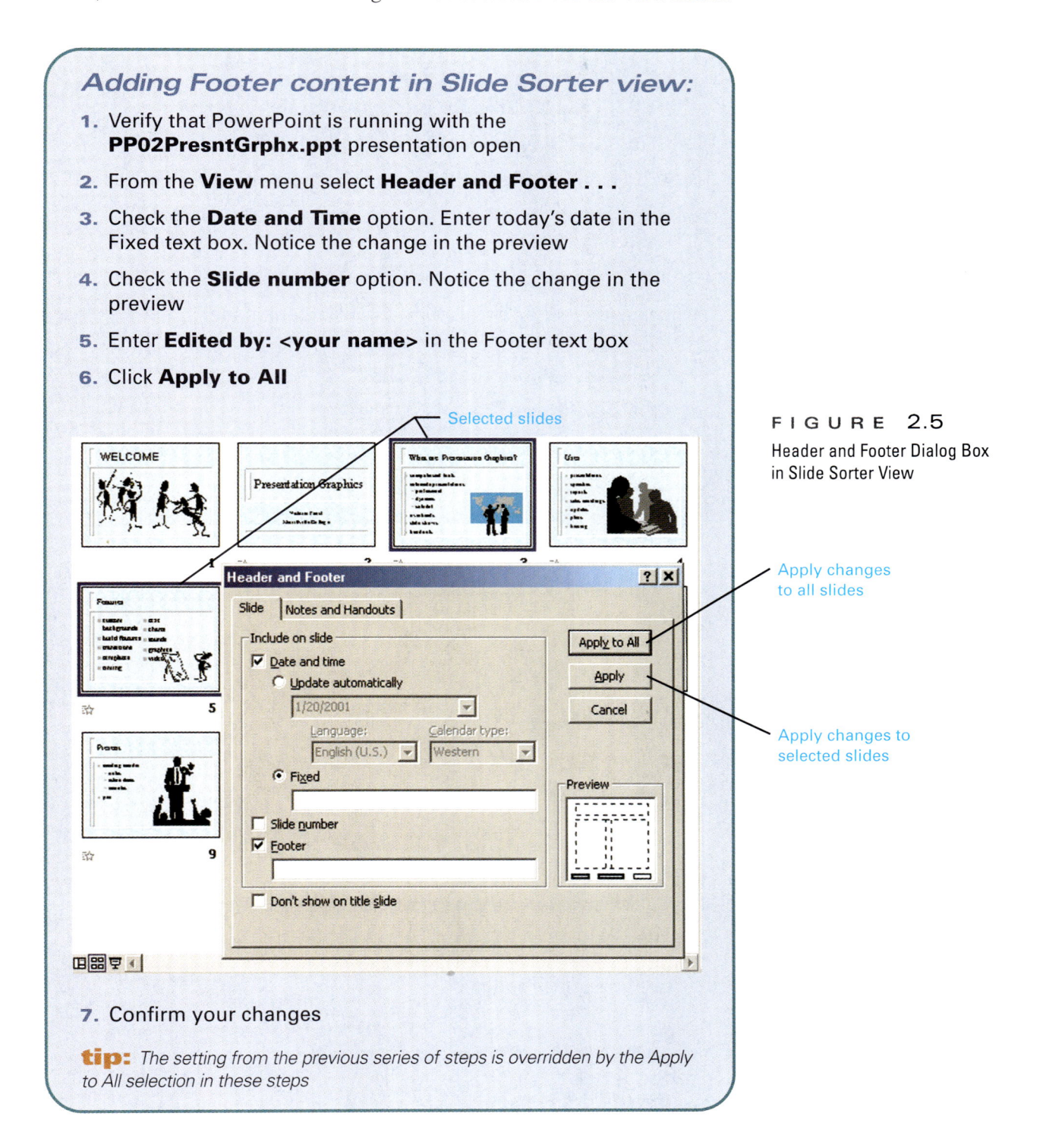

Adding Footer content in Slide Sorter view:

1. Verify that PowerPoint is running with the **PP02PresntGrphx.ppt** presentation open
2. From the **View** menu select **Header and Footer . . .**
3. Check the **Date and Time** option. Enter today's date in the Fixed text box. Notice the change in the preview
4. Check the **Slide number** option. Notice the change in the preview
5. Enter **Edited by: <your name>** in the Footer text box
6. Click **Apply to All**

7. Confirm your changes

tip: *The setting from the previous series of steps is overridden by the Apply to All selection in these steps*

FIGURE 2.5

Header and Footer Dialog Box in Slide Sorter View

Print Preview is also an effective place to edit header/footer contents. Slides, notes, and handouts can all be viewed in Print Preview to determine how they will appear on the printed page. The limitation of this method is that there is no way to select specific slides in Print Preview. Any changes that are made to the header/footer content will be applied to all of the pages of the open document.

> **Adding Footer content in Print Preview:**
>
> 1. Verify that PowerPoint is running with the **PP02PresntGrphx.ppt** presentation open
> 2. Click the **Print Preview** on the toolbar
> 3. Drop down the Options list and choose **Header and Footer** . . .
> 4. Edit the Date and Time option to read **Last Edit Date: <today's date>**
> 5. Verify that the **Slide number** option is checked
> 6. Leave the Edited by: <your name> content in the Footer text box
> 7. Click **Don't show on title slide**
> 8. Click **Apply to All**
>
> Drop-down list with Header and Footer option 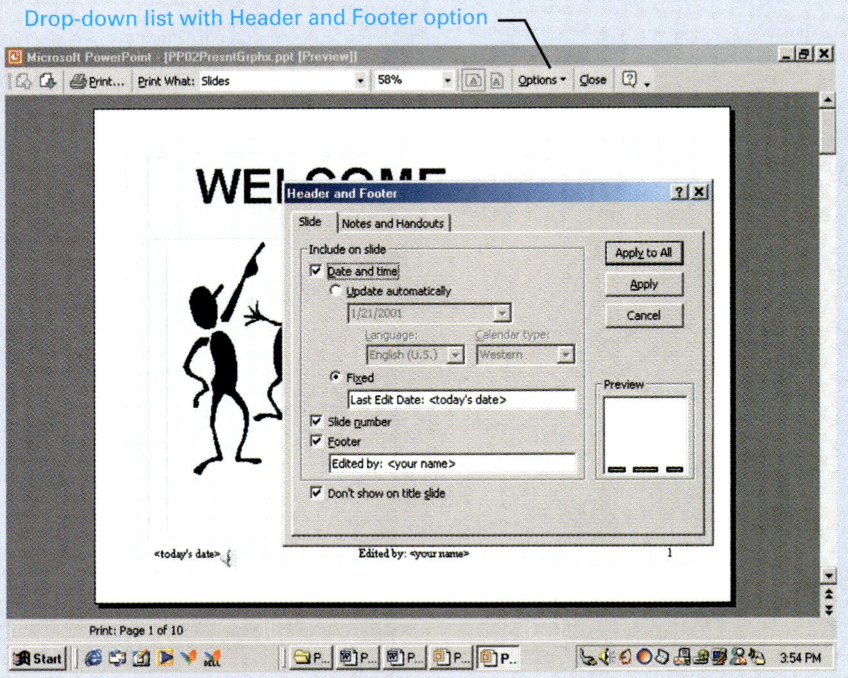
>
> 9. Confirm your changes
>
> **tip:** *The first slide still contains the footer because it does not use the Title slide layout. The second slide does not because it uses Title slide layout*
>
> 10. **Close** Print Preview

FIGURE 2.6

Header and Footer Dialog Box in Print Preview

One behavior of headers/footers that is not intuitive to many users is the Don't show on title slide check box. PowerPoint has a Title slide layout and only suppresses the header/footer on slides with that layout. The first slide of PresntGrphx does not use a Title slide layout (it is Blank layout), and so the header/footer still displays. The second slide does use the Title slide layout, and the footer is correctly suppressed.

Since Victoria does not want the footer to disrupt the opening slide, and Title slide layout is not appropriate, you will remove the header/footer from the first presentation slide.

Removing a Footer from the selected slide:

1. Verify that PowerPoint is running with the **PP02PresntGrphx.ppt** presentation open
2. Click on the first slide to select it
3. Select **Header and Footer** . . . from the **View** menu
4. Deselect all options

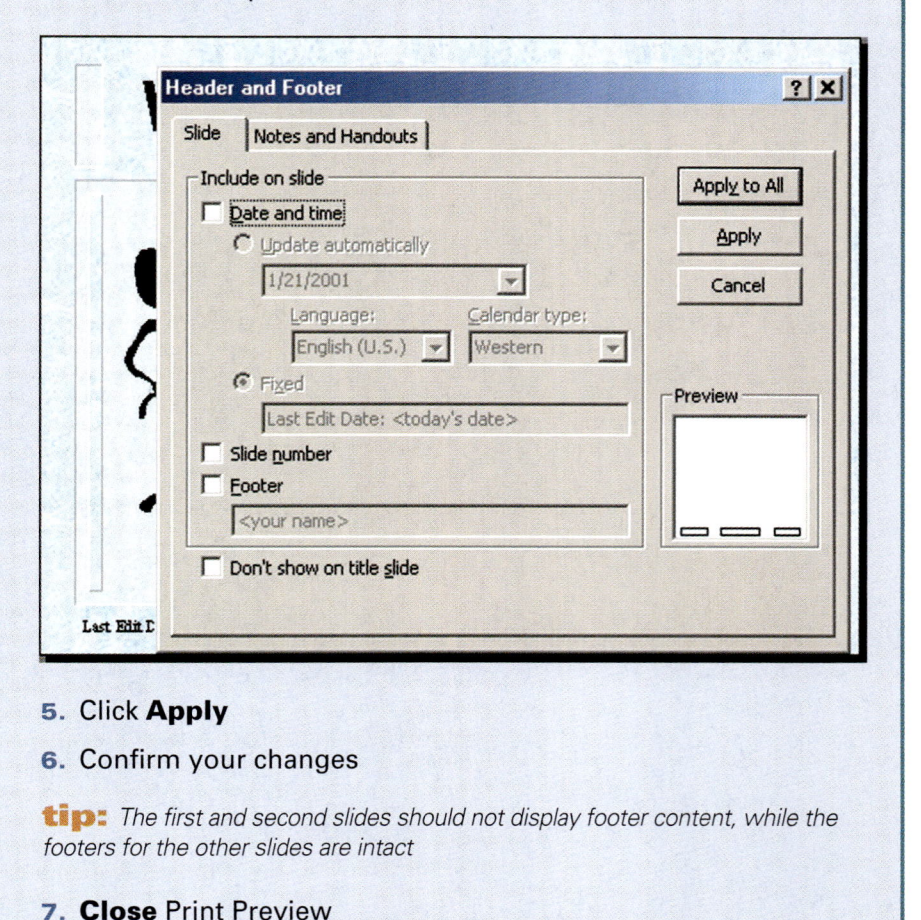

FIGURE 2.7

Updating the Header/Footer of Slide 1

5. Click **Apply**
6. Confirm your changes

tip: *The first and second slides should not display footer content, while the footers for the other slides are intact*

7. **Close** Print Preview

To remove a footer from a slide or slides, deselect all of the components on the Header and Footer dialog box and then select either Apply (to update selected slides) or Apply to all (to remove the header/footer from all slides). When setting headers/footers, apply the content that will be on most of the slides first and then set the individual header/footer content.

Notes and Handouts

Creating header and/or footer content for Notes and Handouts pages applies that material to all print pages. Unlike slides, there are no options for creating different headers/footers on the various output pages. Any headers/footers set for Notes and Handouts will also print with an outline.

Both header and footer content can be set at the same time for Notes and Handouts pages using the Notes and Handouts tab of the Header and Footer dialog box. By default the page number will print as a footer on all pages, but this can be modified or omitted.

All of the methods demonstrated for setting slide headers and footers can also be used to specify Notes and Handouts header/footer text. The Header and Footer dialog box has a Notes and Handouts tab for this purpose. Since most users set up header/footer content just prior to printing, Print Preview is the most common setup locale.

Adding Notes and Handouts header/footer text from Print Preview:

1. Verify that PowerPoint is running with the **PP02PresntGrphx.ppt** presentation open
2. Click on the **Print Preview** button
3. Drop down the **Print What** list and select **Handouts (3 slides per page)**
4. Select **Header and Footer** . . . from the **Options** drop-down list
5. Click the **Notes and Handouts** tab
6. Deselect and select each option and notice the impact on the preview
7. Enter a Fixed Date and Time of **Last Edit Date: <today's date>**

FIGURE 2.8
Notes and Handouts Tab of the Header and Footer Dialog Box

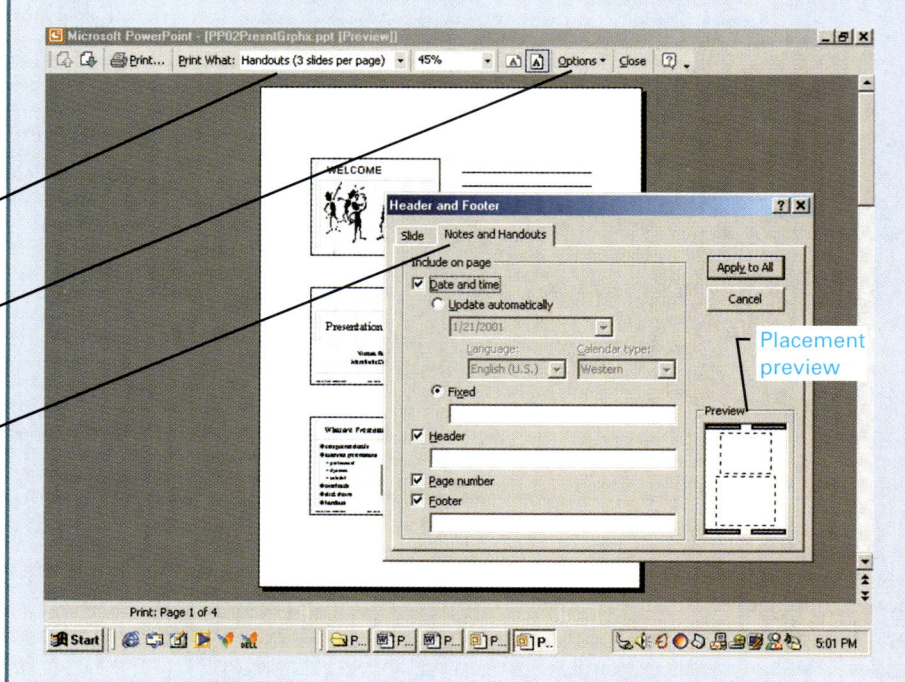

- Select what to print
- Activate Header and Footer dialog box
- Notes and Handouts tab
- Placement preview

8. Enter a Header of **Speech 101**
9. Check the Page number Check Box
10. Type **Edited by: <your name>** in the Footer Text Box
11. Click **Apply to All**
12. Confirm your changes

tip: *Notice that the header and footer appear on each page of the handouts, while the slides display the footers set up in the previous steps*

13. **Close** Print Preview

Text added as a header or footer can be used to provide information like revision (1st Draft, 2nd Draft, . . .), security level (Confidential, Dept. Only, . . .), copyright, credit contributors, or other presentation documentation. When adding headers/footers to slides, be sure that they are concise and do not detract from the main content.

UNDERSTANDING PAGE SETUP

When printing slides, handouts, or notes, the ***Page Setup*** determines how output appears on the printed page. Page Setup is accomplished for all printed output from one dialog box. PowerPoint's default settings are shown in the next figure.

There are seven slide size format selections:

- On-Screen Show is used for an on-screen slide show producing slides 10 × 7.5 in.
- Letter Paper (8.5 × 11 in.) is the correct setting for printing full-page slides
- A4 Paper (210 × 297 mm) is an international paper setting using paper 10.83 × 7.5 in.

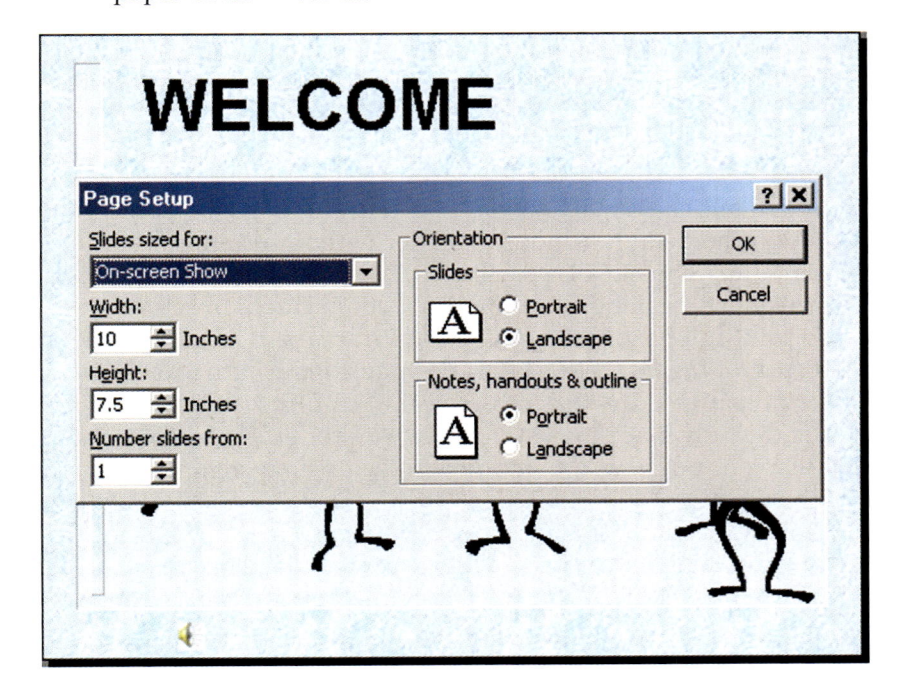

FIGURE 2.9

Page Setup Dialog Box

- 35-mm Slides will size the presentation for conversion to 35-mm slides, which are smaller than the on-screen show setting
- Overhead is the setting for printing standard 8.5 × 11 in. overhead transparencies
- Banner is 8 × 1 in.
- Custom will allow the creation of custom slide sizes

Printing can be accomplished with any of these settings, but will be optimized by selecting the settings appropriate for the print media being used.

another*way*

. . . to Adjust Page Orientation

Print Preview can also be used to change the *page orientation.* Two option button groups are provided to set the page orientation to either portrait or landscape. Unless the placeholders on the output have been resized, it is best not to adjust the page orientation. The Options drop-down list also has a **Scale to fit paper** option that will produce the largest output for the current paper size

Changing PresntGrphx slide size:

1. Verify that PowerPoint is running with the **PP02PresntGrphx.ppt** presentation open
2. On the **File** menu, click **Page Setup**
3. Drop down the **Slides sized for:** list
4. Click **Letter Paper (8.5 × 11 in.)**
5. Notice that the page orientation is set to Landscape for slides and Portrait for all other output
6. Notice the Width and Height settings used to create custom slide sizes
7. Notice the Number slides from option used to control slide numbers
8. Click **OK**

The Page Setup dialog box can only be accessed from the Print option of the File menu. Settings that were noted but not explored in the steps include the ability to customize the beginning slide number and adjusting page orientation. The default page orientation for slides is landscape, while that for all other prints is portrait. PowerPoint uses placeholders that must be modified before changing page orientation of a slide is effective.

EXPLORING THE PRINT DIALOG BOX

Clicking the Printer icon on the standard PowerPoint toolbar will print the presentation on the default Windows printer without prompting for any setup information. The existing settings will be used, so whatever was printed last will print again. If nothing has been printed, the PowerPoint default is to print full-page slides. Using the Print option of the File menu opens the ***Print dialog box,*** which will allow custom printing selections.

Many print features can be accessed from Print Preview, but the Print dialog box is the only place to customize all printer attributes. The available Print dialog box options are outlined in the previous figure, but a few warrant discussion.

The Printer selections include choosing a printer that is known to Windows, customizing that printer's properties, and printing to a file. Printers must be installed in Windows before they are available to applications like PowerPoint. All printers that have been set up in Windows are available on the drop-down list. Once a printer is selected, the Properties

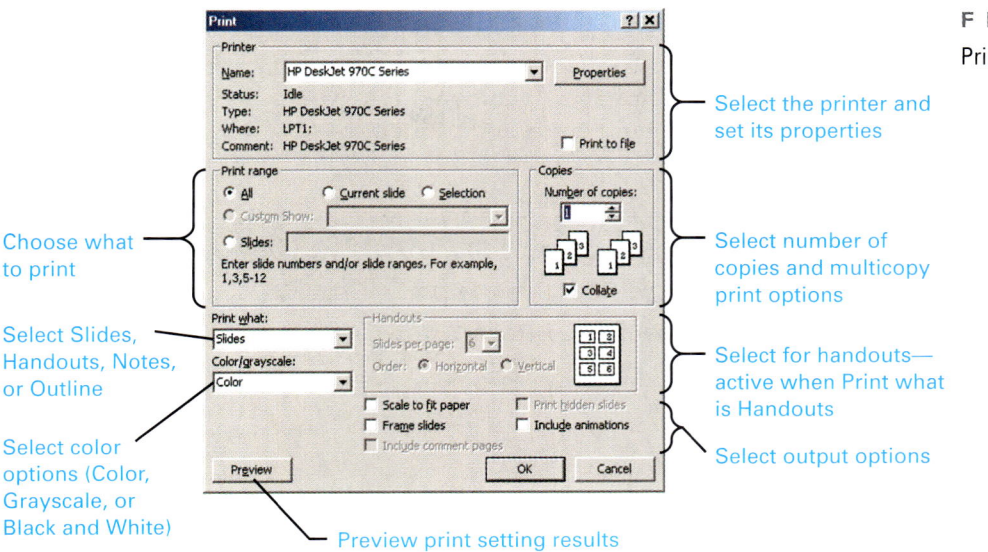

FIGURE 2.10

Print Dialog Box

Choose what to print

Select Slides, Handouts, Notes, or Outline

Select color options (Color, Grayscale, or Black and White)

Select the printer and set its properties

Select number of copies and multicopy print options

Select for handouts—active when Print what is Handouts

Select output options

Preview print setting results

button will allow features specific to that printer model like color, print quality, and duplex printing to be set. The installed printers and their features determine the options available. Shared network printers are usually secured so that settings selected by one user don't impact other users. For that reason, the Properties button of a shared network printer is usually disabled.

The **Print range** section of the Print dialog box allows a page or pages of a presentation to print. The default selection is All, but the current slide, or a group of slides, can be specified. For example, entering 2, 6, 8-10 in the Slides Text Box would print slide 2, slide 6, and slides 8 through 10. The Copies selections control the number of printed copies produced and how those copies are sorted as they print. Multiple copies can be collated (print all of copy 1, then all of copy 2, and so on) or stacked (print all copies of page 1, then all copies of page 2, and so on).

The Print What dialog box allows the user to choose from a drop-down list of slides, handouts, notes, or outline. Choosing slides will print the slides selected in Print range. Similarly, handouts, notes, and outline will print the selected slides in the selected format. When Handouts is selected in the Print What dialog box, the Handouts area is activated so that handout options can be set. The drop-down list includes handouts with one to nine slides per page. Three slides per page is a common option because it provides notes lines for the audience to the right of the screens. It is always a good idea to preview your setup before printing.

Most presentations are designed to be shown in color, but slides and handouts are usually printed in black and white or shades of gray (grayscale). As part of the print process, Microsoft PowerPoint sets the colors in the presentation to match the selected printer's capabilities. For example, if the selected printer is black and white, the presentation will automatically be set to print in *grayscale*. The defaults can be adjusted using the Color/grayscale drop-down list.

It is important to preview the slides as they will be printed because color can cause legibility problems when printed in grayscale or black and white. For example, dark red text against a shaded background displays well in color, but can be illegible in gray tones or black and white. Yellow is effective in a color presentation, but may fade to white in grayscale printing. There are no absolutes in this area since each printer is different.

another*way*

. . . to View Color Options

Use the Color/Grayscale button on the toolbar to see the impact of color selection in Normal view. The advantage of using this method is that the grayscale can be customized. Point to an area of a slide with no text or graphic content, right-click, and select Grayscale Setting. One or more options on this menu can improve the readability of grayscale output—the trick is to find the right one for your presentation.

POWERPOINT

Printing Slides, Handouts, and Notes

Slides can be printed for handouts, to create *transparencies* for an overhead projector, or simply as documentation. Microsoft PowerPoint optimizes slides to print on the selected printer, but you can customize any of the settings using the Page Setup and Print dialog boxes.

---

task reference

Printing a Slide Show:

- From the **File** menu select **Page Setup**
  - In Slides sized for box, click the desired option—usually Letter Paper (8.5 × 11 in.)
- Click **OK**
- Click the **Print Preview** button from the standard toolbar
  - Use **Options** to add **Header and Footer**
  - Use **Options** to change the **Colors/Grayscale**
  - Use **Options** to select **Scale to Fit Paper**
- Click the **Print** button

Printing PresntGrphx slides:

1. Verify that PowerPoint is running with the **PP02PresntGrphx.ppt** presentation open. Page Setup was accomplished in an earlier set of steps
2. Select **Print** from the **File** menu
3. In the Slides Text Box of Print Range enter **1-3**
4. Set the color to **Grayscale** if it is not already
5. Click **Preview** to verify your settings
6. Click **Print**
7. Click **OK**

Notice that the slide header/footer print as you set them up, and that the Notes and Handouts header/footer didn't print with the slides. All slides in a presentation must have the same orientation.

PowerPoint can also print presentation handouts containing between one and nine slides per handout page. The layout selection for handouts can be made in either Print Preview or the Print dialog box. One or two slides per page is the most effective layout for text-heavy presentations when the audience needs to be able to read every word of the content. The three-slide layout has lines for notes. The four-slide layout works best in landscape. Six- and nine-slide layouts are generally too small to be read, but work well for graphic-heavy slides.

Using Print Preview to make layout selections provides a visual advantage. By zooming to 100% the readability of the current selection can be evaluated and zooming out demonstrates how the slides relate to each other on the page. Recall that page layout and header/footer content can also be altered from Print preview.

Printing PresntGrphx handouts:

1. Verify that PowerPoint is running with the **PP02PresntGrphx.ppt** presentation open. Page Setup was accomplished in an earlier set of steps
2. Select **Print** from the **File** menu
3. In the Slides Text Box of Print Range enter **1-9**
4. Set the color to **Grayscale** if it is not already
5. In the Print What drop-down list select **Handouts**
6. Set Slides per page to **9**
7. Click **Preview** to verify your settings
8. Zoom to 100% to see the output at full size
9. In the Print What drop-down list select **Handouts (6 per page)** and evaluate the results
10. In the Print What drop-down list select **Handouts (4 per page)** and evaluate the results. Change the Layout to **Landscape**

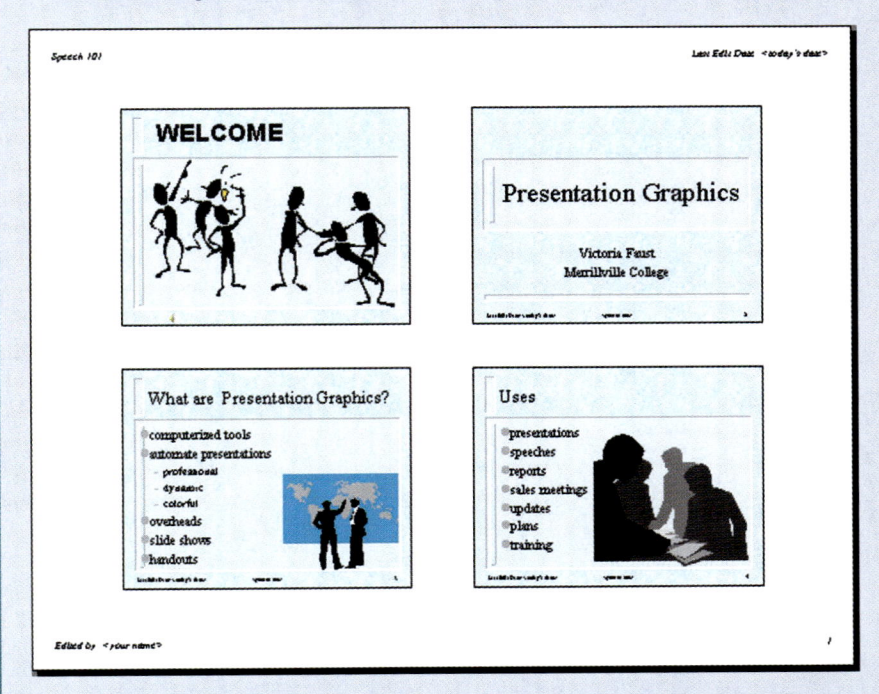

FIGURE 2.11

Print Preview of Handouts (4 per Page), Landscape Page Orientation

11. Evaluate the remaining Handouts settings in Portrait orientation and then return to Handouts (4 slides per page) with Landscape page orientation
12. Click **Print**
13. Enter 1-4 in the Slides Text Box of Print Range and click **OK**

Handouts can be printed in color, but if noncolor copies will be made, it is best to print them in grayscale because the copied results will be easier to read. Sending the PowerPoint handouts to Word can develop additional print layouts.

Notes pages contain the notes that were added to each slide. These notes are usually intended for the speaker, but can also be used as audience handouts providing the detail of the slide topics. Notes pages print one slide per page in either portrait or landscape page orientation.

Printing PresntGrphx notes pages:

1. Verify that PowerPoint is running with the **PP02PresntGrphx.ppt** presentation open. Page Setup was accomplished in an earlier set of steps
2. Select **Print** from the **File** menu
3. In the Slides Text Box of Print Range enter **1-3**
4. Set the color to **Grayscale** if it is not already
5. In the Print What drop-down list select **Notes**
6. Click **Preview** to verify your settings
7. Zoom to 100% to see the output at full size

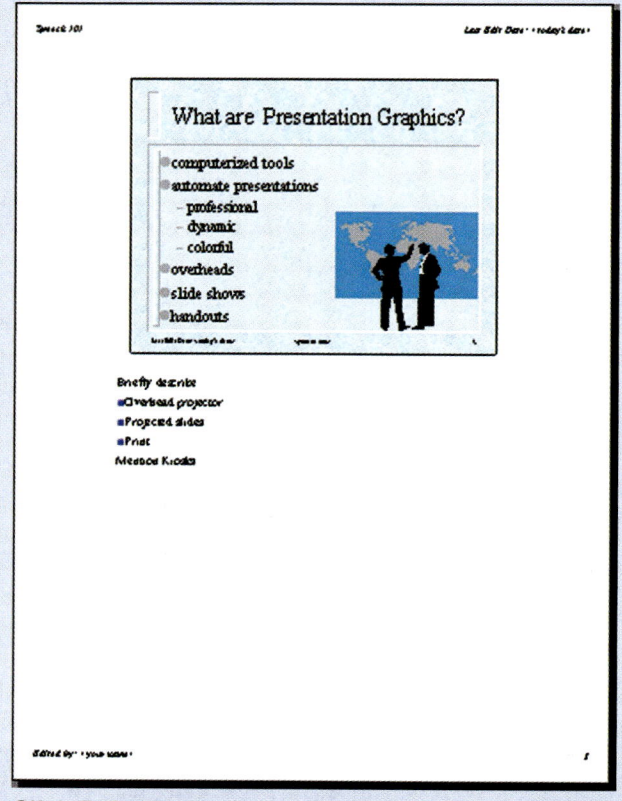

FIGURE 2.12
Print Preview of Notes Page

8. Click **Print**
9. Click **OK**

Notes pages can be designed and formatted with colors, shapes, charts, and layout options. Each notes page includes a copy of the slide it refers to and prints one slide per page, with the notes printed under the slide image. To print two slides per page with the associated notes printed next to the slides, send the presentation to Microsoft Word.

Printing an Outline

Some speakers prefer using a text-only outline of a presentation for speaker's notes and/or handouts. The Outline pane of Normal view displays a text outline of the current project. This outline can be expanded and collapsed using the *Expand All* button on the toolbar. When expanded, all of the slide text displays. When collapsed, only the slide titles display.

Printing PresntGrphx outline:

1. Verify that PowerPoint is running with the **PP02PresntGrphx.ppt** presentation open. Page Setup was accomplished in an earlier set of steps
2. In Normal view click the **Expand All** button to collapse the outline to titles only
3. Click the **Expand All** button again to show all of the text in the outline
4. Select **Print** from the **File** menu
5. Select **All** as the Print Range
6. In the Print What drop-down list select **Outline View**
7. Click **Preview** to verify your settings
8. Zoom to 100% to see the output at full size

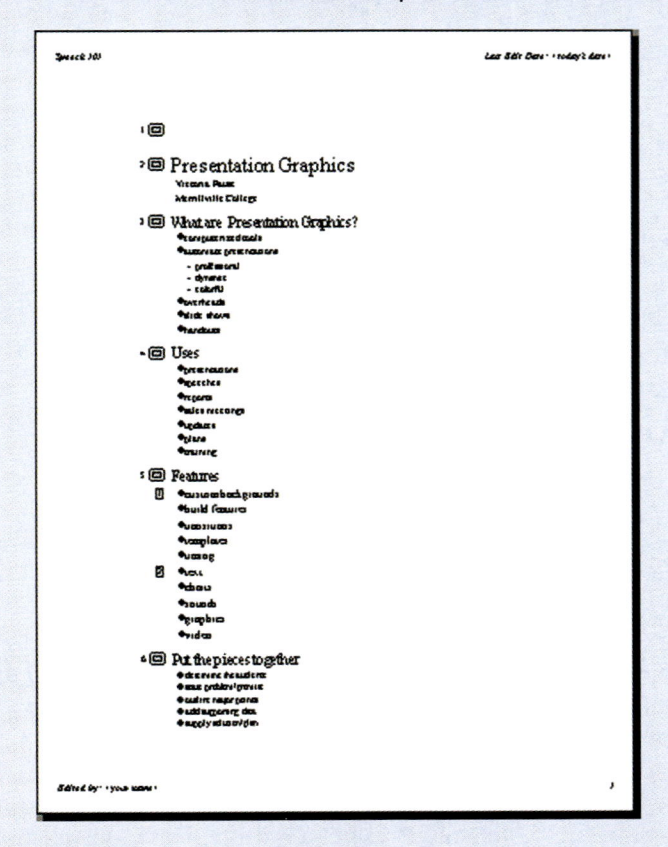

FIGURE 2.13

Print Preview of Outline View Expanded

9. Click **Print**
10. Enter **3** in the Slides Text Box of Print Range and click **OK**

Before printing an outline, expand or collapse to the desired level of detail. Any formatting applied to slide text also displays in the outline print. Like other PowerPoint prints, an outline can be sent to Word for further formatting.

It is sometimes beneficial to print Help topics so that you can more readily follow instructions and work on the computer at the same time. Each page of Help displays the printer icon used to print the topic being displayed. One important Help topic is Troubleshooting Printing. If you are not getting the results that you want, this is a good place to research common print problems and their solutions.

SESSION 2.1 — making the grade

1. What is the benefit of using Print Preview to set up printed output? Limitations?
2. Differentiate between the header/footer settings for slides and notes pages.
3. When the Don't show on title slide option is checked for a header/footer, how does PowerPoint determine where to suppress the header/footer?
4. How is a footer removed?

SESSION 2.2 OUTLINING IDEAS

As you can imagine, organization is an important component of any presentation. Session 1.1 introduced the Outline pane of Normal view as a way to view, edit, and reorganize slide text. This session will concentrate on using the outline view to share data with Microsoft Word documents and format presentation text.

USING POWERPOINT'S OUTLINE VIEW

The value of the outline format when working on a presentation is the ease with which text can be added, moved, formatted, and deleted. Additionally, the outline buttons become available on the Standard and Formatting toolbars to increase or decrease text indents, collapse and expand content, and show or hide text formatting as you work.

Outline View versus Outline Pane

Previous versions of PowerPoint had a separate view called the ***Outline view.*** In the current version of PowerPoint, the Outline view is a customization of the Normal view. Normal view is the main editing view used to develop presentations and contains four panes: the Outline pane, the Slide pane, the Notes pane, and the Task pane. The Outline pane contains two tabs: the Outline tab and the Slides tab. The Outline tab displays an outline of the current presentation consisting of the titles and text from each slide. Besides displaying the flow of a presentation, the Outline tab can be used to make corrections to text, add new text, and rearrange existing text. You can close the Outline pane using the close button at the top right.

In full Outline view, the outline tab is the only open pane. The Task, Slides, and Notes panes are not visible allowing the Outline tab to fill the entire window. There are variations of the Outline view that include a

FIGURE 2.14

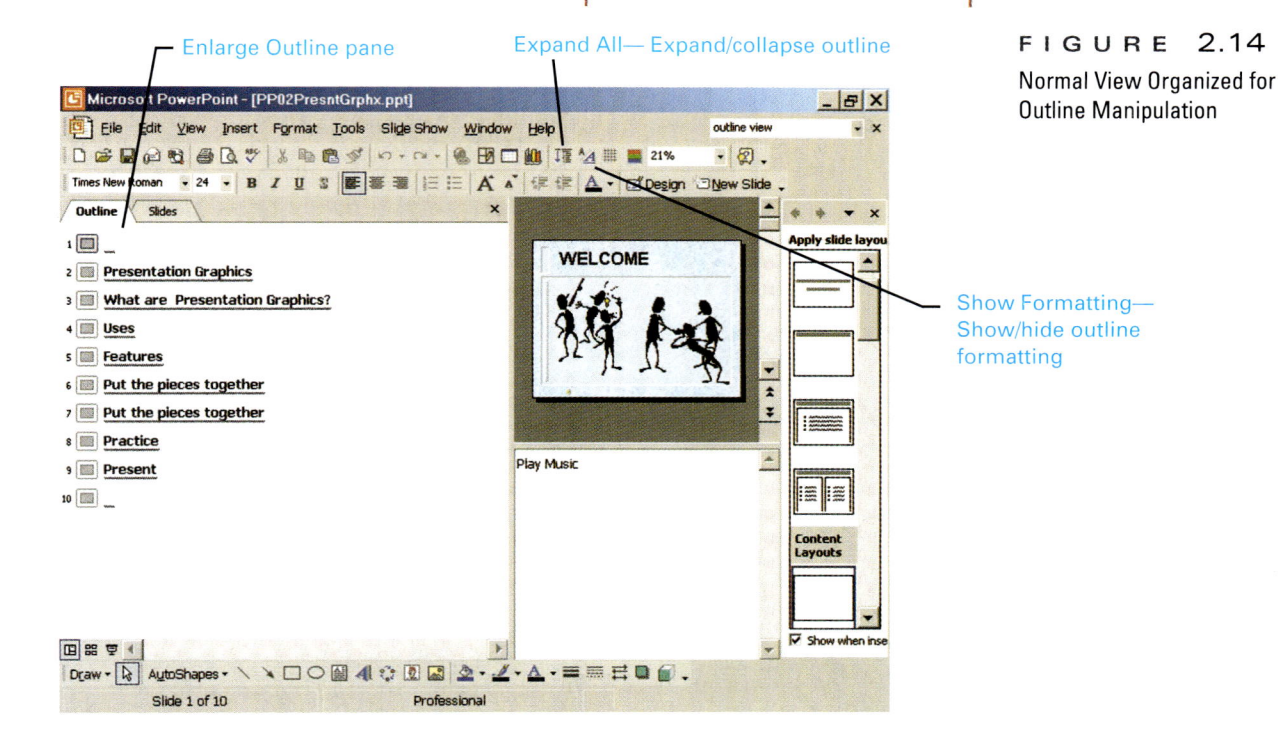

Normal View Organized for Outline Manipulation

small slides and/or notes pane. PowerPoint also has an Outlining toolbar with buttons specifically designed for managing outlines that can be activated from the Toolbars option of the View menu. If you are comfortable with Word outlines, PowerPoint's Outline view and toolbar will be very familiar.

One way to enter an Outline view is to organize the PowerPoint screen manually as shown in Figure 2.14. This arrangement was accomplished by dragging the pane borders to the desired location. Any panes that are not needed can be closed or minimized to provide more space for the outline. Changes made to the size of panes in Outline view are saved and redisplayed with the presentation, but they do not become the default PowerPoint view.

To cause PowerPoint to always open in a particular view or format, select a *default view.* Microsoft PowerPoint will always open new documents in the default view that has been chosen. Default views available include Slide view, Outline view, and several variations on Normal view.

All Microsoft applications use two Tools menu selections, Options and Customize, to personalize the user interface. The View tab of Tools|Options is used to set the default view options used to display a document. Selecting one of the Outline views here will cause all subsequent documents to be opened with the selected view.

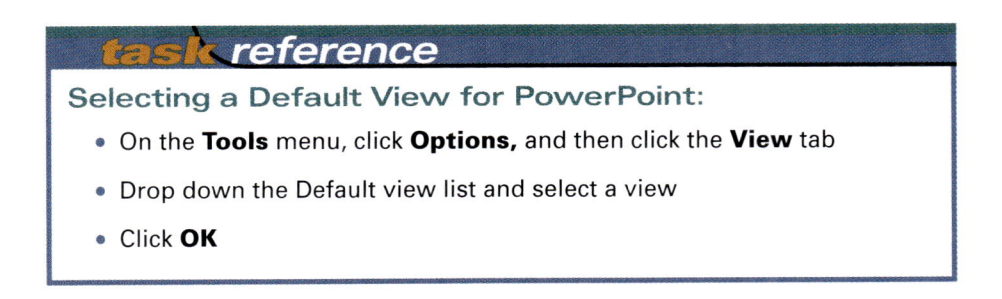

task reference

Selecting a Default View for PowerPoint:

- On the **Tools** menu, click **Options,** and then click the **View** tab
- Drop down the Default view list and select a view
- Click **OK**

POWERPOINT

FIGURE 2.15
Selecting PowerPoint's Default View

FIGURE 2.16
Normal—Outline and Slide Default View

Setting PowerPoint's default view:

1. Verify that PowerPoint is running with the **PP02PresntGrphx.ppt**

2. On the **Tools** menu click **Options,** and then click the **View** tab

3. Review the available Default views and then select **Normal—outline and slide**

tip: *What you are actually doing is defining a new Normal view*

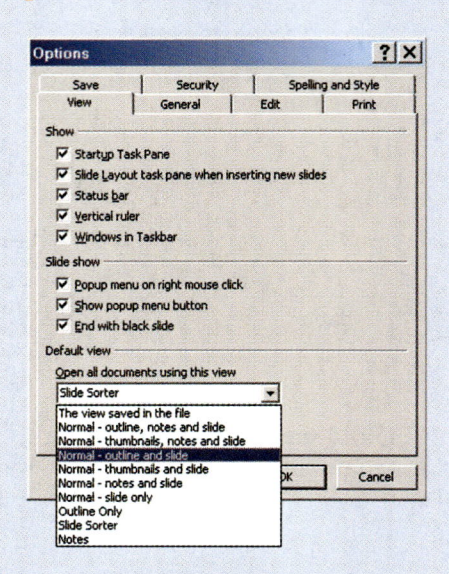

4. Click **OK**

tip: *The new setting does not impact any open documents, but will be in effect when future slide shows are opened*

5. Close PP02PresntGrphx.ppt—you do not need to close PowerPoint

6. Reopen **PP02PresntGrphx.ppt** and observe the new layout

7. Click the **Normal** view button below the outline pane

Although the display was returned to the traditional Normal view in the last step above, the next presentation opened will display in Normal—outline and slide view because it was set as the default. To make the traditional Normal view your default, repeat the previous steps selecting Normal—outline, notes, and slide.

Expanding and Collapsing Outline view

Regardless of how many other panes are open, the Outline pane behaves the same way. The outline can be expanded and collapsed to control how much content displays and prints. The Expand All button is on the Standard toolbar and works to both expand and collapse the displayed outline. Collapsing displays only the slide titles, and expanding displays all text on a slide.

Expanding and collapsing PresntGrphx outlines:

1. Verify that PowerPoint is running with the **PP02PresntGrphx.ppt**
2. Click the **Expand All** button on the Standard toolbar

tip: *If only slide titles were displaying, all of the content should now display. Conversely, if all content was showing before clicking the Expand All button, only the titles should display now*

3. Click the **Expand All** button again to reverse the display

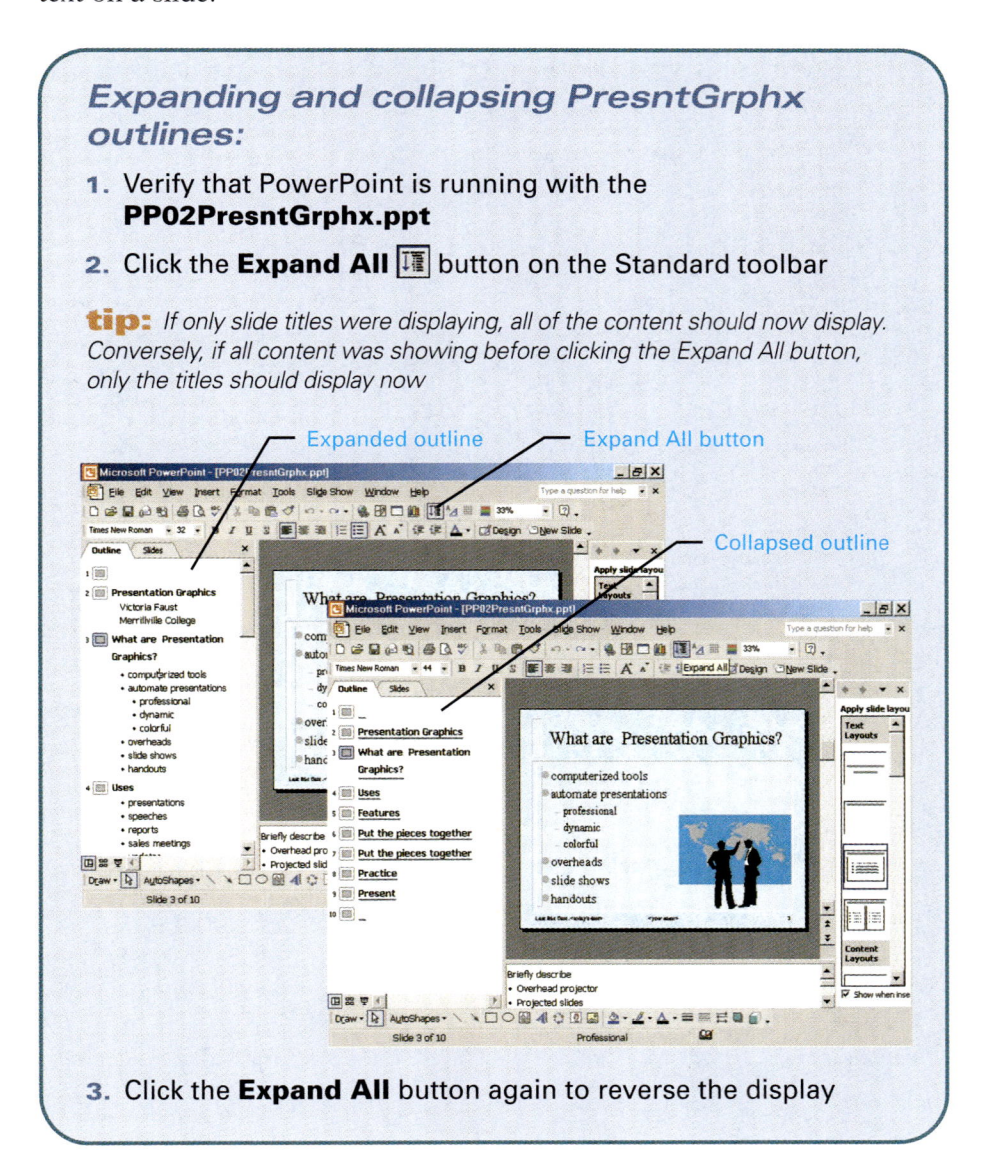

FIGURE 2.17
Expanded and Collapsed Views

Dragging a slide title to a new location when its content is collapsed moves all of the slide content. To move only the bullets from a slide, the view must be expanded so the desired text can be selected and moved. A printed outline will display the expansion level shown on the screen when the print is requested.

Formatting in Outline view

In the Outline view, settings control whether text formatting is displayed or hidden. Text formatting includes the *font, point size, underline, bold,* and *italic.* Other formatting like font color and *shadows* cannot be displayed.

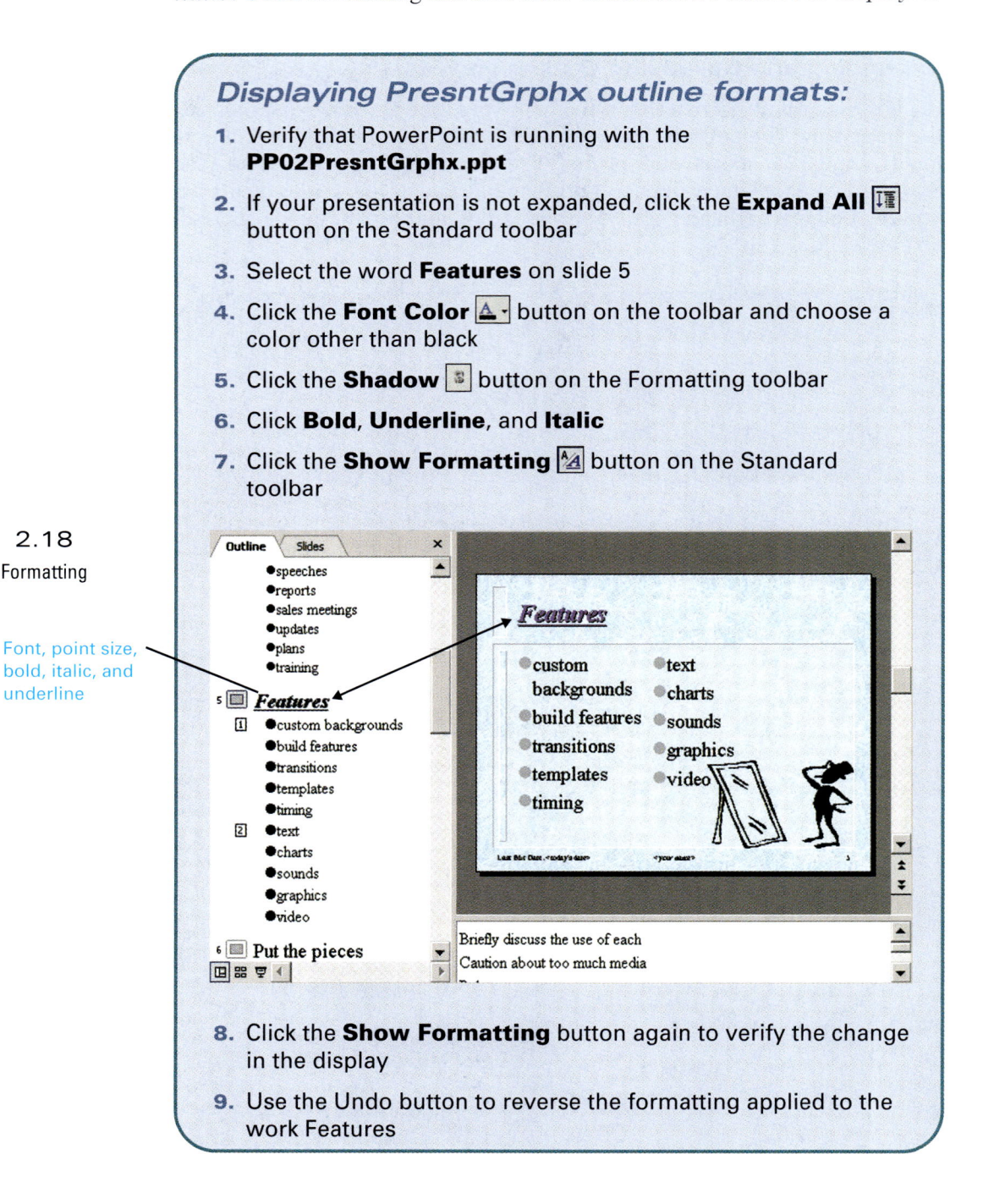

> **Displaying PresntGrphx outline formats:**
>
> 1. Verify that PowerPoint is running with the **PP02PresntGrphx.ppt**
> 2. If your presentation is not expanded, click the **Expand All** button on the Standard toolbar
> 3. Select the word **Features** on slide 5
> 4. Click the **Font Color** button on the toolbar and choose a color other than black
> 5. Click the **Shadow** button on the Formatting toolbar
> 6. Click **Bold**, **Underline**, and **Italic**
> 7. Click the **Show Formatting** button on the Standard toolbar

FIGURE 2.18
Outline Showing Formatting

Font, point size, bold, italic, and underline

> 8. Click the **Show Formatting** button again to verify the change in the display
> 9. Use the Undo button to reverse the formatting applied to the work Features

As was demonstrated in the previous steps, showing text formatting causes the outline to take up more space and display less presentation content. When working in Outline only view, seeing the text formatting that is being applied can be important. Viewing formatting in the outline is not important when both the outline and slide panes are present, since the slide provides a more accurate formatting picture.

INTEGRATING WITH MICROSOFT WORD

The Microsoft office suite is designed for integration. The goal is to make porting documents between applications simple. The Outline format is shared by both Word and PowerPoint, making *importing* Word content an ideal way to rapidly develop PowerPoint presentations.

You have already created and updated original slide content using the Outline pane and used it to maintain prepared text provided by the AutoContent wizard. Presentation content can also be imported from another file format like a Microsoft Word (.doc) file, a text (.txt) file created by a simple text editor like NotePad, a rich text (.rtf) document created by other word processing programs, or HTML (.htm or .html) files designed for Web presentations.

Like most computer users, Victoria has a variety of electronic documents that can provide content for the training presentation. Such documents do not have to be specially designed for the presentation, but it is often helpful to edit them before importing their content to PowerPoint. Candidate documents include topical outlines, descriptive text, and lecture notes covering the subjects to be presented. The desired materials can reside in multiple files and even have different file formats. You will use Victoria's existing material to create a presentation that can be used to teach PowerPoint's features to Randy's trainers.

One way to insert text from these other sources is to use *Copy* and *Paste.* Copy and Paste are features of the Windows clipboard that can be used to copy and move objects between documents and applications. Open the document, select the desired text, and copy the selection to the clipboard using the Standard toolbar button. Move to the new PowerPoint presentation, select the appropriate point in the existing outline, and paste the clipboard content.

Opening a .doc File

When creating a new presentation, any content in Microsoft Word, Excel, or other supported format can directly be opened by PowerPoint. These documents will be converted to slides based on their native formatting. A few *file converters* are included in the standard installation of Microsoft PowerPoint; others require custom installation.

---

task reference

Basing a PowerPoint Presentation on a File in Another Format:

- Open a new PowerPoint presentation
- Use the **Open** button on the Standard toolbar to activate the Open dialog box
- Change the Files of type drop-down list to select all files, **All Outlines**
- Navigate to your file and select it
- Click **Open**

Opening a chapter outline in Word (.doc) format:

1. Use the Start menu to initiate Microsoft Word
2. Click the Open button on the Standard toolbar
3. Navigate to **PP02Chapter2.doc**, select it, and click **Open**
4. Review the document until you are familiar enough with it to understand how it will be imported into PowerPoint
5. Close Microsoft Word
6. Verify that PowerPoint is running
7. Click the **New** button on the Standard toolbar
8. Click the **Open** button on the Standard toolbar
9. Drop down the Files of type list and select **All Files (*.*)**
10. Navigate to the files for this chapter and select **PP02Chapter2.doc**
11. Click **Open**

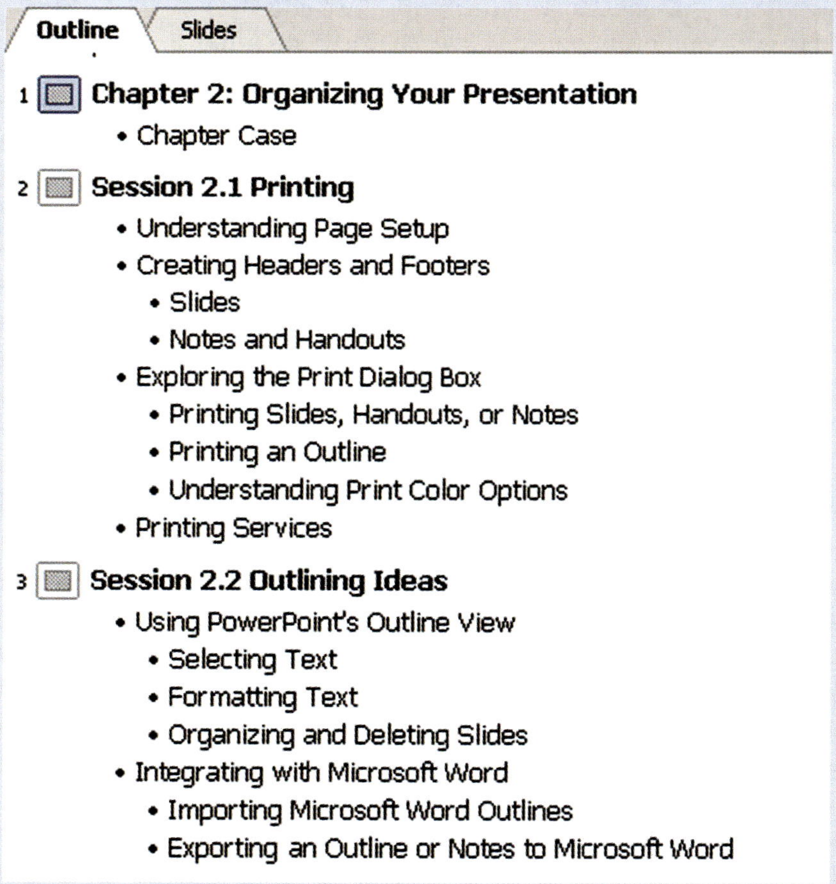

FIGURE 2.19
Chapter 2 Word Outline Opened in PowerPoint

Outline | Slides

1. **Chapter 2: Organizing Your Presentation**
   - Chapter Case
2. **Session 2.1 Printing**
   - Understanding Page Setup
   - Creating Headers and Footers
     - Slides
     - Notes and Handouts
   - Exploring the Print Dialog Box
     - Printing Slides, Handouts, or Notes
     - Printing an Outline
     - Understanding Print Color Options
   - Printing Services
3. **Session 2.2 Outlining Ideas**
   - Using PowerPoint's Outline View
     - Selecting Text
     - Formatting Text
     - Organizing and Deleting Slides
   - Integrating with Microsoft Word
     - Importing Microsoft Word Outlines
     - Exporting an Outline or Notes to Microsoft Word

12. Click through the presentation. Notice that each major header from the Word file has become a slide title
13. Save the presentation as **<yourname>PP02Chapter2.ppt**

Opening a Word file provides very reliable results when the Word document is an outline either created in Word's Outline facility or using Bullets and Numbering. These formats provide a clear-cut way for PowerPoint to convert the content. Text in other formats will be opened and assigned to slides, but with less satisfactory organization.

Once a file has been opened in PowerPoint format, it can be manipulated and reorganized for your presentation. Use the Promote, Demote, Expand All, and Show Formatting buttons that have already been discussed to edit the file or activate the Outline toolbar designed for this purpose.

You decide that the current PP02Chapter2 slides are too busy and that the existing outline doesn't quite match what is needed for the training. You will promote the first level of bullets so that each appears on its own slide.

Customizing Word content:

1. Verify that PowerPoint is running with the PP02Chapter2 presentation open

2. On the **View** menu select **Toolbars** and then select **Outlining**

   tip: The Outlining toolbar's default position is down the left-hand side of the Outline pane. Pause over each button to view its Screen tip

3. Change the title of the first slide to read **Organizing and Printing Your Presentation**

4. Select the **Chapter Case** text, type **Overview,** and press **Enter**

5. Use the **Promote** button to make Overview its own slide

6. Use the **Demote** button to indent under Overview, type **Printing,** and press **Enter**

7. Type **Outlining** and press **Enter**

8. Select all of the bulleted text from Session 2.1 and click the **Promote** button

   tip: This will make four new slides, one for each heading in the selection

9. Click on the Session 2.1 slide and click **Del**

10. Save this file as **<yourname>GettingStarted.ppt**

11. Close the presentation

anotherword

. . . on the Outlining Toolbar

The **Outlining toolbar** is the same as that used in Word's Outline view and may be more comfortable to some users than the PowerPoint toolbar. The only functionality that PowerPoint's Outlining toolbar has above the Standard and Formatting toolbars is the Add Summary button that can be used to insert a summary slide. To remove the Outlining toolbar, reverse the process that initiated it (View|Toolbars|Outlining).

FIGURE 2.20
Updated Word Outline

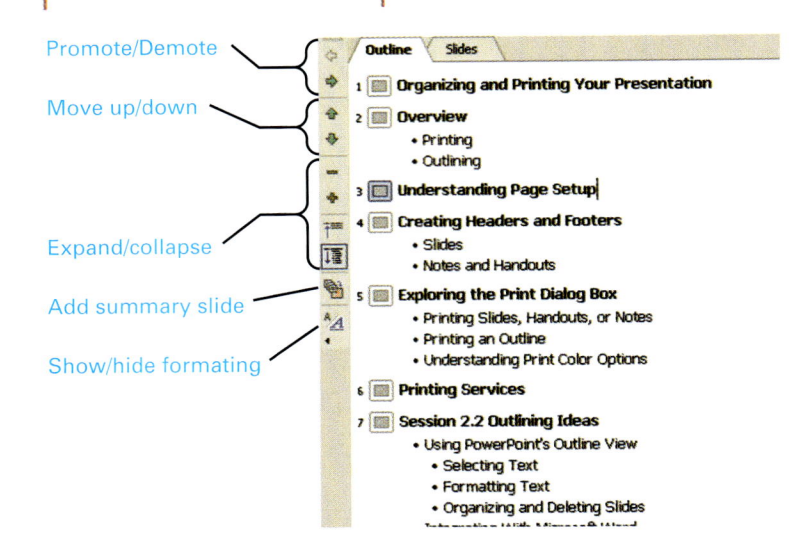

Promote/Demote
Move up/down
Expand/collapse
Add summary slide
Show/hide formating

Outline contents:
1. Organizing and Printing Your Presentation
2. Overview
   - Printing
   - Outlining
3. Understanding Page Setup
4. Creating Headers and Footers
   - Slides
   - Notes and Handouts
5. Exploring the Print Dialog Box
   - Printing Slides, Handouts, or Notes
   - Printing an Outline
   - Understanding Print Color Options
6. Printing Services
7. Session 2.2 Outlining Ideas
   - Using PowerPoint's Outline View
   - Selecting Text
   - Formatting Text
   - Organizing and Deleting Slides

Although PowerPoint supports development of a presentation from start to finish, many users are more comfortable creating and manipulating the outline of their thoughts in Word or another more familiar package. Using existing content can also significantly decrease project development time.

Importing or Exporting a .doc File

Microsoft PowerPoint also provides menu commands to insert content from other files into an existing presentation. Adding slides from another file is as easy as inserting slides from another PowerPoint presentation, which was introduced in Session 1.2. When inserting content from non-PowerPoint files, the slide structure is based on the outline (heading format) used in the imported document. For example, a Heading 1 in the source file becomes a slide title in PowerPoint, and a Heading 2 becomes the first level of body text on a slide.

If the source document does not use heading styles, PowerPoint creates an outline based on paragraphs so that each paragraph becomes a slide. Other formatting like inserted tabs can also impact the conversion. In a text file, text without a tab is treated as a slide title, while text with one tab becomes a bulleted item. An outline can always be modified once it is imported, but it is usually easier to edit the source document formatting to match PowerPoint's import methodology and reduce editing in PowerPoint.

---

task reference

Inserting Slides from a File in Another Format:

- Open a new PowerPoint presentation
- Click the position in the presentation for the new content
- Click the **Insert** menu, **Slides from Outline** option
- Navigate to the file and select it
- Click **Insert**

Inserting slides from Word into PresntGrphx:

1. Use the Start menu to initiate Microsoft Word
2. Click the **Open** button of the Standard toolbar
3. Navigate to **PP02PresentationBasics.doc**, select it, and click **Open**
4. Review the document until you are familiar enough with it to understand how it will be imported into PowerPoint
5. Close Microsoft Word
6. Verify that PowerPoint is running with PresntGrphx open

tip: *It should have still been open from the previous series of steps*

7. In the Outline pane click slide **9**
8. Click the **Insert** menu, **Slides from Outline** option

tip: *Be sure to select **All Outlines** as the type of file to search for*

9. Navigate to the files for this chapter and select **PP02PresentationBasics.doc**
10. Click **Insert**

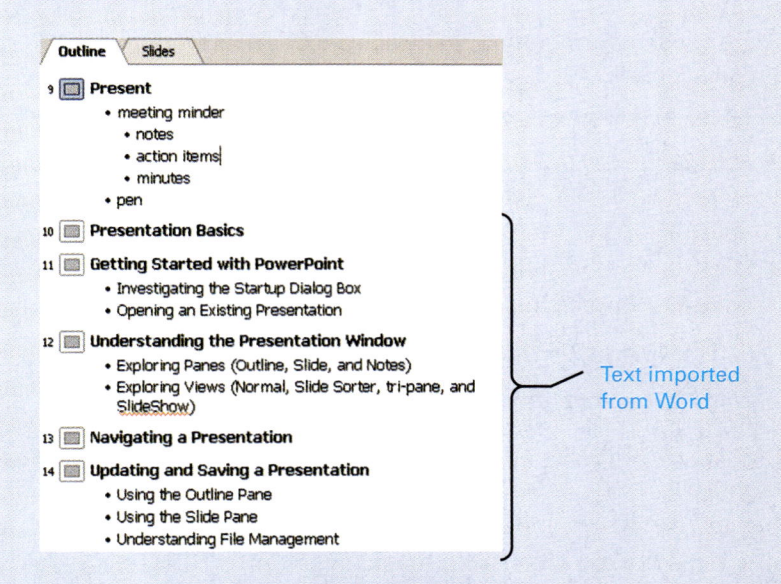

FIGURE 2.21

Word Outline Inserted into PresntGrphx

11. Select all of the PresentationBasics text except the title Presentation Basics
12. Use the **Promote** button to convert the selection to multiple slides

tip: *The Presentation Basics content should now be on slides 10 through 14*

13. Save your changes

Inserting the text component of a presentation from existing documents allows the emphasis to be on creating an appealing presentation rather than on typing. Don't hesitate to use text from other applications to speed the development process.

Exporting An Outline or Notes to Microsoft Word

The Send To option of the File menu is an easy way to **export** data from your current application to another Office application. The Send To option allows the open document to be sent to an e-mail address, an Exchange folder, or a compatible Office application. In Microsoft Word the compatible Send To application is PowerPoint, and in PowerPoint it is Word. The most common reason to import Word data into PowerPoint is to create a presentation from existing materials. The most common reason to export PowerPoint to Word is to have more control over the format of printed output.

task reference

Using Send To:

- Open the document that you would like to send to an e-mail address or another application
- Click the **Send To** option of the **File** menu
- When sending from PowerPoint to Word, select what to send from the Send To Microsoft Word Dialog Box
- When sending to an e-mail, you will need to select or enter a valid e-mail address

FIGURE 2.22
PowerPoint's Send to Word Dialog Box

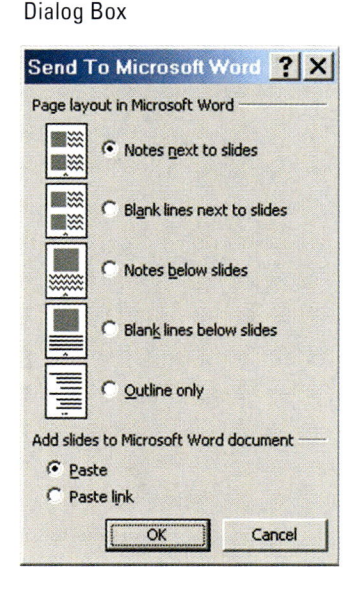

Sending Notes and Slides from PowerPoint to Word:

1. Verify that PowerPoint is running with PresntGrphx open
2. Click the **Send To** option of the **File** menu
3. Select **Microsoft Word**

tip: *Word does need to be installed on the machine, but it does not need to be running*

4. Click the **Notes Next to Slides** (see Figure 2.22)

tip: *This is a layout that can't be accomplished in PowerPoint*

5. Print the Word document and close it without saving

PowerPoint outlines can also be shared with non-Microsoft word processing programs using the Save As option of the File menu. Use the Outline/RTF option of the Save as type drop-down list to create a **rich text format (rtf)** outline that can be opened by most word processing applications.

Sharing data between applications is important to productivity and efficiency. Microsoft office applications are designed to capitalize on the strength of each application while maintaining the flexibility to move from application to application as the need arises.

making the grade — SESSION 2.2

1. Describe how Send To can be useful.
2. What is promoting a bulleted item?
3. Why would you expand an outline?
4. What is the relevance of PowerPoint's default view?

SESSION 2.3 SUMMARY

PowerPoint provides printing facilities for slides, notes, handouts, and outlines. All of the printable output can be previewed using Print Preview. Print Preview provides the ability to zoom in and out on a defined print to evaluate your selections. Changes can be made to the selected output (slides, notes, handouts, and so on), the orientation of the output, and the color scale. Presentations are typically shown in color, but printed in grayscale. Grayscale conversion can be problematic, so it is important to preview prints to verify that all of the content will display.

Headers and footers contain text that is to be printed in the upper and/or lower margins of a document. PowerPoint sets different headers/footers for slides and other output (handouts, notes, and outlines). The slides headers/footers text can be different for each slide or suppressed on specific slides. Only one header/footer text definition can be created that is applied to all handouts, notes, and outlines and that text will print on every page. Since multiple slides can be printed per handout page, each slide on the output page will contain the slide header/footer and each output page will also have the Notes and Handouts header/footer.

The Outline view is designed for manipulating presentation text. This view can also be used to import and export text to and from other applications. Send To from the File menu will send the current presentation to a compatible application like Microsoft Word. The Slides from Outlines option of the Insert menu can be used to import data from an external file. If the file is a compatible format, PowerPoint will convert the text into slides and bulleted items. Once text is imported, it can be edited like native text.

Send To can also be used to send PowerPoint output to Word. Using Word, formatting that is not possible in PowerPoint, like slides with notes beside them, can be printed.

MOUS OBJECTIVES SUMMARY

- PPT2002-1-3—Adding information to the Footer area, Date/Time area, or Number Area of the Slide Master
- PPT2002-2-1—Open a Word outline as a presentation
- PPT2002-5-1—Preview and print slides, outlines, handouts, and speaker notes
- PPT2002-6-4—Saving slide presentations as RTF outlines

task reference roundup

Task	Page #	Preferred Method
Printing a Slide Show	PP 2.14	• From the **File** menu select **Page Setup**
		• In Slides sized for box, click the desired option—usually Letter Paper (8.5 × 11 in.)
		• Click **OK**
		• Click the **Print Preview** button from the standard toolbar
		• Use **Options** to add **Header and Footer**
		• Use **Options** to change the **Colors/Grayscale**
		• Use **Options** to select **Scale to Fit Paper**
		• Click the **Print** button
Selecting a Default View for PowerPoint	PP 2.19	• On the **Tools** menu, click **Options,** and then click the **View** tab
		• Drop down the Default view list and select a view
		• Click **OK**
Basing a PowerPoint Presentation on a File in Another Format	PP 2.23	• Open a new PowerPoint presentation
		• Use the **Open** button on the Standard toolbar to activate the Open dialog box
		• Change the Files of type drop-down list to select all files, **All Outlines**
		tip: Using All Outlines as the File type will display all file types that are supported by PowerPoint
		• Navigate to your file and select it
		• Click **Open**
Inserting Slides From a File in Another Format	PP 2.26	• Open a new PowerPoint presentation
		• Click the position in the presentation for the new content
		• Click the **Insert** menu, **Slides from Outline** option
		• Navigate to the file and select it
		• Click **Insert**
Using Send To	PP 2.28	• Open the document that you would like to send to an e-mail address or another application
		• Click the **Send To** option of the **File** menu
		• When sending from PowerPoint to Word, select what to send from the Send To Microsoft Word Dialog Box
		• When sending to an e-mail, you will need to select or enter a valid e-mail address

chapter two — review of terminology

CROSSWORD PUZZLE

Across

1. Program to interpret other file formats
4. Print ___ shows document as it will print
7. Print in shades of gray
9. Show only outline titles
11. Typeface
12. Show all outline detail
13. Button to add a drop shadow to selected text
15. Send to another application

Down

2. The direction a page will print
3. Clone using the clipboard
5. Formatting to draw a line under text
6. Retrieve from another application
8. View used to open documents
10. Prints in the top margin
14. A text format making text appear darker

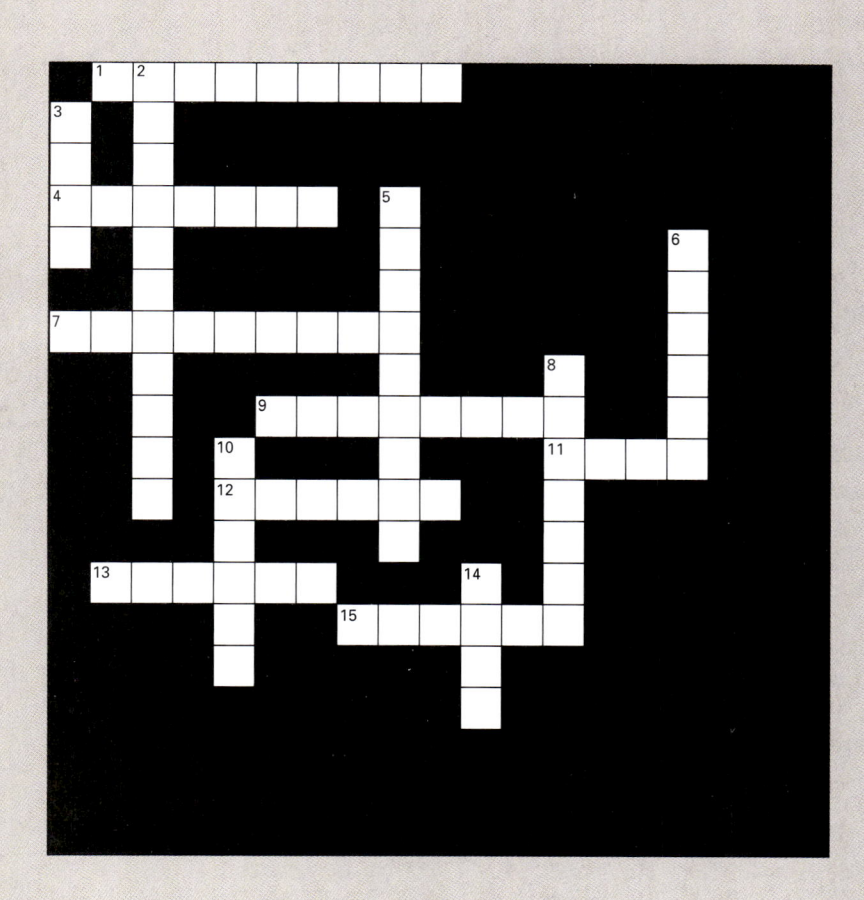

review of concepts

chapter two

FILL-IN

1. A _____ is designed to print in the top margin of a page or pages.
2. The _____ pane displays all text formatting and graphics one slide at a time.
3. Slides that are adjacent are said to be _____.
4. _____ displays output as it will print.
5. _____ can be used to select a specific printer for your output.
6. The _____ Handout format includes lines for taking notes.

REVIEW QUESTIONS

Each of the following topics should be addressed in one to three paragraphs.

1. How would you place all of the data from a file named EOC after the third slide of the open presentation?
2. Who determines what content should be placed in the various headers and footers discussed in this chapter?
3. How would you print pages 5 and 7 through 9 of the open presentation?
4. How would you create handouts with the presentation notes below the slides?
5. How would you print an outline showing only slide titles?

CREATE THE QUESTION

For each of the following answers, create the question.

ANSWER	QUESTION
1. Change the Files of type drop-down list of the Open dialog box to All Outlines.	_____
2. Click a slide in Slide Sorter view and then hold down the Shift key while clicking another slide.	_____
3. Letter Paper (8.5 × 11 in.).	_____
4. Nine slides per page.	_____
5. To apply formatting that is not available in PowerPoint.	_____

FACT OR FICTION

For each of the following determine whether the statement is fact, fiction, or both and present your arguments for that conclusion.

1. Printing handouts in color produces the best results when making photocopies with a noncolor copier.
2. Changing the Open dialog box Files of type value to All Files has the same impact as changing it to All Outlines.
3. Demoting a line of an outline will indent it another level to the right.
4. Imported text is organized in PowerPoint based on the formats of the original document.
5. What is being printed cannot be changed in Print Preview.

chapter two hands-on projects

practice

1. Weekly Status Meeting Presentation for Medical Management Associates

Medical Management Associates facilitates placement of elderly patients to alternative care as their hospital stay draws to a close. Typical assignments may be to their previous living arrangements, assisted living, nursing home, or hospice care. The company employs a staff of nursing personnel who specialize in discharge planning; nursing assistants; social workers; physical, occupational, and speech therapists; and physicians. MMA contracts with hospitals to provide discharge placement and follow-up services. The nursing staff and the supervising physician of the discharge team see patients daily while they are in the hospital. Once the patient is ready for discharge, follow-up care is assigned.

Weekly the discharge teams, consisting of discharge nurse, physician, social worker, and physical therapist, meet to discuss the needs of their team's patients. Here they explore care options and update the group on the patient's condition. Your presentation summarizes the relevant issues of Team Five's patients (only one is illustrated).

1. Use the Task pane to open a blank presentation
2. Save the presentation as **<yourname>MMA.ppt**
3. On the title slide, use two lines to title the presentation **Weekly Discharge Planning Assessment:**
   Team Five
4. Create a footer on the slides with the current day's date. Have the date Apply to All but not show on the title slide
5. Create a header on the Notes and Handouts entitled **125932 Cindy Adams**
6. Create a footer on the Notes and Handouts entitled **Team Five**
7. Use the **New Slide** button on the Formatting toolbar to add a second slide
   a. Make the slide title **Discharge Status**
   b. Add the following bullets:
      - **3 days, imminent**
      - **assisted living possible**
      - **family lives in area; supportive**
8. Use the **New Slide** button on the Formatting toolbar to add a third slide
   a. Make the slide title **Medical Status**
   b. Add the following bullets:
      - **Broken hip knitting well**
      - **Vital signs stable last week**
      - **Breathing problems resolved**
      - **Continued forgetfulness**
9. Use the New Slide button on the Formatting toolbar to add a fourth slide
   a. Make the slide title **Therapy**
   b. Add the following bullets
      - **Physical therapy for ambulation**
      - **Crutches/walker issues**
      - **Assistance caregivers available**
10. In the Notes pane of slide 2 indicate that the family is supportive of the patient's care but unable to take the patient into their home(s). Assisted living arrangement is the best option. Patient is financially able to pay
11. Add relevant notes to each of the other slides
12. Print the presentation as a Handout. Select 3 slides per page
13. If your work is complete, exit PowerPoint, otherwise continue to the next assignment

hands-on projects

chapter two

challenge

1. Westlake Neighborhood Association

Westlake Neighborhood Association was formed two years ago when it became evident that the City of Moosejaw was considering putting in a light rail line directly through the Westlake neighborhood. Westlake is an established, older area with an attractive, well-wooded, semirural neighborhood partly bordered by multifamily properties and commercial corridors. Residents of the area voiced concerns about the character of the neighborhood changing should the rail line be approved. In response, Westlake developed a vision statement, which included maintaining low-density residential areas, improving the appearance and quality of multifamily properties where they exist along the rail line, creating a safer environment through traffic control and protection from crime and violence, and ensuring outstanding parks and recreational facilities for young and old alike. Many months went into developing this vision, and now it is time to present Westlake's goals to the City of Moosejaw. With luck, the plan will be adopted as an amendment to the Moosejaw Comprehensive Plan. You have been asked to develop the presentation illustrating the Westlake goals for the Moosejaw Board Meeting.

1. Using Word, develop your slides using the following sections. Add appropriate bulleted points as you see fit. Save your presentation as **<yourname>Westlake.doc**
    a. Land Use and Property Maintenance
    b. Commercial Corridor Considerations
    c. Traffic Flow
    d. Public Safety
    e. Community Resources and Activities
2. Start PowerPoint and create a new presentation using a Design Template Profile
3. Make the title **Westlake's Vision** and the subtitle **Prepared for the City of Moosejaw**
4. Add a footer entitled **Westlake Neighborhood Association** but don't show it on the title slide
5. Import your Word document into the PowerPoint document
6. Add notes to amplify your presentation
7. Adjust the bulleted text so it is pleasingly centered on the slide
8. Add a concluding slide with your plea for adoption of these goals
9. Preview the presentation and make any necessary corrections
10. Print the presentation as Note Pages
11. Save the presentation as **<yourname>wna.ppt** and exit PowerPoint if your work is complete

FIGURE 2.23
Westlake Neighborhood Association Opening Slide

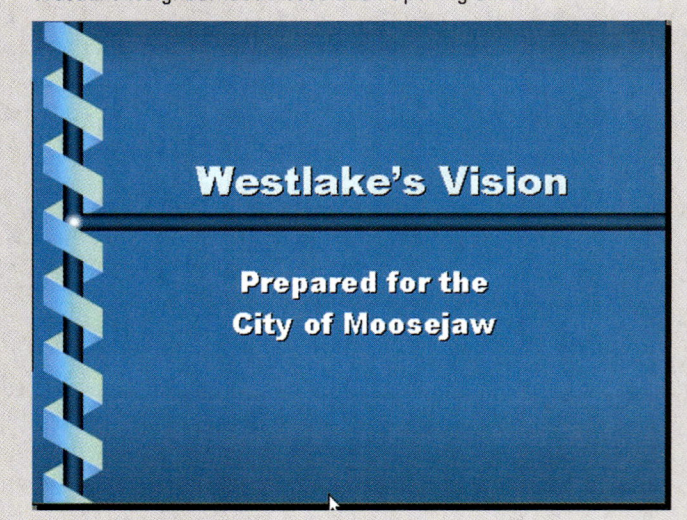

chapter two

hands-on projects

on the web

LEVEL THREE

1. Escape Travel

Escape Travel is an international travel distributor. The company links people up with economy foreign tours. The company handles all types of tours from five-star bus excursions to trips with moderate physical exertion. The continents of Europe, Asia, North and South America, and Africa are their primary focus at present. Escape Travel not only offers a tour or trek but also recommends budget airfares. Travelers subscribing to Escape Travel pay a small 2 percent commission for their services. The tour companies and the airlines pay Escape a commission for the customers. You have been asked by Escape Travel to prepare a presentation to a retired citizens group to encourage them to use Escape Travel. There are over 1,200 retirees in this group, and they all live in a very affluent end of town. Escape has offered a special bonus discount to this group if 10 percent of the group uses Escape Travel in the next 90 days.

1. Open a new PowerPoint presentation and choose the Globe Design Template
2. On the title slide enter **Escape Travel** as the title text and **Your gateway to adventure at a reasonable price!** as the subtitle text
3. Add a second slide to the presentation. Make the slide title **Trips on Four Continents** and add bullets for the continents described in the scenario
4. Add a third slide to the presentation. Make the slide title **All Kinds of Adventure Possible** and add the following bulleted text:
   • **Land and sea excursions**
   • **Motorized, by animal, or trekking**
   • **Exertion ranges from mild to extreme**
   • **All trips ranked and rated**
5. Add a fourth slide to the presentation. Make the slide title **Best Prices Now Available**
6. Using your favorite search engine, identify five trips of varying types and enter them as bullets on slide 4
7. Add a fifth slide with the title **Discounts.** Add bullet text for the Escape Travel advantages outlined in the scenario
8. Add a sixth slide with a title **Contact Us!!** and your contact information
9. Review your presentation and make any changes. Print the presentation in a suitable format for this audience
10. Save the presentation as **<yourname>Escape.ppt** and exit PowerPoint if you are finished

FIGURE 2.24
Escape Travel Opening Slide

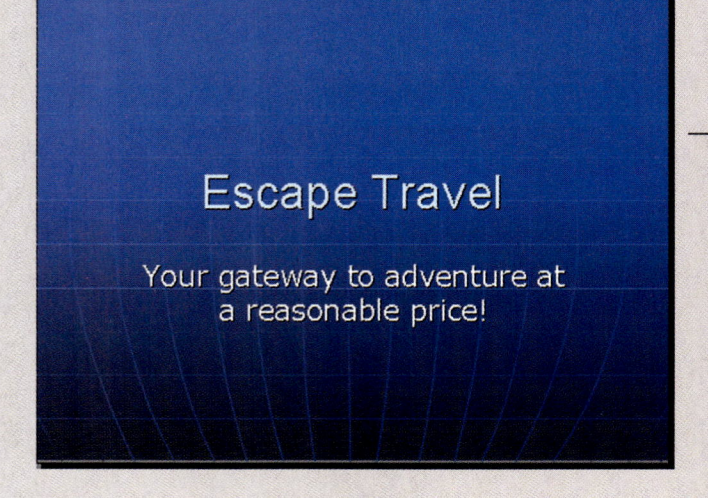

www.mhhe.com/i-series

PP 2.35

POWERPOINT

hands-on projects

e-business

1. Picnic Importers

Picnic Importers is a local company that assembles luscious picnic baskets for duos or groups and delivers them to the door. The baskets include cheeses, fruit, sandwiches, pâtes, desert, and wine or nonalcoholic beverages. A checkered tablecloth, utensils, and goblets are also provided. Picnic Importers prides itself on turning around orders within four hours within a 100-mile radius of the city, seven days a week. Any orders placed on the Web by 8 A.M. will be at the doorstep by noon, just in time for a picnic lunch! You have been asked to prepare a presentation suitable for kiosks that will be placed in downtown business office lobbies.

1. Start PowerPoint and create a new presentation using the Clouds Design Template
2. Save the file as **<yourname>PicnicBasket.ppt**
3. Make the presentation title **Try a Picnic Today!** and the subtitle **Picnic Importers can make it happen**
4. Add a second slide with the title text **Picnic Baskets** and the following bullets
   - Guaranteed delivery in 4 hours
   - You select your picnic from
     - Sandwiches
     - Cheeses and breads
     - Seasonal fruits
     - Luscious deserts
     - Wines or nonalcoholic beverages
   - Tablecloth, utensils, and goblets too!
5. Add a third slide with the title **How to Order**
   - **Orders only through the Internet**
   - **Credits cards accepted**
   - **Secure site**
   - www.picnicbasket.com
6. Add a fourth slide titled **Delivery Guaranteed** and make up the text for the bullets
7. Add a fifth slide titled **Picnic Prices** and create bullets from the following information
   a. Include prices for one, two, four, or each additional person
   b. Add shipping and handling
   c. Tax to be added
   d. Gratuity not included
8. Add a fourth slide titled **More Reasons to Order Your Picnic** and add bullets from the following information
   a. Group discounts available
   b. Ten percent discount for ordering 48 hours or more in advance
   c. Children and senior meals available
9. Preview the presentation and make any corrections
10. Save the presentation and exit PowerPoint if your work is complete

FIGURE 2.25
Picnic Importers Opening Slide

chapter two

hands-on projects

around the world

1. Great Games, Ltd.

Great Games, Ltd., manufactures and distributes arcade machines. Their specialty is classic pinball machines. Originally the company distributed these machines in the United States. However, they have found it more lucrative to market and distribute the machines to third world countries. The arcade machines are generally purchased by the government, then sold at discount to shop owners and distributed in major cities. Recently, Internet cafés have sprung up in coffee shops and small businesses expanding the reach of the computer and gaming as well.

Great Games is now proposing a partnership with several of the companies that produce electronic game consoles. The consoles have sold well in the United States; the foreign market is ripe for expansion. Since Great Games has extensive experience in the international market, the proposal is to use their existing distribution channels to market the consoles produced by the other companies. You have been asked to prepare a professional presentation to the console companies.

1. Start PowerPoint and create a new presentation using the **Recommending a Strategy** AutoContent wizard
2. Set the presentation title to **Gaming in the Foreign Market** and the subtitle text to **It makes sense!** Include the text **First Draft** and the date on each slide. Do not number the slides
3. Adjust the text on the second slide to read: **Partnership Is Win-Win**
   - **Low risk to you**
   - **Sales exceed predictions by 135%**
   - **Government contracts in place**
   - **Marketing expanding countries**
   - **Annual revenues**
4. Add appropriate notes to the second slide
5. Make the title of the third slide **Your Requirements** and use the following bulleted text
   - **You provide; we distribute**
   - **No middleman**
   - **Money back guarantee**
6. Add appropriate notes to the third slide
7. Delete the 4th, 5th, and 6th slides
8. Make the title of the next slide **Key Benefits** and use the following bulleted text
   - **We distribute the product**
   - **Revenues from initial sales and annual revenues**
   - **Not dependent on individual shopkeepers**
   - **Little risk to you**
9. Add appropriate notes to this slide
10. Add another slide titled **Next Steps.** Create appropriate bulleted items and notes
11. Preview the presentation and make any necessary corrections
12. Save the presentation as **<yourname>gg.ppt** and exit PowerPoint if your work is complete

FIGURE 2.26
Great Games Opening Slide

running project

Montgomery-Wellish Foods, Inc: Orienting New Employees

In the previous chapter Daniel Wellish welcomed the new recruits to Montgomery-Wellish Foods as the first part of the training program. Next Daniel will provide an orientation to the company for the new recruits. You have been asked to present a professional PowerPoint presentation from the CEO's outline.

1. Open **<yourname>mwf.ppt.** You will be adding on to your presentation
2. Change the title of the last slide to **About Montgomery-Wellish Foods, Inc.** Add bullets reflecting the following
   a. The company is divided into the National and International business units
   b. Thirty percent of revenues are from international markets
   c. Each business unit contains Marketing, Production, Distribution, and Research and Development divisions
3. In the notes pane indicate that the training program and new recruits fall under Research and Development for the National business unit, and that positions are available for bilingual employees in the International business unit
4. Add another slide to the presentation titled **Marketing Thrust.** Enter the following bulleted items:
   - **Sales force**
   - **Internet Uses**
   - **National contacts**
   - **International contacts**
5. Add another slide titled **Production Thrust.** Enter the following bulleted items:
   - **15% increase in overall products last 5 years**
   - **3% increase in brands**
   - **Greatest increase found in international markets**
6. Add another slide titled **Research and Development.** Enter the following bulleted items:
   - **Training program started six years ago**
   - **Over 1,200 recruits now product managers**
   - **Feedback very positive**
   Add notes that 87 percent of new product managers gave 98 percent approval ratings on program
7. Create a header on the Handouts with the text **Training Program - <today's date>** and **Orientation to the company.** Make the footer **Edited by: <your name>**
8. Preview the presentation and make any necessary corrections
9. Print the presentation as Handouts with two slides per page
10. Save the presentation as **<yourname>mwforient.ppt** and exit PowerPoint if your work is complete

FIGURE 2.27
Marketing Thrust Slide

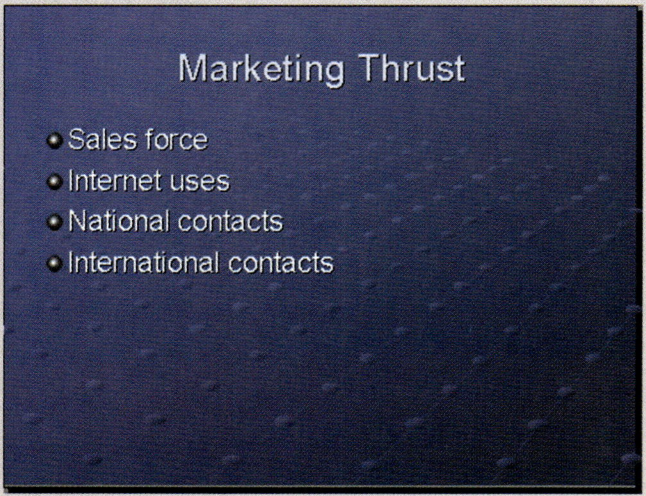

NOTES

www.mhhe.com/i-series

POWERPOINT

NOTES

www.mhhe.com/i-series

did you know?

the average major league baseball is used for five to seven pitches.

the plastic things on the end of shoelaces are called aglets.

the word *samba* means to rub navels together.

the dog Laika became the first living creature to orbit the earth in 1957 aboard the Soviet Sputnik 2.

the feet account for one-quarter of all the bones in a human body.

in 1900 the average age at death in the United States was 47.

each American eats an average of _____ pounds of chocolate per year.

Chapter Objectives

- **Insert, format, and modify text—PPT2002-2-2**
- **Apply formats to presentations—PPT2002-4-1**
- **Use the Meeting Minder to take notes during a presentation**
- **Use proofing tools like Spelling Checker and Find and Replace**
- **Modify PowerPoint Masters—PPT2002-4-5**
- **Add preset animations and transitions—PPT2002-4-3**
- **Create a custom slide template—PPT2002-4-5**

CHAPTER 3

three

Refining Your Presentation

chapter case

Staffing Presentation with PowerPoint

Many high-demand careers are experiencing a shortage of qualified personnel. In scores of health care institutions, the lack of qualified health care workers is becoming critical. Nurses are being recruited from France, England, Germany, and Australia. Hiring bonuses, housing stipends, and retention bonuses are becoming the norm. Ricki Wellington is the Director of Nursing at a large eastern United States hospital where staffing shortages cause one-third of the beds to be closed on any given day.

A shortage of nurses to maintain quality bedside care is the most serious problem. Even with the bed closures, no shift at the hospital is fully staffed. On most days each area is short at least one nurse. Continually working short-staffed is taking its toll on the stable employees, and turnover is becoming a problem. Stress on the floors is very high, and morale is low.

The hospital is the area's Level I trauma center and provides 90 percent of the area's indigent, homeless, underinsured, and uninsured care. It is not possible to shut down more beds to maintain safe staff/patient ratios. Ricki has been instrumental in developing creative staffing alternatives that have allowed the hospital to maintain its safety and care record to date, but she believes the crisis is worsening and patients are at risk.

Based on the hiring history of the past three months and the staffing projections for the next three months, it will not be possible to meet patient care needs. Ricki has been asked to present her perspective on the crisis to the executive board of the hospital. The hope is to create a comprehensive recruiting and retention plan to avert tragedy.

FIGURE 3.1
Staffing Crisis Presentation

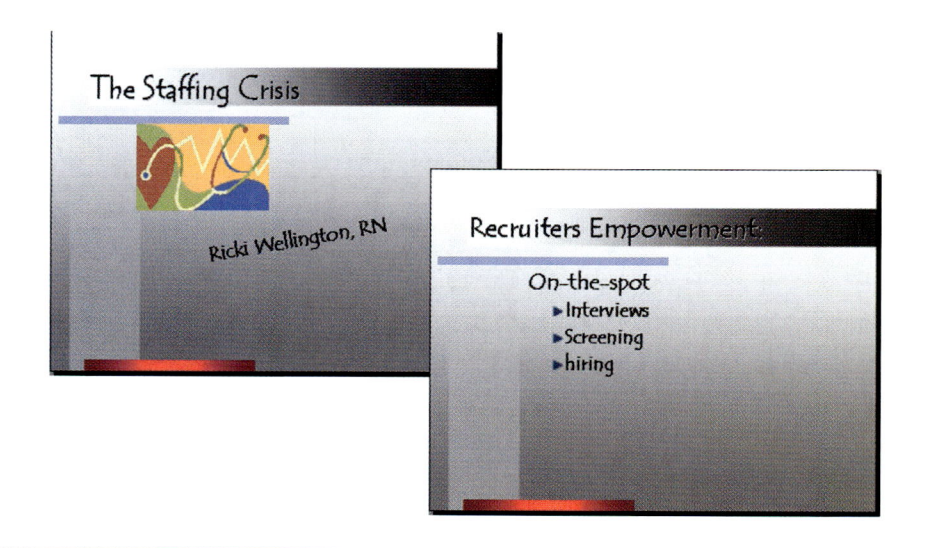

Ricki has used Word to organize her thoughts and imported the outline into PowerPoint. She is not satisfied with the result and is not comfortable enough with PowerPoint to rectify the formatting problems. She has asked you to help make the presentation dynamic and convincing.

SESSION 3.1 ADDING AND MODIFYING OBJECTS

Everything on a PowerPoint slide is an object, and the slide itself is also an object. For our purposes, an ***object*** is anything that can be manipulated like the title of a slide or a graphic. In PowerPoint, each object has ***properties*** that control how it displays and behaves. Text display properties include font, size, and color. Behavior properties are animations and transitions.

UNDERSTANDING POWERPOINT OBJECTS

So far text has been typed into placeholders designed for slide titles, subtitles, and bulleted lists. Text can also be added to a slide using a Text Box or by typing text into a shape. Other objects like graphics, shapes, audio, and video can also be placed on a slide.

Objects often consist of component parts. For example, a graphic is usually a group of shapes, each of which can be selected and formatted individually. Similarly, a Text Box contains a group of characters, each of which can be selected and formatted. Regardless of the object, selecting, placing, and setting properties are very similar.

Selecting and Deselecting Objects

PowerPoint text objects can be selected in two modes. The border surrounding the selected object indicates the selection mode and, therefore,

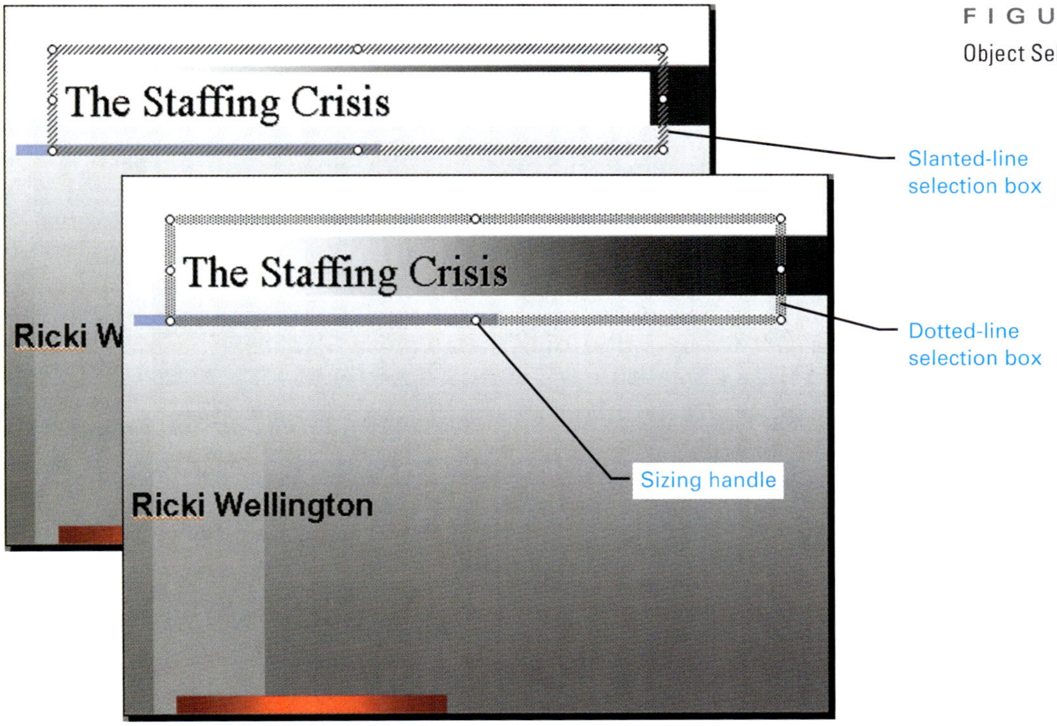

CHAPTER OUTLINE

3.1 Adding and Modifying Objects

3.2 Standardizing Presentations

FIGURE 3.2
Object Selection

PP 3.3

POWERPOINT

FIGURE 3.3
Pointer Shapes

Pointer	Use
I	Click an insertion point in a selected text object
✥	Select the entire object to move, cut, copy, or delete it. If the object is already selected, the four-headed arrow indicates that you can click and drag it to a new location
 ↕ ⬉	Resize the selected object by dragging in the directions indicated

what operations can be performed on that object. A ***slanted-line selection box,*** a border consisting of slanted lines, indicates that the object contents can be edited. For example, a Text Box or placeholder in this mode is ready for text to be edited. A ***dotted-line selection box,*** a border consisting of dots, indicates that the object can be manipulated as a whole. For example, moving and resizing are operations that are performed on the whole object.

The white circles in the selection box are called ***sizing handles.*** Sizing handles are used to drag a border of an object to adjust its size. When the cursor is positioned over a sizing handle, a two-headed arrow appears to tell you what drag direction is valid for that handle. When the cursor pauses over a selected object, a four-headed arrow appears to indicate that the object can be dragged to a new location.

The difference in each selection will be demonstrated using a text placeholder on the title slide of Ricki's presentation. It is important to pay attention to the changes in the pointer shape when selecting. The various pointer shapes are outlined in the previous figure.

Selecting/deselecting a text placeholder:

1. Initiate PowerPoint and open **PP03StaffingPlan.ppt**
2. Save the Presentation as **<yourname>PP03StaffingPlan.ppt**
3. On the first slide, click directly on Ricki's name to initiate a slanted-line selection box
4. Use the I-beam I cursor to click an insertion point in the text
5. Click on the slide away from any object to deselect the text placeholder
6. Position the cursor on the border of the text placeholder with Ricki's name until a four-headed arrow ✥ displays and then click to initiate a dotted-line selection box

tip: *If you miss and get a slanted-line selection box, click the slanted lines and the selection box will change to a dotted-line selection box*

7. Click and drag the I-beam to select Ricki
8. Click away from objects to deselect

A text placeholder contains characters, which can also be selected. PowerPoint supports special clicking options when operating on text. These are the same options that work to select text in Microsoft Word.

FIGURE 3.4
Selecting Text

Action	Result
Double-click word	Select word
Triple-click in paragraph	Select paragraph Triple-clicking a bulleted item will select the entire item and its subordinate items
Ctrl+A	Click a placeholder and then type Ctrl+A to select all text in the placeholder
	Also works for AutoShape or Text Box
	Click in the Outline tab and then type Ctrl+A to select all text in the presentation

Once an object is selected, it can be acted on. Common actions include copying, moving, resizing, deleting, and formatting the selection.

Inserting and Deleting Objects

Placeholders are objects that are placed on a slide based on the slide layout. There are two types of placeholders, those that hold text and those that hold other content (graphics, charts, media clips, tables, and so on). The simplest way to add content to a presentation is to select a slide layout with appropriate placeholders for the desired content.

Placeholder objects can be selected, deleted, moved, and resized. To add subject matter to a placeholder, simply click in it. A content placeholder displays a series of icons that are used to choose the type of content to be added. Adding content with placeholders will be covered in the next chapter.

Ricki has changed the design template of the presentation, and the presentation text does not align appropriately with the new design. She has also decided that the presentation needs some graphics to emphasize her points. To remedy this situation, you will need to move and delete text placeholders and add an image.

another*word*

. . . on Selecting PowerPoint Objects

Sometimes the need arises to format, move, or delete multiple slide objects simultaneously. Click and drag a selection box around all of the objects or hold down the Shift key to select additional objects. Each of the selected objects will display sizing handles.

When selecting text, PowerPoint "helps" by selecting the entire word when you have only selected part of it. If you don't want entire words selected, click the **Tools** menu, then click **Options,** and then click the **Edit** tab. Clear the **When selecting, automatically select entire word** check box.

Inserting a graphic and deleting a text placeholder:

1. Initiate PowerPoint and open **<yourname>PP03StaffingPlan.ppt**
2. On the first slide, click directly on Ricki's name to initiate a slanted-line selection box
3. Click an insertion point after Wellington and type **, RN**

tip: *If you miss and get a dotted-line selection box, move the cursor over the text and click an insertion point, then move the insertion point to the desired location*

PP 3.6   CHAPTER 3 **POWERPOINT**   3.1 Adding and Modifying Objects

4. On the menu click **Insert,** then **Picture,** then **From File,** and then select **HeartHealth.wmf** and click **Insert**

tip: *PowerPoint tries to help formatting by adding a text placeholder when you insert a graphic that is not in a placeholder. It is not needed, so you will delete it*

F I G U R E   3.5
Insert Picture from File

The Staffing Crisis

• Click to add text

Picture added from file

Ricki Wellington, RN

Text placeholder added by PowerPoint

5. Position the cursor over the border of the text placeholder (it says Click to add text). When the pointer becomes a four-headed arrow, click to select the entire object with a dotted-line selection box

6. Click the **Del** key to remove the text placeholder

tip: *Pressing Del with a slanted-line selector box will delete text from the placeholder. If this happens, click the border of the selection box to change to a dotted-line placeholder and press Del again*

7. Click the HeartHealth image to select it

tip: *Since the contents of HeartHealth can't be edited, there will only be sizing handles when it is selected*

8. Drag the image until it sits in the corner created by the blue horizontal line and the light gray vertical bar

9. Use the sizing handles to increase the size of the image to match the length of the blue line

tip: *Drag the bottom right sizing handle down and to the right*

10. Use the four-headed arrow to select the Ricki Wellington text box with a dotted-line selection box

11. Move the text box to the position shown in the next figure

www.mhhe.com/i-series   PP 3.7

FIGURE 3.6
Select and Move Objects

Enlarged and repositioned image

Edited and repositioned text box

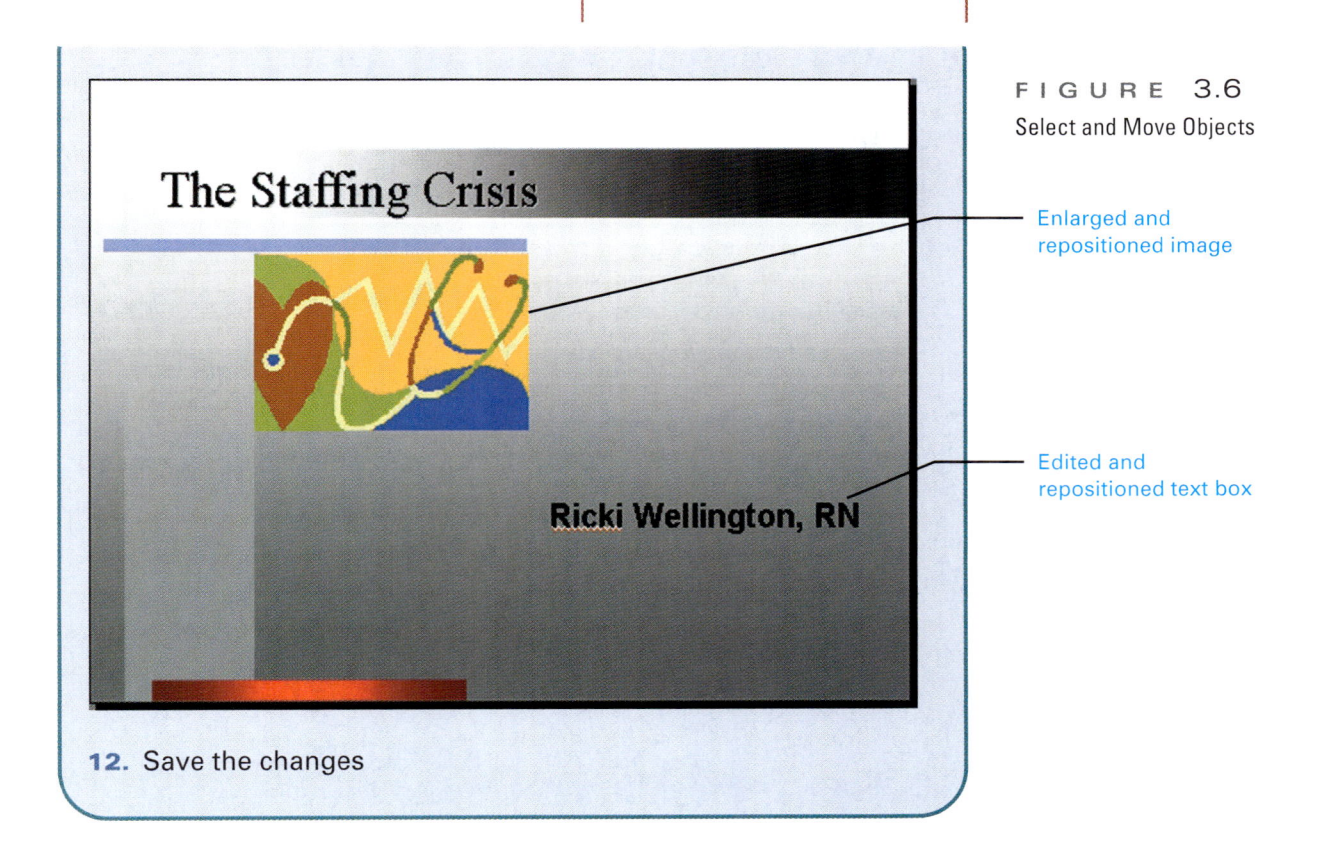

12. Save the changes

Ricki is satisfied with the title slide, so it is time to move on to the other slides in the presentation. Ricki wants the bullets and their text to appear just to the right of the gray vertical bar in the background.

FORMATTING OBJECTS

The text of a presentation is the most important and informative component, but it cannot hold the audience's attention by itself. Choosing appropriate backgrounds, colors, fonts, and bullets is also critical to effective delivery.

Adjusting Object Position

Adjusting the position of an inserted graphic, like that on the title page of Ricki's presentation, is simply a matter of dragging it to a new location. When dealing with text, dragging the text container (placeholder, Text Box, or shape) to a new location is one way to reposition text.

Moving placeholders:

1. Verify that PowerPoint is running with **<yourname>PP03StaffingPlan.ppt** open
2. Move to the second slide
3. Click in the bulleted list
4. Use the left-side sizing handle to move the left border to the right edge of the gray vertical bar

POWERPOINT

FIGURE 3.7
Repositioned Text Placeholder

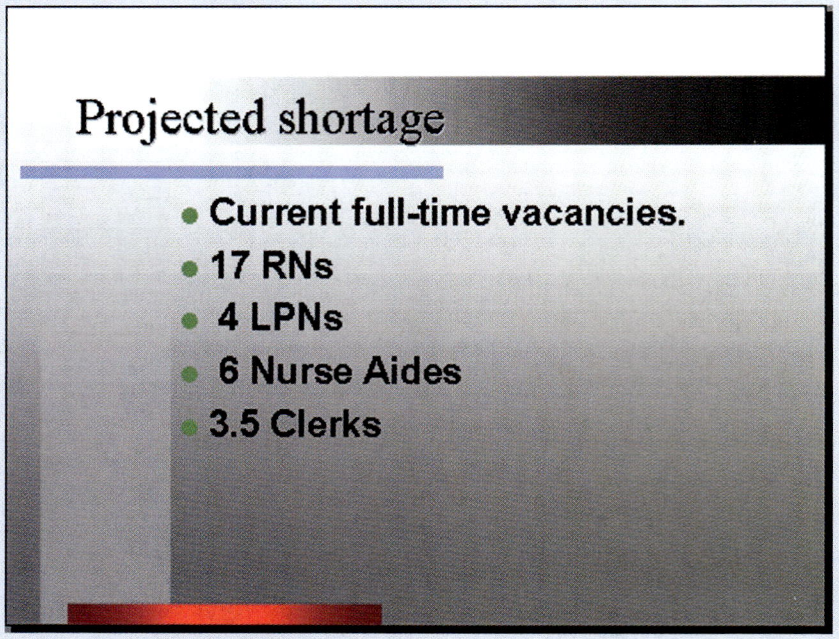
Projected shortage
Current full-time vacancies.
17 RNs
4 LPNs
6 Nurse Aides
3.5 Clerks

5. Repeat the realignment for slides 4 to 6
6. Save your changes

A second way to adjust the position of text is to change its alignment within an object. Text is always contained in a placeholder, Text Box, or shape. The alignment of text controls where it displays in the container. The default alignment is Left, but text can also be centered or right aligned in a container.

Aligning text in a object:

1. Verify that PowerPoint is running with **<yourname>PP03StaffingPlan.ppt** open
2. Move to slide **1**
3. Select the slide title placeholder. Notice that the Left align button on the toolbar is selected
4. Select the placeholder containing Ricki's name. Notice that the Left align button is also selected for this text
5. Click the **Center** alignment button on the Formatting toolbar and observe the adjustment in text position
6. Click the **Right** alignment button on the Formatting toolbar and observe the adjustment in text position
7. Save the changes

PP 3.9

FIGURE 3.8
Right Aligned Text

- Selected text placeholder
- Text right aligned in placeholder
- AutoFit settings

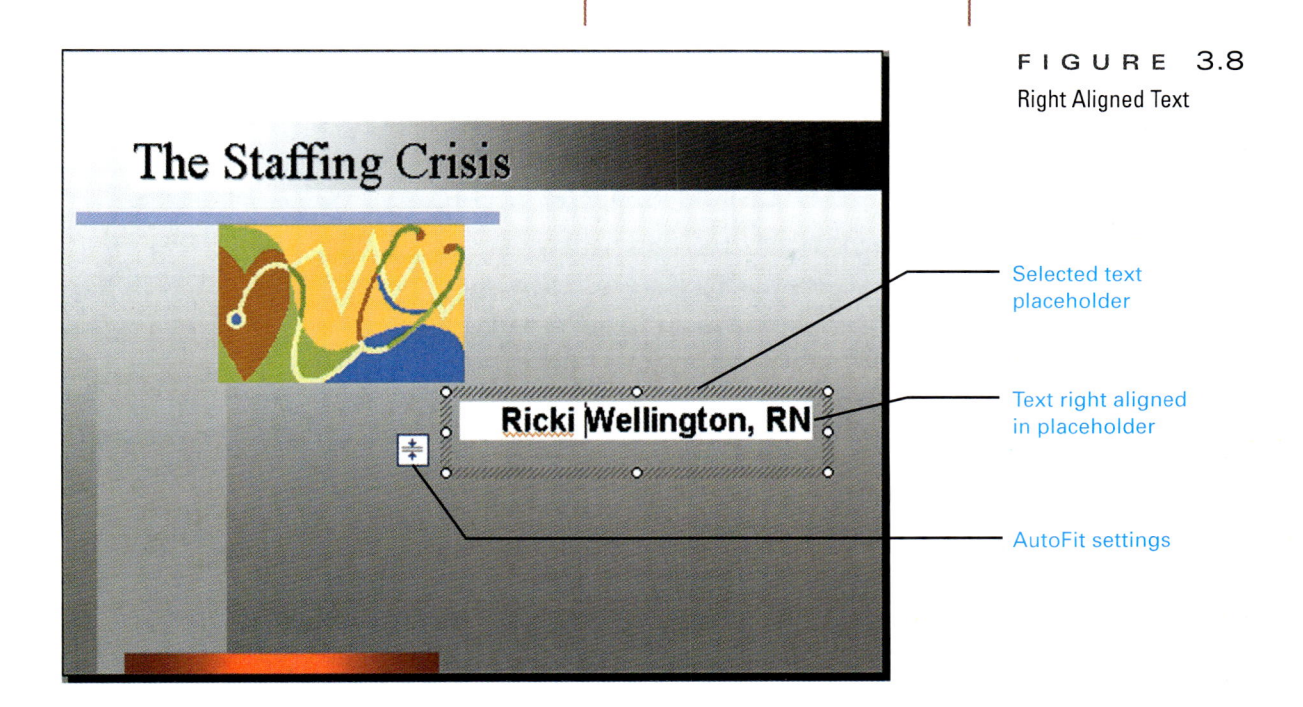

The final way to adjust the position of Text is to use the Increase Indent and Decrease Indent buttons on the toolbar. As you will recall from the outline view, these buttons move the text right or left one tab stop. In the Outline pane, decreasing the indention level of a bullet all the way to the left margin caused it to become a slide title. When working in a text object, like a placeholder, text cannot be moved any farther left than the first level of bullets.

This difference in indent behavior can be demonstrated on the second slide of the presentation. The text Current full-time vacancies is part of a bulleted list, but it should be a subtitle. To resolve this situation, another text object could be added to hold the subtitle, the text under the subtitle can be indented, or the bullet can be removed from the subtitle text. You will demonstrate these options for Ricki.

Increasing and decreasing text indention:

1. Verify that PowerPoint is running with **<yourname>PP03StaffingPlan.ppt** open
2. Move to slide **2**
3. Select the slide bulleted list placeholder
4. Click and drag the I-beam to select the bulleted items under Current full-time vacancies
5. Click the **Increase Indent** button on the Formatting toolbar
6. Select the second-level bulleted items and click the **Decrease Indent** button on the Formatting toolbar to return the text to its original position

tip: *The Undo button could also have been used*

POWERPOINT

FIGURE 3.9
Increased Indent

Indention increased to second-level bullet

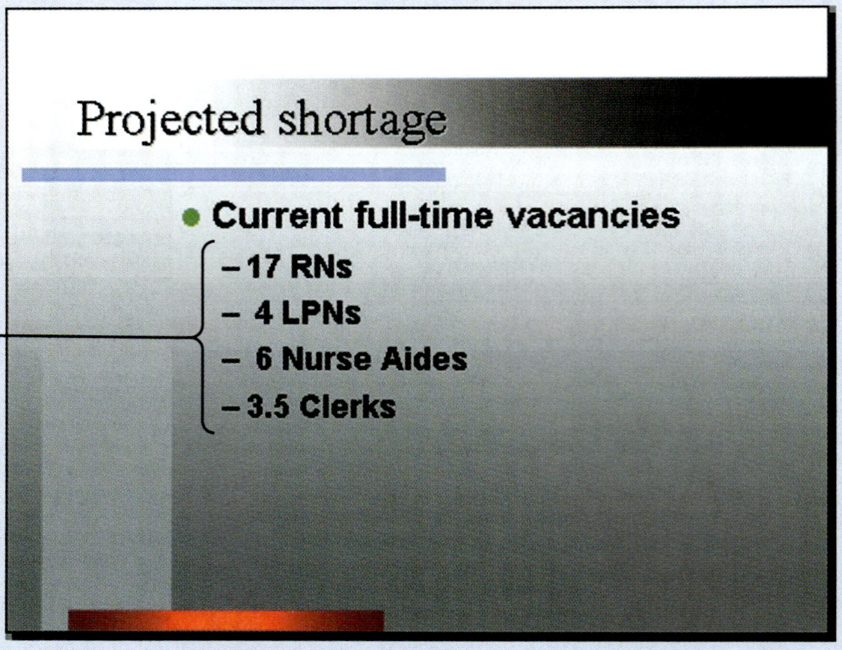

[Slide: Projected shortage — Current full-time vacancies; 17 RNs; 4 LPNs; 6 Nurse Aides; 3.5 Clerks]

7. Click an insertion point to the left of the C in Current
8. Use the **Backspace** key to delete the bullet in front of the item

FIGURE 3.10
Deleted Bullet

Bullet removed from this item

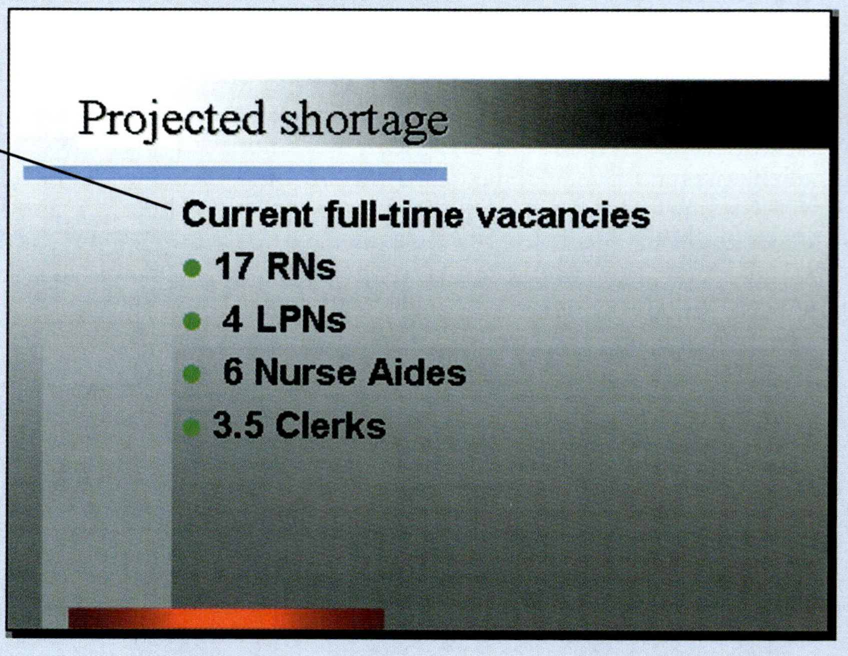

[Slide: Projected shortage — Current full-time vacancies; • 17 RNs; • 4 LPNs; • 6 Nurse Aides; • 3.5 Clerks]

9. Click and drag the I-beam across **Current full-time vacancies** to select it and then use the **Cut** button to remove the text from the slide and place it on the Clipboard
10. Click on the slide to deselect all objects and then click **Paste** to paste a new Text Box containing the cut text onto the slide
11. Click the new Text Box and drag it to the position shown. It will be formatted later

> **tip:** The new Text Box will be pasted in the center of the slide. If you click the bulleted list, the second Text Box will disappear. Deselect and then click the new Text Box

FIGURE 3.11

New Text Box Inserted and Repositioned

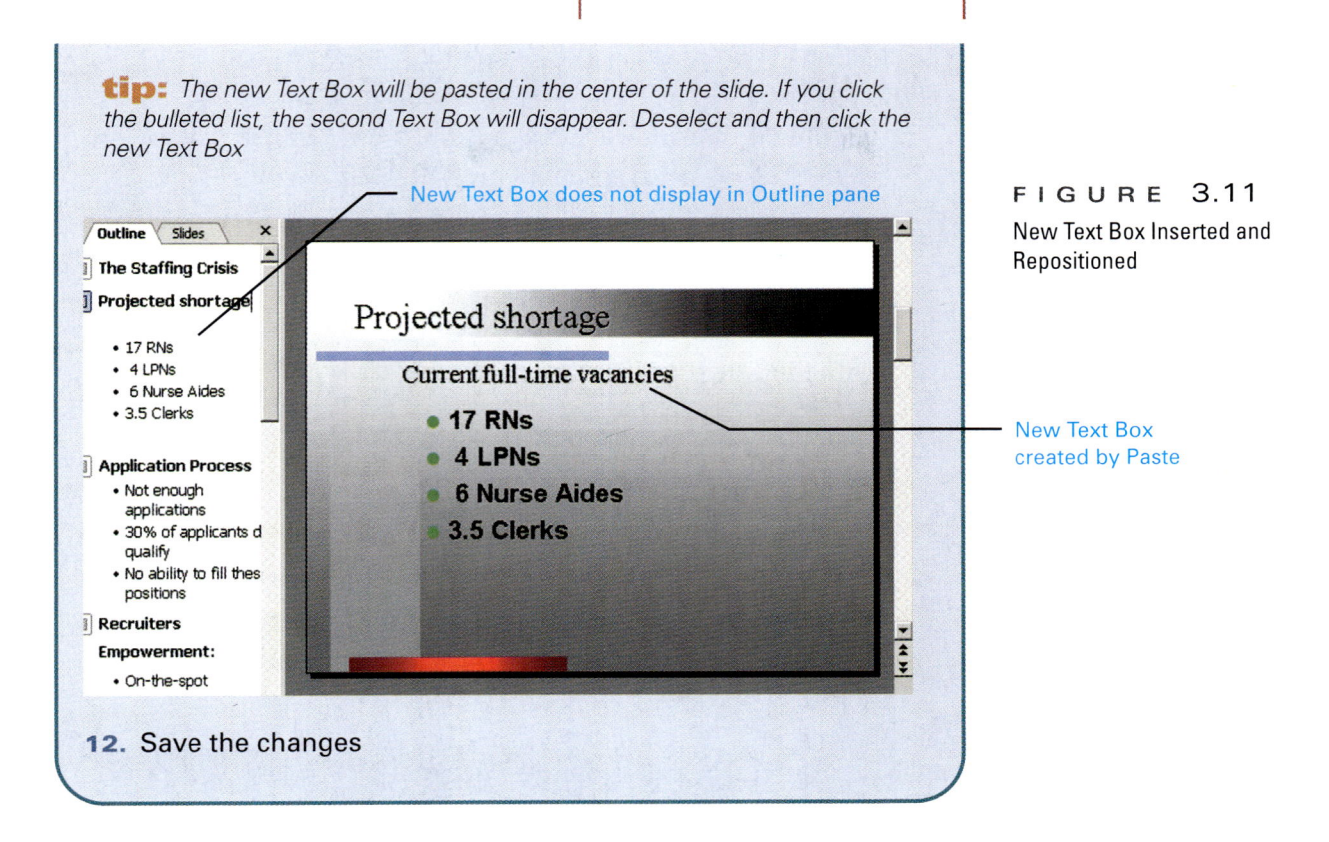

12. Save the changes

The Outline pane only displays text contained in text placeholders. Text added in a Text Box or Shape will not display or print in the outline.

Setting Character Formats

Character formats are those that can be applied to a single character or a group of selected characters. They include **Font, Bold, Italic, Point Size,** and **Shadow.** When developing a slide show, limit the number of font faces used unless the goal is a haphazard or disjointed look. Use point size to indicate the importance of the item. Place titles in larger points and use progressively smaller points for each level of subtitle and bullet. Use the other styles consistently.

The Staffing Plan uses Times New Roman font for the titles and Arial for the bulleted lists. The title text also has a shadow applied. The point size used in placeholders adjusts as you add text. When the text is too large for the placeholder, AutoFit automatically reduces the point size. Clicking in text will cause the Formatting toolbar to display the current character formats. Any of the character formats can be customized to add visual impact to your presentation.

A simple but effective formatting technique is to enlarge the first character in each word of a title. Ricki decides to try this on the title slide. You will build the format and then use the **Format Painter** to copy the format to the remaining characters.

Increasing character point size:

1. Verify that PowerPoint is running with **<yourname>PP03StaffingPlan.ppt** open

2. Move to slide **1**
3. Click in the slide title. Notice the Font, Font Size, Bold, Italic, Underline, and Shadow settings in the Formatting toolbar
4. Select the **T** in The and click the **Increase Font Size** button twice

tip: *The Font Size after this process should be 54*

5. With the T in The still selected, double-click the **Format Painter**
6. Paint the **S** in Staffing and the **C** in Crisis
7. Click the **Format Painter** to turn painting off

FIGURE 3.12
Title Slide without and with Enlarged Letters

Consistent point size

First letters in larger point

8. Save the changes

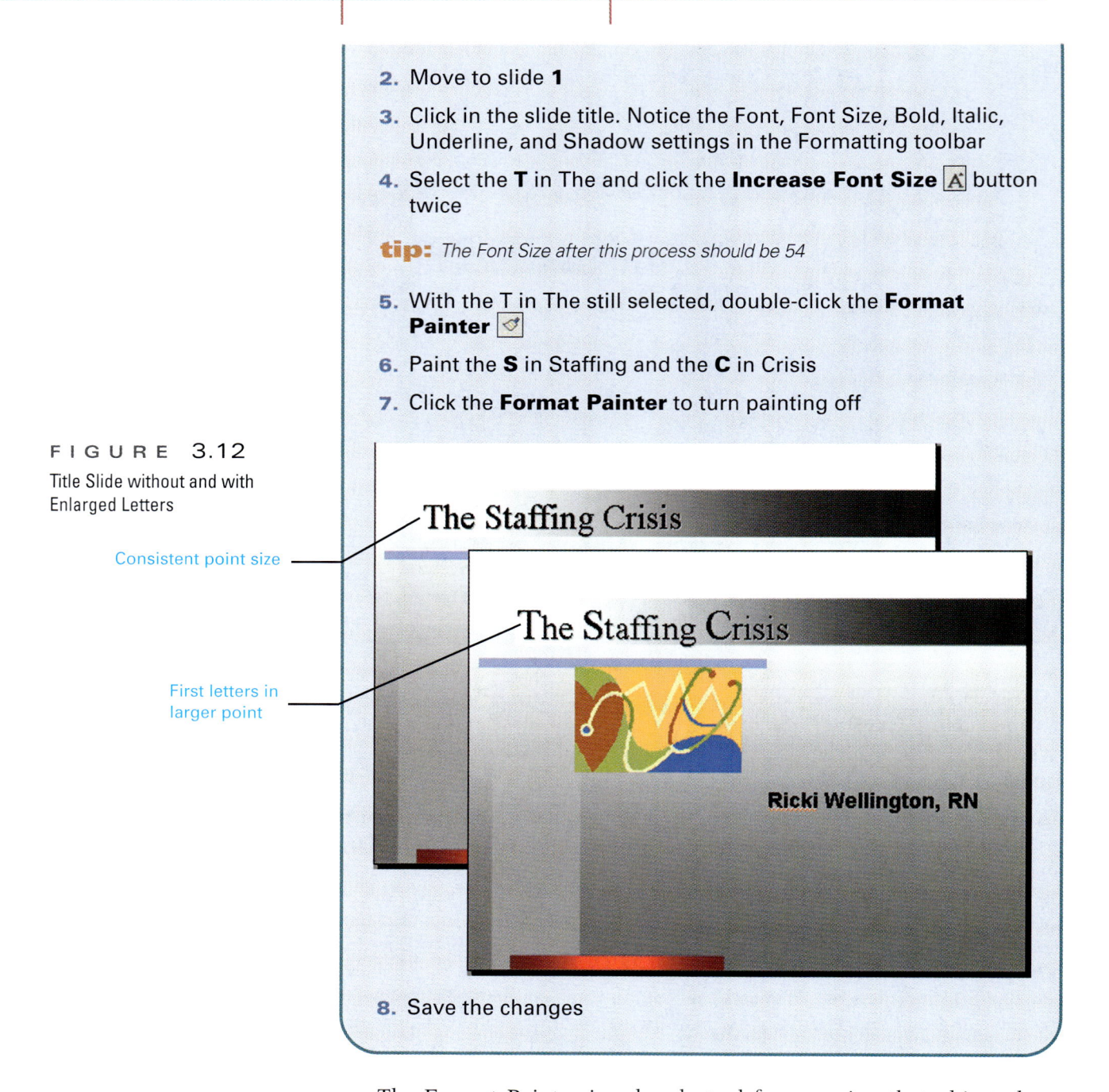

The Format Painter is a handy tool for ensuring that objects have exactly the same format. Format the first object and then use the Format Painter to copy all formatting to other objects. Single-clicking the Format Painter will allow one other object to be painted. Double-clicking the Format Painter allows repeated painting until Format Painter is clicked again to turn it off. Format Painting works on all object types.

The formatting status of selected text displays in the Formatting toolbar. The Bold, Italic, Underline, and Shadow buttons are ***toggle buttons***. If a button is off, clicking it will turn it on for the selection. Vice versa, if it is clicked while on, it will turn off. Clicking

*another*word

. . . on Formatting Text

Sometimes text is entered in the wrong case. To remedy this situation, select the text, click the **Format** menu, and then **Change Case.** There are options for converting the text to sentence case, title case, lowercase, uppercase, and toggling the case.

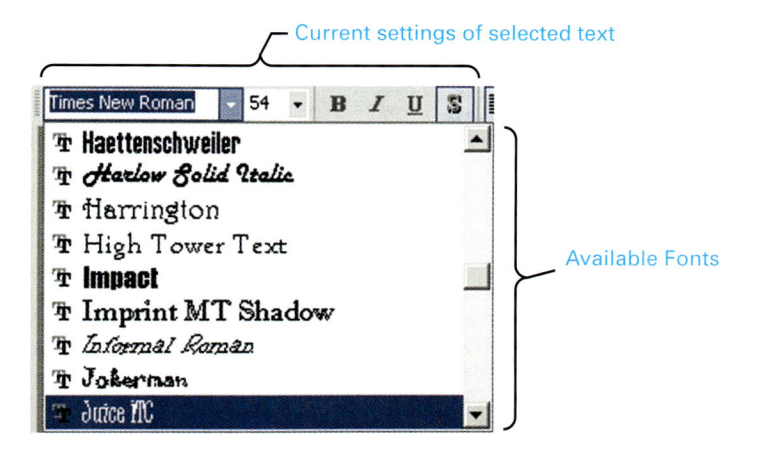

FIGURE 3.13

Font Drop-Down List

— Current settings of selected text

— Available Fonts

the drop-down arrow to the right of the Font will display a list of available fonts. Each font displays as a sample of that font face. The Font Size drop-down box displays a list of valid point sizes for the selected font, but the numbers do not show the impact of the change.

Ricki wants to change the font in the presentation to something that looks a little more technical. Since the audience is small and the quality of the projector is good, she does not need a heavy font for the projection to be readable.

Changing the presentation font:

1. Verify that PowerPoint is running with **<yourname>PP03StaffingPlan.ppt** open
2. Change to Normal view if necessary
3. Click in the Outline pane, click the Outline tab, and then type **Ctrl+A** to select all text in the presentation
4. Drop down the Font list and select **Tempus Sans ITC**

tip: Use a similar font if your computer does not have that one

5. Review the effect of the font change on the remaining slides

tip: Notice that the Text Box was not selected and the new font was not applied to its text

6. Move to slide **2** and select the **Current full-time vacancies** text in the Outline pane
7. Select **Arial** from the font drop-down list
8. Save the changes

Character formats are easy to modify and add visual appeal to any presentation. Be sure the font(s) selected match the tone and delivery method of the presentation. Thin fonts can work well for small audiences, but fade into the background in large rooms. Thick fonts work well in large rooms, but can be overwhelming in small spaces.

FIGURE 3.14

Title Slide with Tempus Sans ITC Font

Adding Numbers and Bullets

The text placeholders for slide body text automatically create a new bulleted item each time you press the Enter key. This formatting property is one of the attributes of a placeholder that can be customized or turned off (covered in AutoCorrect).

Removing or customizing bullets and numbers in a single list is accomplished from the slide containing the list. With the list selected use the Formatting toolbar options to remove the bullets, convert to a numbered list, customize the bullet and number format, or choose a graphic bullet. The same techniques will work to add bullets and numbering to a text box or shape that doesn't have bullets by default.

Ricki has decided that slide 2 should not have bullets and that the other slides should use graphic bullets. She is unsure as to whether to use the same graphic bullet on all of the slides, or to customize each slide. You will show her the available options.

task reference
Change the Bullet Style of a List

- Move to the slide containing the list and select the list (part or all of the list may be selected)
- On the **Format** menu click **Bullets and Numbering**
- Do as many of the following as are needed to implement your change:
  - Select from the standard options on the Bulleted or Numbered tab
  - Select a custom color from the drop-down Color list
  - Increase/decrease the size of the bullet relative to its associated text using the Size scrollbox
  - Click the Picture button to use a picture as the bullet character
  - Click the Customize button to use a Wingding or other special font as the bullet character

Customizing the StaffingPlan bullets:

1. Verify that PowerPoint is running with **<yourname>PP03StaffingPlan.ppt** open

2. Move to slide **2** and select all of the bulleted items

3. Click the **Numbering** button on the Formatting toolbar and observe the changes

4. Click the **Bullets** button on the Formatting toolbar and observe the changes

5. Click the **Bullets** button on the Formatting toolbar and observe the changes

tip: *Many of the Formatting toolbar buttons toggle on and off when repeatedly clicked. Bullets and Numbering are toggle buttons*

6. Move to slide **3** and select all of the bullet items

7. From the **Format** menu select **Bullets and Numbering**

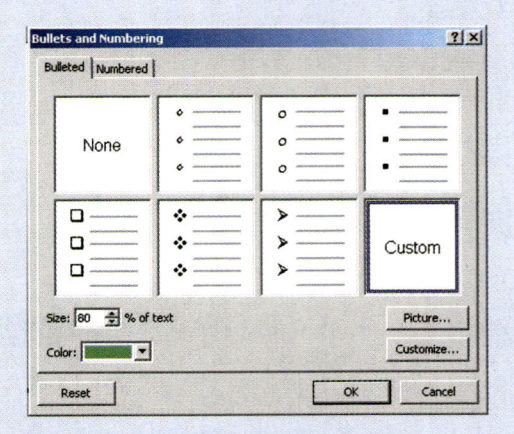

FIGURE 3.15

Bullets and Numbering Dialog Box

8. Select one of the available bullet formats, select a different color, and click **OK**

9. Repeat steps 7 and 8 to review another bullet format

10. From the **Format** menu select **Bullets and Numbering**, select the **Customize** button, and select an available character

11. Click **OK** and **OK** again to view the result of your selection

12. Repeat steps 10 and 11 to explore more of the available characters

tip: *The Font and Subset drop-down lists at the top of the Symbol dialog box allow you to select other character sets*

Ricki has decided that she would like to use a picture as the bullet character. She prefers shades of blue and gray.

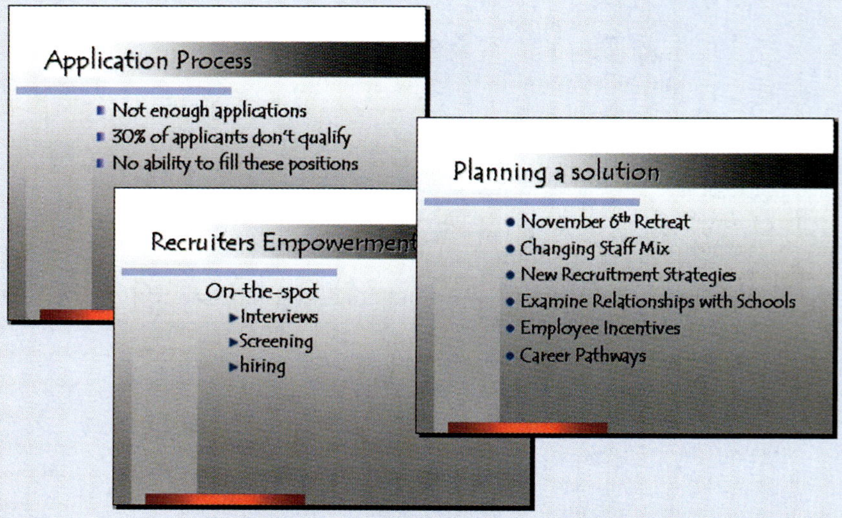

FIGURE 3.16

Pictures Used as Bullet Characters

> *Using a picture as the bullet character:*
>
> 1. Verify that PowerPoint is running with **<yourname>PP03StaffingPlan.ppt** open
> 2. Move to slide **3** and select all of the bulleted items
> 3. From the **Format** menu select **Bullets and Numbering**, select the **Picture** button, and select a square with shades of blue and gray
> 4. Click **OK**
> 5. Move to slide **4** and click in the first bulleted line
> 6. Click the **Bulleted** button on the Formatting toolbar to remove the bullet
> 7. Select the remaining bulleted items
> 8. From the **Format** menu select **Bullets and Numbering**, select the **Picture** button, and select a blue right-pointing arrow
> 9. Move to slide **5** and select all of the bulleted items
> 10. From the **Format** menu select **Bullets and Numbering**, select the **Picture** button, and select a blue circle on a gray background
>
> *[Slide images: Application Process, Recruiters Empowerment, Planning a solution]*
>
> 11. Move to slide **6** and select a bullet that fits the presentation scheme
> 12. Save the changes

Each of the customization options explored for bullets and numbering can be applied to the slide master to change the defaults. Changes made to the slide master are applied to all slides that have not been individually customized.

Other Text Objects

This session has spent a great deal of time formatting placeholders and mentioning that the changes could also be applied to Text Boxes and

FIGURE 3.17
The Drawing Toolbar

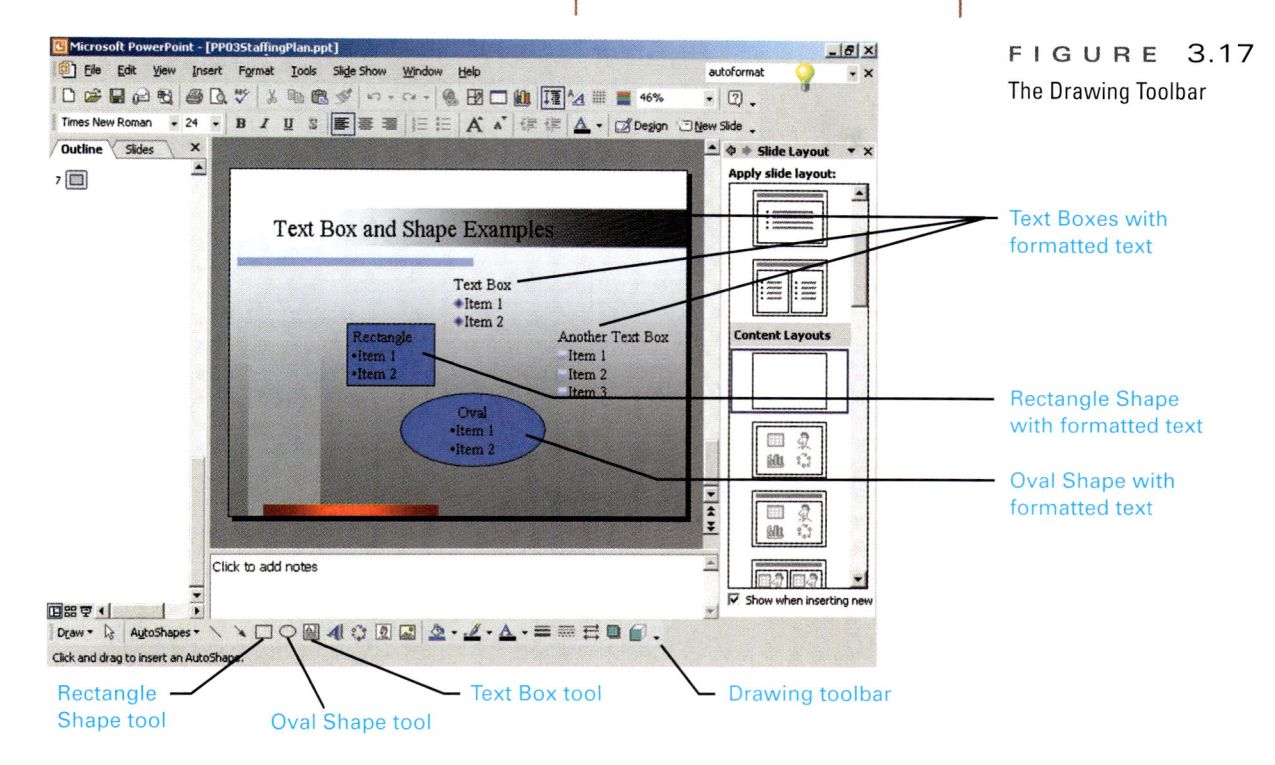

Shapes. Text Boxes can be added by some Paste operations due to the AutoFormat settings. The more common way to add a Text Box is to use the **Text Box tool** of the **Drawing** toolbar. The **Shapes tools** are also located on the Drawing toolbar.

The Drawing toolbar is used to add Text Boxes, lines, shapes, and other art to a slide. It is usually located at the bottom of the PowerPoint screen, but like all toolbars it can float or be anchored on any window edge. To use the Drawing toolbar, select a tool and then click and drag the slide surface to "draw" the selected object. When a shape or Text Box is selected, typing will add text to it.

Adding other text objects:

1. Verify that PowerPoint is running with **<yourname>PP03StaffingPlan.ppt** open

2. Move to slide **6** and click the **New Slide** button from the Formatting toolbar

3. Move to slide **7**, the new slide

4. Select **Blank** slide layout from the Task Pane

5. Click the **Text Box** tool in the Drawing toolbar and then click the slide to position the Text Box for the slide title as shown in the next figure

6. Type the text shown in the next figure for the title

7. Repeat steps 5 and 6 to create the text in the other two Text Boxes

tip: The bullets will be added in the next series of steps. Press Enter at the end of each line

POWERPOINT

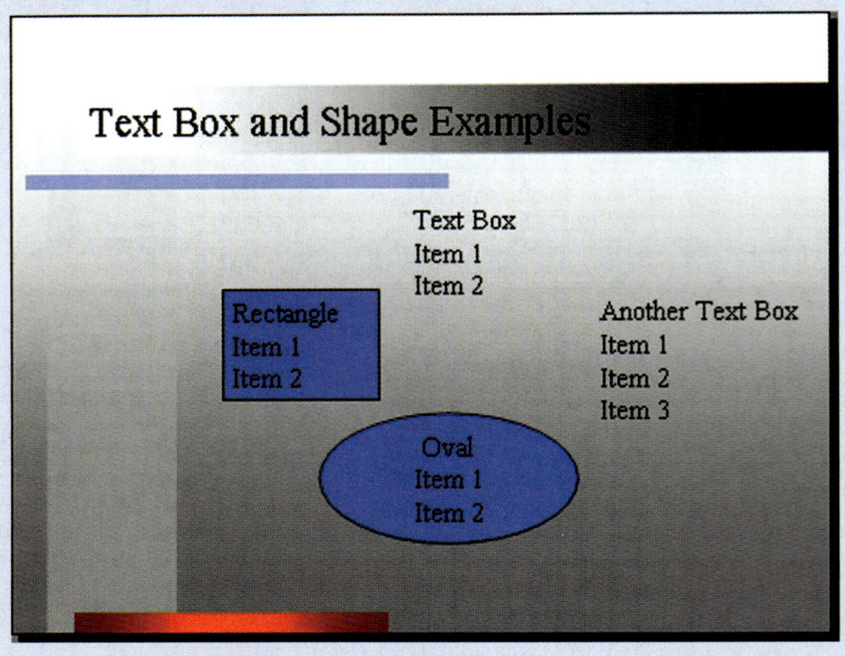

FIGURE 3.18

Shapes and Text Boxes

8. Click the **Rectangle** ☐ tool and then click and drag the rectangle area on the slide

9. Type the rectangle text shown in the next figure. If necessary, click the align left button on the toolbar. Formatting will be applied later

Text Box and Shape Examples

Text Box
Item 1
Item 2

Rectangle
Item 1
Item 2

Another Text Box
Item 1
Item 2
Item 3

Oval
Item 1
Item 2

10. Click the **Oval** ⚪ tool and then click and drag the oval area on the slide

11. Type the oval text shown in the previous figure. Formatting will be applied later

12. Save

Text in AutoShapes and Text Boxes can be formatted with color, font, point size, bullets, and numbers in the same fashion as placeholder text. In addition, the background color can be changed and the object rotated.

Formatting other text objects:

1. Verify that PowerPoint is running with **<yourname>PP03StaffingPlan.ppt** open and slide 7 active

2. Select the Item 1 and Item 2 text in the rectangle and click the **Bullets** button on the Formatting toolbar

3. Select the Item 1 and Item 2 text in the oval and click the **Bullets** button

4. Select the items in Text Box, select **Bullets and Numbering** from the **Format** menu, and click **Picture**

5. Select the picture shown in the figure next and click **OK**
6. Select the items in Another Text Box, select **Bullets and Numbering** from the **Format** menu, and click **Picture**
7. Select the text in the title and click the **Increase Font Size** button until the font size is 36 points
8. Right-click the Text Box and choose **Format Text Box**
9. On the size tab set the rotation to **25**
10. Right-click the Rectangle and choose **Format AutoShape**
11. On the Colors and Lines tab, choose a yellow Fill color. On the size tab set the rotation to **-25**

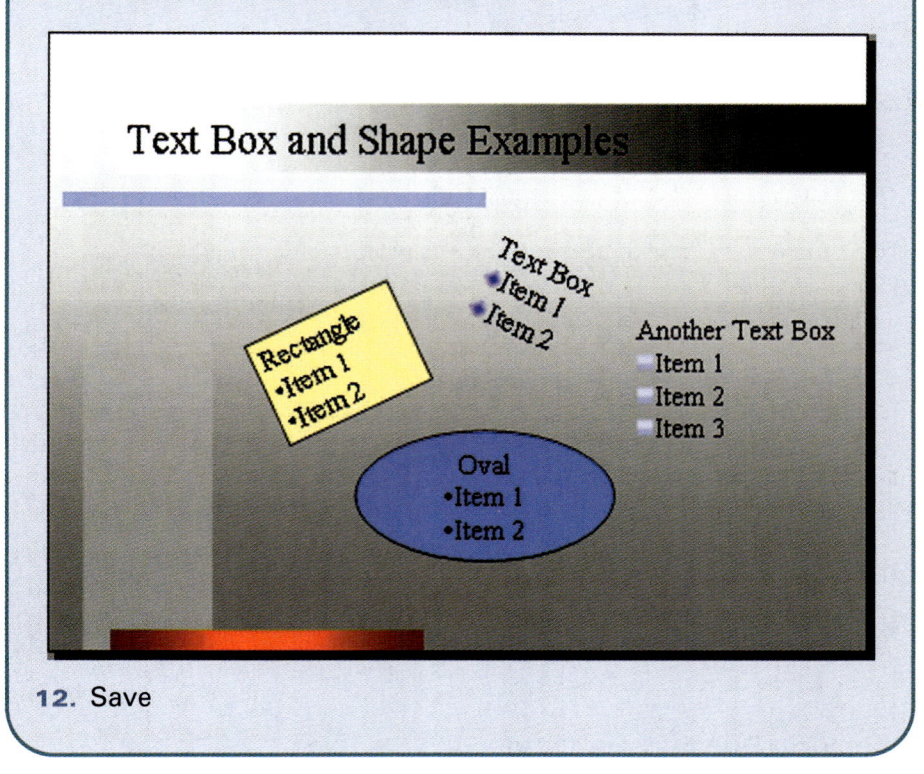

FIGURE 3.19
Rotated Text in Shapes and Text Boxes

12. Save

Rotating a Text Box has the visual appearance of rotating the text it contains. Placeholders can also be formatted by right-clicking the selection border and choosing Format Placeholder. Placeholders have the same formatting options as Text Boxes and AutoShapes.

Formatting placeholders:

1. Verify that PowerPoint is running with **<yourname>PP03StaffingPlan.ppt** open
2. Move to the first slide
3. Select the placeholder holding Ricki's name
4. Right-click on the border of the placeholder and choose **Format Placeholder**

The Staffing Crisis
Ricki Wellington, RN

FIGURE 3.20
Rotated Placeholder

5. Click the Size tab and set the Rotation to **-10**
6. Save

All slide content is made up of objects that can be formatted. Much of this formatting is accomplished using the Formatting toolbar. The complete set of options is available from the pop-up menu activated by right-clicking on an object.

USING PROOFING TOOLS

Microsoft PowerPoint provides an array of tools to help create a consistent and error-free presentation. These tools range from those that work behind the scenes to those that are controlled by the user.

Checking Spelling and Style

The most straightforward tool is the ***Spelling Checker.*** If you are familiar with Microsoft Word, PowerPoint's Spelling Checker works in the same fashion. As you enter text, it is checked against the dictionary. When a word is not found in PowerPoint's dictionary, it is marked with a red wavy underline for your review.

Right-clicking on a word with a red wavy underline will display a list of suggested spellings. The listing will also include options to add the current word to the dictionary, or ignore all occurrences of this word in the current presentation. Adding words to the dictionary is an effective way to handle special terminology, like AutoContent. A word of caution, however: Carefully review spelling before adding a new word to the dictionary. It is easy to add misspelled words to the dictionary, and there is no Undo.

Checking the Style of a presentation is analogous to checking grammar in a word processing document. The ***Style Checker*** helps to correct common stylistic problems that detract from a presentation. The Style Checker works with the Office Assistant by offering tips. If the Office Assistant's Show Tips options have been modified, you may not receive style tips.

Style checking uses style rules to formulate tips. One of the default *style rules* is that text entered into a title placeholder should use title capitalization (the first letter of most words capitalized). When slide content violates one of the style rules, a light bulb appears next to the Microsoft Office Assistant. Clicking the light bulb will provide a list of options for conforming to the style rule, ignoring the style rule, and customizing styles.

The default style rules include:

- Consistent capitalization in titles and body
- Consistent use of end punctuation like periods
- Maximum number of font styles
- Maximum number of bulleted items in a list
- Maximum number of text lines in a list item

task reference
Customize Style and Spelling Checker

- Click **Options** on the **Tools** menu and then click the **Spelling and Style** tab
- Click the appropriate Spelling options
- Set the **Check Style** check box
- Click the **Style Options** button to set Style Checker options
  - On the **Case and End Punctuation** tab select the desired options
  - On the **Visual Clarity** tab, set fonts, point sizes, bullets, and line limits

Setting PowerPoint's Spelling and Style options:

1. Verify that PowerPoint is running with **<yourname>PP03StaffingPlan.ppt** open
2. Click **Tools, Options,** and then the **Spelling and Style** tab
3. Move through the options adjusting them to match those displayed in the next figure
4. Click **OK** until you are back in the presentation
5. Move to slide **2** and click on the **light bulb**

tip: *The message should be about the capitalization of the title. Since this presentation has used sentence capitalization for titles, style setting needs to be changed*

6. Click **Ignore this style rule for this presentation only** and click **OK**
7. Click through the remaining slides and correct other style inconsistencies
8. Save

FIGURE 3.21

Spelling and Style Tab of the Options Dialog Box

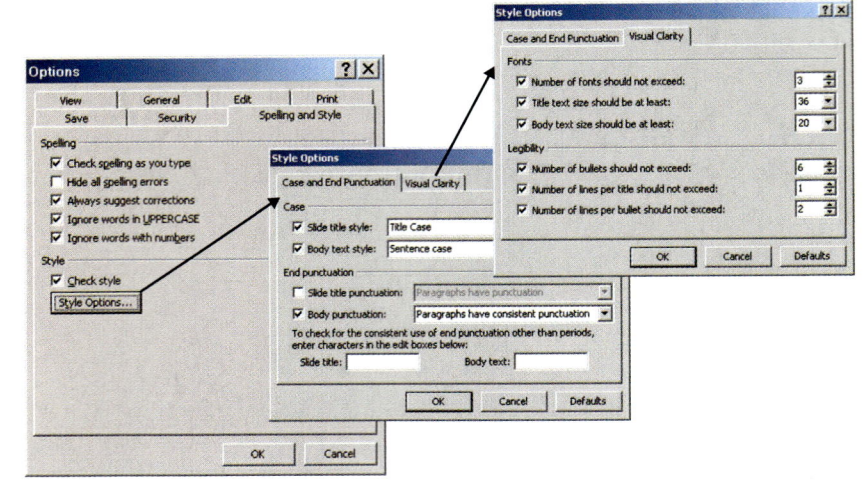

FIGURE 3.22

Style Messages from the Office Assistant

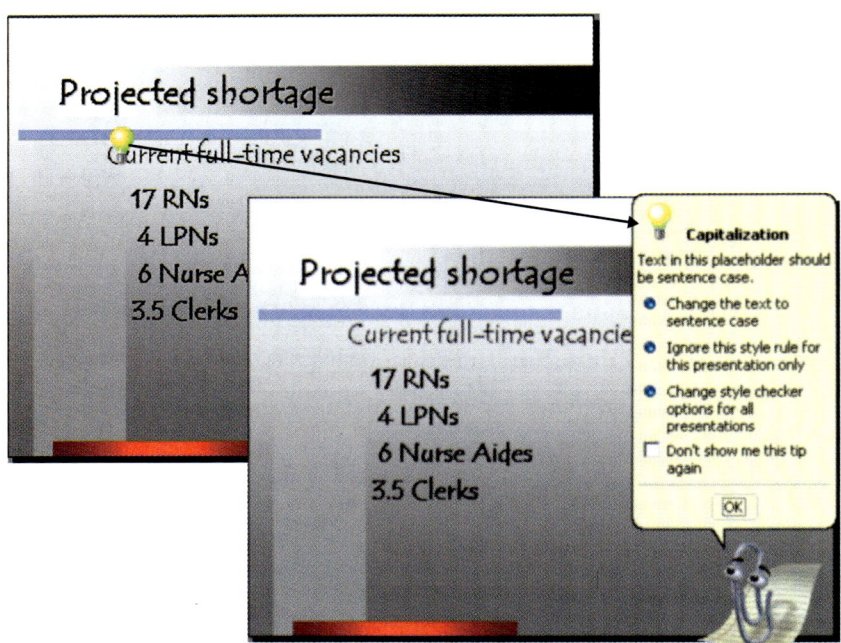

The first slide of your presentation should still have a red wavy line under Ricki's name indicating that this word can't be found in the dictionary. We will introduce another spelling error to demonstrate the use of the Spelling Checker.

task reference
Correct Words Marked by Spelling Checker

- Edit a word with a red wavy underline to correct the spelling manually

  or

- Right-click on a word with a red wavy underline for suggestions and then do one of the following:
  - Select the correct spelling from the list of suggestions
  - Select **Ignore All** to ignore this word in the current presentation
  - Select **Add to Dictionary** to add this word to the dictionary for all presentations

Checking your spelling:

1. Verify that PowerPoint is running with **<yourname> PP03StaffingPlan.ppt** open
2. Move to slide **1**
3. Right-click on Ricki

tip: *Right-clicking will open formatting options rather than spelling options if you have already dealt with the spelling of Ricki*

4. Select **Ignore All** since Ricki is correct, but we do not want to add that spelling to the dictionary
5. Move to slide **2** and change the spelling of vacencies to **vacencies**
6. Click out of the word so that it will be spell checked

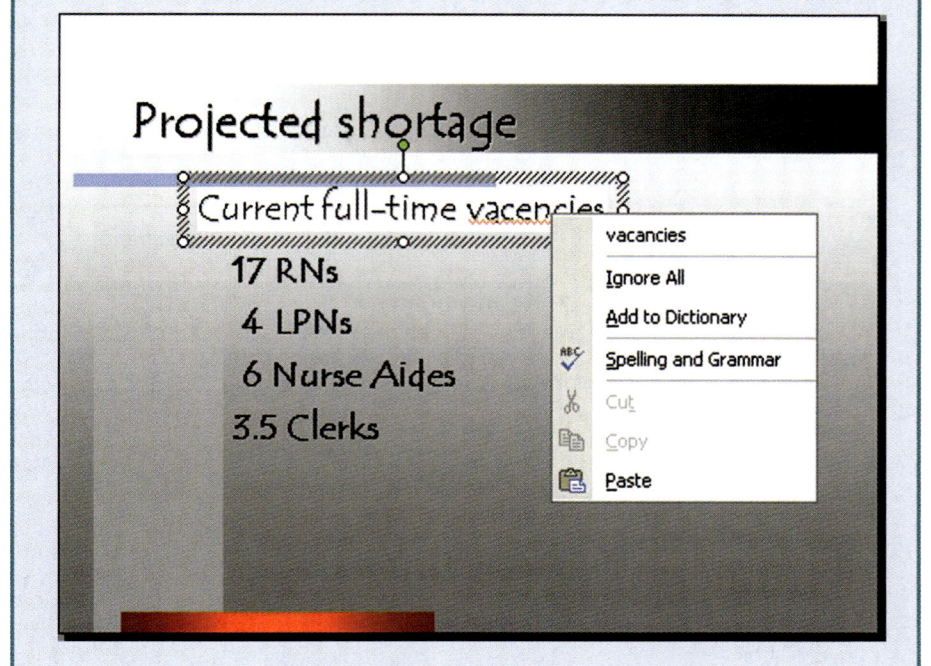

FIGURE 3.23
Spelling Suggestions

7. Right-click on the red wavy line of **vacencies** and select the correct spelling from the list
8. Save

Spelling and Style checkers are very flexible tools because they are easy to customize and override. They prompt with suggestions based on the set profile. Neither tool is foolproof, so it is still necessary to proofread presentations carefully. For example, text that is not contained in a placeholder is not style checked, and spelling checker won't find words that are misused but spelled correctly.

Using Find and Replace

PowerPoint's Find and Replace commands allow a presentation to be searched for specific characters. Aside from finding each occurrence of the specified item, you can also spell out text to replace the found value(s). With Find and Replace, it is easy to consistently adjust wording or correct a consistent error throughout a presentation.

---

task reference

Find Text and/or Formatting

- Click the **Edit** menu and then click **Find**
- Enter the search string and select the appropriate options
- Click the **Replace** button to specify a replacement value
- Do one of the following
  - Click **Find** to locate the next occurrence of the Find what string
  - Click **Replace** to update the current occurrence of the Find what string with the replacement value
  - Click **Replace All** to replace all instances of the Find what string with the Replace with string

---

Replacing text values:

1. Verify that PowerPoint is running with **<yourname>PP03StaffingPlan.ppt** open
2. Click the **Edit** menu and then click **Find**
3. Enter **RN** in the Find what Text Box
4. Click **Find Next** until all instances of RN have been found

FIGURE 3.24
Using Find and Replace

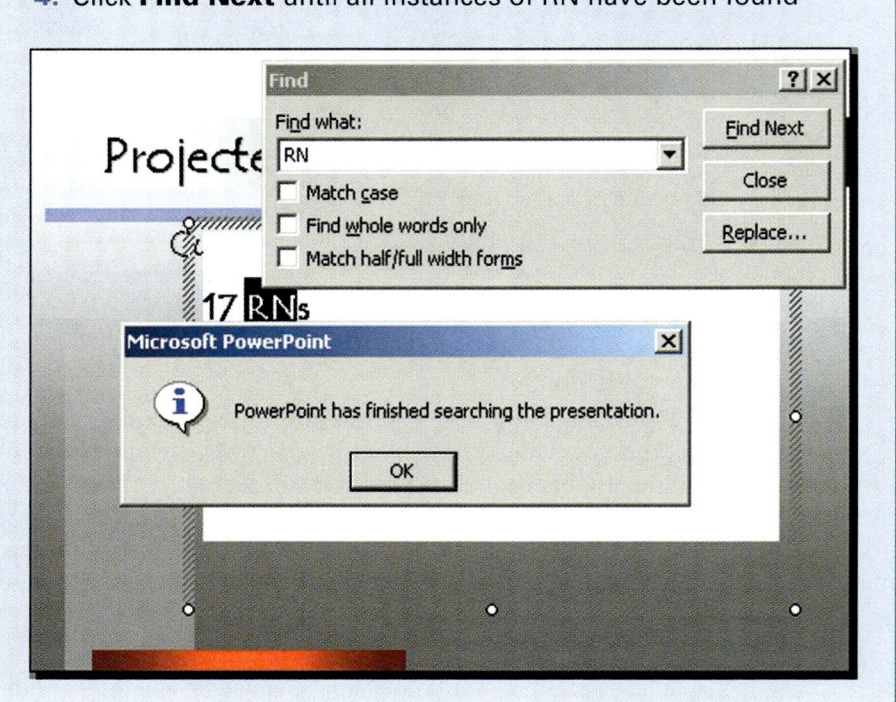

5. Enter **Staff** as the Find what criterion and click the **Replace** button
6. Enter **Nurse** as the Replace with value and click **Find Next**
7. Do not change Changing Staff mix, since Nurse doesn't make sense there
8. Click **Find Next** again
9. Click **Replace** for The Staffing Crisis to change it to The *Nurseing* Crisis
10. Click **OK** and **Close** to close the Find and Replace dialog box
11. Correct the spelling of *Nurseing*
12. Save

Find and Replace is an effective way to search for and change values in large presentations. It is essential to verify each Replace, since it is easy to make undesirable changes by clicking Replace All. Use the Match Case check box to cause the search to return only text that matches the Find what case. Similarly, the Find whole words only check box will only return instances that match the Find what text exactly. In our example of searching for Staff, Staffing would not be considered a match with Find whole words only checked.

Using AutoCorrect

You may have noticed that PowerPoint automatically makes changes to some of your text entries as you type. For example, if you consistently type *teh*, **AutoCorrect** will change it to *the*. AutoCorrect is already set to adjust *teh*, other common typos, and capitalization inconsistencies. AutoCorrect can be customized with your common mistakes.

Backspacing and typing your text again will override AutoCorrect changes. The AutoCorrect option of the Tools menu will allow you to create custom AutoCorrect settings. You may also have noticed an icon that appears next to placeholders using **AutoFit** (a part of AutoCorrect). Clicking this icon will also allow customization.

Customizing AutoCorrect:

1. Verify that PowerPoint is running with **<yourname>PP03StaffingPlan.ppt** open
2. Move to slide **1**
3. Select the placeholder containing Ricki's name. Notice that AutoFit Options icon is displayed

tip: *If there is no icon, type **xx** after RN to initiate AutoFit*

4. Click the **AutoFit** icon
5. Notice that you can turn AutoFit off and on for this placeholder

FIGURE 3.25

Menu Activated by Clicking the AutoFit Icon

6. Click **Control AutoCorrect Options**
7. Review the AutoFormat settings
8. Click the **AutoCorrect** tab and review the options. Be sure to scroll through the list of Replace text as you type pairs

FIGURE 3.26

AutoCorrect Tab of the AutoCorrect Dialog Box

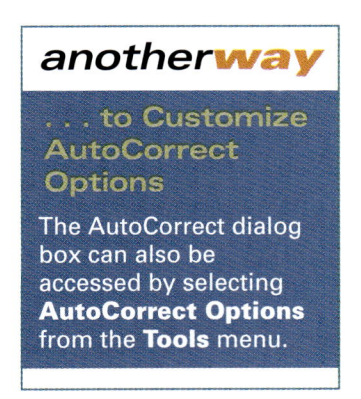

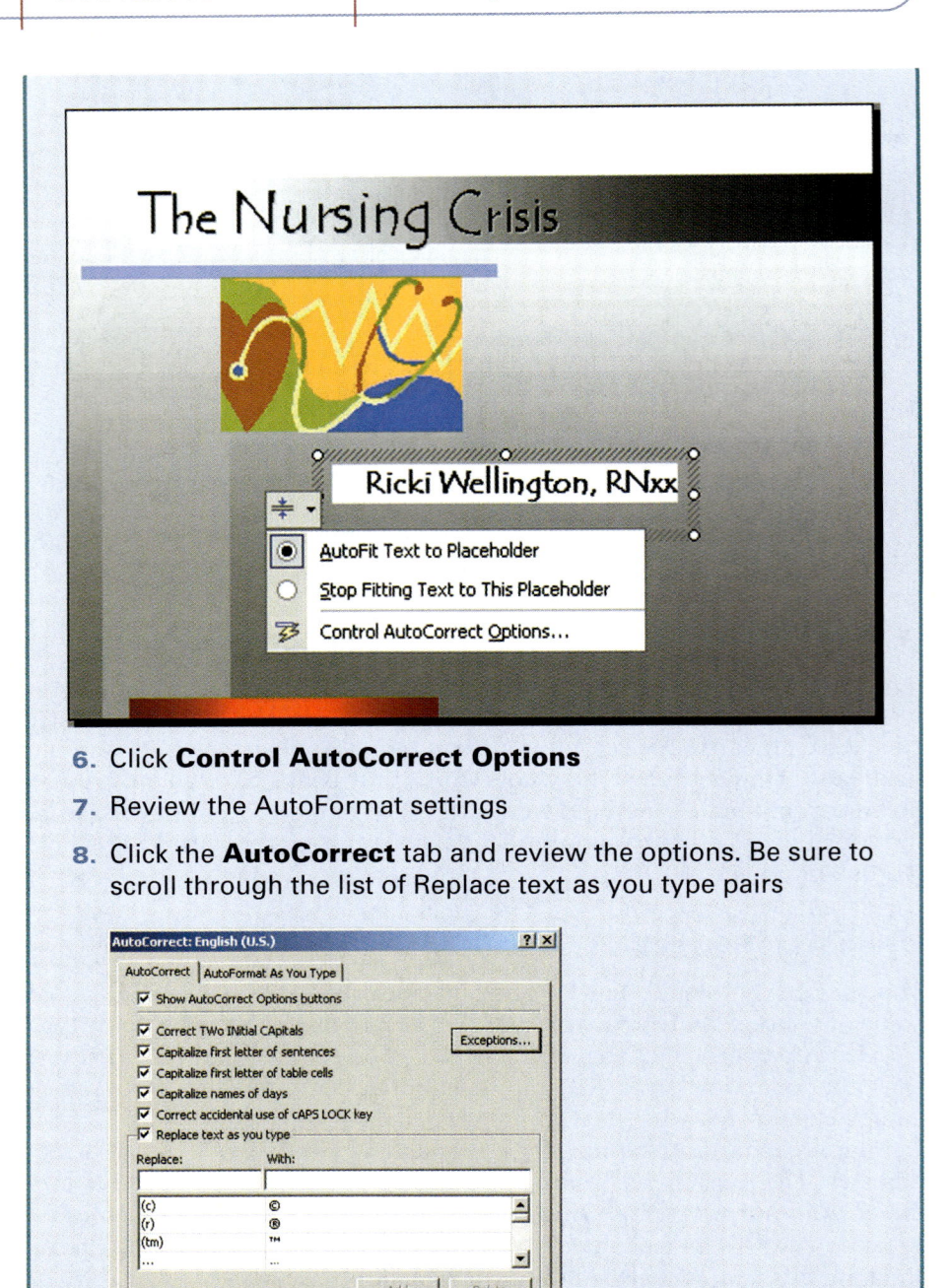

9. If you have a common typing mistake, enter it in the Replace text as you type list. The erroneous text belongs in the Replace box, and the correction belongs in the With box
10. Click **OK**

anotherway

. . . to Customize AutoCorrect Options

The AutoCorrect dialog box can also be accessed by selecting **AutoCorrect Options** from the **Tools** menu.

AutoCorrect is an effective tool for making changes without your intervention, but it can introduce errors in text that does not follow the rules. For example, typing :) results in ☺ when the Replace as you type smiley faces and arrows check box is checked. The Replace as you type list contains entries to convert (c) to ©, (tm) to ™, and (r) to ®. These shortcuts are a handy way to insert symbols into your text. When the actual typed text rather than the symbol is wanted, a single backspace should restore what was typed. If the symbols are never wanted, they can be deleted from the Replace as you type list. Remember that deleting or adding to this list impacts all PowerPoint presentations.

Besides the list of words to AutoCorrect, you should have noticed options to turn off automatic bulleted and numbered lists, create a hyperlink when an address is typed, and capitalize the first letter of a sentence (that includes the first letter of a bulleted item). Any of these options can be changed, but using them can save keystrokes.

Thanks to the automatic bulleted and numbered lists option, you can start a numbered or bulleted list by typing. Asterisk and a tab will initiate a bulleted list, while 1. and a tab will initiate a numbered list. Without the automatic hyperlink setting, you would need to set the link to the Web site or e-mail address manually. Automatic capitalization can save many keystrokes. For example, you do not have to hold the Shift key to capitalize the first letter of a sentence following normal ending punctuation (.?!), the first letter of a bulleted item, or the first letter of text entered into a table cell.

making the grade — SESSION 3.1

1. What is the importance of objects in PowerPoint?
2. Why would you use sizing handles?
3. Describe how text alignment works.
4. What is the purpose of the Format Painter?

SESSION 3.2 STANDARDIZING PRESENTATIONS

Whenever multiple presentations are created, standardization should be considered. Using consistent background, colors, fonts, logos, and object placement can make it simpler for the audience to move from presentation to presentation. When multiple speakers share the same presentation materials, like the slide shows for the chapters of this book, standardization is imperative. Finally, an organization can create a custom look that becomes part of the presenter's image.

CREATING A SUMMARY SLIDE

In large or formal presentations, it is common to include an overview slide early in the presentation and a summary slide late in the presentation. These slides are intended to introduce and summarize the presentation. These slides can be added to the presentation automatically by creating a slide that includes the titles from selected presentation slides. The Summary Slide button available in Slide Sorter view was designed for this task.

task reference
Create a Summary Slide
- Use the **Slide Sorter View** button to change to Slide Sorter View
- Select the slides whose titles will be included on the summary slide (hold down **Ctrl** to select multiples)
- On the Slide Sorter toolbar, click **Summary Slide**

Creating a Summary Slide for Staffing Plan:

1. Verify that PowerPoint is running with **PP03StaffingPlan.ppt** open
2. Click the **Slide Sorter View** button
3. Select slides **2** through **6**

   tip: *Select the first slide and then hold down the **Ctrl** key while selecting the remaining slides*

4. Click the **Summary Slide** button on the Slide Sorter toolbar

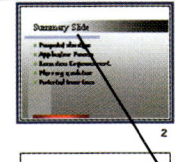

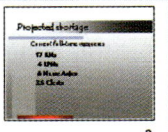

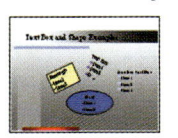

FIGURE 3.27
Summary Slide Created in Slide Sorter View

5. Double-click on the summary slide to see it in Normal view
6. Save

Once created, the summary slide can be edited, moved, and duplicated like any other slide in the presentation. It is always best to create summary slides last so that they reflect the latest version of your presentation. An existing summary slide can also be deleted before maintaining a presentation and then re-created once maintenance is complete.

UNDERSTANDING TEMPLATES

A template is a special file containing color, background, text, and bullet format characteristics. You can create a presentation from a template like the AutoContent wizard, or apply a template to an existing presentation. All template files have a .pot extension. For example, blank.pot is the file used to create a new presentation using the Blank Presentation option.

Viewing Masters

Every Microsoft PowerPoint design template has a set of masters to control the formatting, color, graphics, and text placement of a presentation. Every presentation has one master for each type of output (slides, handouts, and notes).

The **Slide Master** controls the format of each presentation slide. It includes placeholders for slide titles, subtitles, body placeholders, date, slide number, and footer text. The background, text color, font, font size, and other characteristics set on the master will appear on every slide in the presentation. When the Slide Master is edited, those changes will automatically appear on every slide. Custom elements like background artwork or a company logo can be placed on the Slide Master for consistent appearance on all slides.

There are actually two slides called the ***slide-title master pairs*** that define each presentation style. The first slide defines the layout of all slides containing body text. The second, called the **Title Master,** sets the design for slides that use the Title Slide layout (have a subtitle). The Slide Master settings are used as the default, but formatting applied to an individual slide will override the master settings for that slide.

---

task reference

View Masters

- On the **View** menu, point to **Master**
- Select the Master (Slide, Handout, or Notes) that you would like to view

---

Viewing the Slide Masters for the StaffingPlan presentation:

1. Verify that PowerPoint is running with **PP03StaffingPlan.ppt** open

tip: *It is important to return to the original file so that changes made to the individual slides in your copy of the file will not override changes to the Master*

2. On the **View** menu, point to **Master**
3. Click **Slide Master**
4. Select each of the placeholders on the first slide

tip: *There are five of them (title, body, date, footer, and number)*

5. Pause over each of the miniatures in the left-hand pane. A summary of the slides using that master will appear

FIGURE 3.28
Slide Masters

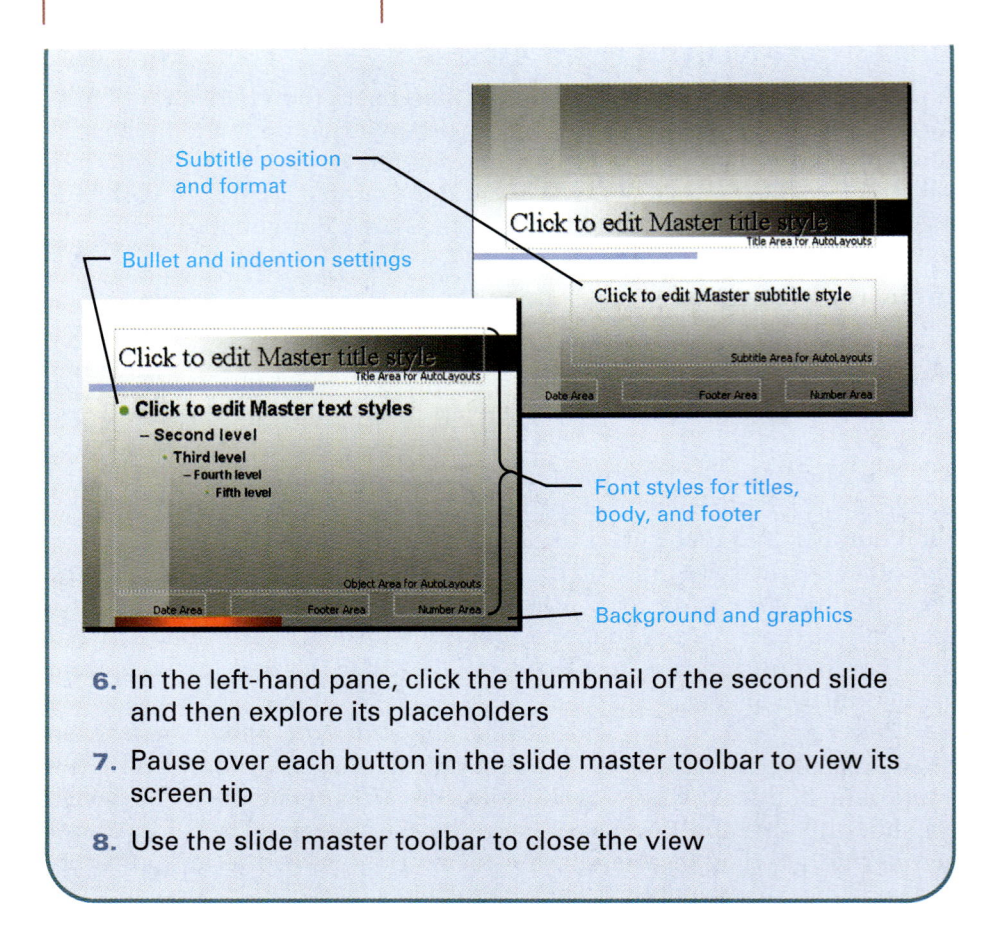

Subtitle position and format

Bullet and indention settings

Click to edit Master title style
Title Area for AutoLayouts

Click to edit Master subtitle style
Subtitle Area for AutoLayouts
Date Area   Footer Area   Number Area

Click to edit Master title style
Title Area for AutoLayouts
• Click to edit Master text styles
  – Second level
    • Third level
      – Fourth level
        · Fifth level

Object Area for AutoLayouts
Date Area   Footer Area   Number Area

Font styles for titles, body, and footer

Background and graphics

6. In the left-hand pane, click the thumbnail of the second slide and then explore its placeholders
7. Pause over each button in the slide master toolbar to view its screen tip
8. Use the slide master toolbar to close the view

Multiple slide masters can be active in a presentation, so the slide master toolbar contains options for working with multiple slide masters. Besides using multiple design templates, it is possible to create a completely new slide master using the commands for inserting, deleting, renaming, duplicating, and preserving masters. When a new master is inserted, it will be displayed in the Task pane with the available design templates. The preserve property of a master protects it from being deleted automatically in certain cases by PowerPoint.

Displaying and navigating the Handout and Notes masters are accomplished using the same steps as viewing the Slides master. Each master consists of placeholders that can be customized. There is only one Notes Master, but each handouts layout (two slide, three slide, and so on) has its own master.

Viewing the Handouts and Notes masters:

1. Verify that PowerPoint is running with **PP03StaffingPlan.ppt** open
2. On the **View** menu, point to **Master**
3. Click **Notes Master**
4. Review the placeholders
5. On the **View** menu point to **Master**

PP 3.31

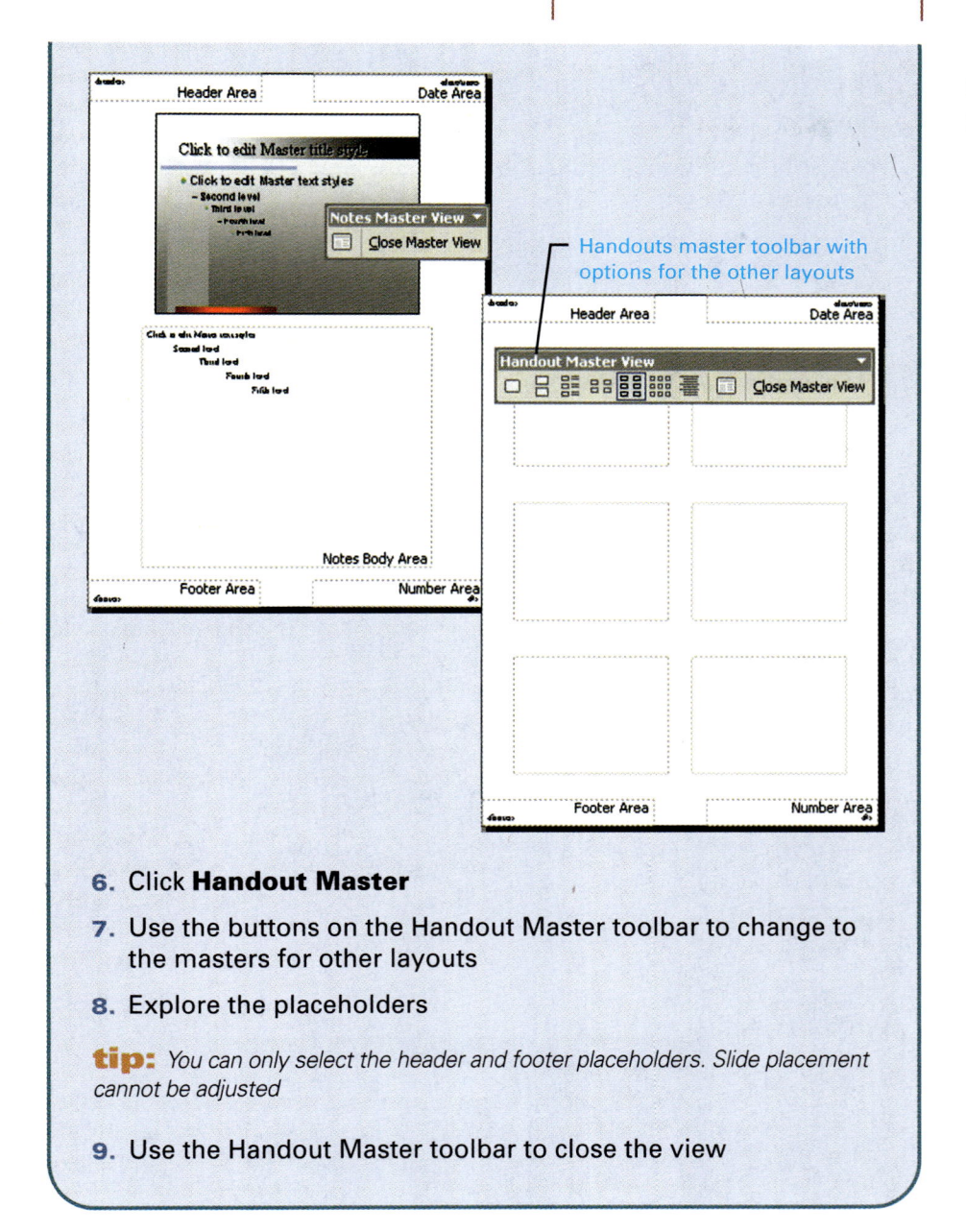

FIGURE 3.29
Notes and Handouts Masters

Handouts master toolbar with options for the other layouts

6. Click **Handout Master**
7. Use the buttons on the Handout Master toolbar to change to the masters for other layouts
8. Explore the placeholders

tip: You can only select the header and footer placeholders. Slide placement cannot be adjusted

9. Use the Handout Master toolbar to close the view

Each presentation has one set of masters for notes and handouts. The masters set the default page layout, but formatting on individual pages can override the settings of the master.

Applying Multiple Design Templates

Sometimes it is effective to use multiple Design Templates in the same presentation. The graphic distinction of a new template can emphasize a change of topic, or the importance of a topic. When a Design Template is clicked in the Task pane, the default is to apply the template to the entire presentation. Pausing over a template will reveal a drop-down button on its right used to select how the design is applied. Ricki is not satisfied with the impact of the current background and wants to experiment. You will apply templates to the first and last slides of the presentation for her to preview.

POWERPOINT

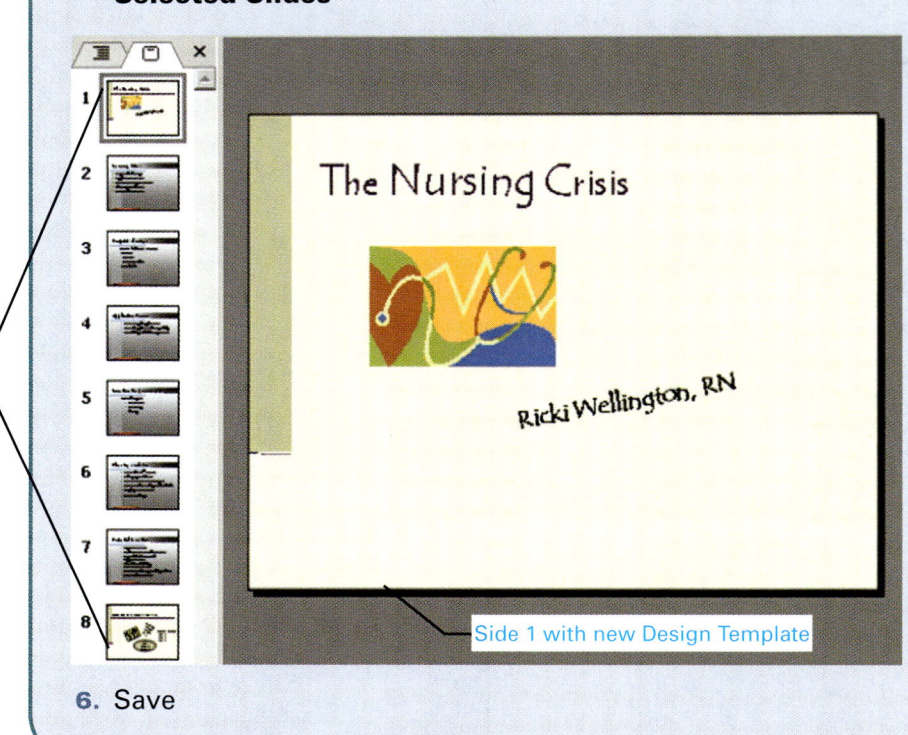

FIGURE 3.30

Design Template Applied to Selected Slides

Selected slides

> **Applying a Design Template to selected slides:**
>
> 1. Verify that PowerPoint is running with **PP03StaffingPlan.ppt** open
> 2. Use the drop-down arrow in the Task pane to choose the **Slide Design—Design Templates** panel
> 3. Select slide **1** and then hold down **Ctrl** to select slides **6–8**
> 4. Locate the Layers.pot template and pause the cursor over it to activate the drop-down arrow
> 5. Click the drop-down arrow of Layers.pot and click **Apply to Selected Slides**
>
> Side 1 with new Design Template
>
> 6. Save

anotherway

. . . to Apply a Design Template to Selected Slides

If no slides are selected when you click a Design Template, the template will be applied to the entire presentation. When specific slides are selected, clicking on a Design Template will apply the template to the selected slides only (there is no need to drop down the list of operations).

Besides the Apply to Selected Slides selection used in the steps, the Design Template drop-down list has selections to

- Apply to Master
- Apply to All slides
- Show Large Previews

Apply to Master will update the Slide Masters with the design of the selected template. Apply to All slides updates the Master and all slides (even those not using the current master). Show Large Previews will display larger thumbnails of the Design Templates. Depending on the resolution of your monitor, this may or may not make them clearer.

When a template is applied to a presentation, PowerPoint copies the slide master information from that template to the corresponding presentation masters. Any applied Design Templates appear in the Slide Design task pane under Used in this presentation. All available Design Templates appear in the same pane under Available for use.

PowerPoint ships with a library of professionally designed templates. Each template can be used as is or modified. Modified templates should be saved under a new name to retain the original template as well as the revised template.

MODIFYING POWERPOINT MASTERS

Design Masters determine the default placeholders, text format, and graphics that will appear on each slide of a presentation. Only the background content of a master can be excluded from individual slides. Customizing master content and formatting is very similar to editing the content of a slide. A standard Design Template can be modified, or a new template created.

Formatting Master Text

Design Masters contain placeholders for the most common presentation text (title, body, subtitle, and footer). Placeholders can be formatted with fonts, text sizes, bullets, and so on. Text that is to appear in the presentation cannot be added to a slide master placeholder unless it is to appear on all presentation slides. The text displaying in the Design Master placeholders is only to demonstrate the impact of applied changes.

Text Boxes and Shapes can be added to a Design Master to create graphics or contain text that is to appear on each presentation slide. As you practiced earlier, adding a Text Box or Shape to a master is accomplished using the Text Box and Shapes tools from the Drawing toolbar.

In <yourname>PP03StaffingPlan.ppt, you used Ctrl+A to select all of the Text placeholders in a presentation and change the font. Although that accomplished the task, applying such changes to the Slide Master has the advantage of simultaneously creating a template that can be used in future presentations. In the following steps, you will apply text formats to the Slide Masters of the original PP03StaffingPlan.ppt and save a new template.

FIGURE 3.31

Design Template Drop-Down List

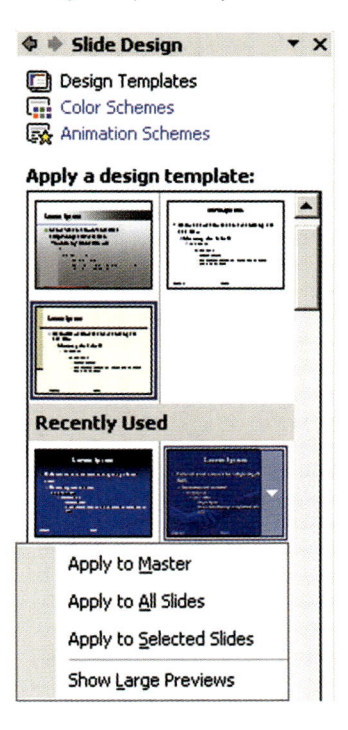

Adjusting Slide Master text formats:

1. Verify that PowerPoint is running with **PP03StaffingPlan.ppt** open

2. Click on slide **1**

   a. Activate the Slide Layout panel of the Task pane

   b. Pause over **Title Slide** layout to activate the drop-down arrow

   c. Click the drop-down arrow and select **Apply to Selected Slides**

   tip: Reapply Layout will remove any formatting applied to a slide and restore it to the formatting of the master. In this case it is being used to remove formatting applied in a previous session

3. On the **View** menu point to **Master** and click **Slide Master**

   tip: You should have two slide-title master pairs—one for each Design Template used in this presentation

FIGURE 3.32

Formatting the Layers Master

4. Click on the subtitle placeholder of the Layers Master
   a. Set the font to **Century Gothic** using the font drop-down list from the Formatting toolbar
   b. Click the **Italic** button on the Formatting toolbar
   c. Drop down the Font Color button on the Formatting toolbar and choose the color matching the bar on the slide background

5. Click the title placeholder
   a. Set the font to **Verdana**
   b. Set the color to brown
6. Click **Close Master View** to preview the changes
7. Move to slide **6** and notice that the changes have not been applied there, since this slide does not use a title layout
8. Review slides 2 through 5 to verify that they have not been impacted because they use a different master
9. Select slides 2 to 5 and set their Design Template to **Layers**
10. Save

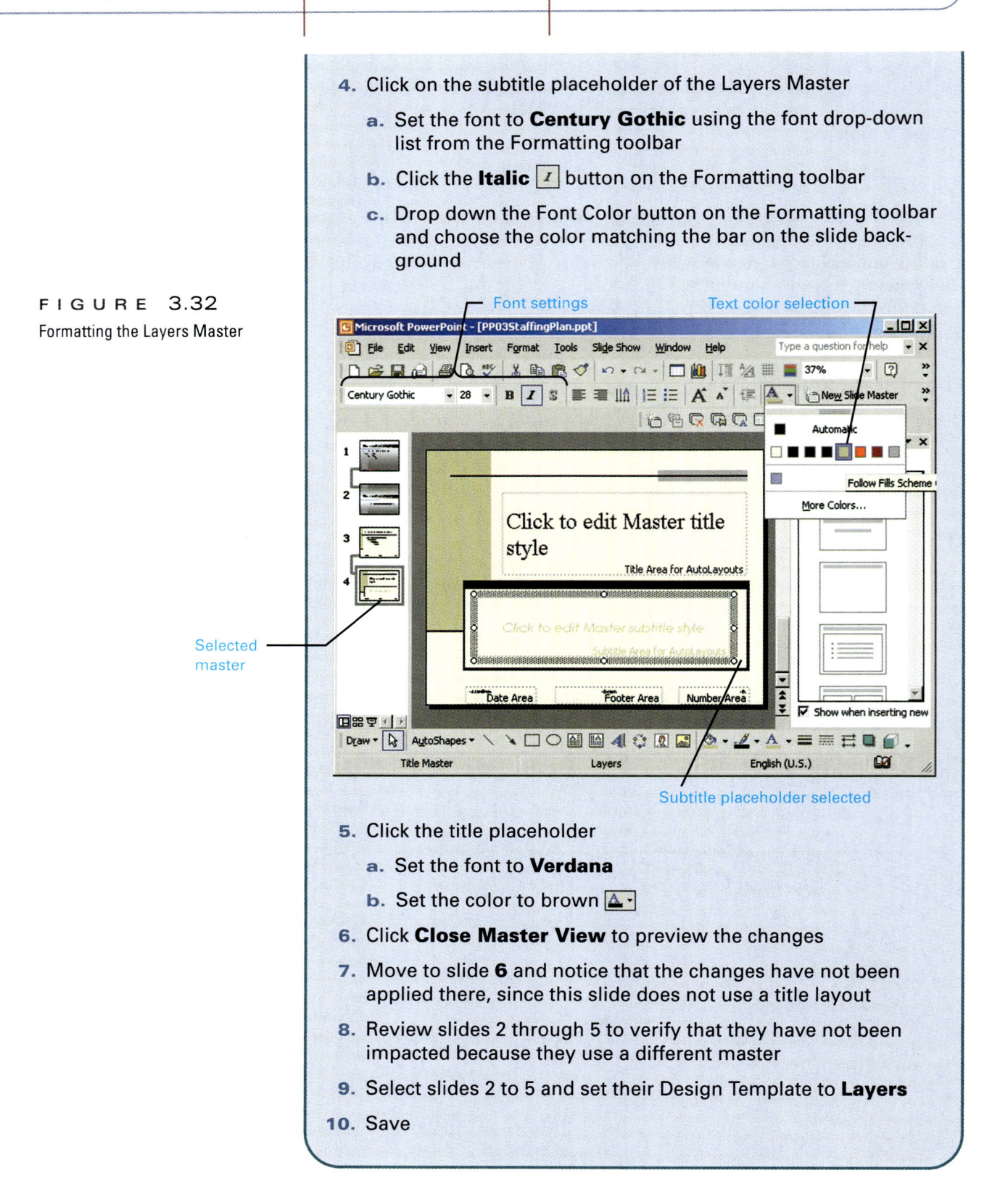

Ricki has decided that she likes the colors and basic design of the Layers template, but she would like to customize the bullets and add a dynamic graphic.

Customizing the Slide Master bullets

Bulleted lists are the default format for body text in each PowerPoint template. You have already created custom bullets for each slide in a presentation. When continuity is important, the bullets can be set in the body placeholder of the Slide Master so that they will be the same on each slide created. The bullets can be sized, customized, and colored. Each of the five bulleted levels can have a unique bullet and indention level. The list can also be converted to a numbered list.

Customizing Slide Master bullets:

1. Verify that PowerPoint is running with **PP03StaffingPlan.ppt** open
2. On the **View** menu point to **Master** and click **Slide Masters**
3. In the **View** menu click **Ruler** so you can see the indention settings
4. Click on the body placeholder in the first bulleted level
    a. Right-click and select **Bullets and Numbering** from the pop-up menu
    b. Click **Customize** and choose **Arial** with a Subset of **Geometric Shapes**
    c. Pick the right-pointing arrow
    d. Click **OK**
    e. Drop down the Color list and choose the **Brown** color
    f. Click **OK**

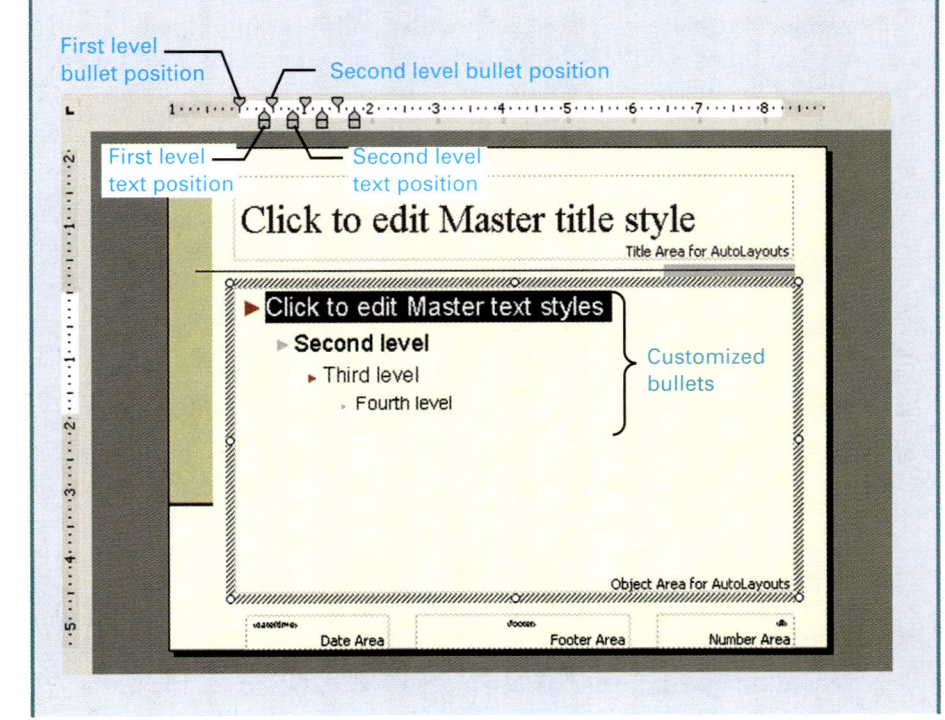

FIGURE 3.33

Formatting Master Bulleted Lists

5. Click in the second bulleted level
   a. Right-click and select **Bullets and Numbering** from the pop-up menu
   b. Click **Customize** and choose **Arial** with a Subset of **Geometric Shapes**
   c. Pick the right-pointing arrow
   d. Click **OK**
   e. Drop down the Color list and choose the **Dark Gray** color
   f. Set the size to **75% of text**
   g. Click **OK**
6. Repeat the process for the third level bullet, setting it to a size of **55% of text** and a color of **Brown**
7. Repeat the process for the fourth level bullet, setting it to a size of **40% of text** and a color of **Dark Gray**
8. Delete the fifth level
9. Close Master View
10. Move through the presentation to view your updates

The ruler holds *indent markers* that control the position of each bullet level and the distance between the bullet and text. If you are familiar with Microsoft Word, adjusting PowerPoint indents work the same way. The upper indent marker controls the bullet position, while the lower indent marker places the text. If the text wraps on more than one line, it will align with the lower marker causing a *hanging indent.*

Dragging the indent markers on the ruler will reposition them. The triangles on the upper and lower markers will move each marker independently. Dragging the box on the lower marker will move the markers in unison.

Repositioning Master indent markers:

1. Verify that PowerPoint is running with **PP03StaffingPlan.ppt** open
2. On the **View** menu point to **Master** and click **Slide Masters**
3. If the ruler is not displaying, click the **View** menu and then click **Ruler**
4. Click in one of the bulleted lists to see the indent markers
5. Move the fourth level indent marker until the upper marker is at 3 inches
6. Move the third level indent marker until the upper marker is at 2 inches
7. Move the second level indent marker until the upper marker is at 1 inch

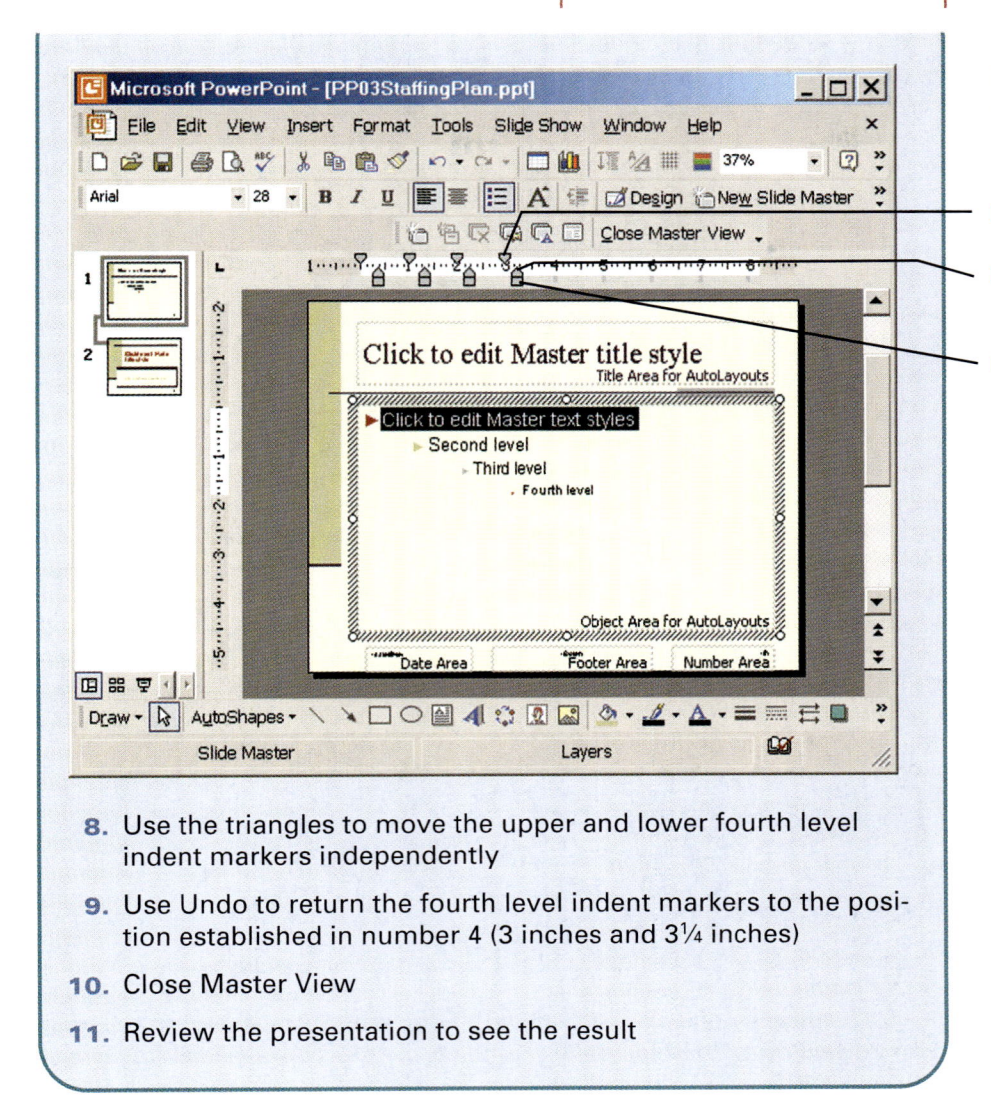

FIGURE 3.34
New Indent Settings

Drag to move upper marker

Drag to move lower marker

Drag to move both markers

8. Use the triangles to move the upper and lower fourth level indent markers independently

9. Use Undo to return the fourth level indent markers to the position established in number 4 (3 inches and 3¼ inches)

10. Close Master View

11. Review the presentation to see the result

anotherword
. . . on Adjusting Indent Markers

Dragging an indent marker into another marker will push the other marker until the mouse button is released. For example, dragging the first level indent marker to 3 inches will push all of the other markers so they remain to the right of the first level marker.

For most presentations the default indent settings are effective. Changing the font or bullet can cause the bullet to crowd the text or appear inappropriately small or large next to the text. In such cases, adjusting the indent is appropriate.

Saving Masters in a Template

After customizing the Masters the presentation can be saved as a new template. The template will display with the other Design Templates for use in future presentations.

POWERPOINT

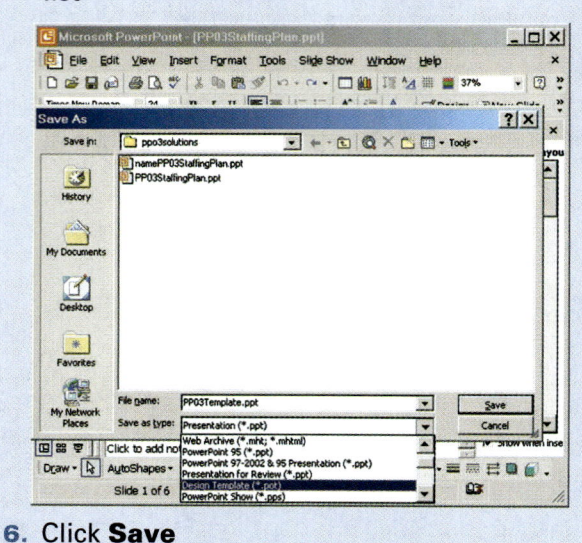

FIGURE 3.35
Save As Template

> **Saving a template:**
> 1. Verify that PowerPoint is running with **PP03StaffingPlan.ppt** open
> 2. On the **File** menu click **Save As**
> 3. Navigate to the folder containing your other practice files
> 4. In the **File Name** box, enter **PP03Template**
> 5. Select **Design Template** from the Save As Type drop-down list
> 6. Click **Save**

Since this template was saved with your other files, it will not display with PowerPoint's templates. All templates are stored in special folders set up when Office is installed. The exact location is determined by the computer's operating system and install options. Find the location of the templates on your computer using the Search (or Find) utility available from the Start menu. Search for *.pot.

Hiding the Master Content

Content and formatting of the Masters is used on each presentation slide. Any formatting applied to a selected object will override the Master settings. The background content of the slide Master can be hidden for a single presentation slide or for all slides in the presentation. The background of a slide includes all Master objects except title, subtitle, and body placeholders. That means that hiding the background hides the header, footer, and graphics from the master.

> **Hiding the background on slide 6:**
> 1. Verify that PowerPoint is running with **PP03StaffingPlan.ppt** open
> 2. Move to slide **6**

3. Click **Format** and then **Background**
4. Click the **Omit Background Graphics From Master** check box
5. Click **Preview** to see the result

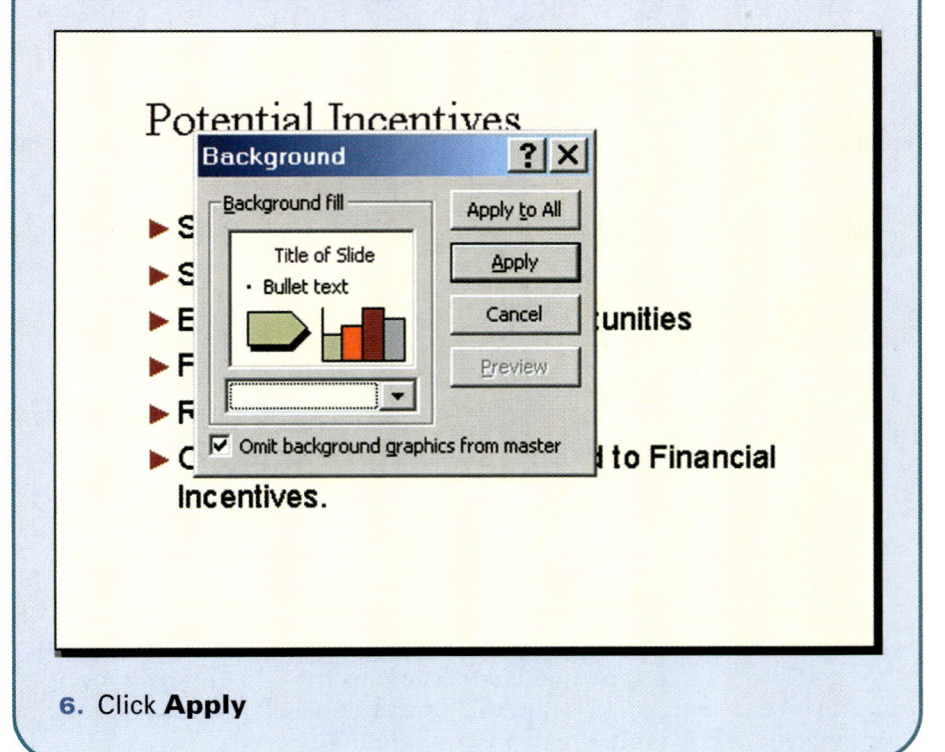

FIGURE 3.36

Omit Background Graphics from Master

6. Click **Apply**

The Background dialog box also provides the ability to apply a custom background color.

Creating a custom background color:

1. Verify that PowerPoint is running with **PP03StaffingPlan.ppt** open
2. Move to slide **6**
3. Click **Format** and then **Background**
4. Click the arrow next to the color bar and select **Fill Effects**
5. Explore each tab
6. On the Gradient tab, select **One Color**
7. Set the color to dark gray
8. Adjust the Dark-Light slider as shown in the next figure
9. Choose **Diagonal down** as the Shading Style
10. Click **OK**
11. Click **Apply**

FIGURE 3.37
Create a Gradient Fill Background

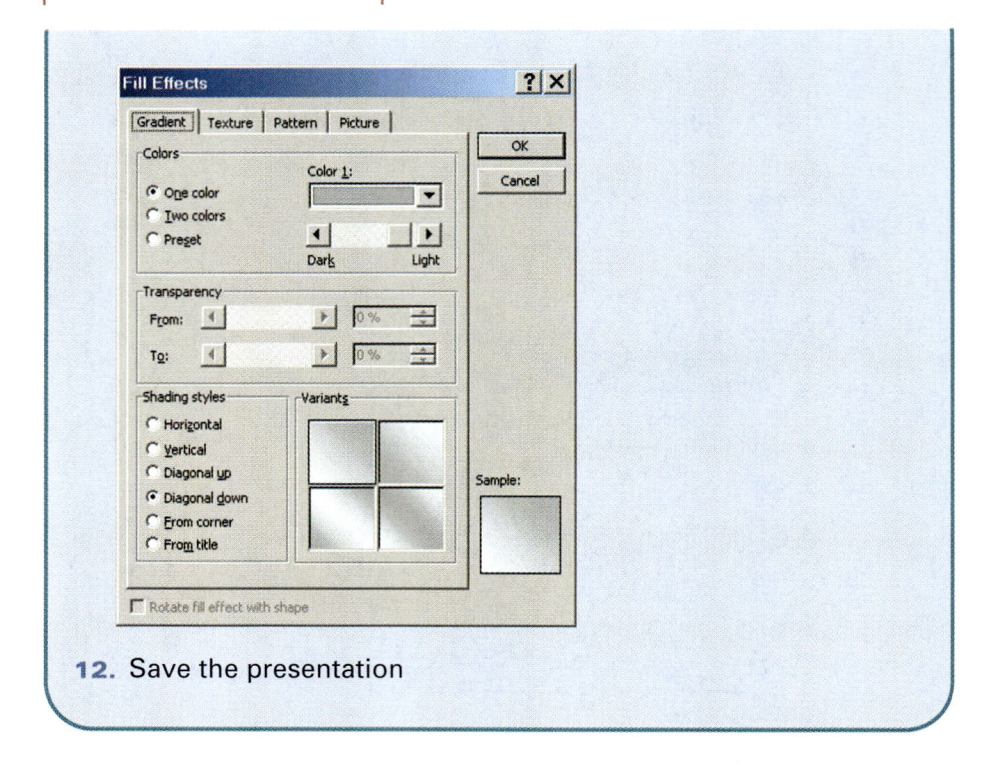

12. Save the presentation

PowerPoint templates use color schemes. The selections automatically displayed by dropping down the color bar are those set by the current color scheme. The More Colors option can be used to select from a broader list of colors or create a custom color. The tabs provide options for applying a texture, a pattern, or a picture as a slide background. The look of your presentation is limited only by your creativity.

USING ANIMATION SCHEMES

Animation Schemes are preset slide transitions with text animations that can be applied to a slide(s) in your presentation to add interest and control presentation flow. A *slide transition* directs how a slide enters and leaves the screen. A *text animation* is a special effect that manages how text enters and leaves a slide. Animations can be accompanied by a sound or other effect. Like all PowerPoint features, preset animation schemes are available or custom settings can be used to create unique animation

task reference
Apply a Preset Animation Scheme
- Open the presentation to be animated
- Use the Task pane drop-down arrow to move to the **Slide Design—Animation Schemes** panel
- Select the slide(s) to animate
- Click the desired Animation Scheme

If Auto Preview is clicked, a preview of the animation will play after you click. Use **Play** to preview the animation setting or **Apply to All Slides** to apply this animation to all slides in the slide show. The **Slide Show** button provides a full-screen preview of the show effects. Custom animations will also allow graphics, diagrams, charts, and other objects to be animated.

Preset animations can be found in the Slide Design—Animation Scheme Task pane. Animation Schemes are applied to text placeholders on the selected slide(s). Animations help to add interest to a presentation and control the flow of the content.

Applying preset animations:

1. Verify that PowerPoint is running with **PP03StaffingPlan.ppt** open
2. Use the drop-down arrow to move to the **Slide Design—Animation Schemes** in the Task pane
3. Move to slide **1**
4. Choose the **Big Title** Animation Scheme from the Exciting group
5. Move to slide **2** and select the **Pinwheel** Animation Scheme

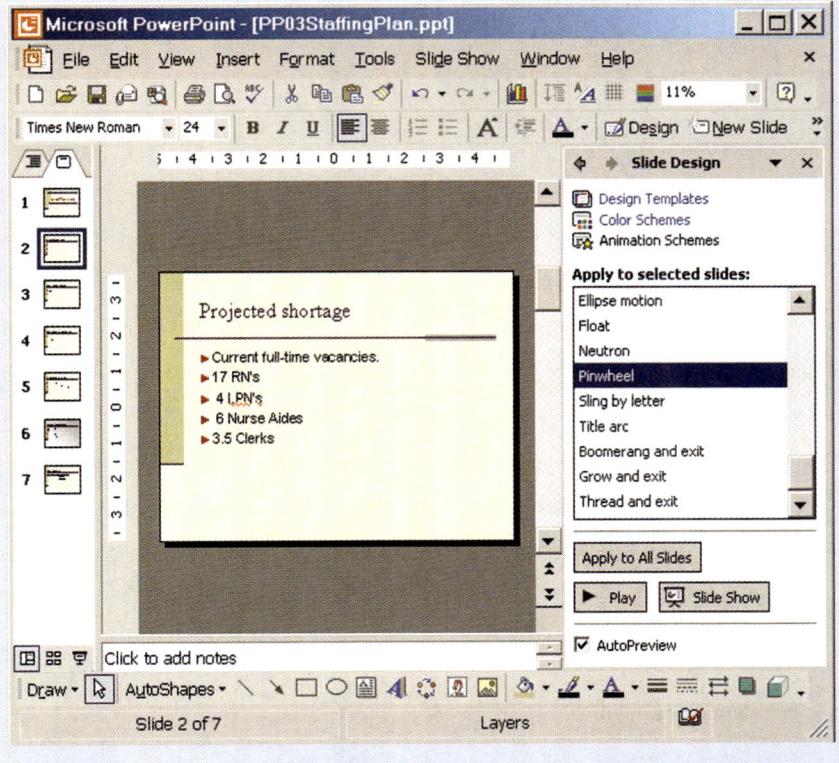

FIGURE 3.38

Preset Text Animations

6. Select slides 3 through 6 by clicking slide **3** in the Outline pane and then holding the **Shift** key while clicking slide **6**
7. Explore other Animation Schemes
8. Choose the **Elegant** Animation Scheme from the Moderate group
9. Click on slide **1** and then use the **Slide Show** button to view the entire show
10. Save the presentation

The Animation Schemes are classified as Subtle, Moderate, and Exciting to help users choose schemes appropriate for the audience and presentation content. Focus on the purpose of the slide show when selecting a scheme. Exciting animations can overshadow presentation content. Custom transitions and animations will be covered in a later session.

USING PRESENTATION TOOLS

PowerPoint has presenter's tools to help manage a slide show while it is being presented. During a slide show the pen can be used to annotate a slide, or the meeting minder used to record notes and track action items. Presenter's notes can also be displayed on a second monitor so that the audience sees the slide show and the presenter can still view content notes for each slide.

Using the Meeting Minder

During business presentations, it is common to need to take minutes and track action items. The *Meeting Minder* is like a notepad available in Slide Show view. Right-clicking on the surface of a slide during a slide show will open a pop-up menu where Meeting Minder is one of the options.

Taking presentation notes:

1. Verify that PowerPoint is running with **PP03StaffingPlan.ppt** open
2. Move to slide **5** and click the **Slide Show** button
3. Click to bring up the first bulleted item
4. Right-click to open the pop-up menu and select **Meeting Minder**
5. Click the **Action Items** tab and enter the following items by entering the data and then clicking **Add**
   a. **Distribute retreat announcements, Mary, 10/10/2002**
   b. **Schedule room and order food, Randy, 10/10/2002**
6. Click the Meeting Minutes tab and type
   Called To Order: 11/6/02 10:33 AM
   Absent members: Sam, Kelsey, and Roger
   1. Introductions
   2. Staffing presentation
7. Move to slide **7** to review the Action Items
8. On the **Tools** menu click **Meeting Minder**
9. Click **Export**

tip: *If the Export button is not active, edit the minutes to activate it*

10. Unclick the Outlook option and click **Export Now**
11. Click **OK**
12. Save the presentation

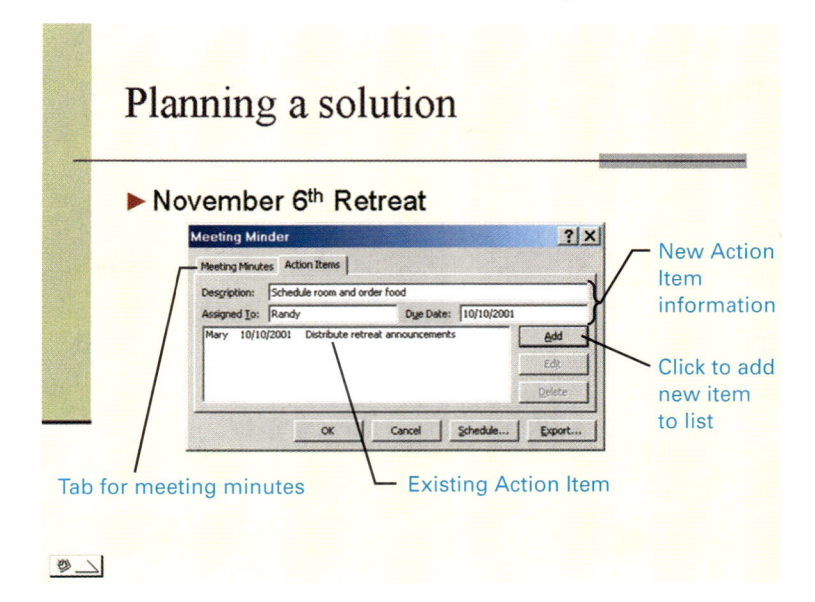

FIGURE 3.39
Action Items

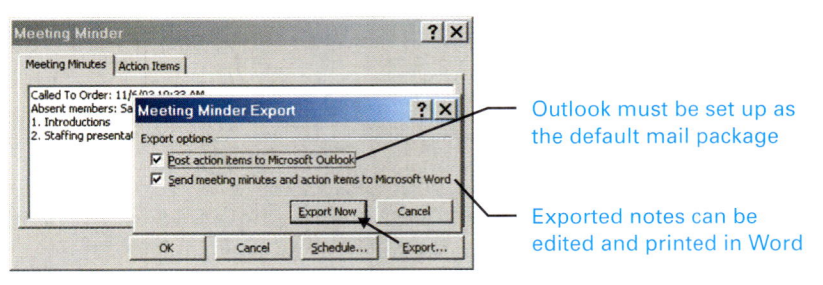

- Tab for meeting minutes
- New Action Item information
- Click to add new item to list
- Existing Action Item

FIGURE 3.40
Meeting Minutes

- Outlook must be set up as the default mail package
- Exported notes can be edited and printed in Word

Using the Meeting Minder allows meeting notes and task assignments to be documented as the meeting progresses. It has the added advantage of displaying to everyone attending so that misunderstandings can be avoided. If Outlook is your e-mail client, meeting notes can be sent directly to attendees as an e-mail attachment.

Navigating in Slide Show View

The pop-up menu from Slide Show view also provides options for navigating the presentation in a nonlinear fashion. Nonlinear navigation allows the presenter or viewer to control the order of slide progressions.

Navigating to specific slides:

1. Verify that PowerPoint is running with **PP03StaffingPlan.ppt** open
2. Move to slide **5** and click the **Slide Show** button
3. Right-click to open the pop-up menu and select **Previous**
4. Click the icon at the bottom left of the screen and select **Go,** then **By Title,** and then slide **2**
5. Click the icon at the bottom left of the screen and select **Help.** Review the shortcuts displayed by Help
6. Right-click and select **End Show**

POWERPOINT

FIGURE 3.41
Slide Show View Pop-Up Menu

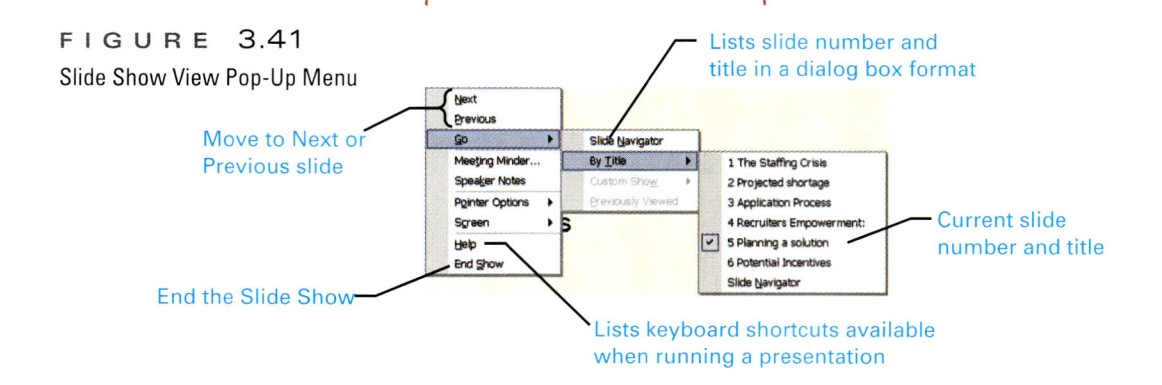

- Move to Next or Previous slide
- End the Slide Show
- Lists slide number and title in a dialog box format
- Current slide number and title
- Lists keyboard shortcuts available when running a presentation

Either right-clicking on a slide or clicking the navigation icon at the bottom left of a slide will activate the Slide show view pop-up menu. Although the menu does allow you to navigate to specific slides, it can disrupt a presentation to continually display the pop-up menu. Most presenters use a mouse click to move linearly through a presentation. The Esc key will stop a presentation, and the Backspace key moves to the previous slide. The complete list of keyboard shortcuts was displayed on the Help screen viewed in the previous steps.

Annotating in Slide Show View

The Slide Show view also provides an annotation tool that will allow the presenter to draw on a slide while the show is running. The *pen tool* is selected from the pop-up menu and controlled by the mouse. Once the pen tool is activated, the pen color is selected and then annotation can begin. When the pen tool is active, the mouse button will not advance the presentation to the next slide (the spacebar will) because it is controlling the pen.

Annotating slides:

1. Verify that PowerPoint is running with **PP03StaffingPlan.ppt** open
2. Move to slide **1** and click the **Slide Show** button
3. Use a left mouse click to advance until the 17RN's bullet of the second slide displays
4. Right-click the slide surface and point to **Pointer Options** on the pop-up menu and then point to **Pen Color**
5. Select **Cyan**
6. Circle the 17 RN's bulleted item
7. Use the **Spacebar** to move to the next slide and annotate there
8. Use the **Backspace** key to move to the previous slide and notice that the annotation was only available while the slide was viewed
9. Use the **Spacebar** to move to the next slide. That annotation has also been erased

You probably noticed other pointer settings in the pop-up menu that can be used to hide the pointer or select the pen tool. In the steps the pen tool was activated by selecting a color. If the Pen menu option is chosen, the default black pen is activated. Pen color can be changed at any point in the annotation process, to multiple colors on the same slide.

making the grade

SESSION 3.2

1. Why would you create a Summary Slide?
2. Differentiate between Templates and Masters.
3. What happens if you type text into a placeholder on a slide Master?
4. How would you customize the bullets used on all slides in a presentation?

SESSION 3.3 SUMMARY

PowerPoint slides consist of objects whose properties can be customized to suit the purpose of the slide show author. Text objects include placeholders, Text Boxes, and Shapes. Each text object contains the text that the author places in it and displays that text in the format specified. Further, the objects themselves can be customized by changing their size, position, background, and rotation.

The standard body text placeholder defines five levels of bulleted list, each with a unique bullet style and indention level. A common customization is to create unique bullets for slide body text. Besides the predefined bullet shapes, characters from any font or a picture can be used as the bullet character. If a character from a font is selected, the color and size of each bullet can be customized.

Custom settings like the bullets can be accomplished on an individual slide, or in the Slide Master. The Slide Masters define the defaults used by all slides. The masters set background content, colors, fonts, bullets, and placeholders applied to each slide in the presentation. Changes applied to an individual slide override the master settings. Reapplying the template will cause the slide to return to the default settings. Masters also define the layout of handouts and notes.

PowerPoint includes a selection of tools to help make presentations professional, consistent, and effective. Find, Spelling Checker, Style Checker, AutoCorrect, Summary Slide, Meeting Minder, and the Pen Tool are a few of the helpful operations introduced in the chapter.

PowerPoint contains an array of professionally designed templates that can be used to create a presentation. The masters for a presentation are copied from the template selected. If a master is customized, the original template can be updated with the changes or a new template created. Animation Schemes are preset slide transitions and text animations that can be applied to a slide, group of slides, or the entire presentation to add interest and help control presentation flow.

MOUS OBJECTIVES SUMMARY

- Insert, format, and modify text—PPT2002-2-2
- Formatting slides differently in a single presentation—PPT2002-4-1
- Modifying presentation templates—PPT2002-4-1
- Applying more than one design template to presentations—PPT2002-4-1
- Applying an animation scheme to a single slide, group of slides, or an entire presentation PPT2002-4-2
- Customizing templates—PPT2002-4-5

task reference roundup

Task	Page #	Preferred Method
Change the Bullet Style of a List	PP 3.14	• Move to the slide containing the list and select the list (part or all of the list may be selected)
		• On the **Format** menu, click **Bullets and Numbering**
		• Do as many of the following as are needed to implement your change:
		• Select from the standard options on the Bulleted or Numbered tab
		• Select a custom color from the drop-down Color list
		• Increase/decrease the size of the bullet relative to its associated text using the Size scrollbox
		• Click the **Picture** button to use a picture as the bullet character
		• Click the **Customize** button to use a Wingding or other special font as the bullet character
Customize Style and Spelling Checker	PP 3.21	• Click **Options** on the **Tools** menu and then click the **Spelling and Style** tab
		• Click the Spelling options that you want
		• Set the **Check Style** check box
		• Click the **Style Options** button to set Style Checker options
		• On the **Case and End Punctuation** tab, select the desired options
		• On the **Visual Clarity** tab, set fonts, point sizes, bullets, and line limits
Correct Words Marked by Spelling Checker	PP 3.22	• Edit a word with a red wavy underline to correct the spelling manually
		or
		• Right-click on a word with a red wavy underline for suggestions and then do one of the following:
		• Select the correct spelling from the list of suggestions
		• Select **Ignore All** to ignore this word in the current presentation
		• Select **Add to Dictionary** to add this word to the dictionary for all presentations

task reference roundup

Task	Page #	Preferred Method
Find Text and/or Formatting	PP 3.24	• Click the **Edit** menu and then click **Find**
		• Enter the search string and select the appropriate options
		• Click the **Replace** button to specify a replacement value
		• Do one of the following:
		• Click **Find** to find the next occurrence of the Find what string
		• Click **Replace** to update the current occurrence of the Find what string with the replacement value
		• Click **Replace All** to replace all instances of the Find what string with the Replace with string
Create a Summary Slide	PP 3.28	• Use the **Slide Sorter View** button to change to Slide Sorter View
		• Select the slides whose titles will be included on the summary slide (hold down Ctrl to select multiples)
		• On the Slide Sorter toolbar, click **Summary Slide**
View Masters	PP 3.29	• On the **View** menu, point to **Master**
		• Select the Master (Slide, Handout, or Notes) that you would like to view
Apply a Preset Animation Scheme	PP 3.40	• Open the presentation to be animated
		• Use the Task pane drop-down arrow to move to the **Slide Design—Animation Schemes** panel
		• Select the slide(s) to animate
		• Click the desired Animation Scheme
		If Auto Preview is clicked, a preview of the animation will play after you click. Use Play to preview the animation setting or Apply to All Slides to apply this animation to all slides in the slide show. The Slide Show button provides a full-screen preview of the show

POWERPOINT

chapter one

review of terminology

LEVEL ONE

CROSSWORD PUZZLE

Across

4. Tool to annotate
7. Toolbar used to add graphic elements
8. Controls how slide presents
10. Indent _____ are adjusted to move bullets and text
11. Buttons that turn properties on and off
12. The second line indents under the first in a _____ indent
14. Control how an object displays and behaves
15. Set the default formats for slides, handouts, and notes
16. The type face of text

Down

1. Allows you to take notes while presenting
2. Format _____ copies formats
3. Updates text as you type
5. Allow you to resize an object
6. Controls how text moves on and off slide
9. Anything that can be manipulated
13. Holds text

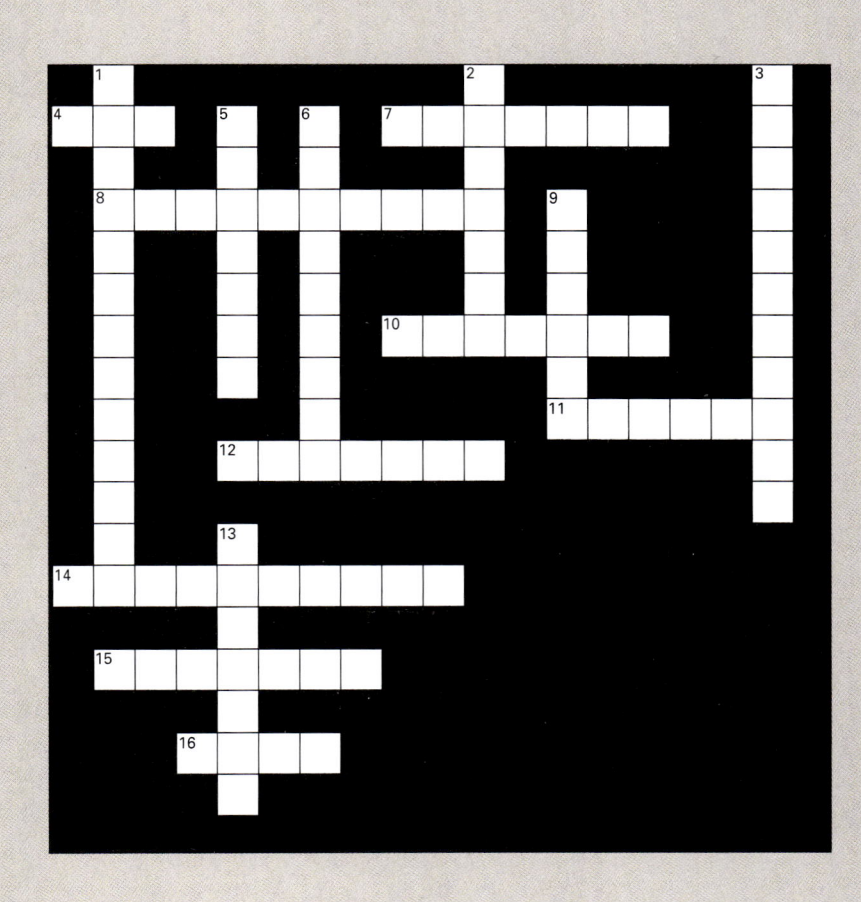

PP 3.49

POWERPOINT

review of concepts

chapter three

LEVEL TWO

FILL-IN

1. The _____ tool can be used to find and replace text in a presentation.
2. _____ is the tool that makes corrections as you type in PowerPoint.
3. A slide that contains the titles of other slides in the presentation is called a(n) _____.
4. A(n) _____ contains the default colors, background, and formatting of a presentation.
5. To change the color of text in the body placeholder of all presentation slides to dark blue, update the _____.
6. Adjusting the _____ can modify the distance between a bullet and its associated text.

REVIEW QUESTIONS

Each of the following topics should be addressed in one to three paragraphs.

1. Discuss the use of indent markers.
2. Discuss the most effective way to change the font of all the body text in a presentation.
3. Describe what happens when you click a new Design Template.
4. What is the difference between displaying text in a text placeholder and in a Text Box?
5. How do you cause a custom template that you have created to be listed with the other PowerPoint templates?
6. Differentiate between transitions and animations. Why are they used?

CREATE THE QUESTION

For each of the following answers, create the question.

ANSWER	QUESTION
1. Object	_____
2. Align text in a container	_____
3. Character formats	_____
4. Toggle buttons	_____
5. Add shapes to a slide	_____

FACT OR FICTION

For each of the following determine whether the statement is fact, fiction, or both and present your arguments for that conclusion.

1. There is no significant difference between the slanted-line selection box and the dotted-line selection box.
2. The only way to modify a slide placeholder is to select a new slide layout.
3. The format painter can be used to pick up a format and paint it multiple times without picking up the format again.
4. Style Checker can only apply preset presentation rules.
5. Red wavy underlines caused by words that are not in the dictionary will display in Slide Show view.

chapter three

hands-on projects

practice

1. United Accounting

United Accounting is a firm that provides accounting services for mortgage lenders. Homeowners direct their mortgage payments to United Accounting where they are processed. The company sets up the payment schedule, provides a payment booklet, and notifies the homeowner when there are delinquent payments or the mortgage is paid off. Monthly, the homeowner department has a planning meeting. As the assistant to the department manager, you have been asked to prepare a PowerPoint presentation for this meeting based on the department manager's outline. During the meeting you will be asked to take notes.

1. Open PowerPoint and select the Cascade Design Template
2. Title the slide **November Department Meeting** and make the subtitle **<yourname>, Department Manager**
3. Add a second slide titled **November Goals** with the following bulleted items
   - Met October processing goals
   - November goal is 2% improvement in accounts receivable from last year
   - One-week turnaround time on late notices
4. In the notes pane of slide 2 type **Excellent job everyone!**
5. Add a third slide with **Software Changes** as the title and the following bulleted items
   - New database software now available
   - Provides additional reporting
   - Amortization schedule available
   - Training begins next week
6. In the notes pane type **Right-click on the payment field to access the amortization schedule**
7. Add a fourth slide titled **Company New Directions** and the following bulleted items
   - Expansion to commercial property as of January 1
   - New division will open
   - Employment opportunities
8. Add the note text: **The commercial property division will begin locally, then expand to the Western, Mid-West, and Eastern Divisions in that order by December 2003**
9. Run the slide show and right-click on the second slide to initiate the Meeting Minder. Enter the following:
   - **November 2, 2002, <your name>, Recorder**
   - **Called to Order at 10:02 a.m.**
   - **Absent: Grace, Bill, Cynthia**
10. Click on the Action Items tab and type **Database training schedule for sections to be posted** in the Description window. In the Assigned To window, type **Karen Blackmond,** and in the Due Date window **12/5/02**
11. Click on Export to transfer this information to WordPad. Save as **MeetingMinder.rtf**. Make PowerPoint the active application and click **OK** in the Meeting Minder dialog box
12. Use **Find** to change the percent goal to 2.5%. Activate the **Edit** menu and click **Find**. Set the Find what criteria to **2%** and click the **Replace** button. Type **2.5%** in the Replace with: window and then click the **Replace** button. Click **Close** and verify the change in slide 2
13. Spell check your presentation; make any corrections and print the presentation as Notes
14. Save your presentation as **NovDeptMtg.ppt** and exit PowerPoint

LEVEL THREE

www.mhhe.com/i-series

PP 3.51

POWERPOINT

hands-on projects

chapter three

challenge

1. Teachers' Web Site

www.WebUse.com is a site that provides online lessons and resources to assist the teachers in understanding and using the Internet. The lessons are free and can be downloaded or used online. The entire series can be completed in 12 hours. Most helpful to the teachers has been the instruction on online collaboration (telecollaboration) and online research (teleresearch). Telecollaboration is a benefit by creating exposure to multiple points of view and interpretations, communicating with a real audience in a written form, and expanding global awareness. Using teleresearch is a benefit when information is not readily available at a local level, information can be viewed in multiple formats, and new information is more readily available.

The site is also a resource for other Web sites built by teachers who have developed curriculum-based collaborative projects. Some projects are e-mail-based involving students from many countries. Other projects offer guidelines, templates, and training materials for teaching activities. Examples of the kinds of activities students might apply using the Internet are global classrooms (groups of students in different classes collectively study a subject); electronic experts (subject matter experts are available to students via e-mail, video-conferencing, etc.); database creation (organize collected information into a database); electronic publishing (create electronic documents and post on the Web); and peer feedback activities (students review other students' answers and post electronically).

You have been asked by WebUse to create a PowerPoint presentation explaining the uses of this site. The presentation will be disseminated to rural school districts across the country, as these areas have the highest percentage of teachers who are unfamiliar with using the Internet.

1. Open PowerPoint and choose the **Satellite Dish** Design template
2. Type **The Internet—a Teaching Resource** as the first slide title and **Teaching the Teachers** as the subtitle
3. Create the footer with today's date and the text **WebUse for Teachers**
4. In five to seven slides, organize and present the information provided in the scenario. Remember that the audience is the teachers who will be using the site. Include using telecollaboration and teleresearch, types of projects that teachers might find and use in their classrooms, and why this is a win-win opportunity. Remember to keep your words in each slide to a 30-word maximum
5. Add art relevant to the classroom/Internet theme for each slide
6. Add animations and transitions to each slide
7. Spell check your presentation
8. Save the presentation as **WebUse.ppt** and exit PowerPoint

chapter three

hands-on projects

on the web

LEVEL THREE

1. Caitlin's Cattery

Caitlin's Cattery is a Web site that is a clearinghouse for all kinds of information about cats. Viewers are encouraged to submit their stories and photos of their own cats. There are links to cats in history, the care of cats, breeders and cat associations, and how to contact a veterinary association for cat health questions. Much of the information on the site is lighthearted. You have been asked to create a short presentation for the Cattery that will eventually be uploaded onto the Cattery's site. You will be using your favorite search engine to find Web sites to fill in the slides.

1. Open PowerPoint and choose a design template. Keep in mind that if the rest of the site has a "busy" look, your design template should be uncluttered
2. Make the first slide title **Caitlin's Cattery.** Make font size **54** to stand out. Add the subtitle text **It's more than a purr.** Add an appropriate graphic
3. Add a second slide titled **A Cat Clearinghouse** with the following bullets
   - Check out these menu items!
     - Your stories and photos of your cat
     - Cats and History
     - Care of Cats
     - Ask the Veterinarian
     - Need to find a Breeder?
     - Cat Societies
4. Add a third slide titled **Owners Tell All** and the following bullets
   - Check out these Web sites for true cat tales
     - Web site(s)
5. Add a fourth slide titled **Cats and History**
   - Egyptian temple cats
     - Web site(s)
   - Choose another historical reference to cats
     - Web site(s)
6. Add a fifth slide titled **Care of Cats**
   - What does the cat eat? From kittens to older cats
     - Web site
   - Hygiene—from claws to teeth
     - Web site
   - Toilet training your cat
     - Web site
7. Add a sixth slide titled **Ask the Veterinarian**
   - E-mail a veterinarian on cat health care
   - Response usually within 24 hours
   - American Veterinary Medical Association
     - Web site
8. Add a seventh slide titled **Need to find a Breeder?**
   - Web site
   - Web site
9. Add an eighth slide titled **Cat Societies**
   - American Cat Fanciers Association
   - Cat Fancier's Association
   - Foot of the Rockies Cat Club
10. Search the Web for cat-related Web sites. Replace at least four of the Web site references in the presentation with the addresses of sites you found
11. Choose an animation scheme for the slide show
12. Save your presentation as **Cattery.ppt** and exit PowerPoint

PP 3.53

www.mhhe.com/i-series

POWERPOINT

hands-on projects

chapter three

e-business

1. Daring Designs

Daring Designs is a cooperative of craftspeople organized to create handmade, custom clothing. Daring works in consultation with a number of prominent fashion designers in exchange for their assistance during the fall season previews. The clothing is hand-dyed, woven, quilted, or embroidered by master craftspeople who have been blue-ribbon winners at the annual Smithsonian Arts and Crafts Fair. Daring Designs markets their clothing to the upscale department stores. You have been asked to review and update a presentation that Daring Designs provided to the department stores that carry their designs. The presentation is in a kiosk format and loops continuously with a 3-second delay between slides. The kiosk will be placed on the Web as well as used in the Daring Design booth at buyers' fairs and expos. A catalog of current products will be added at a later time.

1. Open PowerPoint
2. Open the Microsoft Word document **pp03DaringDesigns.doc** with PowerPoint since it will be used as the outline for the presentation
3. The slide show appears on a white background. Apply the **Kimono** Design template to the show
4. Change the slide layout of the first slide to Title Slide
5. Add **Created by: <yourname>** as a footer on every slide. Do not include the date or slide number in the footer
6. Spell check the presentation
7. Create a summary slide as the second slide in the presentation. Include titles from all but the first slide. Change the title to **Daring Designs Overview**

tip: Use Slide Sorter view for this operation

8. The presentation shows without transitions of any kind. Add the **Thread and Exit** Animation scheme to the first slide and other Exciting Animation schemes to each of the other slides
9. Modify the title slide master
   a. Increase the title size to **44** points and change the font to **Papyrus**
   b. .Increase the subtitle size to **40** points and change the font to **Papyrus**
10. Modify the body slide master
    a. Change the title to **Papyrus** font
    b. Change the first level bulleted text to **Papyrus** font
    c. Change the second level bulleted text to the green from the Font color Drop-down list
11. Run the presentation to view the impact of your changes
12. Save your presentation as **DaringDesigns.ppt** and close

FIGURE 3.42
Daring Design's Opening Slide

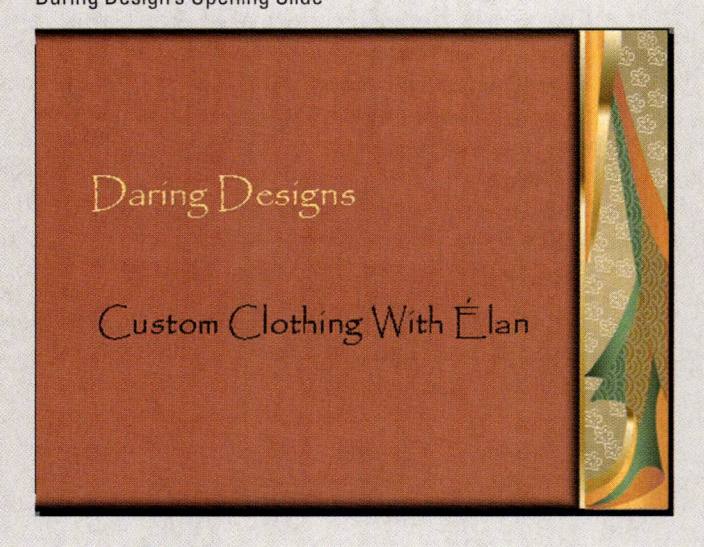

PP 3.54

chapter three

hands-on projects

around the world

1. Global Preservation Alliance

Global Preservation Alliance is a nonprofit organization that produces educational seminars on various environmental issues. GPA is made up of representatives from a wide spectrum of businesses located in the western United States. Funding for the alliance comes from grants from the Department of Energy. GPA focuses on different issues and prepares comprehensive educational seminars on a wide range of environmental topics, mostly renewable energy sources and the fragility of the world's environment. The seminars then travel to major cities across the United States, Europe, and Asia. The seminars are marketed to the public from the Web site, globalpreservationalliances.org, and through a PowerPoint presentation that is sent to public works departments and environmental organizations throughout the world. You have been asked by Global to prepare the public presentation regarding this year's top environmental issues.

1. Start PowerPoint; open a new presentation using the Pixel design template
2. Title the presentation **2003 Environmental Seminars** and use **Global Preservation Alliances** as the subtitle. Make a tag line in Italics: **A Consortium of Businesses dedicated to Environmental Preservation**
3. Center the subtitle text and adjust the font size if necessary
4. Add a second slide titled **Upcoming Seminars.** Make the slide layout Title and 2-Column Text
   a. In the first column enter **U.S. Tour Cities** with each of the following cities as a second level bullet: **San Francisco, Seattle, Phoenix, Denver, Chicago, Philadelphia, Washington DC, New York**
   b. In the second column enter **International Tour Cities** with each of the following cities as a second level bullet: **London, Paris, Frankfurt, Rome, Athens, Cairo, Stockholm, Melbourne**
5. Customize the bullets for all of the cities on this slide. Use the Picture button of the Bullets and Numbering toolbox to select a blue globe
6. Add a third slide titled **Seminar Starting Dates** with the following bullets:
   - **Seminar series starts December 2002**
   - **A new city each month on the 5th**
   - **Complete schedule at GPA Web site**
     www.Globalpreservationalliance.org
7. Add a fourth slide titled **Events.** Choose current environmental topics to list in the bulleted items. For example, solar energy, wind power, global warming, pollution prevention, maintaining a sustainable environment, energy efficient housing, deforestation effects, and so on
8. Add a fifth slide titled **Registration.** Indicate registration can be done online from Global's Web site using a secure server. Scholarships are also available. Confirmation will be given for registration and payment
9. Spell check your presentation
10. Apply a single animation scheme to all slides of the presentation
11. Save your presentation as **GPA.ppt** and exit PowerPoint

LEVEL THREE

www.mhhe.com/i-series

PP 3.55

POWERPOINT

running project

Montgomery-Wellish Foods, Inc.: General Financial and Business Training

This presentation is the third part of the training program. The goal is to give the new business graduate trainees an overview of the training that will occur in depth over the next two weeks. In addition to working with their product managers, the trainees will attend a group of in-service programs. Daniel has provided you with an outline of the subjects to cover. You have been asked to prepare a formal presentation to the trainees.

1. Open PowerPoint
2. Open the Microsoft Word document **pp03MWF.doc** with PowerPoint since it will be used as the outline for the presentation
3. Review the slide content to be sure everything is OK
4. Change the slide layout of the first slide to Title Slide and edit the title to read **Financial and Business Training.** Add your name in the subtitle area with a title of **Training Coordinator**
5. Add a footer with the text **Montgomery-Wellish Foods, Inc.** Leave the date and slide number boxes checked
6. Apply the Studio design template to all slides
7. Edit the first level bulleted list in the Slide Master to be a check box with a check mark in it. Set the size to **65%** of text. Repeat this process for the other bullet levels
8. Save the updates as a new Design template named **pp03MWFoods.pot**

   tip: Use the Customize button of the Bullets and Numbering dialog box

9. Change the title of the Summary slide to **Highlights**
10. Delete the last slide
11. Add a Summary slide with the titles of all but the first slide. Change the title from Summary Slide to **Summary** and make it the last slide of the presentation

    tip: Use Slide Sorter view

12. Spell check, preview, and make any necessary final adjustments to the presentation
13. Save your presentation as **<yourname>pp03MWFoods.ppt** and exit PowerPoint

FIGURE 3.43
Customized Bullets

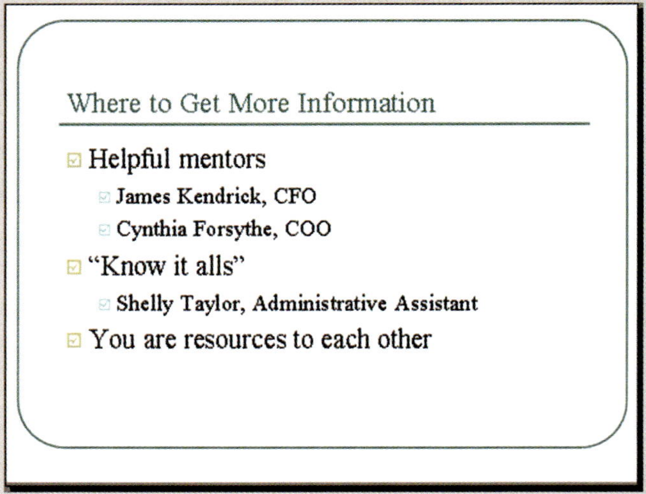

Where to Get More Information

- Helpful mentors
  - James Kendrick, CFO
  - Cynthia Forsythe, COO
- "Know it alls"
  - Shelly Taylor, Administrative Assistant
- You are resources to each other

NOTES

www.mhhe.com/i-series

POWERPOINT

NOTES

www.mhhe.com/i-series

did you know?

according to a Gallup poll, 48 percent of Americans thought the Y2K (computers not understanding dates in the new century) computer problem would cause major problems around the world.

seating on the first scheduled intercity commuter airplane flight consisted of 11 movable wicker chairs.

Sun Microsystems' Java programming language was first used in a handheld remote control.

the only rock that floats in water is pumice.

the word *starboard* originated because astronavigators traditionally stood on a plank on the right side of a boat to get an unobstructed view of the stars.

X-ray technology has shown that there are ___ different versions of the *Mona Lisa under the visible one.*

Chapter Objectives

- Identify the various types of images, their strengths, and limitations
- Insert clip art images to slides—PPT2002-3-1
- Scale and recolor objects
- Add images from files to slides and backgrounds—PPT2002-3-2
- Create and place WordArt—PPT2002-3-3
- Build and format PowerPoint tables and import Word and Excel tables—PPT2002-3-4, PPT2002-6-1, and PPT2002-6-3
- Add Organization Charts and other diagrams to slides—PPT2002-3-1
- Use Microsoft Graph to create bar charts, pie charts, and other numeric graphs—PPT2002-3-1

CHAPTER

4

four

Enhancing Your Presentation with Graphics

chapter case

Phone Minder Sales Presentation with PowerPoint

Chandra Bilker is a sales representative for Phone Minder Systems, Inc. Phone Minder's (PM) primary product is software for routing and tracking phone calls through virtually any existing business phone system. PM will track call volume, chart peak periods, compile frequency distributions for each extension, queue incoming calls, estimate time of wait and inform caller, track callers who disconnect before there is an answer, and assemble many other valuable statistics.

In her work, Chandra travels across four states presenting her products to prospective clients. Her job is to let potential customers know what the Phone Minder is and how it would benefit their organization. She often presents the PM products three or more times a day. She has found that even though she is a motivated and effective presenter, it is easy to leave out important information when repeating the same materials multiple times each day. Additionally, there are frequent upgrades to the product whose features need to be added to her repertoire.

There are seven other sales representatives in the western region experiencing the same presentation difficulties. At their last regional meeting, the seven sales representatives and their technical support staff created a PowerPoint presentation to be used by the sales team when presenting their products. Their goal was to ensure that all sales personnel have the most current product data and the facilities to provide consistent information to all possible clients.

Chandra and the other sales representatives have been using the presentation for several weeks and find it effective, but mundane. The presentation is very text heavy and contains no graphics besides the slide background. There are no transitions or animations.

FIGURE 4.1
Phone Minder Presentation with Graphics

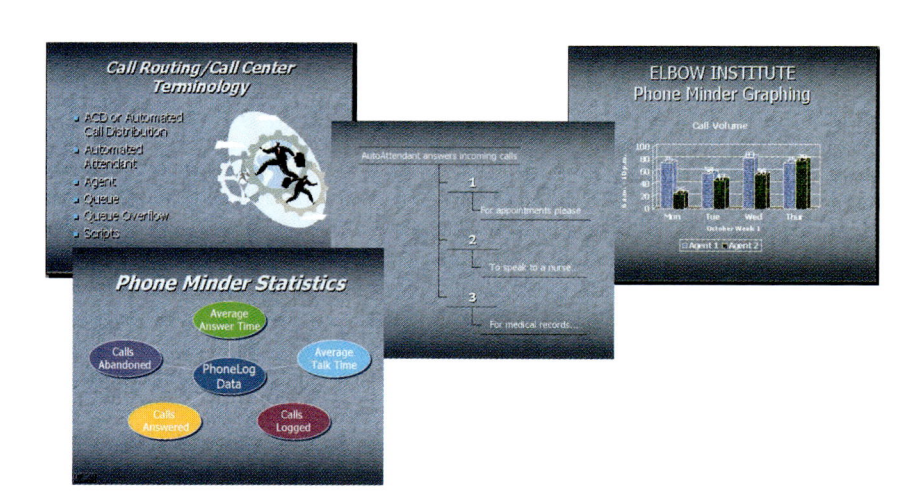

You are an experienced PowerPoint user who has been hired to enhance the presentation for the sales staff. Additionally, you will train them in more effective ways to use the updated presentation.

SESSION 4.1 EFFECTIVELY USING ART

A vital component in any presentation is the supporting artwork. Art can add emphasis, demonstrate a point, set the tone, and provide color. Choosing appropriate artwork can be time-consuming, but research indicates that art improves the attentiveness of the audience and their retention of the presentation content. This means that time selecting suitable artwork is time well spent.

UNDERSTANDING PICTURE TYPES

Although a thorough presentation of the various types of pictures is beyond the scope of this discussion, it is often helpful to understand the basics of picture types. There are two fundamental picture types—bitmaps and drawn pictures—that can be used in PowerPoint. The picture type determines the formatting that can be applied and whether or not it can be edited from PowerPoint.

A *bitmap* or *raster image* is composed of a series of small dots of color. At some point in your educational career you probably colored in specific squares of graph paper to create an image. This is analogous to using dots of ink on a printer or pixels on a monitor of specific colors to create an image. Bitmaps are created and edited in paint programs, such as Microsoft Paint.

Scanners and digital photographs also generate bitmaps. The quality of a bitmap is determined by its size and dot density. Simply stated, more dots provide greater resolution for a sharper picture. Common bitmap file extensions are .bmp, .png, .jpg, and .gif.

Bitmaps can be edited in the program where they originated, or simple changes applied through PowerPoint. Using PowerPoint's bitmap editor the brightness and contrast can be adjusted, transparent areas can be defined, and color bitmaps can be converted to grayscale.

The biggest limitation to bitmaps is their scalability. Since they consist of dots, making an image larger causes it to become grainy as the dots become larger. Making bitmaps smaller can result in loss of detail as dots are dropped when there is no space to display them. Bitmaps can also have very large file sizes, since data on the content of each dot must be stored. High-resolution images with lots of dots require the most storage. File size is important when transporting a presentation or when download times are critical, like on the Web.

Drawn pictures or ***vector graphics*** are created using calculated geometric shapes like circles, lines, curves, and rectangles. Each individual shape can be edited, moved, and rearranged. Resizing drawn pictures does not degrade the picture quality, because the computer recalculates the dimension of each component to retain their original definition and perspective. The AutoShapes available from the Drawing toolbar are drawn pictures as are Windows Metafiles (.wmf extension). Since drawn pictures consist of shapes, they can be grouped and ungrouped, reordered, and each component individually colored.

CHAPTER OUTLINE

4.1 Effectively Using Art

4.2 Adding Other Graphic Elements

FIGURE 4.2

Resized Drawn Picture

PP 4.3

POWERPOINT

INSERTING CLIP ART

All Microsoft Office products share the *Microsoft Clip Organizer.* The media gallery contains drawings, photographs, sounds, videos, and other media that can be inserted into any document. Each media gallery file is referred to as a clip, but *clip art* specifically refers to the drawings contained in the collection.

Inserting Clip Art Images

The number of clips displayed in your Clip Organizer is determined by how Office was installed, and what additional artwork has been placed in the gallery. The default Office install loads only a few pictures to the hard drive to save space. The gallery will display pictures from the entire collection even though they are not available locally. When inserting a picture that has not been installed locally, the user will be prompted to put the install disks in the appropriate drive so that the clip can be retrieved.

Installing more software can add new clips to the Clip Organizer. For example, a computer installed with Microsoft Word, Excel, and Access will have only those clips. Installing Microsoft Publisher and/or Front Page will add more clips to the gallery. Non-Microsoft software can also use the Clip Organizer to store media. Finally, users can insert graphics obtained from their own sources.

In the initial review of the Phone Minder presentation, you and Chandra have modified the presentation to contain fewer words and have a neutral background. Now it is time to add some relevant graphics.

Adding clip art to PhoneMinder:

1. Initiate PowerPoint and open **PP04PhoneMinder.ppt**
2. Save the Presentation as **<yourname>PP04PhoneMinder.ppt**
3. Move to slide **2**
4. Click the **Insert Clip Art** button on the Drawing toolbar
5. In the Insert Clip Art panel of the Task pane enter **phone** as the search criteria and click **Clip Art** and **Photographs** as the media types in the Results Should Be drop-down list
6. Click **Search** (Figure 4.3)

tip: *The graphics available on your computer may differ from those shown*

7. Pause over the picture shown in the next figure and click the drop-down arrow

tip: *If you do not have this picture, choose something similar*

8. Select **Insert** (Figure 4.4)
9. Click and drag the image to the position shown
10. Save

FIGURE 4.3
Insert Clip Art

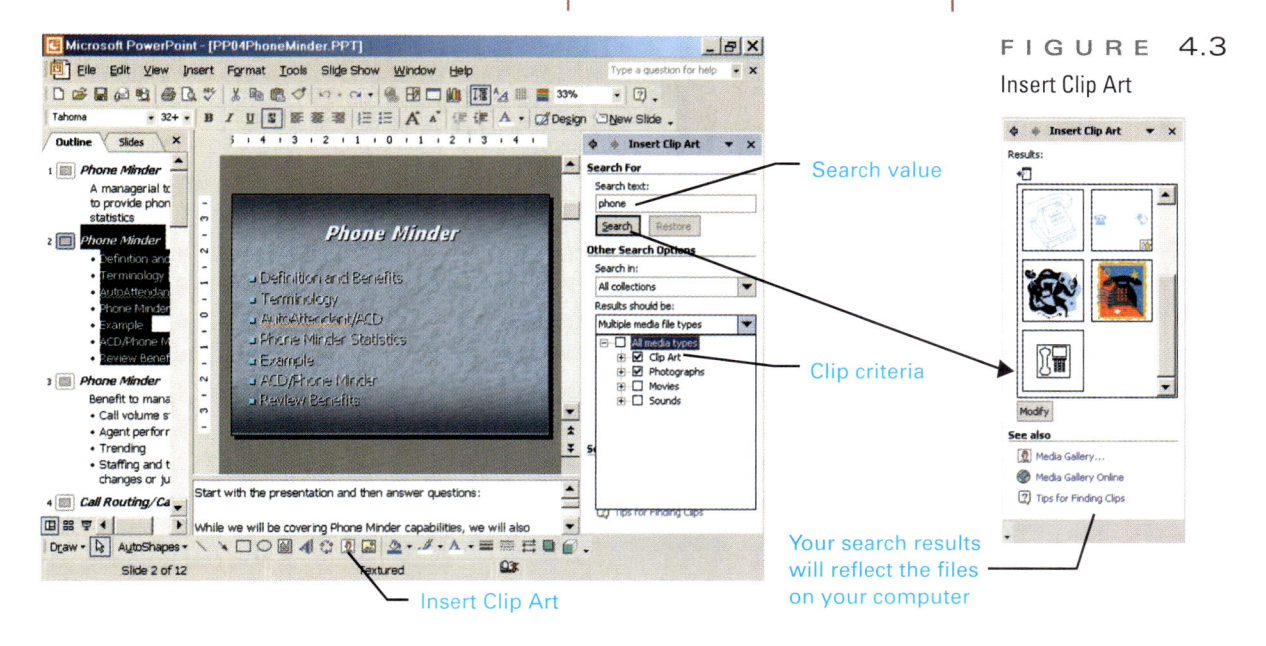

- Search value
- Clip criteria
- Your search results will reflect the files on your computer
- Insert Clip Art

FIGURE 4.4
Clip Art Added to PP04PhoneMinder

On a computer with an active Internet connection, the Clip Organizer will also display clips from Clips Online. These clips carry an icon indicating that they are online. The Insert Clip Art Task pane also has a link to move directly to the Clips Online for a greater clip selection. Although it is not readily apparent, the inserted clip art in the previous steps has been added to a content placeholder. The simplest way to expose the placeholder is to delete the image.

Revealing the media placeholder:

1. Verify that PowerPoint is running with **<yourname>PP04PhoneMinder.ppt** open
2. Select the clip art image on slide **2** by clicking it
3. Press the **Delete** key

FIGURE 4.5

Media Placeholder Revealed by Deleting Clip Art

4. Pause the mouse pointer over each icon in the media placeholder

5. Click the **Insert Clip Art** icon

tip: *The Select Picture dialog box will open.*

6. Enter **phone** as the search text and click **Search**

tip: *You should have the same pictures available as in the previous steps*

7. Click the phone image and then **OK**

8. Save

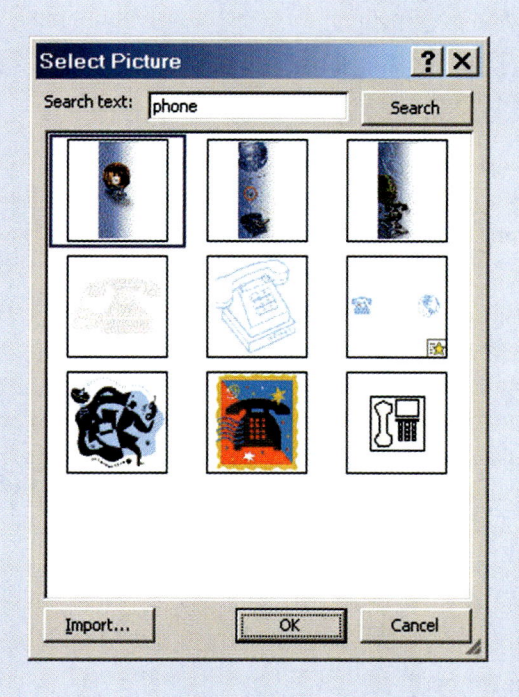

FIGURE 4.6

Select Picture Dialog Box

Notice that inserting the graphic without a placeholder resulted in a default (smaller) image size. When a graphic is added using a content placeholder, the graphic fills the placeholder. The size and position of a content placeholder are determined by the slide layout selected.

Slide layouts are grouped by the type of placeholders they contain. The groupings are

- Text layouts
- Content layouts
- Text and Content Layouts
- Other Layouts

Reviewing slide layout:

1. Verify that PowerPoint is running with **<yourname>PP04PhoneMinder.ppt** open and slide 2 active

2. Activate the Slide Layout panel of the Task pane using the drop-down menu

3. Select each Text and Content layout and evaluate the impact on the slide

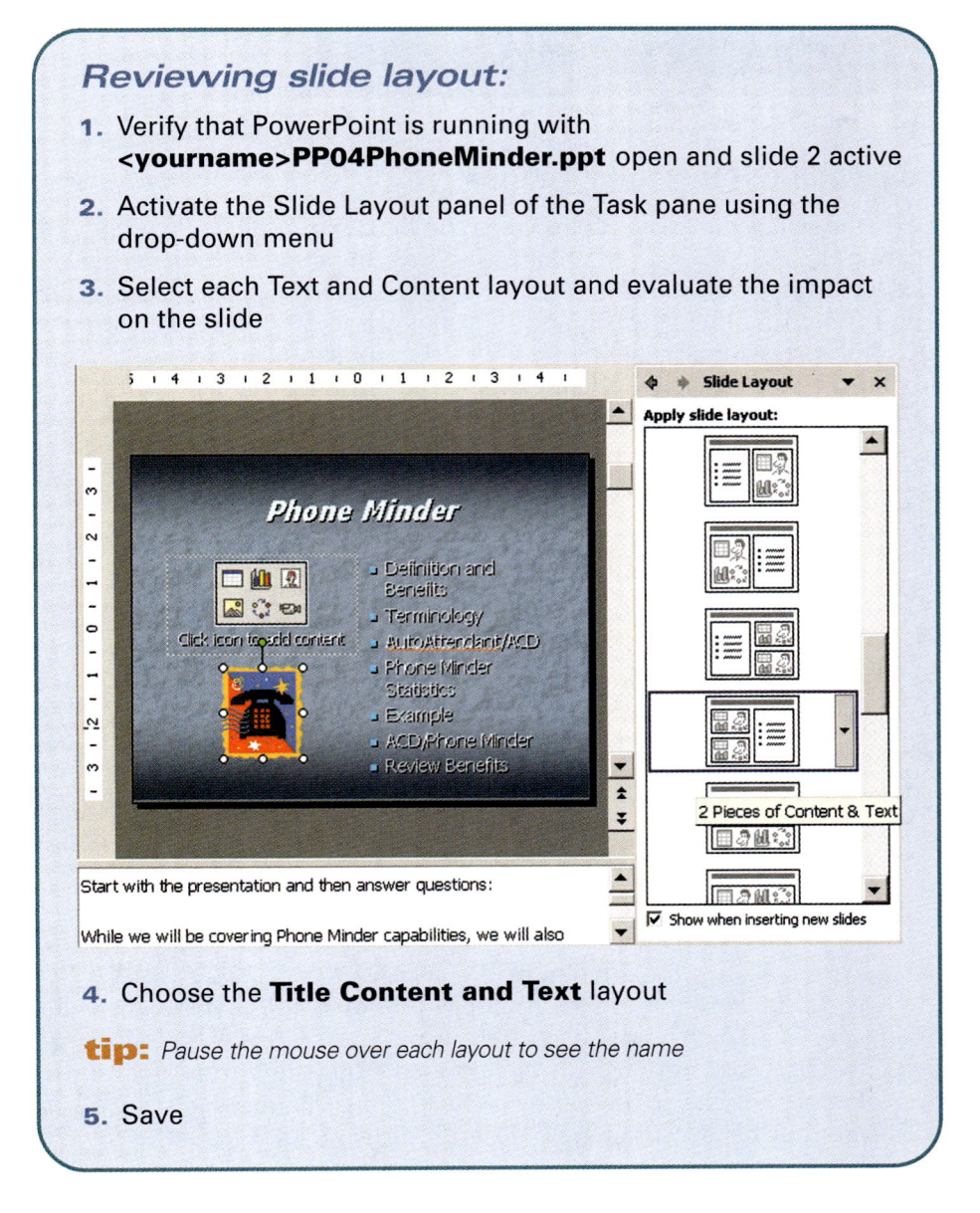

FIGURE 4.7
Slide Layouts with Media Placeholder

4. Choose the **Title Content and Text** layout

tip: *Pause the mouse over each layout to see the name*

5. Save

Although it is not necessary to change the slide layout to insert a graphic, it is probably more effective to choose the slide layout that matches slide content. Remember that slide placeholders can be moved and resized to further accommodate design.

FIGURE 4.8
Content and Text Slide Layout

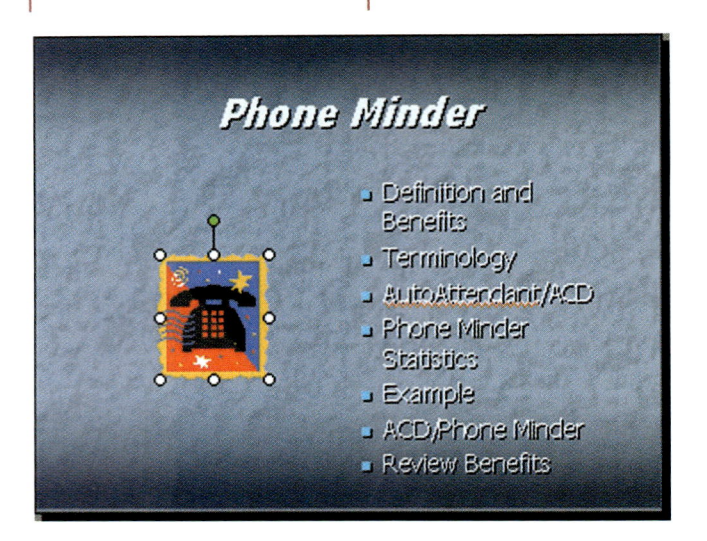

Scaling and Recoloring Images

Since the selected image is a drawn picture, it can be scaled and recolored. Scaling the picture is accomplished by dragging a sizing handle. Images also have a ***rotation handle*** that allows you to drag the image to any angle. The rotation handle is green and typically above the image. Pausing the cursor over a rotation handle changes the cursor to an arrowed circle. Chandra would like a less square look to the presentation and wants to try rotating some of the images.

Resizing and rotating an image:

1. Verify that PowerPoint is running with **<yourname>PP04PhoneMinder.ppt** open
2. Click on the image in slide **2**
3. Use one of the white sizing handles to enlarge the image as shown in Figure 4.9
4. Drag the green rotational handle to angle the image as shown in Figure 4.9
5. Save

It is not uncommon to like an image that does not match your color scheme, or is just too bold. Color controls provide several ways to manage image color. These options can be accessed from the Format Picture or Show Picture Toolbar option of the pop-up menu. Chandra likes the selected image, but believes that it is too bright for the background. You will recolor the picture to better match the color scheme of the presentation.

www.mhhe.com/i-series   PP 4.9

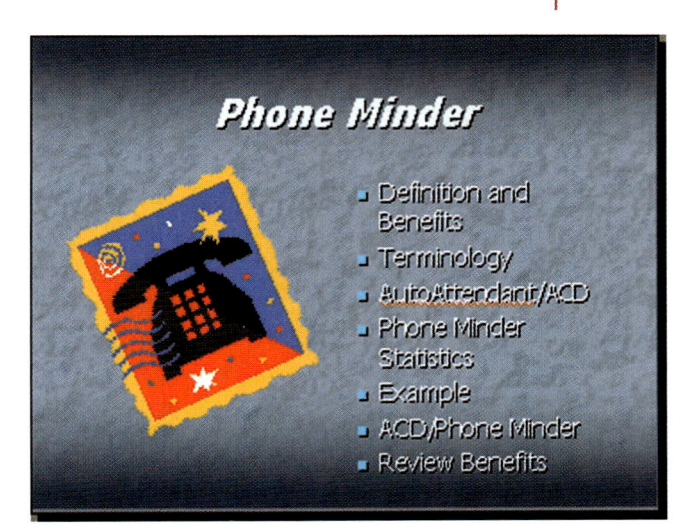

FIGURE 4.9
Resized and Rotated Image

Adjusting image color:

1. Verify that PowerPoint is running with **<yourname>PP04PhoneMinder.ppt** open with slide **2** selected
2. Right-click on the image and select **Format Picture**
3. Drop down the Color list and select **Washout**

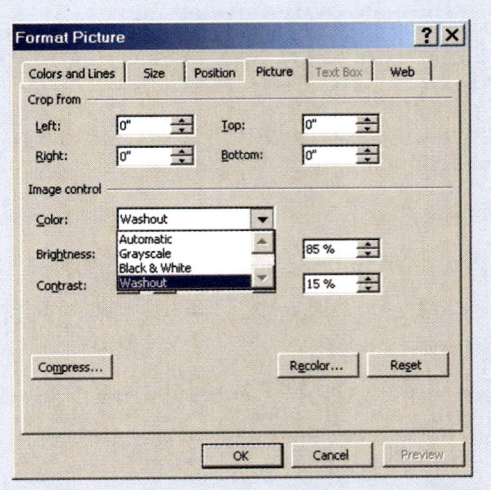

FIGURE 4.10
Format Picture Dialog Box

4. Click **Preview** and move the Format Picture dialog box so that you can see the image
5. Click the **Reset** button to return the image to its original state
6. Set Brightness to **25%** and Contrast to **100%**
7. Click **Preview**
8. Click the **Reset** button to return the image to its original state
9. Click the **Recolor** button

POWERPOINT

FIGURE 4.11
Recolor Picture Dialog Box

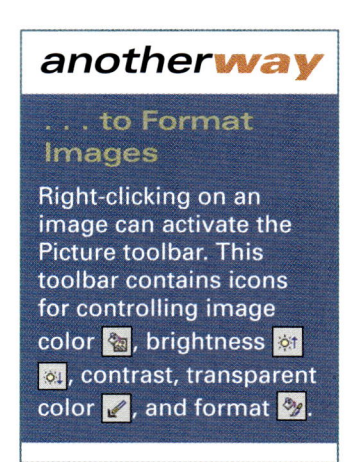

10. Change the red and yellow colors as shown in Figure 4.11

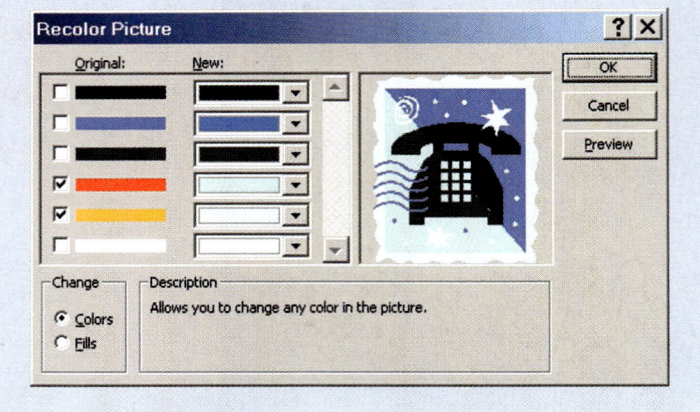

11. Click **OK** and **OK** again
12. Save

anotherway

. . . to Format Images

Right-clicking on an image can activate the Picture toolbar. This toolbar contains icons for controlling image color, brightness, contrast, transparent color, and format.

Chandra would like an image on the next slide too. Since this slide refers to managers, she is looking for a business meeting or management report to enhance the content. You will use keywords to search for a suitable image.

Placing an image on slide 3:

1. Verify that PowerPoint is running with **<yourname>PP04PhoneMinder.ppt** open with slide **3** selected
2. Select the **Title, Text and Content** slide layout
3. Click the **Insert Clip Art** icon in the Content placeholder
4. Enter **communication** as the Search Text in the Select Picture dialog box and click **Search**
5. Select the image shown in Figure 4.12 (use one similar to it if this one is not in your gallery) and click **OK**
6. Position and size the image as shown
7. Move to slide **1** and change to **Slide Show view**
8. Click through the first three slides to preview the images as the audience will see them
9. Right-click on the slide surface and choose **End Show**
10. Save

It is often effective to cluster or stack multiple clip art images to create a more complex image. When images are stacked, selecting a specific

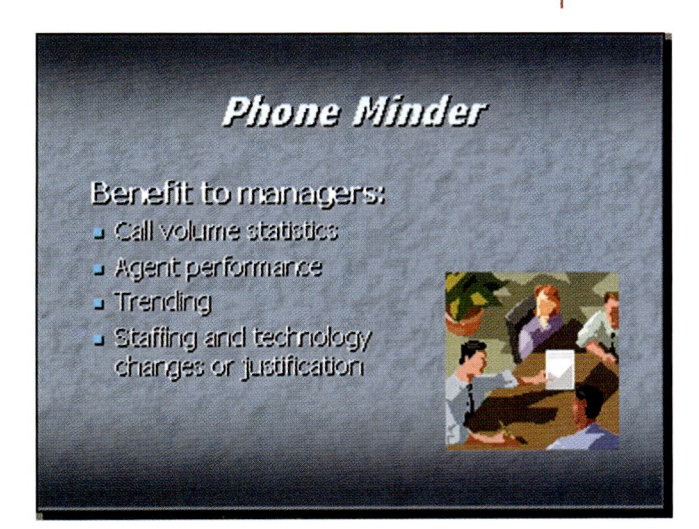

FIGURE 4.12

Slide 3 with Clip Art

image can become more difficult. Remember that by default objects stack in the order that they have been added to the slide. The result is that the first object added is closest to the slide, or in the back. The last object added is on top of the others, or in the front. Objects on top often need to be moved to access an image closer to the bottom.

Updating Image Keywords

Since the Clip Organizer can contain thousands of clips, it is not effective to find media by simply looking through the collection. The search text feature allows clips to be rapidly retrieved using descriptive words. PowerPoint looks through the **keywords** of each clip and displays those having keywords matching the search text entry. Microsoft clips come with keywords already associated, but they may not be effective for all uses. For example, every clip containing a computer does not have *computer* as a keyword. Or images with the keyword *cries* will not be found with a search criteria of crying.

Clips inserted from your own artwork or other media collections will not have any keywords unless you add them. All of this means that there are probably some wonderful images in your collection that will never be retrieved because they do not have appropriate keywords.

Updating image keywords:

1. Verify that PowerPoint is running

tip: The Clip Organizer belongs to Microsoft Office; it is not important which Office product is used to access the gallery for this operation. There is also no need to have a particular document open

2. If the Insert Clip Art panel of the Task pane is not active, click the **Insert Clip Art** icon in the Drawing toolbar

3. If the Search Text Box holds any characters, delete them

POWERPOINT

4. Click **Search** (with no search value all images will be displayed)
5. Pause the mouse over an image to see its keywords and other properties
6. Drop down the arrow on an image and select **Edit Keywords**
7. Use the **Next** button to move through the gallery reviewing keywords

FIGURE 4.13
Editing Image Keywords

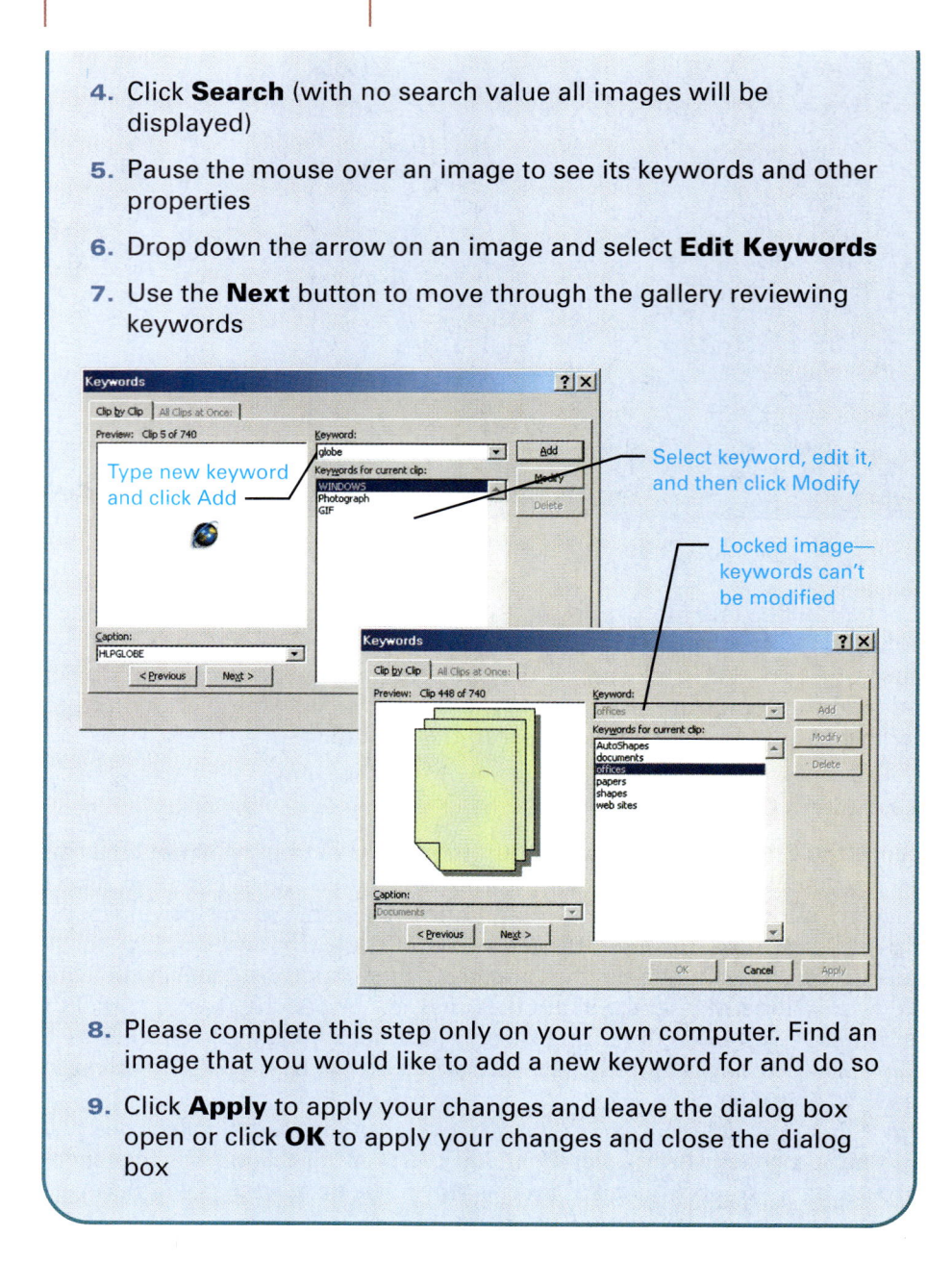

8. Please complete this step only on your own computer. Find an image that you would like to add a new keyword for and do so
9. Click **Apply** to apply your changes and leave the dialog box open or click **OK** to apply your changes and close the dialog box

Exercise caution when adding new keywords to images. Too many keywords can slow the search response time, and inaccurate keywords can retrieve undesirable clip art. There is no way to automatically undo keyword updates, so be sure to apply only appropriate updates.

OPENING FILE ART

Artwork does not have to be stored in the Clip Organizer to be used in Office. Microsoft products understand most common graphic file types. If you have a file of a type that is not directly interpreted by Office products, it can be converted to one of the standard formats with graphics software.

PowerPoint Graphic Formats

In most cases, the graphics that PowerPoint can interpret without filters will provide the best images. PowerPoint can insert the following file formats directly:

- Enhanced Metafile (.emf)
- Graphics Interchange Format (.gif)
- Joint Photographic Experts Group (.jpg)
- Portable Network Graphics (.png)
- Microsoft Windows Bitmap (.bmp, .rle, .dib)
- Windows Metafile (.wmf) graphics

PowerPoint has filters that will convert the file formats discussed below. You will need to install these filters if the PowerPoint's Typical install option was used since these filters are not installed by default. Check the help files for each filter to determine its capabilities and limitations. The available filters include:

- Computer Graphics Metafile (.cgm)
- CorelDRAW (.cdr)
- FlashPix (.fpx)
- Hanako (.jsh, .jah, and .jbh)
- Kodak Photo CD (.pcd)
- Macintosh PICT (.pct)
- PC Paintbrush (.pcx)
- WordPerfect Graphics (.wpg)

Inserting File Images

A file image is any graphic that is *not* stored in the Clip Organizer but is available from a file. File images can be created in graphics packages, purchased on CDs, scanned images, photographs saved as files, or retrieved from the Internet. As long as the image is available and is an appropriate file type, it can be inserted into a PowerPoint presentation. Always adhere to copyright laws when using file art.

Chandra has the company logo and some custom artwork that she wants to include in the Phone Minder presentation.

task reference
Insert an Image from a File

- Position the cursor for insertion
- Click the **Insert Picture** button on the Drawing toolbar
- Navigate to the picture
- Do one of the following:
  - Click **Insert** to embed the image
  - Click the drop-down arrow next to Insert and click **Link to File** to create a link to the picture

FIGURE 4.14

Phones.jpg on Slide 1

> ### Inserting file images:
>
> 1. Verify that PowerPoint is running with **<yourname>PP04PhoneMinder.ppt** open with slide **1** selected
> 2. Click the **Insert Picture** button on the Drawing toolbar
> 3. Navigate to the files for this chapter and select **Phones.jpg** and click **Insert**
> 4. Position the slide and text placeholders as shown in Figure 4.14
>
> *[Slide image: Phone Minder — A managerial tool used to provide phone call statistics]*
>
> 5. Move to the last slide and repeat steps 2 through 4
> 6. Move to slide **4**
> 7. Click **Insert Picture** on the Drawing toolbar, navigate to the files for this chapter, select **Gears.wmf**, and click **Insert**
> 8. Position the slide and text placeholders as shown in Figure 4.15
> 9. Move to slide **6** and insert **Clock.wmf** as shown in the previous figure
> 10. Save

Images added using Insert Picture can be either ***embedded*** or ***linked.*** Clicking the Insert button embeds the image in the presentation with no connection to the image file. Double-clicking an embedded object will open the Format Picture dialog box allowing you to edit that object without impacting the original image. The Format Picture dialog box was introduced in the Clip Art discussion.

Choosing Link to File from the Insert Picture dialog box inserts a link to the image rather than the image itself. Linked images can only be mod-

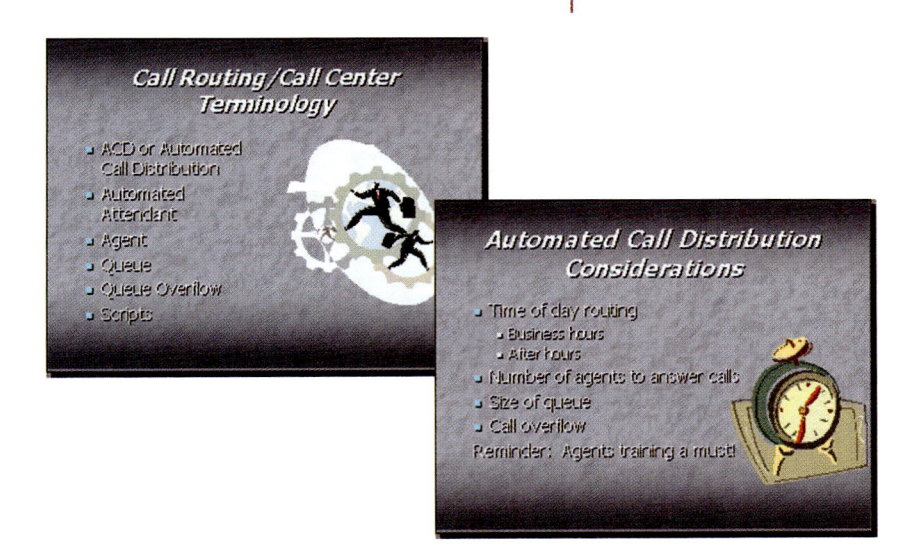

FIGURE 4.15

Image Positioning on Slides 4 and 6

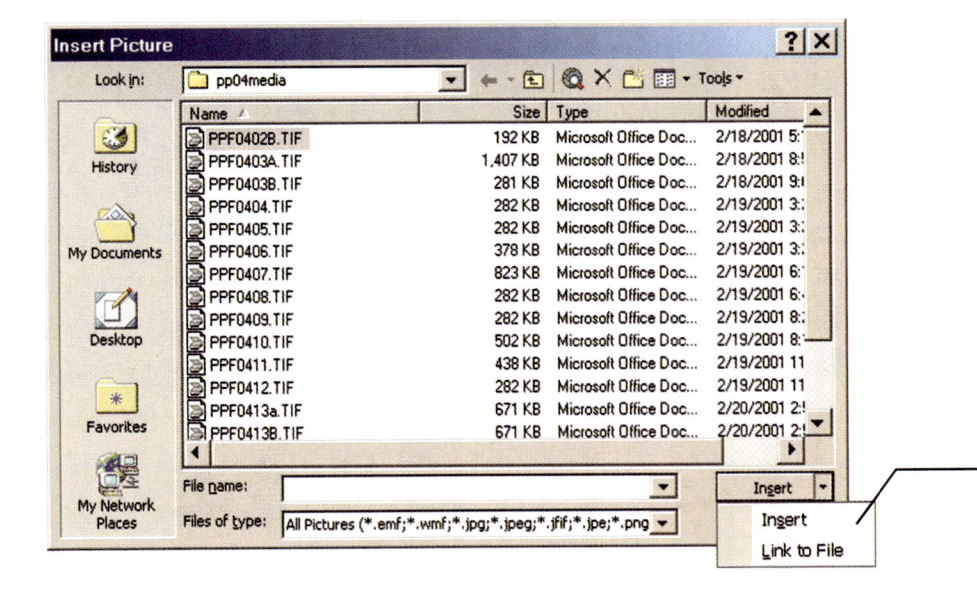

FIGURE 4.16

Linking an Image

Drop down selections

ified by updating the original file. The destination file stores only the location of the source file and displays a representation of the linked data. Use linked objects if file size is a consideration or if it is important to maintain consistency between copies. Linked images should be stored in a common folder for easy retrieval. When presentations with linked files are moved, the linked files must be moved too.

The Insert menu provides more options than are available on the Drawing toolbar. For example, a picture can be directly inserted from a scanner or digital camera using the Insert Picture From Scanner or Camera menu option.

CREATING WORDART

WordArt is a drawing object that is available in all Office applications to create text with special effects. WordArt adds shapes, shadows, colors, and perspectives to text that is not possible with standard fonts.

POWERPOINT

task reference

Insert WordArt

- Click the slide that will contain the WordArt
- Click the **Insert WordArt** icon on the **Drawing** toolbar
- Select a style from the WordArt Gallery
- Click **OK**
- Enter the WordArt text in the Edit WordArt Text dialog box
- Apply formatting as desired to set font, size, bold, or italic
- Click **OK**
- Use the WordArt, shape, color, shadow

Creating WordArt:

1. Verify that PowerPoint is running with **<yourname>PP04PhoneMinder.ppt** open with slide **5** selected
2. Click **Insert WordArt** icon in the **Drawing** toolbar
3. Select the style shown in Figure 4.17 for your WordArt from the WordArt Gallery
4. Click **OK**

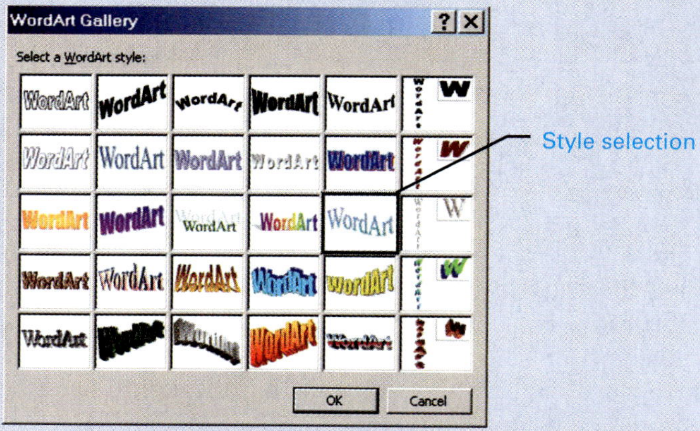

FIGURE 4.17
WordArt Gallery

Style selection

5. Enter **AutoAttendant** in the Edit WordArt Text dialog box
6. Click **OK** to accept the default font, size, bold, and italic settings associated with the selected style
7. Use the WordArt character spacing button to set the character spacing to **Very Tight**
8. Adjust the height and width of your WordArt to match the Figure 4.18

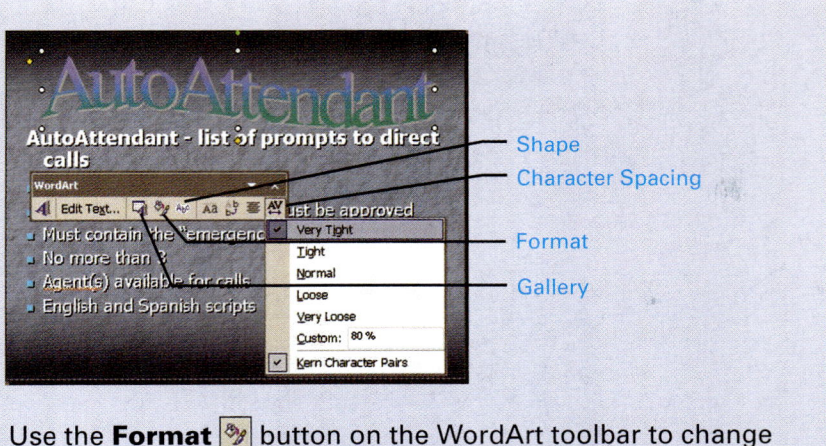

FIGURE 4.18
WordArt Toolbar

9. Use the **Format** button on the WordArt toolbar to change the text color to match those in the presentation
   a. On the Colors and Lines tab, drop down the Fill Color list
   b. Select **Fill Effects**
   c. On the Gradient tab, click one color and set the color to match the bullets on the slide
   d. Click **OK**
   e. Click **OK** again
10. Save

Like other drawing objects, WordArt can be copied, pasted, sized, and edited until satisfactory results are obtained. Chandra would like a shadow effect on this title. Shadows can be added through formatting or by stacking multiple copies of the WordArt object. Formatting is fast, but it is difficult to control multiple colors and perspective between the text and its shadow. Copying and recoloring the WordArt object provides the most control.

Creating multiple copies of WordArt objects:

1. Verify that PowerPoint is running with **<yourname>PP04PhoneMinder.ppt** open and slide **5** selected
2. Delete the title placeholder

tip: The dotted-line selection box will allow you to delete the entire placeholder. If you have a slanted-line selection box, click the box again to obtain a dotted-line selection box

3. Select the WordArt object created in the previous steps
4. Type **Ctrl+C** to copy the object to the Clipboard
5. Deselect the object by clicking outside it
6. Type **Ctrl+V** to paste a copy of the object

tip: The Clipboard buttons on the Standard toolbar could also have been used

FIGURE 4.19
Multiple WordArt Objects

7. Select the top copy of WordArt
   a. Click the **Format** button on the WordArt toolbar
   b. Change the Fill Color to the Dark Blue Green of the color scheme
   c. Click **OK**
8. Position the copies as shown in the figure

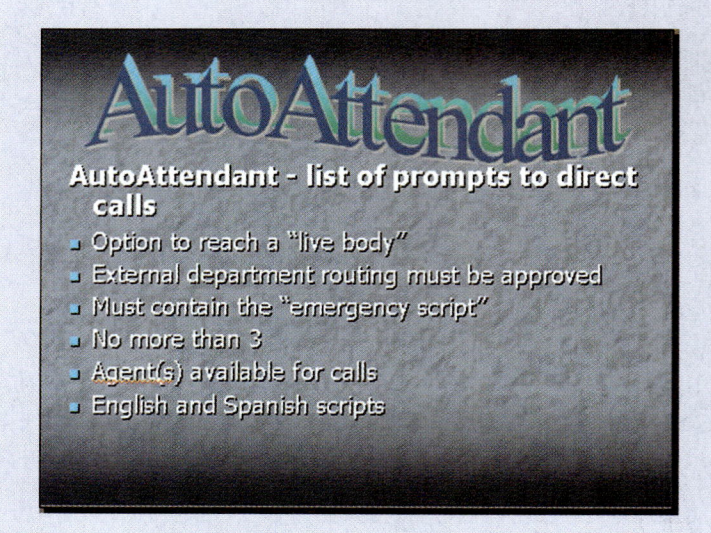

9. Save
10. Move to slide **1** and use Slide Show view to preview the art that has been added

WordArt is an effective way to add impact to a word or two. Too many words in a WordArt image make it difficult to read and detract from the emphasis.

SAVING ART OBJECTS

Any artwork that has been added to a presentation can be stored in the Clip Organizer or saved to a file for easy access from other presentations. Candidates for saving include WordArt, AutoShapes with associated text, and pictures that have been customized.

task reference

Save an Art Object

- Select the picture, WordArt, or AutoShape to save
- Do one of the following:
  - Copy your object to the clipboard and then paste it in the desired collection of the open Media Gallery. You can also set keywords for this new clip
  - Right-click the object and click **Save Picture**. In the Save dialog box, select the format, name the object, and click **Save**

Save Art objects to the Media Gallery:

1. Verify that PowerPoint is running with **<yourname>PP04PhoneMinder.ppt** open with slide **5** selected
2. Select the top copy of WordArt
3. Click **Ctrl+C** to copy the WordArt to the clipboard
4. Click the **Insert Clip Art** button on the Drawing toolbar to activate the Insert Clip Art panel of the Task pane
5. In the See Also section click the **Clip Organizer . . .** link to open the gallery for editing
6. Select the **Favorites** folder in the My Collections folder and click **Ctrl+V** to paste the object

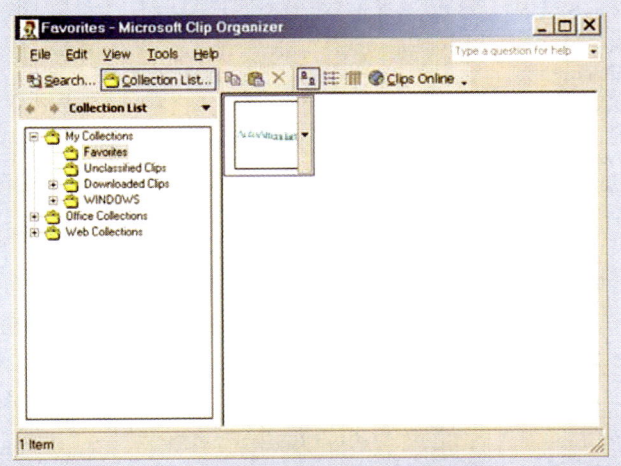

FIGURE 4.20

Art Objects Stored in Your Favorites Folder

7. Minimize the Clip Organizer and move to slide **2** of your presentation
8. Select the custom picture and use **Ctrl+C** to copy it to the clipboard
9. Select the **Clip Art icon** in the Task Bar to activate the Media Gallery window
10. Verify that the Favorites folder is still selected and then click **Ctrl+V** to paste the image into the gallery

Once placed in the Clip Organizer, new clips can be retrieved like any other member of the gallery. Since the clips were placed in the Favorites folder, they can be retrieved from there. Appropriate keywords will need to be added to each clip to facility keyword searches.

Retrieve your Art objects to the Clip Organizer:

1. Verify that PowerPoint is running with **<yourname> PP04PhoneMinder.ppt** open and slide **11** selected

PP 4.20   CHAPTER 4 **POWERPOINT**   **4.1** Effectively Using Art

FIGURE 4.21

Displaying Art in the Favorites Folder

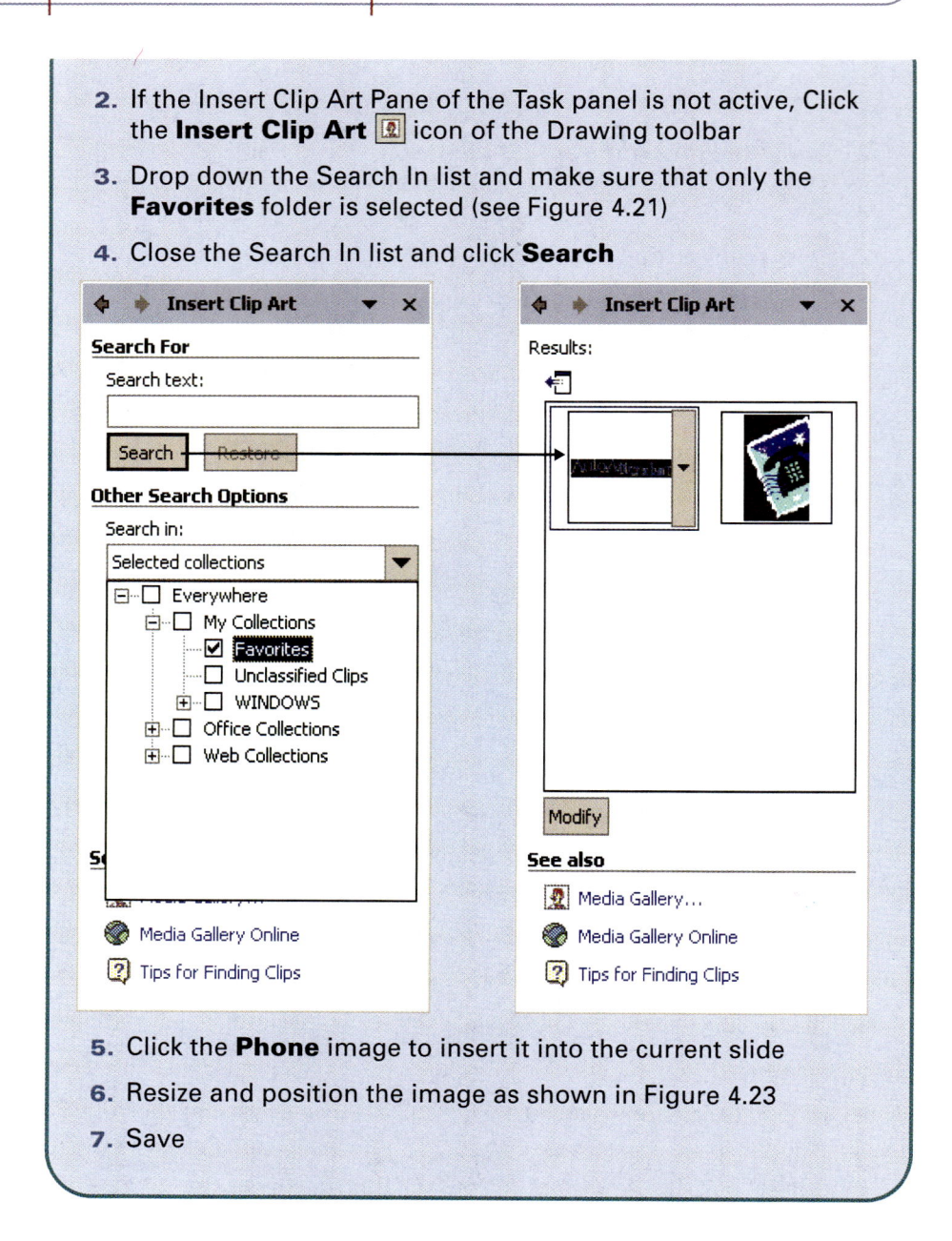

2. If the Insert Clip Art Pane of the Task panel is not active, Click the **Insert Clip Art** icon of the Drawing toolbar
3. Drop down the Search In list and make sure that only the **Favorites** folder is selected (see Figure 4.21)
4. Close the Search In list and click **Search**
5. Click the **Phone** image to insert it into the current slide
6. Resize and position the image as shown in Figure 4.23
7. Save

Depending on the number of images and the user's organizational preferences, storing art to disk may be preferable to using the Clip Organizer.

Save Art objects in a file:

1. Verify that PowerPoint is running with **<yourname>PP04PhoneMinder.ppt** open with slide **5** selected
2. Right-click the top WordArt image
3. Select **Save As Picture**
4. Create a new folder named **SavedImages**

tip: *Use the New Folder button in the Save As Picture dialog box to create and name the new folder*

5. Open SavedImages, name the file **AutoAttendant,** set the Save As Type to **Enhanced Windows Metafile,** and click **Save**

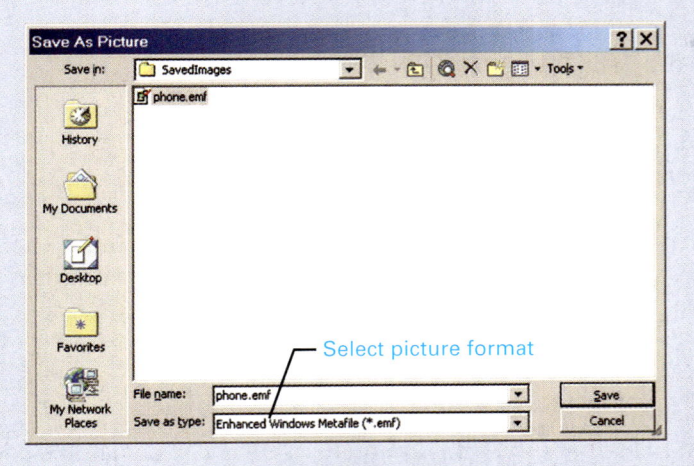

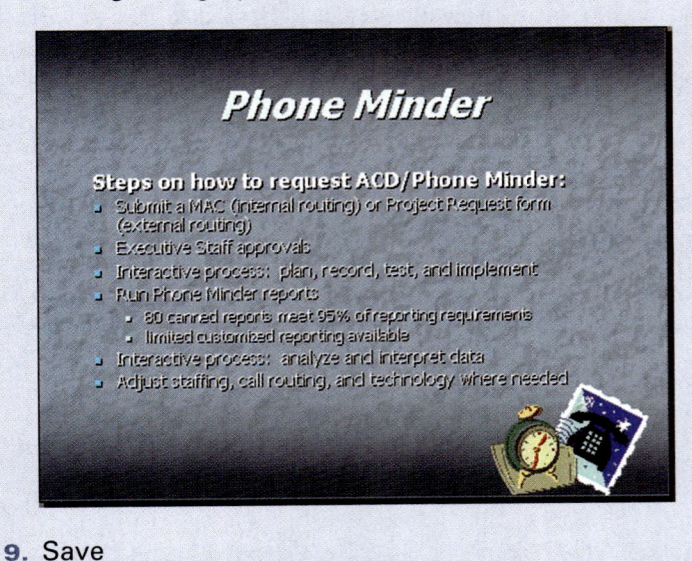

FIGURE 4.22
Save As Picture Dialog Box

6. Repeat the save process for the image on slide 6; name the file **Clock.emf**

7. Move to slide **11** and use the **Insert Picture** button of the Drawing toolbar to insert **Clock.emf**

8. Arrange the graphics as shown in the next figure

FIGURE 4.23
Saved Images Inserted

9. Save

Sometimes it is necessary to save a graphic in several formats to see which provides the best results. In general, the Enhanced Windows Metafile format allows greater flexibility in editing and formatting the retrieved image.

SESSION 4.1

making the grade

1. Discuss the relevance of graphic formats.
2. Why would you use a rotation handle?
3. Explain the difference between linking and embedding objects.
4. List some appropriate applications for WordArt.

SESSION 4.2 ADDING OTHER GRAPHIC ELEMENTS

Chandra is satisfied with the way the graphics are augmenting the text content of the presentation, but the remainder of the presentation is still too text intensive. She would like to explore using tables and charts to deliver the message without so much text.

BUILDING TABLES

Tables are used to format data that do not align correctly using tabs or will present more effectively in a grid. Each cell in a table can have its own formatting including background, border, font, and alignment.

PowerPoint contains its own facilities for building tables, but their formatting abilities are not as complete as those found in Microsoft Word. Complex tables can be created in Word and either linked or embedded in a PowerPoint presentation. Word tables can hold more data and allow special cell formatting like tabs, lists, indents, and nested tables. A workbook from Excel (only one worksheet at a time displays) or data from Access tables can also be displayed on a slide. When tables created in other applications are embedded, the menus and buttons of the source program appear in conjunction with PowerPoint menus. Text stored in a table does not appear in the presentation outline.

PowerPoint Tables

PowerPoint tables can be inserted from the menu or using one of two Standard toolbar buttons. The Insert Table button presents a grid where the user can select the number of rows and columns for the table. The Tables and Borders button opens the Tables and Borders toolbar and converts the cursor to a pen used to draw table cells in the necessary configuration.

task reference
Create a Simple Table
- Select the slide to contain the table
- Click the **Insert Table** button on the Standard toolbar
- Select the desired number of rows and columns by clicking the bottom right cell

www.mhhe.com/i-series   PP 4.23

Build the report table:

1. Verify that PowerPoint is running with **<yourname>PP04PhoneMinder.ppt**
2. Move to slide **10**
3. Select the bulleted list placeholder and delete it

tip: *You need a dotted-line selection box to delete the entire placeholder*

4. Click the **Insert Table** button on the Standard toolbar
5. Select **4 X 4 table**
6. Enter the data for each cell shown in the next figure. Press **Tab** from the last cell in the table to add a new row

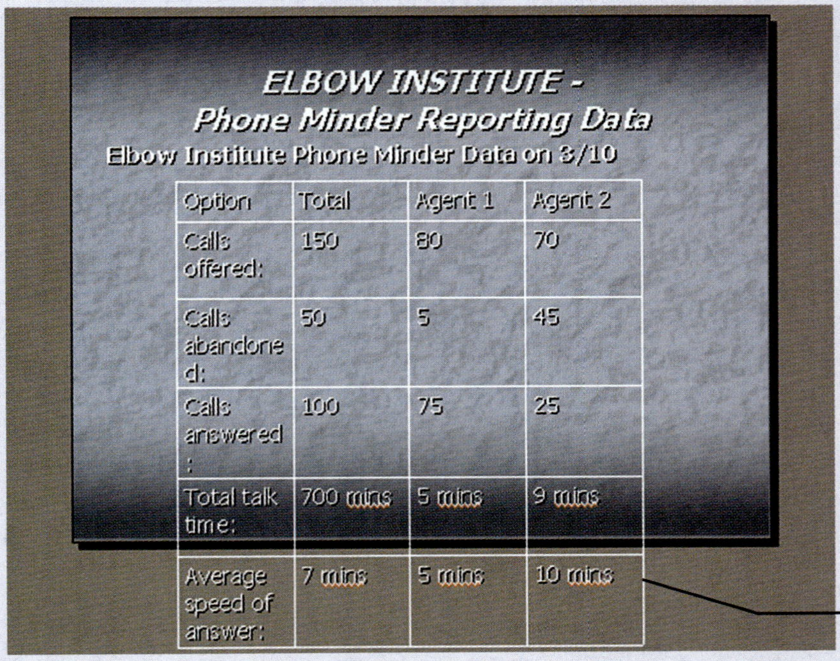

FIGURE 4.24
Initial Table Data Entry

Table cells outside the slide

7. Select the right three columns by clicking and dragging
8. Click the **Align Right** button on the Formatting toolbar
9. Click and drag to select the first row
   a. Click the **Bold** button on the Formatting toolbar
   b. Right-click on the selected row and select **Borders and Fill**
   c. Select the **Fill** tab, choose the dark blue, and click **OK**
10. Drag the borders of the rows and columns to adjust their width/height as shown in Figure 4.25
11. Save

POWERPOINT

FIGURE 4.25
Formatted Table

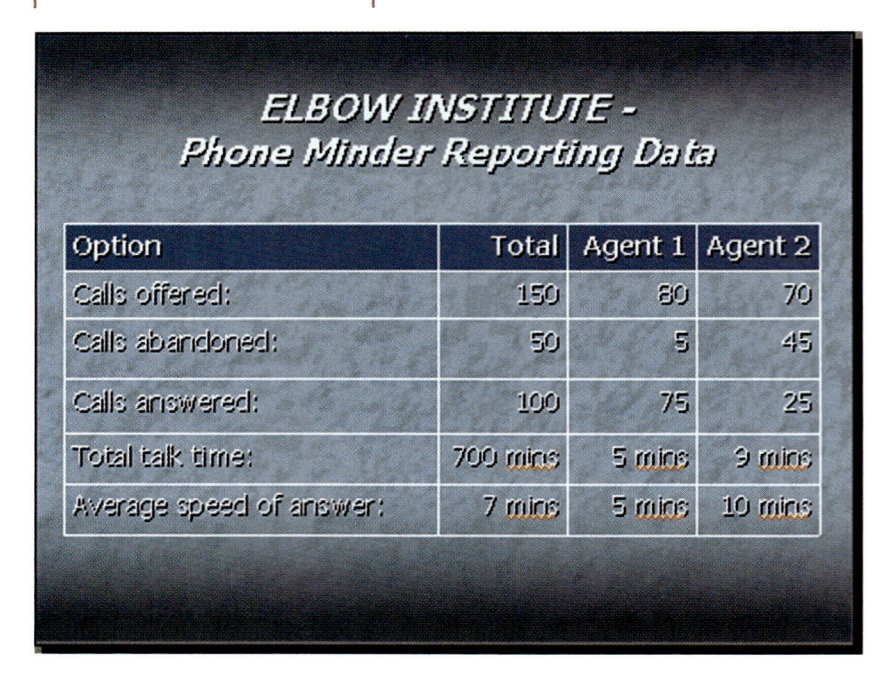

PowerPoint has slide layouts designed to help you quickly create tables. Each of the Content layouts has a table icon that can be clicked to build a table. There is also a Table layout containing only a title and table.

Exploring slide layouts for tables:

1. Verify that PowerPoint is running with **<yourname>PP04PhoneMinder.ppt**
2. Move to the last slide and click the **New Slide** button on the Formatting toolbar
3. Select the **Content** slide layout

FIGURE 4.26
Large Content Slide Layout

tip: *Adding a new slide should activate the Slide Layout panel of the Task pane. If it is not displaying, use the Task panes drop-down menu to activate it*

4. Click the **Insert Table** icon
5. Set the columns to **2** and the rows to **2**
6. Click **OK**
7. Save

For simple tables, choosing the appropriate slide layout is probably the simplest way to insert a table. The Tables and Borders toolbar will allow the creation of complex tables in any configuration that you need.

Drawing tables:

1. Verify that PowerPoint is running with **<yourname>PP04PhoneMinder.ppt** open and the table built in the previous steps active
2. Click the **Tables and Borders** button on the Standard toolbar

tip: *The Tables and Borders toolbar appears and the cursor becomes a pencil*

3. Use the pencil tool to click and drag the new cell lines shown in the next picture

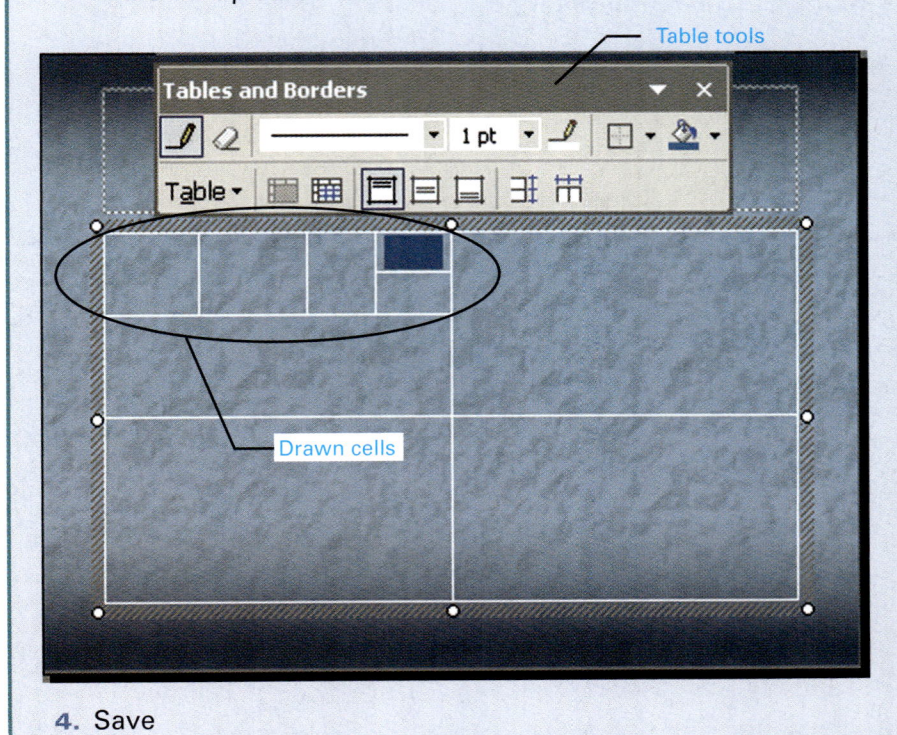

FIGURE 4.27
Drawing New Cells

4. Save

In this example, the pencil tool was used to update an existing table, but it can also be used to create a new table. When creating a new table, draw the first cell, drag it to the size for the whole table, and then draw the cells inside it. The Eraser tool of the Tables and Borders toolbar can be used to erase any line.

Embedding Word Tables and Excel Workbooks

Often the table and data for a slide already exist in a Microsoft Word table. Complex tables with cell indents, tabs, and bullets are also easier to create in Word.

Recall that objects created outside of PowerPoint can be either linked or embedded when placed in a slide. Linked objects are not inserted into the PowerPoint presentation, are updated from the application of origin, reduce the size of the presentation, and must be moved with the presentation. Embedded objects are placed into the PowerPoint file and can be modified without impacting the original object.

Chandra has several call distribution setup examples stored in Microsoft Word files. She would like to link the PowerPoint presentation to the Word files so that only one file needs to be maintained when there are changes to the scripts.

---

task reference

Create a Linked or Embedded Object from an Existing Word or Excel File

- Click the slide that will contain the object
- On the **Insert** menu, click **Object**
- Click the **Create from file** option button
- Click the **Browse** button and navigate to the file
  - Click the **Link** check box to create a linked file
  - Uncheck the Link check box to embed the file
- Click **OK**

Linking a Word table:

1. Verify that PowerPoint is running with **<yourname>PP04PhoneMinder.ppt**
2. Move to slide **9** and delete the bulleted text placeholder
3. On the **Insert** menu, click **Object**
4. Click the **Create from file** option button
5. Click the **Browse** button, navigate to the **WordTable.doc** file, and click **OK**
6. Click the **Link** check box
7. Click **OK**

8. Reposition the linked table if needed

tip: *Resizing a linked object will distort it since the size is determined in the original application*

FIGURE 4.28
Linking a Word Table

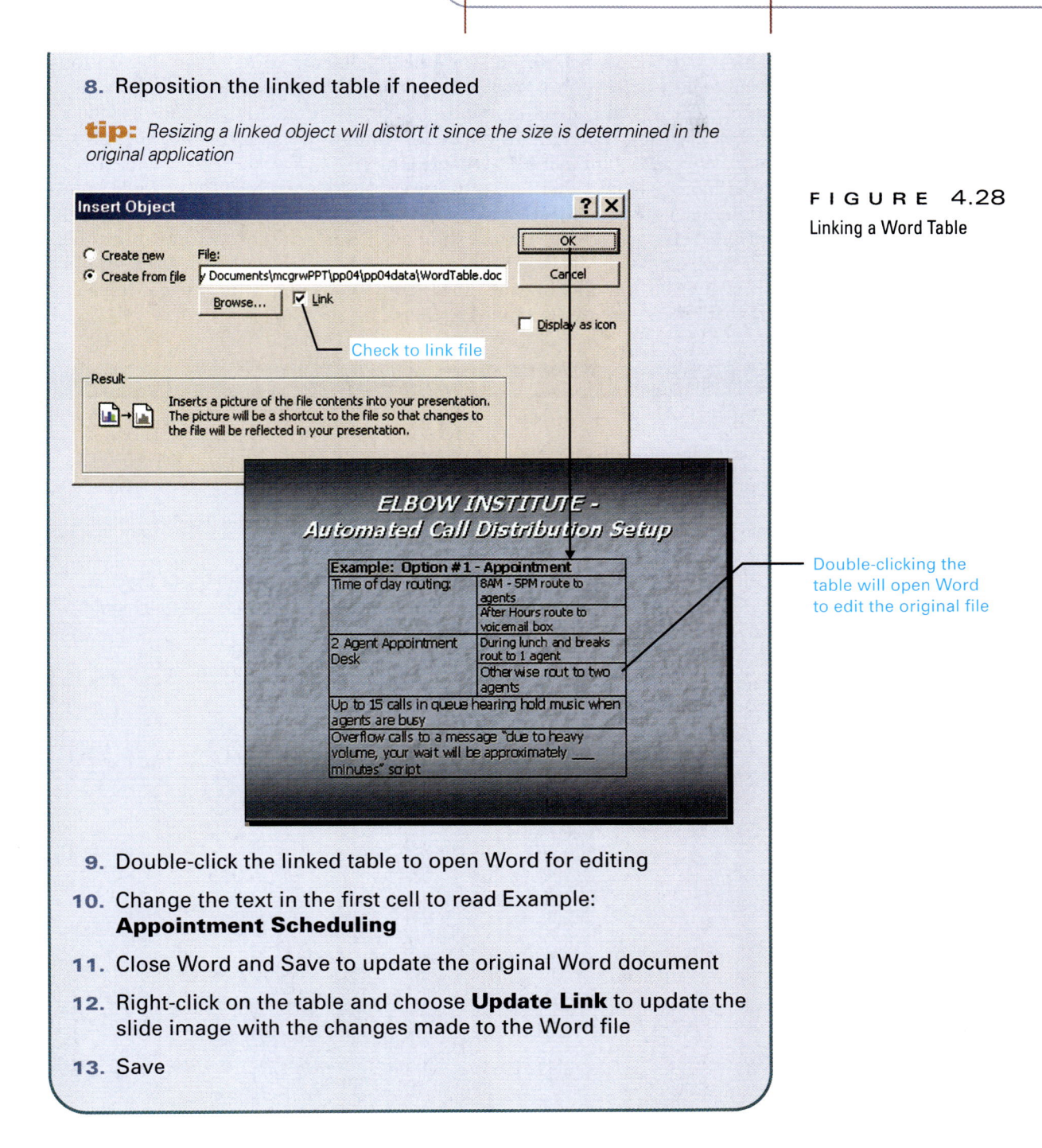

9. Double-click the linked table to open Word for editing
10. Change the text in the first cell to read Example: **Appointment Scheduling**
11. Close Word and Save to update the original Word document
12. Right-click on the table and choose **Update Link** to update the slide image with the changes made to the Word file
13. Save

Inserting an Excel workbook or an object from any other application is accomplished using the steps demonstrated. Use linked objects to reduce PowerPoint file sizes or maintain one version of the content. Use embedded objects when the version of the object displayed in PowerPoint does not need to match the original file. Linked objects are updated each time the presentation opens or when the update link is clicked.

GRAPHING

Charts are used to represent numeric data graphically. Graphs can be built in a presentation using Microsoft Graph or imported from Microsoft Excel. PowerPoint's Insert Chart button will activate Microsoft Graph, which uses a datasheet (table) for entering the data and formatting options used to generate a chart based on the data. When a chart will include large quantities of data, need calculations, or use data that already reside in Excel, creating the chart in Excel and then importing it to PowerPoint is more effective than using Microsoft Graph.

Chandra thinks that an example of a statistical chart that can be created using the Phone Minder data would improve the impact of the presentation. You can add a chart to a slide by clicking the Insert Chart button on the toolbar, by using the Insert menu, or by selecting one of the content slide layouts and clicking the chart icon. Once a chart is started, the steps to specify content and format are the same.

task reference
Create a Microsoft Graph

- Select the most appropriate content layout for the slide that will contain the chart
- Click the **Chart** icon in the Content placeholder to activate Microsoft Graph
- Enter the data to be charted in the datasheet with headings in the first row and column, and data in cells that can be referenced with a letter and number (A1)
- Use the **Chart** menu to select chart type, subtype, and options
- Right-click on any chart object to format it
- Click the slide background to exit Microsoft Graph

Adding a Chart to the Phone Minder presentation:

1. Verify that PowerPoint is running with **<yourname>PP04PhoneMinder.ppt**
2. Move to slide **10** and click the **New Slide** button to create a new blank slide 11
3. Select the Content layout (title and content) for the blank slide
4. In the title placeholder enter

   ELBOW INSTITUTE

   Phone Minder Graphing

5. Click the **Insert Chart** icon in the Content placeholder

   tip: *Microsoft Graph opens with sample data and chart displaying as well as its custom toolbars*

6. Review the sample data and chart to understand how to place data to obtain the results you want
7. Click on the slide background to quit Microsoft Graph

FIGURE 4.29
Microsoft Graph

8. Save

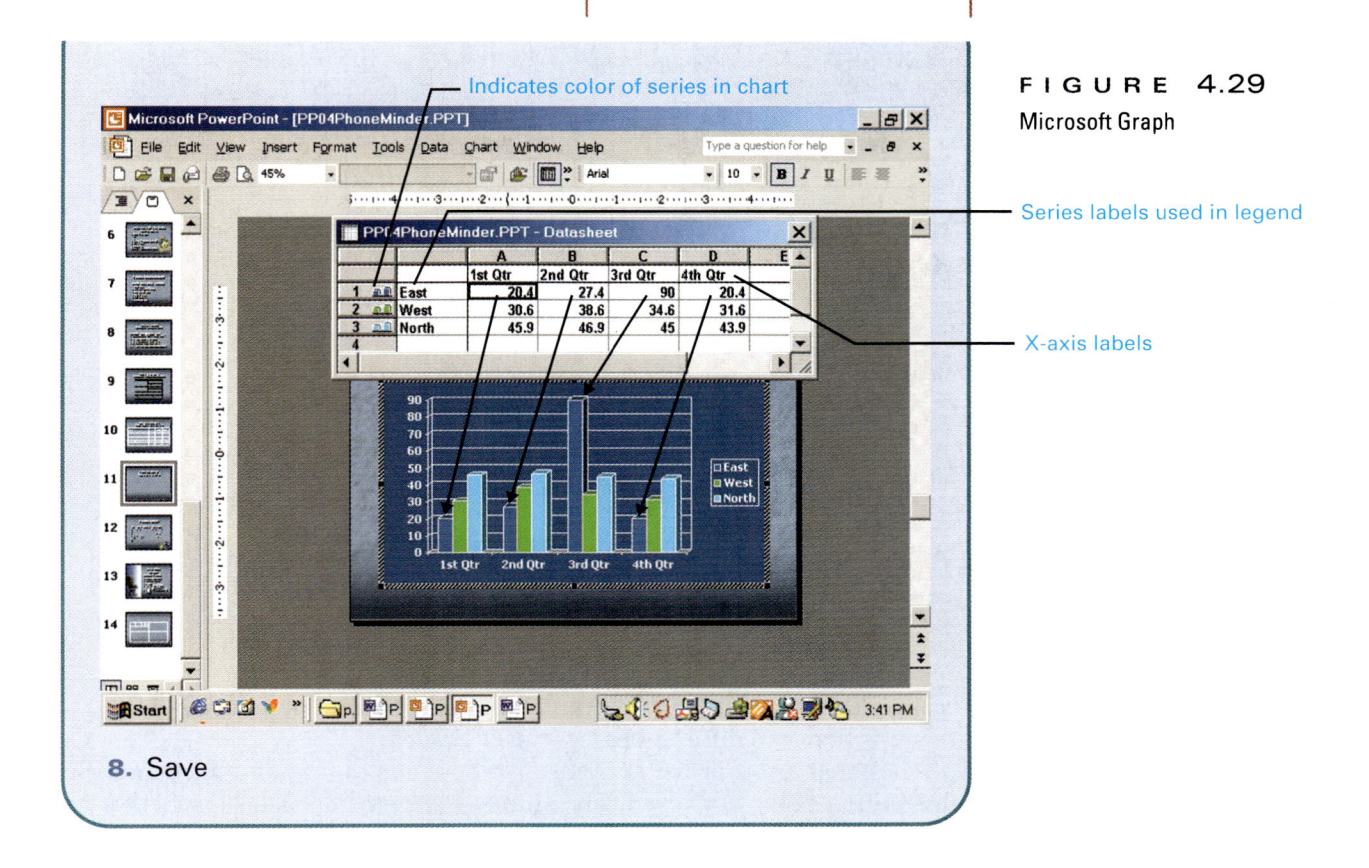

When Microsoft Graph is open, both the datasheet and chart display. The *datasheet* is composed of cells to contain the data used to generate the chart. Each cell contains one *data value.* Data values are plotted on the *y-axis* of bar and column charts. A *data series* contains all of the data values of one type. For example, the first data series in the default datasheet contains the four eastern region sales values for each quarter with each data value plotted in a dark blue column on the chart. The quarter values for West make up the second series, and the quarter values for North make up the third data series. The datasheet row headings define the data series and are used to create the legend text. The column headings describe each data value in the series and display on the *x-axis.*

Microsoft Graph menus and toolbars are designed for manipulating and formatting the datasheet and chart. For example, the Chart menu contains options for changing the chart type, setting chart options that control how the data are charted, and controlling the 3-D view.

Chart Types and Subtypes

Microsoft Graph supports 14 standard chart types that determine how the data are visually displayed. Chart types include pie, line, column, and bar. Each chart type has at least two subtypes to control layout within the type. For example, bar chart subtypes include several 3-D and flat layouts. After a chart and subtype have been selected, use the Press and Hold to View Sample button of the Chart Type dialog box to preview the selections.

Select the chart type that suits the data being plotted and the presentation audience. If you are plotting one data series and want to see how each value in that series relates to the total of all values, use a pie chart. Area and line charts are best to show trends of how data move over time or

FIGURE 4.30

Microsoft Graph Chart Types and Subtypes

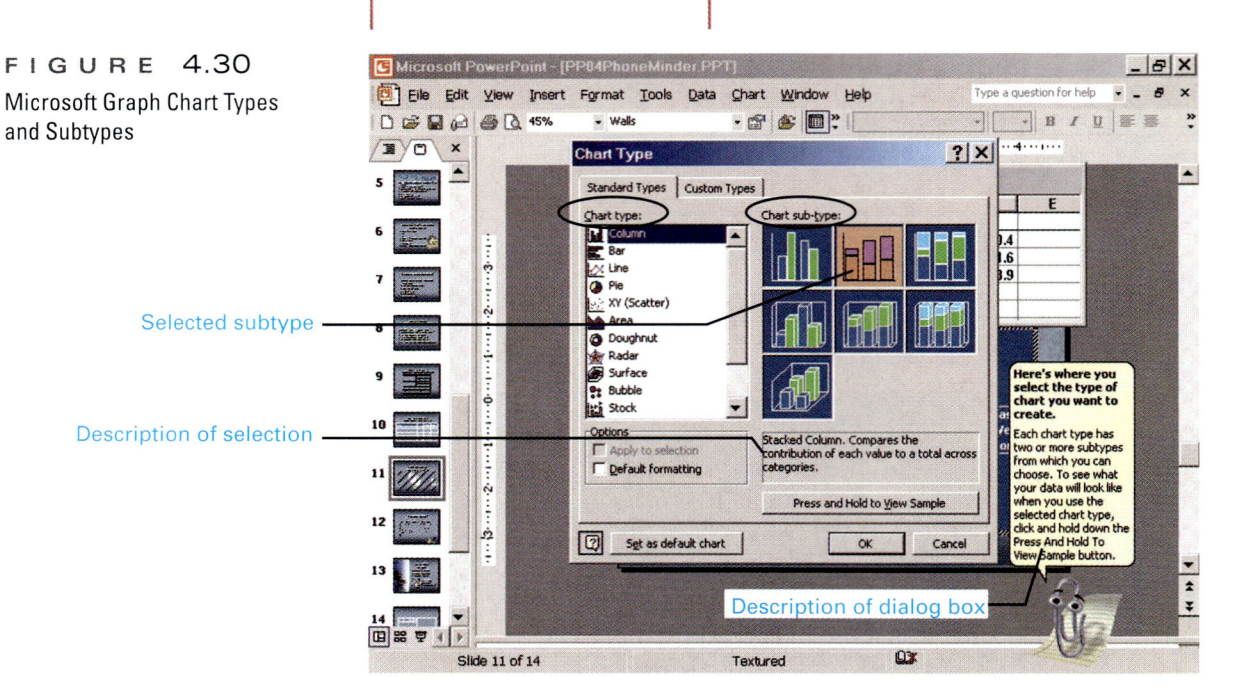

across categories. Bar and column charts are effective at showing the relationships between different categories of values.

The most appropriate subtype also depends on the audience and the information being conveyed. The simplest subtype decision is whether or not to use 3-D visual effects. In most cases 3-D effects improve the visual impact of charts and help the users relate to the quantities represented. 3-D charts can be distracting when there are too many data series or too many data values.

Updating Chart Data

When Microsoft Graph initiates, a default chart and datasheet are inserted into the current slide. Before updating the datasheet, use the default chart and datasheet to determine how to arrange the new data into rows and columns. Typically each datasheet row represents a series of data.

The gray boxes above each datasheet column and to the left of each row are called **control boxes.** Notice that the cells in the datasheet intended to hold data values have letters in the column control box and numbers in the row control box. Refer to data cells by their letter and number, for example C4. The first datasheet column is intended for labels and does not have a letter designator. Likewise, the first row has no number designator and holds x-axis labels.

Control boxes can be used to select rows, columns, or the entire datasheet. Click the control box labeled A to select that entire column of cells. Clicking the control box labeled 7 will select all of row 7. Clicking the top left control box will select all cells in the datasheet. A group of datasheet cells can be selected by clicking the top left cell and then holding the Shift key while clicking the bottom right cell. Once cells are selected, they can be edited, deleted, or formatted.

Moving from cell to cell in the datasheet can be accomplished using the mouse, tab key, or arrow keys. The active cell has a darkened border indicating that it can be acted on. Updating data in a cell is accomplished by typing the new value and moving to another cell.

Chandra has provided data for you to manually enter into the datasheet. You will delete the existing data first and then enter the Phone Minder data.

Adding Phone Minder data to the datasheet:

1. Verify that PowerPoint is running with **<yourname>PP04PhoneMinder.ppt** open
2. Move to slide **11** and double-click the chart to open Microsoft Graph
3. Click the top left control box to select all of the datasheet (see Figure 4.31) and press **Delete**
4. Click in each cell and enter the data shown in Figure 4.31

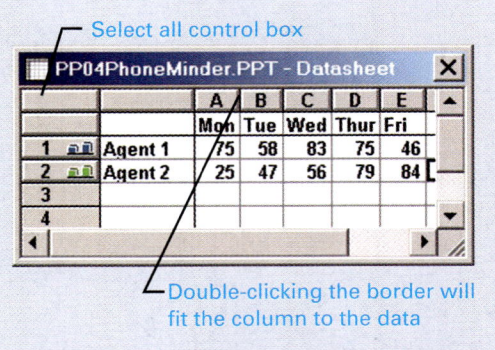

   Select all control box

		A	B	C	D	E
		Mon	Tue	Wed	Thur	Fri
1	Agent 1	75	58	83	75	46
2	Agent 2	25	47	56	79	84
3						
4						

   Double-clicking the border will fit the column to the data

5. Verify your data entry and close the datasheet using the X in the titlebar
6. Save

FIGURE 4.31

Phone Minder Data in Datasheet

As data are entered in the datasheet, they are used to generate a default chart. Chart specifications are used to set chart type, subtype, and format. When the datasheet is not needed, it can be closed to free window space for manipulating the chart. To reopen the datasheet again, use the View Datasheet button on the toolbar.

Customizing a Chart

There are many things that can be done to customize a chart once the datasheet has been updated. Simple changes include adding titles and selecting another chart type or subtype. More complex options are used to control the 3-D rotation and apply custom colors and fills to chart objects. Chandra believes that the column chart is probably the most effective way to present these data, but she would like to see some alternatives.

anotherword

. . . on Charting Data

Sometimes you will want to exclude some data in the datasheet from the chart. This can be accomplished without changing the datasheet by double-clicking the row or column control box corresponding to the data to be excluded. The data will display as grayed out in the datasheet. Double-clicking the control box a second time will include the data in the chart again.

Exploring chart types and subtypes for Phone Minder data:

1. Verify that PowerPoint is running with **<yourname>PP04PhoneMinder.ppt**

FIGURE 4.32
Selecting a Chart Subtype

2. Verify that you are on slide **11** with Microsoft Graph open and the datasheet closed from the last set of steps

   tip: *The chart should be selected and the toolbar and menu for Microsoft Graph displayed. If this is not the case, double-click on the chart and then use the X in the titlebar to close the datasheet window*

3. Select **Chart Type** from the **Chart** menu
4. Review the current chart type and subtype
5. Select the first subtype for a Column chart and press and hold the button to view the sample
6. Select the **Line** chart type and preview the result
7. Experiment with other chart types and subtypes
8. Select **Column** chart type, **3-D** subtype, and click **OK**
9. Save

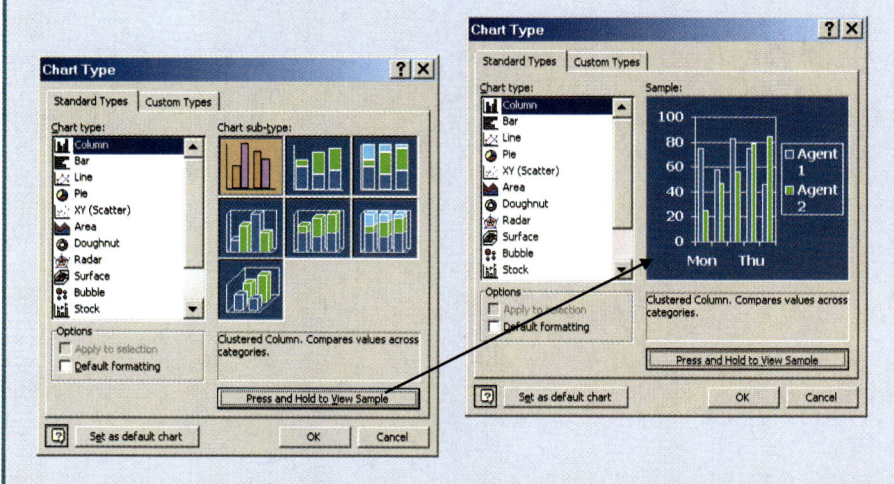

At this point in chart development, there is no chart title or label on either the x- or y-axis to indicate what is actually being measured. The chart does not have a title. Titles and labels can be added using the Chart Options selection of the Chart menu.

Adding a title and axis labels to the Phone Minder chart:

1. Verify that PowerPoint is running with **<yourname>PP04PhoneMinder.ppt**
2. Verify that you are on slide **11** with Microsoft Graph open and the datasheet closed from the last set of steps
3. Click the **Chart Options** selection of the **Chart** menu

4. If necessary, click the **Titles** tab and enter the titles shown in Figure 4.33

5. Click the **Legend** tab and select the **Bottom** option

6. Click the **Data Labels** tab and check **Value**

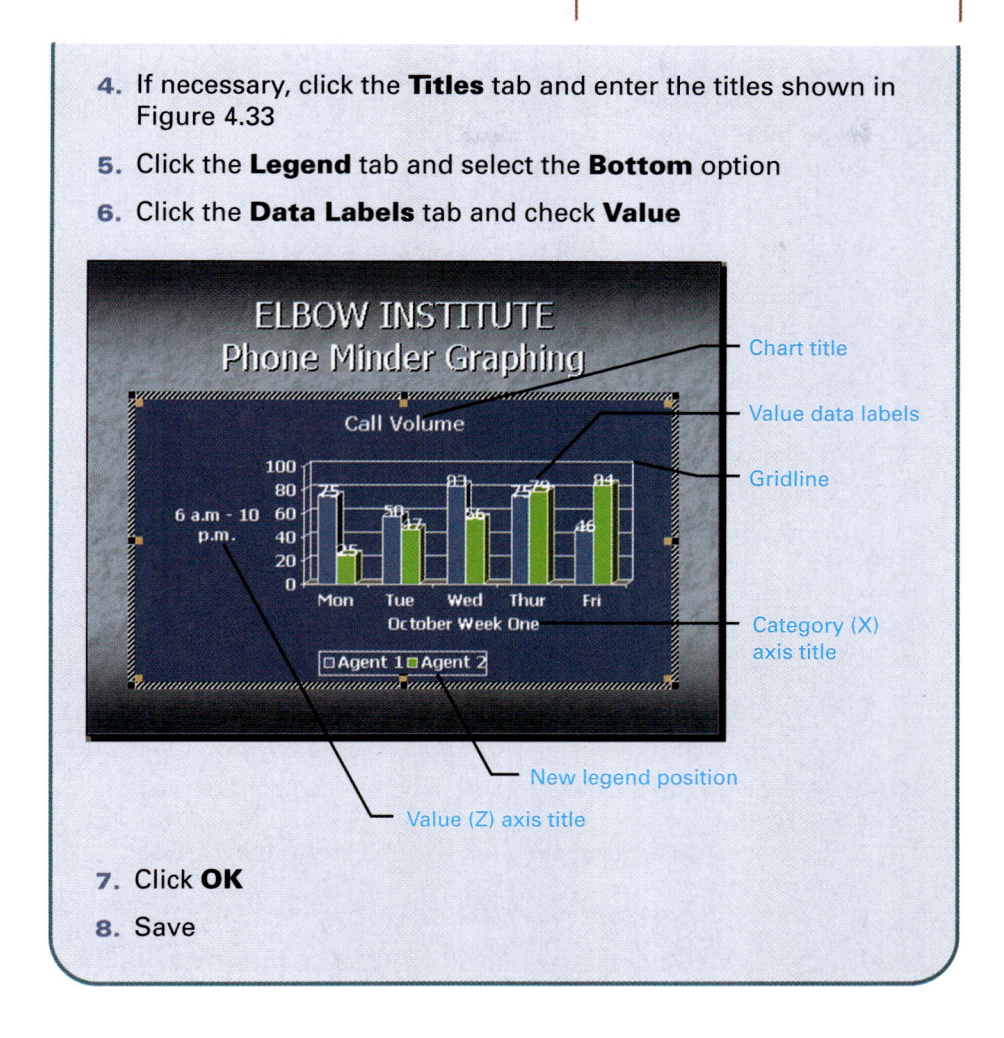

FIGURE 4.33
Customized Legend and Data Labels

7. Click **OK**
8. Save

Chart options provide control over the content and placement of titles, axes, gridlines, legend, data labels, and data table display. The gridlines behind the chart can be turned off or made finer using the Gridlines tab. The chart legend can be turned off or placed in a new location with the Legend tab. Data labels can be added to the chart displaying the value plotted, and the datasheet can be displayed in the slide with the chart.

Each chart object can be modified. Font, size, and orientation can be set for text objects. Shape objects can have fill colors, border colors, and shapes set options. The chart consists of a plot area that holds the graph and a chart area that holds everything else. Both the plot area and chart area can be set to a custom color, fill, or pattern. By default, both are transparent.

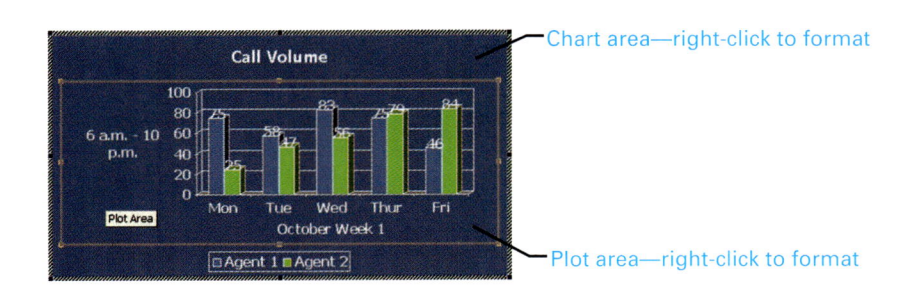

FIGURE 4.34
Chart Area and Plot Area

Customizing chart objects:

1. Verify that PowerPoint is running with **<yourname>PP04PhoneMinder.ppt**
2. Verify that you are on slide **11** with Microsoft Graph open and the datasheet closed from the last set of steps
3. Right-click on one of the green value cubes and select **Format Data Series**
4. Click **Fill Effects**, click the **Texture** tab, select **Green Marble,** and click **OK**
5. Click **OK** again
6. Right-click on one of the blue value cubes and select **Format Data Series**
7. Click **Fill Effects,** click the **Texture** tab, select **Denim,** and click **OK**
8. Click **OK** again
9. Click on the slide background to shut down Microsoft Graph and see the formatting results
10. Right-click on the 6 a.m.—10 p.m. label and select **Format Axis Title**
    a. Click the **Alignment** tab and set the Orientation to **90** degrees
    b. Click the **Font** tab, set the size to **16,** and click **OK**
11. Right-click on October Week 1, select **Format Axis Title,** and set the size to **16**

FIGURE 4.35
Completed Chart

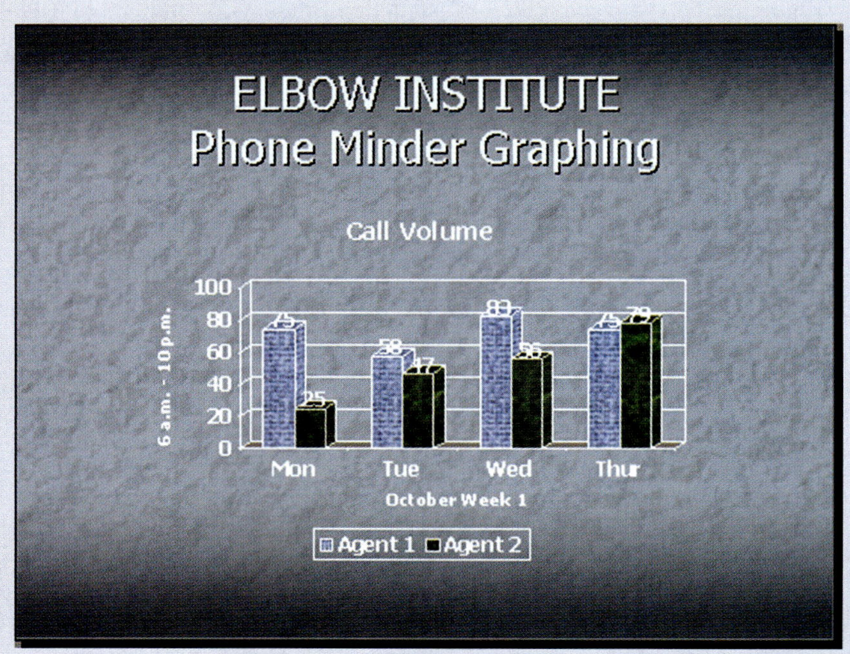

12. Click the slide background to exit Microsoft Graph and Save the presentation

another way

...to Select Chart Objects

Double-clicking on almost any chart object will open it to edit its attributes.

Text can be added to a chart by simply typing. Additional text may be necessary to draw out information or emphasize a point. Typing creates a text box that can be moved, modified, or formatted like any other object.

DEFINING OTHER TYPES OF CHARTS

PowerPoint provides a collection of diagrams to support communicating complex conceptual information and relationships that are not based on numbers. The Insert Diagram or Organization Chart icon opens the Diagram Gallery with the following diagram types:

- *Organization chart*—used to show hierarchical relationships
- *Cycle diagram*—used to show a process with a continuous cycle
- *Radial diagram*—used to show the relationships to a central element
- *Pyramid diagram*—used to show foundational relationships
- *Venn diagram*—used to show overlapping relationships
- *Target diagram*—used to show steps toward a goal

If one of these predefined diagrams won't help build the needed graphical representation, the drawing toolbar provides shapes and connectors that can be used to build custom diagrams including flowcharts.

Building an Organization Chart

Organization charts are most typically used to depict the organization of a company, department, or project. The default chart consists of four connected rectangles for one manager and three subordinates as shown in the next figure. Like other PowerPoint objects, sizing handles appear when a rectangle is selected. Unlike other objects, these sizing handles are often marked with an X because they cannot be used to resize the object.

As the instructions indicate, clicking a chart rectangle will allow text to be added. More rectangles can be added to the chart by selecting an existing rectangle and then accessing the Insert Shape menu of the Organization Chart toolbar. Rectangles can be added as coworkers (the same level),

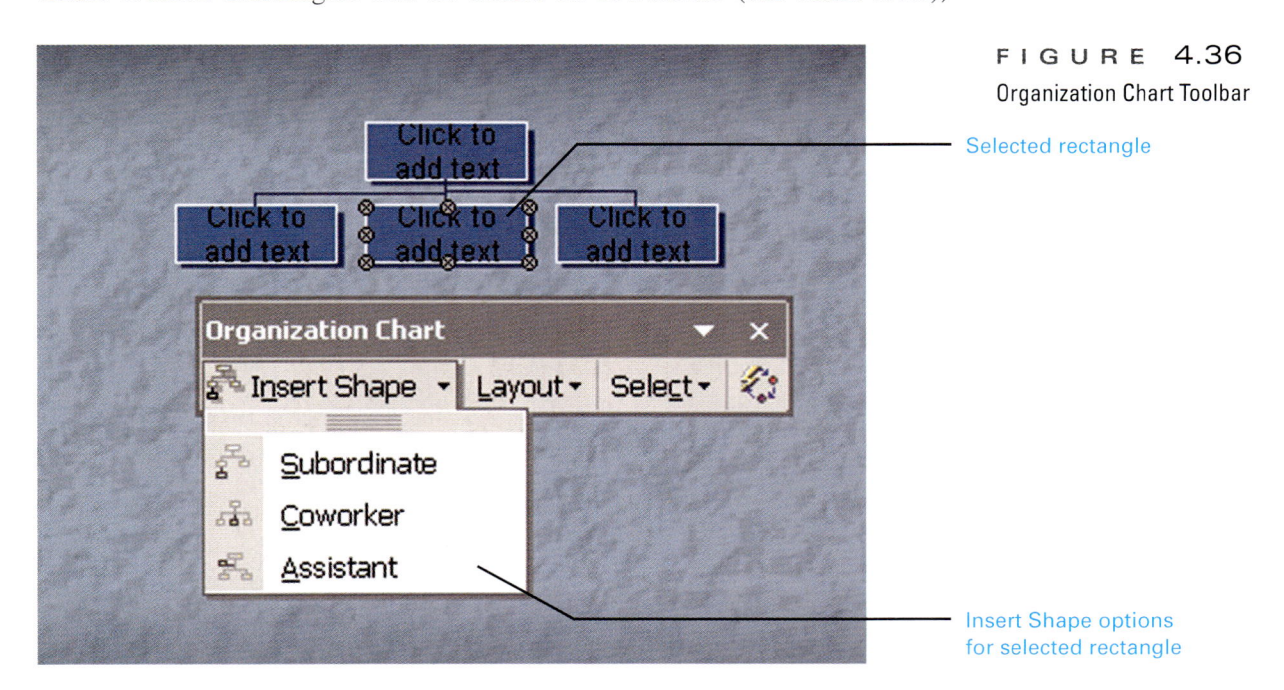

FIGURE 4.36
Organization Chart Toolbar

Selected rectangle

Insert Shape options for selected rectangle

subordinates (below the current rectangle), or assistants (outside the hierarchy). The Layout menu controls how the rectangles are organized on the chart, and the Select menu assists in selecting multiple chart components.

Chandra believes that slide 8 in the presentation, which outlines a sample AutoAttendant script, could be better presented in a hierarchy chart. Although organization charts are designed to depict the management structure of an organization, they can be used for any hierarchical content. The current slide will be deleted and replaced with an organization chart depicting the same information.

task reference
Create an Organization Chart

- Select the most appropriate content layout for the slide that will contain the chart
- Click the **Insert Diagram or Organization Chart** icon in the Content placeholder to activate Microsoft Graph
- Select **Organization Chart** from the Diagram Gallery and click **OK**
- Click in a chart rectangle to add descriptive text
- Select a rectangle and use the Organization Chart toolbar to add coworkers, subordinates, and assistants to build the desired structure
- Use the Layout and Design Gallery menu options to control chart organization
- Click the slide background to exit

Building an organization chart:

1. Verify that PowerPoint is running with **<yourname>PP04PhoneMinder.ppt**
2. Select slide **8** in the Outline pane and press **Delete**
3. Verify that slide **7** is selected and click the **New Slide** button
4. Select the **Large Content** slide layout
5. Click the **Insert Diagram or Organization Chart** button in the content placeholder
6. Select **Organization Chart** and click **OK**
7. Click one of the second-level subordinate rectangles and click **Insert Shape, Subordinate**
8. Repeat step 7 for the other two second-level rectangles
9. Select the top rectangle, click the **Layout** drop-down menu, and select **Right Hanging**
10. Repeat step 9 for each of the second-level rectangles
11. Click the slide background to quit Organization Chart
12. Save

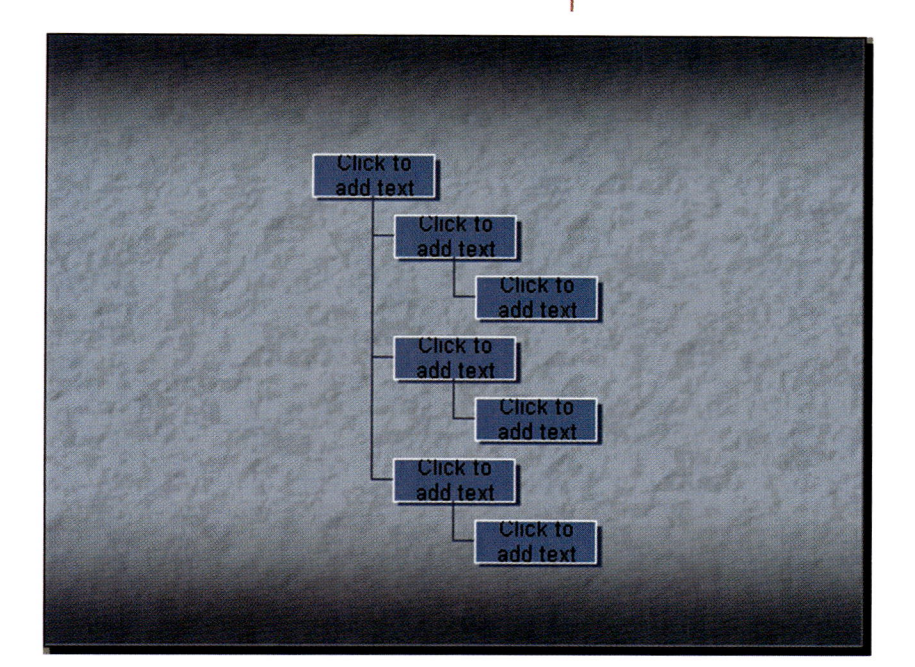

FIGURE 4.37
Right Hanging Subordinates

It is usually easiest to build the hierarchy of the presentation and then add text and formatting. A rectangle inserted in the wrong location can be removed using either Undo or Delete. The Layout option of the Organization Chart toolbar provides control over the orientation of subordinate rectangles in the chart in relation to the selected rectangle. This allows the freedom of setting different layouts for each branch of the chart.

Adding text and formatting to an organization chart:

1. Verify that PowerPoint is running with **<yourname>PP04PhoneMinder.ppt** with slide **8** selected

2. Click the first-level rectangle and type **AutoAttendant answers incoming calls**

3. Click the topmost second-level rectangle; type **1.** Use the Formatting toolbar buttons to make it **bold;** increase the font size to **24** and add a **Shadow**

4. Enter **2** in the next second-level rectangle and format it the same way

5. Enter **3** into the next second-level rectangle and format it the same way

6. Add the text shown in Figure 4.38 to the third-level rectangles

   tip: You may need to preview the slide show for your chart to match the one shown

7. Click the **AutoFormat** (rightmost) button on the Organization Chart toolbar to open the Organization Chart Style Gallery

8. Select a chart style and click **Apply**

FIGURE 4.38

Default and Group Tangle Styles

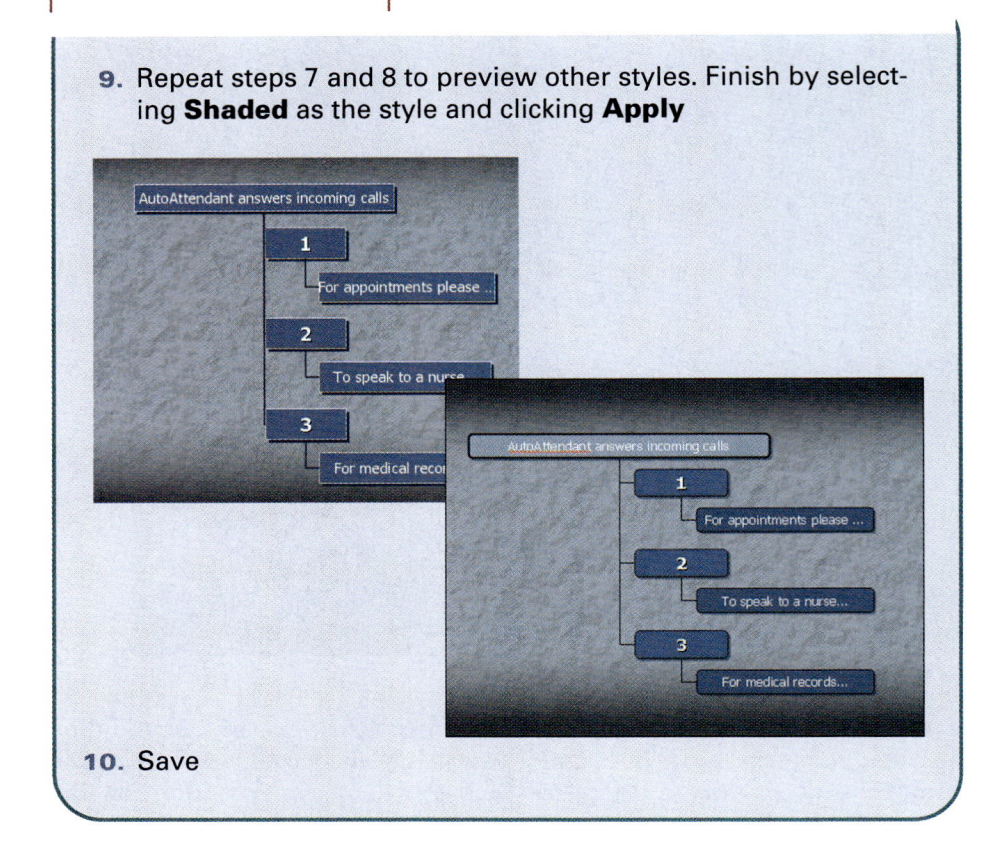

9. Repeat steps 7 and 8 to preview other styles. Finish by selecting **Shaded** as the style and clicking **Apply**

10. Save

The Organization Chart Style Gallery provides a fast and simple way to apply formatting to the chart. If none of the preset formats work effectively, each chart element can be custom formatted by right-clicking it and selecting Format AutoShape.

Adding Diagrams to Your Presentation

The cycle, radial, pyramid, Venn, and target diagrams are each designed to support a different type of process, but their implementation is very similar to that just reviewed for organization charts. To build any diagram, select the appropriate diagram type, add your own text, insert additional chart components, use the style gallery to format the entire chart, and add custom formatting to any chart component.

Chandra would like to replace slide 7's text description of Phone Minder reports with a graphic representation. A radial diagram is used to depict the relationships of multiple elements to a central element. In this case the central element is data gathering with multiple reports created from the data. The layout of slide 7 will be changed to title and content to create the diagram.

Building a radial chart:

1. Verify that PowerPoint is running with **<yourname>PP04PhoneMinder.ppt**

2. Move to slide **7** (Phone Minder Statistics)

3. Select the content placeholder and press **Delete**

4. Select the **Title and Content** slide layout
5. Click the **Insert Diagram or Organization Chart** button in the content placeholder
6. Select **Radial Diagram** and click **OK**

FIGURE 4.39

Initial Radial Diagram

7. Click the **Insert Shape** option of the Diagram toolbar to add a fourth related item
8. Click the **Insert Shape** option of the Diagram toolbar to add a fifth related item
9. Click the slide background to exit the diagram
10. Save

task reference

Create a Diagram (Cycle, Radial, Pyramid, Venn, or Target)

- Select the most appropriate content layout for the slide that will contain the chart
- Click the **Insert Diagram or Organization Chart** icon in the Content placeholder to activate Microsoft Graph
- Select the desired diagram type from the Diagram Gallery and click **OK**
- Click in a chart text placeholder to add descriptive text
- Use the toolbar to build the desired structure
- Use the Layout and Design Gallery menu options to control chart organization
- Click the slide background to exit

The only layout options for radial diagrams impact the size of the diagram box. There are no options to adjust the physical layout.

POWERPOINT

FIGURE 4.40
Formatted Radial Diagram

Adding text and formatting a radial diagram:

1. Verify that PowerPoint is running with **<yourname>PP04PhoneMinder.ppt** with slide **7** selected
2. Select the central circle, type **PhoneLog,** press **Enter** and then type **Data**
3. On the Diagram toolbar select **Layout** and then choose **Scale Diagram**
4. Use the right and left sizing handles to drag the diagram borders to the sides of the slide. Make the diagram as wide as possible without adjusting the height
5. Click each outer circle and enter the text shown in Figure 4.40. You will need to press enter to move to a new line and reduce the font size

tip: *You may need to preview the slide show for your chart to match the one shown*

6. Right-click on each outer shape, choose **Format AutoShape,** and set the colors as shown in Figure 4.40

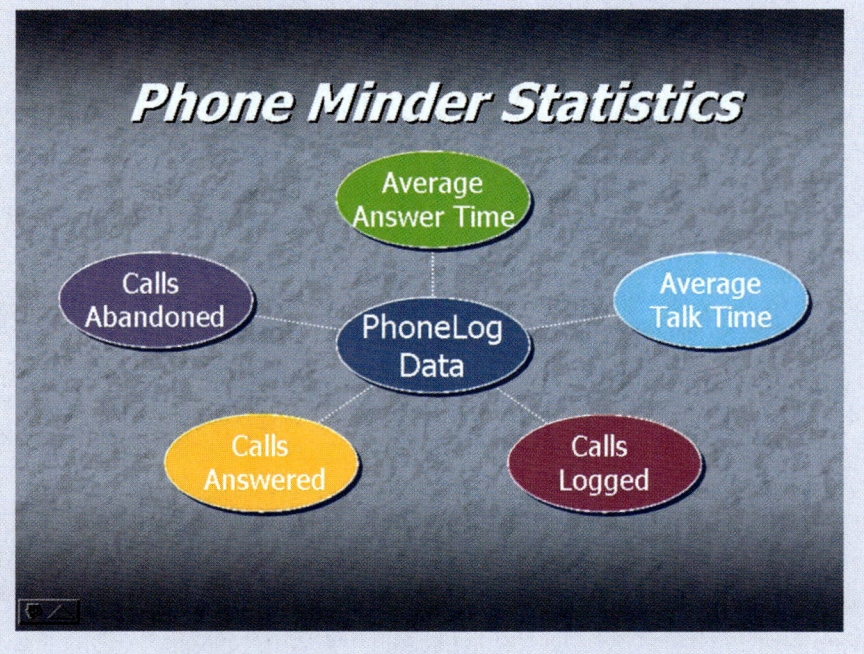

7. Move to slide **1** and use Slide View to preview the presentation
8. Save and close Print

Diagrams are a valuable way to present information without bullets. It takes a little more time to diagram, but graphic representations of relationships are easier for the audience to remember than lists of text. In addition, diagrams are colorful and add visual interest.

making the grade

SESSION 4.2

1. Evaluate the various ways to add a table to a slide.
2. Discuss how you would organize the data to create a column chart comparing the scores of your two favorite sports teams for the past three games.
3. How would you select all values in the third row of a datasheet?
4. Give an example of information not covered in the chapter that could effectively be presented in an Organization Chart.

SESSION 4.3 SUMMARY

Microsoft PowerPoint supports a variety of graphics formats and styles to add emphasis, provide color, and visually demonstrate a point. In addition to looking nice, art elements make a presentation more memorable and help the audience to grasp difficult concepts.

The Microsoft Clip Organizer contains media clips that are added by applications as they are installed or stored in the gallery by users. Media clips are located by entering search words that are matched against the keyword list of each clip. Clips that match the search value are displayed for your evaluation. Keywords can be updated for more effective searches.

Artwork can be added to a slide using the Clip Organizer, the Clip On-line Link, art stored in a file, or directly from a scanner or digital camera. The file type of the art determines whether or not it can effectively be resized and recolored. All images have sizing handles and a rotation handle when selected. The rotation handle is used to rotate the image by dragging.

Tables are an alternative to the traditional bulleted list presentation format and can be created directly on a PowerPoint Slide or retrieved from Word or Excel. Objects retrieved from sources outside PowerPoint can be either linked or embedded. Linked objects do not actually reside in the slide, but have a pointer back to the actual source file. Embedded objects are a copy of the original that can be modified without impacting the source file.

Additional graphic elements available to enhance a presentation include WordArt, charts, and diagrams. WordArt will allow you to create text with special effects like shapes and perspectives that cannot be obtained using standard fonts. Charts are used to generate graphs based on numeric data arranged in a datasheet. Diagrams are used to present relationships like an organizational structure.

MOUS OBJECTIVES SUMMARY

- Creating tables on slides—PPT2002-3-1
- Adding Clip Art images to slides—PPT2002-3-1
- Adding charts and bitmap images to slides—PPT2002-3-1
- Adding bitmap graphics to slides or backgrounds—PPT2002-3-2
- Creating Office Art elements and adding them to slides—PPT2002-3-3
- Applying user-defined formats to tables—PPT2002-3-4

- Inserting Excel charts on slides (as either embedded or linked objects)—PPT2002-6-1
- Inserting Word tables on slides (as either embedded or linked objects)—PPT2002-6-3

task reference roundup

Task	Page #	Preferred Method
Insert an Image From a File	PP 4.13	• Position the cursor for insertion
		• Click the **Insert Picture** button on the Drawing toolbar
		• Navigate to the picture
		• Do one of the following:
		• Click **Insert** to embed the image
		• Click the drop-down arrow next to Insert and click **Link to File** to create a link to the picture
Insert WordArt	PP 4.16	• Click the slide that will contain the WordArt
		• Click the **Insert WordArt** icon on the **Drawing** toolbar
		• Select a style from the WordArt Gallery
		• Click **OK**
		• Enter the WordArt text in the Edit WordArt Text dialog box
		• Apply formatting as desired to set font, size, bold, or italic
		• Click **OK**
		• Use the WordArt, shape, color, shadow
Save an Art Object	PP 4.18	• Select the picture, WordArt, or AutoShape that you want to save
		• Do one of the following:
		• Copy your object to the clipboard and then paste it in the desired collection of the open Media Gallery. You can also set keywords for this new clip
		• Right-click the object and click **Save Picture**. In the Save dialog box, select the format, name the object, and click Save
Create a Simple Table	PP 4.22	• Select the slide to contain the table
		• Click the **Insert Table** button on the Standard toolbar
		• Select the desired number of rows and columns by clicking the bottom right cell
Create a Linked or Embedded Object From an Existing Word or Excel file	PP 4.26	• Click the slide that will contain the object
		• On the **Insert** menu, click **Object**
		• Click the **Create from file** option button

task reference roundup

Task	Page #	Preferred Method
		• Click the **Browse** button and navigate to the file
		• Click the Link check box to create a linked file
		• Uncheck the Link check box to embed the file
		• Click **OK**
Create a Microsoft Graph	PP 4.28	• Select the most appropriate content layout for the slide that will contain the chart
		• Click the **Chart** icon in the Content placeholder to activate Microsoft Graph
		• Enter the data to be charted in the datasheet with headings in the first row and column, and data in cells that can be referenced with a letter and number (A1)
		• Use the **Chart** menu to select chart type, subtype, and options
		• Right-click on any chart object to format it
		• Click the slide background to exit Microsoft Graph
Create an Organization Chart	PP 4.36	• Select the most appropriate content layout for the slide that will contain the chart
		• Click the **Insert Diagram or Organization Chart** icon in the Content placeholder to activate Microsoft Graph
		• Select Organization Chart from the Diagram Gallery and click **OK**
		• Click in a chart rectangle to add descriptive text
		• Select a rectangle and use the Organization Chart toolbar to add coworkers, subordinates, and assistants to build the desired structure
		• Use the Layout and Design Gallery menu options to control chart organization
		• Click the slide background to exit
Create a Diagram (Cycle, Radial, Pyramid, Venn, or Target)	PP 4.39	• Select the most appropriate content layout for the slide that will contain the chart
		• Click the **Insert Diagram or Organization Chart** icon in the Content placeholder to activate Microsoft Graph
		• Select the desired diagram type from the Diagram Gallery and click **OK**
		• Click in a chart text placeholder to add descriptive text
		• Use the toolbar to build the desired structure
		• Use the Layout and Design Gallery menu options to control chart organization
		• Click the slide background to exit

chapter four

review of terminology

CROSSWORD PUZZLE

Across

2. Chart depicting relationships to a central element
6. The less common name for an image created of dots
7. A hierarchical chart
10. A copy of an object placed on a slide is said to be _____
12. An image created using mathematical shapes
13. When an image displays on a slide, but is not part of the PowerPoint file, it is _____
14. Converts numbers to bars, lines, or pies

Down

1. Drawings that can be inserted in a document
2. Type of handle used to turn a graphic on its side
3. The gray buttons that select a row or column of a datasheet
4. Contains the data used to create a graph
5. Type of gallery that holds clips
8. The words used to search for clips in the media gallery
9. Mathematical name for an image created using shapes
11. A type of image created of dots

LEVEL ONE

PP 4.45

POWERPOINT

www.mhhe.com/i-series

review of concepts

chapter four

LEVEL TWO

FILL-IN

1. _____ is a tool on the Drawing toolbar that will create text with effects like shapes and perspectives.
2. When you save customized artwork, it can be placed in _____ or _____ .
3. You can draw the cells of a table using the _____ button of the Standard toolbar.
4. The placeholders on a slide are determined by its _____ .
5. If you do not click the Link check box when inserting an object, it will be _____ .
6. A row of data in a Microsoft Graph datasheet is typically a(n) _____ .

REVIEW QUESTIONS

Each of the following topics should be addressed in one to three paragraphs.

1. Explain how you would graph the weekly price of gasoline at two local stations over the last month.
2. Discuss how to search for and select graphics for a presentation on South America.
3. Discuss how to select a chart type to plot a single data series with four data values representing the total sales for each quarter last year.
4. Create a presentation diagram showing the management structure of your school or workplace.
5. What type of diagram could be used to depict your daily routine (get up, brush teeth, . . .)? Why?
6. What resources can you use to find artwork for your presentations?

CREATE THE QUESTION

For each of the following answers, create the question.

ANSWER	QUESTION
1. Drag the green handle of a selected image until the desired angle is achieved.	_____
2. Because the dots become too visible or grainy as the image size is increased.	_____
3. It stores clip art, photographs, movies, and sounds.	_____
4. A Content placeholder.	_____
5. Right-click the object and choose Format . . . from the pop-up menu.	_____

FACT OR FICTION

For each of the following determine whether the statement is fact, fiction, or both and present your arguments for that conclusion.

1. The same formatting can be applied to all objects on a slide containing multiple object types.
2. When multiple images are stacked, you cannot select the bottom image.
3. Updating keywords can improve the performance of Media Gallery searches.
4. PowerPoint filters will allow you to insert graphics of any known format into a slide.
5. A linked object can be edited directly in PowerPoint.

PP 4.46

chapter four

hands-on projects

practice

1. Preparing for the Triathlon

Cathy Farraday is preparing for her first triathlon. She has been training for months—swimming, biking, and running. Now the big event is almost upon her. The day before the race all participants assemble at a hotel to pick up their race packets, their race chip to verify their times on race day, and have their race number drawn on their arm with indelible ink. Cathy has been asked to speak about her training at the First Timers Seminar. Cathy wants to show the audience that a regular exercise routine really does improve performance.

1. Start PowerPoint and open **pp04TriathlonTraining.ppt**
2. Browse the Microsoft Design Gallery for clip art showing the three sports (running, swimming, and biking). Arrange and size the clips to create a pleasing display on the title slide
3. Move to the second slide titled Starting Training. Browse the Microsoft Design Gallery for clip art showing various workout routines. Add at least two clips to this slide
4. Move to the third slide titled Eating. Below the bulleted text, add a calorie distribution chart using the following data
   a. Right-click outside the chart but within the placeholder. Choose **Chart Type** and select **Pie**
   b. Choose a **3-D** subtype
   c. Click outside the chart to complete the edit
5. Add clip art to the fourth slide related to the last bullet
6. Move to the fifth slide titled Running Progress and insert a table of running times created in Microsoft Word
   a. Choose **Object** from the **Insert** menu
   b. Select the **Create from File** button and browse to the **pp04RunTimes.doc** file. Leave the link box unchecked and click **OK**
   c. Center the table on the slide. Remember, you won't be able to resize the table
7. Move to the sixth slide titled A Month before the Race, and add two copies of the same biking image
8. Move to the seventh slide and add an appropriate graphic
9. Add animation schemes to each slide
10. Save your file as **<yourname>TriathlonTraining.ppt** and exit PowerPoint

FIGURE 4.41

Calorie Distribution Datasheet

	A	B	C	D	E
1 3-D Pie 1	Carbohydr 55%	Fat 30%	Protein 15%		
2					
3					
4					
5					

hands-on projects

chapter four

challenge

1. Alternative Health Services

AHS provides alternative health products across the United States. Its products include herbal and medicinal remedies as well as alternative health books. The company is divided into four divisions: Eastern, Southern, Mid-Western, and Western. Each division has a regional manager responsible for sales reps with designated territories. The sales reps market the products to medical establishments, health stores, and alternative health societies. They are responsible for making the contacts, ordering products and supplies, and delivering them. Monthly, sales reps send in their sales reports to their regional manager. Quarterly, the regional manager presents the sales statistics at the corporate sales meeting.

Jason Middleton, regional manager of the Mid-Western Division, will be presenting a quarterly report to headquarters next week. He has asked you to prepare a PowerPoint presentation for the Fourth Quarter Sales Meeting. Jason is pleased with the improvement in this quarter's results. He believes the division's success is due to a better allocation of his sales reps' time. He now has support staff complete much of the paperwork, thereby freeing up the sales reps to focus on clients.

1. Start PowerPoint and open **pp04AHS.ppt**
2. Insert a second slide with an organization chart depicting the structure of the Mid-Western Division. Start with Jason as the regional manager and include LaDonna Ballet as an assistant with the title of Office Manager. Add four of your friends as subordinates. Use Territory x Sales for your friends' titles where x is a territory number between 1 and 4.
3. Insert a third slide to contain a title and a table. Title the slide **Mid-Western Results** and create and format the table shown in Figure 4.42
4. Insert a fourth slide displaying a 3-D column chart comparing visits and sales by week. Title the slide **Visits and Sales**
5. Insert a fifth slide displaying a 3-D pie chart with each wedge representing one week of products. Title the slide **Products**
6. Add appropriate graphics to the quarterly comparison slide (this should be slide 6)
7. Add graphics to the last slide
8. Insert a summary slide with the titles from all but the first presentation slide
9. Add an animation scheme to each slide
10. Create a summary slide
11. Save your presentation as **<yourname>pp04AHS.ppt** and exit PowerPoint

FIGURE 4.42

Mid-Western Division Sales

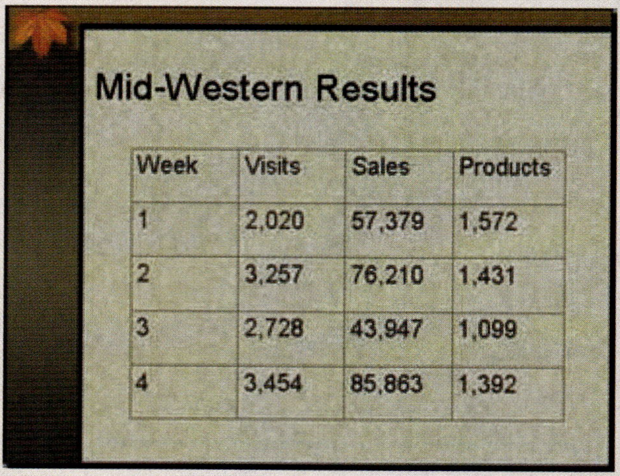

Mid-Western Results

Week	Visits	Sales	Products
1	2,020	57,379	1,572
2	3,257	76,210	1,431
3	2,728	43,947	1,099
4	3,454	85,863	1,392

chapter four
hands-on projects
on the web

LEVEL THREE

1. Chef of the West Cooking School

This school, founded by Scott York, opened three years ago in southern California on four acres of park-like grounds. It consists of 8 state-of-the-art kitchens and 17 full-time faculty. Over 850 classes are offered each year. Classes range from the very basic to preparation of elaborate banquets. In addition to the classes, Chef of the West promotes York's book, *You Can Cook Anything!*, and other products through its Web site, www.ChefWestSchool.com. Scott would like to get an idea of how his school compares with other cooking schools. His areas of interest are the number of kitchens, faculty, and classes given each year. He also wonders if the other schools use the Web to promote their products. He wants you to check Peter Kump's New York Cooking School and at least one other school so he can see how Chef of the West compares. You decide to create a PowerPoint presentation using charts and tables for illustration after searching the Web for the data. You add graphics to enhance your presentation.

1. Start PowerPoint and open **pp04ChefSchool.ppt**
2. Use your favorite Web search engine to locate at least two cooking schools. Document the number of kitchens, the number of faculty, number of classes, and whether or not products are being sold
3. Add **Prepared by: <yourname>** as a footer for the entire presentation
4. Add appropriate graphics to slide 2
5. On slide 3 add the names and URLs for the cooking schools you researched. Add appropriate graphics
6. Open **pp04Kitchens.doc**, a Microsoft Word document with a table. Add your research to the table and save the document as **<yourname>pp04Kitchens.doc**. Use the Insert menu to embed this table in slide 4 and add supporting graphics. Position the table in the center of the slide
7. On slide 5 create a PowerPoint table showing the number of faculty at each school. Add a border to all table cells. Peter Kump's school has 31 faculty. For the column headings, increase the font size and apply both bold and shadow
8. Use Microsoft Graph to create a chart on slide 6 showing the number of classes offered at each school. Peter Kump's school offers 700 classes
9. Update slide 7 with your research and add supporting graphics
10. Adjust the text of slide 8 to reflect your research and add supporting graphics
11. Save your presentation as **<yourname>pp04ChefSchool.ppt** and exit PowerPoint

PP 4.49

POWERPOINT

www.mhhe.com/i-series

hands-on projects

chapter four

e-business

1. Balloon Adventures

Balloon Adventures takes groups of people for rides in hot air balloons. The gondola holds a maximum of 12 people at $100 a person. Included in the price is a champagne breakfast after the ride. Before a balloon ride, the pilot checks the air currents. Takeoff occurs only if the wind is minimal, which will occur early in the morning. While a van drives to hotels to pick up customers, the crew sets up the balloon. After the balloon is airborne, a chase vehicle is used to track it. At the end of the ride when the balloon is close to the ground, the crew grabs lines and secures the balloon to the ground. Balloon Adventures clients come mostly from word of mouth. A kiosk placed in the city's hotels and links from hotel Web sites have also helped to publicize the rides. You have been asked to prepare the presentation for the kiosks and Web links.

1. Start PowerPoint and open **pp04BalloonAdv.ppt**
2. On the first slide
   a. Use WordArt to create an artistic rendering of **Balloon Adventures**
   b. Rotate the WordArt
   c. Search the Microsoft Media Gallery for clips of hot air balloons and insert one on this slide
   d. Add the subtitle Soar the Skies! in a 30-point decorative font and color to complement the WordArt
   e. Add a text box with **Flights daily in summer** in a complementary format
   f. Arrange the content so that two of the text elements overlap the image
3. Move to slide 2, add an appropriate graphic, and copy the title. Use the copy of the title to create a shadow image. Use a light color on the top image and leave the shadow image black
4. Move to slide 3 and add graphics from a source other than the clip gallery like Microsoft online. Use WordArt to create captions related to the clips: for example, **Hear the roar of the fire!** Or, **Feel the ground leave your feet!**
5. On slides 4 through 6 add graphics, set background color, and adjust the text to create the maximum impact for the content
6. On slide 7, add WordArt **We're waiting for you!** Add content-related images. Adjust the background and text to complement the other slide objects
7. Add a moderate animation scheme to each slide
8. Preview
9. Save the presentation as **<yourname>BalloonAdv.ppt** and exit PowerPoint

FIGURE 4.43

Sample Balloon Adventures Opening Slide

chapter four

hands-on projects

around the world

1. Western Reclamation Services

Western Reclamation Services designs hydroelectric plants, drilling tunnels, and diversion systems for water reclamation projects. Its clients can be cities, the government (in conjunction with the Bureau of Reclamation), or even other countries. The City of Hailey has contacted WRS to explore building a hydroelectric plant on the Hailey River. The plant will serve the city with both water and electric power. Since the city has experienced recent rapid growth, the city fathers anticipate increased water and electrical demands. The plant can solve these issues. WRS has researched the feasibility of this project and is now ready to present a preliminary report of its findings to city engineers. Using WRS's outline you have been asked to prepare a PowerPoint presentation for this client meeting.

1. Start PowerPoint
2. Open the Microsoft Word file **pp04PrelimReport.doc** as the outline for your presentation
3. Apply the **Echo** Design Template to the presentation
4. Insert a new first slide with Title slide layout

   tip: *The slide will insert as the second slide. Drag it to the first position*

   a. Select and delete the title placeholder
   b. Use WordArt to create the title **Preliminary Report**
   c. Add the subtitle **Hailey Hydroelectric Plan Prepared by Western Reclamation Services**
   d. Make the second line of the subtitle a smaller size
   e. Right-click on the slide background and use the Fill Effects option of the Background menu to create a gradient background to complement the design template
   f. Insert **pp04HaileyLogo.wmf** from the files for this chapter
   g. Recolor the logo to match the design template's color scheme
   h. Adjust the size and placement of the logo to create a balanced slide
5. Add the footer **Western Reclamation Services** to show on all slides
6. Locate a picture appropriate for the slide 2 background and insert it as the background
7. Delete all of the content of slide 7 and create a Radial chart with Recommendations in the middle with the bulleted points surrounding it. Press Enter after the first word of two-word entries. Apply the 3-D Color style and widen the diagram to fill the page
8. Add content-supporting graphics to each of the remaining slides
9. Add subtle Animation Schemes to each slide
10. Save the presentation as **<yourname>pp04PrelimReport.ppt** and exit PowerPoint

FIGURE 4.44

Sample Preliminary Report Opening Slide

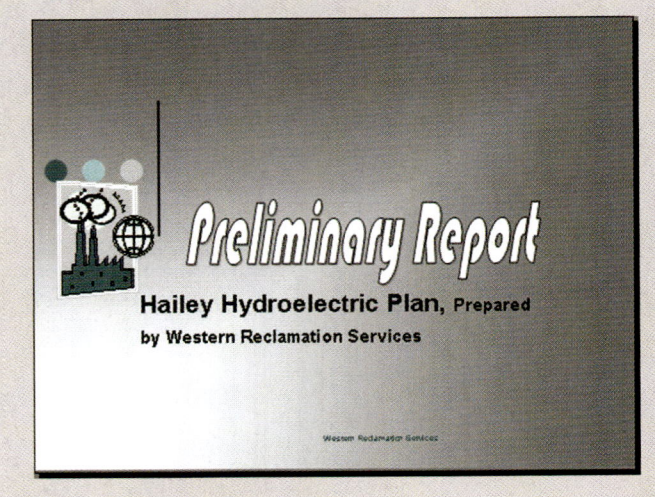

running project

Montgomery-Wellish Foods, Inc.: Presentation Skills

Daniel Wellish believes presentation skills are the single most important attribute a trainee can learn. Managers, by nature, are people oriented. They use their skills not just to prepare reports but to inspire, inform, and persuade. To the degree they can communicate clearly and cogently, they will be successful. Daniel has asked you to prepare a PowerPoint presentation on presentation skills to the new trainees.

1. Open a blank PowerPoint presentation using the Pixel design template. Use the Color Schemes link to evaluate the available color schemes and settle on the second from the last
2. On the title slide delete the title placeholder and create a WordArt title, **Presentation Skills**
3. Add the subtitle
   Montgomery-Wellish Foods, Inc. Training Program
   Adjust the subtitle placeholder
4. Create each of the following slides. Apply at least two content-enhancing graphic elements to each slide
   - Preparation
     - As important as the presentation
     - Know your audience
     - Identify topic purpose
   - Opening
     - Warm to audience
     - Tell what you will tell
     - Convey your enthusiasm
   - Organize
     - Consider topic purpose
     - KISS method
     - Short duration
   - Use Graphics
     - Graphics
     - Charts
     - Sounds
     - Transitions
     - Text
   - Rehearse
     - Ensure a smooth presentation
     - Use gestures
     - Eliminate body mannerisms
     - No "ums" and "ahs"
   - Closing
     - Summarize your points
     - Offer relevant conclusions
     - Audience determines closing
       - Commitment call
       - Inspirational
       - Benefits
5. Add Animation Schemes to each presentation slide
6. Save your file as
   <yourname>pp04MWFoodsPresentation.ppt
   and exit PowerPoint

FIGURE 4.45

Sample Presentation Skills Opening Slide

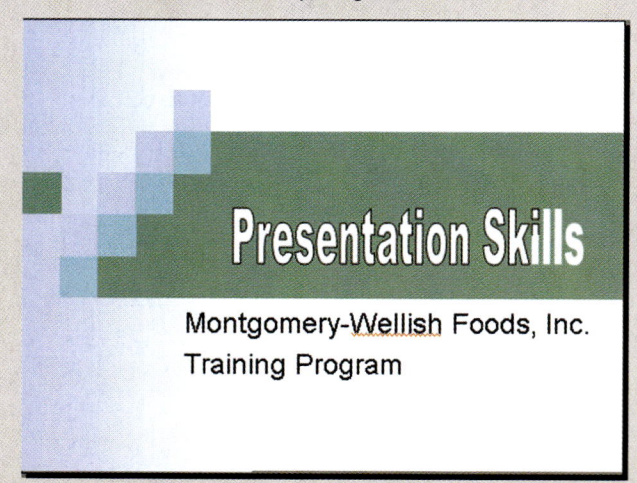

NOTES

www.mhhe.com/i-series

POWERPOINT

NOTES

www.mhhe.com/i-series

did you know?

ants *don't sleep.*

over *80 percent of professional boxers have suffered brain damage.*

the *first Oreo cookie was sold in 1912.*

dragonflies *are one of the fastest insects, flying 50 to 60 mph.*

a *pineapple is a berry.*

there *are 31,557,600 seconds in a year.*

frogs *live on every continent except _____.*

Chapter Objectives

- **Apply and customize slide transitions—PPT2002-4-3**
- **Animate slide objects**
- **Insert and configure sound, movie, and animated gif clips—PPT2002-6-2**
- **Create a self-running presentation**
- **Use presentation rehearsal features—PPT2002-4-7**

CHAPTER

5

five

Creating a Multimedia Presentation

chapter case

Teaching Vital Statistics with PowerPoint

Connor Mackenzie and his partner Margarita Gonzalez are medical trainers who work with families in crisis at the Center for Family Provided Medical Treatment. A wide range of medical events can cause a family member to require medical supervision and care on an ongoing basis. The level of care families need to learn to provide can be as simple as monitoring vital statistics or as complex as ongoing physical therapy or the administration of special medications.

Initially the center provided only individual planning and instruction to each family, but they came to realize that family members giving medical care needed a support group and a way to refresh and update their care skills. While providing individual care plans with training on how to furnish that treatment is critical, contact with other families is an effective way to relieve the stresses of constant care and provide ongoing training.

FIGURE 5.1
Vital Statistics Kiosk

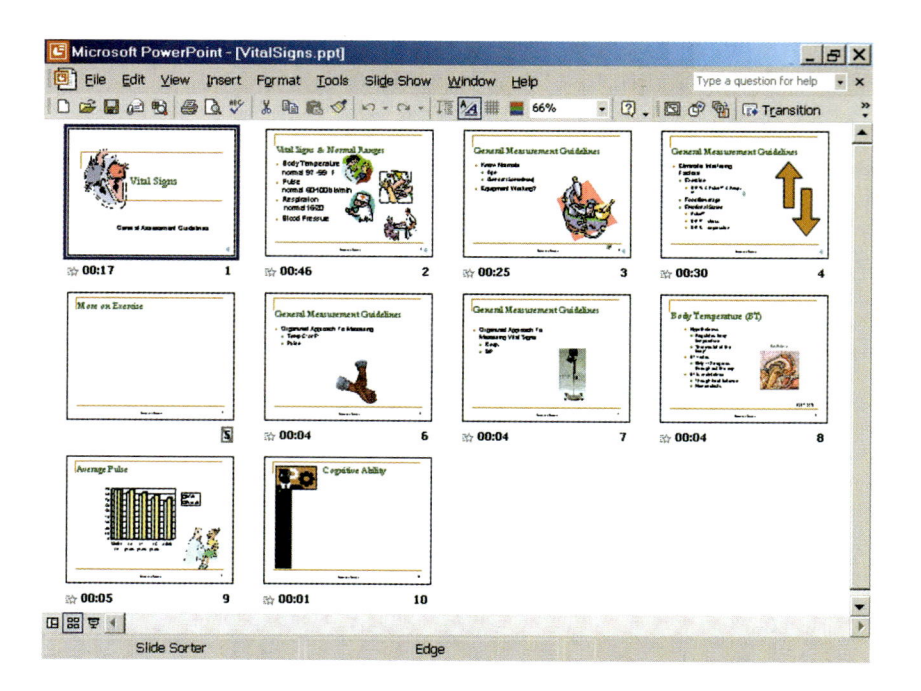

In addition to having gatherings for families, Connor and Margarita have developed short family seminars that encompass the basic skills needed by all family members. Each presentation is 30 minutes or less and covers appropriate skills and statistics for all patient groups.

Since the tradition of family care training has been one-on-one, Connor and Margarita will develop new presentations based on materials they have gathered. The most frequently used presentation describes common vital statistics and their norms. Caregivers must understand this foundational material before moving on to more specific instructions of how to assess a patient. This presentation has been ported to PowerPoint from a Word document and some relevant graphics added. Connor and Margarita want to add animations and sounds to create a self-running kiosk. With a self-running kiosk, family members will be able to review the material at their own convenience.

> **CHAPTER OUTLINE**
>
> **5.1** Using Animations
>
> **5.2** Using Other Audio Multimedia Components

SESSION 5.1 USING ANIMATIONS

Animation is an important component of a compelling PowerPoint presentation. Motion of slide objects helps draw the audience's attention to important presentation points. During a slide show, animations control the way a slide enters and leaves the screen, how text moves on and off the screen, and how other slide objects behave. These behaviors were introduced in Chapter 3 with preset animations called Animation Schemes. While Animation Schemes are easy to apply and add interest to a presentation, they offer no variety and only text is animated. This session will address customized animation of any slide object.

ANIMATING SLIDE OBJECTS

Animation can be used to add motion to any slide object including text, graphics, and charts. Slide objects can be animated individually or in groups. For example, a line of text can be animated as a unit or each character can have motion.

Slide Transitions

The largest PowerPoint object that can be animated is a slide. **Slide Transitions** control the visual effect that displays between slides in a slide show. The available transitions range from mild to dramatic in their impact. All slides can use the same transition, or different transitions can be assigned to each slide.

It is often tempting to use a different transition between each slide, but this can be distracting if dramatic effects are being used. Choose transitions that are appropriate for the audience and presentation content. More importantly strike a balance between using unique transitions to make the presentation interesting and keeping the focus on the content.

PP 5.3

POWERPOINT

task reference
Apply a Slide Transition
- Select the slide(s) the transition will be applied to. If no slide(s) is selected, the transition will be applied to all slides
- From the **Slide Show** menu select **Slide Transition**
- Select a transition effect

FIGURE 5.2

Slide Transition Task Pane

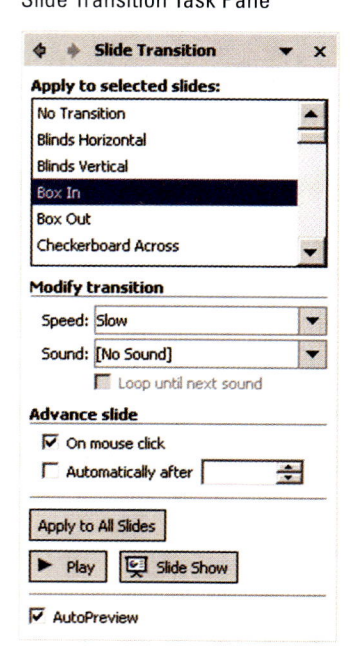

Adding transitions to VitalSigns.ppt:

1. Initiate PowerPoint and open **PP05VitalSigns.ppt**
2. Select the first slide
3. From the **Slide Show** menu select **Slide Transition**
4. In the Slide Transition task pane, choose **Shape Circle**

tip: *If AutoPreview is checked, the selected transition will be demonstrated on the current slide automatically*

5. Click the **Play** button to see the result
6. Click the **Slide Show** button to start the slide show and view a full screen version of the transition
7. Press **Esc** to end the presentation
8. Set the transition for slide 2 to **Newsflash**
9. Set the transition for slide 3 to **Wheel Clockwise, 4 Spokes**
10. Set the transition for slide 4 to **Wheel Clockwise, 3 Spokes**
11. Set transitions that you find appealing for the remaining slides
12. Save the presentation as **<yourname>PP05VitalSigns.ppt**

anotherword
. . . on setting slide transitions
You can create the same transition settings for multiple slides by selecting the slides in the outline pane and then setting the transition. Multiple contiguous slides can be selected by clicking the first slide and then holding the Shift key while clicking the last slide. Noncontiguous slides can be selected by clicking the first slide and then holding down the Ctrl key while clicking subsequent slides.

For most presentations it is best to use the same or similar transitions for each slide. Similar transitions help the presentation to be more cohesive. More dramatic transitions can be used to indicate a topic change or the importance of a particular slide. To improve the effect of a transition, its speed and other ***properties*** can be customized.

Setting VitalSigns.ppt transition properties:

1. Initiate PowerPoint and open **PP05VitalSigns.ppt**
2. Select the first slide and make the following settings in the Slide Transitions panel of the Task pane
   a. Set the Speed to **Fast**
   b. Set the sound to **Click**
   c. Check both Advance Slide options and set the time to 2 seconds

3. Move to slide 2
   a. Set the Speed to **Medium**
   b. Set the sound to **Chime**
   c. Do not set a time option for advancing the slide
4. Move to slide **1** and use Slide Show view to see the impact of these changes
5. Save the presentation

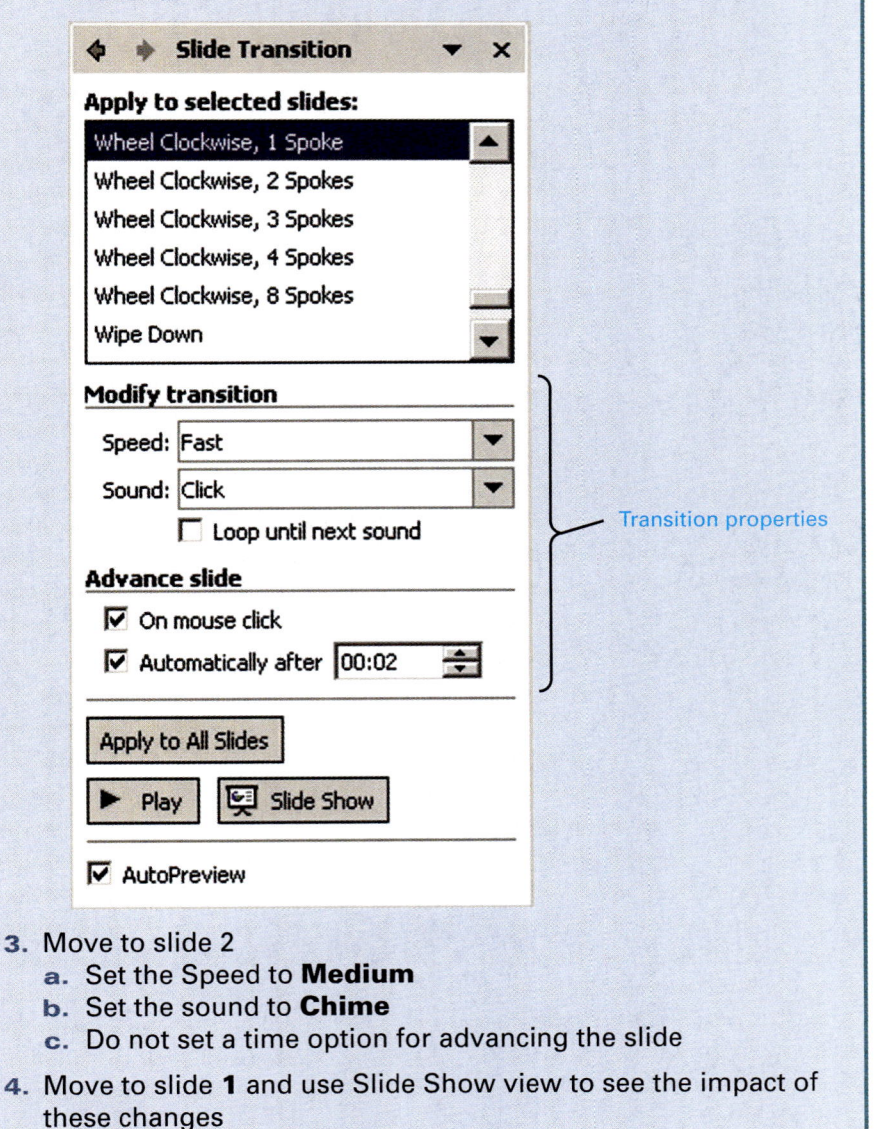

FIGURE 5.3
Setting Transition Properties

To improve their impact, transitions can be modified to control the pace and add a sound. The pace can be matched to a sound so that all of the elements of the transition begin and end together. ***Slide timings*** can be recorded while practicing the presentation or set in the Slide Transition pane. The timing options cause the presentation to advance to the next slide using a mouse click, a preset time period, or both.

task reference
Set Slide Timing While Rehearsing

- Activate the timing feature
  - On the **Slide Show** menu, click **Set Up Show**
  - Under **Advance slides,** click **Use timings, if present**
- Set the time for each slide
  - On the **Slide Show** menu click **Rehearse Timings**
  - Rehearse the show to set timings automatically as you advance
  - At the end of the show, click **Yes** to accept automatic timings or **No** to start again

another way

... to Set Timings for a Slide Show

When you know the speed that is appropriate for a presentation, you can set the times manually by repeating the following steps for each timed slide.

- Select the slide to be timed
- On the **Slide Show** menu, click **Slide Transition**
- In the Task pane under Advance slide, scroll to the desired amount of time

Adding automatic timings to VitalSigns.ppt:

1. Initiate PowerPoint and open **PP05VitalSigns.ppt**
2. On the **Slide Show** menu, click **Set Up Show**
3. Under **Advance slides,** click **Use timings, if present**
4. Select the first slide
5. On the **Slide Show** menu click **Rehearse Timings**
6. Move through the presentation practicing your narration at the desired speed
7. When you reach the end of the slide show, answer **Yes** to save your times

tip: *Answering **No** will not save the times. To set new times return to step 3*

8. Review the times displayed in Slide Sorter view
9. Run the presentation without clicking to review the automatic timing
10. Save the presentation

Automatic timings can be used to keep a speaker-led presentation on task, or to create a self-running kiosk. When the presentation is self-running, it can be initiated by a user or looped to continuously run. Self-running presentations often include sound files with slide narration that can be used to control slide timings as well.

Animating and Dimming Text

Any object on a PowerPoint slide can have motion added to it using **Custom Animation** settings from the Custom Animation panel of the Task pane. The preset animation schemes previously introduced use default settings to animate slide text. Using Custom Animations, each character of text on a slide can be controlled independently, grouped by word, or animated by paragraph.

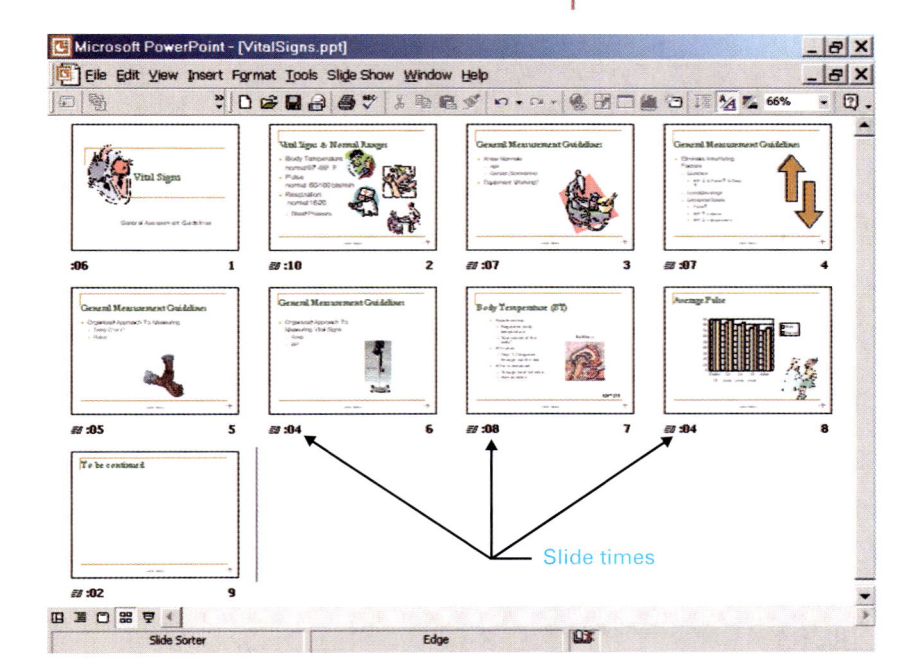

FIGURE 5.4
Timings in Slide Sorter View

Text can be animated on Entrance, Exit, or both using a wide range of standard motion paths or a custom path developed to exactly match slide layout. Emphasis like a font change, color change, spinning, and desaturation can be added. The effects chosen are determined by how dramatic the presentation needs to be.

task reference
Adding Custom Animations to Text
- In Normal view, select the text object to be animated
- From the Task pane drop-down list select **Custom Animation**
- In the custom Animation Task pane click **Add Effects** and select the desired effect(s)

Adding Entrance Animations to VitalSigns text:

1. Initiate PowerPoint and open **PP05VitalSigns.ppt**
2. Move to slide **1** and select the title placeholder containing the text Vital Signs
3. From the **Slide Show** menu, click **Set Up Show**, then set the Advance Slides option to **Manually** to turn off the previously set timings, and then click **OK**
4. If necessary, select Custom Animation from the Task pane drop-down list
5. In the Custom Animation pane, click **Add Effect**, pause over **Entrance,** and choose **More Effects** to view the full list of available entrance effects

POWERPOINT

FIGURE 5.5

Animating the Title Placeholder

Task pane drop-down list selection

Selected text object

Entrance effects

6. Preview several available options

tip: *Check Preview Effect and move the Add Entrance Effect dialog box to preview your selections*

7. Select **Crawl In** and click **OK**

8. On the Custom Animation panel of the Task pane
   a. Set the Direction to **From Left**
   b. Set the Speed to **Medium**
   c. Drop down the complete list of modifications, click **Effect Options,** and set the Animate Text option to **By letter**
   d. Click **OK**

9. Use **Play** to preview the settings

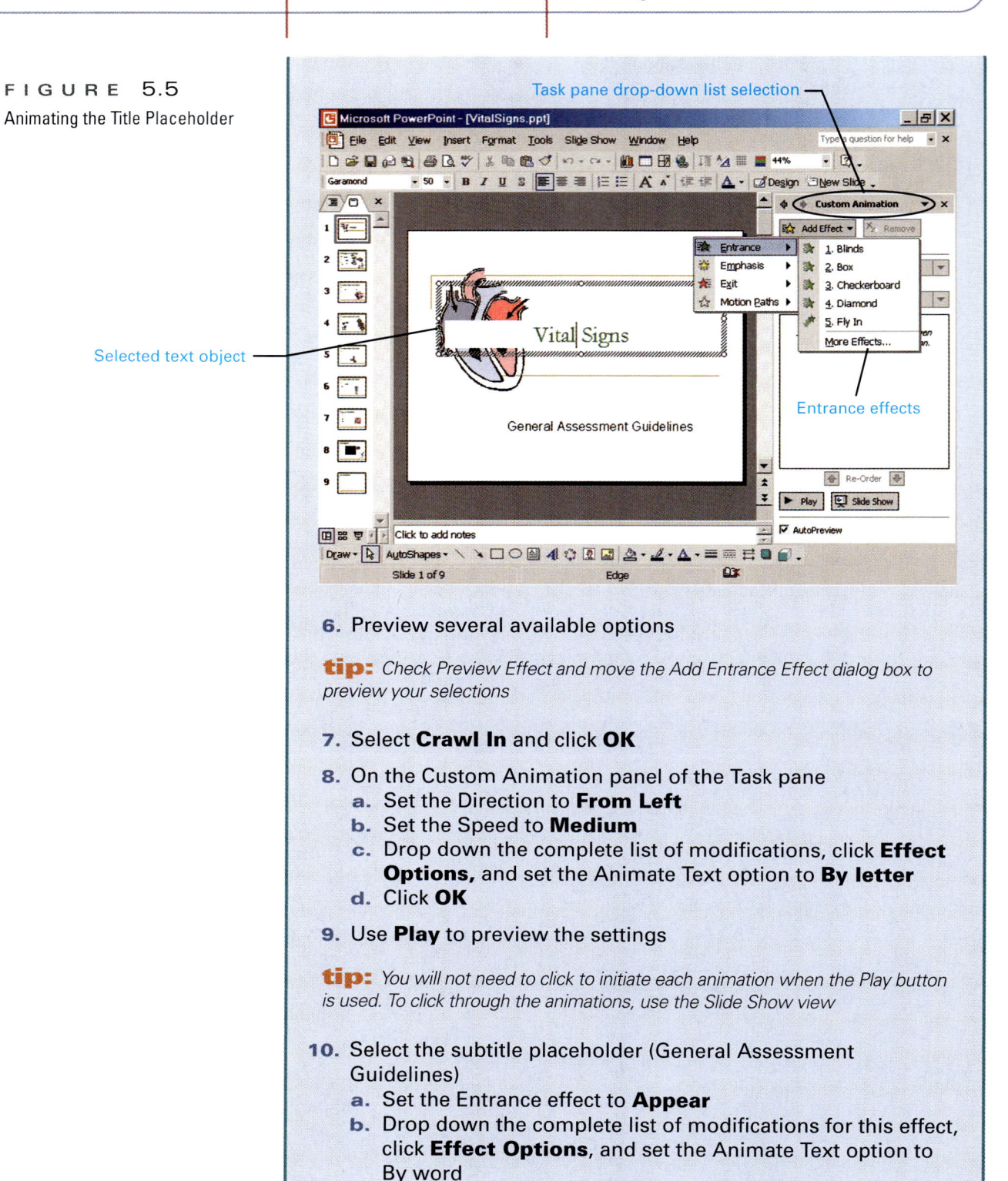

tip: *You will not need to click to initiate each animation when the Play button is used. To click through the animations, use the Slide Show view*

10. Select the subtitle placeholder (General Assessment Guidelines)
    a. Set the Entrance effect to **Appear**
    b. Drop down the complete list of modifications for this effect, click **Effect Options**, and set the Animate Text option to By word

11. Use **Play** to preview the settings

12. Save the presentation

Effects are placed in the Custom Animation list in the order that they are specified. A nonprinting number tag identifies each animation on the slide. The number tag does not display during the slide show, but serves to

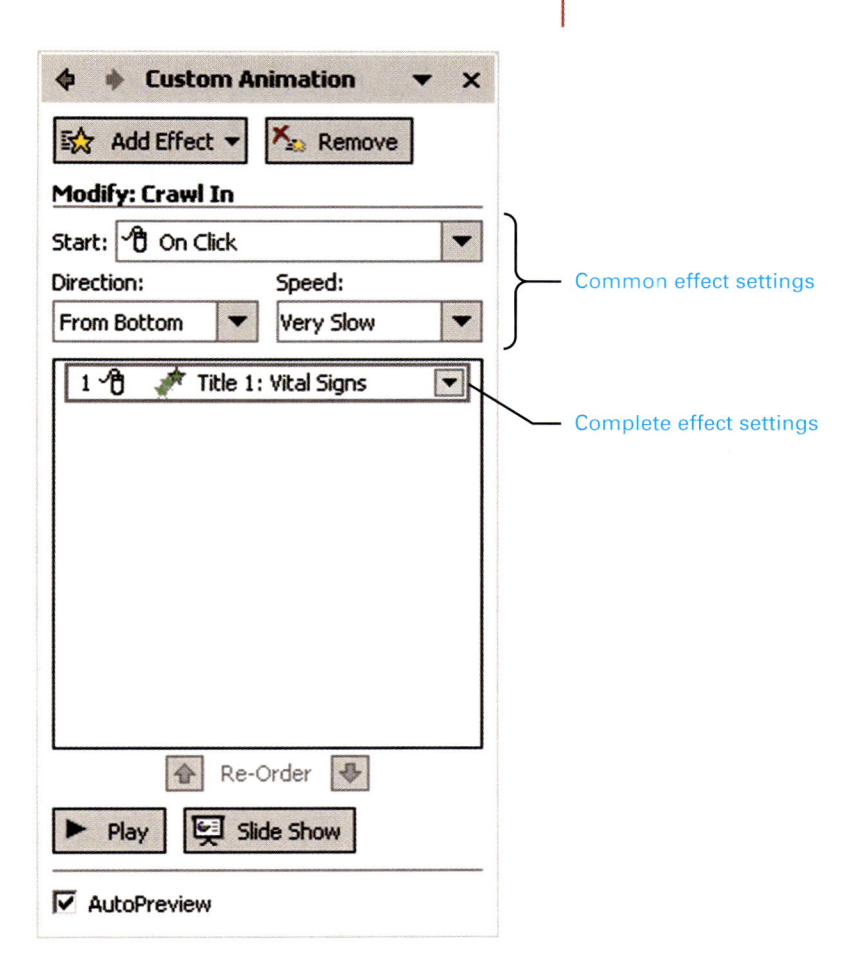

FIGURE 5.6
Modifying Effect Properties

– Common effect settings
– Complete effect settings

uniquely identify each animation. Additional effects like a brush-on underline, change in text color, or spinning text can be applied to the text already displayed on a slide to add further emphasis.

Adding Emphasis Animations to VitalSigns text:

1. Initiate PowerPoint and open **PP05VitalSigns.ppt** with slide 1 active
2. Select the title placeholder
3. If necessary, select **Custom Animation** from the Task pane drop-down list
4. Click the **Add Effect** button in the Task pane, pause over **Emphasis,** and choose **More Effects** to view the full list of available entrance effects
5. Preview several available options
6. Select **Brush On Underline** and click **OK**
7. Use **Play** to preview the animations
8. Save the presentation

FIGURE 5.7
Emphasis Effects

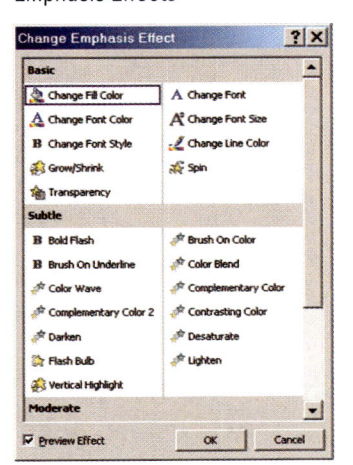

POWERPOINT

The same basic effects that control how text enters a slide can be applied to their exit.

FIGURE 5.8
Exit Effects

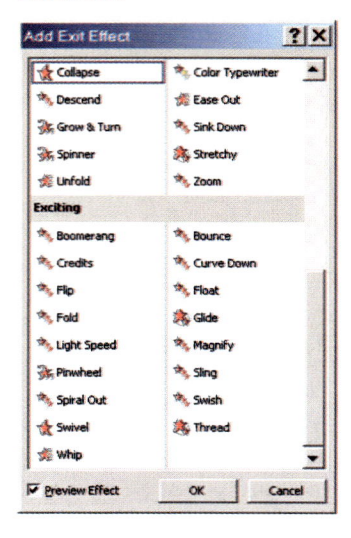

> ### Adding Exit Animations to VitalSigns text:
> 1. Initiate PowerPoint and open **PP05VitalSigns.ppt** with slide 1 active and the title selected
> 2. If necessary, select Custom Animation from the Task pane drop-down list
> 3. Click the **Add Effect** button in the Task pane, pause over **Exit,** and choose **More Effects** to view the full list of available entrance effects
> 4. Preview several available options
> 5. Select **Whip** and click **OK**
> 6. Use **Play** to preview the animations
> 7. Save the presentation

Animated text can have a ***dimming effect*** applied to it by changing its color. This feature is particularly useful in presenter-led or narrated presentations to help keep the audience on topic by dimming text that has already been discussed. Normally dimming is applied to the bulleted text contained in a body text placeholder. When there are multiple bullets, the animation of a bulleted list can be set to load all bullets as a unit, each bullet, or by word or each bullet letter.

> ### Adding dimming effects to VitalSigns text:
> 1. Initiate PowerPoint and open **PP05VitalSigns.ppt**
> 2. Move to slide 2 and click in the body placeholder
> 3. If necessary, select **Custom Animation** from the Task pane drop-down list
> 4. Click the **Add Effect** button in the Task pane, pause over **Entrance,** and choose **Crawl In**
> 5. Use the double carat to expand the Custom Animation list to display all of the components of this animation (see Figure 5.9)
> 6. Drop down the complete list of modifications for this effect and choose **Effect Options** to open the dialog box
>   a. On the Text Animation tab, drop down the Group Text list and review the options (Keep the By 1st level paragraphs selection)
>
>   **tip:** *The As One Object selection will move all bullets simultaneously*
>
>   b. On the Effect tab, set the Direction option to **From Right**, the After Animation color to **gray**, and click **OK**

FIGURE 5.9

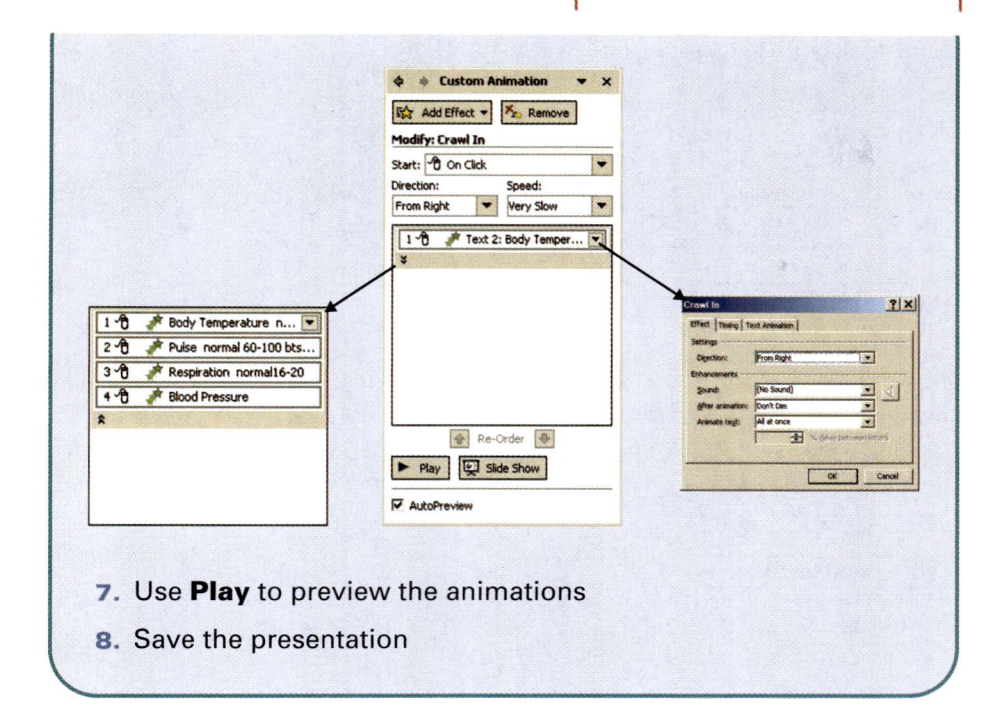

Animating a Bulleted List

7. Use **Play** to preview the animations
8. Save the presentation

The options of the Text Animation tab control how the text is grouped for animation. Set the animation level to correspond with the spoken component of the presentation. As you click through the bullets, the animation for the current bullet plays and any previous bullet will have the After Animation color applied.

Animating Graphic Objects

In addition to animating text, PowerPoint has the ability to animate graphics, charts, and drawn objects. The options for these objects are very similar to those for animating text.

Animating VitalSigns graphics:

1. Initiate PowerPoint and open **PP05VitalSigns.ppt**
2. Move to slide 2 and click in the body temperature image
3. Click the **Add Effect** button in the Task pane, pause over **Entrance,** and choose **Crawl In**
4. Use the Reorder buttons to move this image animation to a position just under the associated bullet (see Figure 5.10)
5. Set the Start option to **With Previous** to cause the bullet content and image to enter simultaneously
6. Use **Play** to preview the animations
7. Repeat steps 3 to 5 to animate the remaining images with the appropriate bullet
8. Use **Play** to preview the animations
9. Save the presentation

anotherway
... to Change the Animation Order

The steps demonstrated the use of the Reorder buttons to change animation order. Selecting an animation and dragging it to a new location will also work.

POWERPOINT

FIGURE 5.10
Reordering Animations

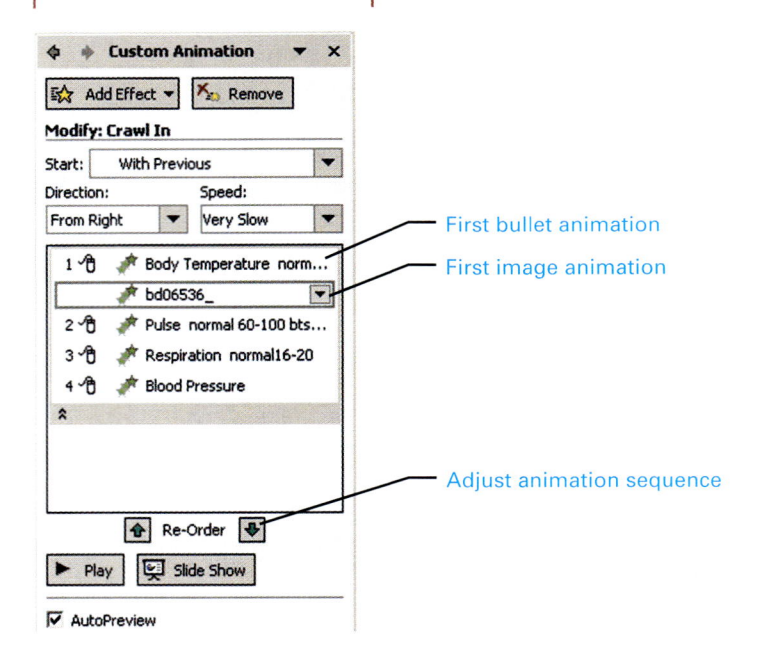

FIGURE 5.11
Final Slide 2 Animations

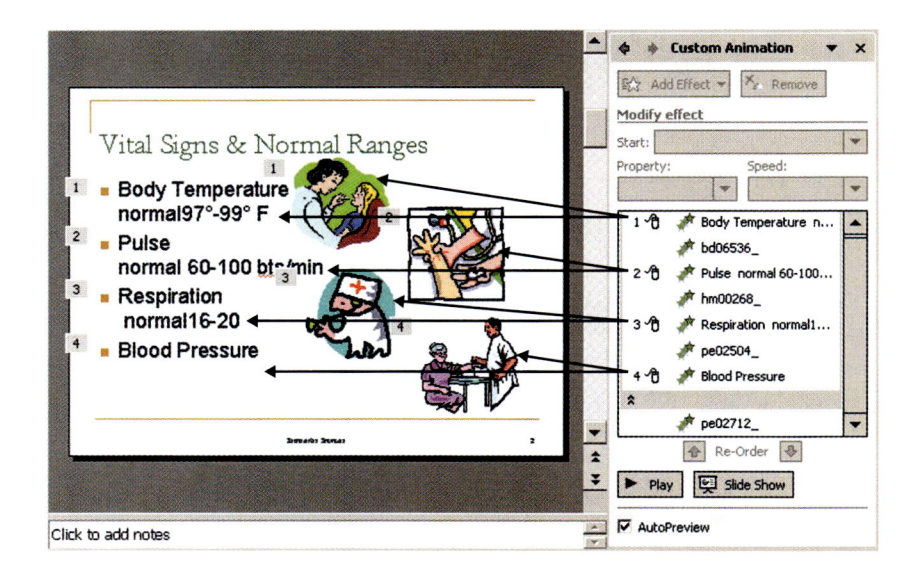

another*word*

...on the Advanced Timeline

When you preview animations, the timeline at the bottom of the Custom Animation list displays the exact timing of each animation. The drop-down list for an animation contains a Show Advanced Timeline option. The Advanced Timeline allows you to control how animations relate to each other by dragging the borders of the timeline marker.

The Start options of an animation are set to control when it begins to play. Using With Previous causes two or more objects to play their animations simultaneously. The After Previous option causes two or more animations to play sequentially. These options reduce the number of mouse clicks required to play all of the animations on a slide.

Other animations options are available from the Timing tab of the Effect Options selection. These options will allow more complete control of start times, delays between animations, the speed of the action, the duration of an animation, how each animation is repeated, and the trigger that initiates the animation.

Animating Chart Objects

Organization charts, numeric charts, and other diagram types are objects on a slide and can be animated in part or as a whole. Animating the component parts of a diagram allows a presenter or narration to address a specific element of the chart, while drawing the audience's attention to that element.

---

task reference

Animating a Chart or Diagram

- In Normal view, select the object to be animated
- From the Task pane drop-down list select **Custom Animation**
- To animate the whole object, in the Custom Animation Task pane click **Add Effects** and select the desired effect(s)
- To animate individual chart elements
  - In the Custom Animation Task pane, select the animation applied to the chart
  - Click the down arrow and select **Effect Options**
  - On the Chart Animation or Diagram Animation tab, select an option from the Group Diagram list

---

Animating the VitalSigns chart:

1. Initiate PowerPoint and open **PP05VitalSigns.ppt**
2. Move to slide **8** and click in the chart
3. On the Custom Animation pane of the Task panel, click the **Add Effect** button, pause over **Entrance,** and choose **Appear**
4. Use the drop-down arrow of the chart animation to open the **Effect Options** dialog box
5. Move to the Chart Animation tab and select **By series** as the Group chart option
6. Use the **Slide Show** button to preview the animation
7. Save the presentation

The Chart Animation tab of the Effect Options dialog box controls how each component of a chart is animated. Choosing *By series* caused the Male data series to present and then the Female data series. Choosing *By category* would cause the Under 10 data to display, then the 12 years, the 14 years, and so on. Choose the group option that corresponds to the narration about the chart.

When animating charts and diagrams, it is most effective to preview the animations in Slide Show view where you will have to click through them. The Play button does not require you to click through and usually

FIGURE 5.12
Animated Chart

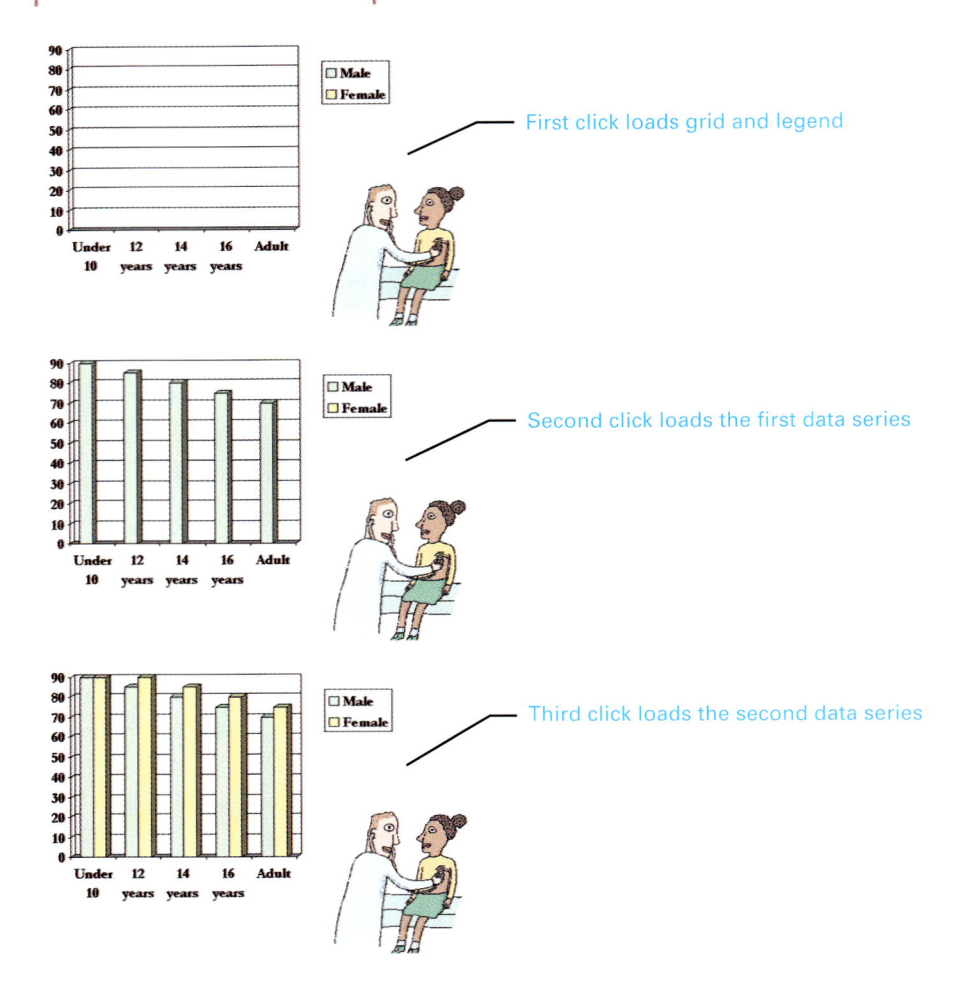

presents the information too rapidly to see the impact of any changes that you have made. The custom effects discussed when animating text and images can also be applied to charts and diagrams. Developers have full control over the Start, Time, Speed, Dimming, and other options.

Media Clips

Another simple way to add motion to a slide is to use a ***media clip*** instead of a static image. Use caution however, because media clips that repeat the same action for a long time can annoy and distract the audience.

Media clips include movies and animated GIF files. An animated GIF file carries a .gif extension like a static gif image, but includes multiple images that stream to create an animation effect. Animated GIFs are common on the Web. Movies are video files (.avi, .mov, .qt, .mpg, and .mpeg) created on a computer. Typical movies can include audio and video.

The Clip Organizer can contain both animated GIF and movie clips. Media can be inserted from any compatible file type. Sources for media clips include the Internet, media CDs that can be purchased anywhere computer software is sold, and custom media created specifically for a presentation. Movie files are linked to your presentation rather than embedded inside it (like images). If a presentation with a movie is ported to another computer, any linked files must also be moved for it to function properly.

All of the clips in the Clip Organizer are short and simple. The media clips available from your computer are determined by the software installed and the options that were selected during the install process. Custom movies can be added using the Movies and Sounds option of the Insert menu.

> **task reference**
> **Inserting a Media Clip**
> - In Normal view, move to the slide that will contain the clip
> - Use the Slide Layout panel of the Task pane to select a layout with a media placeholder
> - Click the **Insert Media Clip** icon
> - Browse through the available selections until you find a clip that you want, click the clip, and click **OK**
> - Use Slide Show view to preview the media clip

> **Adding an Animated Gif to VitalSigns:**
> 1. Initiate PowerPoint and open **PP05VitalSigns.ppt**
> 2. Add a new slide **9** and set the title to **Cognitive Ability**
> 3. Activate the **Insert** menu, select **Movies and Sounds**, click **Movie from File**, and then select **ekg.avi** from the files for this chapter
> 4. Answer **Yes** to play the movie automatically
> 5. Activate the **Insert** menu, select **Movies and Sounds**, click **Movie from File**, and then select **Gears.gif** from the files for this chapter
>
> **tip:** You will need to change Files of type to **All files**
>
> 6. Position the title placeholder and images as shown in the next figure
> 7. Use Slide Show view to preview the motion clips
>
> **tip:** The ekg.avi clip will play once, but it should loop
>
> 8. Right click on ekg.avi and select **Edit Movie Object**
>   a. Check **Loop until stopped**
>   b. Click **OK**
> 9. Use Slide Show view to preview the motion clips
> 10. Save the presentation

These steps demonstrated the insertion of a standard movie clip using an avi format and an animated gif. Both motion clips are simple, but the avi format provides more control. An animated gif cannot be started and stopped: it plays from the time the slide opens until it closes. The avi file

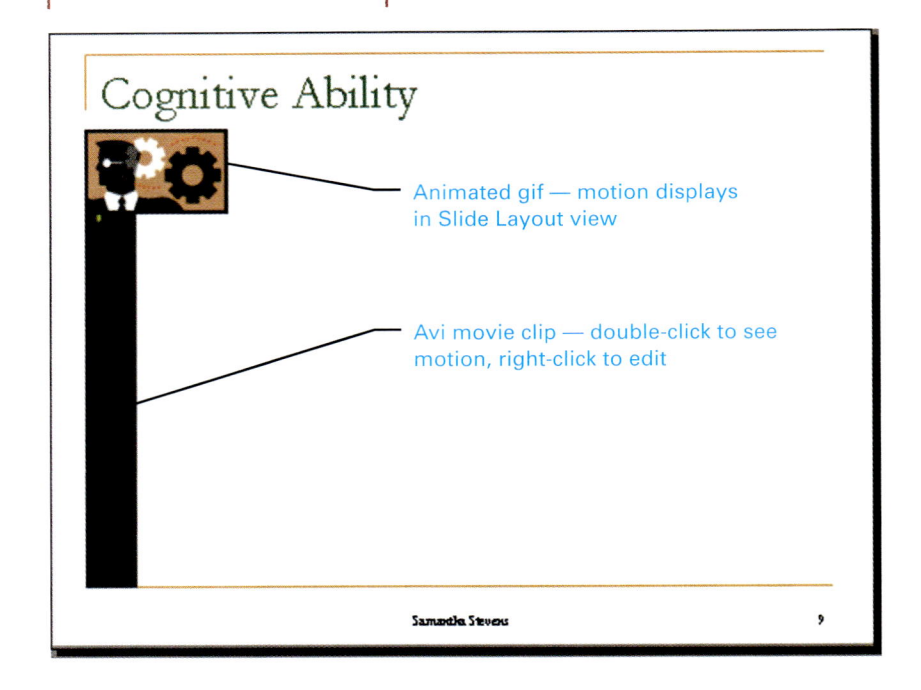

FIGURE 5.13
Motion Clips

Cognitive Ability

Animated gif — motion displays in Slide Layout view

Avi movie clip — double-click to see motion, right-click to edit

Samantha Stevens

can be started automatically, by a mouse click or by using some other trigger. Avi files can also be caused to loop or play a specified number of times. Generally avi files can support all video components and are longer than animated gifs.

If you try to insert a movie and PowerPoint issues a message or won't play it, you may still be able to use the clip through Windows Media Player. Open Windows Media Player (usually in the Accessories menu) and try running the movie. If the movie doesn't play, Windows Media Player will provide diagnostics that can help address the problem.

If the movie will play in Windows Media Player, use the Insert menu to add a Media Clip object to your presentation. A movie played through the Media Player is not controlled through PowerPoint settings but uses the Media Player buttons to start, stop, rewind, and control volume.

anotherword
. . . on Controlling Movies
Custom animation sequences can be applied to media clips to control their play. The Start With Previous option will play the movie automatically after another animation completes, while Timing can be used to start on a mouse click, and Triggers can be used to set a custom event to initiate play.

Hiding a Slide during a Slide Show

Sometimes a single presentation can be customized to meet the needs of multiple audiences or presentation forums. For example, the same presentation could be used for a 30-minute and a 20-minute presentation. The simplest way to accomplish this is to create the 30-minute presentation and then hide some of the slides for the shorter version.

task reference
Hide a Slide
- Select the slide to hide on the Slides tab in Normal view
- On the **Slide Show** menu click **Hide Slide**

Hiding a slide in VitalSigns:

1. Initiate PowerPoint and open **PP05VitalSigns.ppt**
2. Move to slide **4** and insert a new slide with the title **More on Exercise**
3. Select slide **5** (the new slide) and click **Hide Slide** from the **Slide Show** menu
4. Move to slide **4** and use Slide Show view to preview your presentation (it should skip the new slide 5)
5. Right-click on any slide while the Slide Show is running, click **Go**, then **Slide Navigator**, and then select slide **5**
6. Right-click to end the show if necessary
7. Change to Slide Sorter view and locate the Hidden Slide indicator

tip: The Slides tab of Normal view also indicates which slides are hidden

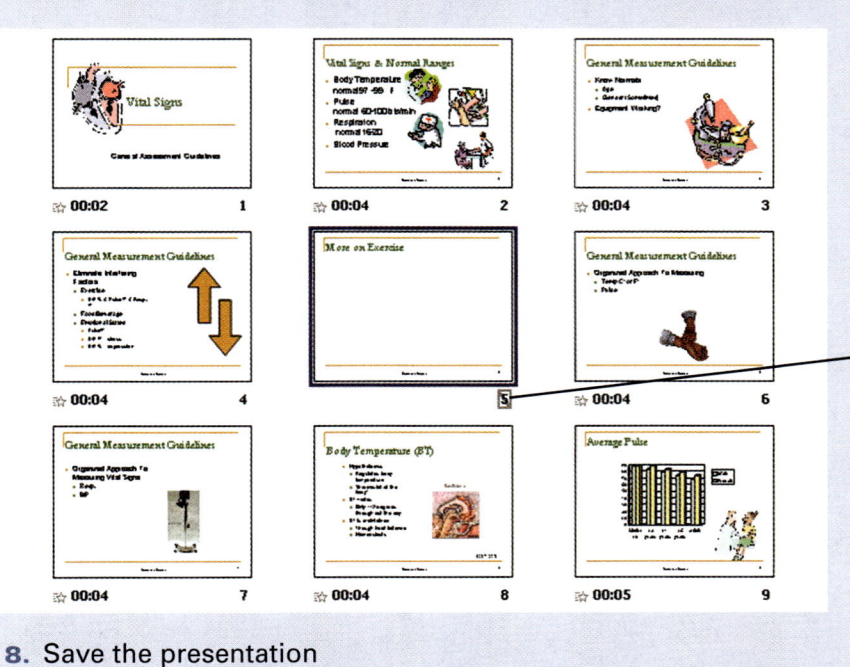

FIGURE 5.14
Hidden Slide

Hidden slide indicator

8. Save the presentation

A hidden slide still resides in the presentation, but will not display in Slide Show view unless you activate the Slide Navigator and select the hidden slide. The only indication that a slide is hidden is the slash through the slide number in Slide Sorter view. Unhiding a slide uses the same process as hiding a slide since the Hide Slide menu option is a toggle.

Creating a Self-Running Slide Show

Self-running slide shows are often called *kiosks.* Kiosks can be used to present product information at a trade show or other high-traffic location. Any presentation that needs to run without human intervention should be treated as a kiosk. Typically such a show is completely self-contained with automatic slide timings, narration, and security to control how the show is stopped.

task reference
Create a Self-Running Presentation
- On the **Slide Show** menu, click **Set Up Show**
- Click **Loop continuously until 'Esc'**

Making VitalSigns a self-running presentation:

1. Initiate PowerPoint and open **PP05VitalSigns.ppt**
2. On the **Slide Show** menu, click **Set Up Show**
   a. In the Show Options area, click **Loop continuously until 'Esc'**
   b. In the Advance slides area, click **Using timings, if present**
   c. Click **OK**

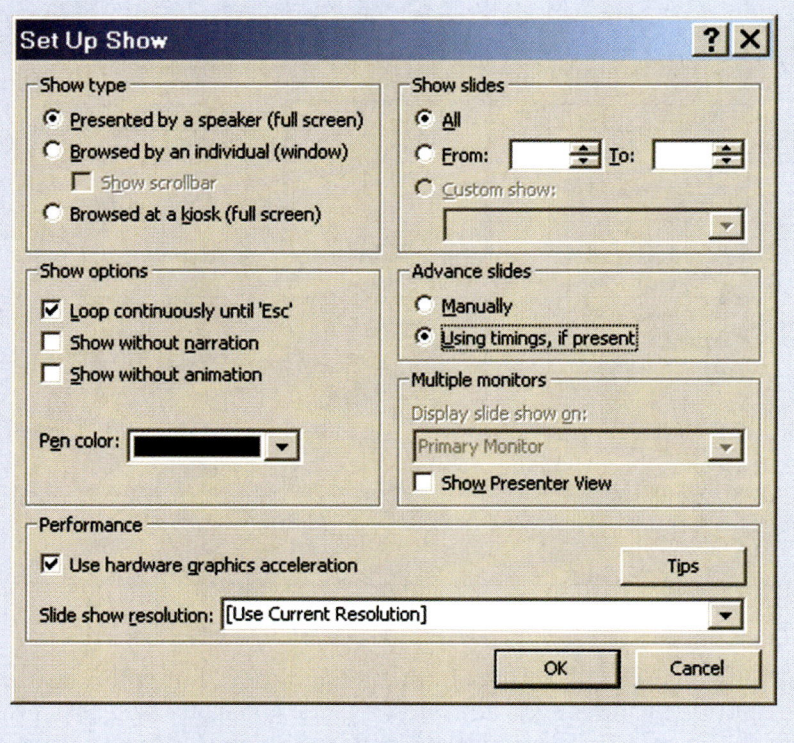

FIGURE 5.15
Set Up Show Dialog Box

3. Move to slide **1** and run the presentation

tip: The timings that have been set by rehearsing the slide show and setting animations will be used to move through the show automatically

4. Use the **Esc** key to stop the presentation
5. Save the presentation

Only the slides that have timings will advance automatically when the Loop continuously until 'Esc' and Using timings, if present options are selected. Timings must be set for all slides and animations for a presentation to run without intervention. Another way to cause a show to loop is to select the Browsed at a kiosk (full screen) from the Set Up Show dialog box. This setting will loop the presentation and restrict users from changing it.

making the grade

SESSION 5.1

1. Differentiate between applying an animation scheme and a custom animation.
2. What are the benefits of using the rehearsal features of PowerPoint?
3. How is a kiosk different from a speaker-led presentation?
4. Differentiate between animating slide objects and adding media clips to a presentation.

SESSION 5.2 USING OTHER AUDIO MULTIMEDIA COMPONENTS

PowerPoint includes intrinsic audio clips that can be applied to transitions, animations, or inserted into a slide and controlled by the presenter. Because audio is a key component in any presentation, PowerPoint supports a variety of ways to create and insert sounds. Audio multimedia components can be inserted from existing sound files, played from a CD, or recorded within PowerPoint.

To preview audio components added to a presentation, you will need speakers and a sound card. If you would like to record sounds, you will also need a microphone. To find out what hardware is installed on your computer, use the Windows Control Panel to check the multimedia and sounds settings.

task reference

Insert a Sound Clip

- On the **Insert** menu, pause over **Movies and Sounds** and click
  - **Sound from Media Gallery** to insert a sound stored in the Microsoft Media Gallery
  - **Sound from File** to insert a sound that you have stored in a file on your computer
  - **Play CD Audio Track** to play a specific track from the CD loaded in your CD tray
  - **Record Sound** to record your own sound or narration
- Right-click on the sound icon and use the Edit Sound Object options to customize the sound settings
- Use the Reorder buttons on the Custom Animation panel of the Task Pane to control the play order of the sound

POWERPOINT

Adding Audio Components

Sounds added to PowerPoint slides can originate in the Microsoft Clip Organizer or be stored in a file on your computer, an available network, the Internet, or a CD. Custom sounds and narrations can be recorded using the features of PowerPoint or any audio recording software. Regardless of how they are created, sound clips are inserted like the other media that have been covered.

Adding a sound clip to VitalSigns:

1. Initiate PowerPoint and open **PP05VitalSigns.ppt**
2. Move to slide **1**
3. On the **Insert** menu, pause over **Movies and Sounds**, and select **Sound from File**
   a. Navigate to the files for this chapter and select **HeartMonitor.wav**
   b. Click **OK**
   c. Answer **Yes** to the Do you want to play the sound automatically prompt

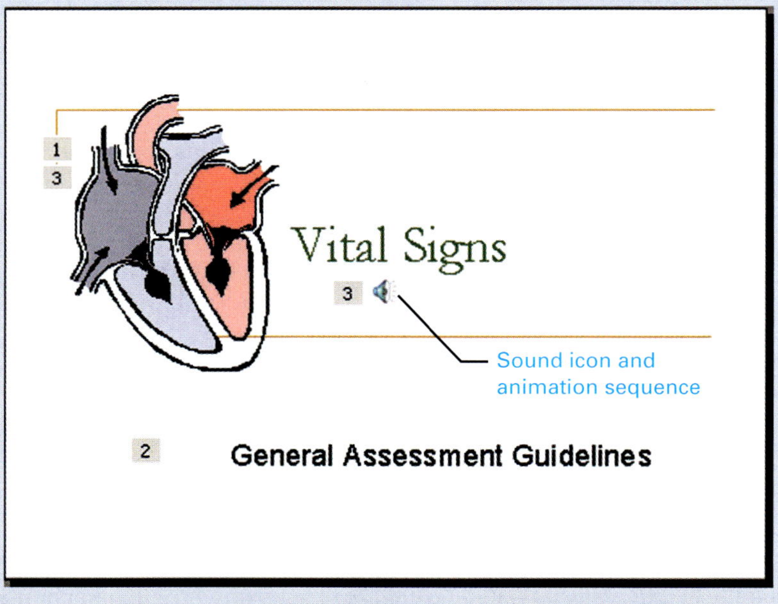

FIGURE 5.16
Sound Icon

4. Right-click on the sound icon and select **Edit Sound Object**
5. Check **Loop until stopped** in the Sound Options dialog box and click **OK**
6. Use the Custom Animation panel of the Task pane to move the sound to the first position on the play list

tip: *You can use the Reorder buttons or drag and drop the sound to relocate it*

7. Use Slide Show view to preview your changes
8. Save the presentation

A sound icon is automatically placed on a slide containing an inserted audio component. If the sound is not set to play automatically, clicking the sound icon will initiate play. If the sound is set to play automatically, the icon can be dragged off the slide so that it does not display during a slide show. Use the Custom Animation Start options to control when an automatic sound starts.

Because sound files can be large, they are usually linked rather than embedded in a presentation. The default is to link all files larger than 100 KB, but the size can be customized using the Options dialog box of the Tools menu. Unless the file size is dramatically increased, most added sound files will need to be moved with your presentation for them to work on another computer.

Intrinsic Sounds

Intrinsic sounds are those that are native to the Microsoft PowerPoint. Intrinsic sounds can be added to a transition, a custom animation, or inserted on a slide. Unless larger sounds have been added to the Microsoft Clip Organizer, the available sounds are very short (small file size) and are usually designed to be looped. As previously discussed, the clips available from the Microsoft Clip Organizer are dependent on the options chosen when Microsoft Office was installed.

---

task reference

Add Sound to a Transition or Animation

The transitions and animations must be set before sounds can be added to them

- Move to the slide where sounds will be added to transitions and/or animations
- Activate the Task Panel pane for Slide Transitions to add a sound to a transition or the pane for Custom Animations to add a sound to an animated object
- Use the sound drop-down list to select the sound

Adding transition and animation sounds to VitalSigns:

1. Initiate PowerPoint and open **PP05VitalSigns.ppt**
2. Move to slide **2**
3. Use the Task pane drop-down button to open the Slide Transition panel
4. Experiment with the available sounds in the Sounds drop-down list before settling on **Whoosh**

tip: *Loop until next slide will cause the sound to loop until the next slide enters the screen*

5. Use **Play** to preview the change

FIGURE 5.17

Adding Sound to a Slide Transition

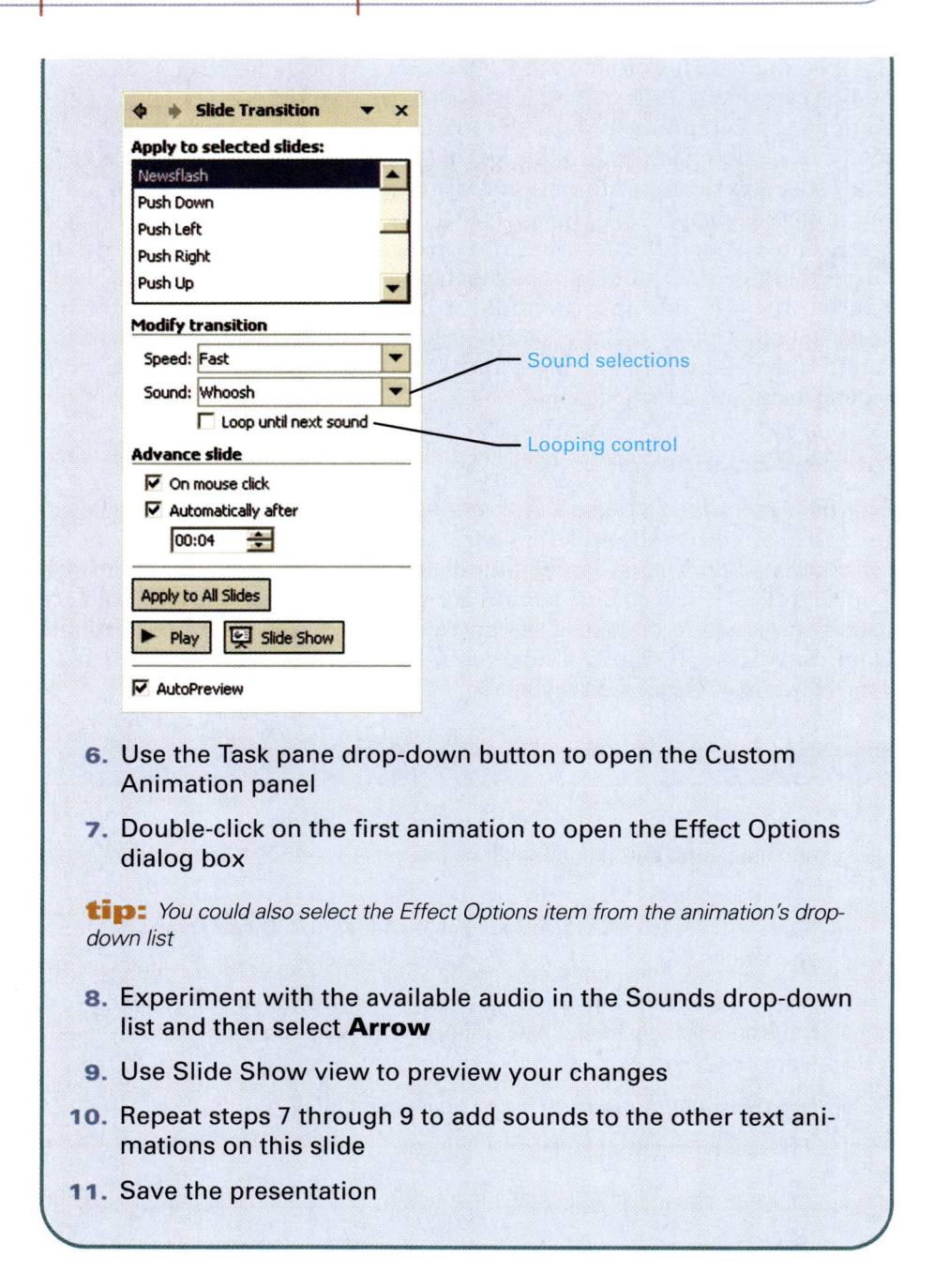

[Slide Transition dialog box showing Sound selections and Looping control]

6. Use the Task pane drop-down button to open the Custom Animation panel

7. Double-click on the first animation to open the Effect Options dialog box

tip: You could also select the Effect Options item from the animation's drop-down list

8. Experiment with the available audio in the Sounds drop-down list and then select **Arrow**

9. Use Slide Show view to preview your changes

10. Repeat steps 7 through 9 to add sounds to the other text animations on this slide

11. Save the presentation

For sounds to be added in this fashion, animations and transitions must already be set. The last option on the list of available sounds is Other sound. This option can be used to add a sound from a file to a transition or animation. This option will allow narration to be added to each animated object.

Sound Files

Using audio content from a CD allows alternate sounds to be played during a slide show without updating the presentation. CD sounds are not embedded in your presentation, but played from their external location. If you specify a track to play from a CD, the presentation will play that track from whatever CD is currently in the tray.

Adding a CD track to VitalSigns:

1. Initiate PowerPoint and open **PP05VitalSigns.ppt**
2. Place an audio CD in the CD tray
3. Move to slide **3**
4. Activate the **Insert** menu, pause over **Movies and Sounds**, and click **Play CD Audio Track**
    a. In the Movie and Sound dialog box select the first and last track(s) to be played (i.e., 5 and 7) and then click **OK**

tip: *Selecting the same Start and End track will cause only that track to play*

   b. Answer **Yes** to have the track(s) play automatically. No would require you to click the icon to play the track(s)
5. Drag the CD icon to the footer portion of the slide to remove it from the main body
6. Use Slide Show view to preview the audio

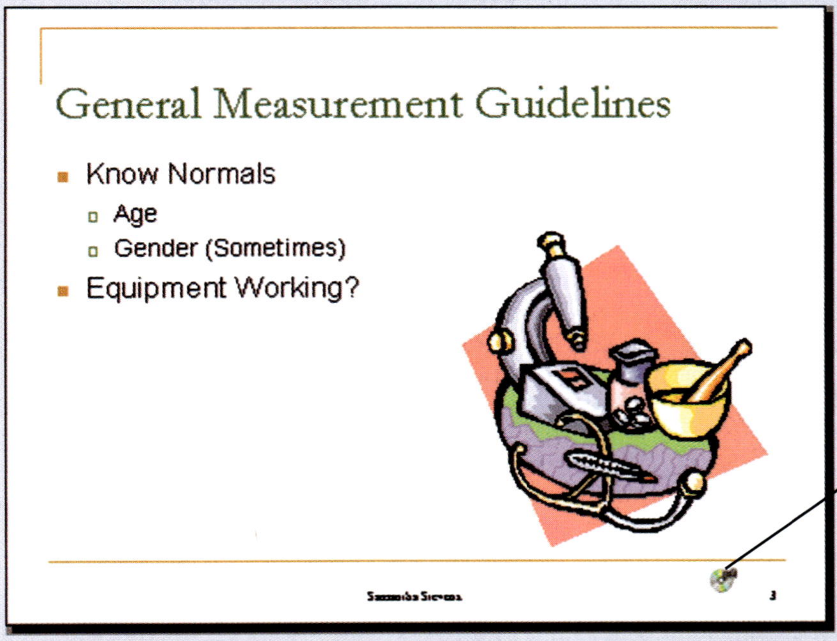

7. Save the presentation

FIGURE 5.18
CD Audio Track Icon

Audio track icon

A music CD must be in the CD-ROM drive during the presentation for a CD audio track to play. This music is always played from the CD, not embedded into your PowerPoint document. Once a CD audio track has been specified, the Custom Animation settings can be used to control how play begins and ends. The default action is to end play on a mouse-click, but other options can cause the clip to play until the current slide is exited or for several slides. To change the CD track that plays or the duration of play, use the Edit Sound Object from the pop-up menu option activated by right-clicking on the CD icon.

Stop or Delete Sound Objects

All sounds inserted from a CD or file display an icon on the slide. Deleting this icon also deletes the sound from the slide. Remember that the icon can be dragged off the edge of the slide so that it is not visible during the presentation.

To remove a sound added to a transition or animation, open the Task Pane panel for the animation containing the sound (either the Slide Transition or Custom Animation panel) and update the Sound selection. The [Stop Previous Sound] option of the Sound drop-down list stops a sound still playing from a previous transition or animation. The [No Sound] option removes any sound currently associated with this animation.

The Edit Sound Object dialog box can be used to stop a sound from playing without removing it from the presentation using the Edit Sound Object settings. Right-click on the sound icon to open the pop-up menu with the Edit Sound Object option. Set the sound object to play on a specific triggering event so that you can decide whether or not to play it during a show.

Narration

Most presentations rely on narration to deliver the bulk of their content. When there is a live presenter, the narration is spoken during the slide show. Self-running presentations, Web presentations, and kiosks need to contain recorded narration so that the audience receives all of the available information without adding more text to the slides than can be easily read.

Voice narration can be created in a sound studio, using a PC-based recording software like Sound Recorder that ships with Windows, or from within the presentation itself. The sound quality desired determines the recording method. A sound studio costs the most and provides the best quality sound. Recording from within PowerPoint is easy, but produces the lowest sound quality and least control. The biggest advantage of recording narration from within PowerPoint is that it can be accomplished during a live presentation and can include audience comments as well as the basic narrative.

FIGURE 5.19
CD Audio Track Icon off the Edge of the Slide

CD icon positioned not to display during show

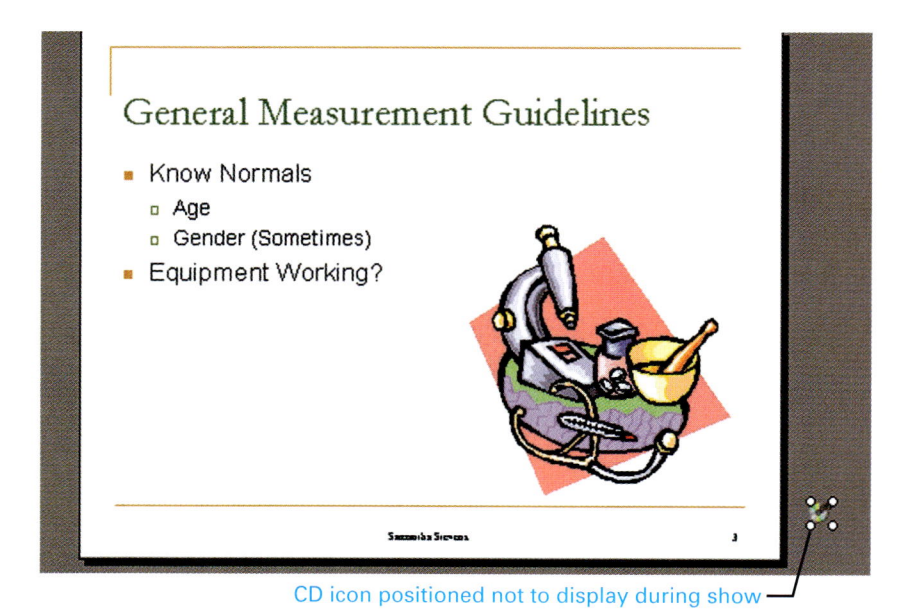

Narration recorded from within PowerPoint places a sound icon on the slide(s) with associated sound. Like other types of sound files, narration can be set to play automatically or when triggered by a mouse click or other event. Narration can be created for each slide, or for the entire presentation. When multiple sounds are set for a slide, narration takes precedence.

When only a portion of the slide show is to be narrated, it is useful to record a voice comment or narration on individual slides in a slide show. This is a simple way to ensure that the voice directly relates to the slide content being displayed.

Adding a narration to a VitalSigns slide:

1. Initiate PowerPoint and open **PP05VitalSigns.ppt**
2. Move to slide **4**
3. On the **Insert** menu, point to **Movies and Sounds**, and then click **Record Sound**
   a. Name the sound **Exercise**
   b. Click the **Record** button and speak the following narration into your microphone **Exercise causes blood pressure to decrease while increasing pulse and respiration. Vital signs should not be taken within 30 minutes of vigorous exercise if it can be at all avoided**
   c. Click the **Stop** button
   d. Click **OK**

tip: To complete this step, you must have a sound card and microphone on your computer

4. Use Slide Show view to preview the audio

tip: You will need to click on the sound icon

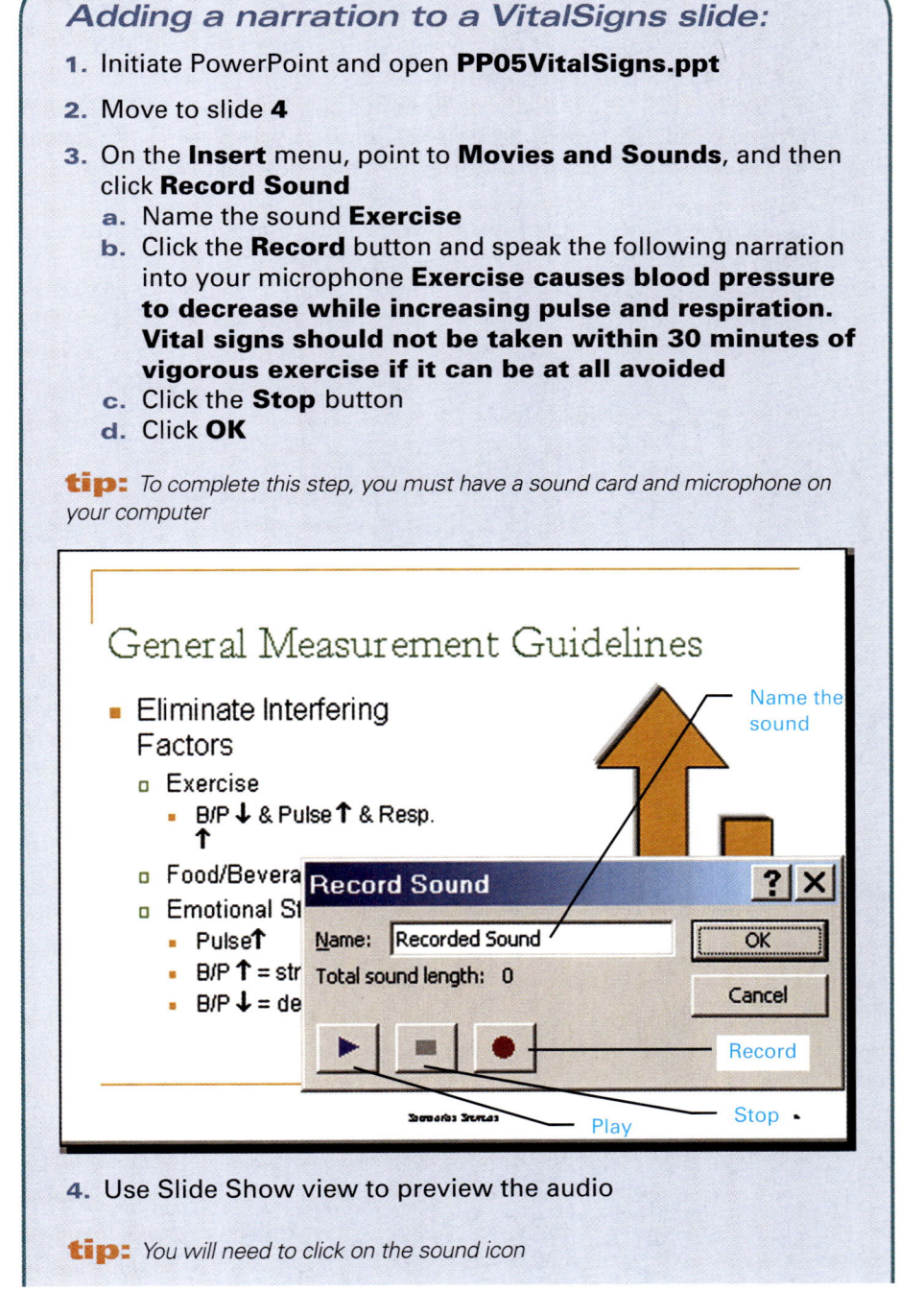

FIGURE 5.20
Recording Narration

POWERPOINT

5. Open the Custom Animation panel of the Task pane
6. Drop down the list for the sound object and select **Timing**
7. On the Timing tab, set the Start option to **With Previous** and click **OK**

tip: *This will start the sound when the slide opens*

8. Use Slide Show view to preview the audio
9. Save the presentation

The Timing options set in the previous steps control the narration. The Start settings control when the narration begins, while the Repeat settings control when it ends. Since this narration is associated with this slide, its timings relate to the slide also. Repeat settings include playing the narration a specific number of times, until the user clicks again, or until the slide is exited.

If you would like the narration to continue throughout a self-running presentation, the Slide Show menu has an option that will record your narration and save the timings of each mouse click so that your presentation is perfectly synchronized.

Adding a timed narration to the VitalSigns presentation:

1. Initiate PowerPoint and open **PP05VitalSigns.ppt**
2. Move to slide **1**
3. In the **Slide Show** menu select **Record Narration**
   a. Click the **Set Microphone Level** button, read the text as instructed, and click **OK**
   b. Click the **Change Quality** button, select **CD Quality** from the Name drop-down list, and click **OK**

tip: *The CD setting will produce the best sound file possible with your recording situation. The resulting file size is large and may cause a problem if you do not have much disk space*

   c. Click **OK** to close the Record Narration dialog box and begin recording
   d. Read the content of each slide as you click through the show

tip: *You can pause and reinitiate the recording process by right-clicking and selecting either Pause Narration or Resume Narration. The Esc key will stop the recording process*

   e. When you come to the end of the show, click **Save** to store the timings as well as the narration

tip: *Normally the narration would contain much more information than just reading the slides. This was done for demonstration purposes only*

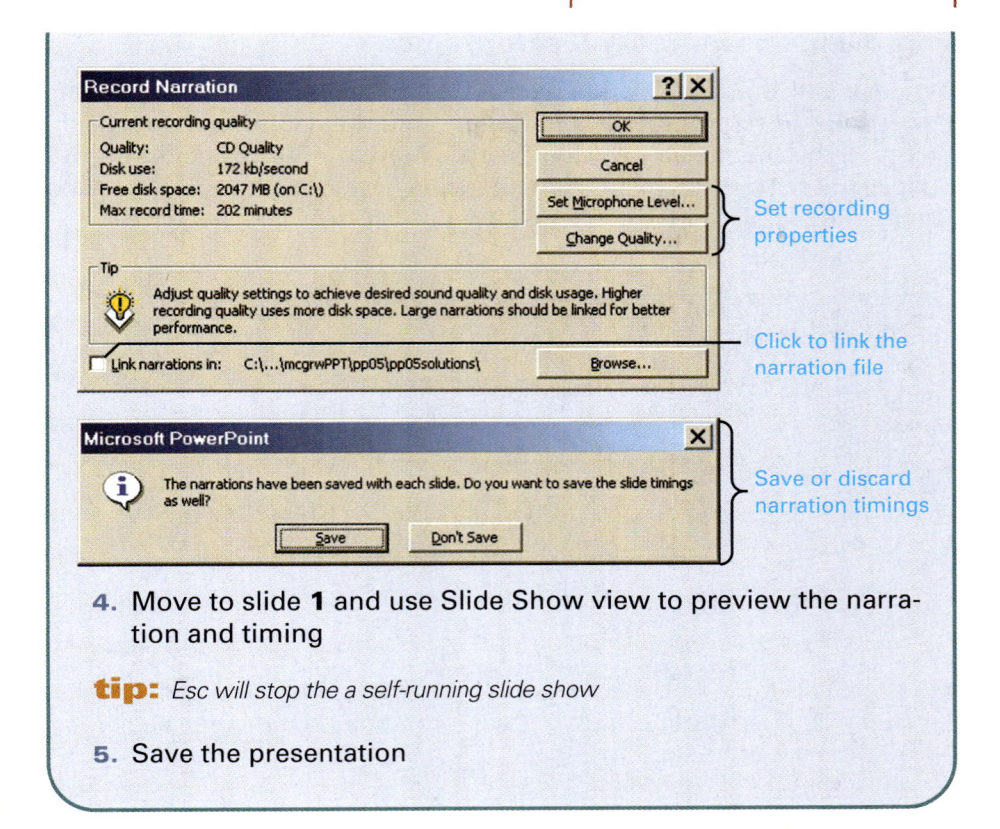

FIGURE 5.21

Recording Narration for an Entire Presentation

- Set recording properties
- Click to link the narration file
- Save or discard narration timings

4. Move to slide **1** and use Slide Show view to preview the narration and timing

tip: Esc will stop the a self-running slide show

5. Save the presentation

The timings created as the narration is recorded are usually the most appropriate for a self-running slide show. If the initial timings or narration are not effective, the process can be repeated to record a new narration. There is no mechanism to update only a portion of the narration. The narration sound icon appears on the first slide only. Deleting that icon will remove the narration from the entire presentation. Only one sound can play at a time when running a slide show. If there are multiple sounds on a slide, the narration will take precedence.

A presentation narration can be ***embedded*** or stored in a ***linked*** file. Embedded narrations are the default, but result in large PowerPoint file sizes. Linked sound files yield smaller PowerPoint file sizes, but the sound file must be ported with the presentation.

To create a linked narration, click Link narrations in the check box of the Record Narration dialog box (see Figure 5.21) before beginning to record. You will be prompted for a location to store the linked sound file and a file name. A further advantage of linked sound is that it will play faster.

A narrated presentation can be run with or without the narration. The Set Up Show option of the Slide Show menu contains the options that control whether or not a narration is played. Click Show without narration. Recall that this dialog box can also be used to advance slides manually or using the timings.

IDENTIFYING SOURCES FOR MEDIA

The Microsoft Clip Organizer is a starting point for locating high-impact media for your presentation. Other sources will be needed for presentations about unique topics or to obtain the most professional look.

Improving Presentation Performance

As more and more media are added to a presentation, the size of the PowerPoint file will increase and the presentation can become sluggish. Compressing the media can significantly decrease file size and improve performance. This is especially true if media have been added and deleted to obtain the desired look and feel.

> **Compressing VitalSigns graphics:**
>
> 1. Initiate PowerPoint and open **PP05VitalSigns.ppt** in Normal view
> 2. Move to slide **1**
> 3. Right-click on the heart image and choose **Show Picture Toolbar**
> 4. On the picture toolbar, click the **Compress Pictures** button
> 5. Verify the compression settings with those shown in the next figure and click **OK**
> 6. Select the **Apply** button when prompted about the possibility of reduced image quality
>
> 7. Save the presentation

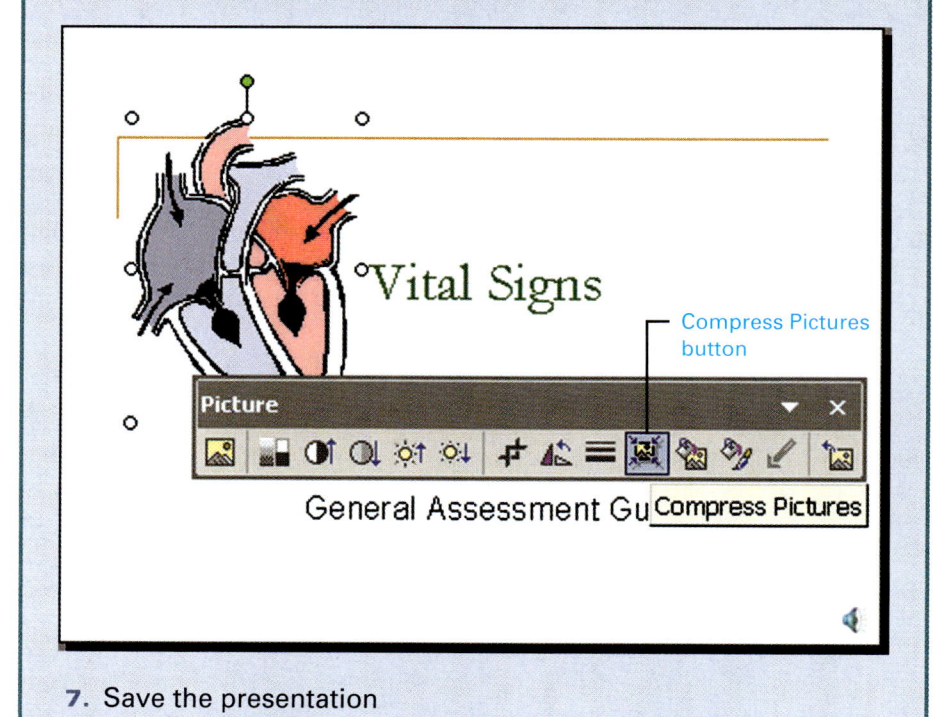

FIGURE 5.22
Compressing Pictures

The settings chosen have optimized the presentation for delivery using a screen or via the Web. This provides the greatest compression available. If a presentation is to be printed, use the settings that will best support printing. The performance improvement and file size reduction experienced will depend on how much media are in your presentation and the settings that you select.

Other Sources for Media

The Microsoft Design Gallery Live is a Web-based collection of media available to licensed Microsoft Office users. This collection contains the same types of media as the Microsoft Clip Organizer installed with Office, but is continually updated. This is a good place to locate seasonal art and clips that follow the style and color schemes available from the Clip Organizer. The simplest way to reach online clips is to use the link from the Insert Clip Art pane of the Task panel.

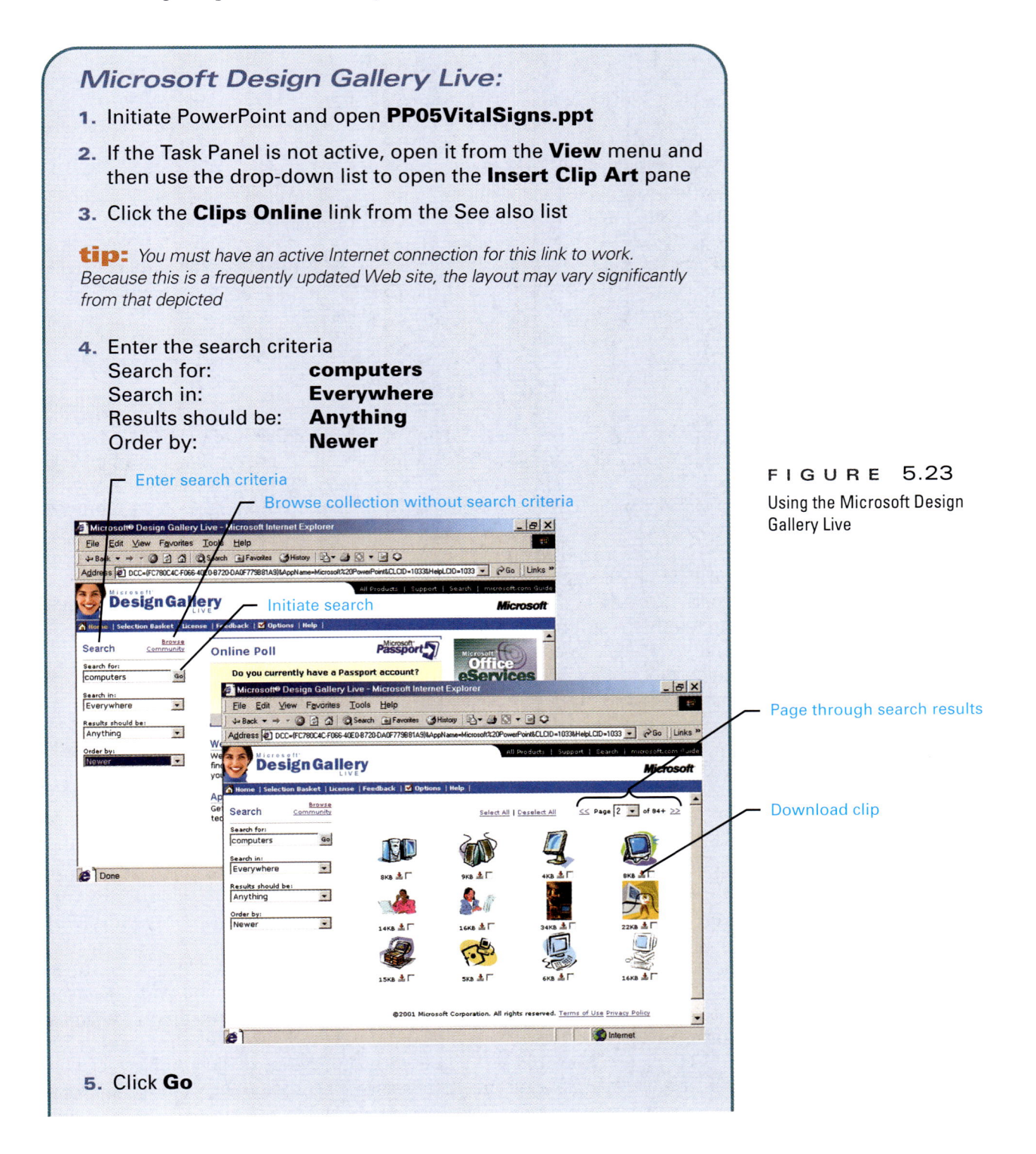

Microsoft Design Gallery Live:

1. Initiate PowerPoint and open **PP05VitalSigns.ppt**

2. If the Task Panel is not active, open it from the **View** menu and then use the drop-down list to open the **Insert Clip Art** pane

3. Click the **Clips Online** link from the See also list

   tip: You must have an active Internet connection for this link to work. Because this is a frequently updated Web site, the layout may vary significantly from that depicted

4. Enter the search criteria
   - Search for: **computers**
   - Search in: **Everywhere**
   - Results should be: **Anything**
   - Order by: **Newer**

5. Click **Go**

FIGURE 5.23

Using the Microsoft Design Gallery Live

*another*way

. . . to Use Microsoft Design Gallery Live

If you have a live Internet connection, online clips are available from the Microsoft Clip Organizer. Online clips have an online logo, but are listed with the rest of the media clips as long as the Search in criteria is set to Everywhere.

---

6. Select a clip and click its download button

tip: Be sure to control the folder that will hold the downloaded clip and to remember the file name

7. Use the **Insert Picture** button of the Drawing toolbar to insert your clip into slide 5

8. Save the presentation

The World Wide Web interface of Design Gallery Live allows online media searches using an interface similar to the Clip Organizer. When media of interest are located, clicking them will provide a larger preview. Each clip has a check box that can be used to select multiple clips for simultaneous download, or a clip's download button can be used to store a single clip locally. Once a clip has been downloaded, it can be added to the Clip Organizer or inserted as a file.

There are many other sources of free and low-cost media on the Internet. Any **Internet search engine** (Yahoo!, WebCrawler, AskJeeves, etc.) can be used to locate artwork. The search criteria are determined by the presentation content. Searches for wide-open topics like *free art* will return many possible matches, while specific searches like *free Christmas gif* are more likely to retrieve appropriate art.

Most software stores carry a selection of CDs that contain sounds, graphics, pictures, movies, and animations that are suitable for use in presentations. CDs traditionally contain media that are similar in some fashion, such as style, topic, or artist. The **royalty** for using these media can be covered by the cost of the CD, or additional payment can be required based on how the media are used.

Custom images can also be created using a digital still camera, a digital video camera, or a scanner. Using these methods to create your own custom media is more difficult than it would initially appear. The digital media that result from these methods are rarely usable without using specialty software to edit, retouch, crop, and restore the images and sounds. Each media type requires access to and knowledge of specialty software used to create professional media.

Remember to allow a significant portion of development time for research when planning to locate media on CDs or the Web. Previewing vast quantities of artwork is very time consuming.

All media, regardless of how they are displayed, are covered by **copyright law.** Copyright laws give the owner of the art all rights to control its distribution and use. A **license agreement** is used to legally outline the rights and responsibilities of anyone who uses copyrighted materials. Most artwork available for download can be used in private presentations without charge, but carefully read the license agreements before you download. Commercial use of most works requires acknowledgment of the creator and a payment. Some media licenses have a time limit or quantity restriction that determines when payment needs to be made. Most licenses also preclude using any part of the work as the foundation of another work for profit.

There are also many Web sites that provide media for hire. Media prices vary widely, but typically increase with the quality and uniqueness of the work. Web-based graphic art studios are similar to online shopping sites that allow shoppers to browse merchandise and add art for purchase to a shopping cart. If you cannot find exactly the right clip, the work can be commissioned. These sites protect the media from download until payment is received and often embed digital signatures to protect media copyrights.

making the grade
SESSION 5.2

1. Differentiate between animation/transition sounds and sound clips.
2. When a CD track is set to play on a slide, what happens if the wrong CD is in the CD tray?
3. How can you remove a sound icon from the slide without removing the sound?
4. How do you determine what method to use when recording a narration in PowerPoint?

SESSION 5.3 SUMMARY

Animation Schemes were introduced in Chapter 3 as a simple way to apply preset movements to slide text. This chapter covers custom animations that can be applied to any slide object. Slide objects include the slide itself and any text, chart, image, or drawing object. Animations can be applied to control the way the object enters, exits, or displays on the slide. The properties of each animation are set in the Task panel and control the speed, order, sound, and other effects that control animation behavior.

When multiple slide objects are animated, the Animation pane of the Task panel is used to control the order of play. Animations can play simultaneously, sequentially, or the Advanced Timeline can be used for more complete control. Animated gif files and movies can also be inserted to add motion to a presentation.

Voice narration can be recorded for a slide, a group of slides, or the entire presentation. When the narration is for a slide, the sound icon is stored on the slide and animation settings control when the narration is played. Narration for the entire presentation displays an icon on the beginning slide. The simplest way to record a complete voice narration with slide timings is to record the presentation while clicking through it. This feature is activated using the Record Narration from the Slide Show menu.

A presentation can be customized to meet the needs of a new audience or presentation time reduced by hiding slides. Hidden slides can still be edited, but will not play during a normal presentation. Right-clicking will allow you to navigate to a hidden slide. Slide sorter view and the slide panel of Normal view display a slash through the slide number, but there is no visible difference in other views.

The Slide Show menu contains a number of options for setting up a presentation. One option is to create a self-running presentation or a kiosk. When this is done, the presentation can run without intervention or as the user clicks through it. Typically options are selected to keep the viewer from interrupting the presentation or making changes to it.

MOUS OBJECTIVES SUMMARY

- Apply and customize slide transitions—PPT2002-4-3
- Insert and configure sound, movie, and animated gif clips—PPT2002-6-2
- Use presentation rehearsal features—PPT2002-4-7

task reference roundup

Task	Page #	Preferred Method
Apply a Slide Transition	PP 5.4	• Select the slide(s) the transition will be applied to
		tip: *No selection is needed if the transition will be applied to all slides*
		• From the **Slide Show** menu select **Slide Transition**
		tip: *The Task pane menu can also be used*
		Select a transition effect
Set Slide Timing while Rehearsing	PP 5.6	• Activate the timing feature
		• On the **Slide Show** menu, click **Set Up Show**
		• Under **Advance slides**, click **Use timings, if present**
		• Set the time for each slide
		• On the **Slide Show** menu click **Rehearse Timings**
		• Rehearse the show to set timings automatically as you advance
		• At the end of the show, click **Yes** to accept automatic timings or **No** to start again
Adding Custom Animations to Text	PP 5.7	• In Normal view, select the text object to be animated
		• From the Task pane drop-down list select **Custom Animation**
		• In the custom Animation Task pane click **Add Effects** and select the desired effect(s)
Animating a Chart or Diagram	PP 5.13	• In Normal view, select the object to be animated
		• From the Task pane drop-down list select **Custom Animation**
		• To animate the whole object, in the Custom Animation Task pane click **Add Effects** and select the desired effect(s)
		• To animate individual chart elements
		• In the Custom Animation Task pane, select the animation applied to the chart
		• Click the down arrow and select **Effect Options**
		• On the Chart Animation or Diagram Animation tab, select an option from the Group Diagram list

task reference roundup

Task	Page #	Preferred Method
Inserting a Media Clip	PP 5.15	• In Normal view, move to the slide that will contain the clip
		• Use the Slide Layout panel of the Task pane to select a layout with a media placeholder
		• Click the **Insert Media Clip** icon
		• Browse through the available selections until you find a clip that you want, click the clip, and click **OK**
		• Use Slide Show view to preview the media clip
Hide a Slide	PP 5.16	• Select the slide to hide on the Slides tab in Normal view
		• On the **Slide Show** menu click **Hide Slide**
Create a Self-Running Presentation	PP 5.18	• On the **Slide Show** menu, click **Set Up Show**
		• Click **Loop continuously until 'Esc'**
Insert a Sound Clip	PP 5.20	• On the **Insert** menu, pause over **Movies and Sounds** and click
		• **Sound from Media Gallery** to insert a sound stored in the Microsoft Media Gallery
		• **Sound from File** to insert a sound that you have stored in a file on your computer
		• **Play CD Audio Track** to play a specific track from the CD loaded in your CD tray
		• **Record Sound** to record your own sound or narration
		• Right-click on the sound icon and use the Edit Sound Object options to customize the sound settings
		Use the Reorder buttons on the Custom Animation panel of the Task pane to control the play order of the sound
Add Sound to a Transition or Animation	PP 5.21	The transitions and animations must be set before sounds can be added to them
		• Move to the slide where sounds will be added to transitions and/or animations
		• Activate the Task Panel pane for Slide Transitions to add a sound to a transition or Custom Animations to add a sound to an animated object
		• Use the sound drop-down list to select the sound

www.mhhe.com/i-series — PP 5.33

POWERPOINT

chapter five
review of terminology

CROSSWORD PUZZLE

Across

1. Laws that control the legal rights of media owners
6. Member of Microsoft Media Gallery
7. Used to locate information and media on the Internet
8. Motion added to a presentation object
9. Sound files that come with Microsoft Office
11. An external file that becomes part of a PowerPoint file
15. Determine how long each slide in a self-running show is on the screen

Down

2. Attributes that control an object's behavior
3. Effects added to a slide entering or exiting the screen
4. Legal agreement for copyrighted materials
6. The smallest unit of text that can be animated
10. Fee for use of copyrighted materials
12. Color change after animation
13. A self-running presentation
14. A file that is visible from PowerPoint but not part of the presentation

review of concepts

chapter five

LEVEL TWO

FILL-IN

1. The _____ animation timing option is used to play multiple animations at the same time.
2. _____ images will reduce the overall size of a PowerPoint presentation.
3. _____ is a Web site of media provided for licensed Microsoft Office users.
4. The agreements that govern legal use of copyrighted media are called _____.
5. The _____ menu contains the option to set a slide transition.

REVIEW QUESTIONS

Each of the following topics should be addressed in one to three paragraphs.

1. Discuss how you would find appropriate graphics for a presentation used to recruit high school girls for sports teams.
2. How would you apply the same transition to slides 2, 4, 7, and 9 of a presentation?
3. How effective is it to add an intrinsic sound like camera to each animation and transition in a presentation?
4. Why use multimedia in a slide show?
5. How would you select and add a range of CD tracks to a slide?

CREATE THE QUESTION

For each of the following answers, create the question.

ANSWER	QUESTION
1. Custom Animation panel.	_____
2. Speed property.	_____
3. Rehearse Timings and recording a narration.	_____
4. Font, color, spinning, and desaturation, for example.	_____
5. Reorder button.	_____

FACT OR FICTION

For each of the following determine whether the statement is fact, fiction, or both and present your arguments for that conclusion.

1. The grid background of a bar chart cannot be animated.
2. Most sounds inserted from files are linked, not embedded, in a presentation.
3. When a narration is recorded from the Slide Show menu, a sound icon is placed on each slide with the narration for that slide.
4. The intrinsic sounds added to a transition or animation do not have to be moved to play when the presentation is placed on another computer.
5. PowerPoint provides the best quality recorded sound available.

chapter five — hands-on projects

practice

Heap Collectors

Heap Collectors is a company that collects donated vehicles and delivers them to their final resting place. The recipient business organizations will typically pay the towing fee. However, non-profit organizations usually do not. In that case, Heap Collectors is able to collect most of its fee from grants, a small portion of which comes as a pass-through when donors contribute to charities. You have been asked to create a PowerPoint presentation to be viewed at community centers.

1. Start PowerPoint and open **pp05HeapCollectors.ppt**
2. On slide 1 add a car graphic retrieved from a CD or an online gallery and then add a **Fly from Left** entrance animation with an appropriate sound. Make the sound occur first and then the title **Fly from Left** (After previous)
3. On slide 2 arrange several graphics of vehicles to look "junky" and then group them into a single object. Set the animation for the grouped car graphic to **Dissolve In**, Very Fast, then have the title **Dissolve In**, Very Fast, and finally set the text to **Dissolve In** line by line on mouse click
4. On slide 3, add a graphic of a motorcycle, an older car, and the sound of a motorcycle starting up. Set the following in the order presented
   a. Set a **Newsflash** Slide Transition
   b. Set the title to **Fly In** with **driveby.wav** as the simultaneous sound
   c. The remaining text should **Fly In** Very Fast after the mouse is clicked
   d. Add an exit effect for the motorcycle graphic causing it to **Fly Out** playing the motorcycle sound simultaneously
5. On slide 4, add the graphic of a donkey pulling a car (Clips Online), and insert sounds of a horse snorting and galloping (Clip Organizer). Set the following in the order presented
   a. Play the horse snort first
   b. Set the title to **Dissolve In**, Very Fast
   c. Set the text to **Wipe, From Top**, Very Fast
   d. Set the graphic to move off the screen with the galloping sound
6. On slide 5 insert a graphic of coins and the sounds of coins dropping (Clip Organizer). Set the following in the order presented
   a. Add a Flash Bulb emphasis effect to the title
   b. Have the text enter line-by-line by clicking the mouse as the coins dropping sound plays
7. On slide 6 insert a graphic of helping hands and the clip **Happy open** sound clip (Clips Online). Set the following in the order presented
   a. Set the title to **Dissolve In**
   b. Play the music clip
   c. Make the text display as a group using **Wipe, From Left**, All at Once
8. Drag the sound icons off each slide so that they do not display during the presentation
9. Save the presentation as **<yourname>HeapCollectors.ppt**

hands-on projects

chapter five

LEVEL THREE

challenge

Plaza at the Mall

The covered mall has replaced stand-alone shopping areas. These cities-within-a-city favor block-long shops punctuated with a corner or intersection. Intersections are an opportunity to entertain the public, and frequently there will be performers, trade shows, and other displays to draw people. By keeping the public within the mall, there is a greater likelihood they will continue to shop. Hence the vitality of the mall is ensured. Plaza at the Mall is a consulting company that designs activities for those intersections at malls across the United States. Their focus is multifold, including decorations for all occasions, exhibits, and entertainment of all kinds. When mall retailers subscribe to Plaza's services, they are guaranteed events for every month of the year. You have been asked to prepare a PowerPoint presentation to illustrate what Plaza at the Mall can provide.

1. Start PowerPoint and open **pp05PlazaMall.ppt**
2. Open the Slide Master, add a **Zoom** Entrance effect to the Firework graphic, and **Close Master View**
3. On slide 1 add a **Pinwheel** Entrance effect to the title that spins each letter individually
4. Move to slide 2
    a. Add the **Faded Swivel** Entrance effect to the title and set it to play without a mouse click
    b. Add the **Fly In** Entrance effect to the bulleted text. Adjust the settings so that each bullet enters after a mouse click and becomes a medium gray after the next mouse click
5. Move to slide 3
    a. Add the **Compress** Entrance effect to the title and set it to play without a mouse click
    b. Add the **Checkerboard** Entrance effect to the bullets and set the options to load each major bullet (1st level paragraph) on a mouse click
6. Move to slide 4
    a. Add the **Box** In Entrance effect to the title and set it to play automatically
    b. Set the bulleted text to **Fly In** From Bottom by 1st level paragraph
7. Move to slide 5
    a. Add the **Pinwheel** Entrance effect to the title and set it to play automatically
    b. Cause the bulleted text to **Dissolve In** by 1st level paragraph
8. Add a **Bounce** Entrance effect to the title of slide 6. Add graphic(s) and sound(s) to convey the idea of a festival or fun atmosphere
9. Add transitions and animations of your own choosing to slides 7 and 8
10. Test the presentation and save it as **<yourname>pp05PlazaMall.ppt**

chapter five — hands-on projects

on the web

EU Currency

Twelve European countries are in the process of changing or have changed their currency to European Union (EU) notes and coins. The coins have one side that is standard among all countries. On the obverse, each country will decorate the coins with their own designs. The notes will be uniform. Making this change is a tremendous undertaking, and one that has not been entirely well received. For most, a change can be frightening. To ease the transition, the Web site www.EUnotesandcoins.com has been designated. You have been asked to prepare a presentation that will help American travelers understand and use the new currency.

1. Visit the Web site listed above and the use search engines to locate data and graphics for this presentation
2. Open PowerPoint and create a new presentation with the **Watermark** Design Template
3. Save the presentation as **<yourname>pp04EuroCurrency.ppt**
4. Add a currency-related graphic to the first slide
    a. Set a **Diamond** In Entrance Effect for both the title and graphic. Cause the animations to play simultaneously after the slide loads
    b. Set a **Fly In** Entrance Effect for the subtitle that plays automatically after the title animation is completed
5. Move to the second slide and add graphics (at least two) representing the euro countries
    a. Add a **Diamond** In Entrance effect to the slide title that plays automatically
    b. Add a **Shimmer** Emphasis effect to the country names. No mouse click should be required
    c. Use a **Spin** Emphasis effect to animate the graphics. Do not require a mouse click
6. Move to slide 3 and add graphics depicting the use of coins
    a. Add a **Dissolve In** Entrance effect to the title that plays automatically
    b. Use a **Checkerboard** Entrance effect to have the bullets enter one at a time by mouse click
7. Move to slide 4 and add graphics of paper notes and coins. Set the following animations to occur without mouse clicks
    a. Animate the coins to drop into position with an appropriate sound
    b. Set the title animation to **Fly In** From Bottom Right
    c. Set the bulleted text to have a **Grow/Shrink** Emphasis effect
8. Move to slide 21
    a. Insert appropriate graphics
    b. Animate all slide elements
9. Using images from your research, add graphics to at least three of the remaining slides to complete the information being presented
10. Test the presentation and make any needed adjustments. Save

hands-on projects

chapter five

e-business

Exotic Flora

Exotic Flora is an international association of florists that was introduced in Chapter 1. The basic presentation was created to introduce the organization's services, but no graphics or animations were added. The goal is to place self-running kiosks on the Web site and in malls around the world. The purpose of the kiosk is to present the floral arrangements that can be purchased through the network. Now you will add photographs to go with the text, develop transitions, and set the presentation to run automatically.

1. Start PowerPoint and open **pp05ExoticFlora.ppt**
2. Search for photographs of exotic flower arrangements to be used on two of the slides. Try to find some of the flowers listed on the slides
3. Move to slide 3
   a. Refer to Figure 5.24 as you add a 3-D rectangle to frame the picture. Insert **splash.jpg** from the files for this chapter
   b. Size and arrange the image and frame
   c. Copy both the image and frame and paste them on slide 1
4. Move to slide 4. Using the techniques from the previous step, insert and frame **HA2.jpg**. Copy and paste the image and frame to slide 1
5. Move to slide 6. Using the same techniques, insert and frame **KeaMix.jpg**
6. Move to slide 7. Using the same techniques, insert and frame **OhanuMix.jpg**
7. On slides 2 and 5 add a rectangle with 3-D effect to frame the picture. Insert one of the images that you located. Adjust the frame and image and then group them. Copy one of the groups to slide 1
8. Arrange the three frames and images on slide 1 to create a display similar to that shown in Figure 5.25. Be sure to control the stacking order
9. Set transitions and animations for each slide. Set the slide show to automatically advance after 4 seconds on each slide
10. Save the presentation as **<yourname>ppt05ExoticFlora.ppt**

FIGURE 5.24
3-D Rectangle Framing splash.jpg

FIGURE 5.25
Grouping Framed Images

PP 5.40

chapter five

hands-on projects

around the world

Golden Globe, Inc.

Golden Globe is a successful exploration company that contracts with development companies across the world to locate gold ore. Gold ores are frequently found in association with various copper minerals such as malachite, copper sulfate, copper carbonate, chalcopyrite (copper iron sulfide), or silver. Golden Globe's business strategy has been to identify areas through geologic maps that correspond to known gold ore locations in association with copper or silver veins. Once an area has been identified, Golden Globe sends its geologists into the field to explore more fully. If substantial veins of gold are found, Golden Globe is given a bonus of 15 percent of the profits from the tonnage collected during the first year. With this in mind, Golden Globe has become a top-ranking gold exploration company in the world. Golden Globe has been hired to complete a preliminary assessment of the feasibility of marketable gold ore in the northwest sector of Australia. You have been asked to prepare a PowerPoint presentation for the Queensland Development Company on Golden Globe's preliminary report.

1. Start PowerPoint and open **pp05GoldenGlobe.ppt**
2. Set all slides to have a **Box Out** slide transition
3. Move to slide 1 and add an intrinsic sound. Set the sound to play without clicking
   a. Add an intrinsic sound that will play without clicking. Move the sound icon off the slide
   b. Add an **Unfold** Entrance effect to the title that plays automatically
   c. Add the **Rise Up** Entrance effect to the subtitle that plays automatically after the title
4. Move to slide 2 and add a graphic
   a. Set the Box Out Slide Transition to have a Chime
   b. Add the **Box In** animation to both the title and the graphic. Make the animations play simultaneously
5. Move to slide 3. Add the **Fold** Entrance effect to the bulleted text
6. Move to slide 4. Animate the chart to appear **By series** on mouse click
7. Move to slide 5. Add an appropriate graphic. Animate the graphic and title to **Spiral In** simultaneously
8. Repeat step 7 for slides 6 through 8
9. Move to slide 9
   a. Add and organize several relevant graphics
   b. Animate the bullets with a **Fly In** From Bottom Right Entrance effect
   c. Dim the text to light blue
10. Test the presentation and make any adjustments
11. Save your presentation as **<yourname>pp05GoldenGlobe.ppt**

LEVEL THREE

www.mhhe.com/i-series

PP 5.41

POWERPOINT

running project

Montgomery-Wellish Foods, Inc.: Preparing MWF FoodsPresentation to Be Self-Running

In the last chapter, you created a presentation designed to instruct new trainees on effective presentation skills. It was shown at one of the training meetings. Daniel Wellish would now like that presentation to be adapted so that it can run automatically at future training seminars or for trainees to review. You will need to make some adaptations to fit these new circumstances.

1. Open **<yourname>pp04MWFoodsPresentation.ppt** in PowerPoint
2. Locate an appropriate animated gif for the first slide, insert it, and configure it to play automatically
3. Use the techniques from this chapter to improve the graphics on each remaining slide of your presentation
4. Set animations on each slide
   a. Set each title to **Fly In** From Right without a mouse click
   b. Set bulleted text to Box In by 1st level paragraph when triggered by a mouse click
   c. Animate the graphics and set the animation to play at the same time as the title animation
   d. Dim text from previous bullets
5. Record a narration for the presentation using MWFscript.doc as your guide. Print the script for the best results. Use the options from the Slide Show menu. Remember to speak slowly and distinctly and pause between points. If necessary, rerecord
6. Save the presentation as **<yourname>PP05MWFoodsPresentation.ppt**

did you know?

the *most abundant metal in the Earth's crust is aluminum.*

seventy-five *percent of the hacking victims—most often corporations and government agencies—have found that it costs an average of $1 million per intrusion to investigate, repair, and secure their systems once they've been hacked.*

the *Wright brothers' historic flight covered a distance less than the length of today's Space Shuttle.*

"any *sufficiently advanced technology is indistinguishable from a rigged demo," James Klass*

nearly *60 percent of women say they receive at least 11 e-mails a day, whereas only _____ percent of men say they do.*

Chapter Objectives

- **Create and add Office Art elements to slides using the Drawing toolbar—PPT2002-3-3**
- **Modify PowerPoint Design Templates using Color Schemes**
- **Create and apply custom Color Schemes**
- **Customize slide backgrounds using bitmaps—PPT2002-3-2**
- **Add graphic elements to presentation notes**

CHAPTER

6

six

Color Schemes and Drawing

chapter case

Using PowerPoint to Report Progress

For the past year Ian Matubo has been the vice president of Human Resources for Aggregate Petroleum, a large oil and gas company with holdings in the United States, Canada, and Mexico. Aggregate has offices, filling stations, refineries, and oil wells throughout the North American continent with over 10,000 employees.

The organization is divided into 12 regions for management, distribution, and reporting purposes. Each region has a director of Human Resources who reports to Ian. Each director manages a staff responsible for all personnel issues in their region. Responsibilities include advertising for new employees, interviewing potential employees, screening résumés, managing employee benefits, documenting employee performance, resolving work-related conflicts, sponsoring employee recreational activities, monitoring disciplinary actions, and supervising terminations.

Large businesses like Aggregate use operations and procedures manuals to ensure common practice and equitable treatment of employees across the entire organization. Such manuals outline exactly what steps must be taken to hire, interview, fire, or discipline an employee. Actions that an employee must take to resolve conflict with another employee, a manager, or with the organization as a whole are also documented. Aggregate's current manual is over three years old and no longer reflects up-to-date practice or law.

FIGURE 6.1
Artwork for Ian's Presentation

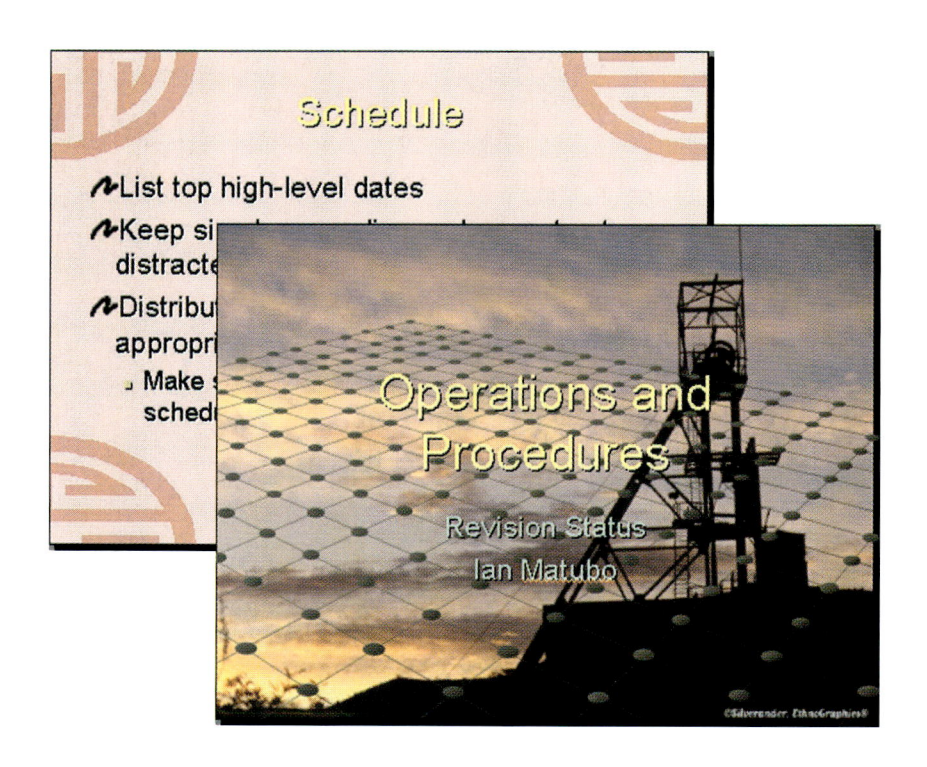

For the past month Ian and the Human Resource directors have been evaluating the updates that need to be applied to the operations and procedures manual. They have estimated that the update process will require four to six months, and they believe that it is important to involve the rest of Aggregate's employees in the process. Toward this end, Ian will begin presenting the status of this project at each region's monthly managers' meeting. For the first report, Ian will travel to each region and update the managers using a projected PowerPoint presentation. The remaining status updates will use PowerPoint's Web and broadcast capabilities so that Ian can present without traveling.

Ian has begun to develop his initial presentation using the AutoContent Wizard's template for reporting on the progress or status of a project. He believes that this template will be very effective in guiding him in the creation of slide content. Since he will be presenting to a large professional audience, he would like a customized business look for the slide show and has asked you to work on colors and graphics that would be effective.

SESSION 6.1 CHOOSING A COLOR SCHEME

Making a presentation aesthetically pleasing is an important component in maintaining audience attention and producing a professional-looking slide show. PowerPoint templates use a ***color scheme*** to control the colors for the slide background, body text, lines, shadows, title text, fills, hyperlinks, and accents. PowerPoint's features make it easy to evaluate various color schemes until you find the one that will best suit current needs.

USING COLOR SCHEMES

Selecting an effective color scheme or ***palette*** involves evaluating the audience and the presentation forum. Color sets the tone of a presentation and must be appealing to viewers. The method of delivery (projected, printed, or computer monitor) impacts the value of selected colors.

A great deal of research has been compiled on the most effective use of color. Consider the audience, tone, speaker's personality, and what is being communicated when selecting colors. A complete discussion of color theory is beyond the scope of this chapter; please refer to art and color theory materials for guidance in these matters.

Intrinsic Color Schemes

The slide template of a presentation determines the initial color scheme applied to a slide show. Each design template, including the blank template, has a default color scheme and several alternate color schemes referred to as ***intrinsic color schemes***. Alternate schemes display in the Slide Design—Color Schemes panel of the Task pane. Each scheme has

CHAPTER OUTLINE

6.1 Choosing a Color Scheme

6.2 Creating Custom Art

6.3 Summary

FIGURE 6.2

Title Page with Various Color Schemes

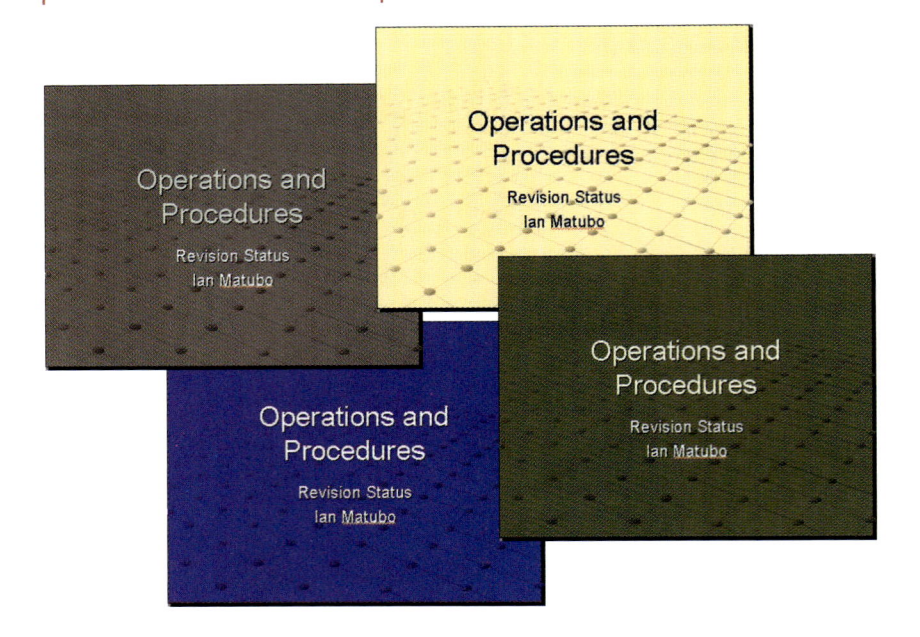

been developed by artists with color theory, audience appeal, and effective content delivery in mind. Additionally, custom colors can be used with any palette or a completely custom palette can be developed. Ian would like to use the colors of Aggregate's logo for his presentation, if they will work effectively.

---

task reference

Select a Color Scheme

- Select a Design Template
- Select the slide(s) the color scheme will be applied to
- Use the drop-down menu of the Task pane to activate the Slide Design—Color Scheme panel
- Click a Color Scheme

Changing the pp06StatusReport.ppt Color Scheme:

1. Initiate PowerPoint and open **PP06StatusReport.ppt**

   tip: *The Digital Dots Design Template has already been applied to all slides in the presentation*

2. Select the first slide

3. Use the drop-down menu of the Task pane to activate the Slide Design—Color Scheme panel

   tip: *Use the View menu to activate the Task pane if it is not already displaying*

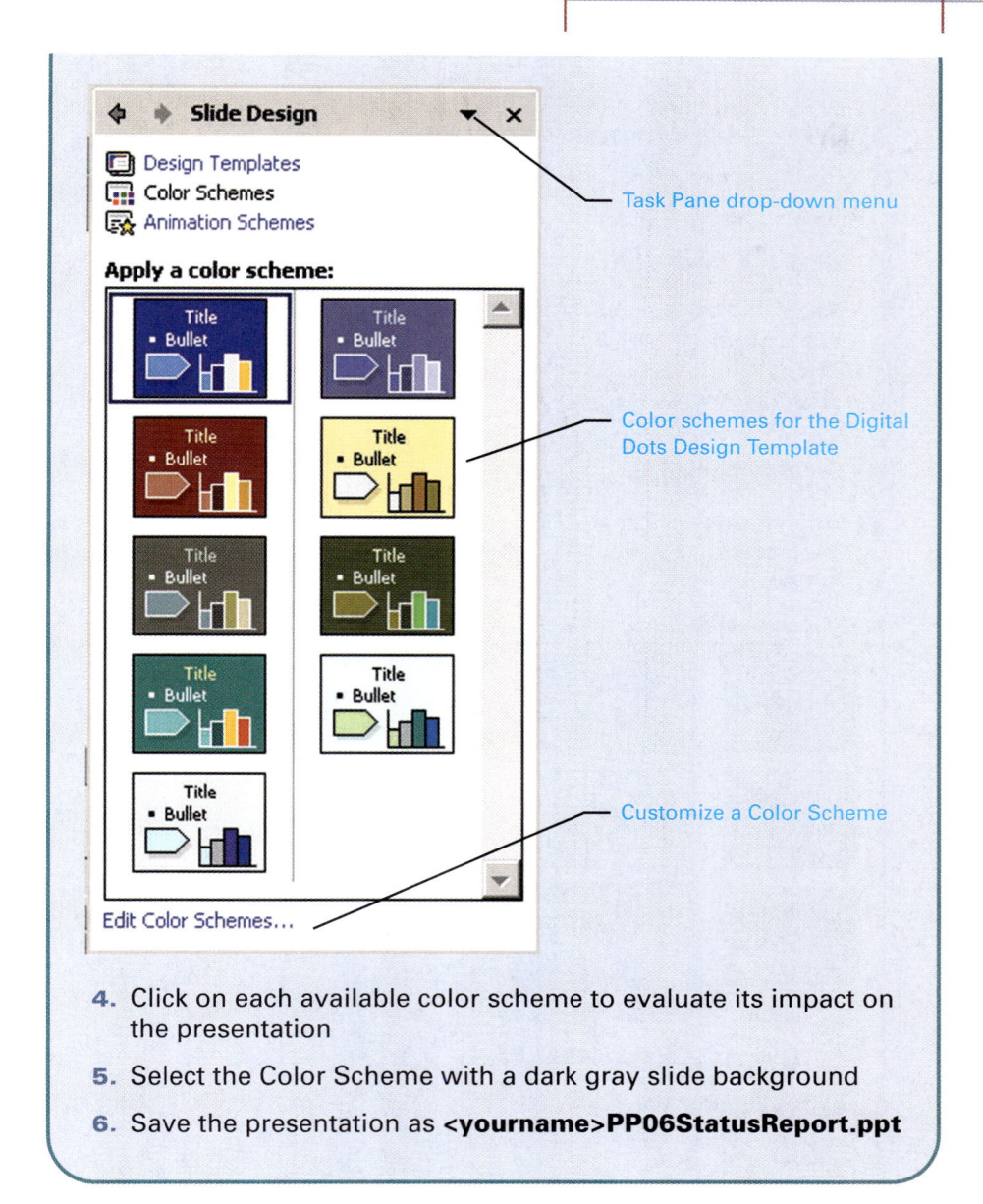

FIGURE 6.3
Digital Dots Color Schemes

- Task Pane drop-down menu
- Color schemes for the Digital Dots Design Template
- Customize a Color Scheme

4. Click on each available color scheme to evaluate its impact on the presentation
5. Select the Color Scheme with a dark gray slide background
6. Save the presentation as **<yourname>PP06StatusReport.ppt**

The Color Scheme selected impacts the personality and readability of the presentation. In general, light backgrounds are best for printed presentations and dark backgrounds work best for on-screen or projected presentations. Regardless of how the presentation will be delivered, legible text always requires high contrast between the text and background.

Projected presentations should be previewed with the projector that will be used whenever possible. Projection can introduce unpredictable color distortions such as brown tones appearing orange in the projected image. These distortions vary from projector to projector and can cause the audience to be unable to read slide text and decipher images. Colors that work well for projection can look very unappealing on the presenter's monitor but still provide the most effective viewing environment for the audience.

Sometimes it is essential to draw attention to an important topic or to visually let the audience know that a new subject is being introduced. One way to accomplish this is by using different color schemes within the same presentation.

POWERPOINT

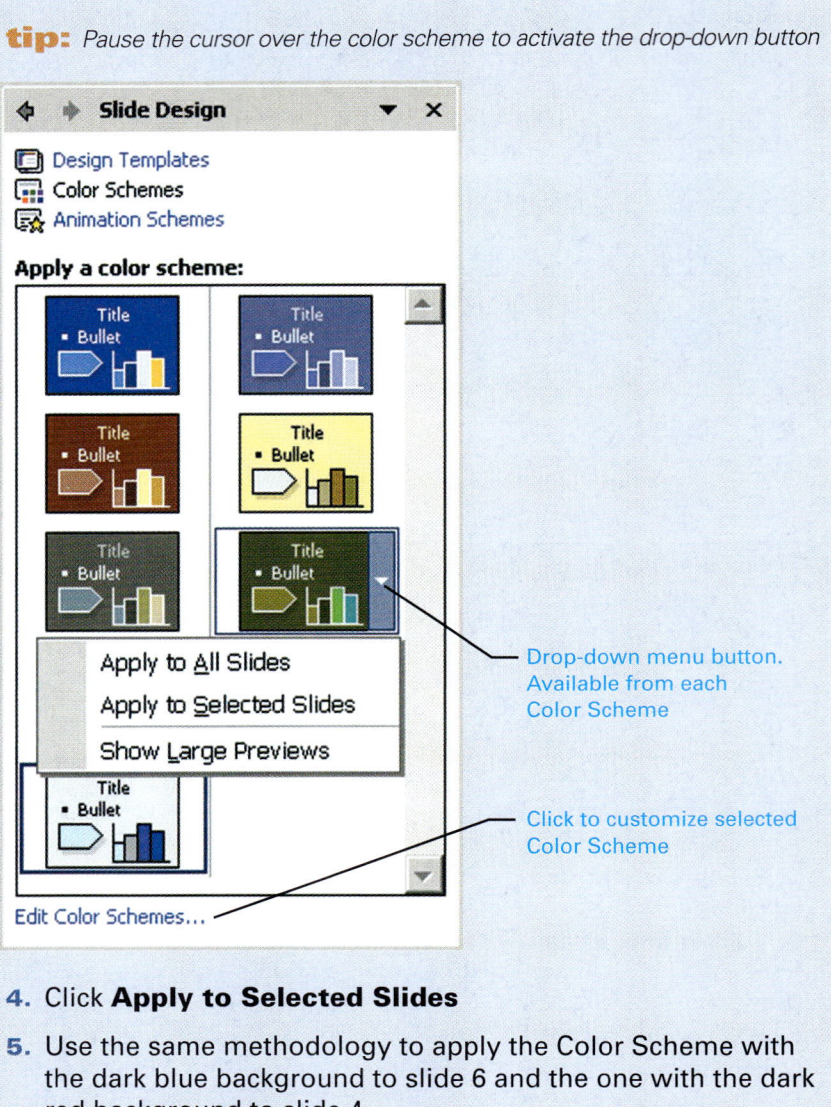

FIGURE 6.4
Color Scheme Drop-Down Button

Using multiple Color Schemes in pp06StatusReport.ppt:

1. Verify that PowerPoint is running with **PP06StatusReport.ppt** open
2. Select the third slide
3. Activate the Color Scheme drop-down menu with a teal background

tip: *Pause the cursor over the color scheme to activate the drop-down button*

— Drop-down menu button. Available from each Color Scheme

— Click to customize selected Color Scheme

4. Click **Apply to Selected Slides**
5. Use the same methodology to apply the Color Scheme with the dark blue background to slide 6 and the one with the dark red background to slide 4
6. Save the presentation

A Color Scheme can be applied to the entire slide show, a single slide, or multiple slides. Multiple adjacent slides are selected by clicking the first slide and holding the Shift key while clicking the last slide. Multiple non-contiguous slides are selected by clicking the first slide and then holding the Ctrl key while clicking each of the remaining slides.

FIGURE 6.5

Color Scheme Applied to Notes and Handouts

Although it is unusual, Color Schemes can be applied to notes pages and handouts. Use the Notes View to apply a scheme to notes or use the Handout Master to update handouts. Since notes and handouts are usually printed, a color printer is needed to see the full impact of selected color schemes. When selecting color schemes for printed materials, it is important to consider that background colors consume large quantities of ink and significantly slow printing time.

Customizing a Color Scheme

The palette of an individual presentation is automatically updated when the color of a font, or other palette object, is changed. The new color appears below the eight colors of the Color Scheme (slide background, body text, lines, shadows, title text, fills, hyperlinks, and accents) on all color menus. The ability to view colors that have already been applied in a presentation helps you to be consistent.

When different colors are frequently used for a component or two of a Design Template, customizing the color scheme simplifies the process and ensures uniformity. Customizing the color scheme is an efficient way to change a color component that does not display well on a monitor or projector throughout a presentation. Color Schemes can also be adapted to an event theme that is relevant to a presentation. Any of the eight template colors can be modified using the Color Schemes Task pane.

The result of modifying any or all slide colors is a new color scheme. The eight Color Scheme elements (slide background, body text, lines, shadows, title text, fills, hyperlinks, and accents) will change or update if a new Color Scheme is selected, while other custom colors that have been applied to a presentation will not change.

FIGURE 6.6
Edit Color Scheme Dialog Box

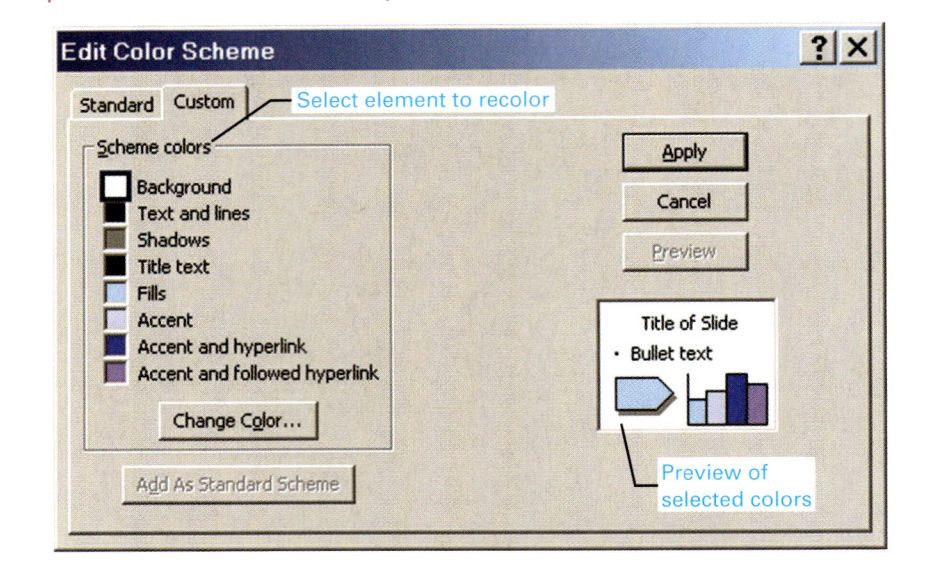

task reference
Customize a Color Scheme

- Use the Task pane drop-down list to activate the **Slide Design—Color Scheme** panel
- Click the **Edit Color Schemes** link in the Slide Design—Color Scheme panel
- On the **Standard** tab of the Edit Color Scheme dialog box, select the Standard Color Scheme to be customized
- On the **Custom** tab, select the Color Scheme element to customize and click **Change Color**
  - Use either the Standard or Custom tab of the Background Color dialog box to select a new color
  - Click **OK**
- Repeat the previous step for each element to be customized
- Use the **Preview** button to view the new colors on your slide
- Click **Apply** to permanently apply the changes

Customizing the pp06StatusReport.ppt Color Scheme:

1. Verify that PowerPoint is running with **PP06StatusReport.ppt** open
2. Select the first slide
3. Use the Task pane drop-down list to activate the **Slide Design—Color Scheme**
4. Click the **Edit Color Schemes** link

5. On the **Standard** tab of the Edit Color Scheme dialog box, select the Standard Color Scheme that matches the current slide (dark gray background)

6. On the **Custom** tab of the Edit Color Scheme dialog box, click the **Title Text** element and click **Change Color**

7. On the Standard tab of the Title Text Color dialog box, choose the color indicated in the next figure and click **OK**

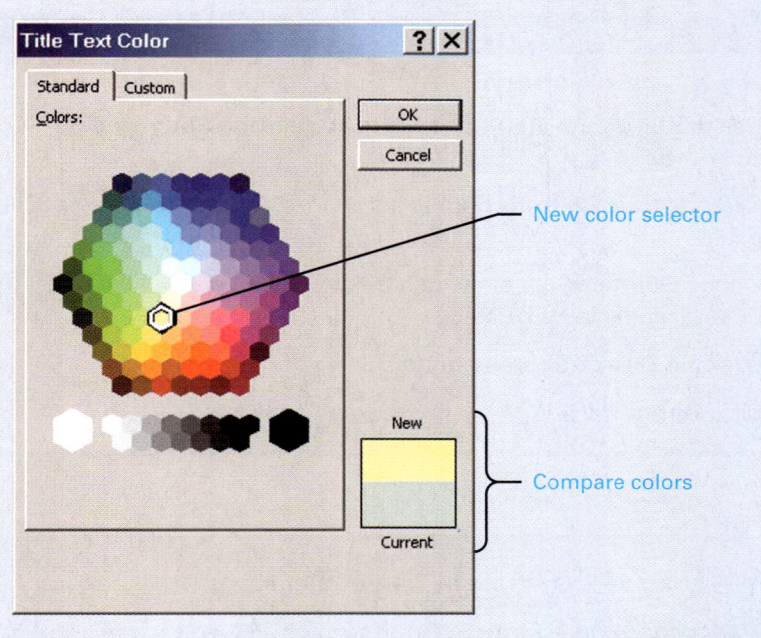

FIGURE 6.7
Selecting a New Title Color

8. Repeat the process to choose a light blue color for Text and Lines

9. Use the Preview button to evaluate the impact on your slide

10. Click **Apply** to apply the revised color scheme to the presentation and create a custom scheme

11. Save the presentation

Each time a standard color scheme is modified a new color scheme is created. A total of 16 color schemes can be stored for each design template. Custom color schemes display along with the standard schemes in the color gallery in the Slide Design—Color Schemes Task pane. Custom schemes are available to any presentation using the design template that was updated.

Painting and Deleting a Color Scheme

PowerPoint's format painting feature can be used to copy the color scheme from one slide to another slide within a presentation or to copy schemes between presentations. Click the slide with the format that you would like to copy and then activate the Format Painter button of the Standard toolbar. Single-click the button to apply the format to one additional slide, or double-click it to apply the format to multiple slides. The Esc key will cancel format painting initiated by double-clicking. When a color scheme is copied from another presentation, it becomes available in the Slide Design—Color Schemes Task pane of the destination presentation.

Color Schemes can be deleted from the list of Standard schemes using the Edit Color Scheme dialog box. It is important to remove any color schemes that are created by mistake or are not used for another reason. An unnecessary color scheme will be created and deleted to demonstrate this concept.

task reference
Delete a Color Scheme

- Use the Task pane drop-down list to activate the **Slide Design—Color Scheme** panel
- Click the **Edit Color Schemes** link in the Slide Design—Color Scheme panel
- On the **Standard** tab of the Edit Color Scheme dialog box, select the Color Scheme to be deleted
- Click the **Delete Scheme** button
- Click **Apply**

Deleting a custom Color Scheme:

1. Verify that PowerPoint is running with **PP06StatusReport.ppt** open
2. Select the first slide
3. Use the Task pane drop-down list to activate the **Slide Design—Color Scheme**
4. Click the **Edit Color Schemes** link
5. On the **Standard** tab of the Edit Color Scheme dialog box, select the Standard Color Scheme with a dark green background
6. On the **Custom** tab of the Edit Color Scheme dialog box, click the **Background** element and click **Change Color**
7. Choose a bright green, click **OK,** and then **Apply**

tip: The bright green Color Scheme has now been added to the Standard Schemes gallery

8. Click the **Edit Color Schemes** link to reactivate the Edit Color Scheme dialog box
9. On the **Standard** tab of the Edit Color Scheme dialog box, select the Standard Color Scheme with a light green background
10. Click the Delete Scheme

tip: The scheme will also be removed from the presentation

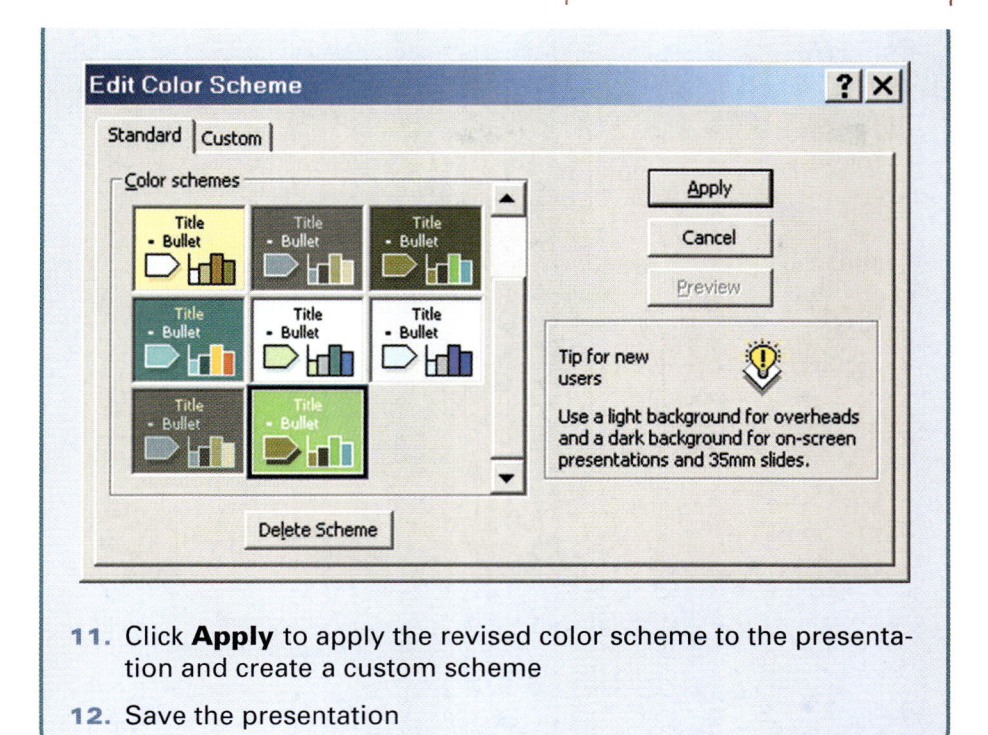

FIGURE 6.8
Deleting a Color Scheme

11. Click **Apply** to apply the revised color scheme to the presentation and create a custom scheme
12. Save the presentation

A mistakenly deleted color scheme can be restored using the Undo button of the standard toolbar. Reinstalling PowerPoint may be required to restore standard color schemes once the application has been shut down. Deleting a color scheme makes it unavailable to other presentations using the updated design template.

CUSTOMIZING THE COLOR MENUS

The eight colors defined by the selected Color Scheme are automatically applied to the appropriate components of each slide. These colors will display on all color menus. Other colors are added to these menus as you apply them to slide components. Colors added to one of the menus, for example the Font Color Menu, will appear on all of the other menus. This feature allows you to apply the same custom color to various objects throughout the presentation.

Adding new colors to the Color Menus:

1. Verify that PowerPoint is running with **PP06StatusReport.ppt** open

2. Move to slide **2** and select the text box in the top triangle containing **The Future**

   tip: You will need a dotted line selection box around the object or to select the text

3. Drop down the **Font Color** selections from the Formatting toolbar
   a. Click **More Colors** to activate the Colors dialog box

PP 6.12 CHAPTER 6 **POWERPOINT** **6.1** Choosing A Color Scheme

FIGURE 6.9
Color Menus

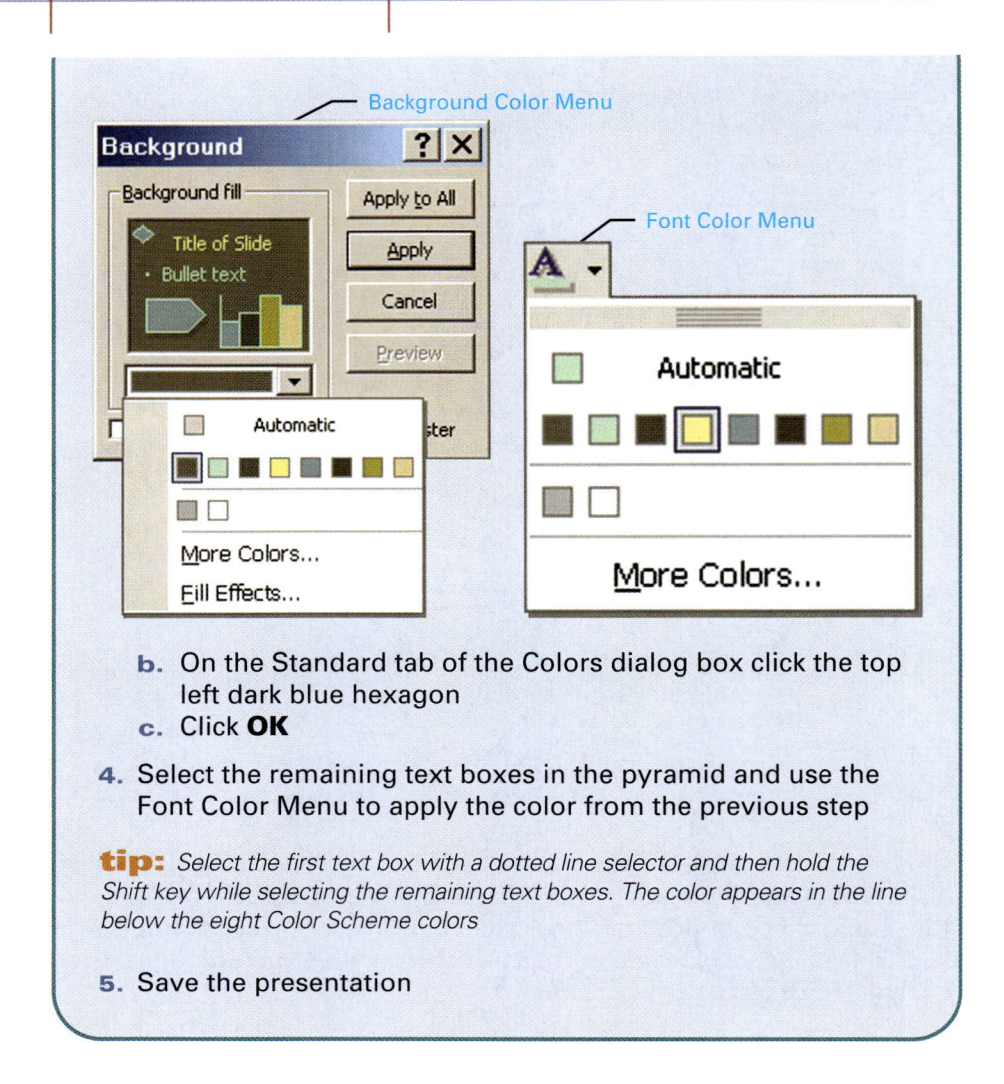

b. On the Standard tab of the Colors dialog box click the top left dark blue hexagon
c. Click **OK**

4. Select the remaining text boxes in the pyramid and use the Font Color Menu to apply the color from the previous step

tip: *Select the first text box with a dotted line selector and then hold the Shift key while selecting the remaining text boxes. The color appears in the line below the eight Color Scheme colors*

5. Save the presentation

As was previously mentioned, the Color Menus are palettes that display colors already in use for a presentation. Up to eight custom colors display below the eight colors of the active color scheme. If more than eight custom colors are used in a presentation, the ninth color displays in the first slot replacing the first custom color used. The tenth color will display in the second slot, and so on.

CUSTOMIZING SLIDE BACKGROUNDS

Changing the color of a slide background can be accomplished by adjusting the Background component of the color scheme, or using the Background Color menu. The Background Color menu can also be used to change the slide background to a texture, fill pattern, or picture.

Gradient and Texture Backgrounds

Gradient and Texture backgrounds add a depth and professionalism to a presentation. Gradient backgrounds merge two or more colors to create the illusion of light. Gradients and textures can be added using the preset selections or colors from the presentation's Color Scheme, or they can be completely customized.

www.mhhe.com/i-series   PP 6.13

task reference
Define a Gradient Background
- Right-click on the slide to contain the gradient background
- Click the **Background** pop-up menu option
- Click **Fill Effects**
- Click the **Gradient** tab
- Select the desired gradient effects and click **OK**
- Click either
  - **Apply to All** to set this as the background for all presentation slides
  - **Apply** to set this as the background for the selected slides only

Adding a gradient background to pp06StatusReport.ppt:

1. Verify that PowerPoint is running with **PP06StatusReport.ppt** open
2. Select the third slide
3. Right-click on the slide background and select **Background** from the pop-up menu
4. Drop down the Color Menu and select **Fill Effects**
5. Activate the Gradient tab and refer to the next figure for the settings
   a. Select the **Two Colors** option button
   b. Match the Color 1 and Color 2 selections shown in Figure 6.10
   c. Click the **From Corner** Shading Style option button
   d. Click **OK** to accept the default variant

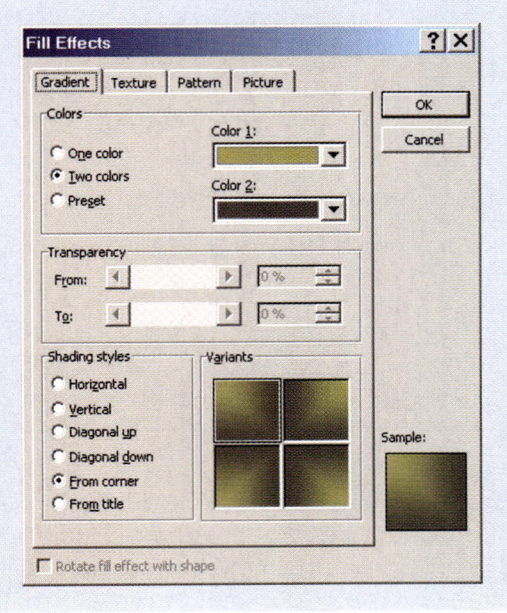

FIGURE 6.10
Gradient Settings

POWERPOINT

6. Click **Apply** to apply the gradient to the current slide
7. Save the presentation

The gradient background just applied should appear behind the graphic of the Digital Dots Design Template. In this case the gradient effect works well with the template graphic and slide text. Sometimes the result could be too busy for a readable slide, and one solution is to omit the graphic. The Background option of the slide pop-up menu has a check box that will omit any background graphics from the Slide Master.

task reference
Select a Texture Background
- Right-click on the slide to contain the texture background
- Click the **Background** pop-up menu option
- Click **Fill Effects**
- Click the **Texture** tab
- Select the desired texture and click **OK**
- Click either
  - **Apply to All** to set this as the background for all presentation slides
  - **Apply** to set this as the background for the selected slides only

FIGURE 6.11

Selecting the Purple Mesh Texture

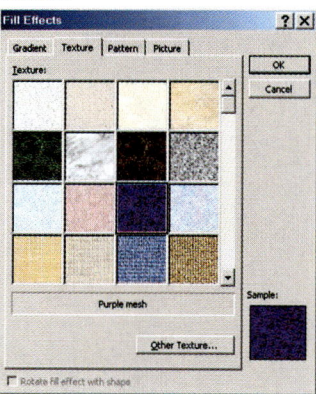

Adding a texture background to pp06StatusReport.ppt:

1. Verify that PowerPoint is running with **PP06StatusReport.ppt** open
2. Select the second slide
3. Right-click on the slide background and select **Background** from the pop-up menu
4. Drop down the Color Menu and select **Fill Effects**
5. Activate the Texture tab, select the **Purple Mesh** texture, and click **OK**
6. Click **Apply** to apply the texture to the current slide
7. Save the presentation

Many of the available textures are busy and can detract from the text in a presentation. Be sure to select textures that are appropriate for your audience and topic, while still providing the high contrast necessary for readable text. When changing the text color does not improve readability, adding a solid panel behind the text will usually allow text to be read. This technique, called *matting*, will be demonstrated with a busy picture background in the next topic.

Picture Backgrounds

Pictures can also be used as slide backgrounds. Appropriate background images typically are related to the presentation topic and will not interfere with the text of the presentation. The Microsoft Clip Organizer contains a few background images. A broader image selection is available from the online gallery, or images from other sources can be used.

---

task reference

Apply a Picture Background

- Locate and save an appropriate picture
- Right-click on the slide to contain the picture background
- Click the **Background** pop-up menu option
- Click **Fill Effects**
- Click the **Picture** tab
- Click the **Select Picture** button, choose the picture file, click **Insert**, and then click **OK**
- Click either
  - **Apply to All** to set this as the background for all presentation slides
  - **Apply** to set this as the background for the selected slides only
  - **Preview** to evaluate the effect of the background without applying it

---

Adding a picture background to pp06StatusReport.ppt:

1. Verify that PowerPoint is running with **PP06StatusReport.ppt** open
2. Select the first slide
3. Right-click on the slide background and select **Background** from the pop-up menu
4. Drop down the Color Menu and select **Fill Effects**
5. Activate the **Picture** tab
6. Click the **Select Picture** button, navigate to the files for this chapter, select **pp06SunriseOil.jpg**, and click **Insert**
7. Click **Apply** to apply the picture to the current slide
8. Move to slide **4**, make **pp06Background2.jpg** the background picture, and check **Omit background graphics from master**

FIGURE 6.12

Title Slide with SunriseOil Picture Background

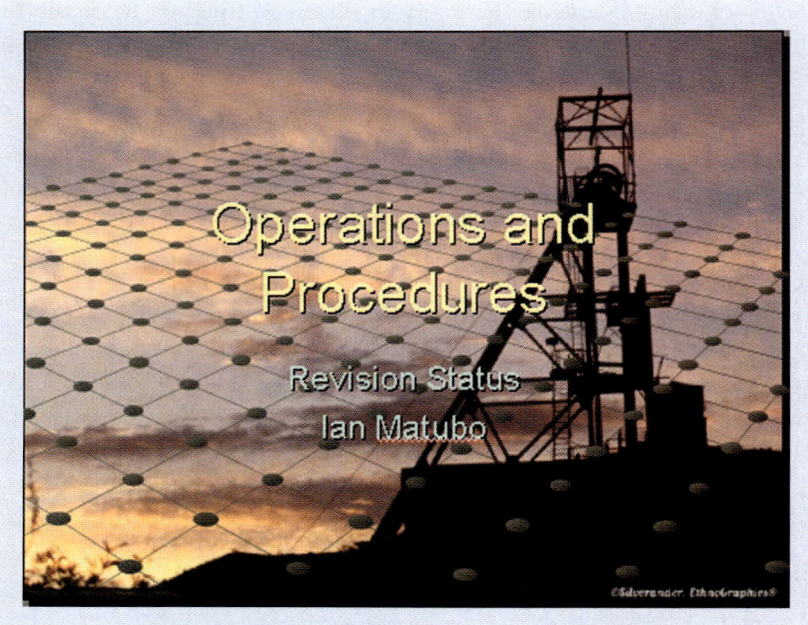

9. Move to slide **5**, make **pp06Background2.wmf** the background picture, and check **Omit background graphics from master**
10. Adjust the text color in slides 4 and 5 to black
11. Save the presentation

Any picture format that can be accessed by PowerPoint can be used as a background. Most of the sources already mentioned for graphics have images specifically designed to be used as backgrounds. The images used in the previous steps were downloaded from the Microsoft Media Gallery online.

The fourth slide is still not as readable as Ian would like, so you decide to apply a mat effect behind the text. Matting can be accomplished using shape objects from the drawing toolbar or by simply formatting each placeholder.

Adding a mat background to pp06StatusReport.ppt text:

1. Verify that PowerPoint is running with **PP06StatusReport.ppt** open
2. Select the fourth slide
3. Right-click on the title placeholder and select **Format Placeholder** from the pop-up menu
4. Drop down the Fill Color Menu and select the **White** color square
5. Select a dark gray (not black) line color and set the line weight to **2.5 pt**
6. Click **OK**

7. Repeat steps 3 through 6 for the bulleted list placeholder

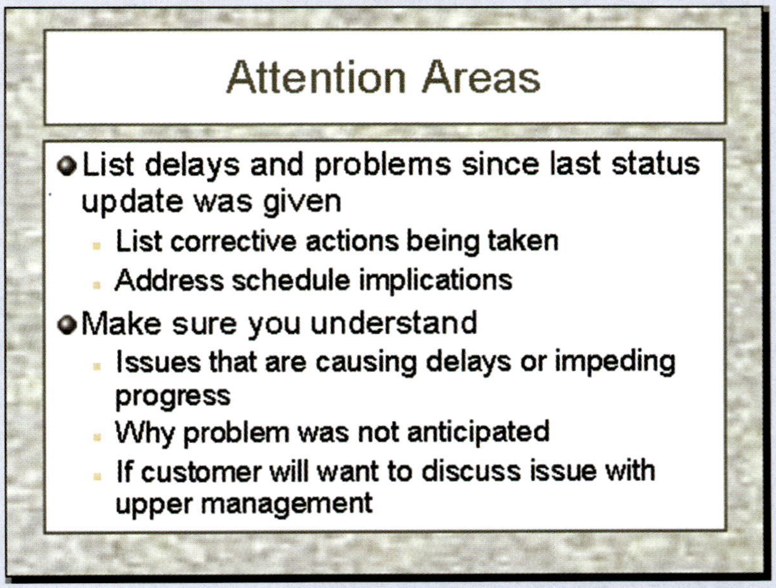

FIGURE 6.13
Formatted Text Placeholders

Attention Areas
- List delays and problems since last status update was given
  - List corrective actions being taken
  - Address schedule implications
- Make sure you understand
  - Issues that are causing delays or impeding progress
  - Why problem was not anticipated
  - If customer will want to discuss issue with upper management

8. Use the formatting toolbar to remove the shadow from all slide text

tip: *Select the text and click the* **Shadow** *button*

9. Save the presentation

When matting text by formatting the placeholder background, select a color that compliments the background image on the slide while maintaining high contrast between the mat and text. Adding a line around the mat provides a 3-D effect. Experiment with different line colors and weights until you achieve the desired look. All of the custom background effects that have been applied to slides can also be applied to notes pages.

Pictures as Bullets

You have seen pictures used as bullets in the PowerPoint templates. Custom bullets can be selected to match the theme or color scheme of any presentation. The Clip Organizer contains several images that make suitable bullets, and more are available online.

task reference
Apply a Picture as a Bullet
- Select the text or list that will contain the picture bullet
- On the **Format** menu, click **Bullets and Numbering**, and then click the **Bulleted** tab
- On the Bulleted tab, click the **Picture** button
  - Select a picture from the Picture Bullet dialog box
  - Click **OK**

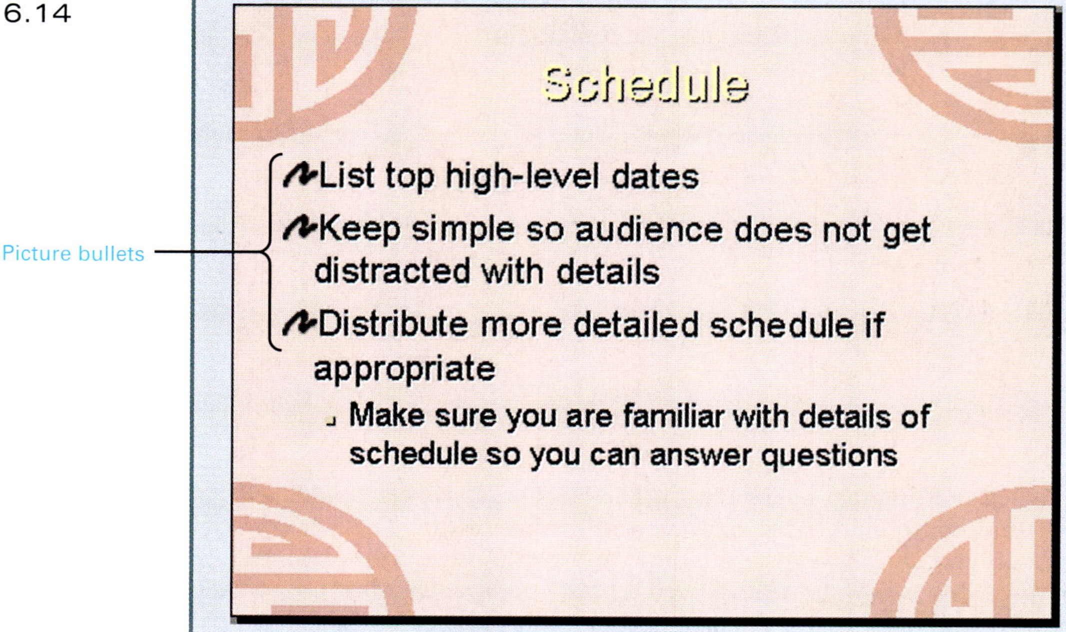

FIGURE 6.14
Picture Bullets

Adding a picture bullet to pp06StatusReport.ppt:

1. Verify that PowerPoint is running with **PP06StatusReport.ppt** open
2. Select the fifth slide
3. Select the first three bullets
4. On the **Format** menu, click **Bullets and Numbering**, and then click the **Bulleted** tab
5. On the Bulleted tab, click the **Picture** button
6. Select the picture shown in the next figure

[Slide image showing "Schedule" with picture bullets:]
- List top high-level dates
- Keep simple so audience does not get distracted with details
- Distribute more detailed schedule if appropriate
  - Make sure you are familiar with details of schedule so you can answer questions

Picture bullets

7. Click **OK** to apply the picture to the selected text
8. Save the presentation

Pictures used as bullets should match the color scheme and topic of the presentation. Custom photographs and scanned images can be used a bullets with the Import button of the Picture Bullet dialog box. Imported images will appear as a choice in the dialog box. Custom bullets set in the Slide Master will be applied to all slides based on that master.

SESSION 6.2 CREATING CUSTOM ART

Shapes, pictures, and clip art are critical components of a compelling presentation. Although large collections of stock artwork are readily available, the ability to create and modify custom images can greatly enhance any slide show.

making the grade

SESSION 6.1

1. What are intrinsic color schemes?
2. Assume that you are creating a presentation for parents of brain injured children. The content has three distinct parts: types of injuries, financial resources, and support groups. What color scheme would be appropriate?
3. How many custom colors can be displayed on the Color Menu palette?
4. How can you make the text more readable when using pictures, textures, and fill effects on slide backgrounds?

CREATING AND MODIFYING DRAWING OBJECTS

The drawing toolbar allows standard objects such as lines, rectangles, and shapes to be drawn, edited, customized, and combined to create complex artwork. Each shape can be resized, rotated, flipped, colored, and combined into complex shapes. To draw an object, select the drawing tool or AutoShape from the drawing toolbar; then drag on the slide to create the object.

Draw and Format Objects

The Drawing toolbar displays the most commonly used shapes so they can be readily selected. The AutoShapes menu contains the full array of drawing objects categorized as lines, connectors, Basic Shapes, Block Arrows, Flowchart, Stars and Banners, Callouts, and more. Additional shapes can be accessed from the Clip Organizer.

task reference
Using the AutoShape Button of the Drawing Toolbar

- Select the slide that will contain the AutoShape
- Click the **AutoShapes** menu of the **Drawing** toolbar
- Select the shape category and then the shape to be applied
- Click and drag on the slide surface to create the shape

Adding an AutoShape object to pp06StatusReport.ppt:

1. Verify that PowerPoint is running with **PP06StatusReport.ppt** open
2. Select the tenth slide
3. Activate the **AutoShapes** menu, select **Block Arrows**, and then select the upward pointing arrow from the first row

4. Refer to the next figure as you click and drag the shape on the bottom right-hand corner of the slide

tip: *You are creating the upward pointing light gray arrow from the figure*

5. With the object selected, click the **Fill Color** tool of the Drawing toolbar and choose a light gray

6. Select the downward pointing block arrow from the AutoShapes menu and draw an arrow below the current one

tip: *You are creating the orange arrow in the figure*

7. Use the **Fill Color** tool to color the new arrow orange

8. Use the clipboard to copy and paste a second orange arrow

9. Use the **Fill Color** tool to make the copy gold and drag it to the location shown

10. Create, color, and position the straight left and right pointing arrows

11. Create, color, and position the left and right curved arrows

12. Save the presentation

FIGURE 6.15

Block Arrow Object

The previous steps created and formatted the group of objects that will be used as a single graphic on the Goals slide. To create the final graphic, these individual objects will be combined into one object, rotated, and have 3-D effects applied.

Customizing Objects

All objects from the AutoShapes menu are drawn, colored, and positioned in the same fashion as the arrows manipulated in the previous steps. Each drawn object can be moved, copied, pasted, and resized as you practiced with the arrows. In addition, all objects can be rotated, many objects can contain text, and some objects include ***adjustment handles*** that can be used to change the object's prominent features.

Text can be added to most objects. Text added to a shape becomes part of the shape and will rotate and flip as those options are applied to the shape. Once a shape has been added to the slide, the shortcut menu contains the Add Text option. Text added to an object can be selected and formatted like any other text on the slide.

task reference

Adding Text to an AutoShape

- Select the AutoShape
- Right-click the **AutoShape** and select **Add Text** from the shortcut menu
- Type and format the text

FIGURE 6.16

Text Added to a Block Arrow Object

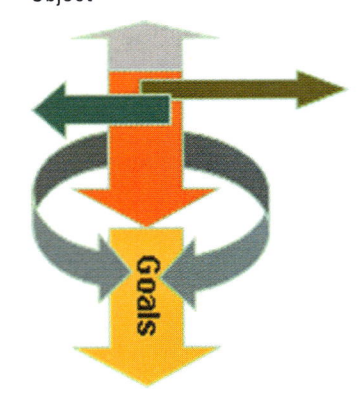

Adding text to an AutoShape object in pp06StatusReport.ppt:

1. Verify that PowerPoint is running with **PP06StatusReport.ppt** open
2. If you are not already at the tenth slide, move to it
3. Right-click on the downward pointing gold arrow and select **Add Text** from the pop-up menu
4. Type **Goals** in the arrow's text box
5. Select the text and use the toolbar to bold it and change the color to dark gray
6. Save the presentation

Notice that the text added to the downward pointing arrow in the previous steps is oriented with the arrow. All drawn objects have a default text orientation that can be adjusted 90 degrees using the formatting options of the object. As a drawn object is rotated, the text will also reorient. In the next steps these techniques will be used to create a graphic slide title.

To add interest to the presentation, Ian would like to use an image to contain the title on slide 8. The ribbon with the title will run down the left edge of the slide.

Rotating text in an AutoShape object:

1. Verify that PowerPoint is running with **PP06StatusReport.ppt** open
2. Move to slide 8
3. Select the title placeholder containing the text Technology and delete it
4. Activate the AutoShapes menu from the Drawing toolbar and select **More AutoShapes**
5. Locate the light blue Sharp Ribbon Object and add it to your slide

tip: *Pause the cursor over the image to see its name*

6. Right-click on the ribbon, choose **Add Text**, and type **TECHNOLOGY**
7. Select TECHNOLOGY and use the toolbars to center it, and make it **Bold** and **28** point
8. Right-click on the ribbon and choose **Format AutoShape** from the pop-up menu
9. Click the Text Box tab, check both Resize AutoShape to fit text and Rotate text within shape by 90°, and click **OK**

FIGURE 6.17
Rotated Text in a Ribbon

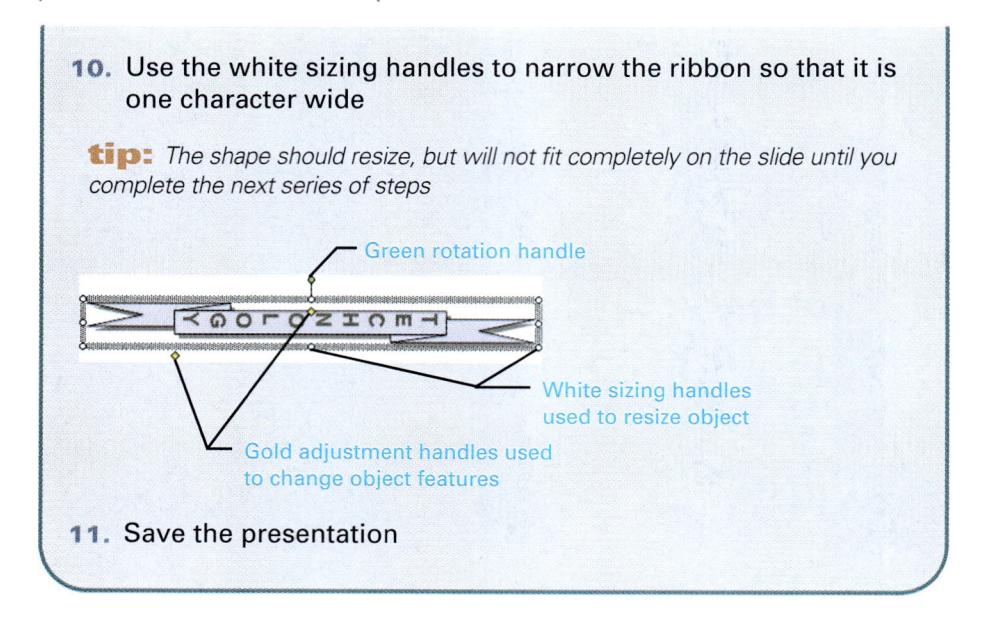

10. Use the white sizing handles to narrow the ribbon so that it is one character wide

   tip: *The shape should resize, but will not fit completely on the slide until you complete the next series of steps*

   — Green rotation handle
   — White sizing handles used to resize object
   — Gold adjustment handles used to change object features

11. Save the presentation

Most objects contain eight white resizing handles. The four corner handles can be used to adjust height and width simultaneously, while the remaining handles will only adjust one dimension. The green handle, called the ***rotation handle***, controls the rotation of an object. Clicking and dragging the rotation handle will adjust the orientation of the object on the slide. The TECHNOLOGY ribbon needs to be rotated to a vertical rather than horizontal orientation.

FIGURE 6.18
Rotated Ribbon

Using the ribbon object's rotation handle:

1. Verify that PowerPoint is running with **PP06StatusReport.ppt** open
2. If slide 8 is not the active slide, move to it
3. Select the TECHNOLOGY ribbon by clicking on it
4. Click and drag the green rotation handle down and to the left until the ribbon is vertical as shown in the next figure
5. Click outside the object to set the rotation
6. Save the presentation

another way
. . . to rotate an object

Rotating an object by 90 degrees to the left or right can also be accomplished using the Draw menu of the Drawing toolbar. From the Draw menu select Rotate or Flip and then use either Rotate Left or Rotate Right to achieve the desired result. This process can be reversed with the Undo menu or repeated to rotate an additional 90 degrees.

The gold handles shown in Figure 6.17 are called adjustment handles and will modify the prominent features of an object. For example, the adjustment handles for a block arrow object will change the size of the arrow head, and those of a parallelogram will adjust the wall angle. In the ribbon object, the adjustment handles control how long the ribbon tails are and how far offset the center of the ribbon is from the tails. Adjusting the ribbon will help it to fit on the slide effectively.

> **anotherword**
>
> **. . . on rotating objects**
>
> Sometimes the freedom of an object's rotation handle can be difficult to control precisely. Hold down the **Shift** key while rotating to limit the rotation to 15-degree angles, making the rotation process easier to manage.

Adjusting the ribbon object's prominent features:

1. Verify that PowerPoint is running with **PP06StatusReport.ppt** open
2. If slide 8 is not the active slide, move to it
3. Select the TECHNOLOGY ribbon by clicking on it

tip: *You may need to click the object again to activate the gold adjustment handles*

4. Drag the upper golden adjustment handle to the left until the ribbon is rectangular and then drag it back to the right to make it as narrow as possible
5. Drag the bottom golden adjustment handle up to lengthen the tails of the ribbon and then down until the ribbon fits properly on the slide

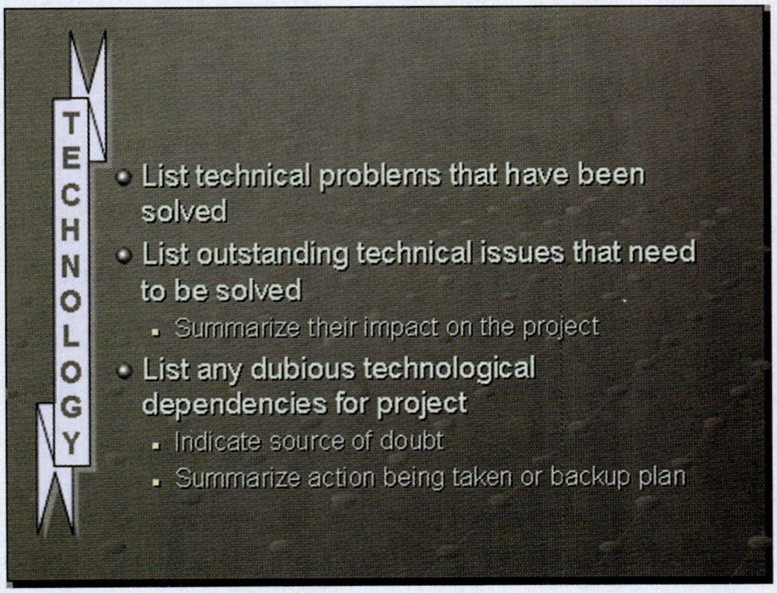

FIGURE 6.19
Adjusted Ribbon AutoShape

6. Adjust the size and position of the bulleted placeholder and the ribbon until their orientation matches the figure
7. Adjust the text color if necessary
8. Save the presentation

The prominent features of each AutoShape object are different, but the adjustment techniques are the same. The adjustment handles will change the shape of a prominent feature while holding the object size constant. As an adjustment handle is moved, a dotted outline of the object indicates how the object will be changed when the mouse button is released. When you have a concept of the shape that you would like to use, find the AutoShape that is closest to your ideal, and then manipulate the adjustment handles to achieve the desired effect.

Positioning Objects

When two or more objects are placed on a slide, aligning them manually can pose a problem. The Draw menu of the Drawing toolbar has options to position objects relative to each other. Another useful feature allows shapes to be flipped either horizontally or vertically.

Aligning objects:

1. Verify that PowerPoint is running with **PP06StatusReport.ppt** open
2. Move to slide 9
3. Use the **More AutoShapes** option of the **AutoShapes** menu to place a Scanner, a Printer, and a Computer with Tower in the top right-hand corner of the slide
4. Position the scanner to the left of the computer and the printer to the right with the images overlapping slightly
5. Select all three AutoShape objects by selecting the first and then holding the **Shift** key while clicking the others
6. Open the **Draw** menu of the Drawing toolbar, point to **Align or Distribute,** and then select **Align Middle**. Repeat the process selecting **Align Bottom** to demonstrate alignment differences
7. Open the **Draw** menu of the Drawing toolbar, point to **Align or Distribute,** and then select **Distribute Horizontally**
8. Left align the title text
9. Adjust the position of the bulleted placeholder and the aligned objects until they are similar to the next figure
10. Save the presentation

You may have noticed that there are two alignment groupings from the Align or Distribute menu. The first group includes Align Left, Align Center, and Align Right. These options are to align vertically organized objects. The second group includes Align Top, Align Middle, and Align Bottom. This group is designed to operate on horizontally organized objects. The Distribute Horizontally and Distribute Vertically options are used to evenly distribute selected objects along the horizontal or vertical axis, respectively.

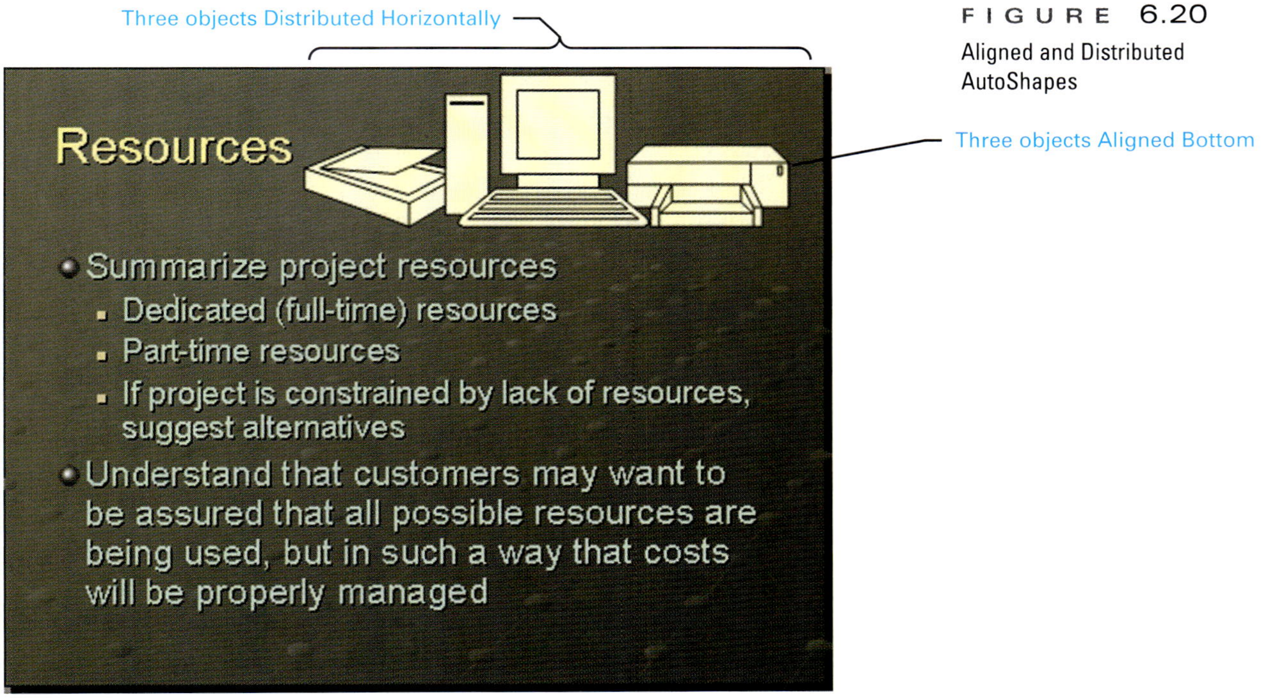

Three objects Distributed Horizontally

FIGURE 6.20

Aligned and Distributed AutoShapes

Three objects Aligned Bottom

If you prefer to align objects manually, ***grids*** and ***guides*** can be helpful. Dotted lines display at regular intervals on each slide when grids are turned on. Grids can be used as visual aids or have the snap-to option activated so that objects align to the nearest grid. The spacing between gridlines can be set from a list of preset measures.

When guides are activated, one horizontal and one vertical line are added to the slide to be positioned as needed to align slide objects. Guides can be moved by dragging. An unwanted guide can be deleted by dragging it off the edge of a slide. New guides are added by holding the CTRL key while dragging an existing guide.

task reference
Adding Grids and Guides to a Presentation

- Use the **Toolbars** option of the **View** menu to activate the **Drawing** toolbar, if it is not already visible
- Click the **Draw** drop-down list of the Drawing toolbar and click **Grid and Guides**
- Adjust the Snap to, Grid, and Guide settings in the Grid and Guides dialog box and then click OK

Using Grids and Guides when drawing:

1. Verify that PowerPoint is running with **PP06StatusReport.ppt** open
2. Move to slide 6

3. From the **Draw** drop-down menu of the Drawing toolbar select **Grid and Guides**
4. In the Grid and Guides dialog box check
   a. Snap objects to grid
   b. Display grid on screen
   c. Display drawing guides on screen
   d. Click **OK**
5. Drag the vertical guide to **1.53** and the horizontal guide to **1.97**

tip: *Refer to Figure 6.21. The position displays in a pop-up box as you drag. The Snap To Grid feature controls the numbers that appear as you drag and may need to be disabled (see step 4) to get these exact settings*

6. Use the left sizing handle of the Title placeholder to align it with the vertical guide at 1.53 and then move the vertical guide to **4.33**
7. Select the **Rectangle** tool from the Drawing toolbar and draw the trailer of the semi
8. Select the **Parallelogram** from the **Basic Shapes** option of the **AutoShapes** menu and draw the cab of the semi
9. Stack a second smaller parallelogram on the first to make the window. Use the Fill Color tool of the Drawing toolbar to make this object white
10. Use the Oval tool of the Drawing toolbar to draw a tire. Stack a white oval on top of the blue one to complete the tire

tip: *With both ovals for one tire selected, use the **Align Middle** and **Align Center** options of the Draw button's Align and Distribute option to center the inner oval inside the outer oval*

11. Repeat step 9 for the remaining wheels
12. Select the **Lightning Bolt** from the **Basic Shapes** option of the **AutoShapes** menu and add it to the trailer of the semi
13. Save the presentation

The Grid and Guides dialog box allows a designer to choose the alignment options that best suit the situation. By returning to the dialog box, any or all selected options can be reversed. When the snap-to grid option is selected, the grids do not need to be visible for objects to align with the nearest grid. The default is to have snap-to active and both guides and grids hidden. Guides and grids display as slides are developed, but are not visible in slide show view and will not print with the presentation.

Using 3-D Effects

Drawn objects can be modified to look three-dimensional. The 3-D options control the depth, rotation, angle, lighting direction, color, and texture of an object. Multiple objects can be selected to apply the same effects to each.

FIGURE 6.21
Drawing with Grids and Guides

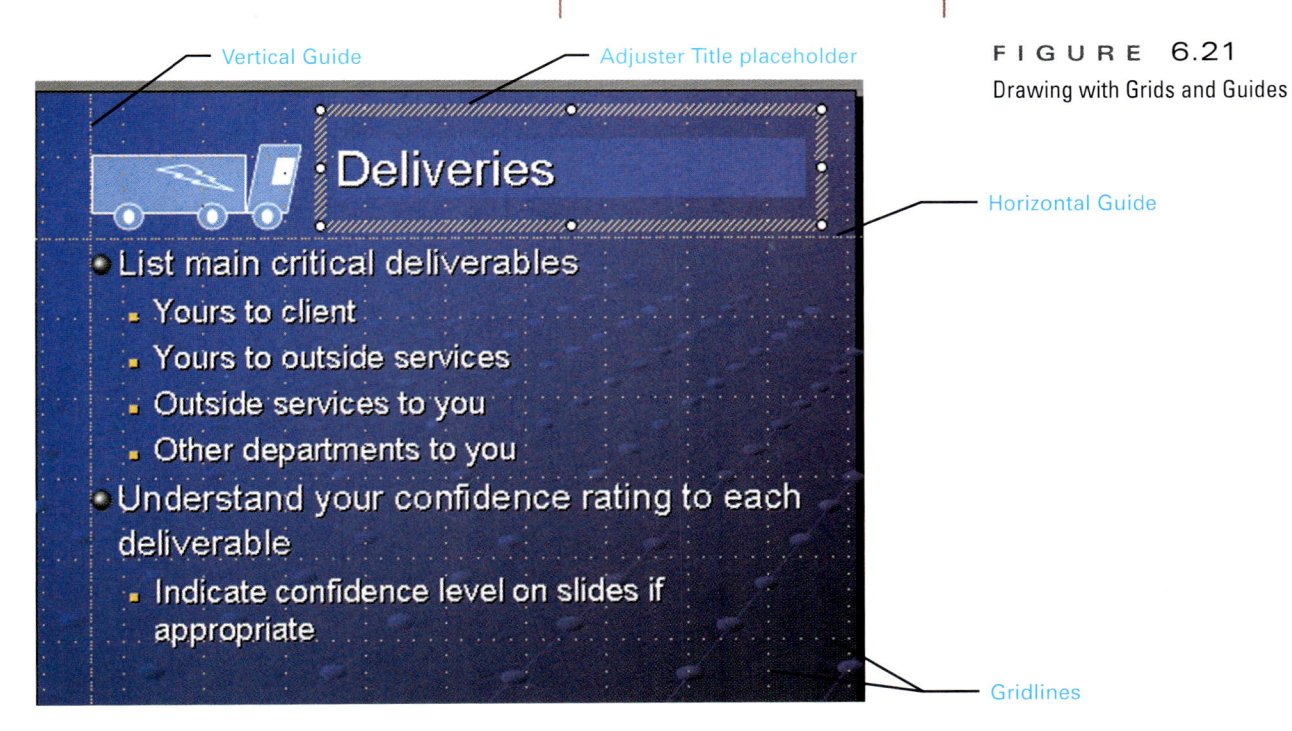

— Vertical Guide   — Adjuster Title placeholder   — Horizontal Guide   — Gridlines

task reference

Adding 3-D Effects to an Object

- Select the object(s) that will have 3-D effects
- Choose the desired 3-D effects from the 3-D Style button of the Drawing toolbar

Applying 3-D effects to arrow objects:

1. Verify that PowerPoint is running with **PP06StatusReport.ppt** open
2. Move to slide 10
3. Select all of the arrows except the left and right curved arrows, which don't support 3-D effects

   tip: Hold down the Shift key to select additional objects

4. Activate **3-D Style** button from the drawing toolbar and try some of the options. When you are finished exploring, select **3D Style 6**
5. Save the presentation

FIGURE 6.22
Arrows with 3-D Effects

As you just saw, there are 20 predefined 3-D effects that can be added to objects that support 3-D. Not all objects support 3-D effects. If a selected object does not allow 3-D effects, the 3-D Styles will display in gray as an indication that they cannot be applied. When the predefined effects do not match your needs, you can create your own effect using the 3-D Settings toolbox.

POWERPOINT

> ### *Exploring the 3-D Settings toolbox:*
>
> 1. Verify that PowerPoint is running with **PP06StatusReport.ppt** open
> 2. Move to slide 7
> 3. From the Stars and Banners option of the AutoShapes menu, select Explosion 2
>
> **tip:** *Pause over the shapes to see their names*
>
> 4. Click to the right of the title to add the object to the slide at its default size
> 5. Right-click the explosion, choose **Add Text** from the pop-up menu, and type **$$$**
> 6. From the Drawing toolbar, open the **3-D Style** options and select **3-D Style 16** as the foundation for the 3-D effect being built
> 7. Click **3-D Style** on the Drawing toolbar and select **3-D Settings** to open the 3-D Settings toolbox. Refer to the next figure and
>   a. Click the **Tilt Up** option of the 3-D Setting toolbox several times to adjust the length of the explosion's tail
>   b. Click the Tilt Right option several times to adjust the angle of the explosion's tail
>   c. Explore the Depth and Direction settings of the 3-D Setting toolbox leaving them at their original settings
>   d. Use the Lighting options to reverse the angle of light (click the right-center light)
> 8. Use the explosion's rotation handle to angle it to the right
> 9. Use the top right sizing handle to increase the explosion's dimension
> 10. Make the dollar signs ($$$) 32 point
> 11. Save the presentation

At this point the object created from the explosion is in front of the text on the slide. This situation will be remedied by restacking the objects in later steps.

EDITING OBJECTS

Many of the familiar editing techniques can readily be applied to drawn objects. Setting the attributes of text or the background color of an object is the same regardless of the object involved. Drawn objects are selected by clicking and deselected by clicking elsewhere on the slide. Multiple objects can be simultaneously edited.

Duplicating Objects

Although you have been duplicating objects for some time, there are details to these operations that have not been addressed. Drawn objects can

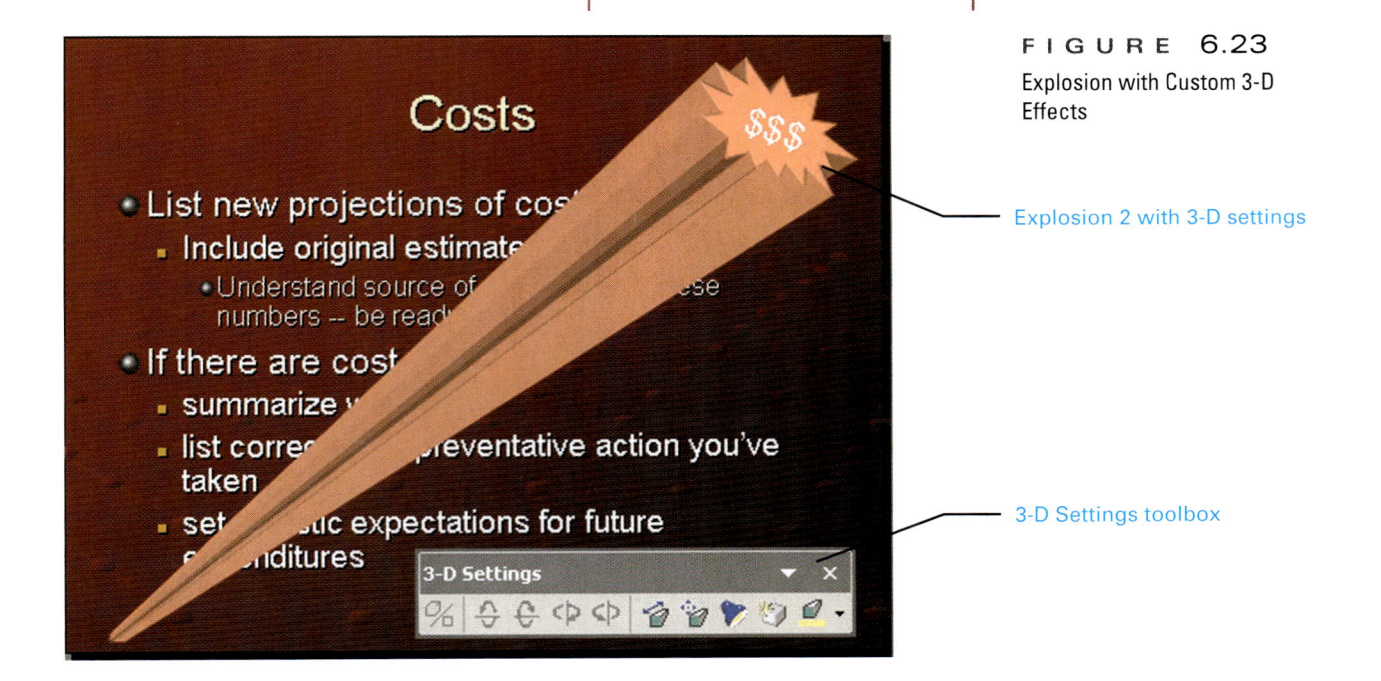

FIGURE 6.23

Explosion with Custom 3-D Effects

Explosion 2 with 3-D settings

3-D Settings toolbox

be deleted, copied, and pasted using the familiar Cut, Copy, and Paste buttons of the Standard toolbar, but other techniques can be more effective. The Edit menu contains a Duplicate option that can be used to copy objects. This menu selection can be accessed with the shortcut keys Ctrl+D.

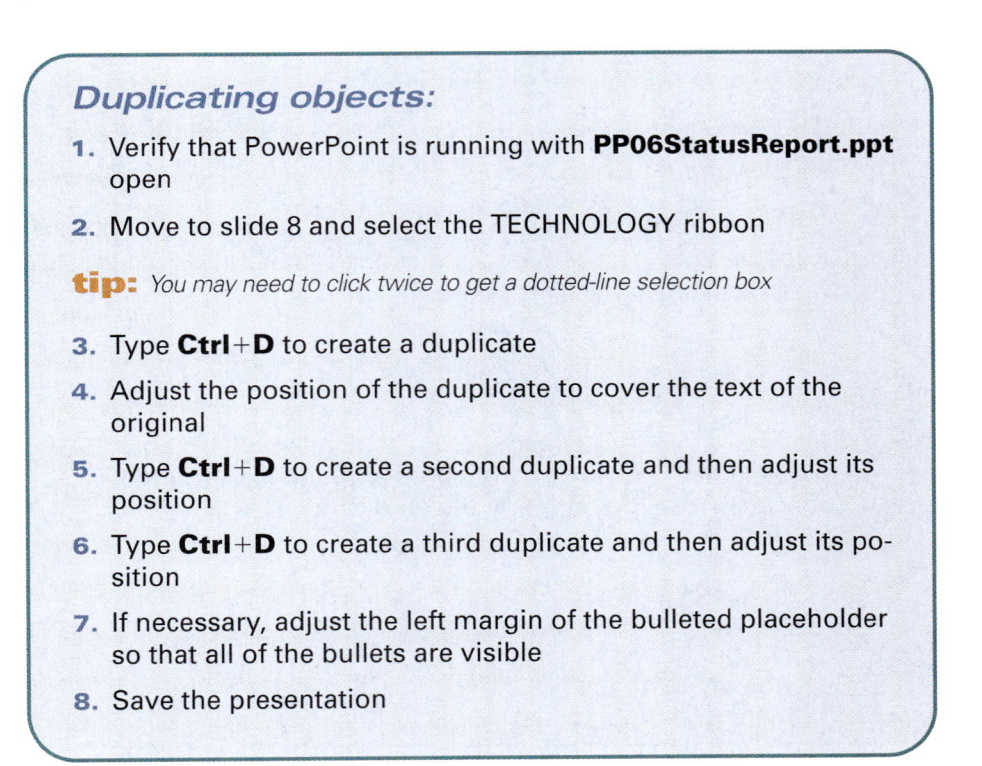

Duplicating objects:

1. Verify that PowerPoint is running with **PP06StatusReport.ppt** open
2. Move to slide 8 and select the TECHNOLOGY ribbon

tip: *You may need to click twice to get a dotted-line selection box*

3. Type **Ctrl+D** to create a duplicate
4. Adjust the position of the duplicate to cover the text of the original
5. Type **Ctrl+D** to create a second duplicate and then adjust its position
6. Type **Ctrl+D** to create a third duplicate and then adjust its position
7. If necessary, adjust the left margin of the bulleted placeholder so that all of the bullets are visible
8. Save the presentation

Stacking duplicate objects like the ribbons is a simple way to add interest to a graphic element. Lines are another method for adding interest and can also separate topics on a slide. Creating straight lines can be difficult unless the Shift key is used. The Shift key restricts the movement of an

PP 6.30 CHAPTER 6 **POWERPOINT** **6.2** Creating Custom Art

FIGURE 6.24
Duplicate Ribbons Stacked

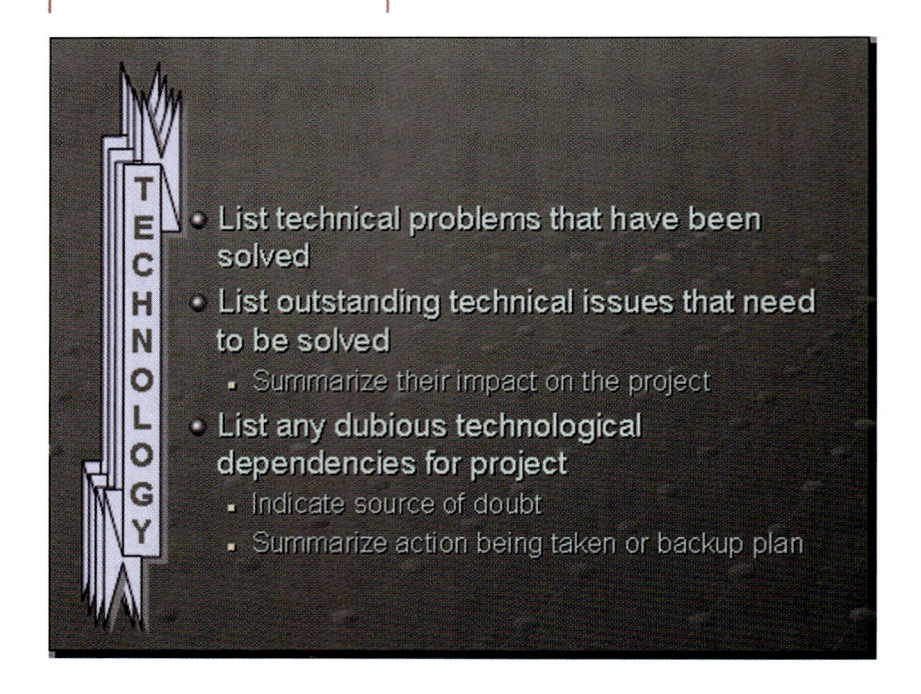

object being drawn or resized to either horizontal or vertical movement. Using the Ctrl key to drag duplicates makes it easier to align them and is faster than using the Office Clipboard buttons (Cut, Copy, and Paste).

> **Using the Shift and Ctrl keys when drawing and duplicating objects:**
>
> 1. Verify that PowerPoint is running with **PP06StatusReport.ppt** open
> 2. Move to slide 6
> 3. Select the **Line** tool from the drawing toolbar and hold the **Shift** key while drawing a horizontal line below the semi and title
>
> **tip:** The Shift key constrains the drawing motion to one direction ensuring a straight line
>
> 4. Hold the **Ctrl** key while dragging the existing line to create a duplicate of the line. Position the duplicate half way up the semi tires
>
> **tip:** When using Ctrl to drag a duplicate object, the pointer has a box and a plus sign to indicate that duplication is active
>
> 5. Save the presentation

Ctrl+drag is the fastest way to create a replica of an object. When multiple objects are selected, Ctrl+drag will copy all selected objects simultaneously. Ctrl+click is used to select multiple objects. Clicking outside the multiple selection will deselect everything. Ctrl+clicking on an already selected object will deselect just that object.

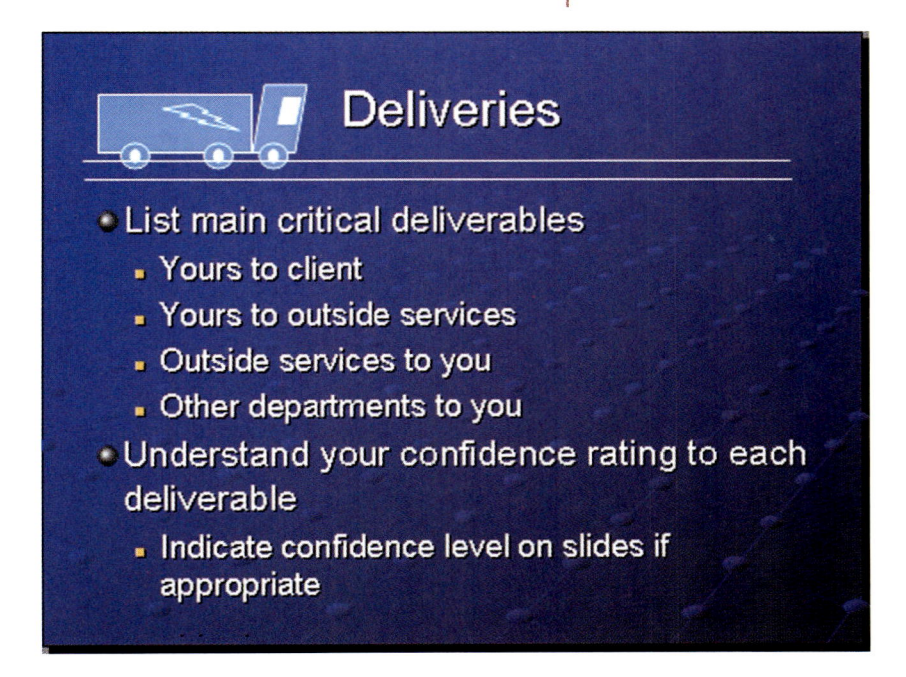

FIGURE 6.25

Lines Created Using the Shift and Ctrl Keys

The work on slide 6 is nearly completed, but the line through the semi's tires needs to be placed in the background. This will be accomplished in the Grouping and Stacking Objects topic.

Changing an Object's Shape

Using AutoShapes to create drawn art often involves trial and error. You may begin with one shape and then decide that another shape is better suited for your purpose. Fortunately PowerPoint provides a menu option for changing a shape. Ian has decided that the lightning bolt emblem on the semi in slide 6 is inappropriate for the audience. You will change it to an inverted moon shape.

Changing the shape of a Lightning Bolt:

1. Verify that PowerPoint is running with **PP06StatusReport.ppt** open
2. If slide 6 is not the active slide, move to it
3. Select the lightning bolt on the semi
4. Click the **Draw** menu of the Drawing toolbar, pause the cursor over **Change AutoShape**, pause the cursor over **Basic Shapes,** and then select the **Moon** object
5. With the moon still selected, click the **Draw** menu of the Drawing toolbar, pause the cursor over **Rotate or Flip**, and choose **Flip Horizontal**
6. Save the presentation

FIGURE 6.26

Lightning Bolt Changed to a Moon

Multiple objects can be selected and changed to a new shape. The original objects do not have to be the same shape, but the goal should be to convert all selected objects to the same new object. You have decided that

POWERPOINT

the round inner ring of the semi tires is boring and want to convert all three objects to octagons.

> **Changing the shape of multiple objects simultaneously:**
>
> 1. Verify that PowerPoint is running with **PP06StatusReport.ppt** open
> 2. If slide 6 is not the active slide, move to it
> 3. Use the zoom box of the standard toolbar to make the slide 100% or greater so that you can select these small objects
> 4. Deselect any selected objects and then hold the **Ctrl** key while selecting each of the inner white circles on the semi tires
> 5. With three circles selected, click the **Draw** menu of the Drawing toolbar, pause the cursor over **Change AutoShape**, pause the cursor over **Basic Shapes,** and then select the **Octagon** object
>
> — Oval shape converted to Octagon
>
> 6. Save the presentation

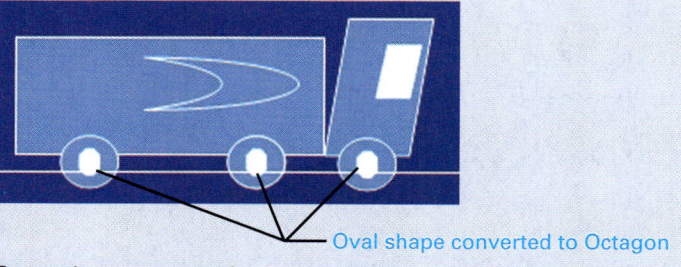

FIGURE 6.27

Multiple Circles Changed to Octagons

Most of the clip art in the Media Gallery is constructed using objects from the AutoShapes menu. The basic concept is that altering existing shapes to suit the current need is less time intensive than custom drawing each new work. Although the most dramatic changes to an object are accomplished using the techniques already reviewed, there are a few more subtle tricks that can improve the artwork in any presentation.

Other Object Attributes

The attributes of an object determine how it displays on the slide. The graphic attributes include fill, line, shape, and shadow. Text attributes include font, color, embossment, and shadow. All of the features covered for slides in the first session of this chapter are available for individual objects on the slide. Custom colors can be created using the More Fill Colors option of the Fill Color button. The Fill Effects option of the Fill Color button includes gradients, textures, patterns, and pictures that can be added to any object.

> **Creating and copying object fill effects:**
>
> 1. Verify that PowerPoint is running with **PP06StatusReport.ppt** open

2. If slide 6 is not the active slide, move to it
3. Select the semitrailer
4. Choose **Fill Effects** from the **Fill Color** button
5. In the Gradient tab of the Fill Effects dialog box
   a. Click **Two colors**
   b. Set the Shading styles to **Diagonal Up**
   c. Select the bottom left Varian
   d. Click **OK**
6. With the trailer selected click the **Format Painter** button of the Standard toolbar and then click the cab of the semi

tip: The cursor will change to a paintbrush when a format can be painted

7. Select the inverted moon on the semitrailer, choose the **Fill Color** button, and then click **Fill Effects**
8. From the Texture tab of the Fill Effects dialog box, choose the **Bouquet** (it is blue with some pink in it) pattern and click **OK**

tip: The pattern name for the selected texture displays in the box below the textures

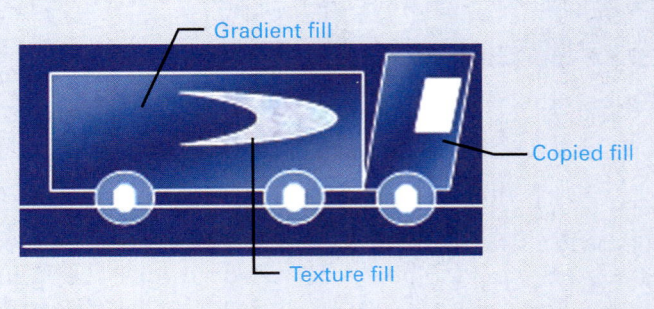

- Gradient fill
- Copied fill
- Texture fill

9. Save the presentation

FIGURE 6.28
Object Fill Effects

The Format Painter can be used to transfer the formatting of one object to another. Single-clicking the Format Painter allows one object to be painted, while double-clicking will allow multiple objects to be painted. When Format Painter is double-clicked, painting must be turned off by either hitting Esc on the keyboard or clicking the Format Painter button again.

For many audiences and tasks, dramatic formatting is not appropriate. Such simple changes can improve the dynamics of an object without overshadowing other slide elements. The shadow attribute can be used to create a subtle 3-D effect, while line color, style, and weight help to differentiate art components.

Adding shadows and setting line color:

1. Verify that PowerPoint is running with **PP06StatusReport.ppt** open
2. If slide 6 is not the active slide, move to it

FIGURE 6.29
Shadow and Line Adjustments

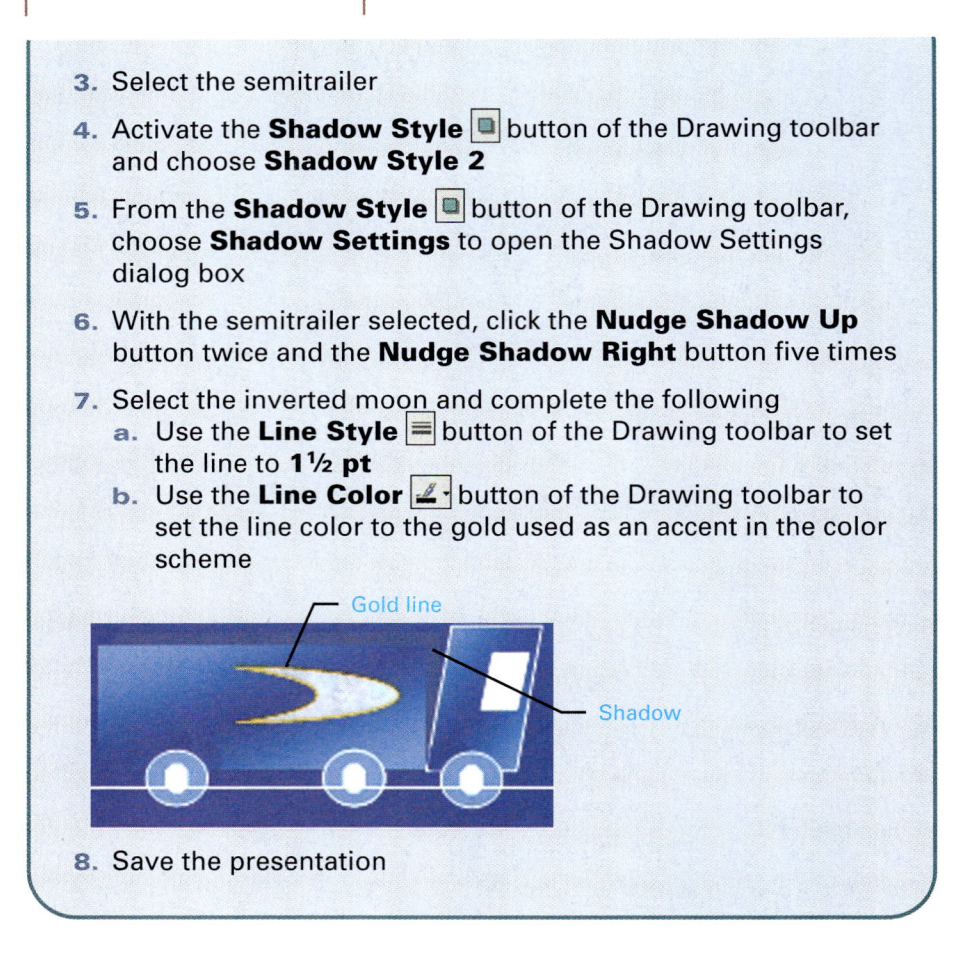

3. Select the semitrailer
4. Activate the **Shadow Style** button of the Drawing toolbar and choose **Shadow Style 2**
5. From the **Shadow Style** button of the Drawing toolbar, choose **Shadow Settings** to open the Shadow Settings dialog box
6. With the semitrailer selected, click the **Nudge Shadow Up** button twice and the **Nudge Shadow Right** button five times
7. Select the inverted moon and complete the following
   a. Use the **Line Style** button of the Drawing toolbar to set the line to **1½ pt**
   b. Use the **Line Color** button of the Drawing toolbar to set the line color to the gold used as an accent in the color scheme

Gold line

Shadow

8. Save the presentation

Shadowing can be added to most slide objects such as text characters, AutoShapes, and images. Once a shadow is added to an object, the Nudge features of the Shadow Setting toolbox can be used to adjust the width and length of the shadow. The color and transparency of a shadow can be adjusted in the same fashion. A transparent shadow allows background colors and objects to show through. The Shadow Style button can also be used to remove existing shadow settings.

Objects Outside the Slide Area

Objects can be created and manipulated in the background portion of the presentation window. Objects outside the slide area are used to provide information to developers since they do not display during a slide show and will not print.

Viewing objects outside the slide area:

1. Verify that PowerPoint is running with **PP06StatusReport.ppt** open
2. Move to slide 1
3. Click in the Slide pane and use the Zoom drop-down to **Fit**
4. Notice the notes to developers in the rectangle to the right of the first slide

PP 6.35

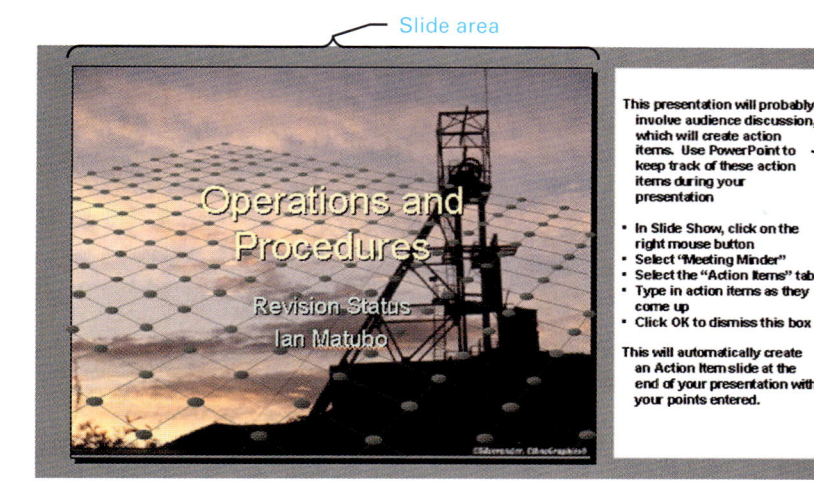

FIGURE 6.30

A Rectangle Object in the Presentation Window

The notes from slide 1 of this slide show are part of the AutoContent template that was used to build the presentation. It contains tips for anyone using the template. The rectangle can be edited or deleted to suit your needs. You can add your own background objects by changing the zoom to expose the background and then drawing.

STACKING AND GROUPING OBJECTS

As more and more objects are added to a slide, it becomes critical to control their positioning. The stacking order determines what object(s) display in the foreground and background. Grouping allows multiple objects to be treated as a single object when moving, formatting, and editing.

Controlling Z-Order

To make editing, moving, and combing objects easier, each object added to a presentation is placed in its own layer. The layers stack on top of each other with the first object added being closest to the slide and the last object added the farthest away. This stacking order is also referred to as the *z-order* referencing the z-axis of a three-dimensional chart.

Ideally, each object would be created in the correct order so that it could be freely edited and never touched again. In practice most of us fall short of the ideal and need to adjust the stacking order of objects. There are a series of Send and Bring options used to control z-order.

---

task reference

Changing the Z-Order of an Object

- Select the object(s) to be moved in the stack of objects
- From the Drawing toolbar, click **Draw**, pause over **Order**, and then select the appropriate movement option

POWERPOINT

FIGURE 6.31
Bulleted List Placeholder Brought to Front

Changing z-order in PP06StatusReport slides:

1. Verify that PowerPoint is running with **PP06StatusReport.ppt** open
2. Move to slide 6
   a. Select the line that is in front of the semi tires
   b. Click the **Draw** button of the Drawing toolbar, pause the cursor over **Order**, and select **Send to Back**
3. Move to slide 7
   a. Click the bulleted list placeholder
   b. Click the **Draw** button of the Drawing toolbar, pause the cursor over **Order**, and select **Bring to Front**
4. Move to slide 8
   a. Select any slide object

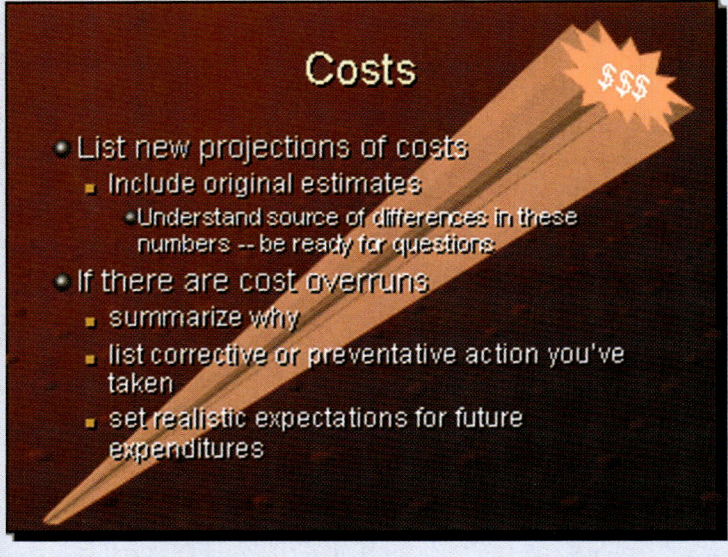

tip: *You may need to click again to get a dotted-line selection box*

   b. Use the Tab key to move through the slide objects
   c. Use Shift+Tab to move backward through slide objects
5. Save the presentation

anotherway

... to change z-order

The Order menu options can be accessed by right-clicking an object.

When ordering objects on a slide, it is important to remember that each slide element, including text and placeholders, is an object. The Send to Back and Bring to Front options of the Order menu were demonstrated in the previous steps. Regardless of how many layers there are, these options will place the selected object on the bottom or top, respectively. The remaining options of the Order menu will move an object one layer at a time. Bring Forward will move the object one layer toward the top of the stack, while Send Backward will move the object one layer toward the bottom of the stack.

Layering can sometimes make an object difficult to select because it is behind other objects. For example, selecting the second stacked TECH-

NOLOGY ribbon on slide 8 would be particularly arduous. Sometimes the desired object can be reached by zooming in until each object's borders are distinct. PowerPoint can zoom to 400 percent to support this type of selection. Another option is to move the layers that are in front of the desired object. Depending on the number of layers, this option is also tedious. The Tab and Shift+Tab keys are usually the easiest way to move from object to object on a slide.

Grouping Objects

When objects have been combined or stacked to achieve a desired effect, it is a good idea to finish the process by grouping the discrete objects into one object. *Grouping* ensures that the work is not accidentally ruined by inadvertently moving a component. It also makes moving, copying, editing, and setting attributes much simpler.

---

task reference

Grouping Objects

- Select all objects to be grouped
- From the Drawing toolbar, click **Draw** and then select the appropriate grouping (Group, **Ungroup**, or **Regroup**) option

---

Working with grouped objects:

1. Verify that PowerPoint is running with **PP06StatusReport.ppt** open

2. Move to slide 6
   a. Select all of the objects the make up the tractor and trailer by clicking and dragging a selection box around the semi

   tip: *A selection box does not select objects not completely contained in its area. Be sure to include all of the semi parts and exclude both lines and the title placeholder*

   b. Click the **Draw** button of the Drawing toolbar and select **Group**
   c. With the semi group selected, hold down the **Ctrl** key and select both lines
   d. Click the **Draw** button of the Drawing toolbar and select **Group**
   e. With the group selected, click on the inverted moon on the semitrailer

   tip: *Although we will not set any attributes for the inverted moon, selecting it would allow you to do so*

   f. Click off the group to deselect

3. Move to slide 8
   a. Group all of the TECHNOLOGY ribbons into one object using the techniques from the previous steps
   b. Use the rotation handle for the group to angle all of the ribbons a few degrees to the left

FIGURE 6.32
Doubly Grouped Object with One Element Selected

- Individual group elements can be selected
- The slide title is not part of the group
- The first group contains all of the semi objects
- The second group contains the first group and the lines

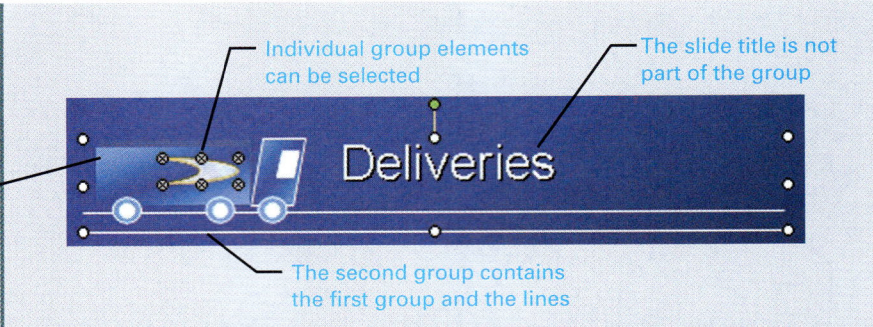

tip: *If all of the ribbons do not rotate, they are not properly grouped. Ungroup, adjust your selection, and then Regroup*

4. Move to slide 9
    a. Select and group the computer equipment
    b. Use the Fill Color button of the Drawing toolbar to change the color to the gray brown of the background
    c. Use the Line Color button of the Drawing toolbar to match the line color to the title text color

5. Move to slide 10
    a. Select and group all of the arrows
    b. Use the Ctrl+drag method to create a copy of the group
    c. Select the **Goals** text in the copy and delete it
    d. Reduce the size of the copy
    e. Use the rotation handle to rotate the copy to the right (clockwise)
    f. Position the copy to the left of the title

FIGURE 6.33
Copied Arrow Group

Copied, resized, and rotated arrow group

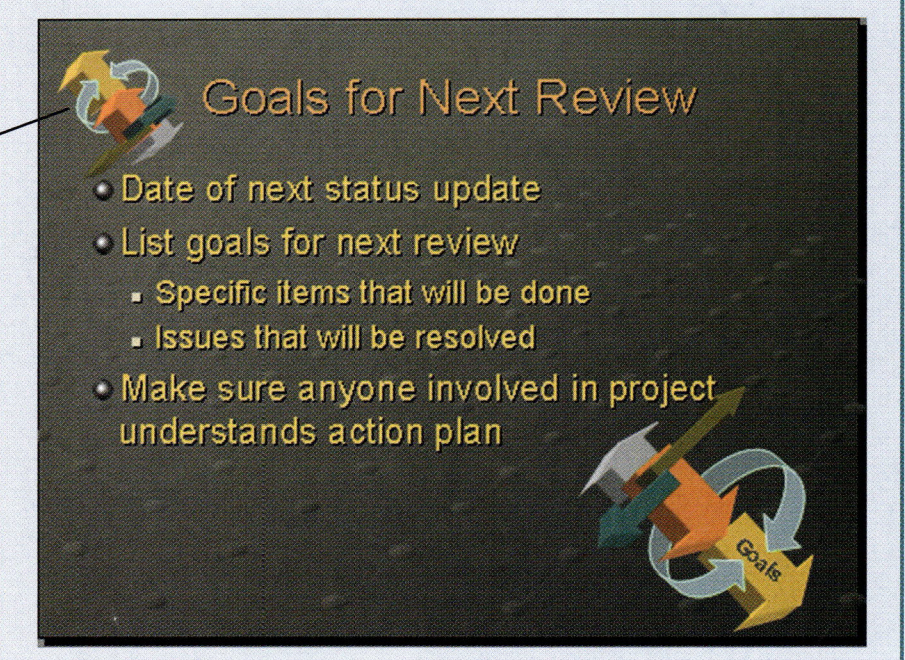

6. Save the presentation

The attributes of all grouped objects can be changed simultaneously. For example, the same fill or shadow can be applied to all group objects. Flip, resize, rotate, and 3-D effects also work well with groups. Individual objects from a group can be selected without ungrouping to have unique attributes set. Grouped objects can be ungrouped when it is necessary to work exclusively with a single object from the group and regrouped when those tasks are completed. The Ungroup and Regroup options are available from the Draw menu. A group can be included in other groups to create even more complex objects.

making the grade

SESSION 6.2

1. What is the difference between the rectangle shape on the drawing toolbar and the one available from the Basic Shapes option of the AutoShapes button?
2. How can you create a mirror image of an object?
3. How are adjustment handles valuable?
4. A slide contains three rectangles stacked top to bottom whose left sides need to be aligned. How would you accomplish this?

SESSION 6.3 SUMMARY

Color is a critical component of any presentation. The colors used impact the mood and readability of the presentation. When choosing a color scheme, consider the audience, presentation topic, and how the presentation will be delivered. Projected presentations and kiosks have very different color requirements.

A color scheme is a palette of eight colors used as the presentation default colors for the slide background, body text, lines, shadows, title text, fills, hyperlinks, and accents. Each PowerPoint Design template has a selection of intrinsic color schemes that have been developed by artists. Color schemes can be applied to an entire presentation or to selected slides. New slides and objects created in a presentation follow the active color scheme. You can customize the color of individual objects or the entire color scheme. When custom colors are applied to an object, the new color displays below those of the color scheme in all of the color menus. When a color or colors of a color scheme are customized, a new color scheme is added to the Design template. Deleting a color scheme removes it from the Design template.

Most PowerPoint objects, including slides and AutoShapes, can use special fills such as gradient, texture, and picture. These custom fills add distinction to objects and present a more professional image. Be sure, however, that the fills do not detract from readability or presentation content.

The Drawing toolbar supplies an array of standard objects that can be used to create more complex objects and drawings. Select a drawing tool and then click and drag the shape on a slide. As new objects are added, they are stacked so that the first object is closest to the slide and the last object added is on top. Tab and Shift+Tab usually provide the easiest navigation between stacked slide objects. Objects that will display together should be grouped to avoid accidental alterations to their arrangement.

MOUS OBJECTIVES SUMMARY

- Create and add Office Art elements to slides using the Drawing toolbar—PPT2002-3-3
- Customize slide backgrounds using bitmaps—PPT2002-3-2

task reference roundup

Task	Page #	Preferred Method
Select a Color Scheme	PP 6.4	• Select the slide(s) the color scheme will be applied to **tip:** Select a Design Template before choosing a Color Scheme
		• Use the drop-down menu of the Task pane to activate the Slide Design—Color Scheme panel
		Click a Color Scheme
Customize a Color Scheme	PP 6.8	• Use the Task pane drop-down list to activate the **Slide Design—Color Scheme** panel
		• Click the **Edit Color Schemes** link in the Slide Design—Color Scheme panel
		• On the **Standard** tab of the Edit Color Scheme dialog box, select the Standard Color Scheme to be customized
		• On the **Custom** tab, select the Color Scheme element to customize and click **Change Color**
		• Use either the Standard or Custom tab of the Background Color dialog box to select a new color
		• Click **OK**
		• Repeat the previous step for each element to be customized
		• Use the **Preview** button to view the new colors on your slide
		• Click **Apply** to permanently apply the changes
Delete a Color Scheme	PP 6.10	• Use the Task pane drop-down list to activate the **Slide Design—Color Scheme** panel
		• Click the **Edit Color Schemes** link in the Slide Design—Color Scheme panel
		• On the **Standard** tab of the Edit Color Scheme dialog box, select the Color Scheme to be deleted
		• Click the **Delete Scheme** button
		• Click **Apply**
Define a Gradient Background	PP 6.13	• Right-click on the slide to contain the gradient background
		• Click the **Background** pop-up menu option
		• Click **Fill Effects**
		• Click the **Gradient** tab
		• Select the desired gradient effects and click **OK**

task reference roundup

Task	Page #	Preferred Method
		• Click either
		• **Apply to All** to set this as the background for all presentation slides
		• **Apply** to set this as the background for the selected slides only
Select a Texture Background	PP 6.14	• Right-click on the slide to contain the texture background
		• Click the **Background** pop-up menu option
		• Click **Fill Effects**
		• Click the **Texture** tab
		• Select the desired texture and click **OK**
		• Click either
		• **Apply to All** to set this as the background for all presentation slides
		• **Apply** to set this as the background for the selected slides only
Apply a Picture Background	PP 6.15	• Locate and save an appropriate picture
		• Right-click on the slide to contain the picture background
		• Click the **Background** pop-up menu option
		• Click **Fill Effects**
		• Click the **Picture** tab
		• Click the **Select Picture** button, choose the picture file, click **Insert**, and then click **OK**
		• Click either
		• **Apply to All** to set this as the background for all presentation slides
		• **Apply** to set this as the background for the selected slides only
		• **Preview** to evaluate the effect of the background without applying it
Apply a Picture as a Bullet	PP 6.17	• Select the text or list that will contain the picture bullet
		• On the **Format** menu, click **Bullets and Numbering**, and then click the **Bulleted** tab
		• On the Bulleted tab click the **Picture** button
		• Select a picture from the Picture Bullet dialog box
		• Click **OK**
Using the AutoShape Button of the Drawing Toolbar	PP 6.19	• Select the slide that will contain the AutoShape
		• Click the **AutoShapes** menu of the **Drawing** toolbar
		• Select the shape category and then the shape to be applied

task reference roundup

Task	Page #	Preferred Method
Adding Text to an AutoShape	PP 6.20	• Click and drag on the slide surface to create the shape • Select the AutoShape • Right-click the **AutoShape** and select **Add Text** from the shortcut menu • Type and format the text
Adding Grids and Guides to a Presentation	PP 6.25	• Use the **Toolbars** option of the **View** menu to activate the **Drawing** toolbar, if it is not already visible • Click the **Draw** drop-down list of the Drawing toolbar and click **Grid and Guides** • Adjust the Snap to, Grid, and Guide settings in the Grid and Guides dialog box, and then click OK
Adding 3-D Effects to an Object	PP 6.27	• Select the object(s) that will have 3-D effects • Choose the desired 3-D effects from the 3-D Style button of the Drawing toolbar
Changing the Z-Order of an Object	PP 6.35	• Select the object(s) to be moved in the stack of objects • From the Drawing toolbar, click **Draw**, pause over **Order**, and then select the appropriate movement option
Grouping Objects	PP 6.37	• Select all objects to be grouped • From the Drawing toolbar, click **Draw** and then select the appropriate grouping (Group, Ungroup, or Regroup) option

chapter six

review of terminology

LEVEL ONE

CROSSWORD PUZZLE

Across

3. Object stacking order
8. Color schemes that ship with PowerPoint
10. Combining two or more objects into one object
14. Key that will duplicate during a drag operation
16. Allows an object to be rotated by dragging

Down

1. Improving text readability by adding a solid background
2. Returning grouped objects to their individual state
4. Returning ungrouped objects to their grouped state
5. The number of custom colors that can be displayed in a palette
6. Standard toolbar button to copy formats
7. The number of color schemes that can be stored with a design template
9. Controls the default colors of presentation components
10. Evenly spaced lines to help size and align objects
11. User placed lines for sizing and alignment
12. Visual presentation of the available colors
13. Key that constrains a drag operation to one dimension
15. The number of color schemes that can be applied to a slide

PP 6.43

POWERPOINT

www.mhhe.com/i-series

review of concepts

chapter six

FILL-IN

1. Ctrl+_____ can be used to create a duplicate of the selected object.
2. _____ lines can be moved to facilitate object alignment.
3. The _____ (color) handle of an object is used to rotate it.
4. A _____ fill effect merges colors to create the illusion of light.
5. The _____ (color) handles of an object are used to resize it.

REVIEW QUESTIONS

Each of the following topics should be addressed in one to three paragraphs.

1. What should be considered when selecting a color scheme and graphics for a retirement planning presentation?
2. Describe how the Format Painter is helpful.
3. How many backgrounds should be used in a single presentation?
4. Discuss techniques that could be used to improve the readability of text on a busy slide background.
5. Discuss how you would locate graphics for an educator's seminar on using PowerPoint in the classroom.

CREATE THE QUESTION

For each of the following answers, create the question.

ANSWER	QUESTION
1. Use the Fill Color button on the Drawing toolbar.	_____
2. Select the item and then Ctrl+drag.	_____
3. Use the Shift key.	_____
4. Format Painter.	_____
5. The 3-D style selected.	_____

FACT OR FICTION

For each of the following determine whether the statement is fact, fiction, or both and present your arguments for that conclusion.

1. All drawn objects can have 3-D effects applied.
2. The Align or Distribute options of the Draw menu (Drawing toolbar) are the only way to align slide objects.
3. Adjustment handles change feature(s) of an AutoShape object.
4. Individual components of a grouped object cannot be formatted.
5. Objects outside the slide area have no real function.

chapter six
hands-on projects

practice

LEVEL THREE

Story Weavers

This nonprofit organization teaches others how to tell a story in a way that captivates an audience. From scary to hilarious topics, Story Weavers teaches others to hold audiences in the palm of their hands even with the driest of material. Audiences cry for more! Story Weavers' instructors are retired drama teachers, playwrights, authors, and fine arts directors—those who work with the written and acted word. Schools, libraries, private parties, and churches are popular recipients of Story Weavers' services. You have been asked to prepare a PowerPoint presentation to publicize Story Weavers.

1. Start PowerPoint and open **pp06StoryWeavers.ppt**
2. On slide 1, create a web and spider similar to that shown in Figure 6.34
   a. Right-click on the first slide, select **Background**, check **Omit background graphics from master**, and click **Apply**
   b. Using the **Line** tool from the Drawing toolbar, create a spider web
   c. Use the **Oval** tool to create a body and head for a spider. Use the Fill tool to fill the spider in dark gray
   d. Use the **Arc** Basic Shape to create curved spider legs. You will need to Flip four of the legs
   e. Select the spider components, right-click, and group them into a single object
   f. Select all of the web and spider components, right-click, and group them into a single object
   g. Add another relevant graphic to the slide
3. Copy the spider and web to the clipboard
   a. Use the **View** menu to open the Slide Master
   b. Paste the spider and web on the slide master (not the Title slide master)
   c. Right-click on the graphic and use the Format Graphic option to change the image color to medium gray
   d. Place a second copy of the recolored image near the center of the slide
   e. Artistically arrange the images and **Close Master View**
4. Add relevant graphics to each of the other slides. Arrange the graphics to appear as part of the background. For example, place the image over one of the spiders
5. Copy two extra webs to the final slide of your screen and change the color of each new spider by adding a Texture Fill Effect
6. Save the presentation as **<yourname>pp06StoryWeavers.ppt**

FIGURE 6.34

Spider and Web

PP 6.45

POWERPOINT

www.mhhe.com/i-series

hands-on projects

LEVEL THREE

challenge

Preview Specialists

Across America before each movie shows, a "captive audience" sits. Usually the viewer sees a slide show of ads for local businesses. Some theaters run quizzes to engage the audience. However, frequently these presentations show little design aptitude, and many times they are quite ignored. Using market research, Preview Specialists discovered that audiences prefer preshows that provide information about current local events. With this technique in mind, the Preview Specialists' shows have been distributed across the United States tailored to each community, at the major movie chains. You have been asked to create such a presentation for your locale.

1. Open PowerPoint and select a blank screen
2. Save your presentation as **<yourname>PreviewSpecialists.ppt**
3. Title your presentation "Events in <name of your city or state>" and subtitle text "What to Do and See"
4. Locate a photograph to use as the background for this slide and apply it. Adjust the text color, size and font to achieve optimal readability
5. Create at least five additional slides using photos you own or have found; select activities characteristic to your community
   a. Add titles and information for each slide to highlight the activity
   b. Include slides about local sports, social events, and culture
   c. Demonstrate matting on at least one of the slides
6. Select animations for the information and slide transitions
7. Choose a sound or sounds to punctuate the slides
8. Set the show to run continuously
9. Preview your presentation, make adjustments, save, and exit PowerPoint

FIGURE 6.35
Sample Opening Slide

FIGURE 6.36
Sample Matting

chapter six

hands-on projects

on the web

LEVEL THREE

World Horizons

History is usually taught by exploring an event as it occurs across time. For example, students are exposed to a civilization as it progresses century after century. Events or cultures unrelated to that civilization are minimized. World Horizons is a Web site that doesn't ignore this discrepancy. Students can now discover the world concurrently rather than in date-oriented fashion. When a student enters a year or range of years, the Horizon Timeline for that time period is displayed. Major events in history, literature, religion, visual arts, music, science, and daily life across all cultures are represented on the time line. Each event is hot-linked to an encyclopedic reference. Other links are also available by category. At World Horizons' inception a handful of schools subscribed to its services. Now, two years later, World Horizons is available in 90 percent of the schools in the United States and internationally in 23 countries. You have been asked by World Horizons to prepare a presentation that will be used at educational conventions to inform teachers of World Horizons' subscription service.

1. Start PowerPoint and open **pp06WorldHorizons.ppt**
2. Save the presentation as **<yourname>pp06WorldHorizons.ppt**
3. Move to slide 1
   a. Place an image of a globe in the center of the slide
   b. Make the globe as large as possible without hanging off the slide and send it behind the slide text

   tip: *You may need to recolor the image to match the presentation. Right-click, choose Format object, and use the Recolor button. Customizing the color scheme may also be necessary to improve readability*

4. Move to slide 2 and create two images
   a. Use multiple block arrows with 3-D effects to represent latitude. Group the component parts and animate it to load with the associated text
   b. Use multiple block arrows with 3-D effects to represent both latitude and longitude. Group the component parts and animate it to load with the "History is" text
5. Use a search engine to locate a picture of a solar eclipse and use this image as a background on slide 3
6. Create a representative time line on slide 4. Use a double-headed horizontal arrow across the width of the slide. Add six or seven Callouts from the AutoShapes menu to indicate how historical data would be displayed. Group all of the objects into a single image
7. Locate or create art to illustrate the remaining slides
8. Preview the presentation, make any needed adjustments, and save

FIGURE 6.37

Solar Eclipse Background

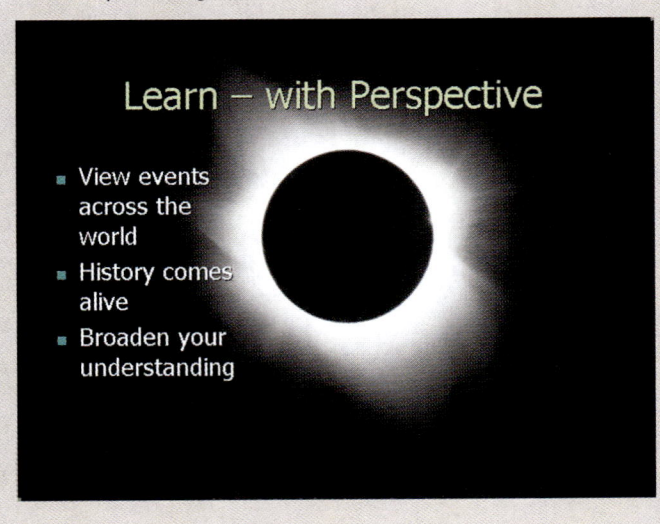

PP 6.47

POWERPOINT

www.mhhe.com/i-series

hands-on projects

e-business

Trekking Assistant

Trekking is a getaway vacation involving slow, prolonged travel by foot, ox, or other beast of burden. Trekking Assistant (TA) is a full-service trekking administrator. Working closely with clients TA is able to plan treks of any length through hundreds of locations around the world. TA provides carefully planned routes with detailed maps and orienting photographs. After the route is determined, TA identifies and provides equipment, food, and porters, if desired. The cache areas are mapped, and all supplies are transported to cache sites. Once the trek is in progress, TA makes sure all goes smoothly. Clients can be as involved in their planning as they choose. You have been asked to prepare a PowerPoint kiosk presentation about the services offered by Trekking Assistant. The kiosk will be distributed at recreational and sporting goods stores, travel agencies, malls, and posted to the TA Web site.

1. Start PowerPoint and open **pp06TrekkingAssistant.ppt**
2. Use your favorite search engines to find 10 pictures of locations suitable for trekking (mountains, forests, deserts, and so on). Some of the pictures should include people walking. Images of pack animals could also be appropriate
3. On slide 1, insert a background picture with blue sky. Use the Cloud Callout from the AutoShapes menu to create a mat for the slide title. Send the cloud behind the text. Use the gold adjustment handle and sizing handles to adjust the shape as necessary
4. For slides 2 through 9
    a. Apply one of the background pictures
    b. Use matting techniques to make the slide text stand out without obscuring the photograph
    c. Customize slide colors as needed to obtain optimal visual impact and readability
5. Set slide transitions with varying delays depending on the slide content. Be sure to set the show to loop continuously
6. Preview the slide show, make any needed adjustments, and save

FIGURE 6.38

Sample Trekking Assistant Slide

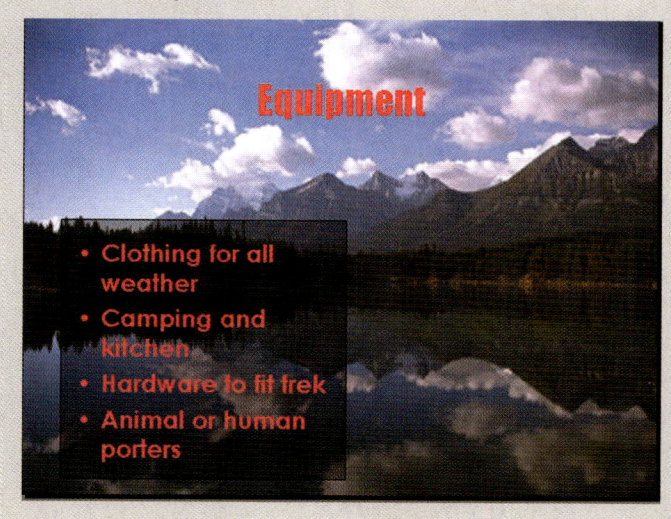

chapter six

hands-on projects

around the world

LEVEL THREE

Arrow Briefings

Arrow Briefings (AB) produces efficiency products to assist executives in improving productivity. While Arrow Briefings produces tangible products such as extremely rapid Internet access and a user-friendly operating system for their computers, the most valuable product is their two-day seminar teaching patented techniques to improve the decision-making process. Arrow Briefings' clients are top executives of businesses from all over the world. All are Fortune 500 companies.

The seminar is always located in an elegant hotel. Here all the trimmings are provided, down to meals on fine china. Topics include studies on the effects of productivity, how professionals spend (or waste) their time, human factors in productivity, effectiveness of corporate executives in decision making, communicating decisions in today's complex world, and AB's state-of-the-art technology. You have been asked to prepare a PowerPoint presentation at conventions that will introduce the seminar to executives.

1. Start PowerPoint and open **pp06ArrowBriefings.ppt**
2. Save the presentation as **<yourname>pp06ArrowBriefings.ppt**
3. Select the light blue Color Scheme for this template
4. Use shapes from the Drawing toolbar to create a logo for the company. Include the company name. Use shadow and 3-D effects. Group the finished logo into one object
5. Position the logo on the first slide
6. Use AutoShapes to create a moon and stars on the second slide. Arrange and color artistically and then group the finished work
7. Use a lightning bolt with other graphics to illustrate slide 3. Add a custom fill to the lightning bolt
8. Apply a Texture background to slide 4. Mat text and/or customize colors to obtain optimal readability. Place a reduced size logo on this slide
9. Apply a picture background to slide 5 reflecting leisure activities. Mat text and /or customize colors to obtain optimal readability
10. Use stacked ovals to create a target on slide 6. The largest circle is white, the next is red, and the center is black. Align the centers of the circles. Draw an arrow approaching the bull's-eye. Group the component parts into one object
11. Add effective graphics to each of the remaining slides
12. Set slide transitions and custom animations for the bulleted items and graphics
13. Test your presentation, make needed adjustments, and save

FIGURE 6.39

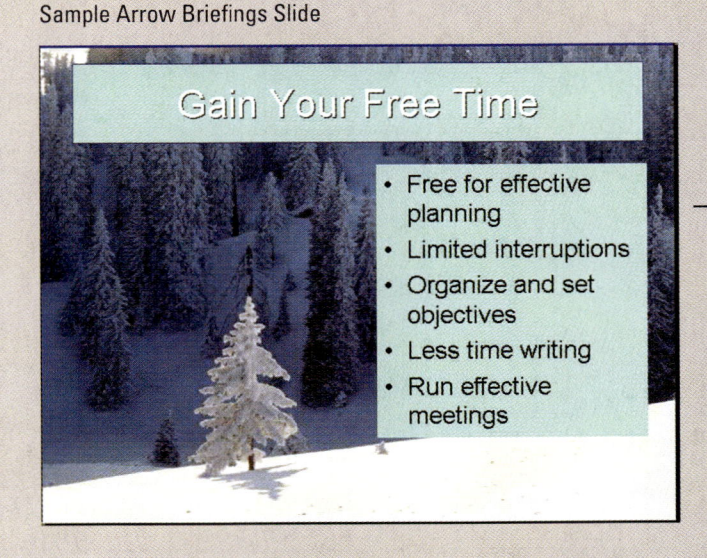

Sample Arrow Briefings Slide

www.mhhe.com/i-series

PP 6.49

POWERPOINT

running project

Montgomery-Wellish Foods, Inc.: Spice Tracking Presentation

One of the first lessons the new Montgomery-Wellish trainees learn is to pick a product and follow it throughout its life cycle. There are several steps to a product's life cycle. The trainee receives a request to buy food from a producer. A number of cases or palettes are purchased. The goods are then shipped to MWF's warehouse. Once there, the warehouse is responsible for placing the goods in storage and then sending the goods out to the supermarkets. The trainee not only authorizes the purchase of the product but also is responsible for tracking the shipment every step of the way. If the food isn't available to the supermarket in a timely fashion (e.g., for seasonal display), supermarkets may not purchase from MWF at a later date. Mary Einhorn has been charged with tracking spices. Mary's data show that there are delays in the shipping and handling of spices all along the way. You have been asked to prepare a PowerPoint presentation that illustrates Mary Einhorn's tracking of spices, which she will present to the trainees.

1. Start PowerPoint and open **pp06MWFTracking.ppt**
2. Save the presentation as **<yourname>pp06MWFTracking.ppt**
3. Use various gradient combinations of the presentation color scheme to vary the background of slides 2 through 8 while maintaining a consistent look
4. Add pictures of herbs and spices to the first slide
5. Search for art that will enhance each of the remaining slides
6. Title the sixth slide Transport Timetable Averages. Construct a chart (graph) that shows the expected time and actual time in days for delivery to the warehouse, storage processing time, and delivery to the market, using data from the next figure. Title the chart **Shipping and Handling Days January–June 2002**
6. Set custom animation for the title, bulleted text, and chart. Establish slide transitions
7. Preview your presentation, make adjustments, save, and exit PowerPoint

FIGURE 6.40
Sample Opening Slide

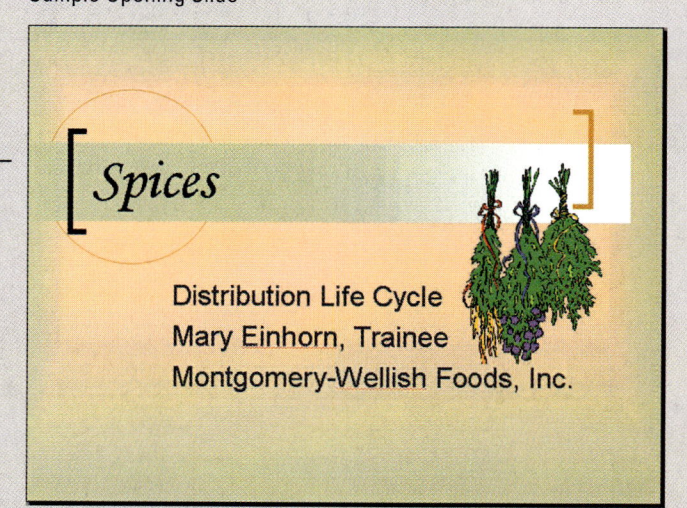

FIGURE 6.41
Chart Data

Shipping to Warehouse		Storage		Delivery to Market	
Expected	Actual	Expected	Actual	Expected	Actual
3	5	.5	1.5	1	2.5

did you know?

vanilla is the extract of fermented and dried pods of several species of orchids.

if the sun stopped shining suddenly, it would take eight minutes for people on earth to be aware of the fact.

almonds, peaches, and apricots belong to the rose family.

the oldest living thing in existence is a bristlecone pine in the White Mountains of California, dated to be 4,600 years old.

ten inches of snow equals one inch of rain in water content.

the first woman to qualify for the Indianapolis 500 was Janet Guthrie in 1977.

one organ donor can save up to _____ lives.

Chapter Objectives

- Add hyperlinks to slides—PPT2002-4-10
- Publish presentations to the Web (Save as HTML)—PPT2002-7-5
- Save a presentation as a Web page (Publish)—PPT2002-8-4
- Manage files and folders for Presentations—PPT2002-7-3

CHAPTER 7

seven

Internet/Intranet Presentations

chapter case

Using PowerPoint to Build a Donor Information Kiosk

Lauda Simmons is the coordinator of several donor organizations in the southern United States. These organizations are responsible for tracking the need for donated organs and tissue, educating the public about these needs, and coordinating the donation process.

Lauda spends a considerable amount of her time speaking at public events to promote organ and tissue donation. She has a PowerPoint presentation that she typically modifies to suit the technical understanding of the audience. For example, when speaking to the general public, the presentation typically contains very few medical terms, but when speaking to the medical or legal community, the terms and definitions must be included.

Keeping multiple copies of the presentation and updating each time she speaks is becoming tedious and too time-consuming. Lauda has asked you to help her create an interactive presentation that will allow her to choose what content to include in her production as the slide show is running. She envisions a linked slide show that contains all of the information that she might need to address. As she is speaking, she would like to be able to choose or ignore links based on audience interest and available time.

FIGURE 7.1
Organ Donor Presentation Links

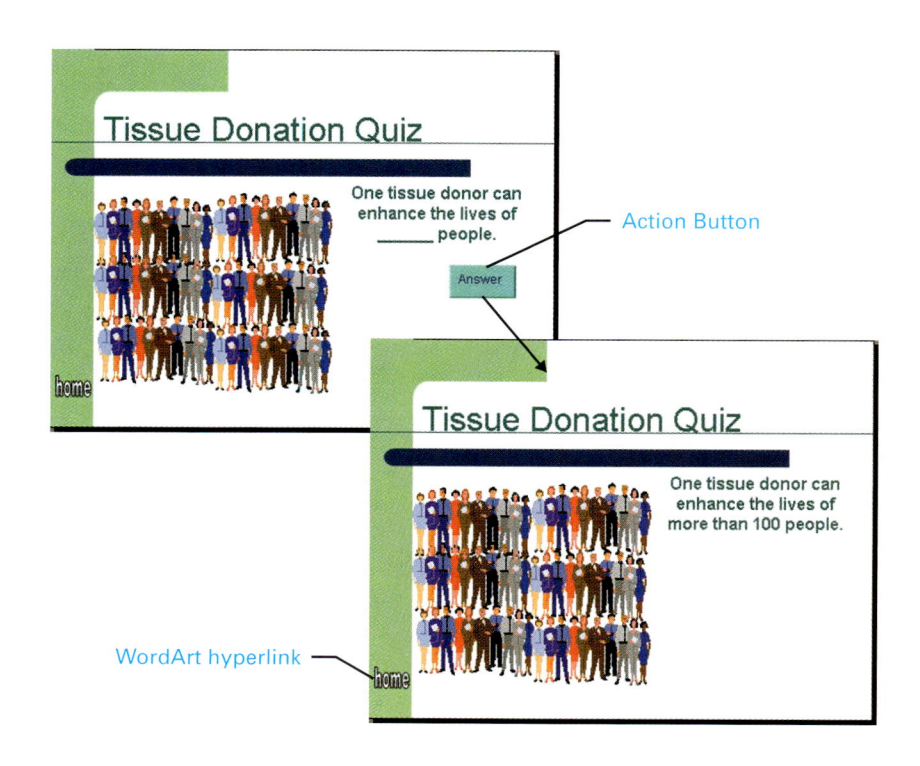

PP 7.2

Lauda would also like to promote organ and tissue donation to a wider audience than just those she can personally present to. The organization she represents has a Web site that is currently used to promote the organization. Lauda would like to put a version of her presentation on the Web site to more specifically address the information needs of potential organ and tissue donors.

Finally, Lauda believes that a Web site could be used by hospital personnel like an informational kiosk. Because the presentation would be Web-based, there would be no need for a dedicated computer. The kiosks would not replace the medical professional speaking to family members, but could serve as on-demand reinforcement of information provided at a very stressful time.

CHAPTER OUTLINE

7.1 Interactive Presentations

7.2 Using PowerPoint to Publish Web Pages

SESSION 7.1 INTERACTIVE PRESENTATIONS

The linear presentations that have been developed up to this point are very effective for short speaker-led slide shows or any presentation that is always run from beginning to end. Linear presentations make use of the basic navigation provided by PowerPoint. Such a presentation can move forward and backward one slide at a time or use pop-up menus and shortcuts to move to a specific slide. By contrast, interactive presentations allow the order of a slide show to be determined by the viewer. Interactive slide shows are effective as kiosks, Web sites, and presentations that change based on the audience.

ADDING NAVIGATION TO YOUR PRESENTATION

Before looking at adding nonlinear navigation to Lauda's Organ Donor presentation, you will need to review the slides and evaluate how well they work with PowerPoint's default navigation features. PowerPoint's native navigation methods are outlined in the next figure. Although it is possible to move to any slide without using special features, the way to accomplish such movement is not intuitive to a novice user and can be visually disturbing to an audience.

Navigating PP07OrganDonor:

1. Initiate PowerPoint and open **PP07OrganDonor.ppt**
2. Use the **Slide Show** button to run the show
3. Press the **spacebar** to advance one slide and then press the **spacebar** again after the slide's animations have completed
4. Press **Enter** to advance one slide and then press **Enter** again when the slide animations are completed
5. Press **Backspace** to move back one animation and then continue pressing backspace until you are on the first slide

tip: You will need to backspace twice for slides containing animations—once to move to the slide and the second time to initiate the animation

6. Type **9** and press **Enter** to move to slide 9

FIGURE 7.2
Slide Show Navigation

Slide Show Navigation

Go to the next slide	Click the mouse.
	Press Spacebar or Enter.
	Right-click, and on the shortcut menu, click Next
Go to the previous slide	Press Backspace.
	Right-click, and on the shortcut menu, click Previous.
See a specific previously viewed slide	Right-click, point to Go on the shortcut menu, and then click Previously Viewed
Go to a specific slide	Type the slide number, and then press Enter.
	Right-click, point to Go on the shortcut menu, then point to By Title, and click the slide you want.

7. Right-click on the slide and use the **Go** menu to move to slide **5**

tip: *Either the Slide Navigator or By Title option of the Go menu is appropriate*

8. Use **Esc** to end the slide show

Nonlinear navigation is added to a presentation using hyperlinks and action buttons. These features provide an intuitive way for users to move directly to materials of interest. Each hyperlink or action button is linked to a specific slide, another slide show, a Web page, or a file. Presentations with links are typically hierarchical in structure with several paths the user can choose. The audience may view every slide in the presentation, or just those of current interest.

Designing Hierarchical Presentations

When you are accustomed to creating linear presentations, it is important to take some time to review the design of nonlinear presentations. Nonlinear presentations are usually hierarchical with several branches or fingers that the viewer can follow. If you have visited Web sites, you are familiar with the methodology. By clicking, you can choose what topic(s) to view and how much to view about it.

Hierarchical structures typically have a menu page of topics with each topic having additional options for as many levels as are necessary for the materials. The menu may be the opening page or can follow introductory materials. Any page layout that provides the user with clickable options can be considered a menu. The next figure shows the hierarchical structure that will be applied to the Organ Donor presentation.

The hierarchy chart in the previous figure effectively defines the paths that should be available to the viewer when moving through the presentation. To determine an appropriate structure, review the slides of a presen-

FIGURE 7.3

Organ Donor Presentation Structure

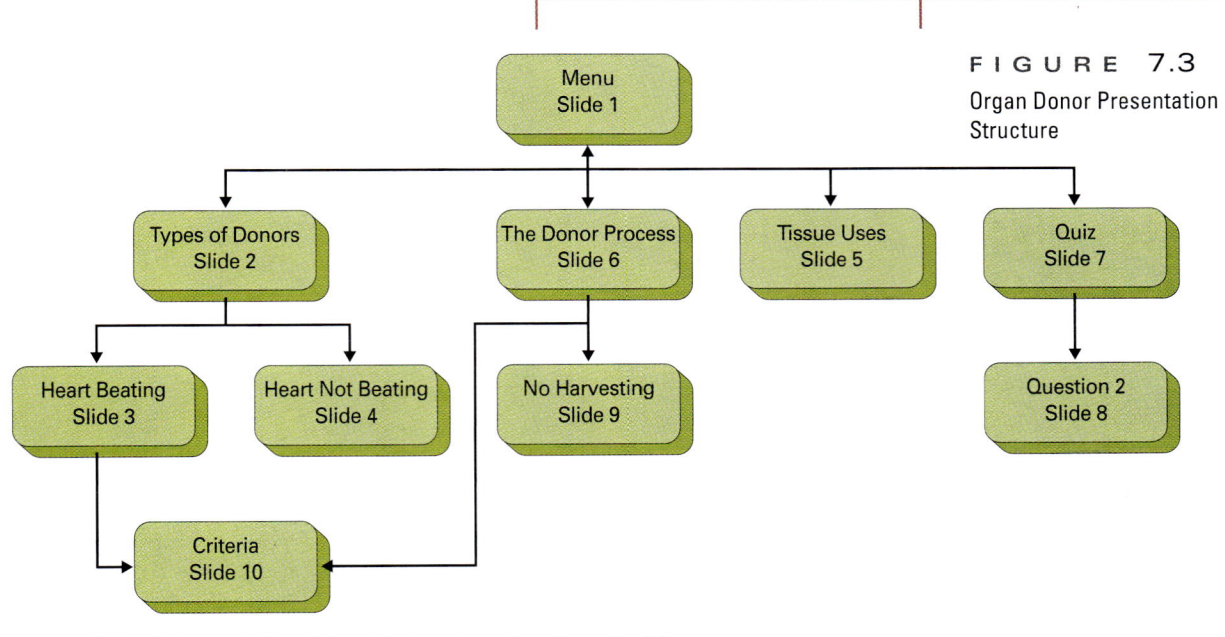

Slides 2 through 10 will be able to return directly to the Menu

tation and group them by topic. Each topic will become a menu item on the opening slide. Repeat this process for the slides in each topic to determine what lower level links will need to be added.

When the hierarchy has been established, it is time to determine the direction of navigation. The arrow heads in the previous figure represent the direction of navigation. It is rare to have a hierarchy that can only be navigated from top to bottom. It is common to allow the user to return to the menu from every slide, but sometimes additional movement between slides and topics is desirable. For the Organ Donor presentation, Lauda would like to be able to access the menu from every slide but have linear progression through each topic.

Creating Hyperlinks

A *hyperlink* is a connection from one slide in a presentation to another location. The other location can be another slide in the current presentation, a slide in another presentation, a file, a Web page address, or an e-mail address. The hyperlink can be any text or object on the slide including a Clip Art, WordArt, graph, or image. Hyperlinks are not active in any of the PowerPoint views used to develop slide shows, but become clickable when the show is run.

When a link to another PowerPoint slide is clicked, the slide is displayed as part of the PowerPoint presentation. If the link is to a Web page and an active Internet connection is available, the page will open in your default browser. Links to other types of files will open in the source application.

Adding hyperlinks to an Internet resource like a Web page or e-mail address is simple. Just type the address, called a ***uniform resource locator*** (URL), of a Web page or an e-mail address as part of the content of a slide; PowerPoint automatically creates a hyperlink to those external locations. This is because Internet addresses contain all of the information needed to locate a particular Web page or e-mail account. Other types of hyperlinks must be specifically defined. You will begin this process by building the opening page for Lauda's presentation, which will contain links to Web resources and specific locations within the slide show.

task reference

Insert a Hyperlink
- Select the object that will initiate the hyperlink. The object can be text, WordArt, a graphic, or any other clickable object
- Click the **Insert Hyperlink** button in the Standard toolbar
- Select the location of the link and then set the link options

Building the PP07OrganDonor opening page:

1. Verify that PowerPoint is running with **PP07OrganDonor.ppt** open
2. Move to slide 1 if necessary
3. Add a Textbox to the bottom right of the slide as shown in the next figure
   a. Type **www.organdonor.com**
   b. Press enter and type your e-mail address (if you don't have an e-mail address, use yourname@mailserver)
4. Select the subtitle placeholder containing Lauda's name and type the following text in its place

   Types of Donors

   The Donor Process

   Tissue Uses

   Quiz

5. Adjust the subtitle placeholder as needed to match your positioning of the menu items to the figure
6. Select the **Types of Donors** text
   a. Click the **Insert Hyperlink** button in the Standard toolbar
   b. Click the **Place in This Document** option
   c. Select **Slide 2** and click **OK**

tip: The Types of Donors text is now formatted as a hyperlink. The link will not become active until the slide show is run

7. Repeat actions outlined in step 6 to
   a. Link **The Donor Process** to **slide 6**
   b. Link **Tissue Uses** to **slide 5**
   c. Link **Quiz** to slide 7
8. Save your changes as **<yourname>pp07OrganDonor.ppt**
9. Use Slide Show view to test each of the links

tip: You will need to right-click and use the Go menu to return to the first slide since that navigation has not been added to the presentation

Referring back to Figure 7.3, notice that the first level of downward links from the hierarchy chart has now been added to your presentation. It

www.mhhe.com/i-series   PP 7.7

FIGURE 7.4
Organ Donor Menu Page

— Hyperlinked menu options

— Web and e-mail addresses

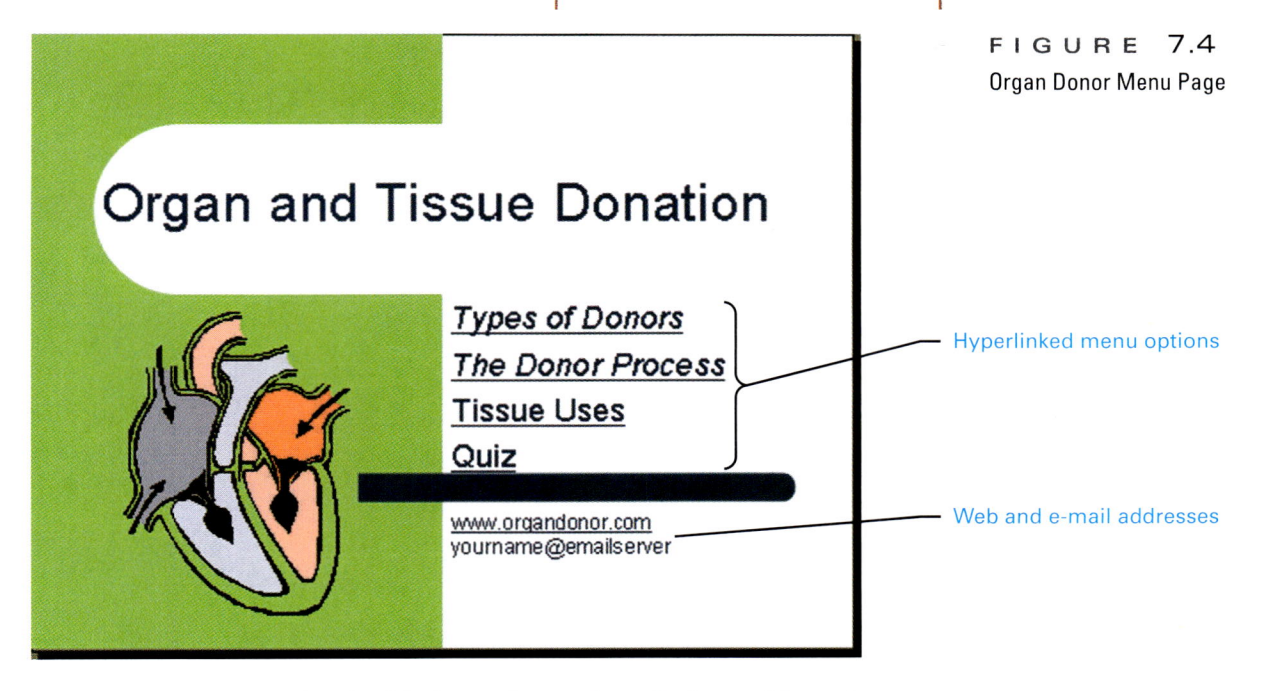

is easiest to add one level of links and test them before adding the next level of links. For the menu, specific text was created to be used as the link text. The next level of links uses existing slide content as the link text.

Building the PP07OrganDonor second level links:

1. Verify that PowerPoint is running with **PP07OrganDonor.ppt** open
2. Move to slide 2 if necessary
3. Select **Heart Beating,** click the **Insert Hyperlink** button, and add a hyperlink to slide 3
4. Select **Non-Heart Beating,** click the **Insert Hyperlink** button, and add a hyperlink to slide 4
5. Select **Brain Dead,** click the **Insert Hyperlink** button, and add a hyperlink to slide 10
6. Move to slide 6
7. Select **Brain Death,** click the **Insert Hyperlink** button, and add a hyperlink to slide 10
8. Move to slide 4, select Only, remove the underline, and add italic formatting
9. Save your changes
10. Run the presentation and test the new links

Underlining and color are both used to indicate text that can be clicked. The visited and unvisited text hyperlink colors are set by the active color scheme. Other hyperlinked objects like pictures, WordArt, or shapes are not formatted to indicate that they are hyperlinked.

POWERPOINT

FIGURE 7.5
Slide 2 Second-Level Links

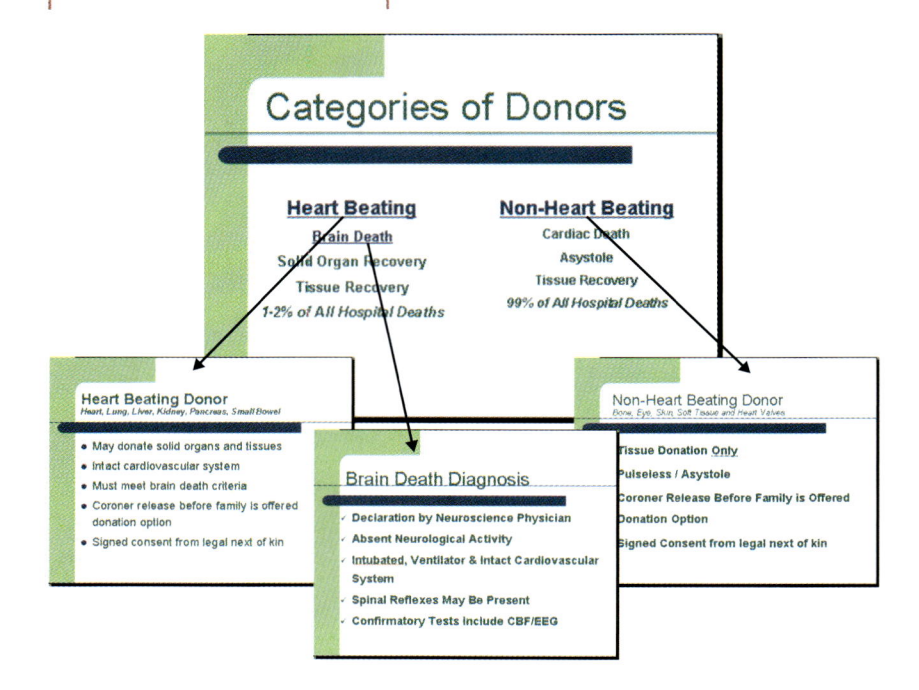

The underline was removed from Only in the previous steps because it confuses users to have underlines used for emphasis in a presentation with hyperlinks. Although the mouse pointer changes to a pointing finger when it is over a clickable object, many users don't notice this change and will try to click any underlined text. Try to make navigation as intuitive as possible to avoid confusing users.

Since hyperlinks can be applied to any text or object, text, shapes, tables, graphics, and pictures can link to other locations. Although clicking is the most common way to initiate a link, other actions, like pausing over a link, can be used to start the action. When linking compound objects like text within a shape or grouped objects, each component can have a unique link attribute set. Editing a hyperlinked object does not impact the hyperlink, but deleting a hyperlinked object removes the associated hyperlink.

Using the Insert Hyperlink Dialog Box

The Insert Hyperlink dialog box has already been used to add hyperlinks to the Organ Donor slide show, but a closer look at its capabilities is warranted. In the original evaluation of the donor presentation, a reference to brain death on slide 3 was missed. That text needs to be linked to the brain death criteria on slide 10.

Exploring the Insert Hyperlink dialog box:

1. Verify that PowerPoint is running with **PP07OrganDonor.ppt** open

2. Move to slide 3 if necessary

3. Select **Brain Death** in the third bulleted item and click the **Insert Hyperlink** button

4. Click **Existing File or Web Page**

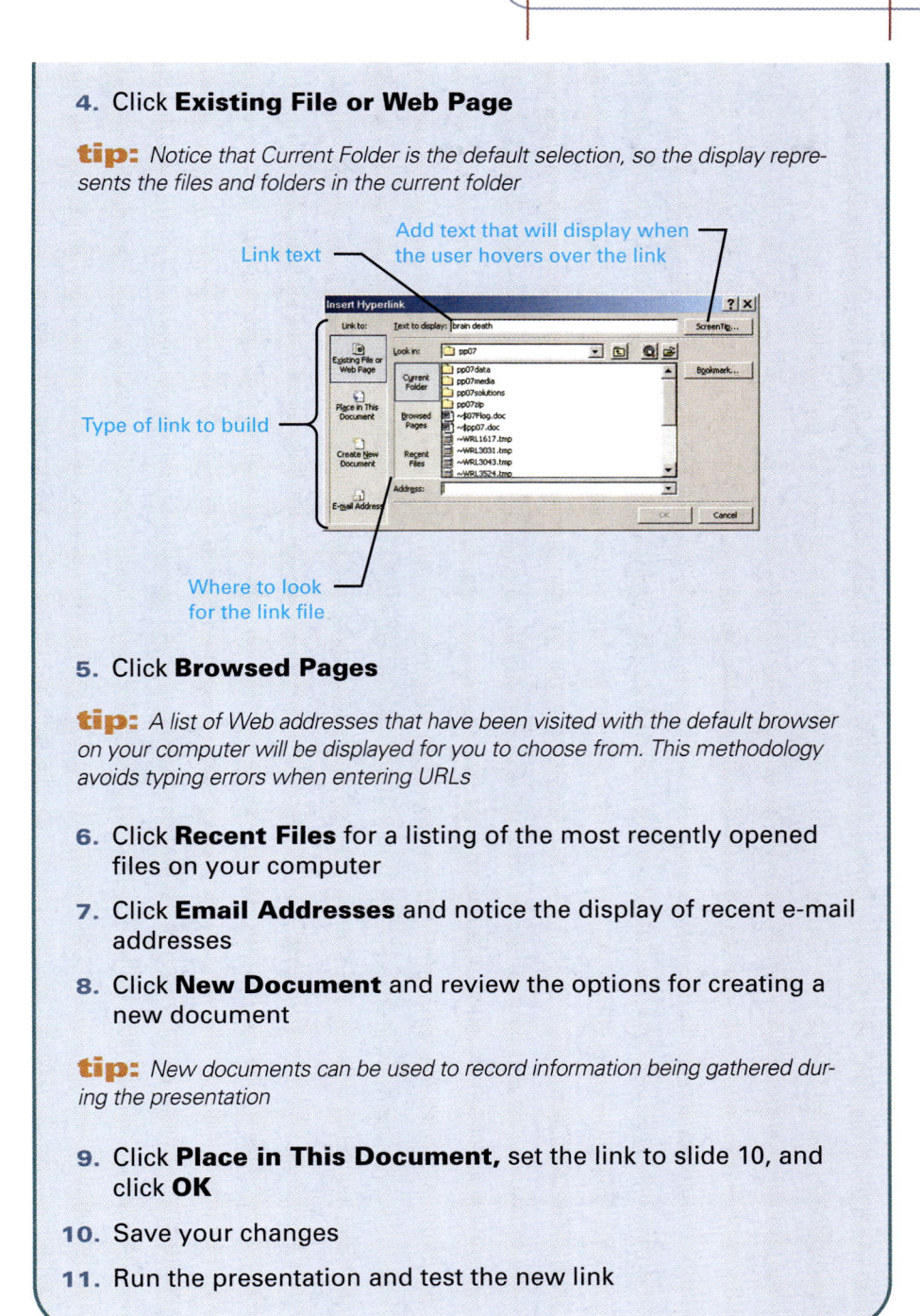

   tip: *Notice that Current Folder is the default selection, so the display represents the files and folders in the current folder*

   FIGURE 7.6
   Insert Hyperlink Dialog Box

   Link text — Add text that will display when the user hovers over the link

   Type of link to build

   Where to look for the link file

5. Click **Browsed Pages**

   tip: *A list of Web addresses that have been visited with the default browser on your computer will be displayed for you to choose from. This methodology avoids typing errors when entering URLs*

6. Click **Recent Files** for a listing of the most recently opened files on your computer

7. Click **Email Addresses** and notice the display of recent e-mail addresses

8. Click **New Document** and review the options for creating a new document

   tip: *New documents can be used to record information being gathered during the presentation*

9. Click **Place in This Document,** set the link to slide 10, and click **OK**

10. Save your changes

11. Run the presentation and test the new link

When an e-mail or Web address is known, it is convenient to just type it in and let PowerPoint take care of making the link. This method was demonstrated on the first slide of Organ Donor. When a site has been visited but the URL was not committed to memory, the Insert Hyperlink dialog box will display a selectable list of recently viewed addresses. Similarly, the Current Folder and Recent Files selections display files for you to select from.

Changes can be made to an existing hyperlink by selecting the link and clicking the Insert Hyperlink button. This action opens the Edit Hyperlink dialog box. Lauda would like screen tips added to some of the hyperlinks in the presentation.

FIGURE 7.7
Setting a Screen Tip

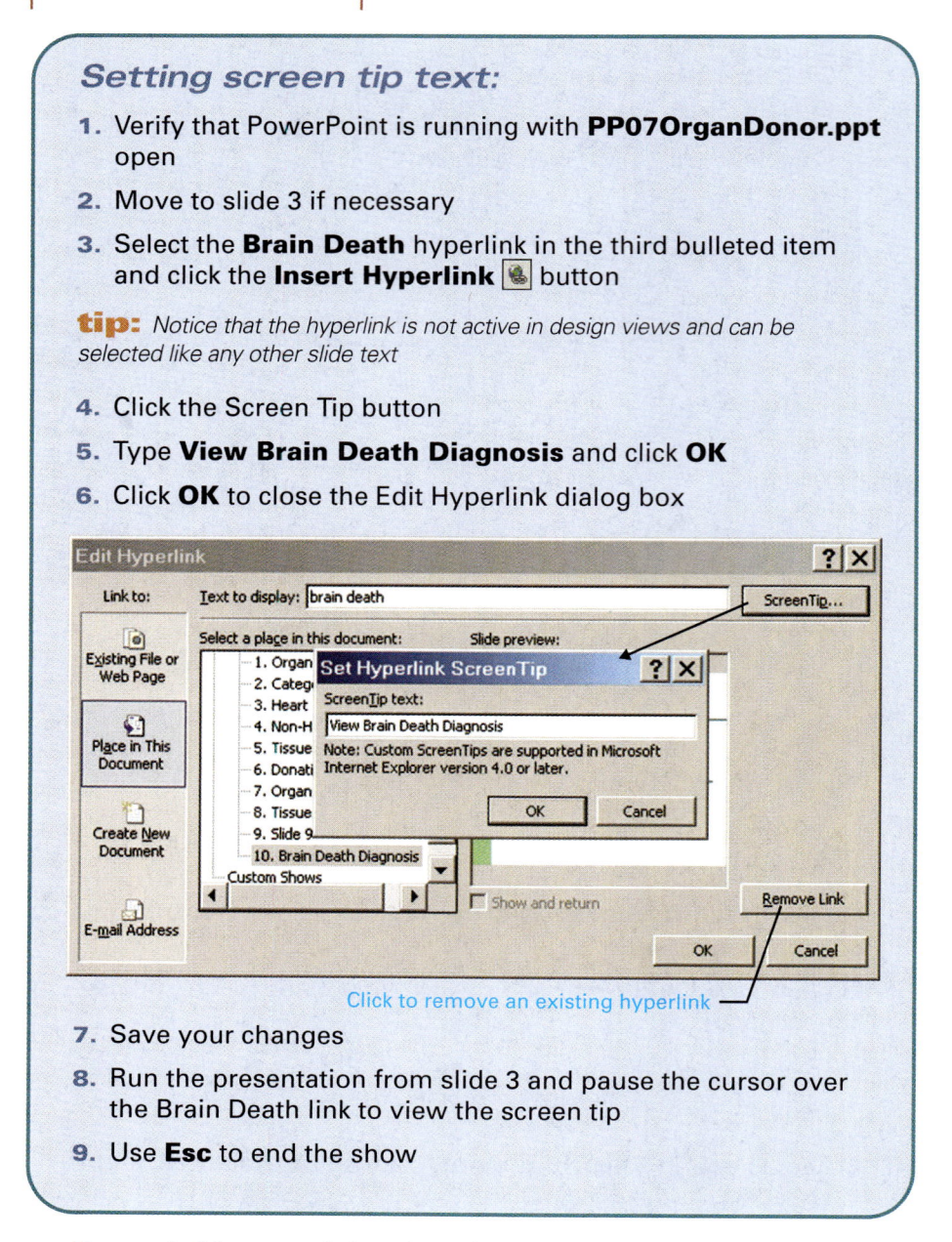

Setting screen tip text:

1. Verify that PowerPoint is running with **PP07OrganDonor.ppt** open
2. Move to slide 3 if necessary
3. Select the **Brain Death** hyperlink in the third bulleted item and click the **Insert Hyperlink** button

tip: Notice that the hyperlink is not active in design views and can be selected like any other slide text

4. Click the Screen Tip button
5. Type **View Brain Death Diagnosis** and click **OK**
6. Click **OK** to close the Edit Hyperlink dialog box

Click to remove an existing hyperlink

7. Save your changes
8. Run the presentation from slide 3 and pause the cursor over the Brain Death link to view the screen tip
9. Use **Esc** to end the show

You probably noticed that the Edit Hyperlink dialog box is very similar to the Insert Hyperlink dialog box. The most significant difference is the Edit Hyperlink option for removing the hyperlink while leaving the hyperlinked object intact. The Edit Hyperlink dialog box can also be used to update link text and change the link address.

When presentations are moved to a new computer, it is common to have **broken hyperlinks.** It is always best to test all hyperlinks before running a slide show, but this is critical if the show has been moved to a new folder or computer. A broken hyperlink is one that has an invalid destination causing an error to display when it is clicked. The cause might be as simple as a URL that was mistyped, or a hyperlink to a destination that was moved or deleted. Update broken hyperlinks with the Edit Hyperlink features just discussed.

Noticeably absent from the Edit Hyperlink dialog box is the ability to change the color of the hyperlinks. That is because hyperlinks are controlled by the eight colors of the color scheme. Updating the colors of the color scheme is the only way to change hyperlink colors.

HYPERLINKING OTHER OBJECTS

All other linking methods are based on hyperlinks. The first step is to build the object that will be used to initiate the link. Once an object is built, it is made clickable by adding a hyperlink to it.

Placing Links on the Slide Master

The original hierarchy designed for the Organ Donor presentation noted that slides 2 through 10 were to provide navigation back to the menu. The first slide in a presentation is often referred to as the home slide. Lauda would like to use WordArt to create a navigation icon for this purpose. This icon will be placed on the Slide Master so that it will appear on all slides that do not use the Title Slide format.

Adding a link to the Slide Master:

1. Verify that PowerPoint is running with **PP07OrganDonor.ppt** open
2. Open the **View** menu, pause over **Master,** and click **Slide Master**
3. Select the slide master with the bulleted list
4. Click the **WordArt** button on the Drawing toolbar
   a. Select the top-left style and click **OK**
   b. Type **home** and click **OK**
   c. Position and size the WordArt as shown in the next figure

   tip: *Use the Align options from the Draw menu of the Drawing toolbar*

5. With the WordArt still selected
   a. Click the **Insert Hyperlink** button, select **Place in This Document** and then **Slide 1**
   b. Click the **Screen Tip** button, type **Return to menu slide,** and click **OK**
   c. Click **OK**
   d. Click **Close Master View**
6. Run the presentation and test the Home links
7. Use **Esc** to end the show
8. Save your changes

Any object placed on a Slide Master will appear on all slides in the presentation based on that master. The Home link could have been text or any other object placed on the master. If a presentation uses multiple templates, each set of masters would need to be updated to place an item on all pages.

Using Action Buttons

Action buttons are ready-made buttons that can be placed on a slide to intuitively control slide progressions. Once the button is placed on a slide, it is assigned a hyperlink that controls its action. Action buttons are available from the AutoShapes menu of the drawing toolbar and are added to a slide by selecting the button and then clicking and dragging in onto the slide.

FIGURE 7.8
WordArt Link Added to Slide Master

Linked WordArt

Action buttons are effective when a simple pictorial interface is needed for moving between slides, playing movies, and playing sounds.

Lauda would like to use Action buttons for the navigation in the quiz component of Organ Donor. The plan is to add a few more questions and make the quiz more interactive. The first step of this process is to duplicate each quiz slide and remove the answer from the first slide. Action buttons will be added to the question slide so the user can see the answer and move to the next question.

task reference
Create and Link an Action Button

- Select the slide to contain the Action Button
- If needed, use the View menu to activate the Drawing toolbar
- Click the **AutoShapes** button of the Drawing toolbar, pause over **Action Buttons**, and select the desired button
- Click and drag the button on the slide surface
- Click the Action Button and follow the steps to set a hyperlink

Adding Action Buttons to the quiz:

1. Verify that PowerPoint is running with **PP07OrganDonor.ppt** open
2. Move to slide 7 if necessary
3. Use the **Duplicate** option of the **Edit** menu to create a copy of this slide
4. Return to slide 7, delete the answer text, and reduce the size of the question placeholder

5. Click **AutoShapes** on the Drawing toolbar, select **Action Buttons,** then click the **Custom** (blank) Action Button, and draw it on the slide using the next figure as your guide

6. On the Mouse Click tab, click the **Hyperlink to** option button, then select **Next Slide** and click **OK**

7. Type **Answer** in the Action Button

8. Move to slide 8, delete the answer text, and replace the underline with **up to 8**

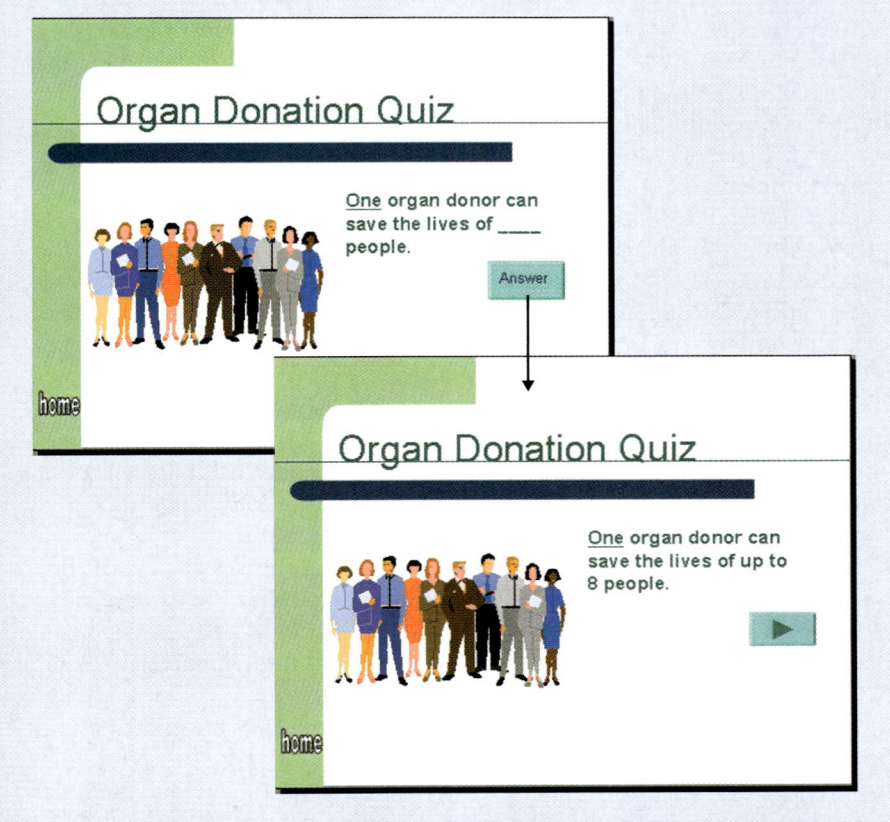

FIGURE 7.9
Action Buttons with Hyperlinks

9. Add a **Next** Action Button to slide 8 that advances to slide 9

10. Repeat steps 3 through 6 to duplicate, edit, and add Action Buttons to slide 9

tip: You can copy and paste action buttons that suit your needs

11. Move to slide 10 and replace the underline with **more than 100**

12. Run the slide show from slide 7 and test the Action Buttons

13. Use **Esc** to end the show

If a mistake is made when attaching a hyperlink to an object such as WordArt or an Action button, the Insert Hyperlink button can be used to open the Edit Hyperlink dialog box and make adjustments. When using objects other than text for a hyperlink, there are no visual indications to the user like the change in text color and underline used for text links. It is important that hyperlinked objects look clickable. Clickable objects can be distinguished by color, background, and position on the slide. In general, buttons should be placed on the bottom or down the left of the slide.

Linking to External Resources

One of the most powerful features of hyperlinked presentations is the ability to draw in external resources as you need them. When linking to an external resource, its location is described with a uniform resource locator (URL). When the hyperlink is to a page or file on a local computer or network, the location is represented by the path to the file. The path contains the drive name and all of the folders that must be opened to reach the file. For example, C:\My Documents\Presentation\Notes.doc describes the location of the Word file, Notes.doc, as being on the C: drive in the Notes folder, which can be found in the My Documents folder. Similarly www.microsoft.com describes the default Web page (since no file name is included) found on the Microsoft.com server.

The hyperlinks that are connected to resources outside a slide show can use either absolute or relative paths. ***Absolute links*** state all of the information required to find the resource, so for a file it would contain the drive, path, and file name. ***Relative links*** usually don't include a drive and path, but depend on the file being in the same folder as the presentation or in a folder that has been specified as the hyperlink base.

Relative linking allows the presentation and base folder to be moved to another computer without breaking any links. When delivering a presentation from a stand-alone computer, it is best to place all linked files in the same folder as your presentation. If the presentation is moved to another computer, all of the linked files must be moved as well.

When a presentation is stored on a server with links to several files, it is a good practice to put the files in a common location on a server and set a ***hyperlink base.*** If the server URL changes, updating the hyperlink base will repair any broken links without editing each link. If you need this feature, please refer to PowerPoint Help for instructions.

When presenting to certain audiences, Lauda has found that she likes to use slides from some of her other presentations. In the past she has stopped the current slide show and opened another to retrieve the data. To avoid this juggling, she wants to place links to other shows in the Organ Donor presentation.

Linking to another PowerPoint file:

1. Verify that PowerPoint is running with **PP07OrganDonor.ppt** open
2. Move to slide 5
3. Build a WordArt object with the first style from the style gallery. The text should be **case**
4. Position the new WordArt object above the home object as shown in the figure

tip: *The home object is on the Slide Master and cannot be manipulated from slide 2*

5. Select the case WordArt
   a. Click the **Insert Hyperlink** button
   b. Click **Existing File or Web page**
   c. Click **Current Folder** and navigate to the file **pp07DonorPresentation2.ppt**
   d. Click the **Bookmark** button, select slide **4** of the presentation, and click **OK**
   e. Click **OK** again to exit the Insert Hyperlink dialog box

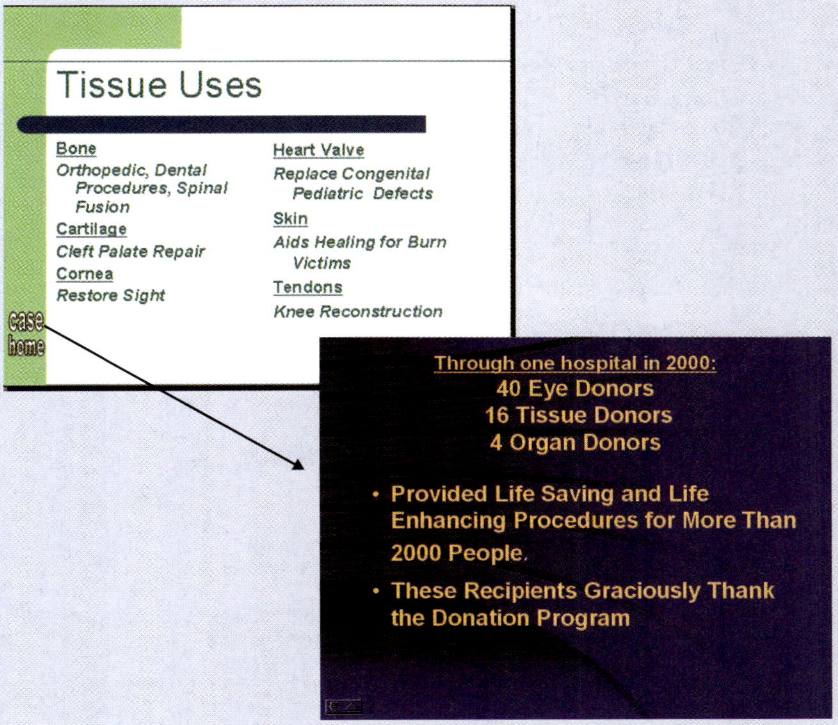

FIGURE 7.10

Hyperlink to Slide 4 in Another Presentation

6. Run the slide show from slide 5 and test the case link
7. Use **Esc** to end the pp07DonorPresentation2.ppt show
8. Use **Esc** again to end your show

The *bookmark* used in the previous steps is similar to a bookmark left in a book to mark your place, but this one kept track of which slide to display when the hyperlink was clicked. With the slide show running you clicked the case link causing pp07DonorPresentation2 to open as a separate presentation. The bookmark caused slide 4 to be active when the presentation opened, but navigation can be used to move to any slide in the presentation. Since two slide shows were open, both needed to be closed.

Links can also open files of other types. Lauda has created a chart in Excel that she would like to access from a link in the slide show.

Linking to an Excel file:

1. Verify that PowerPoint is running with **PP07OrganDonor.ppt** open

2. Move to slide 2 if necessary
3. Build a WordArt object with the first style from the style gallery containing the text **chart**
4. Position the new WordArt objects above the home object as shown in Figure 7.11

tip: *The home object is on the Slide Master and cannot be manipulated from slide 2*

5. Select the chart WordArt
   a. Click the **Insert Hyperlink** button
   b. Click **Existing File or Web page**
   c. Click **Current Folder** and navigate to the Excel file **pp07DonorStats.xls**
   d. Click **OK**

FIGURE 7.11
Hyperlink to an Excel File

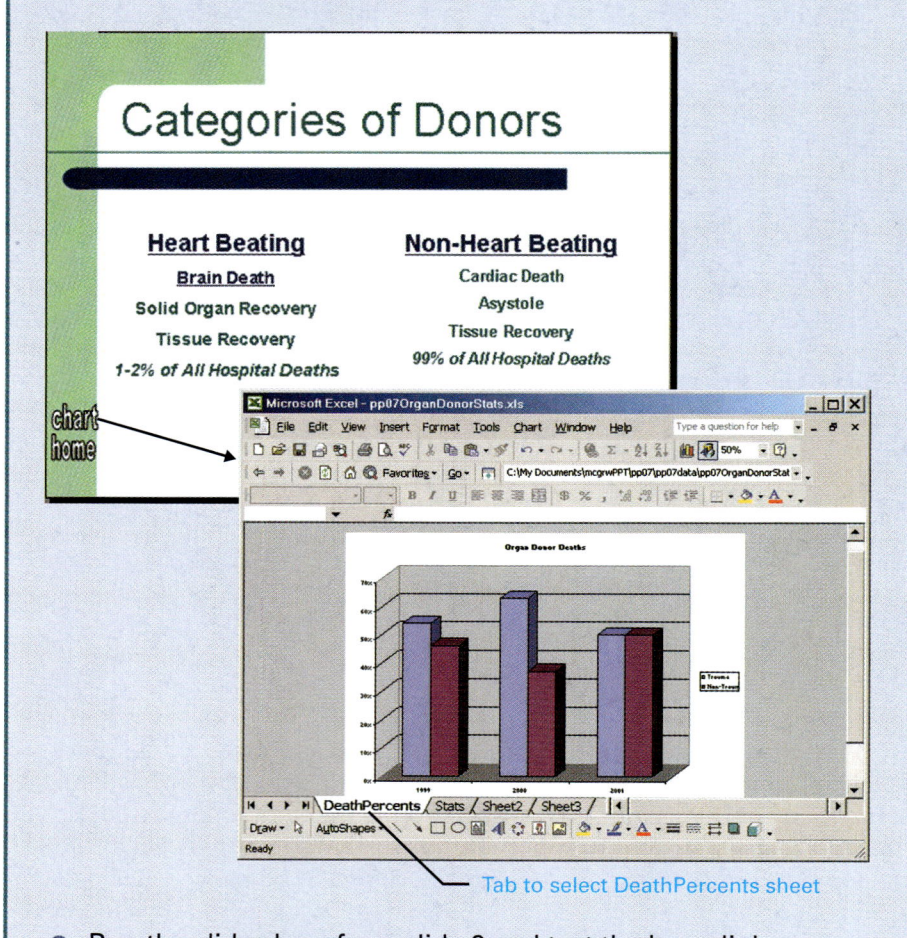

Tab to select DeathPercents sheet

6. Run the slide show from slide 2 and test the hyperlink

tip: *You may need to click the DeathPercents tab*

7. Close the Excel file
8. Use **Esc** to end the slide show
9. Use the **Save** as option of the **File** menu to save the presentation as **<yourname>OrganDonor.ppt**

The procedure demonstrated can be used to open files created in any application. When a link to a file created in another application is clicked, the native application is opened to display the file. For this to work properly, the file type must be recognized by Windows. Any needed operations can be performed in the native application before closing it. Lauda is happy with the presentation and understands how to add more links to external documents as she needs them.

making the grade — SESSION 7.1

1. What are the advantages of using nonlinear navigation?
2. What objects can have hyperlinks added to them?
3. How do you remove a hyperlink but leave the object?
4. Where can a hyperlink take you?

SESSION 7.2 USING POWERPOINT TO PUBLISH WEB PAGES

PowerPoint makes creating a Web publication as easy as building a speaker-led presentation. Web presentations can be designed specifically for Web publication, or an existing presentation can be converted to a Web format. Even though Web publishing is easy, there is some Web-specific knowledge necessary to fully control the published results.

PREPARING FOR WEB PUBLISHING

Web formatted documents, called **Web pages,** rely mostly on **hypertext markup language (HTML),** a scripting language that describes how to format the content of the page. **HTML tags** are enclosed in <> throughout page content describing how the browser will display the content. For example Hello would cause the browser to bold the text between the tags, resulting in **Hello.** Using PowerPoint, Web pages can be created without knowing HTML, because it is generated without user intervention. At least some HTML skill is needed to maintain and customize the generated pages. There are many good HTML tutorials available on the World Wide Web.

Publishing Web Pages

The motivations for publishing PowerPoint presentations as Web pages are as varied as the people and organizations using this feature. Published pages provide an easy way to share documents without face-to-face contact. Web pages can be viewed using any browser, making a presentation more portable. Pages can be published to either an intranet or the Internet. **Intranets** are networks serving an organization and are used to share documents within that organization. The **Internet** is a worldwide network of computers used to support the **World Wide Web** (www), a network of Web documents, and other services such as e-mail. Although World Wide Web sites can be secured to restrict access, they are generally intended to reach a larger audience than intranet publications.

Publishing a presentation involves creating the presentation, converting the presentation to a Web format, and then placing the files on a shared server. A server is a computer that provides services to a network. A shared server can be a *local server,* meaning that it provides services within an organization, or a *Web server* that provides computing services to access the World Wide Web. Publishing a presentation to a local server makes the content available locally, while publishing to a Web server makes the presentation available from the Internet. The steps to create the Web pages are the same, regardless of where the converted files are placed.

Navigation is a critical element of any Web presentation. To avoid mystery navigation, PowerPoint adds a *navigation bar* to all Web publications. PowerPoint's navigation bar provides linear movement through pages, while a hierarchical structure like that built for Organ Donor in the previous session is usually better suited to Web presentations.

Speaker's notes are visible in a Web publication and can be used to provide slide captions and explanatory notes. Depending on the browser being used, animations, movies, and sound files will play. Sound files can be used to narrate a Web presentation in a manner similar to that explored for a stand-alone kiosk.

Selecting a Web Browser

A *Web browser* is the software application used to view Web pages. The browser reads and interprets HTML and other scripting languages to determine how the page content should be laid out on the screen. The two most popular browsers are Microsoft Internet Explorer and Netscape Navigator. Many *internet service providers (ISPs)* provide a custom browser highlighting their Web services. America on Line (AOL) and AT&T@Home are examples of ISPs with custom browsers.

The browser used by those viewing your published pages has an impact on how well the presentation works. PowerPoint is a Microsoft product, and the HTML code that it generates is optimized for Microsoft Internet Explorer 4.0 or above. This format provides the best fidelity, fastest performance, and smallest file size. During the publication process, a selection is available to save files for other browsers, but the result is larger files and slower performance. Additionally, not all of the browsers support all of the features published by PowerPoint. For example, older versions of Internet Explorer and all versions of Netscape Navigator will not display slide animations, transitions, sounds, or movies. If all of these features are needed, it is best to encourage your audience to use the current version of Internet Explorer.

CREATING A PERSONAL WEB PAGE

There are several ways to create a Web site using PowerPoint. Choose the method that best suits your skills and goals. The AutoContent Wizard can be used to create any of the standard presentations supported as Web pages. When Web page is chosen as the output type, the wizard will automatically select a color scheme appropriate for Web browsing. The AutoContent Wizard also has a template that can be used to create a Group Home Page. This template is designed to allow a group of people working on a project or projects to update Web pages to reflect project status.

Microsoft provides a wizard that will publish your site on an organizational server or to a number of popular ISPs. The wizard is initiated from the Add Network Place option of the New Document Task pane in any Office Application. Since this wizard is available from any Office application, it can publish content from any Office application to the Web. You must have an account with the ISP before Web pages can be stored to their server.

task reference

Build an AutoContent Web Page

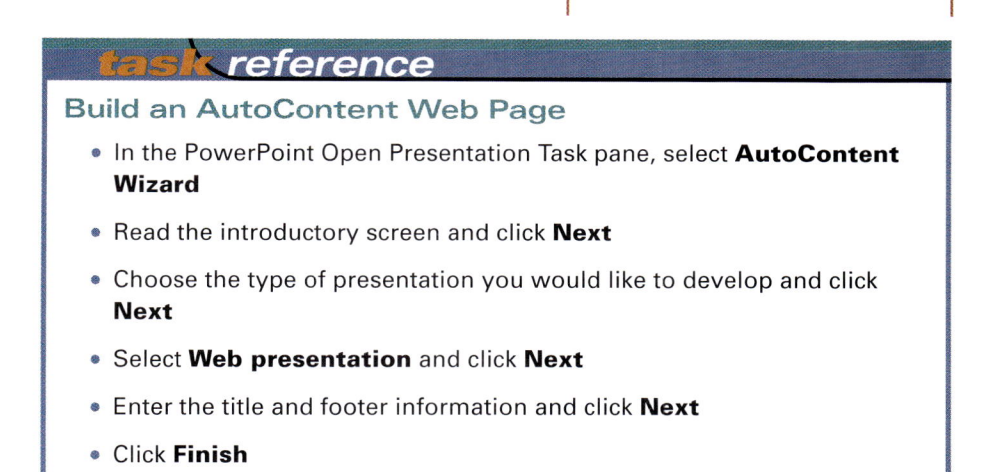

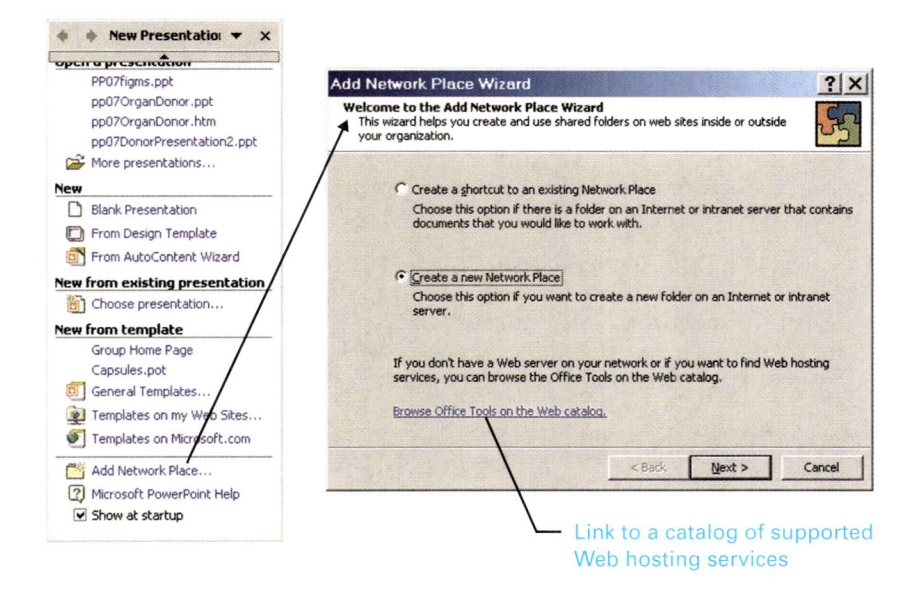

- In the PowerPoint Open Presentation Task pane, select **AutoContent Wizard**
- Read the introductory screen and click **Next**
- Choose the type of presentation you would like to develop and click **Next**
- Select **Web presentation** and click **Next**
- Enter the title and footer information and click **Next**
- Click **Finish**

FIGURE 7.12

Accessing Microsoft Web Publishing Wizard

Link to a catalog of supported Web hosting services

The simplest way to create a Web page is to use the Save As option of the File menu. If direct access to a file or network server is available, the files can be stored in a shared location using the Save As process. If direct access is not available, *file transfer protocol (FTP)* software can be used to place a copy of the Web files on the appropriate server.

Building your Home page:

1. Verify that PowerPoint is running and close any open presentations
2. On the **File** menu click **New** to open the New Presentation Task pane
3. Click **From Design Template** in the New Presentation Task pane
4. Select the **Textured** template

tip: *Pause the cursor over each template to see its name*

5. Use the drop-down arrow to switch to the **Slide Layout** panel of the Task pane and choose **Blank** layout

6. Refer to the next picture as you use the Drawing toolbar to
   a. Add a text box. Type your name in the text box, position it as shown, and size the characters to 36 point
   b. Add another text box. Type **My aspirations are . . .** , press **Enter**, click the **Bullets** button on the Formatting toolbar, and type at least four aspirations, pressing Enter after each
   c. Use the **Insert Picture** button of the Drawing toolbar to insert a picture of yourself. If you don't have a digital image of yourself, the image shown is in the Clip Organizer
   d. Copy and paste the bulleted list text box and then edit the text to read **My hobbies are . . .** Edit the bullets to reflect your hobbies and areas of interest
   e. Add a third text box and type any other information you would like to share about yourself
   f. Add a fourth text box and enter at least two Web URLs and descriptions for sites you like to visit

7. Use the **Align or Distribute** options of the **Draw** menu on the Drawing toolbar to align your objects

8. From the File menu select **Web Page Preview**

tip: *The page will display in your default browser. If your browser is not Internet Explorer 4.0 or above, your results may be very different. Visit www.microsoft.com to download the latest Internet Explorer version*

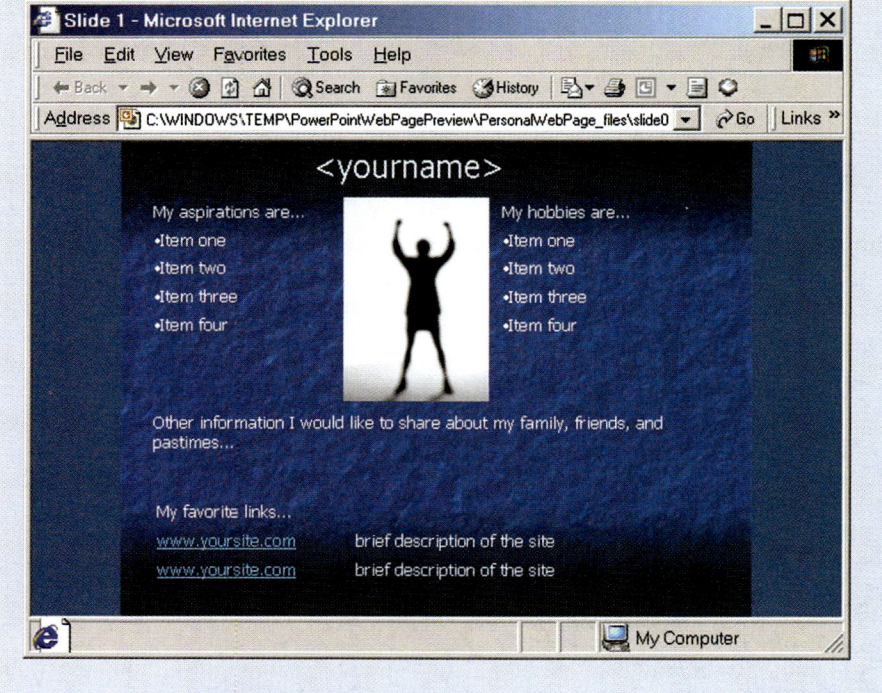

FIGURE 7.13
Personal Home Page

9. Close the browser window

In the previous steps you were able to preview your work in the browser as it was being developed, but the presentation is still in PowerPoint format. Before placing the files on a server, they must be converted to HTML format that can be understood by all browsers. The conversion to Web format can be accomplished using the Save As Web Page option of the File menu.

Saving your Home page as a Web page:

1. Verify that PowerPoint is running with **<yourname>pp07OrganDonor.ppt** open

2. On the **File** menu click **Save As Web Page**

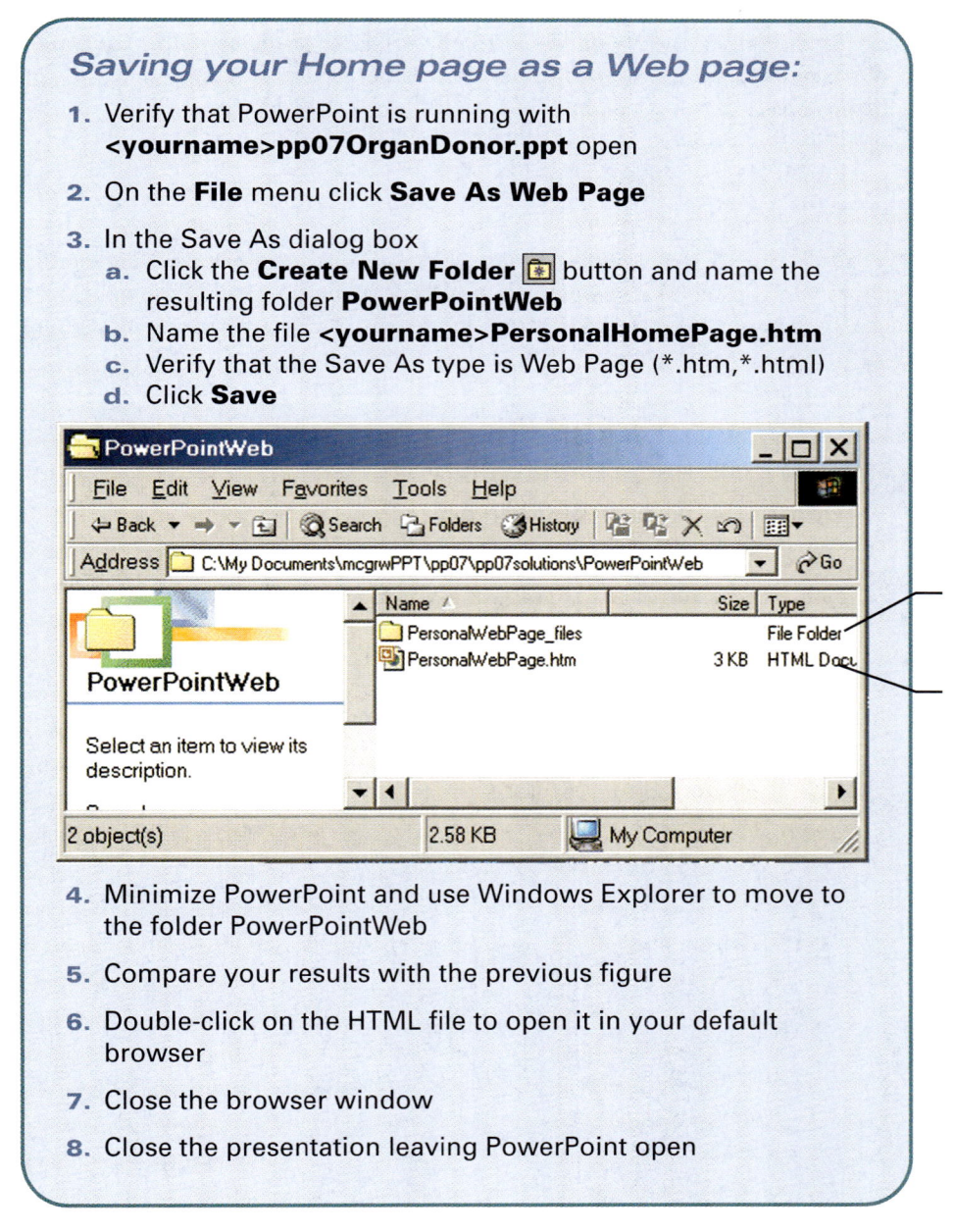

3. In the Save As dialog box
   a. Click the **Create New Folder** button and name the resulting folder **PowerPointWeb**
   b. Name the file **<yourname>PersonalHomePage.htm**
   c. Verify that the Save As type is Web Page (*.htm,*.html)
   d. Click **Save**

FIGURE 7.14
Files Created by Save As Web Page

Folder containing graphics and scripts needed by the HTML file

HTML file that can be opened by a browser

4. Minimize PowerPoint and use Windows Explorer to move to the folder PowerPointWeb

5. Compare your results with the previous figure

6. Double-click on the HTML file to open it in your default browser

7. Close the browser window

8. Close the presentation leaving PowerPoint open

The Save As Web Page process creates files with .htm extensions that can be opened by Web browsers. The .htm extension indicates that the file is in HTML format. Other files, such as the graphics in the presentation and a style sheet, are stored in a folder. The folder carries the name of the presentation plus _files. For this presentation to work from a server, the .htm file and the associated folder with all of its files must be on the server.

PowerPoint does not provide a way to directly edit any of the files created in the Save As Web Page process. The .htm file can be edited in any text editor, such as Notepad, or in a code generator such as Microsoft

Front Page. PowerPoint can open the .htm file as a presentation so that it can be edited and the Save As Web Page process repeated to replace the original files.

SAVING EXISTING PRESENTATIONS AS WEB PAGES

When saving a multi-slide presentation in HTML format, a Web site with a home page is create. A ***Web site*** is a group of organized Web pages that cover a topic area and are stored in a specific electronic location. Typically the ***home page*** is the opening page of the site and contains general information about the site and navigational links to access the various topics. Each slide becomes a page in the Web site.

The Organ Donor presentation built in Session 7.1 was designed to be placed on a shared server in HTML format. Since there are 10 slides in the presentation, there will be 10 Web pages created in the Save As Web Page operation. By default, PowerPoint creates the presentation with frames. On the Web, ***frames*** allow multiple Web pages to display simultaneously. Frames are similar to the panels in the PowerPoint development environment.

task reference
Preview a Presentation as a Web Site
- Open the presentation in PowerPoint
- Select **Web Page Preview** from the **File** menu

Previewing the Organ Donor Web site:

1. Verify that PowerPoint is running
2. On the **File** menu click **Open**
3. Use the Open dialog box to navigate to **<yourname>OrganDonor.ppt** and open it
4. Click in the Notes pane of the first slide and type **Click underlined text**

   tip: Notes must be present for the Notes pane to display in your Web presentation

5. Choose **Web Page Preview** from the **File** menu
6. Use the links in the Navigation frame to click to several presentation slides
7. Test the functionality of each of the buttons outlined in the previous figure
8. Close the browser window

The Web Page Preview displays a Web site as it would appear created with the default settings. When there are multiple slides in the presentation, a Navigation frame is created displaying the title of each slide. The notes frame will display when there are notes in the Notes panel of the presentation. The navigation bar across the bottom of the presentation allows the viewer to customize the display to suit his or her needs.

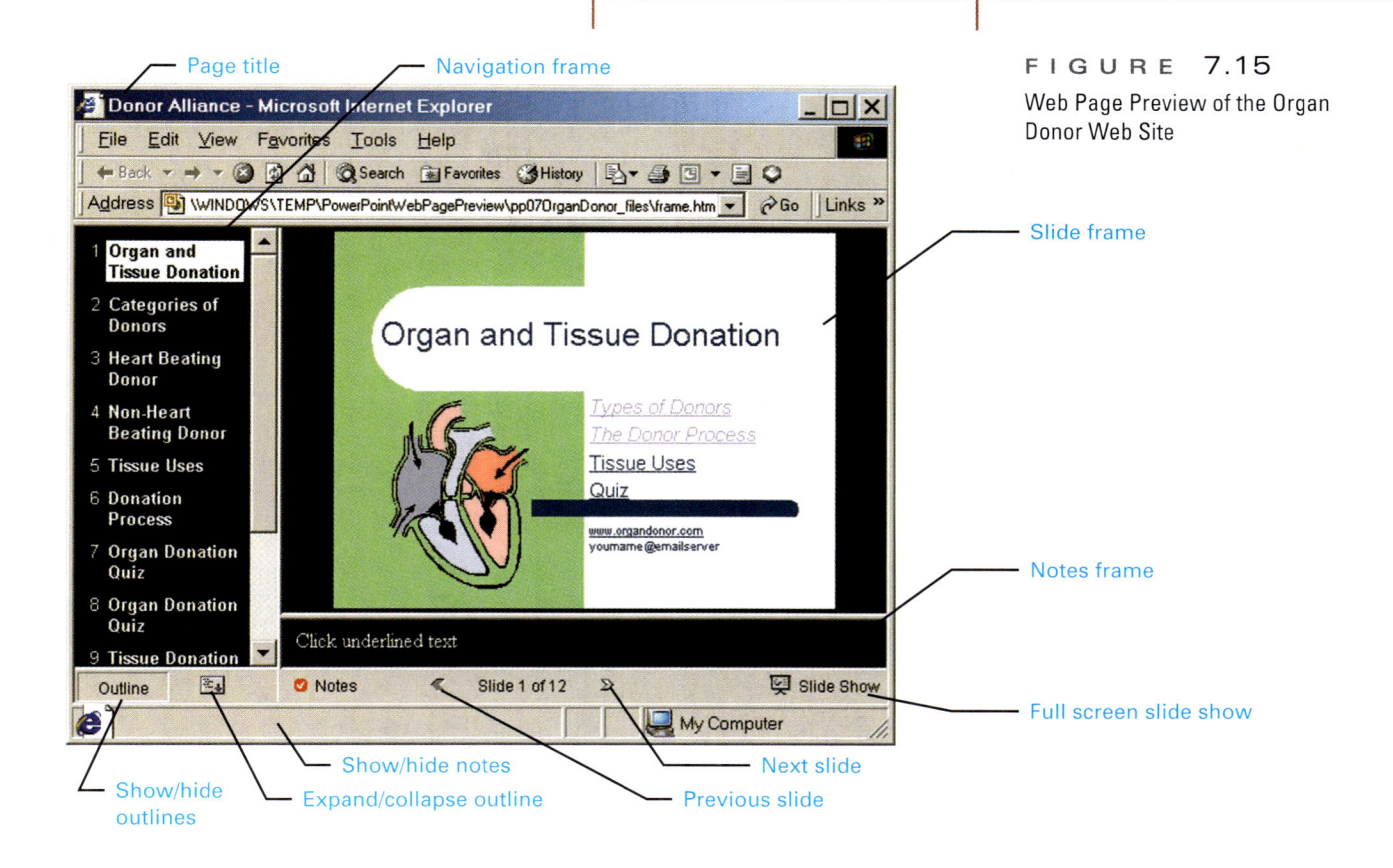

FIGURE 7.15
Web Page Preview of the Organ Donor Web Site

Labels on figure: Page title, Navigation frame, Slide frame, Notes frame, Full screen slide show, Next slide, Previous slide, Show/hide notes, Expand/collapse outline, Show/hide outlines

task reference

Save a Presentation in Web Format

- Open the presentation in PowerPoint
- From the **File** menu select **Save As Web Page**
- Use the Save As dialog box Publish button to customize the Save As settings
- Click **Publish** when the settings are complete

Creating the Organ Donor Web site:

1. Verify that PowerPoint is running with **<yourname>pp07OrganDonor.ppt** open
2. On the **File** menu click **Save As Web Page**
3. Click the **Publish** button to open the Publish as Web Page dialog box (see Figure 7.16)
    a. Click the **Web Options** button (see Figure 7.17)
        i. On the General tab, unclick Add slide navigation controls
        ii. On the General tab, click **Show slide animation while browsing**
        iii. On the Browser tab, select **Microsoft Internet Explorer 5.0 or later** as the target browser
        iv. Explore the other tabs and then click **OK**

> b. Click the **Change** button to the right of Page Title, type your first name in front of Donor Alliance, and click **OK**
> c. Check **Open published Web page in browser**
> d. Click **Publish**
>
> 4. Use the links to navigate through the presentation
> 5. Close the browser

By customizing the publication settings, the Web presentation was optimized for a specific browser. Optimizing for newer browsers results in smaller file sizes, but the pages will not view appropriately on older browsers. Optimize for the oldest browser in use by your intended audience.

FIGURE 7.16
Save as Web Page Dialog Box

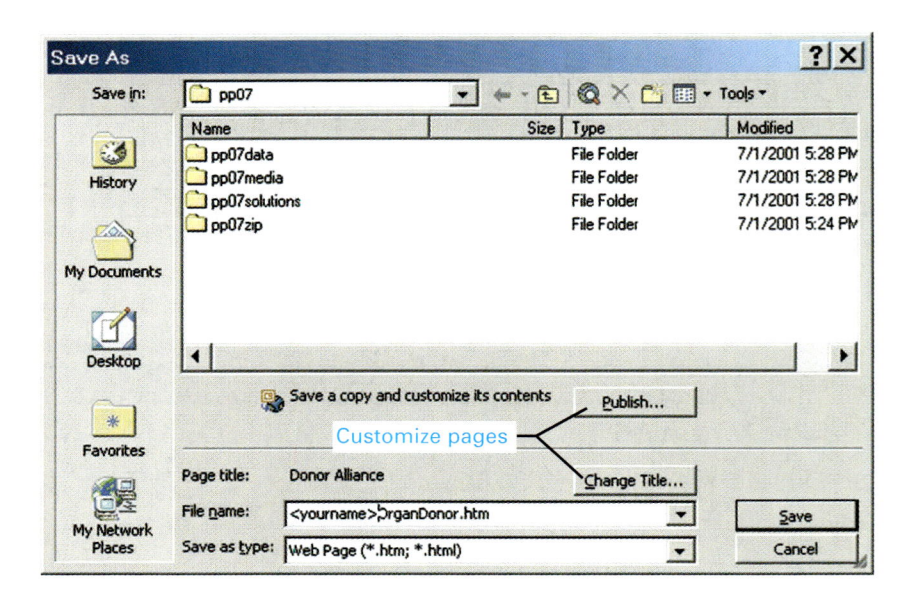

FIGURE 7.17
Web Options Dialog Box

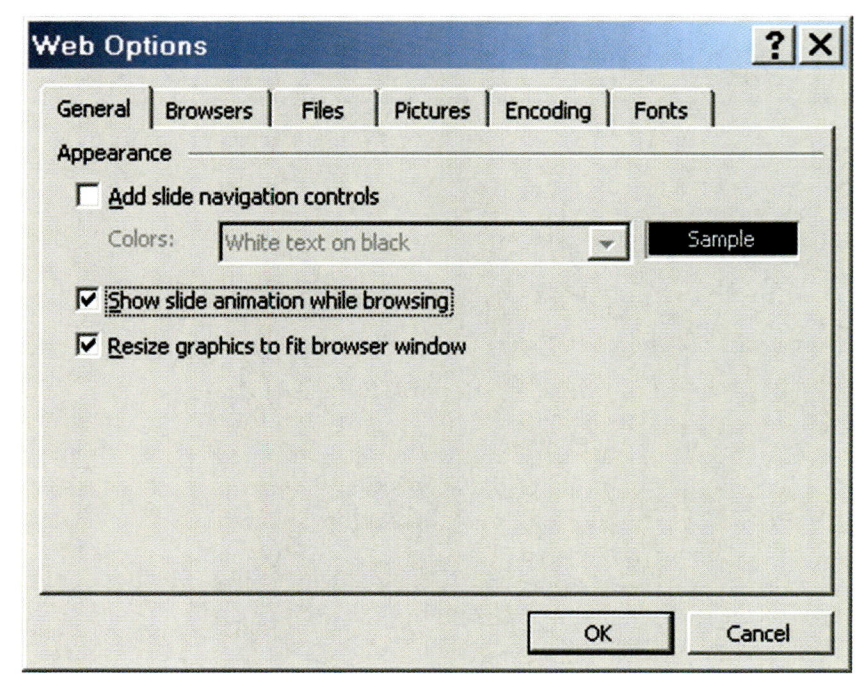

The customization process also allows adjustments to be made for the intended audience and presentation style. For instance, the default Save as Web Page options do not display slide animations or transitions. By clicking that option, the final product includes all animation that would play if the presentation were run in PowerPoint. The title of the presentation can also be customized. The title may seem insignificant, but this text displays in the title bar of the browser when the page is open. If a site is stored in a browser history or favorites list, the title text is what displays, so it is important for the title to be descriptive.

WEB ACCESS FROM POWERPOINT

Like all Microsoft Office Applications, PowerPoint supports Internet and intranet browsing without opening another application. If you have access and permissions on the local network to allow it, the Web toolbar has many of the same features as Internet Explorer.

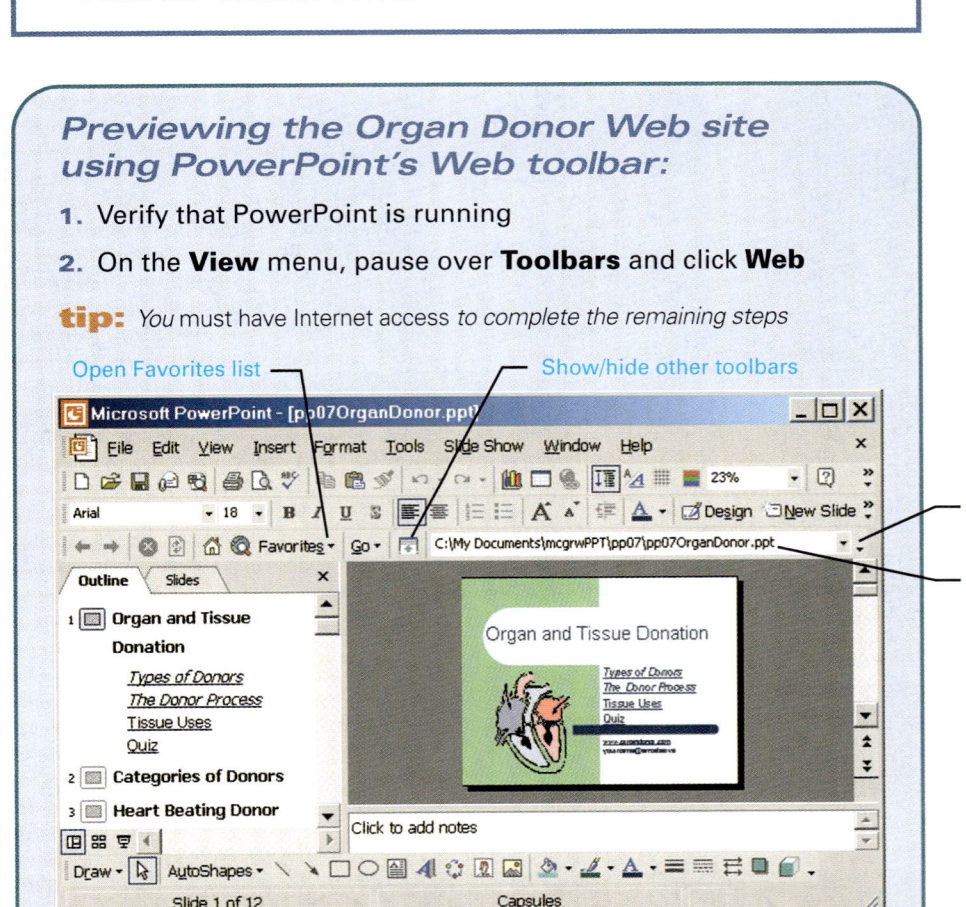

task reference
Showing the Web Toolbar
- Click the **View** menu
- Pause over **Toolbars** and click **Web**

another way
...to Show the Web Toolbar

Right-clicking any toolbar will open the list of available toolbars. Clicking Web in this list will show the Web toolbar. Repeating the process will hide the Web toolbar again.

Previewing the Organ Donor Web site using PowerPoint's Web toolbar:

1. Verify that PowerPoint is running
2. On the **View** menu, pause over **Toolbars** and click **Web**

tip: You must have Internet access to complete the remaining steps

FIGURE 7.18

Web Toolbar in PowerPoint

3. Click the **Show Only Web Toolbar** button on the Web toolbar

4. Drop down the address bar list by clicking the down arrow on its right and select an address to visit

tip: *The most recently viewed Web addresses should display*

5. Select the address currently in the address bar, type www.microsoft.com over the selection, and press **Enter** to visit the Microsoft Web site

6. Drop down the **Favorites** list and select one of the sites to visit

tip: *If you have not added addresses to your Favorites list, nothing will display*

7. Click the **Go** button

tip: *The Open Internet Address dialog box should open. Depending on where you clicked, you may need to click Open Hyperlink also*

   a. Use the Browse button to open a file from any available local or network drive
   b. Click **OK** to open the file

8. Use the **Back** and **Forward** buttons to move through the pages that have been browsed this session

9. Click the **Favorites** button, then click **Add to Favorites**, select a favorites category, and then click **Add** to add the open file to your favorites list for quick future access

10. Use the **Show Only Web Toolbar** button to display the Standard and Formatting toolbars

11. Use the **Toolbars** option of the **View** menu to remove the Web toolbar

Adding a presentation to the Favorites list is an easy way to find it again. The Favorites list is also a good place to store Web sites that need to be available for a presentation. It is important to have valid addresses to avoid broken links.

GETTING HELP ON THE WEB

The Ask a Question box and the Office Assistant are the most common tools used to look up helpful information about a task. Both of these tools are search engines that use the Help files installed with PowerPoint. The latest tools for PowerPoint and other Office applications can be found on the Microsoft Web site. Additionally there are tips, techniques, free stuff, product news, answers to frequently asked questions (faq), and online support for licensed Microsoft products.

task reference

Accessing Microsoft Online Support

- Click the **Help** menu
- Click **Office on the Web**

> **Accessing Office on the Web:**
>
> 1. Verify that PowerPoint is running
> 2. On the **Help** menu click **Office on the Web**
>
> **tip:** You must have Internet access to complete the remaining steps
>
> [screenshot of Microsoft Office Assistance Center web page]
>
> 3. Explore the available resources
> 4. Close the browser window

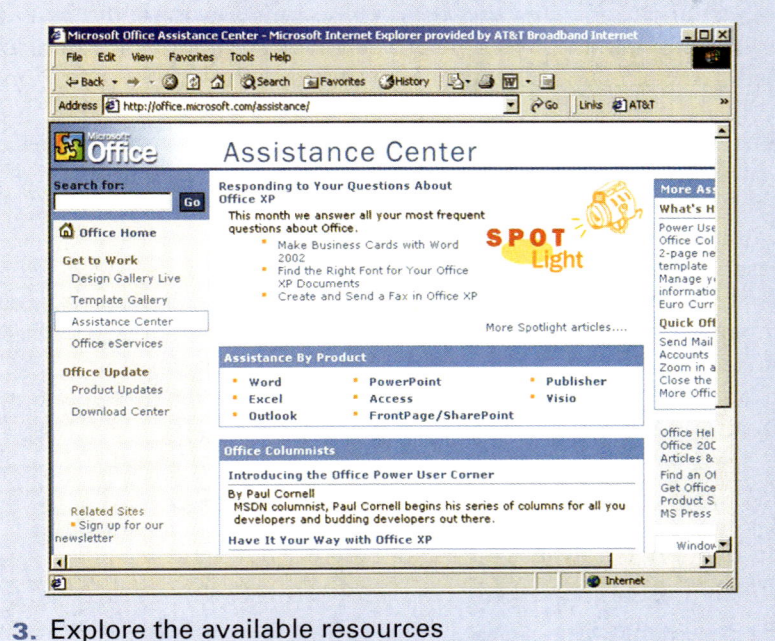

FIGURE 7.19
Microsoft Office on the Web

Microsoft is known for frequent updates to its site, so the pages you visit may look different from the figure and from any previous visits. Even though the look and organization change, extensive online support for all licensed copies of Microsoft products will be available. The support Web site is the best place to get up-to-date information about products as well as tips and techniques.

making the grade — SESSION 7.2

1. Why use PowerPoint to create Web pages?
2. How would you choose whether to publish your Web pages on the Internet or an intranet?
3. What browser is most effective for viewing PowerPoint Web publications?
4. How do you update Web pages published from PowerPoint?

SESSION 7.3 SUMMARY

Interactive presentations are typically hierarchical in structure. The opening page or home page outlines the viewing options as hyperlinks. Hyperlinks are clickable objects that allow the user to click and move to another slide in the current document, a slide in another presentation, a file, or any Web resource. Most commonly the hyperlinks on the opening page will move to a topic overview that presents linear navigation through the pages of topical material. The user should be able to return to the opening page from at least some of the other presentation pages.

Before a hyperlink can be set, the hyperlink object must be built. Hyperlink objects can be any clickable object like text, WordArt, charts, graphs, Action Buttons, and images. Hyperlinks are created by selecting the link object and then using the Insert Hyperlink button on the Standard toolbar to set the link attributes. The Insert Hyperlink button can also be used to edit an erroneous hyperlink or delete a link that is no longer needed.

Hyperlinks to Web addresses are called uniform resource locators and can be added to a presentation by typing the address. Hyperlink colors are controlled by the color scheme of the project. Links placed on the slide master will be active on all slides using that master.

A presentation created in PowerPoint can be saved in HTML format and published on an intranet or the Internet. HTML uses tags contained in <> to control the display of a page in the Web browsers. Once a presentation is in HTML format, it can be moved to a server so that it can be shared. The presentation must be placed on a Web server to make it available through the World Wide Web.

MOUS OBJECTIVES SUMMARY

- Add hyperlinks to slides—PPT2002-4-10
- Publish presentations to the Web (Save as HTML)—PPT2002-7-5
- Save a presentation as a Web page (Publish)—PPT2002-8-4
- Manage files and folders for Presentations—PPT2002-7-3

task reference roundup

Task	Page #	Recommended Method
Insert a Hyperlink	PP 7.6	• Select the object that will initiate the hyperlink. The object can be text, WordArt, a graphic, or any other clickable object
		• Click the **Insert Hyperlink** button in the Standard toolbar
		• Select the location of the link and then set the link options
Create and Link an Action Button	PP 7.12	• Select the slide to contain the Action Button
		• Click the **AutoShapes** button of the Drawing toolbar, pause over Action Buttons, and select the desired button
		tip: *Use the View menu to activate the Drawing toolbar if it is not already visible*
		• Click and drag the button on the slide surface
		• Click the Action Button and follow the steps to set a hyperlink
Build an AutoContent Web Page	PP 7.19	• In the PowerPoint Open Presentation Task pane, select **AutoContent Wizard**
		• Read the introductory screen and click **Next**

task reference roundup

Task	Page #	Preferred Method
		• Choose the type of presentation you would like to develop and click **Next**
		• Select **Web presentation** and click **Next**
		• Enter the title and footer information and click **Next**
		• Click **Finish**
Preview a Presentation as a Web Site	PP 7.22	• Open the presentation in PowerPoint
		• Select **Web Page Preview** from the **File** menu ***tip:*** *This will take some time to create the pages and then display the presentation in your default browser*
		• Close the browser window when you have completed your tasks
Save a Presentation in Web Format	PP 7.23	• Open the presentation in PowerPoint
		• From the **File** menu select **Save As Web Page**
		• Use the Save As dialog box Publish button to customize the Save As settings ***tip:*** *Be sure to check the box to open the presentation in the browser so that you can review your results*
		• Click Publish when the settings are complete
Showing the Web Toolbar	PP 7.25	• Click the **View** menu
		• Pause over **Toolbars** and click **Web** ***tip:*** *The same steps will close the Web toolbar when it is no longer needed*
Accessing Microsoft Online Support	PP 7.26	• Click the **Help** menu
		• Click **Office on the Web**

POWERPOINT

NOTES

chapter seven

review of terminology

CROSSWORD PUZZLE

Across

1. Software that displays Web pages
4. A computer that provides internet services
9. Used to link to a specific page of another document
10. Allows the user to jump to another location
11. A hyperlink that doesn't work is said to be _____
12. Documents created to display from the World Wide Web
14. <b> and <i> are examples
15. A link that contains a partial address

Down

2. A worldwide network of documents
3. Multiple Web windows are called _____
5. A link that contains a complete address
6. The opening page of a Web site is called _____
7. The address of a Web resource
8. An organization that provides Internet services
13. The language used to specify Web pages

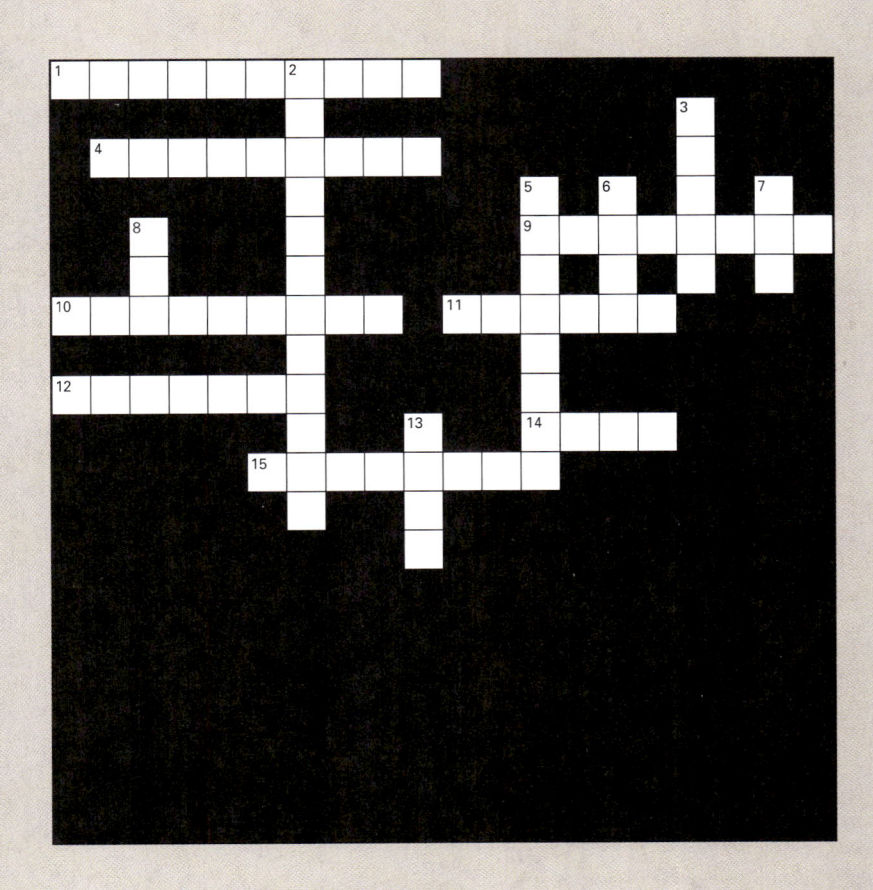

LEVEL ONE

PP 7.31

POWERPOINT

review of concepts

chapter seven

LEVEL TWO

FILL-IN

1. The most widely used scripting language to create Web pages is _____.
2. A hyperlink with a _____ is used to open to a specific location in the hyperlinked document.
3. Typing a _____ on a PowerPoint slide will automatically create a hyperlink.
4. _____ and _____ are used to add nonlinear navigation to a presentation.
5. Hyperlinks placed on the _____ are available to all slides.

REVIEW QUESTIONS

Each of the following topics should be addressed in one to three paragraphs.

1. Discuss the various native navigation options available in PowerPoint.
2. Discuss how custom navigation is added to a PowerPoint presentation.
3. How do you determine what custom navigation to add to a presentation?
4. What information must be provided for a functioning hyperlink?
5. How do you determine what HTML format to use when creating Web pages from a PowerPoint presentation?

CREATE THE QUESTION

For each of the following answers, create the question.

ANSWER	QUESTION
1. Any clickable object.	_____
2. URL.	_____
3. Esc.	_____
4. Place the link on the Slide Master.	_____
5. A link that includes all information needed to find a resource.	_____

FACT OR FICTION

For each of the following determine whether the statement is fact, fiction, or both and present your arguments for that conclusion.

1. The latest PowerPoint tips and techniques can be found in the Help files that ship with PowerPoint.
2. Only the Standard and Formatting toolbars can be open simultaneously.
3. When a PowerPoint presentation is saved as Web pages, only the default Navigation bar can be used to move through the slides.
4. Web pages can be viewed using PowerPoint's Web toolbar.
5. Presentations saved in a Web format must be placed on a Web server to be viewed from the World Wide Web.

chapter seven

hands-on projects

practice

LEVEL THREE

Wildlife Management Associates

Wildlife Management Associates (WMA) contracts with the U.S. Fish and Wildlife Department to perform population counts and assess the health of wildlife. WMA has put together a presentation that illustrates their study areas and the results of their assessments. WMA has decided the best approach is an interactive presentation with the following menu items: Home, Assessments, About Us, Fish Program, and Contact Us. WMA has provided you with a map of the presentation and a Word document to help you understand its layout and text. For now you will develop the Aquatic Division's assessment of Colorado Brook Trout population. Although the other divisions only have data pending, you will still create the pages. At a later date, the data can be added.

1. Start PowerPoint and open pp07WildlifeMgmt.ppt
2. Save the presentation as **<yourname>pp07WildlifeMgmt.ppt**
3. Open the Slide Master
   a. Create a text box containing the word *Home* in 20 point Tahoma bold
   b. Use the Fill option of the Format Text Box dialog box to set a two-color (dark blue and white) horizontal gradient fill for the text box
   c. Set a hyperlink to slide 1 for the text box (not the text)
   d. Close Master view

FIGURE 7.20
Wildlife Management Site Map

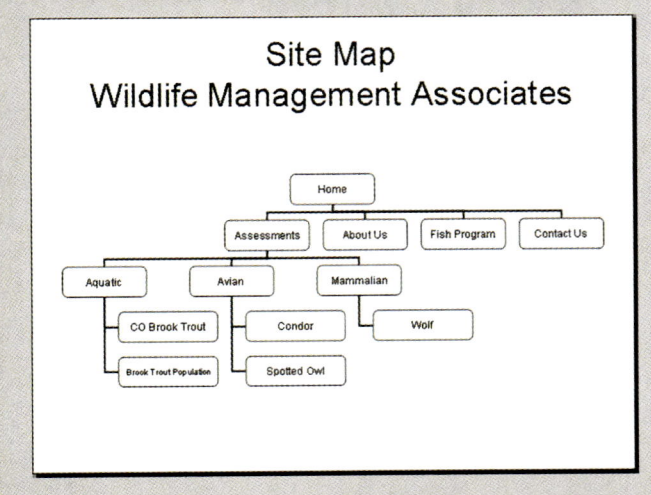

4. Use techniques outlined in step 3 to create Assessments, About Us, Fish Program, and Contact Us buttons. Arrange the buttons as shown in Figure 7.21
   a. Hyperlink the Assessments text box to slide 2
   b. Hyperlink the About Us text box to slide 9
   c. Hyperlink the Fish Program text box to slide 7
   d. Hyperlink the Contact Us text box to slide 8
5. Align and distribute the buttons
6. Move to slide 2
   a. Hyperlink the text Aquatic Division to slide 3
   b. Hyperlink Avian Division to slide 5
   c. Hyperlink Mammalian Division to slide 6
   d. Copy the relevant navigation buttons from slide 1
7. Move to slide 3, copy the navigation buttons from slide 1, and create a Next button linked to slide 4
8. Move to slide 4, copy the navigation buttons from slide 1, and add a Back button linked to slide 3
9. Add the navigation buttons to the remaining slides
10. Test the presentation, make any needed adjustments, and save

FIGURE 7.21
Wildlife Management Navigation Buttons

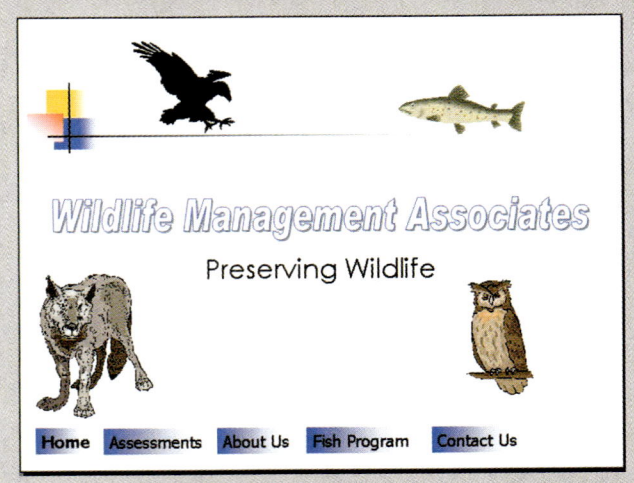

PP 7.33

www.mhhe.com/i-series

POWERPOINT

hands-on projects

chapter seven

challenge

Safe Foods

Safe Foods is an informational Web site designed to educate the consumer about food preparation and handling. It provides links to other Web sites about eating foods safely. In addition, at the Safe Foods site you can document a possible food poisoning episode through a hyperlink to a Word document. The viewer can print the online form, fill in the information, and mail or fax it back to Safe Foods. You have been asked to prepare this Web site.

1. Start PowerPoint and open **pp07SafeFoods.ppt**
2. Save the presentation as **<yourname>pp07SafeFoods.ppt**
3. Refer to Figure 7.22 for the overall site organization and navigation
4. On slide 1 create three navigation buttons
   a. Hyperlink the Safe Handling button to slide 2
   b. Hyperlink the Register Poisoning button to slide 10
   c. Hyperlink the Other Site References button to slide 9
5. On slide 2
   a. Hyperlink the Restaurants text to slide 5
   b. Hyperlink the In the kitchen text to slide 4
   c. Hyperlink the Traveling text to slide 3
   d. Hyperlink the Preparing food text to slide 6
6. Add a Home button to slides 2 through 10
7. Add the Next buttons to the slides in the Safe Handling Tips sequence (refer to Figure 7.22)
8. Use your favorite search engine to locate Web sites to be included on slide 9. Add the URLs to the slide
9. Test the presentation, make any needed adjustments, and save
10. Save the presentation as a Web page
    a. Suppress PowerPoint navigational controls using the Web Options button from the Publish dialog box
    b. Set the title to **Safe Food Handling and Preparation**
    c. Test the result using Microsoft Internet Explorer

FIGURE 7.22
Safe Foods Site Map

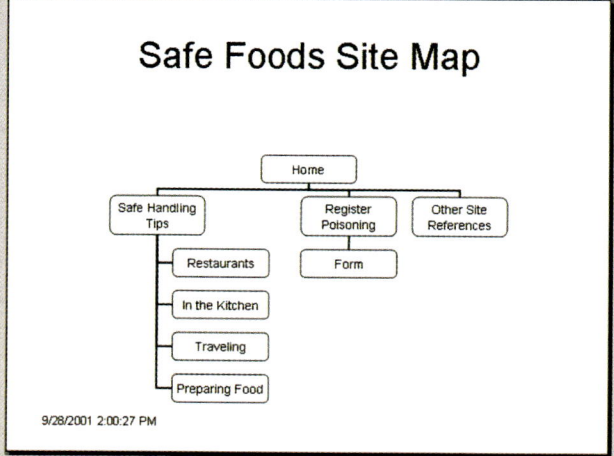

FIGURE 7.23
Safe Foods Opening Page

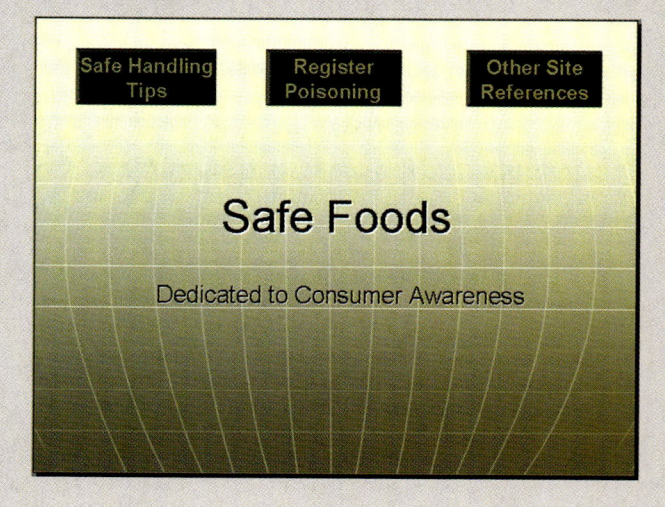

PP 7.34

chapter seven

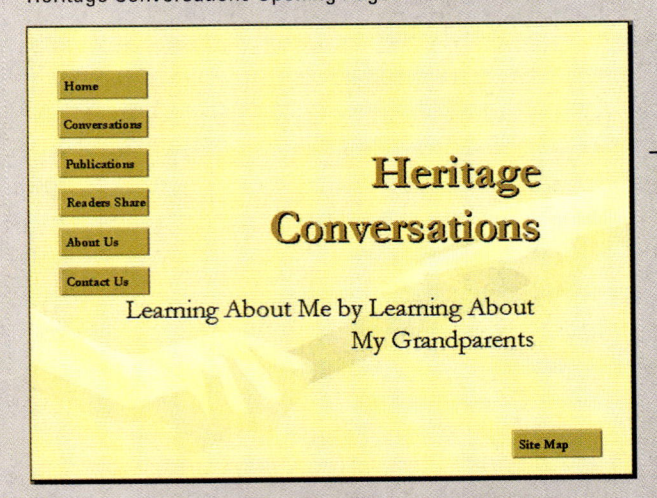

hands-on projects

on the web

LEVEL THREE

Heritage Conversations

What if you had a tool to help you understand and learn about your grandparents? And in doing so you learned a lot about yourself. That's the premise for Heritage Conversations. This company publishes a book with questions, worksheets, and helpful suggestions to make the interviewing process with your grandparent successful. Heritage Conversations' Web site lets others know about its product. You have been asked to build this Web site using PowerPoint.

1. Start PowerPoint and open **pp07Heritage.ppt**
2. Save the presentation as **<yourname>pp07Heritage.ppt**
3. Review the site map on slide 2 to understand the navigational structure you will build
4. Add slide 9 with a Blank layout. This slide will be used as a work space to create buttons and then deleted
    a. Use the Custom Button from the Action Buttons selection of the AutoShapes menu on the Drawing toolbar to create nine buttons
    b. Click on each button and type one of the following labels: Home, Next, Back, Conversations, Publications, Readers Share, About Us, Contact Us, and Site Map
    c. Place the Next button on the lower right-hand corner of the Conversations slide and hyperlink it to the next slide
    d. Place the Back button on the lower right-hand corner of the Sample Questions slide and hyperlink it to the previous slide
    e. Place the Site map button on the lower right-hand corner of the Home slide and hyperlink it to the second slide
    f. Place the six remaining buttons down the left-hand side of both the Title Master and Slide Master. Use distribution and alignment options to adjust their position. Hyperlink each appropriately
    g. Delete slide 9
5. Visit each slide and adjust content as necessary for readability and alignment
6. On slide 3 adjust the e-mail screen tip to read **Email Heritage Conversations** and the Web site screen tip to read **Visit Heritage Conversations home page**
7. Use your favorite search engine to locate at least two Web sites appropriate for slide 5. Add the URLs to the slide
8. Test the presentation, make any needed adjustments, and save
9. Save the presentation as a Web page
    a. Suppress PowerPoint navigational controls using the Web Options button from the Publish dialog box
    b. Set the title to **Heritage Grandparent Conversations**
    c. Test the result using Microsoft Internet Explorer

FIGURE 7.24
Heritage Conversations Opening Page

www.mhhe.com/i-series

PP 7.35

POWERPOINT

hands-on projects

e-business

Chuska Photos

For years Harold Chuska has traveled around the world capturing photographs of nature, people, and places. His photographs have consistently won top prizes in photography contests. Now Chuska has decided to set up an interactive kiosk that will provide a taste of his photography. Chuska wishes to start locally, and then expand later to the Web. With luck, he will be able to sell his photographs and finance additional trips around the world. You have been asked to prepare the kiosk presentation that will appear in malls in Chuska's home city.

1. Start PowerPoint and open **pp07Photos.ppt**
2. Save the presentation as
   <yourname>pp07Photos.ppt
3. Create four Custom Action Buttons on the first slide. Select each button and type to add a label. Label the buttons Nature, People, Contact Me, and Places. Make the button text Comic Sans MS, 28 point, bold
   a. Hyperlink the Nature button to slide 4
   b. Hyperlink the People button to slide 3
   c. Hyperlink the Contact Me button to slide 2
   d. Hyperlink the Places button to slide 5
4. On slide 4 arrange three to five thumbnail (reduced-size) nature photographs that you have located
   a. Place full-size versions of each of these photographs on separate slides
   b. Hyperlink from each thumbnail photograph on slide 4 to the slide containing the full-size photograph
   c. On each slide with a full-size photograph, place a Back button that returns to slide 4
5. On slide 3 arrange three to five thumbnail (reduced-size) photographs of people that you have located. Use the techniques from step 4 to create links from the thumbnail photographs to their full-size versions and back
6. On slide 5 arrange three to five thumbnail (reduced-size) Places photographs that you have located. Use the techniques from step 4 to create links from the thumbnail photographs to their full-size versions and back
7. Create and add a Home button to every slide but slide 1. Hyperlink this button to return to slide 1
8. Test your presentation, make any needed adjustments, and save
9. Save the presentation for Web delivery
   a. Suppress PowerPoint navigational controls using the Web Options button from the Publish dialog box
   b. Set the title to **Chuska Photos**
   c. Test the result using Microsoft Internet Explorer

FIGURE 7.25

Chuska Photos Opening Page

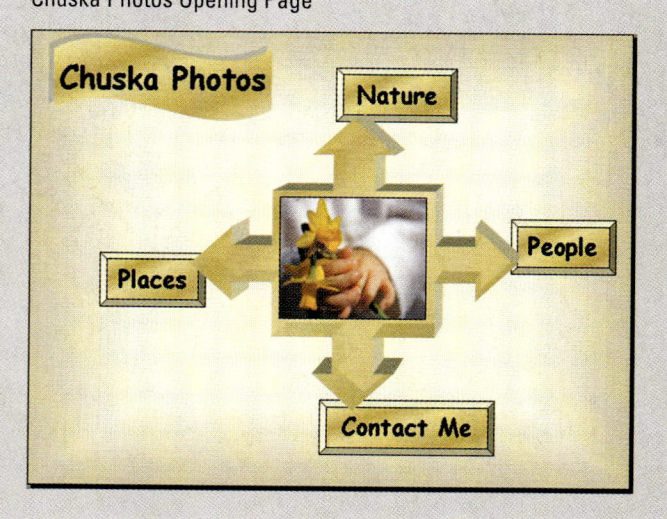

chapter seven — hands-on projects

around the world

LEVEL THREE

Sonic Strategies

Sonic Strategies manufactures and sells the Sonic 5 throughout the world. The Sonic 5 device identifies anything in the atmosphere of import: comets, meteors, catastrophic weather, or explosions are some examples. The device produces an infrasound wave of low frequency into the atmosphere. When it encounters compressed air, it returns a frequency wave. Each atmospheric event has its own characteristic wave shape. The wave data are recorded, entered into a database, and returned to Sonic Strategies' database headquarters for analysis. The resulting assessment is distributed to governmental agencies such as NASA, NCAR, and the Department of Defense. Monitoring of the Sonic 5 outside the United States occurs through Sonic Strategies' International Division. International teams are located on all seven continents. Sonic Strategies wants the international teams to preview the Sonic 9 that will replace the Sonic 5 next year. You have been asked to prepare a PowerPoint presentation for the teams.

1. Start PowerPoint and open **pp07Sonic Strategies.ppt**
2. Save the presentation as **<yourname>pp07SonicStrategies.ppt** in a folder named **SonicStrategies**
3. Use the **Oval** tool of the Drawing toolbar to create four buttons on the home page
   a. Apply **Shadow Style 4** from the Shadow Style menu of the Drawing toolbar to each
   b. Type one of the following labels on each button. Bold the text and use Enter to cause each word to be on a new line
      - Int'l Division
      - U.S. Division
      - Specs
      - Training
4. Hyperlink each of the buttons as follows
   a. Int'l Division to slide 3
   b. U.S. Division to slide 2
   c. Specs to slide 4
   d. Training to slide 5
5. Create and place a Home button on all slides except the title slide. Hyperlink this button to return to the first slide
6. Test your presentation, make any needed adjustments, and save
7. Save the presentation for Web delivery
   a. Suppress PowerPoint navigational controls using the Web Options button from the Publish dialog box
   b. Set the title to **Announcing the Sonic 9**
   c. Test the result using Microsoft Internet Explorer

FIGURE 7.26

Sonic Strategies Opening Page

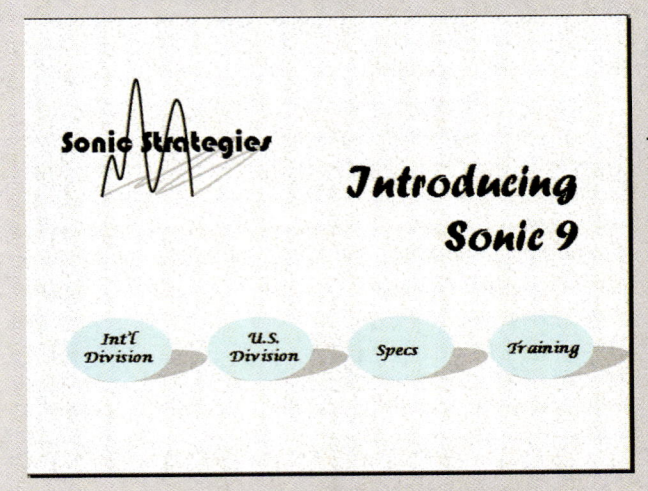

PP 7.37

POWERPOINT

www.mhhe.com/i-series

running project

Montgomery-Wellish Foods, Inc.: Understanding Critical Time Lines

Well designed and implemented training materials are critical to the success of MWF employees. Time lines are a particularly difficult concept for trainees. Daniel Wellish has developed the skeleton for a PowerPoint slide show to present time lines and quiz trainees in the following areas: Order Confirmation, Warehouse Stocking and Transport, and Foreign Shipments. You have been asked to complete this PowerPoint presentation.

1. Start PowerPoint and open **pp07TrainingQuiz2.ppt**
2. Save the presentation as **<yourname>pp07TrainingQuiz2.ppt**
3. Use the Rectangle tool to create seven buttons to navigate this presentation
   a. Type each of the following headings in one of the buttons
      - Home
      - Order
      - Order Quiz
      - Warehouse
      - Warehouse Quiz
      - Foreign
      - Foreign Quiz
   b. Arrange the buttons as shown in Figure 7.27
   c. Hyperlink as follows
      - Home to slide 1
      - Order to slide 2
      - Order Quiz to slide 3
      - Warehouse to slide 11
      - Warehouse Quiz to slide 12
      - Foreign to slide 7
      - Foreign Quiz to slide 8
   d. Group the buttons and use copy and paste to place them in the Slide Master. Verify that they display correctly on all of the slides
4. Develop **Try Again** and **Next Question** buttons to be used in the quiz portion of the presentation
5. On slide 3 hyperlink as follows:
   a. Hyperlink the 2 hours text to slide 4
   b. Hyperlink the 4 hours text to slide 5
   c. Hyperlink both the 8 hours and 12 hours text to slide 6
6. Add Try Again buttons to bottom right-hand side of slides 4 and 6 that return the trainee to slide 3 for another try
7. Add a Next Question button to the bottom of slide 12 that hyperlinks to slide 13
8. The rest of the hyperlinks have already been constructed. Test your presentation, make any needed adjustments, and save
9. Save the presentation for Web delivery
   a. Suppress PowerPoint navigational controls using the Web Options button from the Publish dialog box
   b. Set the title to **Time Lines Quiz**
   c. Test the result using Microsoft Internet Explorer

FIGURE 7.27

Training Quiz Opening Page

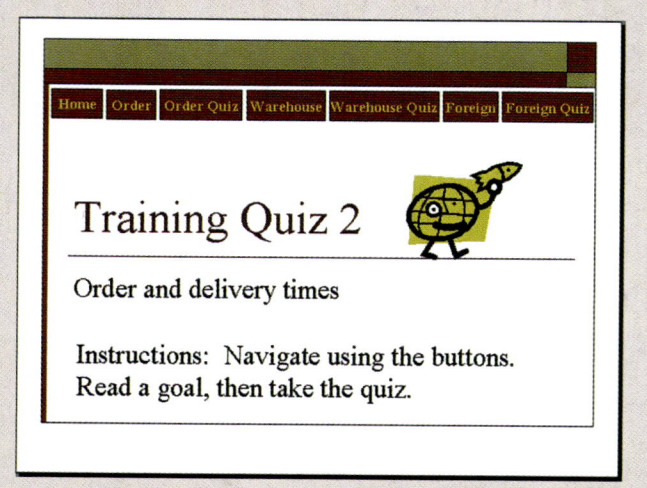

NOTES

www.mhhe.com/i-series

POWERPOINT

NOTES

www.mhhe.com/i-series

did you know?

the first true calculator, the abacus, originated in China during the sixth century B.C.

the last thing to happen is the ultimate. The next-to-last is the penultimate, and the second-to-last is the antepenultimate.

the plastic things on the end of shoelaces are called aglets.

the "O" when used as a prefix in Irish surnames means descendant of.

every human spent about half an hour as a single cell.

the blood of mammals is red, the blood of insects is yellow, and the blood of lobsters is blue.

of the Atlantic and Pacific oceans, which is saltier?

Chapter Objectives

- Set up presentations for delivery—PPT2002-7-1
- Deliver presentations—PPT2002-7-2
- Work with embedded fonts—PPT2002-7-4
- Use Pack and Go—PPT2002-7-6
- Use Workgroup Collaboration—PPT2002-8

CHAPTER

8

eight

PowerPoint Power Features

chapter case

Collaborating and Sharing the PhonePerformance Presentation

Parks Industries is a large privately held company that produces consumer plastics. The publicly marketed products include everything from plastic dinnerware to skateboard wheels. One of the company's divisions also produces custom molded plastic parts used in manufacturing.

The various manufacturing facilities used to produce different types of plastic products are scattered throughout the Midwest. In the past, each site has had a manager who coordinated all local operations including computing and telephone services. As the company has grown and competition on the plastics arena has become intense, the need to share resources and reduce overhead has become critical to the success of Parks.

Walter Pauls is the son of the founder and current CEO. Each of the remote production facilities is managed by a division president who is also a family member. As one of the initiatives to consolidate efforts and reduce costs, Parks executive officers decided to standardize computing services and implement a central phone system that would meet all of their needs while reducing overhead.

FIGURE 8.1
PowerPoint Web Communication

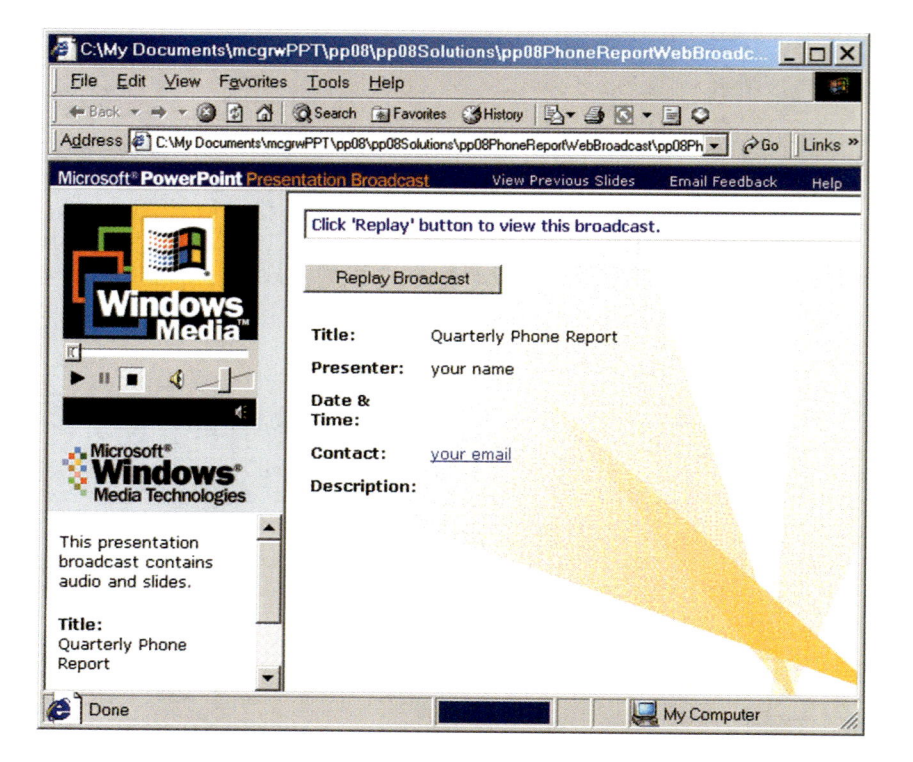

Computer Services elected to use Microsoft products across the board. Each site has a Microsoft NT network with all of the features needed to support the workgroup capabilities of Microsoft Office products. The various sites are also connected so that Microsoft Outlook can be used to coordinate planning, set appointments, share client contact files, and send e-mail.

Catherine Witt has been charged with coordinating the phone efforts among the various locations and reporting back to the executive officers in their monthly meeting. She has created a PowerPoint presentation to use in reporting and has asked you to help implement all of the necessary features. She will need PowerPoint collaboration features to retrieve comments from the phone system managers at the remote sites and incorporate them into the presentation for the executives. To accomplish this reporting task, it is essential to understand how PowerPoint can be used to share documents, collaborate effectively, take a presentation on the road, and add custom functionality.

CHAPTER OUTLINE

8.1 PowerPoint Power User Features

8.2 Sharing Presentations

SESSION 8.1 POWERPOINT POWER USER FEATURES

Many presentations are developed on one computer and presented on another. PowerPoint's viewer will allow slide shows to display on a computer that does not have PowerPoint, while the Pack and Go Wizard prepares the presentation for travel.

TAKING YOUR SHOW ON THE ROAD

There are many things to consider when moving a PowerPoint presentation from the development computer to another environment. For a successful presentation, it is critical that all files required to run the slide show have been moved to the new computer and a backup plan has been prepared. Catherine has developed the presentation on her desktop computer and will need to run it on a laptop for the presentation to the Parks executives.

Backup Planning

Backup plans are often forgotten when preparing to present but are essential to a successful show. In most instances everything will run smoothly, but spending a little time planning for difficulties can ensure a smooth show even when things go wrong.

Any component that is critical for the show should be considered when backup planning. It is always a good idea to have a second copy of the presentation files on a separate media. A second computer capable of running the slide show and extra projector bulbs are a must. Copies of the files can be placed on the backup computer if the original presentation fails. Having a spare projector bulb, and knowing how to replace the bulb, allows the completion of repairs that would otherwise have to wait for a technician.

For critical projected presentations, consider having additional projector units available. Sometimes scheduling a backup speaker is also a good idea. The importance of the presentation determines how much effort should be spent ensuring success.

Whenever possible arrive at the presentation site early enough to test all of the equipment, preview the presentation colors, and ensure proper visibility for all attendees. In most instances, improperly functioning equipment will be discovered and can be repaired before the presentation should start.

Introducing the PowerPoint Viewer

When preparing to take a presentation on the road, you must decide whether or not to use the Microsoft **PowerPoint viewer.** The viewer is a software program that will run PowerPoint presentations on computers that do not have PowerPoint installed. If the viewer is installed on your computer, it can be added to the presentation in the packaging process. When you unpackage the presentation, the viewer is also loaded.

The viewer is stored in the file Ppview32.exe, is distributed at no cost, and will operate files created in either PowerPoint for Windows or PowerPoint for the Macintosh. As a backup, the viewer can also be downloaded at no cost from the Microsoft Office Web site. The viewer allows the creation of *playlists* so that multiple presentations can be run automatically. A few of the PowerPoint 2002 features, like picture bullets and new animation effects, are not supported by the viewer.

Using the Pack and Go Wizard

When taking a presentation on the road, the most effective way to ensure that it will run properly on another computer is to use the **Pack and Go Wizard.** The Pack and Go Wizard packages all of the required files into one file that can be placed on a disk or network. In the packaging process, there are options to include any linked files and embed TrueType fonts. Embedding the fonts ensures that the fonts used by your presentation are available when running on a different computer.

The packed files must be unpacked to load all of the files onto the destination computer that will host the presentation. A presentation must be repackaged using the Pack and Go Wizard each time it is updated.

---

task reference

Package a Presentation

- Open the presentation to be packaged
- If you are saving the presentation to a storage media, insert it
- Click the **File** menu and then **Pack and Go**
- Make appropriate selections on each Wizard screen
    - Clicking **Other Presentations** will allow you to package multiple presentations
    - Use the **Viewer for Microsoft Windows** option to include the Microsoft PowerPoint Viewer in the package. If this option is not available, the viewer is not installed

Packaging PP08PhoneReport:

1. Start PowerPoint and open **PP08PhoneReport.ppt**
2. Click the **File** menu and then **Pack and Go**

FIGURE 8.2
Pack and Go Wizard Opening Page

3. Click **Next**
4. Verify that **Active Presentation** is checked and click **Next**
5. Click **Choose Destination,** use the **Browse** button to navigate to the storage location for your files, and click **Select**
6. Click **Next**
7. Click **Include Linked Files** and **Embed TrueType fonts** and then click **Next**
8. If you do not have the viewer installed and have access to the Internet, click the Download button and follow the instructions to install

tip: *The browser will open the Office Web site, and you will need to use the search facility to locate the download. There is no viewer for PowerPoint 2002*

9. Click **Viewer for Microsoft Windows** and click **Next**
10. Click **Finish**
11. Close PowerPoint

In order to view a packaged presentation, it must be unpackaged. Unpackaging returns the presentation file to PowerPoint format, installs necessary fonts, and places linked files in the destination folder.

FIGURE 8.3
Including the Microsoft PowerPoint Viewer

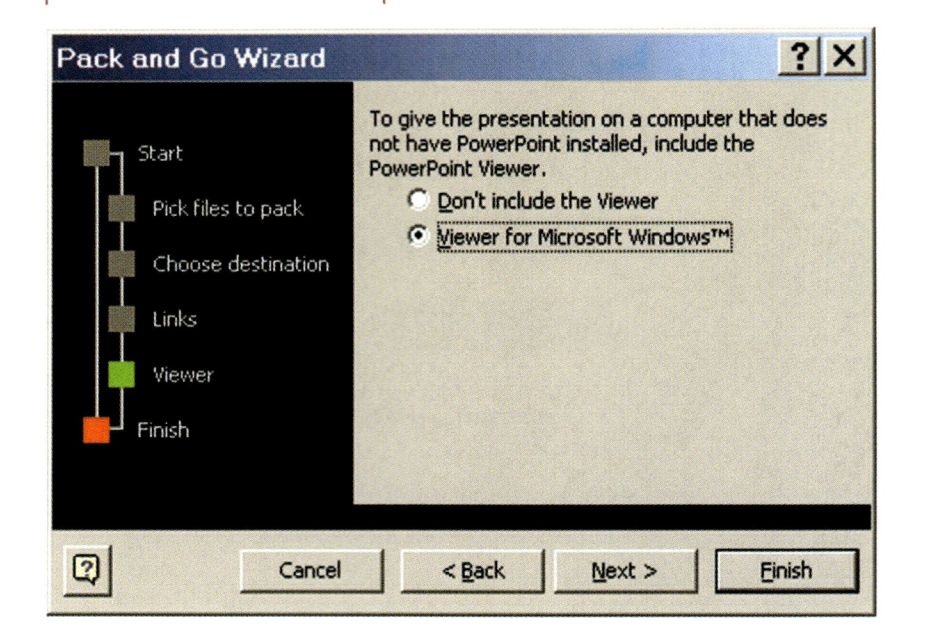

task reference
Unpackage a Presentation

- Insert the disk containing the presentation or connect to the shared device
- Use Windows Explorer to locate the packaged presentation folder and double-click **pngsetup.exe**
- In the Pack and Go Setup dialog box
  - Browse to the new location for the presentation
  - Click **OK**
- To run the presentation now click **Yes,** or to run the presentation later click **No**

Reviewing PP08PhoneReport:

1. Verify that PowerPoint is closed
2. Use Windows Explorer to locate the packaged presentation folder
   a. Create a folder for the unpackaged presentation named **Unpkpp08PhoneReport**
   b. Double-click **pngsetup.exe** to start unpacking

tip: *If you do not remember where you placed the packaged presentation, the Search or Find command of the Windows Start menu can be used to locate pngsetup.exe*

3. Select **Unpkpp08PhoneReport** as the destination folder for your unpackaged presentation and click **OK**
4. Select **Yes** to run the presentation now

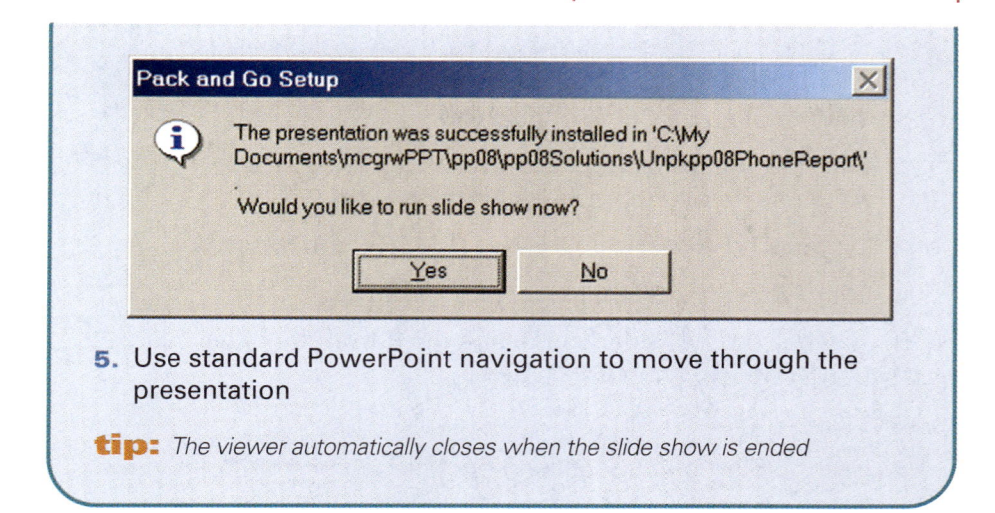

FIGURE 8.4
Run the Unpacked Presentation

5. Use standard PowerPoint navigation to move through the presentation

tip: *The viewer automatically closes when the slide show is ended*

The Start menu can be used to initiate the viewer after it has been unpackaged. Right-clicking on a PowerPoint file in Windows Explorer will display both Show and Open options in the pop-up menu. Selecting Show will run the presentation in the viewer while Open will open the file in PowerPoint.

CREATING AND MANAGING PLAYLISTS

A powerful feature of the Viewer for Microsoft Window is the ability to run multiple presentations in sequence. The order of the presentations is controlled by a playlist created in a text editor such as Notepad. The playlist contains the name and location of each file that will play. The effect is a series of kiosks that play without intervention.

task reference
Create and Use a Playlist

- Open Microsoft Notepad
- Type the name of each file
  - For files in the same folder as the playlist, simply type the filename with extension
  - For files in a different folder than the playlist, type the entire path including the drive, folder, filename, and extension
  - Filenames containing spaces must be enclosed in double quotes ("")
- Click **File,** then **Save**, provide a filename with a **.lst** file extension, and click **Save**
- Use the Start menu to run the PowerPoint viewer
  - Click **Using Timings, if present** to automatically run the slide shows
  - In the Files of type box, click **Playlists,** click the playlist file, and then click **Show**
  - Click **Esc** to end the show

Creating a playlist:

1. Verify that PowerPoint is closed
2. Click the **Start** menu, pause over **Programs**, select **Accessories,** and then click **Notepad**
3. Type **pp08PhoneReportb.ppt pp08OrganDonor.ppt**
4. Click **File** and then **Save**
5. Navigate to the folder containing the PowerPoint files, name the list **pp08.lst,** and click **Save**
6. Close Notepad
7. Use the Start menu to initiate the Microsoft PowerPoint viewer
8. Set the Files of type to **Playlist(*.lst),** select **pp08.lst** as the playlist file
9. Click the **Options** button, click **Override saved settings,** and then click **Loop continuously until 'Esc'**
10. Click **OK** and then **Show**

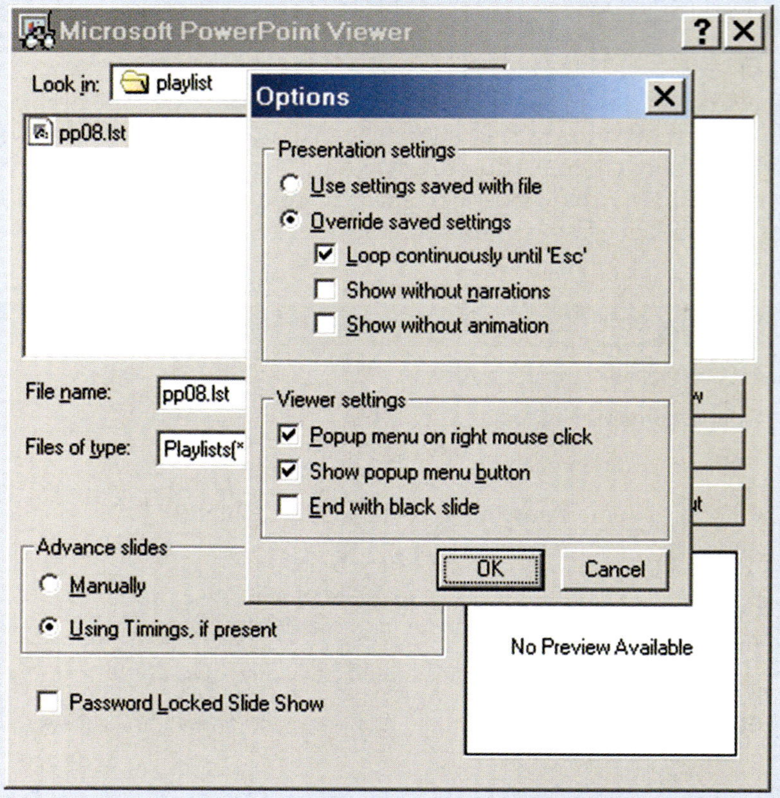

11. Watch the shows loop using their automatic timings and then press **Esc** to end the show
12. Close Microsoft PowerPoint viewer

FIGURE 8.5
Setting Up a Playlist

The slide shows included in this playlist both contained automatic timings that allowed the list to play without user intervention. If the slide shows have no automatic timings, the audience will have to click through the shows, which will still run sequentially. Commands can be included in the playlist file to control how the multifile show will play.

AUTOMATING TASKS WITH MACROS

A *macro* can be created in any Microsoft Office product to store common tasks. Macros are recorded commands that are stored in a Microsoft Visual Basic module attached to the presentation. Macros should be created for frequently repeated operations to save time and reduce errors. Special security features are included in Office 2002 to safeguard against macro viruses that can be spread when sharing macros.

Macros are recorded using a process that is similar to creating an audio recording. Once recording starts, all keyboard and mouse operations performed on the computer are stored. When recording stops, the recorded operations are given a name so they can be replayed. If you make a mistake while recording a macro, it is usually easiest to rerecord the steps from the beginning. The Visual Basic code of a macro can be directly edited, if you are familiar with the language.

Catherine has reviewed the PhonePerformance presentation and would like the letter grades assigned to each task to stand out more. She would like to see a larger text size and yellow text color. You will build a macro to simplify applying the same formats multiple times.

---

task reference
Record and Play a Macro

- On the **Tools** menu, point to **Macro,** then click **Security,** and select appropriate Security Level settings and add Trusted Sources
- On the **Tools** menu, point to **Macro,** then click **Record New Macro**
  - Select the storage location for the macro, enter the macro name in the Macro name box, and click **OK** to begin recording
  - Perform the actions to be recorded
- Click **Stop Recording** on the Stop Recording toolbar

Recording and using a macro to format text:

1. Start PowerPoint and open **pp08PhoneReport.ppt**
2. Move to slide **4** and select the **F** rating of the Appointment notification system
3. On the **Tools** menu, point to **Macro,** then click **Security**, read about the security setting, and click the **Medium** setting
4. On the **Tools** menu, point to **Macro,** then click **Record New Macro**
   a. Name the macro **GradesFormat**
   b. In the Description box, replace default with your name
   c. Click **OK**

5. Use the Font Size drop-down of the Formatting toolbar to increase the font size to **28** points and the **More Colors** option of the Font Color drop-down to set the text color to yellow
6. Click the **Stop Recording** ■ button in the Stop Recording toolbar
7. Select the **D** score for Call Management, click **Tools**, pause over **Macro**, and click **Macros**
8. In the Macro dialog box, verify that **GradesFormat** is selected and click **Run**

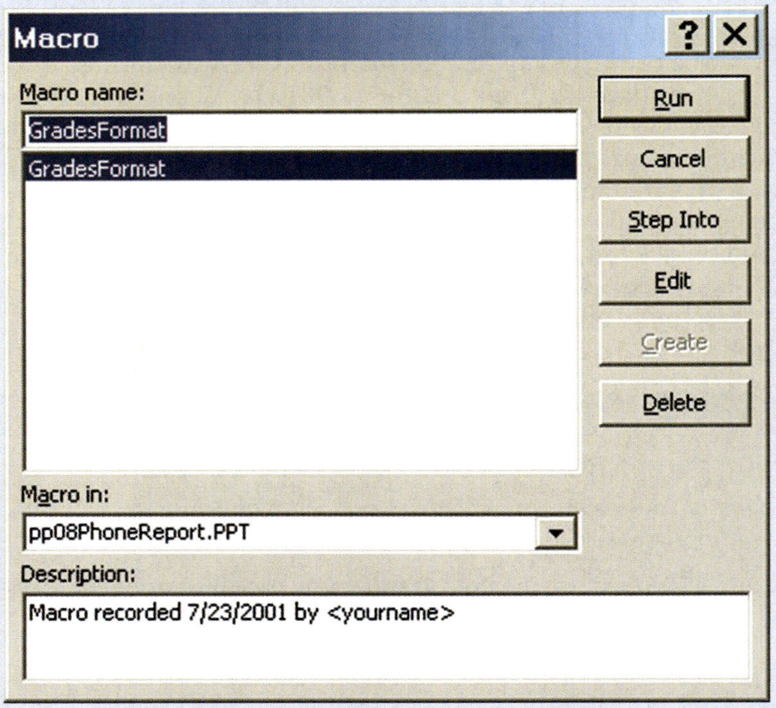

FIGURE 8.6
The Macro Dialog Box

9. Repeat steps 7 and 8 for the **B** of Disaster Recovery
10. Save

Macros can be recorded for any combination of mouse and keyboard operations that are frequently performed and then stored with a particular presentation or shared across presentations. Macro names must begin with a letter and cannot contain spaces. Macros can be edited as well as run from the Macro dialog box. Macros are often contained in PowerPoint files from other people or add-in software used to expand Office functionality.

A *macro virus* is a computer virus stored in a macro, an add-in, or template. Such viruses are spread by sharing files containing macros. Although virus protection software can isolate and reverse the damage of most macro viruses when their virus profiles are regularly updated, there is no guarantee. Microsoft Office XP provides *macro security levels* and *digital signatures* to further reduce the risk of macro virus infection. Both are controlled from the Security option of the Macro menu demonstrated in the previous steps.

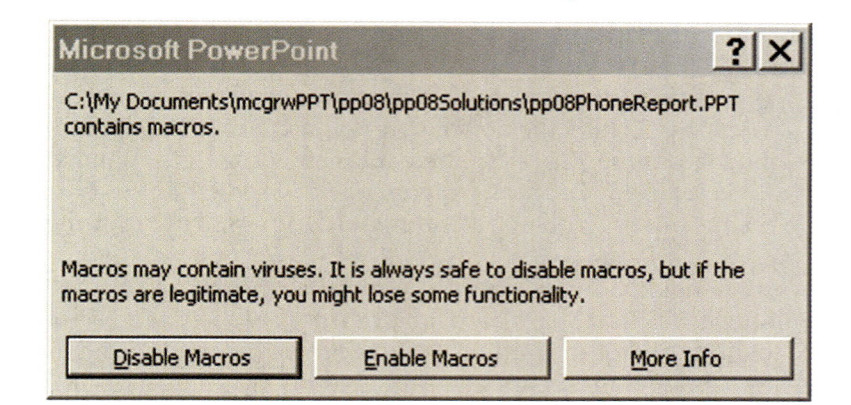

FIGURE 8.7
Enabling Macros

When Office XP is installed, the default macro security level is High. With this setting only macros that have been digitally signed and that appear on the trusted source list can be run. Unsigned macros are disabled, and the file is opened without a warning message. The security level can be adjusted to medium or low. The medium setting will display the message shown in the next figure when questionable macros are encountered. The low setting enables all macros without verifying sources.

Digital signatures are used to verify the source of a macro and that it has not been tampered with. When a file or an add-in containing a digitally signed macro is opened, the digital signature appears on the computer monitor as a certificate. The certificate names the macro's source, plus additional information about the identity and integrity of that source. A digital signature does not necessarily guarantee the safety of a macro, so users must still decide whether to trust a macro that has been digitally signed. For example, don't trust unknown sources, but macros signed by someone known or by a well-established company are probably safe. When unsure about a file or add-in that contains digitally signed macros, carefully examine the certificate before enabling macros or, to be even safer, disable the macros. If there are individuals and organizations that can always be trusted, they can be added to the list of trusted sources when a file is opened or add-in loaded.

Running macros from the Tools menu was demonstrated in the previous steps, but does not save enough keystrokes to make creating macros for simple operations effective. Faster access to macros is provided by assigning the macro to a toolbar button, a keyboard shortcut, or an object in a presentation.

MODIFYING MENUS AND TOOLBARS

Like all Office applications, PowerPoint can be completely customized to suit the work habits of each user. Using the Customize option of the Tools menu, the content and placement of each toolbar can be adjusted, or new custom toolbars developed. Since the Standard and Formatting toolbars are frequently used, most users choose not to customize them to avoid confusion.

Standard Menus and Toolbars

All Microsoft Office applications provide menus and toolbars as the primary method for users to control the application. Most users view menus and toolbars as different tools, but both are actually toolbars. A toolbar can contain buttons, menus, or a combination of the two.

POWERPOINT

Microsoft Office XP menus and toolbars automatically customize themselves based on how they are used. When an application is first used, only the most basic commands appear on the menus. Full menus appear after a short delay or by clicking the downward-pointing arrows at the bottom of the menu. Once a menu is expanded, all menus remain expanded until a command is selected. The selected command is added to the short version of the menu. Infrequently used commands are removed from the short menu.

When an Office application is first used, multiple toolbars share the same row without room to display all of the buttons. Since there is not enough space to display all of the buttons, only the most recently used buttons will display. Complete toolbars are available by clicking the right-pointing chevrons on the right end of the toolbar. The settings that control how Microsoft Office customizes menus and toolbars can be adjusted from the Customize option of the Tools menu.

task reference
Personalize Menu and Toolbar Settings
- On the **Tools** menu, click **Customize**
- Adjust Options tab settings

Personalizing Menu and toolbar settings:

1. Verify that PowerPoint is running. There is no need to have a particular presentation open for this operation
2. Click the **Customize** from the **Tools** menu
3. If necessary, select the **Options** tab of the Customize dialog box
4. Review the available settings

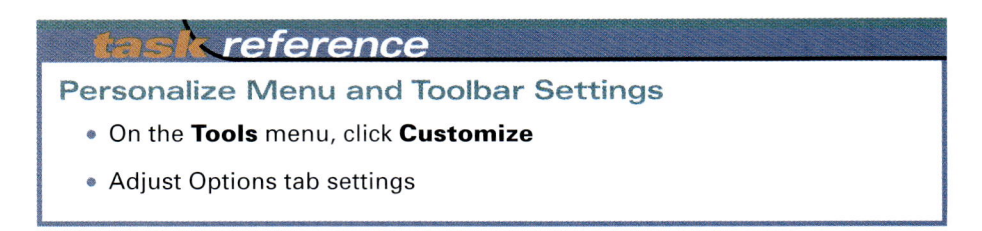

FIGURE 8.8
The Customize Dialog Box

5. Click **Show Standard and Formatting toolbars on two rows**

6. Click the **Always show full menus** check box

7. Click the **Large icons** check box

tip: *You should be able to see the icons increase in size behind the dialog box*

8. Uncheck **Large icons**

9. Click **Close**

The Customize dialog box settings impact the behavior of menus and toolbars throughout all Office applications. The Reset my usage data button restores the menus and toolbars to their just installed settings by deleting the user history. A new user history will be created as the applications are used. The Show Standard and Formatting toolbars on two rows check box takes up more screen real estate, but ensures that all buttons show. The Always show full menus option checked in the steps stops Office from customizing menus based on use. When this is clicked, all menu options will display.

Custom Toolbars

Users can customize menus and toolbars by adding and removing buttons and menus or even creating completely new toolbars. The menu bar and any toolbar are updated following the same procedures. Options added to menus or toolbars can be attached to either existing PowerPoint commands or macros created by the user.

task reference
Customize an Existing Toolbar

- Click the **Toolbar Options** downward-pointing arrow at the right end of the toolbar
- Point to **Add or Remove Buttons,** and then click **Customize**
- In the **Categories** box select the type of command to be added. For example, Macro
- From the **Commands** box, click and drag the command to the toolbar

Adding the GradesFormat macro to the Formatting toolbar:

1. Verify that PowerPoint is running with pp08PhoneReport.ppt open

2. On the Formatting toolbar, click the **Toolbar Options** arrow (downward-pointing arrow at the right end of the toolbar)

3. Point to **Add or Remove Buttons,** and then click **Customize**

4. Verify that the Commands tab is active
5. In The Categories box select **Macro**
6. Click and drag GradesFormat from the Commands box to the Formatting toolbar

FIGURE 8.9

Dragging GradesFormat to the Formatting Toolbar

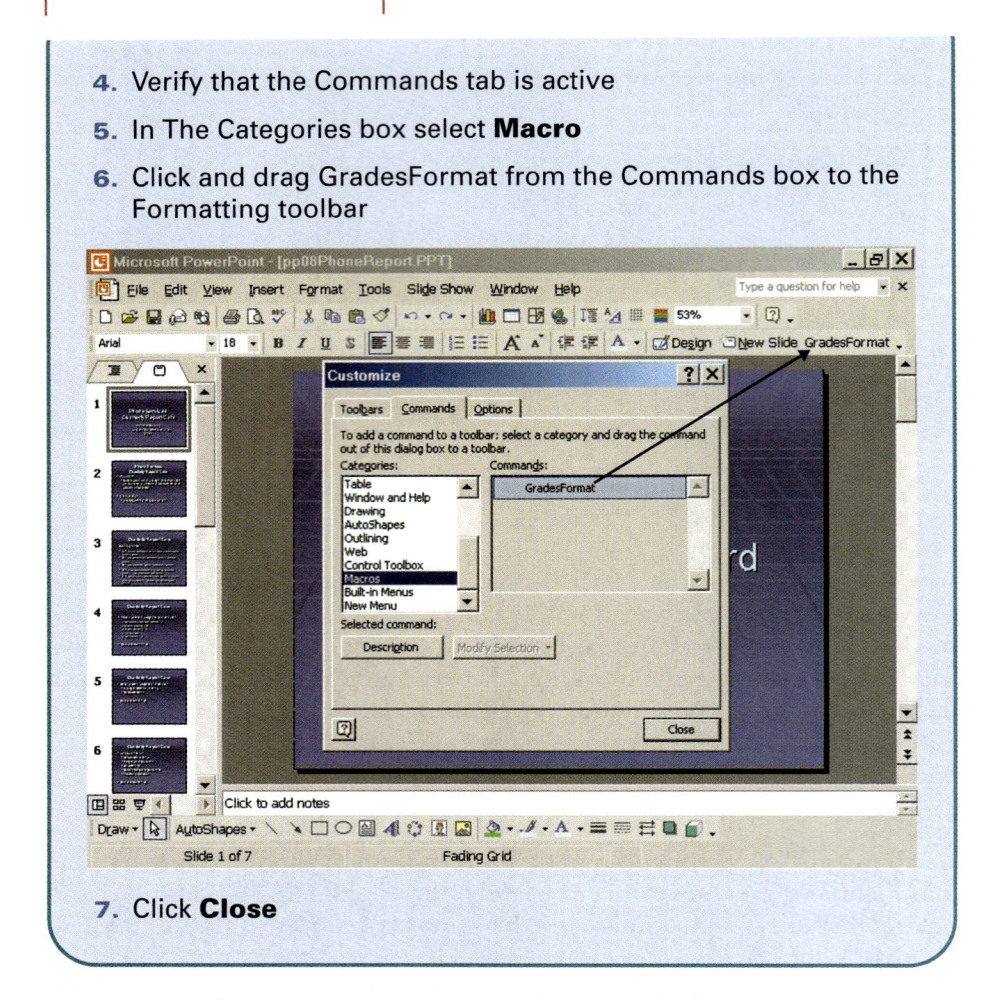

7. Click **Close**

Some security conscious organizations restrict the ability to customize toolbars. If you were unable to complete these steps, it may be because customization has been disabled. The GradesFormat button acts like the toolbar's intrinsic buttons; select text and click the button to activate the GradesFormat macro.

Removing the GradesFormat macro from the Formatting toolbar:

1. Verify that PowerPoint is running with pp08PhoneReport.ppt open
2. On the Formatting toolbar, click the **Toolbar Options** downward-pointing arrow at the right of the toolbar
3. Point to **Add or Remove Buttons,** and then click **Customize**
4. Click the **Toolbars** tab
5. Select the **Formatting** toolbar
6. Click the **Reset** button
7. Click **Close**

As was previously mentioned, it is best to create custom toolbars for your favorite commands and macros. Creating a custom toolbar avoids the confusion of customizing the Standard and Formatting toolbars, while allowing commonly used tasks to be readily available.

Creating the Custom Formats toolbar:

1. Verify that PowerPoint is running with pp08PhoneReport.ppt open
2. From the **Tools** menu, select **Customize**
3. Click the **Toolbars tab**
4. Click the **New** button
5. Name the new toolbar **Custom Formats** and click **OK**
6. Reposition the Customize dialog box until the new toolbar is visible. Adjust their position so that commands can be dragged from the dialog box to the toolbar

tip: *The Custom Formats toolbar will not contain any buttons and is usually floating near the center of the screen*

7. Click the **Commands** tab of the dialog box
8. In The Categories box select **Macro**
9. Click and drag GradesFormat from the Commands box to the Custom Formats toolbar

FIGURE 8.10

Dragging GradesFormat to the Custom Formats Toolbar

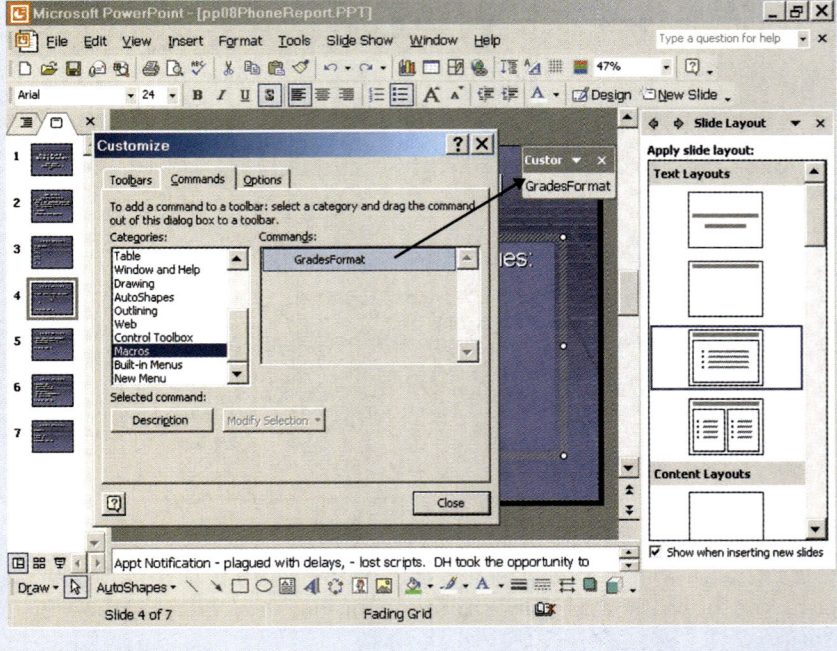

10. Click **Close**
11. Move to slide 4, select the **F** grade for PBX Upgrades, and click the **GradesFormat** button of the Custom Formats toolbar
12. Repeat step 11 for the remaining scores in the presentation. Do not use this format for the Overall scores on each slide

Adding macros to toolbar buttons is the most effective way to save keystrokes and maintain consistency. Any number of buttons and menus can be added to a custom toolbar. Like built-in toolbars, custom toolbars can be moved and anchored to any window edge. When the toolbar is no longer functional, the Toolbars tab of the customize dialog box contains a Delete button.

REVISING POWERPOINT SETTINGS

Many of the ways to customize PowerPoint have been addressed as each related topic was covered. The most common place to adjust settings is the Options selection of the Tools menu. Properties of individual PowerPoint files can be adjusted from the Properties option of the File menu.

Changing PowerPoint Defaults

The Options selection of the Tools menu is a multi-tabbed dialog box with settings to control the behavior of most critical PowerPoint operations. This dialog box contains options to control save, print, view, security, edit, spelling, and style. It is not possible in a text of this nature to cover every customization situation, so this review is intended to point you in the right direction to find the necessary options.

Exploring the Options dialog box:

1. Verify that PowerPoint is running. No particular file is needed for this operation
2. From the **Tools** menu, select **Options**
3. Click the **Save** tab and explore the available options
4. Click the **Security** tab and explore the available options
5. Click the **Spelling and Style** tab and explore the available options
6. Click the **View** tab and explore the available options
7. Click the **General** tab and explore the available options
8. Click the **Edit** tab and explore the available options
9. Click the **Print** tab and explore the available options
10. Click **OK**

All Office applications use the Customize option of the Tools menu to control toolbars and the Options choice to control other critical operations.

Customizing File Properties

Each Office file is saved with properties including the author, file type, and file size. Pausing the cursor over a filename in Windows Explorer will display the author and file size from these properties. Other properties are maintained and can be customized.

> ### Exploring the File Properties dialog box:
> 1. Verify that PowerPoint is running with pp08PhoneReport.ppt open
> 2. On the **File** menu, click **Properties**
> 3. Review contents of the **General** tab
> 4. Click on the **Statistics** tab and review the contents
> 5. Review the **Contents** tab
> 6. Click on the **Summary** tab
>   a. Update the title to reflect the current month and the title Phone Report
>   b. Set the subject to **Unsatisfactory phone support services**
>   c. Update the author to reflect your full name
>   d. Add your instructor's name as the Manager
> 7. Click **OK**

Most users don't override the default settings for author and title. The other settings on the Summary tab can be very useful for published or shared presentations. The Custom tab contains settings for adding the names of reviewers, checking out files, and adding custom comment fields.

ENHANCING POWERPOINT WITH ADD-INS

Add-ins are additional software programs that augment the capabilities of an existing application like PowerPoint. Many add-ins are available from the Microsoft Office Web site, while others can be obtained from third-party vendors. Visual Basic for Applications can also be used to write add-ins. All PowerPoint add-ins have the file extension .ppa.

Loading Add-Ins

Add-ins can be as simple as expanded templates and help files, or they can include complex programming like the kiosk creator or interactive Web add-in. Visit www.microsoft.com, go to the PowerPoint home page, and look through the PowerPoint downloads for add-ins. Currently the site has more than 50 add-ins available at no charge. The exact installation process varies from add-in to add-in, but the general process is reflected in the following steps.

> ### Loading an add-in:
> 1. Visit www.microsoft.com, locate a PowerPoint add-in, and download it
> 2. Place the add-in file on a disk available to your system
> 3. Verify that PowerPoint is running. No particular file is needed for this operation
> 4. On the **Tools** menu, click **Add-Ins**

FIGURE 8.11
Add-Ins Dialog Box

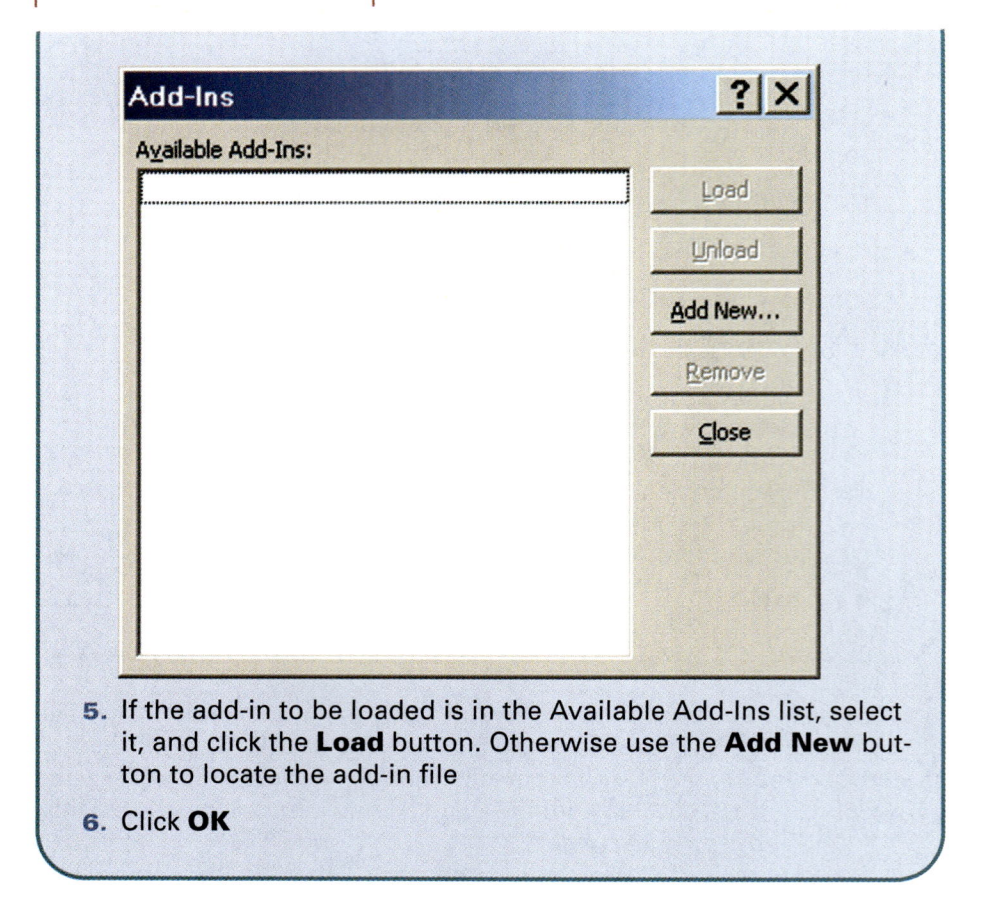

5. If the add-in to be loaded is in the Available Add-Ins list, select it, and click the **Load** button. Otherwise use the **Add New** button to locate the add-in file

6. Click **OK**

The features of the add-in are available when the load operation is completed. How the features are accessed varies from add-in to add-in. Additional templates and help files simply display with the built-in versions. Others may be accessed from custom menus and toolbars. Read the available documentation for details on a specific add-in.

Unloading Add-Ins

In general, add-ins should be loaded, used, and then unloaded unless the features are needed on a continual basis. Unloading an add-in does not remove the file from the computer, but stops it from loading with PowerPoint. Unloading saves memory and improves application performance.

Unloading an add-in:

1. Verify that PowerPoint is running. No particular file is needed for this operation

2. On the **Tools** menu, click **Add-Ins**

3. Click **Unload**

tip: *Clicking Remove will cause the add-in not to show in the list*

4. Click **OK**

Since the unload process does not remove the add-in from your computer, it can be reloaded whenever it is needed. Add-ins that will not be used again should be removed, and then the install file deleted from the disk.

> **making the grade** — **SESSION 8.1**
>
> 1. Discuss the importance of creating presentation backups.
> 2. Why use the PowerPoint viewer?
> 3. What is the advantage of packaging a presentation before it is delivered?
> 4. Explain the advantage of using macros. Of attaching macros to toolbar buttons.
> 5. What is the difference between settings in the Customize dialog box and the Options dialog box?

SESSION 8.2 SHARING PRESENTATIONS

When creating a presentation needs to be a team effort or a presentation must play simultaneously in diverse locations, the workgroup and integration features of PowerPoint provide the necessary functionality. In the previous chapter we began to look at using Web publishing to share documents. Besides publishing in Web format, presentations can also be sent via e-mail and broadcast during an online meeting. When using a computer attached to a network or the Internet, a presentation can be run on any computer on that network.

UNDERSTANDING ONLINE COLLABORATION TOOLS

A presentation being created by multiple people must support gathering team member input and tracking comments. Software that supports such collaboration is called *workgroup software*. There are several ways that e-mail can be used to collaborate.

Sending a Presentation for Review via e-mail

The simplest ways to share any document is to give it to reviewers on a disk or send it as an e-mail attachment. Almost any e-mail software will support attaching files, but the exact methodology will vary from package to package. Simply sending a PowerPoint file on disk as an attachment has the disadvantage of requiring one of the team members to coordinate the review process, collect suggestions, and apply updates to the original presentation.

Before sending a presentation to others on a disk or as a simple e-mail attachment, it is important to take care of any linked files. Linked files include any large sound files that the presentation plays and non-Internet files that the presentation needs to run effectively. If linked files are not changed to embedded files, they must be transported with the presentation.

Parks Industries' PhoneReport does not contain any linked files, so no special processing to deal with links is needed. The presentation does need input from each of the phone system managers at the remote sites before it can be finalized. To simulate this process, you will create two review files that could be distributed to reviewers, edit the files yourself, and then merge the updates with the original file.

task reference
Prepare a Presentation for Review
- Open the presentation to be reviewed
- For each reviewer:
  - Click **Save As** on the **File** menu
  - Change the name in the **File name** box to indicate whose review copy it is
  - Change the **Save as type** to **Presentation for Review**
  - Click **Save**
- Distribute the files to reviewers on disk or as e-mail attachments

Reviewing PP08PhoneReport:

1. Verify that PowerPoint is running with **PP08PhoneReport.ppt** open
2. Click the **Save as** option of the **File** menu
3. In the Save as dialog box
   a. Change the File name to **Reviewer1PP08PhoneReport.ppt**
   b. Change the Save as type to **Presentation for Review**
   c. Click **Save**
4. Repeat step 3 saving the file as **Reviewer2PP08PhoneReport.ppt**

tip: *Notice that the file name in the title bar does not change as it would with a typical Save as operation*

5. Open **Reviewer1PP08PhoneReport.ppt**

tip: *Respond **No** if the dialog box to merge changes appears*

   a. Place your name on the line above the date on the first slide
   b. Move to slide 2 and change ??? to **with Parks Industries**
   c. Close the presentation saving your changes

6. Open **Reviewer2PP08PhoneReport**
   a. On slide 1 add the name **Walter Pauls** on the line above the date
   b. Move to slide 2 and change ??? to **with Parks Industries**
   c. Close the presentation saving your changes

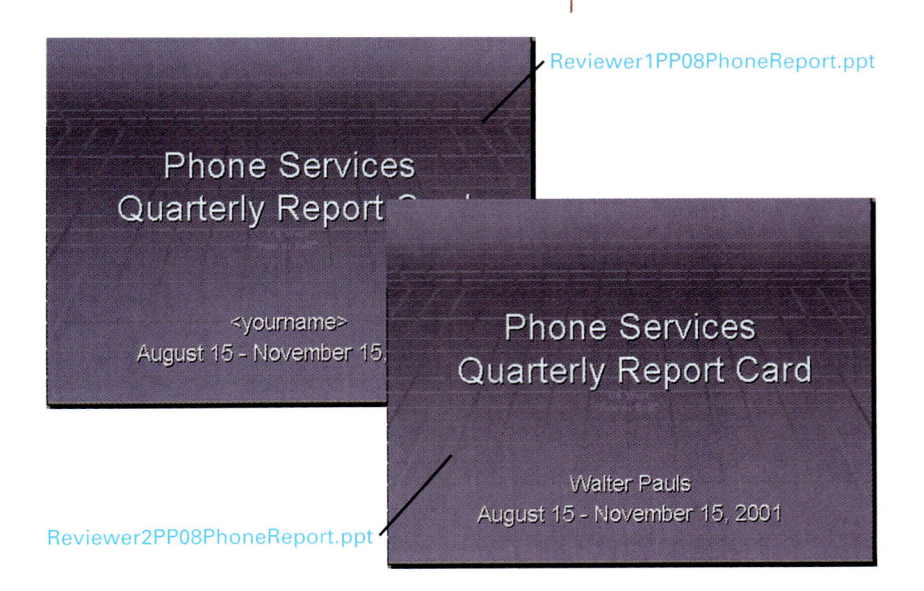

FIGURE 8.12
Reviewer Changes

Reviewer1PP08PhoneReport.ppt

Reviewer2PP08PhoneReport.ppt

Once all review copies have been created, they can be distributed to the intended reviewers as an attachment in any e-mail program or on disk. As was demonstrated in the steps, each reviewer can open their copy of the file, make changes, and then return the file to the coordinator. The coordinator is responsible for distributing the review files, ensuring that the reviewed files are returned, and accepting/rejecting reviewers' suggestions.

Applying PP08PhoneReport reviews:

1. Verify that PowerPoint is running with **PP08PhoneReport.ppt** open
2. On the **Tools** menu select **Compare and Merge Presentations**
3. Click **Reviewer1PP8PhoneReport.ppt,** then hold the **Shift** key to select **Reviewer2PP8PhoneReport.ppt,** and click **Merge**
4. Read the warning and then click **Continue**
5. Move to slide **1**
   a. In the Revisions pane select the slide with yourname (see Figure 8.13)
   b. Click the Apply button on the Reviewing toolbar
6. Move to slide 2 and apply the revisions
7. Click the **End Review** button on the Reviewing toolbar
8. Read the warning and click **Yes**
9. Save the project

When the End Review button is clicked, the ability to combine revisions from the reviewer file is permanently terminated. Many of the review tools are not available with simple attached e-mail files. Full reviewing functionality is available to users of Microsoft Outlook.

POWERPOINT

FIGURE 8.13
Viewing Revisions

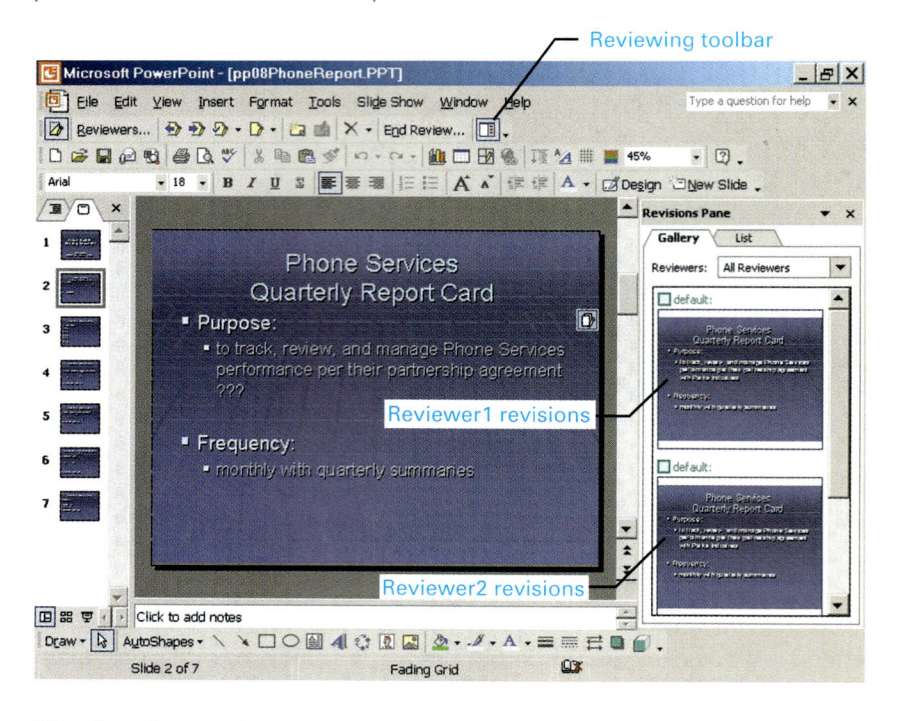

Reviewing with Microsoft Outlook

Microsoft Outlook is software designed to coordinate workgroup activities by providing e-mail, calendars, contacts, and other shared and personal support. If all parties involved in the collaboration are using Microsoft Outlook, features for coordinating and tracking the presentation review are available. When PowerPoint is used to send a presentation for review through Outlook, other team members can add comments and make changes in their personal review copy of the presentation. The reviews are returned to the author, who combines them with the original file and then uses reviewing tools to apply or reject suggested updates.

Outlook will automatically generate a review request e-mail message with appropriate text, create a follow-up flag, and track changes made by reviewers. Some of this functionality is available using other 32-bit e-mail programs compatible with the Messaging Application Programming Interface (MAPI).

Parks Industries has implemented all of the Microsoft product features needed to collaborate using Outlook. Since it is anticipated that the reader does not have all of these features and there is no actual Phone Services group to interact with, this topic includes discussion and Task References to indicate how each task could be completed, but Steps are not included for the reader to follow.

---

task reference

Use Outlook to Send a Presentation for Review

- Open the presentation to be reviewed
- On the **File** menu, point to **Send To,** and then click **Mail Recipient (for Review)**
- In the e-mail that opens enter the To and Cc e-mail addresses of your reviewers
- Click **Send**

Sending PP08PhoneReport for review:

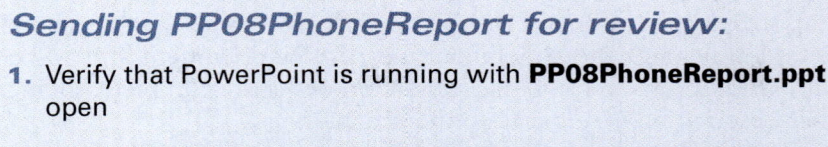

1. Verify that PowerPoint is running with **PP08PhoneReport.ppt** open

tip: You must be running Outlook to complete the remaining steps

2. Click the **File** menu, point to **Send To,** and then click **Mail Recipient (for Review)**

3. Enter your e-mail addresses

tip: In an actual review process you would enter the e-mail addresses of the reviewers

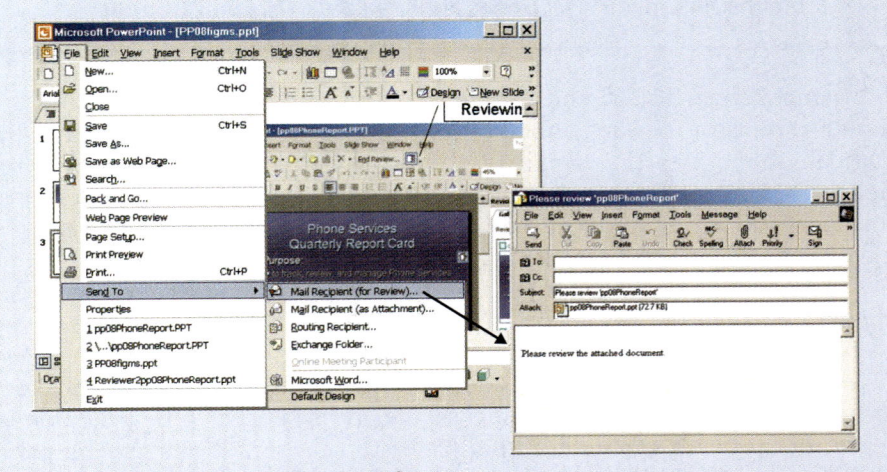

4. Set any other desired options
5. Click **Send**

FIGURE 8.14

Send To Mail Recipient (for Review)

Microsoft Outlook provides an array of e-mail options that can be useful when tracking revisions. A pivotal feature of Outlook is the address book. Besides being able to keep individual information in the address book, e-mail lists and groups can be created so that clicking one address book entry sends e-mails to all members of that group. Other valuable options include:

- Setting the importance level from low to high
- Flags to remind yourself to follow up and reviewers to respond by a specific due date
- The ability to mark the message private, personal, or confidential. Private messages cannot be modified after they are sent
- Adding security to messages
- Tracking messages and replies
- Delaying message delivery or causing the message to expire on a specified date

Deadlines and follow-ups are particularly useful in review cycles. They help to keep the project on track without further intervention by the coordinator. If you are not familiar with these features, please refer to Outlook's Help facilities for further information.

The reviewers will receive e-mail with an individual copy of the presentation attached. When a reviewer opens the e-mail, he or she will be able to double-click the attachment to open the document and add comments. Once a reviewer's changes and comments are complete, their copy of the presentation is returned to the originator.

---

task reference

Review a Presentation Sent with Outlook

- Open e-mail and double-click on the presentation to be reviewed
- Edit the presentation in the normal fashion
- Use the Comments button of the Reviewing toolbar to add comments
- From the **File** menu click **Send,** and then click **Original Sender**

Using Return To Original Sender has some advantages over using the standard reply or forward e-mail buttons. Return To Original Sender automatically generates the e-mail text indicating that the file has been reviewed. Additionally, the correct return address and file attachment are ensured. The review request e-mail can be deleted, saved, or moved to a specific folder, just like any other e-mail.

When you, the originator, receive the reviewers' e-mails, combine their updated presentations with your original presentation so that you can see everything at once. Each reviewer's comments and changes are identified in your presentation by a color-coded comment or a change icon with a description of the change. All reviewers' files do not need to be available to begin this process since additional reviewed presentations can be combined with the original presentation until the review is ended.

As the author of the slide show, it is up to you to make the final edit of the presentation. Comments and changes from reviewers can be ignored, applied individually, by slide, or by reviewer. If reviewers have made con-

FIGURE 8.15
Returning a Reviewed Presentation

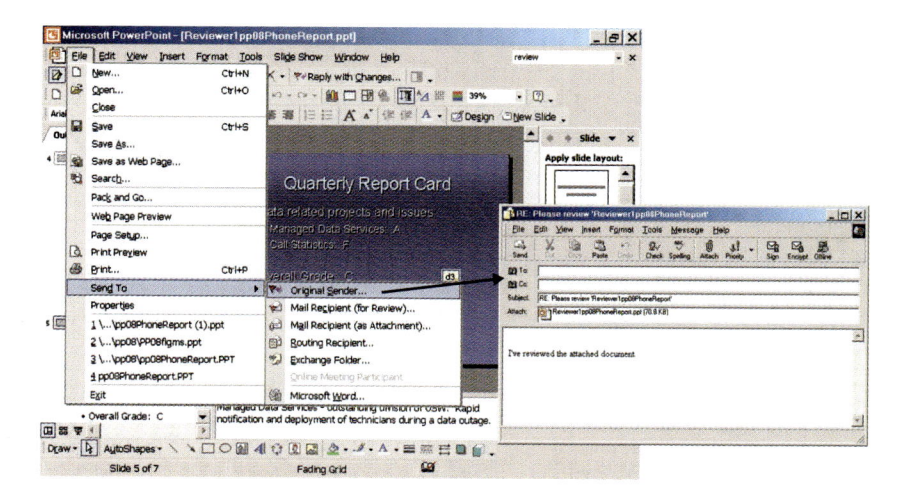

FIGURE 8.16
Combining Reviewed Presentations

> **task reference**
>
> **Use Outlook to Combine Reviewed Presentations**
>
> - Open the Outlook e-mail containing the reviewed presentation
> - Double-click the attached reviewed presentation
> - Click **Yes** in the alert box so that PowerPoint will automatically combine the reviewed presentation with your original presentation
> - Close the e-mail and repeat the process for any other reviews

flicting changes, the various updates are displayed and the coordinator must select which changes to apply.

Changes made by reviewers and combined with the original presentation will display as a change icon on the original presentation slide or in the Revisions pane of the Task panel. There are several effective ways to view, evaluate, and apply changes. Moving through the combined presentation one slide at a time displays what each reviewer suggested about each slide. Alternatively a single reviewer can be selected from the Reviewers list of the Reviewing toolbar to follow just one person's comments. The Next Item and Previous Item buttons of the Reviewing toolbar will move from comment to comment in the presentation. The Apply and Unapply buttons are used to make and unmake the suggested changes to the original presentation.

When working through the combined presentation, changes that won't be applied can be deleted. To remove unwanted icons from the combined presentation, select them and click the Delete button. Removing unneeded icons unclutters the slide and allows the originator to concentrate on issues that need to be addressed. The check boxes representing each task performed by each reviewer can be checked and unchecked to indicate which revisions to retain. When multiple reviewers have made conflicting changes, click Multiple Reviewers and select the changes to retain.

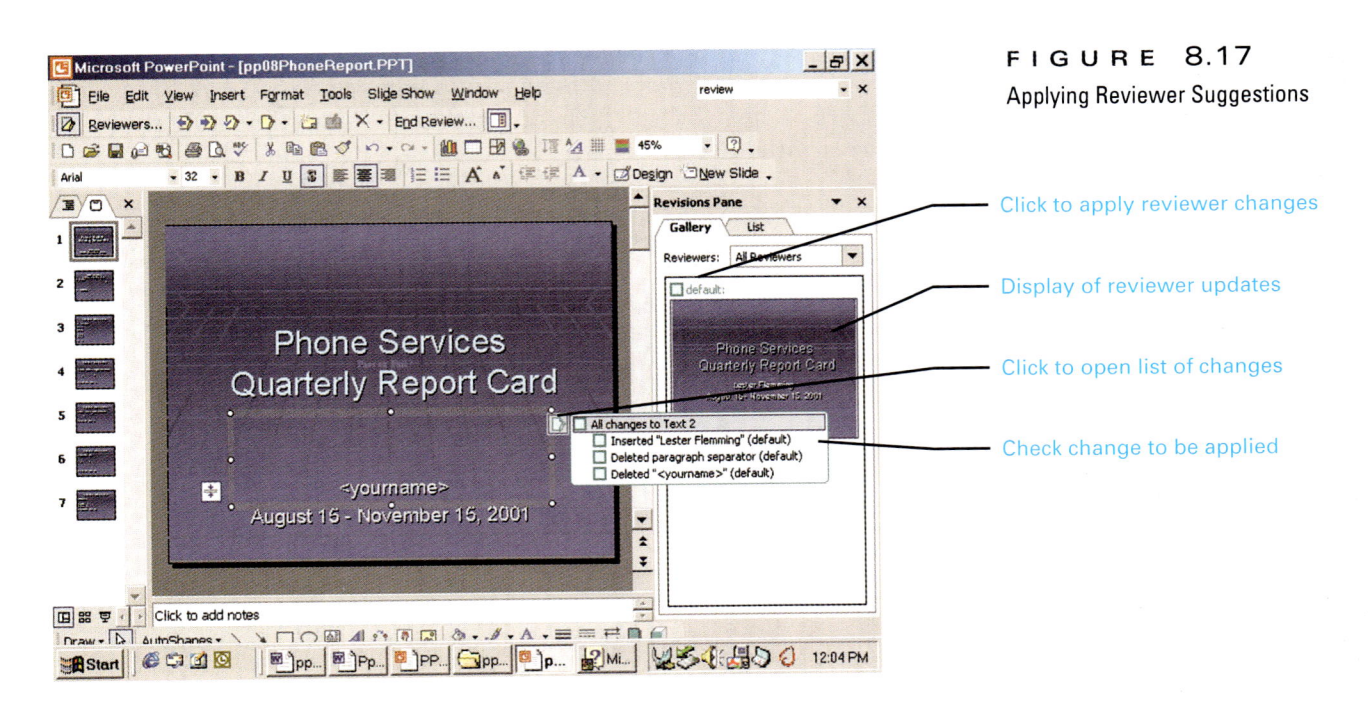

FIGURE 8.17

Applying Reviewer Suggestions

- Click to apply reviewer changes
- Display of reviewer updates
- Click to open list of changes
- Check change to be applied

If any presentation reviewers made changes to the slide master, those suggestions must be reviewed separately. Use the View menu to open the Slide Master so that reviewer notes will display. Apply or ignore Slide Master updates as you would any other update and then close the view.

When all desired reviews have been applied, end the review. Once the review is ended, it will not be possible to combine any more reviewed presentations with the original presentation.

task reference
End a Review
- On the Reviewing toolbar, click **End Review**

Often multiple review cycles are required to complete presentation development. The completed cycle should be ended and another one begun each time feedback is solicited. By combining the power of multiple Microsoft applications, coordinating a review cycle is greatly simplified. This scenario assumes that Outlook has been installed with the configuration options necessary to support online collaboration.

Routing a Presentation

Routing a file is another use of Microsoft e-mail software to facilitate collaboration. Routing typically e-mails one attached file to a group of reviewers in sequence. Using this method, the file is sent to the first recipient, who adds comments and then sends it on to the next person on the routing slip. This process is repeated until each address on the routing slip has been used and the presentation is returned to the originator. With the sequential strategy, each recipient can see the comments made by previous reviewers. Routing can also be set to present files to multiple reviewers simultaneously and allows you to set deadlines, deliverables, and status checks.

Parks Industries has all of the e-mail and networking options needed to fully implement routing, so this is a valid option for the Phone Status project. Personal preference, available time, and group style determine whether or not routing is the best choice. In general, sequential routing requires more review time than using Outlook to send a project for review. Since there is no workgroup to interact with, this topic contains Task References without Steps.

FIGURE 8.18
Routing a Presentation

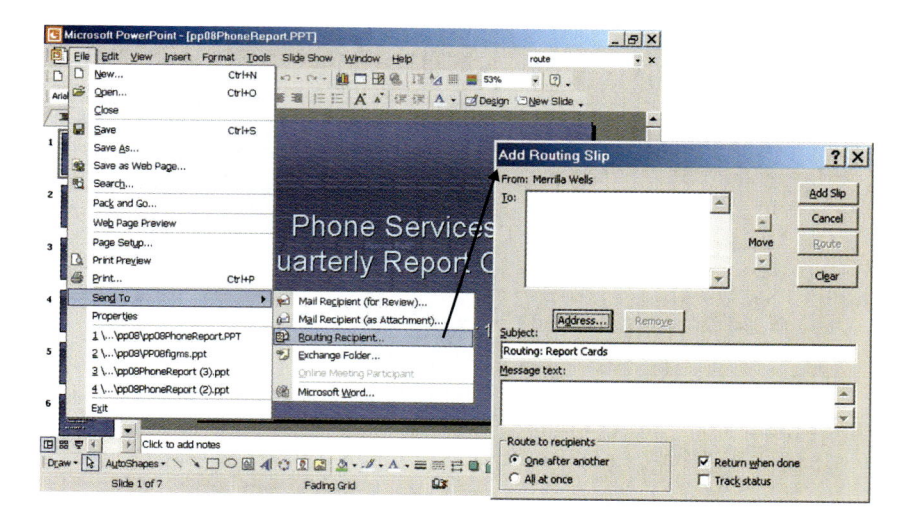

task reference

Route a Presentation

- Open the presentation to be routed
- Activate the **File** menu, point to **Send To,** and then click **Routing Recipient**
- Click the **Address** button to access your address book
  - Select the desired addresses in order of receipt
  - Close the address book
- Type the Message text
- Select the routing options such as Track Status and how to distribute
- Click **Route** to start the process

or

- Click **Add Slip** to close the dialog box without starting the routing process. At a later time, click **File, Send To,** and then **Next Routing Recipient** to start the routing process

Since routing is a serial course of action, it depends on each recipient to be responsive and complete their tasks in a timely fashion. The Track status option is designed to help the originator keep track of who has the project and determine when intervention is needed.

Sometimes the composition of a project team changes or a mistake is made on the routing list. When this occurs, the routing slip needs to be edited to reflect the changes.

task reference

Update a Routing Slip

- Open the presentation to have its routing updated
- Activate the **File** menu, point to **Send To,** and then click **Other Routing Recipient**
- If you are the originator of the file, you can change any option
  - Use the **Address** button to add a new recipient
  - Select a recipient and click the **Remove** button to remove it from the routing list
  - Select a recipient and click the up or down arrow to change the order of receipt
  - Update the options as needed
- If you are a recipient of the routed file, you can only change the routing order by selecting a recipient and using the up or down arrows to change its rank in the list
- Click **Route** to send the updated file or **Add Slip** to save the changes without sending

POWERPOINT

The recipient of a routed file will get an e-mail request with an attached file. After the attached file is opened, the reviewer adds comments and then sends the e-mail to the next reviewer on the routing list. After sending the file to the next reviewer, the e-mail can be deleted or filed in the same manner used for any other e-mail.

---

task reference

Send a Routed File to the Next Reviewer

- Open the presentation to have its routing updated
- Add your comments to the file
- Click the **File** menu option, point to **Send To**
  - Click **OK** to accept the next routing recipient

  or

  - Click **Other Routing Recipient** to send the file to someone not on the list, click **OK,** then enter the e-mail address, and click **Send**

When a routed file has been through all of the recipients on the routing slip, it returns to the originator. At this point, the presentation contains comments from all of the reviewers that the author must evaluate and apply. The updated file can be routed again to gather a second round of input.

WEB BROADCASTING

Complete presentations including video and audio narration can be delivered over the World Wide Web. Web broadcasts can be live or recorded. Recorded broadcasts can be rebroadcast at scheduled times or configured for on-demand viewing. Web broadcasts are ideal for large geographically dispersed audiences or when multiple conference rooms are required to handle the volume of people.

Viewing a Web Broadcast

The contents of a Web broadcast are saved in HTML format so that viewers need a Web browser to view the presentation. Microsoft Internet Explorer 5.1 or later is the recommended browser since it supports all of the features that might be included in a broadcast. The viewer must know how to access the server where the broadcast is stored.

Web broadcasts are similar in appearance to presentations saved as Web pages. The broadcast consists of multiple frames as follows:

- The current slide displayed in a browser frame
- A clickable table of contents so the audience can view previous slides or skip ahead
- Live video displayed in its own browser frame
- Audience tools like Help, E-mail, and View Previous

Most business presentations using Web broadcasting are initiated via e-mail. The participant receives an e-mail with the broadcast time and URL. It is best to join a live broadcast early to verify the URL and check for any last-minute changes.

FIGURE 8.19
Web Broadcast

task reference
View a Web Broadcast

- To view a live broadcast, open the e-mail with the broadcast invitation and click the URL

- To view a recorded broadcast, go to the start page provided by the presenter and click **Replay Broadcast**

Preparing for Web Broadcast

Web broadcasts should be set up and tested well in advance of the scheduled presentation delivery. In most situations, the presenter is responsible for organizing and delivering the broadcast. Setting up small-group presentations on a local intranet or the Internet does not require much technical expertise and can usually be completed by the presenter alone.

The minimum requirements for Web broadcasting are PowerPoint 2002 and Internet Explorer 5.1 or later. If the live broadcast is to contain audio, video, or both, a video camera and microphone must be properly connected to the presentation computer. Microsoft Outlook or another e-mail client will be needed to distribute the live broadcast invitations. PowerPoint creates e-mail invitations during the online broadcast setup process.

For a successful presentation involving 10 or more audience computers, Microsoft Windows Media Server is necessary. Microsoft Media Server can be purchased and locally installed, or provided through a third party. Whether these services are provided locally or through a service provider, the setup will require additional time and coordination before the presentation can be delivered. See the *Tips for broadcasting* Help topic for more broadcasting resources.

Setting Up a Recorded Web Broadcast

All of the PowerPoint setup for an online broadcast is accomplished from the Online Broadcast selection of the Slide Show menu. As has been mentioned, Web broadcasts can be recorded for later delivery or presented live. Live broadcasts can begin immediately or be scheduled for later. Each of these delivery methodologies requires a slightly different setup.

task reference
Set Up a Recorded Web Broadcast

- Open the presentation to be broadcast on a computer with functioning audio and/or video equipment
- On the **Slide Show** menu, point to **Online Broadcast** and select **Record and Save a Broadcast**
- Complete the information for the broadcast lobby
- Click **Settings** and update the audio/video, presentation display, speaker notes, and file location
- Click **OK**
- Click **Record** to prepare the presentation for recording
- Click **Start** to begin recording the broadcast
    - Narrate each slide speaking clearly and staying positioned in front of the camera, if there is one
    - Click to progress to the next slide
- When you have recorded through all of the slides in the presentation, you will be presented with an option to Replay the Broadcast
- Move all broadcast files to a shared folder on your intranet or to the Internet and notify your audience of the location

Recording the PP08PhoneReport Web broadcast:

1. Open **PP08PhoneReport.ppt**
2. On the **Slide Show** menu, point to **Online Broadcast** and select **Record and Save a Broadcast**
3. Change the Title to **Quarterly Phone Report**, insert your name as the speaker, and place your e-mail address in the E-mail text box
4. Click **Settings**
    a. Select the Audio/Video setting appropriate for your computer

    tip: *Be sure to use the Test button if you are using either audio or video*

    b. Click **Display speaker notes with the presentation**
    c. Change the Save broadcast files in location to reflect where you are storing your work
    d. Click **OK**

5. Click the **Tips for Broadcast** button, review the tips, and then close the window

6. Click **Record**, wait for the presentation to be prepared, perform any requested checks, and then click **Start**

7. Click through the presentation reading highlights of the slide content for audio and video presentation

tip: When you click to end the presentation, PowerPoint saves the broadcast and displays a dialog box with an option to view the broadcast

8. Click the **Replay Broadcast** button and watch the show

tip: If you included audio or video, you should see and hear it as the presentation plays

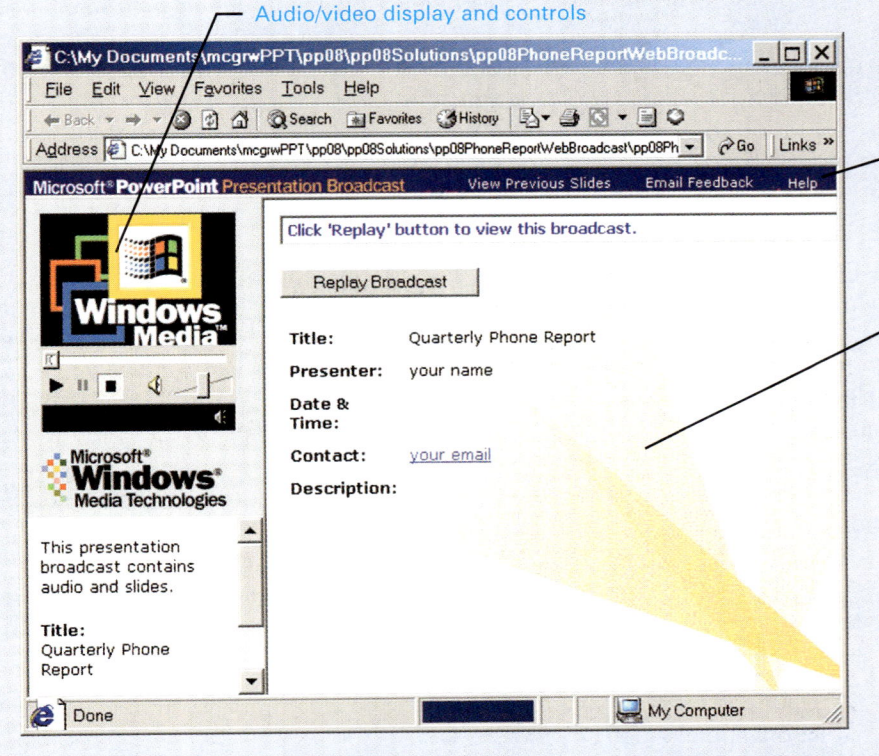

FIGURE 8.20
PP08PhoneReport Lobby with Audio Recorded

- Audio/video display and controls
- Viewer toolbar including Help
- Slide window

9. Close the Web browser window when you are done viewing the broadcast

anotherword

...on Broadcast Settings

In these steps, you used the Settings button to set options for the presentation media, display, and storage location. These options are available on the Presenters tab of the Broadcast Settings dialog box. The Advanced tab of this dialog box can be used to set up Windows Media Encoder, a chat room URL, or Windows Media Services. These options use the resources of other computers and the network that must be set up by a technician.

FIGURE 8.21
Setting Up a Live Broadcast

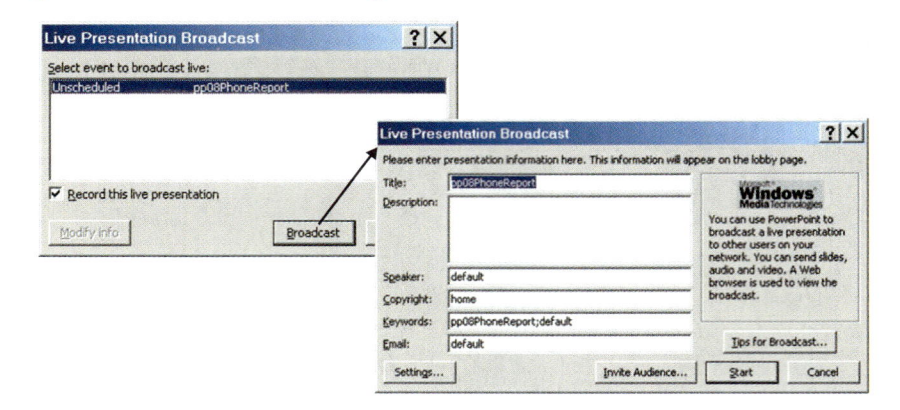

In the preceding steps the recorded broadcast was saved locally but the files can still be moved to a shared location for audience browsing. During the recording process, Microsoft PowerPoint creates the opening or lobby page using the name of the PowerPoint presentation with the .htm file extension of an HTML file. All of the pages of the presentation, graphics, audio, and video files are stored in a folder with the same name as the presentation plus _files. The .htm file and the folder of supporting files must be moved or copied to the same location for the broadcast to work correctly.

Setting Up a Live or Scheduled Web Broadcast

A live Web broadcast is viewed by the audience at the same time that it is being produced by the speaker. Viewing and creating the broadcast are very similar to the experience of creating a recorded broadcast, but the setup is somewhat different. An unscheduled live broadcast can be started at any time, but you are responsible for inviting and organizing the participants. A scheduled broadcast will use your e-mail software to invite people you select to the future event.

As with recorded presentations, functioning audio and video equipment are required to include those components in your broadcast, and

task reference

Start a Live Web Broadcast

- Open the presentation to be broadcast on a computer with functioning audio and/or video equipment
- On the **Slide Show** menu, point to **Online Broadcast** and select **Start Live Broadcast Now**
- In the Live Presentation Broadcast dialog box, select the presentation, check the record option if you want a recorded copy for on-demand viewing, and click **Broadcast**
- Enter the information to create the lobby
- Click **Settings** and update the audio/video, presentation display, speaker notes, and file location. A shared file location must be specified to continue
- Click **OK**
- If you want to invite participants, click **Invite Audience** to send e-mails
- Click **Start** to begin recording the broadcast
- Click **Start** again to begin streaming audio and video

broadcasting to 10 or more computers requires additional resources. Live presentations must be saved to a shared intranet or Internet drive as they are created so that the audience can view them.

It is wise to check the settings prior to each broadcast, because they apply to all broadcasts from a particular computer, not just to the current broadcast. The actual presentation of a scheduled broadcast is initiated using the live broadcast procedure just explored. Scheduled presentations will be listed in the selection box of the opening Live Presentation Broadcast dialog box. The steps to scheduling a broadcast should be completed a week or more before the broadcast to verify hardware and accommodate participants' needs.

task reference
Schedule a Live Web Broadcast
- Open the presentation to be broadcast on a computer with functioning audio and/or video equipment
- On the **Slide Show** menu, point to **Online Broadcast** and select **Schedule a Live Broadcast**
- Enter the information to create the lobby
- Click **Settings** and update the audio/video, presentation display, speaker notes, and file location. A shared file location must be specified to continue
- Click **OK**
- Click **Schedule** in the Schedule Presentation Broadcast dialog box

Live Web broadcasts are an effective way to communicate across distances to multiple concurrent audiences. Saving the live presentation allows participants to review its content and those who were unable to attend the live broadcast the ability to participate.

MAKING ONLINE MEETINGS WORK FOR YOU

PowerPoint presentations can be shared online using Microsoft NetMeeting. All computers participating in an online meeting must be connected to a network and have NetMeeting installed and properly configured. Such online meetings are called *collaborative meetings* and are usually conducted when members of an organization are unable to convene at a central location.

The act of initiating an online meeting automatically starts NetMeeting in the background. NetMeeting is capable of delivering the presentation and allowing the distributed audience to exchange information in real time (as if everyone were in the same room). ***Chat*** can be used to send text messages, and the ***Whiteboard*** is visible to all users. Collaboration settings will allow multiple audience members to work in Chat or on the Whiteboard simultaneously. Only one user at a time can work on the presentation, however.

Scheduling Online Meetings

Online meeting attendees can have the role of either host or participant. All meeting participants must have access to a server that will be used to present the meeting. Only the meeting host needs to have the shared document and its host application installed.

Online meetings can be scheduled in advance or started immediately. All participants can see a shared document such as a PowerPoint presentation, but the host has control of who can update the document. As the host makes changes to the document, other meeting attendees can watch the work. When attendees are updating a document, the host cannot use the pointer for any purpose. Multiple attendees can use Chat and the Whiteboard at any time during the meeting.

task reference
Host an Online Meeting with PowerPoint

- Open the presentation to be broadcast on a computer with functioning audio and/or video equipment
- On the **Tools** menu, point to **Online Collaboration** and select either **Meet Now** or **Schedule Meeting**
- Complete the NetMeeting dialog box and click **OK**
- On the Online Meeting Toolbar, click **Call Participant** and use the Find Someone dialog box to invite attendees
- Participate in the meeting
- On the Online Meeting Toolbar click **End Meeting**

Only the host of a meeting can use the Online Meeting Toolbar to invite attendees, open the Whiteboard, or initiate Chat. Once a participant has joined a meeting, they can see the shared document, use the Whiteboard and Chat if they are open, and use the End Call option of the Online Meeting Toolbar to leave the meeting.

FIGURE 8.22

Initiating an Online Meeting

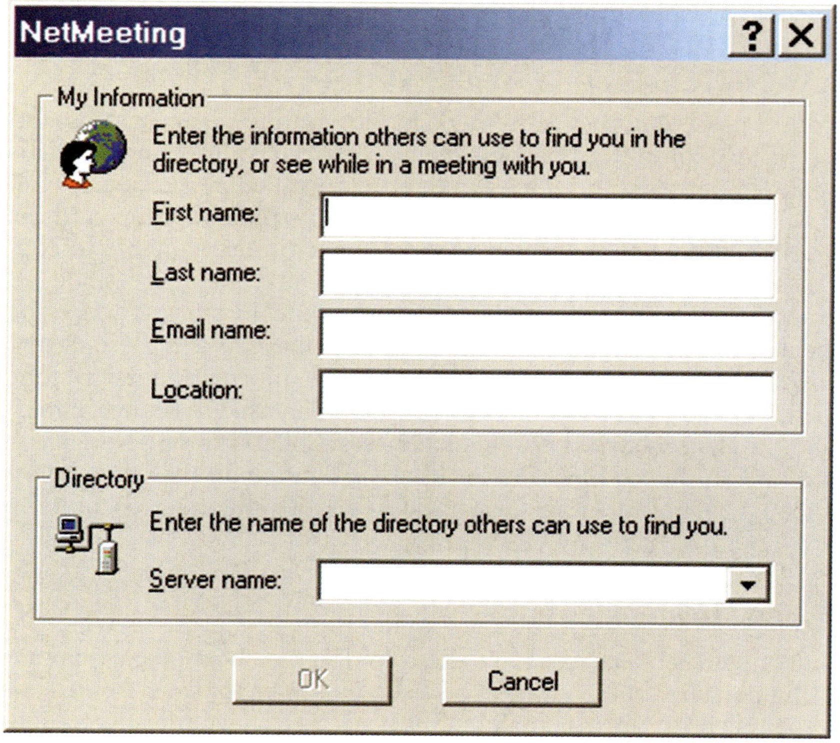

Collaborating on the Web

Microsoft Office also provides tools for collaborating on the Web. Some Web collaboration features will work on a network that supports Microsoft Office Server Extensions, but many require a server running Microsoft SharePoint Team Services. The network administrator can tell you whether these services are available to you.

Web discussions can be used to add comments to any document that can be opened with a Web browser. The discussions are threaded and display with the page in the browser. Anyone with permission to discuss a document can use the Web Discussion button on the toolbar to add general discussions about the entire document or inline discussions about a particular paragraph. These discussions are asynchronous so that participants do not have to be online simultaneously. The Web Discussions toolbar is available in Microsoft Internet Explorer 4.0 and later.

Team Web sites are designed to help groups share files, participate in discussions, and communicate effectively from the Web. Although these sites are built and accessed from Microsoft Office products, Microsoft SharePoint Team Services software must be installed on a network supporting team Web sites.

If the support software is functioning properly, creating a team Web site is simple. The New File Task Pane of any Microsoft Office product contains an Add Network Place link that initiates a wizard. A basic team site can be functioning in a few minutes. A team Web site can contain:

- Libraries of documents to share
- Discussion boards for team communication
- Web document discussions
- Announcements
- Upcoming events
- Surveys to gather data
- Shared favorites listing Web sites of interest
- Custom lists for any purpose
- Subscriptions to notify members of file and folder changes

Team Web sites can be created from any Office application and easily customized using Microsoft FrontPage. Each team member is assigned a role that determines what operations they can perform. The SharePoint team member Web site roles are:

- Browser—A member who can view pages, documents, and Web document discussions
- Discussion Participant—A member who can view pages and documents and participate in Web document discussions
- Author—A team member who can view pages, participate in Web document discussions, and modify pages, documents, or tasks
- Advanced Author—A team member who can create content, contribute to Web document discussions, change themes and borders, and update hyperlinks
- Content Manger—The team member responsible for advanced authoring tasks like managing subscription lists and Web document discussions
- Administrator—The network person responsible for managing server settings and accounts

Team Web sites are ideal for communicating information to a geographically dispersed group of people, or facilitating discussions and documenting project progress.

SESSION 8.2 — making the grade

1. Why is a simple e-mail attachment not the most effective way to send a presentation to a reviewer?
2. T F A review must be ended before applying the reviewer suggestions.
3. How are reviewer suggestions represented in the original file?
4. What is needed for a successful Web broadcast?

SESSION 8.3 SUMMARY

When creating a presentation, it is important to consider storing backups of the involved files. Backups can be simple copies of the files on a separate media. If the presentation is critical, multiple backups can be created and one stored off-site. Backups are used to restore files that become damaged due to user error or mechanical failure.

PowerPoint contains many features to make presenting on the road easier. The PowerPoint viewer will allow a presentation to be run on a computer that does not have PowerPoint installed. The Pack and Go Wizard will consolidate and packages all project files for transport. The viewer can be packaged with the files, and multiple disks can be used for a single presentation. Pack and Go can also be used to create a playlist of multiple presentations to be run sequentially. Packed presentations must be unpacked before viewing.

Macros are recorded mouse and keyboard operations that can be replayed any time the actions need to be repeated. Microsoft Office XP provides added security features including security levels and digital signatures to help protect against macro viruses. Toolbars and menus can be customized to contain options configured by the user including macros.

The default behavior of Office XP applications is updated from the Options selection of the Tools menu. Updatable categories include Print, Edit, Save, and Security.

Add-ins are special software that enhance the capabilities of an application like PowerPoint. PowerPoint add-ins can be found on the Microsoft Office Web page or from third-party vendors.

Collaborative or workgroup tools support groups of people working together. These tools range from the ability to control and track presentation review cycles to creating complex Web sites. Web broadcasts are used to present recorded presentations with audio and video over the Internet. Such broadcasts can be live or stored for on-demand review.

MOUS OBJECTIVES SUMMARY

- Set up presentations for delivery—PPT2002-7-1
- Deliver presentations—PPT2002-7-2
- Work with embedded fonts—PPT2002-7-4
- Use Pack and Go—PPT2002-7-6
- Use Workgroup Collaboration—PPT2002-8

task reference roundup

Task	Page #	Preferred Method
Package a Presentation	PP 8.4	• Open the presentation to be packaged
		• If you are saving the presentation to a storage media, insert it
		• Click the **File** menu and then **Pack and Go**
		• Make appropriate selections on each Wizard screen
		• Clicking **Other Presentations** will allow you to package multiple presentations
		• Use the **Viewer for Microsoft Windows** option to include the Microsoft PowerPoint Viewer in the package
		tip: *The option will not be available if the viewer is not installed on your computer*
Unpackage a Presentation	PP 8.6	• Insert the disk containing the presentation or connect to the shared device
		• Use Windows Explorer to locate the packaged presentation folder and double-click pngsetup.exe
		• In the Pack and Go Setup dialog box
		• Browse to the new location for the presentation
		• Click **OK**
		• To run the presentation now click **Yes,** or to run the presentation later click **No**
Create and Use a Playlist	PP 8.7	• Open Microsoft Notepad
		• Type the name of each file
		• For files in the same folder as the playlist, simply type the filename with extension
		• For files in a different folder than the playlist, type the entire path including the drive, folder, filename, and extension
		• Filenames containing spaces must be enclosed in double quotes ("")
		• Click **File,** then **Save,** provide a filename with a **.lst** file extension, and click **Save**
		• Use the Start menu to run the PowerPoint viewer
		• Click **Using Timings, if present** to automatically run the slide shows
		• In the Files of type box, click **Playlists,** click the playlist file, and then click **Show**
		• Click **Esc** to end the show
Record and Play a Macro	PP 8.9	• On the **Tools** menu, point to **Macro,** then click **Security,** and select appropriate Security Level settings and add Trusted Sources
		• On the **Tools** menu, point to **Macro,** then click **Record New Macro**
		• Select the storage location for the macro, enter the macro name in the Macro name box, and click **OK** to begin recording

POWERPOINT

task reference roundup

Task	Page #	Preferred Method
		• Perform the actions to be recorded
		• Click **Stop Recording** on the Stop Recording toolbar
Personalize Menu and Toolbar Settings	PP 8.12	• On the **Tools** menu, click **Customize**
		• Adjust Options tab settings
Customize an Existing Toolbar	PP 8.13	• Click the **Toolbar Options** arrow at the right end of the toolbar
		• Point to **Add or Remove Buttons,** and then click **Customize**
		• In the **Categories** box select the type of command to be added. For example, Macro
		• From the **Commands** box, click and drag the command to the toolbar
Prepare a Presentation for Review	PP 8.20	• Open the presentation to be reviewed
		• For each reviewer:
		• Click **Save As** on the **File** menu
		• Change the name in the **File name** box to indicate whose review copy it is
		• Change the **Save as type** to **Presentation for Review**
		• Click **Save**
		• Distribute the files to reviewers on disk or as e-mail attachments
Use Outlook to Send a Presentation for Review	PP 8.22	• Open the presentation to be reviewed
		• On the **File** menu, point to **Send To** and then click **Mail Recipient (for Review)**
		• In the e-mail that opens, enter the To and Cc e-mail addresses of your reviewers
		• Click **Send**
Review a Presentation Sent with Outlook	PP 8.24	• Open e-mail and double-click on the presentation to be reviewed
		• Edit the presentation in the normal fashion
		• Use the Comments button of the Reviewing toolbar to add comments
		• From the **File** menu click **Send,** and then click **Original Sender**
		tip: To edit the e-mail message before replying, use **Reply with Changes** on the Reviewing toolbar
Use Outlook to Combine Reviewed Presentations	PP 8.25	• Open the Outlook e-mail containing the reviewed presentation
		• Double-click the attached reviewed presentation

task reference roundup

Task	Page #	Preferred Method
		• Click **Yes** in the alert box so that PowerPoint will automatically combine the reviewed presentation with your original presentation
		• Close the e-mail and repeat the process for any other reviews
End a Review	PP 8.26	• On the Reviewing toolbar, click **End Review** **tip:** *PowerPoint automatically ends the review when you have applied reviewer changes, deleted all change markers, and saved your presentation*
Route a Presentation	PP 8.27	• Open the presentation to be routed
		• Activate the **File** menu, point to **Send To,** and then click **Routing Recipient**
		• Click the **Address** button to access your address book
		• Select the desired addresses in order of receipt
		• Close the address book
		• Type the Message text
		• Select the routing options such as Track Status and how to distribute
		• Click **Route** to start the process *or*
		• Click **Add Slip** to close the dialog box without starting the routing process
		At a later time, click **File, Send To,** and then **Next Routing Recipient** to start the routing process
Update a Routing Slip	PP 8.27	• Open the presentation to have its routing updated
		• Activate the **File** menu, point to **Send To,** and then click **Other Routing Recipient**
		• If you are the originator of the file, you can change any option
		• Use the **Address** button to add a new recipient
		• Select a recipient and click the **Remove** button to remove it from the routing list
		• Select a recipient and click the up or down arrow to change the order of receipt
		• Update the options as needed
		• If you are a recipient of the routed file, you can only change the routing order by selecting a recipient and using the up or down arrows to change its rank in the list
		• Click **Rout** to send the updated file or **Add Slip** to save the changes without sending
Send a Routed File to the Next Reviewer	PP 8.28	• Open the presentation to have its routing updated
		• Add your comments to the file

POWERPOINT

task reference roundup

Task	Page #	Preferred Method
		• Click the **File** menu option, point to **Send To**
		• Click **OK** to accept the next routing recipient
		or
		• Click **Other Routing Recipient** to send the file to someone not on the list, click **OK**, then enter the e-mail address, and click **Send**
View a Web Broadcast	PP 8.29	• To view a live broadcast, open the e-mail with the broadcast invitation and click the URL
		tip: *You can also open your browser and type the URL in the address bar*
		• To view a recorded broadcast, go to the start page provided by the presenter and click **Replay Broadcast**
Set Up a Recorded Web Broadcast	PP 8.30	• Open the presentation to be broadcast on a computer with functioning audio and/or video equipment
		• On the **Slide Show** menu, point to **Online Broadcast** and select **Record and Save a Broadcast**
		• Complete the information for the broadcast lobby
		• Click **Settings** and update the audio/video, presentation display, speaker notes, and file location
		• Click **OK**
		• Click **Record** to prepare the presentation for recording
		• Click **Start** to begin recording the broadcast
		• Narrate each slide speaking clearly and staying positioned in front of the camera, if there is one
		• Click to progress to the next slide
		• When you have recorded through all of the slides in the presentation, you will be presented with an option to Replay the Broadcast
		• Move all broadcast files to a shared folder on your intranet or to the Internet and notify your audience of the location
Start a Live Web Broadcast	PP 8.32	• Open the presentation to be broadcast on a computer with functioning audio and/or video equipment
		• On the **Slide Show** menu, point to **Online Broadcast** and select **Start Live Broadcast Now**
		• In the Live Presentation Broadcast dialog box, select the presentation, check the record option if you want a recorded copy for on-demand viewing, and click **Broadcast**
		• Enter the information to create the lobby
		• Click **Settings** and update the audio/video, presentation display, speaker notes, and file location
		tip: *A shared file location must be specified for setup to continue*
		• Click **OK**

task reference roundup

Task	Page #	Preferred Method
		• If you want to invite participants, click **Invite Audience** to send e-mails
		tip: *If you have Outlook, this will allow you to use the meeting request feature*
		• Click **Start** to begin recording the broadcast
		• Click **Start** again to begin streaming audio and video
Schedule a Live Web Broadcast	PP 8.33	• Open the presentation to be broadcast on a computer with functioning audio and/or video equipment
		• On the **Slide Show** menu, point to **Online Broadcast** and select **Schedule a Live Broadcast**
		• Enter the information to create the lobby
		• Click **Settings** and update the audio/video, presentation display, speaker notes, and file location
		tip: *A shared file location must be specified for setup to continue*
		• Click **OK**
		• Click **Schedule** in the Schedule Presentation Broadcast dialog box
		tip: *If you have Outlook, this will allow you to use the meeting request feature*
Host an Online Meeting with PowerPoint	PP 8.34	• Open the presentation to be broadcast on a computer with functioning audio and/or video equipment
		• On the **Tools** menu, point to **Online Collaboration** and select either **Meet Now** or **Schedule Meeting**
		• Complete the NetMeeting dialog box and click **OK**
		• On the Online Meeting Toolbar, click **Call Participant** and use the Find Someone dialog box to invite attendees
		• Participate in the meeting
		• On the Online Meeting Toolbar, click **End Meeting**

POWERPOINT

NOTES

chapter eight — review of terminology

CROSSWORD PUZZLE

Across

2. A computer infection stored in a macro
5. Stored keyboard and mouse operations
8. Software to allow multiple people to work on the same document
10. Settings of low, medium, and high used to enable macros
11. Used to authenticate the creator

Down

1. The Wizard that prepares presentations for transport
3. Software to facilitate working in groups
4. Used to control the sequential presentation of multiple PowerPoint files
6. Electronic equivalent of a classroom chalkboard
7. Web-based communication that does not occur in real time
8. Text messages sent over the Internet in real time
9. Used to view presentations without PowerPoint

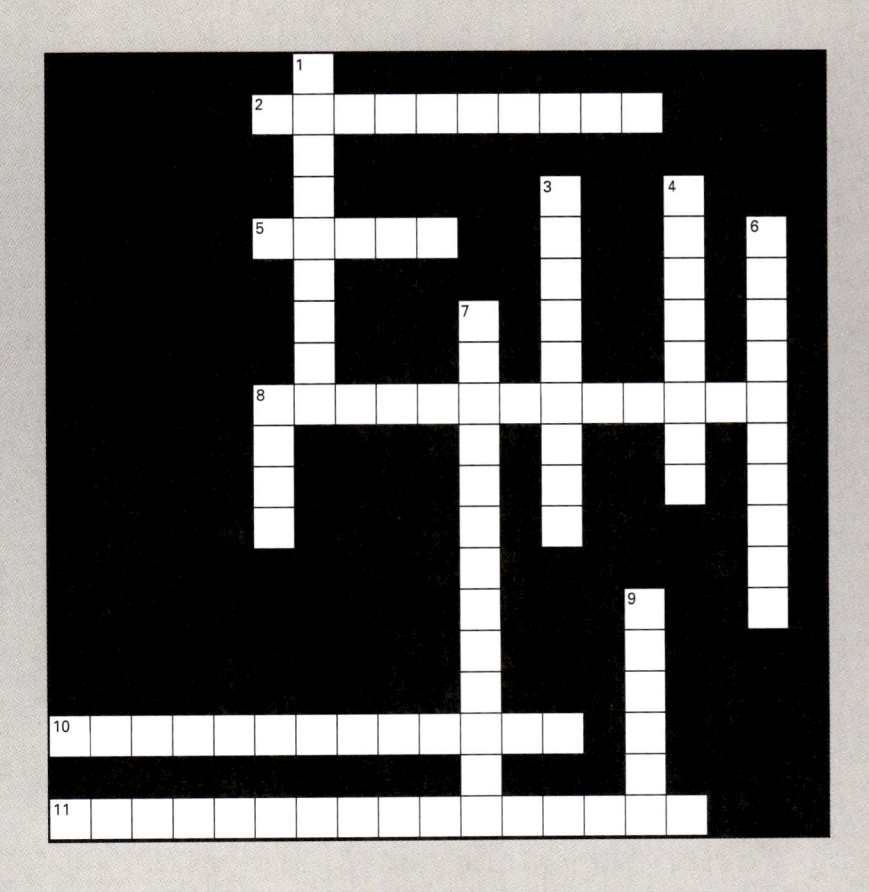

review of concepts

LEVEL TWO

chapter eight

FILL-IN

1. Web-based meetings using Microsoft NetMeeting are called _____.
2. A _____ is created in NotePad to control the order that presentations will play in the PowerPoint viewer.
3. _____ are recorded mouse and keyboard actions that can be replayed.
4. A _____ is a plan to handle things that could go wrong while presenting.
5. The default Office security level setting is _____.

REVIEW QUESTIONS

Each of the following topics should be addressed in one to three paragraphs.

1. Explain how digital signatures help to protect against macro viruses.
2. Where would you go to customize PowerPoint and what types of things can be customized?
3. Discuss the benefits of using macros.
4. Why do linked files used in a presentation need to be moved with it?
5. How are the comments from various reviewers differentiated in a routed file?

CREATE THE QUESTION

For each of the following answers, create the question.

ANSWER	QUESTION
1. PowerPoint viewer.	_____
2. Linked file and fonts.	_____
3. Controls the behavior of menus and toolbars throughout Office.	_____
4. Digital signatures.	_____
5. Add-ins.	_____

FACT OR FICTION

For each of the following determine whether the statement is fact, fiction, or both and present your arguments for that conclusion.

1. The best way to get comments on a presentation from multiple people is to e-mail each person a copy of the presentation.
2. A routed presentation must always be sent to the next reviewer on the routing list.
3. A Web broadcast allows live audio and video to be transmitted with a PowerPoint presentation.
4. All Web broadcast participants must be online simultaneously.
5. It is always a good idea to customize toolbars to match your personal preferences.

www.mhhe.com/i-series

PP 8.44

chapter eight

hands-on projects

practice

LEVEL THREE

Triathlon Training Part I

Meghan Owens is a personal trainer who specializes in exercise and nutrition programs for competitive athletes. She is a successful triathlon competitor who has trained several winning triathletes. Meghan has firsthand knowledge of what strategies work best in the months before a competition—nutrition, swimming, biking, and running. It is important for trainers to understand the unique nature of this training, so a new qualification in triathlon is being offered to degreed personal trainers. Meghan has been asked to present an overview of the program, which will be placed on the Web and used to market the new qualification to the trainers. The same program will be used to open each seminar where Meghan is the keynote speaker. She has developed a draft PowerPoint presentation, but needs help obtaining feedback on the content, preparing it for delivery, and setting up the broadcast.

1. Start PowerPoint and open **PP08TriathlonWebBroadcast.ppt**
2. Save the presentation as **<yourname>pp08TriathlonWebBroadcast.ppt**
3. Use the **Pack and Go** option of the **File** menu to package Meghan's presentation for travel on a floppy disk

FIGURE 8.23
New Toolbar with PhotoAdjust Button

4. Create a backup of the package files
5. Unpackage the presentation on another computer to verify that it will work when ported
6. Meghan has decided that some presentation graphics need to be adjusted. Develop a macro activated by a button on a custom toolbar
   a. On slide 1 select the graphic of swimmers
   b. On the **Tools** menu, pause over **Macro** and click **Record New Macro**
      i. Name the macro **PhotoAdjust**
      ii. Right-click on the selected swimmers and click **Format Object**
      iii. On the Picture tab set the Brightness to **40**, the Contrast to **70**, and click **OK**
      iv. Click off the object to deselect it
      v. Stop recording
   c. Use the **Customize** option of the **Tools** menu to create a new toolbar
      i. Select **New** on the **Toolbars** tab of the **Customize** menu
      ii. Name the toolbar **<yourname>** and click **OK**
      iii. On the Commands tab of the Customize dialog box, select Macros and then click and drag the PhotoAdjust command to your new toolbar

tip: You may need to move the Customize dialog box to see the new toolbar

      iv. Close the Customize dialog box
   d. Move to slide 2 and use the PhotoAdjust button to modify each color graphic
   e. Use the Customize dialog box to remove the new toolbar from your computer
   f. Save the presentation

www.mhhe.com/i-series

PP 8.45

POWERPOINT

hands-on projects

chapter eight

challenge

Triathlon Training Part II

Meghan Owens' triathlon slide show was introduced in the Practice project for this chapter. If you did not complete the Practice project, please do so now.

1. Start PowerPoint and open **<yourname>PP08TriathlonBroadcast.ppt**
2. Prepare this presentation for review by saving two review formatted copies. Name the first copy **PP08TriathlonReviewer1.ppt** and the second **PP08TriathlonReviewer2.ppt**
   a. Close <yourname>pp08TriathlonBroadcast.ppt
   b. Pretend that you are reviewer 1 and open that presentation. On slide 2 add a bullet to begin Nutritional regimen. Close and save the presentation
   c. Pretend that you are reviewer 2 and open that presentation. On slide 3 edit Eat between workouts to read **Eat 6-8 times per day.** Close and save the presentation
   d. Reopen <yourname>PP08TriathlonBroadcast.ppt
   e. Select Compare and Merge Presentations from the Tools menu. Review the suggested changes, but do not apply any. Save the merged presentation as **<yourname>TriathlonMerge.ppt** and close it
   f. Do not end the review so that your instructor can evaluate the reviews
3. Record and Save a Web Broadcast. You will need the ability to record sounds to successfully complete this broadcast
   a. Open **<yourname>PP08TriathlonBroadcast.ppt**
   b. Use the Notes pane to create a short script for each slide of the presentation. You will need to print this before recording
   c. Complete the setup necessary to record and save a Web broadcast with audio (video can be used if your computer has the appropriate hardware)
      i. Create a folder **PP08TriathlonTraining** and set the Web broadcast to save there
      ii. Set the Title to **Training Triathletes**
      iii. List **Meghan Owens** as the speaker
      iv. Insert your e-mail address
      v. Display the speaker notes
   d. Record the Web broadcast and replay it to verify your work. Rerecord if needed
4. Close <yourname>pp08TriathlonBroadcast.ppt

chapter eight

hands-on projects

on the web

Culinary Arts Referrals

This online referral service is headed by Sarah Silverman and opened last year in Colorado to provide evaluation and ranking of culinary arts programs nationwide. The service is funded by subscription. Each evaluated school subscribes to the service and is listed in Culinary Arts reports. The schools are ranked based on the number of kitchens, faculty, and classes given each year. You will be using PowerPoint to create a Web broadcast for potential subscribers.

1. Start PowerPoint and open **PP08CulinaryArts.ppt**
2. Use your favorite Web search engine to locate at least two cooking schools. Document the number of kitchens, the number of faculty, number of classes, and whether or not products are being sold
3. Add **Prepared by: <yourname>** as a footer for the entire presentation
4. On slide 3 add the names and URLs for the cooking schools you researched
5. Add your research to the table on slide 4
6. Add your research to slide 5
7. Update the graph on slide 6 with your research
8. Update slide 7 with your research
9. Adjust the text of slide 8 to summarize your research
10. Save the presentation as **<yourname>PP08CulinaryArts.ppt**
11. Record and Save a Web broadcast. You will need the ability to record sounds to successfully complete this broadcast
    a. Use the Notes pane to create a short script for each slide of the presentation. You will need to print this before recording
    b. Complete the setup necessary to record and save a Web broadcast with audio (video can be used if your computer has the appropriate hardware)
        i. Create a folder **PP08CulinaryArts** and set the Web broadcast to save there
        ii. Set the Title to **Evaluating Culinary Arts Education**
        iii. List **Sarah Silverman** as the speaker
        iv. Insert your e-mail address
        v. Display the speaker notes
    c. Record the Web broadcast and replay it to verify your work. Rerecord if needed
12. Collaborate with two of your classmates to create a presentation review. Save review copies and distribute them to your classmates, who must make comments. Merge the review files with your original presentation
13. Close <yourname>PP08CulinaryArts.ppt

LEVEL THREE

PP 8.47

POWERPOINT

hands-on projects

chapter eight

e-business

Balloon Adventures

Balloon Adventures was introduced in Chapter 4 where the assignment was to create a presentation that would later be converted to a Web kiosk. The kiosk has been updated with content from the remaining chapters and is now ready to be placed on the Web as a recorded Web broadcast. Additionally, the presentation needs to be packaged so that it can be transported and used as a speaker-led presentation at various gatherings where Balloon Adventures' services can be marketed.

1. Start PowerPoint and open **PP08BalloonAdventures.ppt**
2. Save the presentation as **<yourname>PP08BalloonAdv.ppt**
3. Review the slides to familiarize yourself with their content
4. Record and Save a Web broadcast. You will need the ability to record sounds to successfully complete this broadcast
   a. Use the Notes pane to create a short script for each slide of the presentation. You will need to print this before recording
   b. Complete the setup necessary to record and save a Web broadcast with audio (video can be used if your computer has the appropriate hardware)
      i. Create a folder **PP08BalloonAdv** and set the Web broadcast to save there
      ii. Set the Title to **Come Fly With Us**
      iii. List **Glenn Bachmann** as the speaker
      iv. Insert your e-mail address
      v. Display the speaker notes
   c. Record the Web broadcast and replay it to verify your work. Rerecord if needed
5. Collaborate with two of your classmates to create a presentation review. Save review copies and distribute them to your classmates, who must make comments. Merge the review files with your original presentation
6. Use the Pack and Go wizard to package this presentation and place it on a disk. Create a backup
7. Close <yourname>PP08BalloonAdv.ppt

chapter eight

hands-on projects

around the world

Holistic Health Services

Holistic Health Services is an organization that markets alternative health products through local vendors around the world. Its products include herbal and medicinal remedies, and alternative health books. Terri Lane, the director of Sales, has asked you to prepare a PowerPoint presentation for the Quarterly Sales Meeting. Terri is pleased with the improvement in this quarter's results. She believes the success is due in part to a better allocation of her sales reps' time. Travel is being reduced by holding online meetings, and support staffs have been employed to complete much of the paperwork, thereby freeing up the sales reps to focus on clients.

1. Start PowerPoint and open **PP08HolisticHealth.ppt**
2. Save the presentation as **<yourname>PP08HolisticHealth.ppt**
3. Review the slides to familiarize yourself with their content
4. Record and Save a Web broadcast. You will need the ability to record sounds to successfully complete this broadcast
    a. Use the Notes pane to create a short script for each slide of the presentation. You will need to print this before recording
    b. Complete the setup necessary to record and save a Web broadcast with audio (video can be used if your computer has the appropriate hardware)
        i. Create a folder **PP08HolisticHealth** and set the Web broadcast to save there
        ii. Set the Title to **Excellent Quarter! Let's keep it up.**
        iii. List **Terri Lane** as the speaker
        iv. Insert your e-mail address
        v. Display the speaker notes
    c. Record the Web broadcast and replay it to verify your work. Rerecord if needed
5. Collaborate with two of your classmates to create a presentation review. Save review copies and distribute them to your classmates, who must make comments. Merge the review files with your original presentation
6. Use the Pack and Go wizard to package this presentation and place it on a disk. Create a backup
7. Close <yourname>PP08HolisticHealth.ppt

LEVEL THREE

www.mhhe.com/i-series

PP 8.49

POWERPOINT

running project

Montgomery-Wellish Foods, Inc.: Presentation Skills

In Chapter 4, a slide show covering the important skills a trainee needs to acquire in order to present effectively was developed. Daniel Wellish believes presentation skills are the single most important attribute a trainee can learn. Managers, by nature, are people-oriented and must use their skills not just to prepare reports but to inspire, inform, and persuade. To the degree they can communicate clearly and cogently, they will be successful. Daniel has asked you to prepare a PowerPoint presentation outlining the skills necessary for successful Web broadcasts to the new trainees.

1. Start PowerPoint and open **PP08MWFWebPresentation.ppt**
2. Save the presentation as **<yourname>PP08WebPresentation.ppt**
3. Review the slides to familiarize yourself with their content and then update them with pertinent Web broadcasting information from this chapter
4. Record and Save a Web broadcast. You will need the ability to record sounds to successfully complete this broadcast
    a. Use the Notes pane to create a short script for each slide of the presentation. You will need to print this before recording
    b. Complete the setup necessary to record and save a Web broadcast with audio (video can be used if your computer has the appropriate hardware)
        i. Create a folder **PP08MWF** and set the Web broadcast to save there
        ii. Set the Title to **Web Broadcasting Skills**
        iii. List **Daniel Wellish** as the speaker
        iv. Insert your e-mail address
        v. Display the speaker notes
    c. Record the Web broadcast and replay it to verify your work. Rerecord if needed
5. Collaborate with two of your classmates to create a presentation review. Save review copies and distribute them to your classmates, who must make comments. Merge the review files with your original presentation
6. Use the Pack and Go wizard to package this presentation and place it on a disk. Create a backup
7. Close <yourname>PP08WebPresentation.ppt

NOTES

www.mhhe.com/i-series

POWERPOINT

NOTES

reference 1

PowerPoint File Finder

PowerPoint file finder

Location in Chapter	Data File to Use	Student Saves Data File as . . .
CHAPTER 1		
Opening a file	PP01PresntGrphx.ppt	
Views	PP01PresntGrphx.ppt	
Modifying	PP01PresntGrphx.ppt	PP01PresntGrphx.ppt
Undo and Redo	PP01PresntGrphx.ppt	
Saving	PP01PresntGrphx.ppt	<yourname>PP01PresntGrphx.ppt
Slide layout		<yourname>Blank.ppt
AutoContent		<yourname>Wizard.ppt
Editing AutoContent	<yourname>Wizard.ppt	<yourname>Wizard.ppt
Templates	<yourname>Blank.ppt	<yourname>DesignTemplate.ppt
Editing outline		<yourname>EditExercise.ppt
Slide sorter	PP01AccessFigures.ppt	<yourname>PP01AccessFigures.ppt
Inserting slides	<yourname>DesignTemplate.ppt (PP01PresntGrphx.ppt)	<yourname>DesignTemplate.ppt
Inserting notes	<yourname>DesignTemplate.ppt	<yourname>DesignTemplate.ppt
Formatting slides		<yourname>Curbside.ppt
Building a presentation		<yourname>LWSH.ppt
AutoContent		<yourname>WHHA.ppt
Design templates		<yourname>ExoticFlora.ppt
Inserting Slides	(PP01PresntGrphx.ppt)	<yourname>AGC.ppt
Design template		<yourname>MWF.ppt
CHAPTER 2		
Print preview	PP02PresntGrphx.ppt	
Adding footer	PP02PresntGrphx.ppt	
Removing footer	PP02PresntGrphx.ppt	
Adding notes	PP02PresntGrphx.ppt	
Changing slide size	PP02PresntGrphx.ppt	
Printing slides	PP02PresntGrphx.ppt	

REF 1.1

REFERENCE

REF 1.2 — **REFERENCE 1** — PowerPoint File Finder

Location in Chapter	Data File to Use	Student Saves Data File as . . .
Printing handouts	PP02PresntGrphx.ppt	
Printing notes	PP02PresntGrphx.ppt	
Printing outline	PP02PresntGrphx.ppt	
Setting default view	PP02PresntGrphx.ppt	
Expanding and collapsing outlines	PP02PresntGrphx.ppt	
Displaying outline formats	PP02PresntGrphx.ppt	
Basing presentation on another file format	(PP02Chapter2.doc)	<yourname>GettingStarted.ppt
Inserting slides from Word	(PP02PresentationBasics.doc)	
Presentation/Handouts		<yourname>MMA.ppt
Word content		<yourname>Westlake.doc
Importing Word		<yourname>wna.ppt
Design Template		<yourname>Escape.ppt
Template		<yourname>PicnicBasket.ppt
AutoContent		<yourname>gg.ppt
Notes	<yourname>mwf.ppt	<yourname>mwforient.ppt
CHAPTER 3		
Placeholder	PP03StaffingPlan.ppt	<yourname>PP03StaffingPlan.ppt
Inserting a graphic	(HeartHealth.wmf)	<yourname>PP03StaffingPlan.ppt
Moving a placeholder	<yourname>PP03StaffingPlan.ppt	<yourname>PP03StaffingPlan.ppt
Aligning text	<yourname>PP03StaffingPlan.ppt	<yourname>PP03StaffingPlan.ppt
Indentation	<yourname>PP03StaffingPlan.ppt	<yourname>PP03StaffingPlan.ppt
Character size	<yourname>PP03StaffingPlan.ppt	<yourname>PP03StaffingPlan.ppt
Font	<yourname>PP03StaffingPlan.ppt	<yourname>PP03StaffingPlan.ppt
Bullets	<yourname>PP03StaffingPlan.ppt	<yourname>PP03StaffingPlan.ppt
Bullet character	<yourname>PP03StaffingPlan.ppt	<yourname>PP03StaffingPlan.ppt
Adding text objects	<yourname>PP03StaffingPlan.ppt	<yourname>PP03StaffingPlan.ppt
Formatting text objects	<yourname>PP03StaffingPlan.ppt	<yourname>PP03StaffingPlan.ppt
Formatting placeholders	<yourname>PP03StaffingPlan.ppt	<yourname>PP03StaffingPlan.ppt
Spelling and style	<yourname>PP03StaffingPlan.ppt	<yourname>PP03StaffingPlan.ppt
Spelling	<yourname>PP03StaffingPlan.ppt	<yourname>PP03StaffingPlan.ppt
Replacing	<yourname>PP03StaffingPlan.ppt	<yourname>PP03StaffingPlan.ppt
AutoCorrect	<yourname>PP03StaffingPlan.ppt	<yourname>PP03StaffingPlan.ppt

Location in Chapter	Data File to Use	Student Saves Data File as . . .
Creating a summary slide	<yourname>PP03StaffingPlan.ppt	<yourname>PP03StaffingPlan.ppt
Viewing a slide master	<yourname>PP03StaffingPlan.ppt	<yourname>PP03StaffingPlan.ppt
Viewing a handout and note master	<yourname>PP03StaffingPlan.ppt	<yourname>PP03StaffingPlan.ppt
Applying a design template	<yourname>PP03StaffingPlan.ppt	<yourname>PP03StaffingPlan.ppt
Adjusting Slide master text formats	<yourname>PP03StaffingPlan.ppt	<yourname>PP03StaffingPlan.ppt
Customizing slide master bullets	<yourname>PP03StaffingPlan.ppt	<yourname>PP03StaffingPlan.ppt
Repositioning master indent markers	<yourname>PP03StaffingPlan.ppt	<yourname>PP03StaffingPlan.ppt
Saving template	<yourname>PP03StaffingPlan.ppt	<yourname>PP03StaffingPlan.ppt
Hiding background	<yourname>PP03StaffingPlan.ppt	<yourname>PP03StaffingPlan.ppt
Creating custom background	<yourname>PP03StaffingPlan.ppt	<yourname>PP03StaffingPlan.ppt
Applying preset animations	<yourname>PP03StaffingPlan.ppt	<yourname>PP03StaffingPlan.ppt
Taking presentation notes	<yourname>PP03StaffingPlan.ppt	<yourname>PP03StaffingPlan.ppt
Navigation	<yourname>PP03StaffingPlan.ppt	<yourname>PP03StaffingPlan.ppt
Export RTF		Meeting Minder.rtf
Bullets		NovDeptMtg.ppt
Web		WebUse.ppt
Templates		Cattery.ppt
Using other file formats	PP03DaringDesigns.doc	DaringDesigns.ppt
Presentation exercise		GPA.ppt
Presentation exercise	PP03MWF.doc	PP03MWFoods.ppt (PP03MWFoods.pot)
CHAPTER 4		
Adding clip art	PP04PhoneMinder.ppt	<yourname>PP04PhoneMinder.ppt
Reveal placeholder	<yourname>PP04PhoneMinder.ppt	<yourname>PP04PhoneMinder.ppt
Reviewing slide layout	<yourname>PP04PhoneMinder.ppt	<yourname>PP04PhoneMinder.ppt
Resizing and rotating	<yourname>PP04PhoneMinder.ppt	<yourname>PP04PhoneMinder.ppt
Adjusting image color	<yourname>PP04PhoneMinder.ppt	<yourname>PP04PhoneMinder.ppt
Inserting image	<yourname>PP04PhoneMinder.ppt	<yourname>PP04PhoneMinder.ppt
Inserting images (more)	<yourname>PP04PhoneMinder.ppt (Phones.jpg) (Gears.wmf) (Clock.wmf)	<yourname>PP04PhoneMinder.ppt
Creating WordArt	<yourname>PP04PhoneMinder.ppt	<yourname>PP04PhoneMinder.ppt
Creating WordArt objects (more)	<yourname>PP04PhoneMinder.ppt	<yourname>PP04PhoneMinder.ppt
Save art objects to media gallery	<yourname>PP04PhoneMinder.ppt	<yourname>PP04PhoneMinder.ppt

REF 1.4 — REFERENCE 1 — PowerPoint File Finder

Location in Chapter	Data File to Use	Student Saves Data File as . . .
Retrieving art objects from media gallery	<yourname>PP04PhoneMinder.ppt	<yourname>PP04PhoneMinder.ppt
Save art objects in file	<yourname>PP04PhoneMinder.ppt	<yourname>PP04PhoneMinder.ppt (Clock.emf)
Build table	<yourname>PP04PhoneMinder.ppt	<yourname>PP04PhoneMinder.ppt
Exploring layouts	<yourname>PP04PhoneMinder.ppt	<yourname>PP04PhoneMinder.ppt
Drawing tables	<yourname>PP04PhoneMinder.ppt	<yourname>PP04PhoneMinder.ppt
Linking Word table	<yourname>PP04PhoneMinder.ppt (WordTable.doc)	<yourname>PP04PhoneMinder.ppt
Adding chart	<yourname>PP04PhoneMinder.ppt	<yourname>PP04PhoneMinder.ppt
Adding data to datasheet	<yourname>PP04PhoneMinder.ppt	<yourname>PP04PhoneMinder.ppt
Exploring chart types and subtypes	<yourname>PP04PhoneMinder.ppt	<yourname>PP04PhoneMinder.ppt
Adding title and axis labels to a chart	<yourname>PP04PhoneMinder.ppt	<yourname>PP04PhoneMinder.ppt
Customizing chart objects	<yourname>PP04PhoneMinder.ppt	<yourname>PP04PhoneMinder.ppt
Building an organization chart	<yourname>PP04PhoneMinder.ppt	<yourname>PP04PhoneMinder.ppt
Adding text and formatting to an organization chart	<yourname>PP04PhoneMinder.ppt	<yourname>PP04PhoneMinder.ppt
Building radial chart	<yourname>PP04PhoneMinder.ppt	<yourname>PP04PhoneMinder.ppt
Adding text and formatting a radial diagram	<yourname>PP04PhoneMinder.ppt	<yourname>PP04PhoneMinder.ppt
Clip art	PP04TriathlonTraining.ppt (PP04RunTimes.doc)	<yourname>TriathlonTraining.ppt
Charts	PP04AHS.ppt	<yourname>PP04AHS.ppt
Charts & tables	PP04ChefSchool.ppt (PP04Kitchens.doc)	<yourname>PP04ChefSchool.ppt (<yourname>PP04Kitchens.doc)
WordArt	PP04ChefSchool.ppt	<yourname>BalloonAdv.ppt
Design template	(PP04PrelimReport.doc) (PP04HaileyLogo.wmf)	PP04PrelimReport.ppt
Art & template		<yourname>PP04MWFoodsPresentation.ppt
CHAPTER 5		
Adding transitions	PP05VitalSigns.ppt	<yourname>PP05VitalSigns.ppt
Setting transition properties	PP05VitalSigns.ppt	PP05VitalSigns.ppt
Adding automatic timings	PP05VitalSigns.ppt	PP05VitalSigns.ppt
Adding entrance animations	PP05VitalSigns.ppt	PP05VitalSigns.ppt
Adding emphasis animations	PP05VitalSigns.ppt	PP05VitalSigns.ppt

Location in Chapter	Data File to Use	Student Saves Data File as . . .
Adding exit animations	PP05VitalSigns.ppt	PP05VitalSigns.ppt
Adding dimming effects	PP05VitalSigns.ppt	PP05VitalSigns.ppt
Animating graphics	PP05VitalSigns.ppt	PP05VitalSigns.ppt
Animating a chart	PP05VitalSigns.ppt	PP05VitalSigns.ppt
Adding an animated gif	PP05VitalSigns.ppt (ekg.avi) (Gears.gif)	PP05VitalSigns.ppt
Hiding a slide	PP05VitalSigns.ppt	PP05VitalSigns.ppt
Making a self-running presentation	PP05VitalSigns.ppt	PP05VitalSigns.ppt
Adding a sound clip	PP05VitalSigns.ppt (HeartMonitor.wav)	PP05VitalSigns.ppt
Adding transition and animation sounds	PP05VitalSigns.ppt	PP05VitalSigns.ppt
Adding a CD track	PP05VitalSigns.ppt	PP05VitalSigns.ppt
Adding a narration	PP05VitalSigns.ppt	PP05VitalSigns.ppt
Adding a timed narration	PP05VitalSigns.ppt	PP05VitalSigns.ppt
Compressing graphics	PP05VitalSigns.ppt	PP05VitalSigns.ppt
MS Design Gallery Live	PP05VitalSigns.ppt	PP05VitalSigns.ppt
Hands-On Project	PP05HeapCollectors.ppt	<yourname>HeapCollectors.ppt
Challenge	PP05PlazaMall.ppt	<yourname>PP05P1azaMall.ppt
On the Web		<yourname>PP04EuroCurrency.ppt
E-Business	PP05ExoticFlora.ppt (splash jpg) (HA2.jpg) (KeaMix.jpg) (OhanuMix.jpg)	<yourname>PP05ExoticFlora.ppt
Around the World	PP05GoldenGlobe.ppt	<yourname>PP05GoldenGlobe.ppt
Running Project	PP05MWFoodsPresentation.ppt	<yourname>PP05MWFoodsPresentation.ppt
CHAPTER 6		
Changing the color scheme	PP06StatusReport.ppt	<yourname>PP06StatusReport.ppt
Using multiple color schemes	PP06StatusReport.ppt	PP06StatusReport.ppt
Customizing a color scheme	PP06StatusReport.ppt	PP06StatusReport.ppt
Deleting a color scheme	PP06StatusReport.ppt	PP06StatusReport.ppt
Adding new colors	PP06StatusReport.ppt	PP06StatusReport.ppt
Adding a gradient background	PP06StatusReport.ppt	PP06StatusReport.ppt
Adding a texture background	PP06StatusReport.ppt	PP06StatusReport.ppt

REF 1.6   **REFERENCE 1**   Access File Finder

Location in Chapter	Data File to Use	Student Saves Data File as . . .
Adding a picture background	PP06StatusReport.ppt (PP06Sunrise0il.jpg) (PP06Background2.jpg) (PP06Background2.wmf)	PP06StatusReport.ppt
Adding a mat background	PP06StatusReport.ppt	PP06StatusReport.ppt
Adding a picture bullet	PP06StatusReport.ppt	PP06StatusReport.ppt
Adding an AutoShape object	PP06StatusReport.ppt	PP06StatusReport.ppt
Adding text to an AutoShape object	PP06StatusReport.ppt	PP06StatusReport.ppt
Rotating text in an AutoShape object	PP06StatusReport.ppt	PP06StatusReport.ppt
Using the ribbon object's rotation handle	PP06StatusReport.ppt	PP06StatusReport.ppt
Adjusting the ribbon object's prominent features	PP06StatusReport.ppt	PP06StatusReport.ppt
Aligning objects	PP06StatusReport.ppt	PP06StatusReport.ppt
Using grids and guides	PP06StatusReport.ppt	PP06StatusReport.ppt
Applying 3-D effects to arrow objects	PP06StatusReport.ppt	PP06StatusReport.ppt
Exploring the 3-D Settings toolbox	PP06StatusReport.ppt	PP06StatusReport.ppt
Duplicating objects	PP06StatusReport.ppt	PP06StatusReport.ppt
Using Shift and Ctrl keys	PP06StatusReport.ppt	PP06StatusReport.ppt
Changing the shape of a lightning bolt	PP06StatusReport.ppt	PP06StatusReport.ppt
Changing the shape of multiple objects simultaneously	PP06StatusReport.ppt	PP06StatusReport.ppt
Creating and copying object fill effects	PP06StatusReport.ppt	PP06StatusReport.ppt
Adding shadows and settling line color	PP06StatusReport.ppt	PP06StatusReport.ppt
Viewing objects outside the slide area	PP06StatusReport.ppt	
Changing z-order	PP06StatusReport.ppt	PP06StatusReport.ppt
Working with grouped objects	PP06StatusReport.ppt	PP06StatusReport.ppt
Hands-on project	PP06StoryWeavers.ppt	<yourname>PP06StoryWeavers.ppt
Challenge		<yourname>PreviewSpecialists.ppt
On the Web	PP06WorldHorizons.ppt	<yourname>PP06WorldHorizons.ppt
E-Business	PP06TrekkingAssistant.ppt	PP06TrekkingAssistant.ppt
Around the World	PP06ArrowBriefings.ppt	<yourname>PP06ArrowBriefings.ppt
Running Project	PP06MWFTracking.ppt	<yourname>PP06MWFTracking.ppt
CHAPTER 7		
Navigating	PP07OrganDonor.ppt	

Location in Chapter	Data File to Use	Student Saves Data File as . . .
Insert a hyperlink	PP07OrganDonor.ppt	<yourname>PP07OrganDonor.ppt
Building second level links	PP07OrganDonor.ppt	PP07OrganDonor.ppt
Exploring the Insert Hyperlink dialog box	PP07OrganDonor.ppt	PP07OrganDonor.ppt
Setting screen tip text	PP07OrganDonor.ppt	PP07OrganDonor.ppt
Adding a link	PP07OrganDonor.ppt	PP07OrganDonor.ppt
Adding Action Buttons	PP07OrganDonor.ppt	
Linking to another PowerPoint file	PP07OrganDonor.ppt (PP07DonorPresentation2.ppt)	
Linking to an Excel file	PP07OrganDonor.ppt (PP07OrganDonorStats.xls)	<yourname>OrganDonor.ppt
Saving your Home page as a Web page	<yourname>PP07OrganDonor.ppt	<yourname>PersonalHomePage.htm
Previewing the Web site	<yourname>PP07OrganDonor.ppt	
Creating the Web site	<yourname>PP07OrganDonor.ppt	
Hands-On Project	PP07WildlifeMgmt.ppt	<yourname>PP07WildlifeMgmt.ppt
Challenge	PP07SafeFoods.ppt	<yourname>PP07SafeFoods.ppt
On the Web	PP07Heritage.ppt	<yourname>PP07Heritage.ppt
E-Business	PP07Photos.ppt	<yourname>PP07Photos.ppt
Around the World	PP07SonicStrategies.ppt	<yourname>PP07SonicStrategies.ppt
Running Project	PP07TrainingQuiz2.ppt	<yourname>PP07TrainingQuiz2.ppt
CHAPTER 8		
Packaging	PP08PhoneReport.ppt	
Recording and using a macro to format text	PP08PhoneReport.ppt	PP08PhoneReport.ppt
Adding the GradesFormat macro	PP08PhoneReport.ppt	
Removing the GradesFormat macro	PP08PhoneReport.ppt	
Creating the Custom Formats toolbar	PP08PhoneReport.ppt	
Exploring the File Properties dialog box	PP08PhoneReport.ppt	
Reviewing	PP08PhoneReport.ppt Reviewer1PP08PhoneReport.ppt Reviewer2PP08PhoneReport.ppt	Reviewer1PP08PhoneReport.ppt Reviewer2PP08PhoneReport.ppt
Applying reviews	PP08PhoneReport.ppt (Reviewer1PP08PhoneReport.ppt) (Reviewer2PP08PhoneReport.ppt)	

REFERENCE 1: Access File Finder

Location in Chapter	Data File to Use	Student Saves Data File as . . .
Sending report for review	PP08PhoneReport.ppt	
Recording a Web broadcast	PP08PhoneReport.ppt	
Hands-On Project	PP08TriathlonWebBroadcast.ppt	<yourname>PP08TriathlonWebBroadcast.ppt
Challenge	<yourname>PP08TriathlonWebBroadcast.ppt	PP08TriathlonReviewer1.ppt PP08TriathlonReviewer2.ppt <yourname>TriathlonMerge.ppt
On the Web	PP08CulinaryArts.ppt	<yourname>PP08CulinaryArts.ppt
E-Business	PP08BalloonAdventures.ppt	<yourname>PP08BalloonAdv.ppt
Around the World	PP08HolisticHealth.ppt	<yourname>PP08HolisticHealth.ppt
Running Project	PP08MWFWebPresentation.ppt	<yourname>PP08WebPresentation.ppt

reference 2

MOUS Certification Guide

MOUS Certification Guide

MOUS Objective	Task	Session Location	End-of-Chapter Location
CHAPTER 1	**Presentation Basics**		
PP2002-1-1	Create presentations, manually and using automated tools	1.2	1.38
PP2002-1-2	Add and delete slides from presentations	1.1	1.38
PP2002-2-2	Insert, format, and modify text	1.2	1.38
PP2002-4-8	Rearrange slides	1.1	1.38
CHAPTER 2	**Organizing Your Presentation**		
PP2002-1-3	Adding information to the footer area, Date/Time area, or Number area of the Slide Master	2.1	2.29
PP2002-2-1	Open a Word outline as a presentation	2.2	2.29
PP2002-5-1	Preview and print slides, outlines, handouts, and speaker notes	2.1	2.29
PP2002-6-4	Saving slide presentations as RTF outline	2.2	2.29
CHAPTER 3	**Refining Your Presentation**		
PP2002-2-2	Insert, format, and modify text	3.1	3.46
PP2002-4-1	Formatting slides differently in a single presentation	3.1	3.46
PP2002-4-1	Modifying presentation templates	3.2	3.46
PP2002-4-1	Applying more than one design template to presentations	3.2	3.46
PP2002-4-2	Applying an animation scheme to a single slide, group of slides, or an entire presentation	3.2	3.46
PP2002-4-5	Customizing templates	3.2	3.46
CHAPTER 4	**Enhancing Your Presentation with Graphics**		
PP2002-3-1	Creating tables on slides	4.2	4.41
PP2002-3-1	Adding ClipArt images to slides	4.1	4.41
PP2002-3-1	Adding charts and bitmap images to slides	4.1	4.41
PP2002-3-2	Adding bitmap graphics to slides or backgrounds	4.1	4.41
PP2002-3-3	Creating Office Art elements and adding them to slides	4.1	4.41
PP2002-3-4	Applying user-defines formats to tables	4.2	4.41
PP2002-6-1	Inserting Excel charts on slides (as either embedded or linked objects)	4.2	4.42
PP2002-6-3	Inserting Word tables on slides (as either embedded or linked objects)	4.2	4.42

REF 2.1

REFERENCE

MOUS Objective	Task	Session Location	End-of-Chapter Location
CHAPTER 5	**Creating a Multimedia Presentation**		
PP2002-4-3	Apply and customize slide transitions	5.1	5.4
PP2002-6-2	Insert and configure sound, movie, and animated gif clips	5.1–5.2	5.14, 5.22
PP2002-4-7	Using presentation rehearsal features	5.2	5.24
CHAPTER 6	**Color Schemes and Drawing**		
PP2002-3-3	Create and add Office Art elements to slides using the Drawing toolbar	6.2	6.19
PP2002-3-2	Customize slide backgrounds using bitmaps	6.1	6.15
CHAPTER 7	**Internet/Intranet Presentations**		
PP2002-4-10	Adding hyperlinks to slides	7.1	7.5
PP2002-7-5	Publish presentations to the Web (Save as HTML)	7.2	7.22
PP2002-8-4	Save a presentation as a Web page (Publish)	7.2	7.23
PP2002-7-3	Manage files and folders for Presentations	7.2	7.21
CHAPTER 8	**PowerPoint Power Features**		
PP2002-7-1	Set up presentations for delivery	8.1	8.3
PP2002-7-2	Deliver presentations	8.1	8.6
PP2002-7-4	Work with embedded fonts	8.1	8.5
PP2002-7-6	Use Pack and Go	8.1	8.3
PP2002-8	Use Workgroup Collaboration	8.2	8.19

reference 3

Task Reference RoundUp

Task reference roundup

Task	Page #	Preferred Method
Opening a PowerPoint Presentation	PP 1.5	• If the presentation you would like to open is listed in the Open a presentation list of the Task Pane, click it
		• If your presentation is not listed, click **More presentations** in the Open a presentation list of the Task pane
		• Navigate to the drive and folder containing your presentation
		• Select the presentation and click **Open**
Navigating in Normal View	PP 1.10	• Go to next slide—Using the Outline pane, click in the next slide's outline or icon
		• Go to a specific slide—Using the Slides pane, drag the scrollbox until the Screen Tips show the slide that you want
		• Move one slide at a time—Use the Next and Previous buttons at the bottom of the Slides pane scrollbar
Navigating in Slide Show View	PP 1.11	• Go to next slide—click the mouse
		• Go to the previous slide—Press **Backspace**
		• Go to a specific slide—Type the slide number and press **Enter**
		• End the slide show—**Esc**
Activating the AutoContent Wizard	PP 1.25	• With PowerPoint running select **New** from the **File** menu to activate the New Presentation Task pane
		• From the New option of the Task pane select **From AutoContent Wizard**
Getting Help	PP 1.36	• Click in the Ask A Question drop-down text box in the PowerPoint menu
		• Type in keywords relevant to your topic. Full sentences are not necessary and do not improve the performance of the search
		• Press **Enter**
		• Select from the topics provided or adjust the keywords and search again
Printing a Slide Show	PP 2.14	• From the **File** menu select **Page Setup**
		• In Slides sized for box, click the desired option—usually Letter Paper (8.5 × 11 in.)
		• Click **OK**
		• Click the **Print Preview** button from the standard toolbar
		• Use **Options** to add **Header and Footer**
		• Use **Options** to change the **Colors/Grayscale**

REF 3.1

REFERENCE

Task reference roundup

Task	Page #	Preferred Method
		• Use **Options** to select **Scale to Fit Paper**
		• Click the **Print** button
Selecting a Default View for PowerPoint	PP 2.19	• On the **Tools** menu, click **Options**, and then click the **View** tab
		• Drop down the Default view list and select a view
		• Click **OK**
Basing a PowerPoint Presentation on a File in Another Format	PP 2.23	• Open a new PowerPoint presentation
		• Use the **Open** button on the Standard toolbar to activate the Open dialog box
		• Change the Files of type drop-down list to select all files, **All Outlines**
		tip: *Using All Outlines as the File type will display all file types that are supported by PowerPoint*
		• Navigate to your file and select it
		• Click **Open**
Inserting Slides From a File in Another Format	PP 2.26	• Open a new PowerPoint presentation
		• Click the position in the presentation for the new content
		• Click the **Insert** menu, **Slides from Outline** option
		• Navigate to the file and select it
		• Click **Insert**
Using Send To	PP 2.28	• Open the document that you would like to send to an e-mail address or another application
		• Click the **Send To** option of the **File** menu
		• When sending from PowerPoint to Word, select what to send from the Send To Microsoft Word Dialog Box
		• When sending to an e-mail, you will need to select or enter a valid e-mail address
Changing the Bullet Style of a List	PP 3.14	• Move to the slide containing the list and select the list (part or all of the list may be selected)
		• On the **Format** menu click **Bullets and Numbering**
		• Do as many of the following as are needed to implement your change:
		• Select from the standard options on the Bulleted or Numbered tab
		• Select a custom color from the drop-down Color list
		• Increase/decrease the size of the bullet relative to its associated text using the Size scrollbox
		• Click the **Picture** button to use a picture as the bullet character

Task reference roundup

Task	Page #	Preferred Method
		• Click the **Customize** button to use a Wingding or other special font as the bullet character
Customizing Style and Spelling Checker	PP 3.21	• Click **Options** on the **Tools** menu and then click the <yourname>**Spelling and Style** tab
		• Click the Spelling options that you want
		• Set the **Check Style** check box
		• Click the **Style Options** button to set Style Checker options
		• On the **Case and End Punctuation** tab, select the desired options
		• On the **Visual Clarity** tab, set fonts, point sizes, bullets, and line limits
Correcting Words Marked by Spelling Checker	PP 3.22	• Edit a word with a red wavy underline to correct the spelling manually *or*
		• Right-click on a word with a red wavy underline for suggestions and then do one of the following:
		• Select the correct spelling from the list of suggestions
		• Select **Ignore All** to ignore this word in the current presentation
		• Select **Add to Dictionary** to add this word to the dictionary for all presentations
Finding Text and/or Formatting	PP 3.24	• Click the **Edit** menu and then click **Find**
		• Enter the search string and select the appropriate options
		• Click the **Replace** button to specify a replacement value
		• Do one of the following
		• Click **Find** to find the next occurrence of the Find what string
		• Click **Replace** to update the current occurrence of the Find what string with the replacement value
		• Click **Replace All** to replace all instances of the Find what string with the Replace with string
Creating a Summary Slide	PP 3.28	• Use the **Slide Sorter View** button to change to Slide Sorter View
		• Select the slides whose titles will be included on the summary slide (hold down Ctrl to select multiples)
		• On the Slide Sorter toolbar, click **Summary Slide**
Viewing Masters	PP 3.29	• On the **View** menu, point to **Master**
		• Select the Master (Slide, Handout, or Notes) that you would like to view
Apply a Preset Animation Scheme	PP 3.40	• Open the presentation to be animated
		• Use the Task pane drop-down arrow to move to the **Slide Design—Animation Schemes** panel

REFERENCE

Task reference roundup

Task	Page #	Preferred Method
		• Select the slide(s) to animate
		• Click the desired Animation Scheme If Auto Preview is clicked, a preview of the animation will play after you click. Use Play to preview the animation setting or Apply to All Slides to apply this animation to all slides in the slide show. The Slide Show button provides a full-screen preview of the show
Inserting an Image From a File	PP 4.13	• Position the cursor for insertion
		• Click the **Insert Picture** button on the Drawing toolbar
		• Navigate to the picture
		• Do one of the following:
		• Click **Insert** to embed the image
		• Click the drop-down arrow next to Insert and click **Link to File** to create a link to the picture
Inserting WordArt	PP 4.16	• Click the slide that will contain the WordArt
		• Click the **Insert WordArt** icon on the **Drawing** toolbar
		• Select a style from the WordArt Gallery
		• Click **OK**
		• Enter the WordArt text in the Edit WordArt Text dialog box
		• Apply formatting as desired to set font, size, bold, or italic
		• Click **OK**
		• Use the WordArt, shape, color, shadow
Saving an Art Object	PP 4.18	• Select the picture, WordArt, or AutoShape that you want to save
		• Do one of the following:
		• Copy your object to the clipboard and then paste it in the desired collection of the open Media Gallery. You can also set keywords for this new clip
		• Right-click the object and click **Save Picture**. In the Save dialog box, select the format, name the object, and click Save
Creating a Simple Table	PP 4.22	• Select the slide to contain the table
		• Click the **Insert Table** button on the Standard toolbar
		• Select the desired number of rows and columns by clicking the bottom right cell
Creating a Linked or Embedded Object From an Existing Word or Excel File	PP 4.26	• Click the slide that will contain the object
		• On the **Insert** menu, click **Object**

Task reference roundup

Task	Page #	Preferred Method
		• Click the **Create from file** option button
		• Click the **Browse** button and navigate to the file
		• Click the Link check box to create a linked file
		• Uncheck the Link check box to embed the file
		• Click **OK**
Creating a Microsoft Graph	PP 4.28	• Select the most appropriate content layout for the slide that will contain the chart
		• Click the **Chart** icon in the Content placeholder to activate Microsoft Graph
		• Enter the data to be charted in the datasheet with headings in the first row and column, and data in cells that can be referenced with a letter and number (A1)
		• Use the **Chart** menu to select chart type, subtype, and options
		• Right-click on any chart object to format it
		• Click the slide background to exit Microsoft Graph
Creating an Organization Chart	PP 4.36	• Select the most appropriate content layout for the slide that will contain the chart
		• Click the **Insert Diagram or Organization Chart** icon in the Content placeholder to activate Microsoft Graph
		• Select Organization Chart from the Diagram Gallery and click **OK**
		• Click in a chart rectangle to add descriptive text
		• Select a rectangle and use the Organization Chart toolbar to add coworkers, subordinates, and assistants to build the desired structure
		• Use the Layout and Design Gallery menu options to control chart organization
		• Click the slide background to exit
Creating a Diagram (Cycle, Radial, Pyramid, Venn, or Target)	PP 4.39	• Select the most appropriate content layout for the slide that will contain the chart
		• Click the **Insert Diagram or Organization Chart** icon in the Content placeholder to activate Microsoft Graph
		• Select the desired diagram type from the Diagram Gallery and click **OK**
		• Click in a chart text placeholder to add descriptive text
		• Use the toolbar to build the desired structure
		• Use the Layout and Design Gallery menu options to control chart organization
		• Click the slide background to exit

REFERENCE

task reference roundup

Task	Page #	Preferred Method
Apply a Slide Transition	PP 5.1	• Select the slide(s) the transition will be applied to **tip:** *No selection is needed if the transition will be applied to all slides*
		• From the **Slide Show** menu select **Slide Transition** **tip:** *The Task pane menu can also be used*
		Select a transition effect
Set Slide Timing while Rehearsing	PP 5.6	• Activate the timing feature
		• On the **Slide Show** menu, click **Set Up Show** • Under **Advance slides**, click **Use Timings, if present**
		• Set the time for each slide
		• On the **Slide Show** menu click **Rehearse Timings**
		• Rehearse the show to set timings automatically as you advance
		• At the end of the show, click **Yes** to accept automatic timings or **No** to start again
Adding Custom Animations to Text	PP 5.7	• In Normal view, select the text object to be animated
		• From the Task pane drop-down list select **Custom Animation**
		• In the custom Animation Task pane click **Add Effects** and select the desired effect(s)
Animating a Chart or Diagram	PP 5.13	• In Normal view, select the object to be animated
		• From the Task pane drop-down list select **Custom Animation**
		• To animate the whole object, in the Custom Animation Task pane click **Add Effects** and select the desired effect(s)
		• To animate individual chart elements
		• In the Custom Animation Task pane, select the animation applied to the chart
		• Click the down arrow and select **Effect Options**
		• On the Chart Animation or Diagram Animation tab, select an option from the Group Diagram list
Inserting a Media Clip	PP 5.15	• In Normal view, move to the slide that will contain the clip
		• Use the Slide Layout panel of the Task pane to select a layout with a media placeholder
		• Click the **Insert Media Clip** icon
		• Browse through the available selections until you find a clip that you want, click the clip, and click **OK**
		• Use Slide Show view to preview the media clip

task reference roundup

Task	Page #	Preferred Method
Hide a Slide	PP 5.16	• Select the slide to hide on the Slides tab in Normal view
		• On the **Slide Show** menu click **Hide Slide**
Create a Self-Running Presentation	PP 5.18	• On the **Slide Show** menu, click **Set Up Show**
		• Click **Loop continuously until 'Esc'**
Insert a Sound Clip	PP 5.20	• On the **Insert** menu, pause over **Movies and Sounds** and click
		• **Sound from Media Gallery** to insert a sound stored in the Microsoft Media Gallery
		• **Sound from File** to insert a sound that you have stored in a file on your computer
		• **Play CD Audio Track** to play a specific track from the CD loaded in your CD tray
		• **Record Sound** to record your own sound or narration
		• Right-click on the sound icon and use the Edit Sound Object options to customize the sound settings
		Use the Reorder buttons on the Custom Animation panel of the Task Pane to control the play order of the sound
Add Sound to a Transition or Animation	PP 5.21	The transitions and animations must be set before sounds can be added to them
		• Move to the slide where sounds will be added to transitions and/or animations
		• Activate the Task Panel pane for Slide Transitions to add a sound to a transition or Custom Animations to add a sound to an animated object
		• Use the sound drop-down list to select the sound
Select a Color Scheme	PP 6.4	• Select the slide(s) the color scheme will be applied to
		tip: *Select a Design Template before choosing a Color Scheme*
		• Use the drop-down menu of the Task pane to activate the Slide Design—Color Scheme panel
		Click a Color Scheme
Customize a Color Scheme	PP 6.8	• Use the Task pane drop-down list to activate the **Slide Design—Color Scheme** panel
		• Click the **Edit Color Schemes** link in the Slide Design—Color Scheme panel
		• On the **Standard** tab of the Edit Color Scheme dialog box, select the Standard Color Scheme to be customized
		• On the **Custom** tab, select the Color Scheme element to customize and click **Change Color**
		• Use either the Standard or Custom tab of the Background Color dialog box to select a new color
		• Click **OK**

REF 3.7

www.mhhe.com/i-series

REFERENCE

task reference roundup

Task	Page #	Preferred Method
		• Repeat the previous step for each element to be customized
		• Use the **Preview** button to view the new colors on your slide
		• Click **Apply** to permanently apply the changes
Delete a Color Scheme	PP 6.10	• Use the Task pane drop-down list to activate the **Slide Design—Color Scheme** panel
		• Click the **Edit Color Schemes** link in the Slide Design—Color Scheme panel
		• On the **Standard** tab of the Edit Color Scheme dialog box, select the Color Scheme to be deleted
		• Click the **Delete Scheme** button
		• Click **Apply**
Define a Gradient Background	PP 6.13	• Right-click on the slide to contain the gradient background
		• Click the **Background** pop-up menu option
		• Click **Fill Effects**
		• Click the **Gradient** tab
		• Select the desired gradient effects and click **OK**
		• Click either
		• **Apply to All** to set this as the background for all presentation slides
		• **Apply** to set this as the background for the selected slides only
Select a Texture Background	PP 6.14	• Right-click on the slide to contain the texture background
		• Click the **Background** pop-up menu option
		• Click **Fill Effects**
		• Click the **Texture** tab
		• Select the desired texture and click **OK**
		• Click either
		• **Apply to All** to set this as the background for all presentation slides
		• **Apply** to set this as the background for the selected slides only
Apply a Picture Background	PP 6.15	• Locate and save an appropriate picture
		• Right-click on the slide to contain the picture background
		• Click the **Background** pop-up menu option
		• Click **Fill Effects**
		• Click the **Picture** tab

task reference roundup

Task	Page #	Preferred Method
		• Click the **Select Picture** button, choose the picture file, click **Insert**, and then click **OK**
		• Click either
		• **Apply to All** to set this as the background for all presentation slides
		• **Apply** to set this as the background for the selected slides only
		• **Preview** to evaluate the effect of the background without applying it
Apply a Picture as a Bullet	PP 6.17	• Select the text or list that will contain the picture bullet
		• On the **Format** menu, click **Bullets and Numbering**, and then click the **Bulleted** tab
		• On the Bulleted tab click the **Picture** button
		• Select a picture from the Picture Bullet dialog box
		• Click **OK**
Using the AutoShape Button of the Drawing Toolbar	PP 6.19	• Select the slide that will contain the AutoShape
		• Click the **AutoShapes** menu of the **Drawing** toolbar
		• Select the shape category and then the shape to be applied
		• Click and drag on the slide surface to create the shape
Adding Text to an AutoShape	PP 6.20	• Select the AutoShape
		• Right-click the **AutoShape** and select **Add Text** from the shortcut menu
		• Type and format the text
Adding Grids and Guides to a Presentation	PP 6.25	• Use the **Toolbars** option of the **View** menu to activate the **Drawing** toolbar, if it is not already visible
		• Click the **Draw** drop-down list of the Drawing toolbar and click **Grid and Guides**
		• Adjust the Snap to, Grid, and Guide settings in the Grid and Guides dialog box, and then click OK
Adding 3-D Effects to an Object	PP 6.27	• Select the object(s) that will have 3-D effects
		• Choose the desired 3-D effects from the 3-D Style button of the Drawing toolbar
Changing the Z-order of an Object	PP 6.35	• Select the object(s) to be moved in the stack of objects
		• From the Drawing toolbar, click **Draw**, pause over **Order**, and then select the appropriate movement option
Grouping Objects	PP 6.37	• Select all objects to be grouped

REF 3.9

www.mhhe.com/i-series

REFERENCE

task reference roundup

Task	Page #	Preferred Method
		• From the Drawing toolbar, click **Draw** and then select the appropriate grouping (Group, Ungroup, or Regroup) option
Insert a Hyperlink	PP 7.6	• Select the object that will initiate the hyperlink. The object can be text, WordArt, a graphic, or any other clickable object
		• Click the **Insert Hyperlink** button in the Standard toolbar
		• Select the location of the link and then set the link options
Create and Link an Action Button	PP 7.12	• Select the slide to contain the Action Button
		• Click the **AutoShapes** button of the Drawing toolbar, pause over Action Buttons, and select the desired button
		tip: *Use the View menu to activate the Drawing toolbar if it is not already visible*
		• Click and drag the button on the slide surface
		• Click the Action Button and follow the steps to set a hyperlink
Build an AutoContent Web Page	PP 7.19	• In the PowerPoint Open Presentation Task pane, select **AutoContent Wizard**
		• Read the introductory screen and click **Next**
		• Choose the type of presentation you would like to develop and click **Next**
		• Select **Web presentation** and click **Next**
		• Enter the title and footer information and click **Next**
		• Click **Finish**
Preview a Presentation as a Web Site	PP 7.22	• Open the presentation in PowerPoint
		• Select **Web Page Preview** from the **File** menu
		tip: *This will take some time to create the pages and then display the presentation in your default browser*
		• Close the browser window when you have completed your tasks
Save a Presentation in Web Format	PP 7.23	• Open the presentation in PowerPoint
		• From the **File** menu select **Save As Web Page**
		• Use the Save As dialog box Publish button to customize the Save As settings
		tip: *Be sure to check the box to open the presentation in the browser so that you can review your results*
		• Click Publish when the settings are complete
Showing the Web Toolbar	PP 7.25	• Click the **View** menu
		• Pause over **Toolbars** and click **Web**

task reference roundup

Task	Page #	Preferred Method
		tip: *The same steps will close the Web toolbar when it is no longer needed*
Accessing Microsoft Online Support	PP 7.26	• Click the **Help** menu
		• Click **Office on the Web**
Package a Presentation	PP 8.4	• Open the presentation to be packaged
		• If you are saving the presentation to a storage media, insert it
		• Click the **File** menu and then **Pack and Go**
		• Make appropriate selections on each Wizard screen
		• Clicking **Other Presentations** will allow you to package multiple presentations
		• Use the **Viewer for Microsoft Windows** option to include the Microsoft PowerPoint Viewer in the package
		tip: *The option will not be available if the viewer is not installed on your computer*
Unpackage a Presentation	PP 8.6	• Insert the disk containing the presentation or connect to the shared device
		• Use Windows Explorer to locate the packaged presentation folder and double-click pngsetup.exe
		• In the Pack and Go Setup dialog box
		• Browse to the new location for the presentation
		• Click **OK**
		• To run the presentation now click **Yes,** or to run the presentation later click **No**
Create and Use a Playlist	PP 8.7	• Open Microsoft Notepad
		• Type the name of each file
		• For files in the same folder as the playlist, simply type the filename with extension
		• For files in a different folder than the playlist, type the entire path including the drive, folder, filename, and extension
		• Filenames containing spaces must be enclosed in double quotes ("")
		• Click **File**, then **Save**, provide a filename with a **.lst** file extension, and click **Save**
		• Use the Start menu to run the PowerPoint viewer
		• Click **Using Timings, if present** to automatically run the slide shows
		• In the Files of type box, click **Playlists**, click the playlist file, and then click **Show**

REFERENCE

REF 3.12   **REFERENCE 3**   Task Reference RoundUp

task reference roundup

Task	Page #	Preferred Method
		• Click **Esc** to end the show
Record and Play a Macro	PP 8.9	• On the **Tools** menu, point to **Macro**, then click **Security**, and select appropriate Security Level settings and add Trusted Sources
		• On the **Tools** menu, point to **Macro**, then click **Record New Macro**
		• Select the storage location for the macro, enter the macro name in the Macro name box, and click **OK** to begin recording
		• Perform the actions to be recorded
		• Click **Stop Recording** on the Stop Recording toolbar
Personalize Menu and Toolbar Settings	PP 8.12	• On the **Tools** menu, click **Customize**
		• Adjust Options tab settings
Customize an Existing Toolbar	PP 8.13	• Click the **Toolbar Options** arrow at the right end of the toolbar
		• Point to **Add or Remove Buttons**, and then click **Customize**
		• In the **Categories** box select the type of command to be added. For example, Macro
		• From the **Commands** box, click and drag the command to the toolbar
Prepare a Presentation for Review	PP 8.20	• Open the presentation to be reviewed
		• For each reviewer:
		• Click **Save As** on the **File** menu
		• Change the name in the **File name** box to indicate whose review copy it is
		• Change the **Save as type** to **Presentation for Review**
		• Click **Save**
		• Distribute the files to reviewers on disk or as e-mail attachments
Use Outlook to Send a Presentation for Review	PP 8.22	• Open the presentation to be reviewed
		• On the **File** menu, point to **Send To** and then click **Mail Recipient (for Review)**
		• In the e-mail that opens, enter the To and Cc e-mail addresses of your reviewers
		• Click **Send**
Review a Presentation Sent with Outlook	PP 8.24	• Open e-mail and double-click on the presentation to be reviewed
		• Edit the presentation in the normal fashion
		• Use the Comments button of the Reviewing toolbar to add comments
		• From the **File** menu click **Send**, and then click **Original Sender**

task reference roundup

Task	Page #	Preferred Method
		tip: To edit the e-mail message before replying, use **Reply with Changes** on the Reviewing toolbar
Use Outlook to Combine Reviewed Presentations	PP 8.25	• Open the Outlook e-mail containing the reviewed presentation
		• Double-click the attached reviewed presentation
		• Click **Yes** in the alert box so that PowerPoint will automatically combine the reviewed presentation with your original presentation
		• Close the e-mail and repeat the process for any other reviews
End a Review	PP 8.26	• On the Reviewing toolbar, click **End Review**
		tip: PowerPoint automatically ends the review when you have applied reviewer changes, deleted all change markers, and saved your presentation
Route a Presentation	PP 8.27	• Open the presentation to be routed
		• Activate the **File** menu, point to **Send To**, and then click **Routing Recipient**
		• Click the **Address** button to access your address book
		• Select the desired addresses in order of receipt
		• Close the address book
		• Type the Message text
		• Select the routing options such as Track Status and how to distribute
		• Click **Route** to start the process
		or
		• Click **Add Slip** to close the dialog box without starting the routing process
		At a later time, click **File**, **Send To**, and then **Next Routing Recipient** to start the routing process
Update a Routing Slip	PP 8.27	• Open the presentation to have its routing updated
		• Activate the **File** menu, point to **Send To**, and then click **Other Routing Recipient**
		• If you are the originator of the file, you can change any option
		• Use the **Address** button to add a new recipient
		• Select a recipient and click the **Remove** button to remove it from the routing list
		• Select a recipient and click the up or down arrow to change the order of receipt
		• Update the options as needed

task reference roundup

Task	Page #	Preferred Method
		• If you are a recipient of the routed file, you can only change the routing order by selecting a recipient and using the up or down arrows to change its rank in the list
		• Click **Route** to send the updated file or **Add Slip** to save the changes without sending
Send a Routed File to the Next Reviewer	PP 8.28	• Open the presentation to have its routing updated
		• Add your comments to the file
		• Click the **File** menu option, point to **Send To**
		• Click **OK** to accept the next routing recipient
		or
		• Click **Other Routing Recipient** to send the file to someone not on the list, click **OK**, then enter the e-mail address, and click **Send**
View a Web Broadcast	PP 8.29	• To view a live broadcast, open the e-mail with the broadcast invitation and click the URL
		tip: *You can also open your browser and type the URL in the address bar*
		• To view a recorded broadcast, go to the start page provided by the presenter and click **Replay Broadcast**
Set up a Recorded Web Broadcast	PP 8.30	• Open the presentation to be broadcast on a computer with functioning audio and/or video equipment
		• On the **Slide Show** menu, point to **Online Broadcast** and select **Record and Save a Broadcast**
		• Complete the information for the broadcast lobby
		• Click **Settings** and update the audio/video, presentation display, speaker notes, and file location
		• Click **OK**
		• Click **Record** to prepare the presentation for recording
		• Click **Start** to begin recording the broadcast
		• Narrate each slide speaking clearly and staying positioned in front of the camera, if there is one
		• Click to progress to the next slide
		• When you have recorded through all of the slides in the presentation, you will be presented with an option to Replay the Broadcast
		• Move all broadcast files to a shared folder on your intranet or to the Internet and notify your audience of the location
Start a Live Web Broadcast	PP 8.32	• Open the presentation to be broadcast on a computer with functioning audio and/or video equipment
		• On the **Slide Show** menu, point to **Online Broadcast** and select **Start Live Broadcast Now**

REF 3.15

task reference roundup

Task	Page #	Preferred Method
		• In the Live Presentation Broadcast dialog box, select the presentation, check the record option if you want a recorded copy for on-demand viewing, and click **Broadcast**
		• Enter the information to create the lobby
		• Click **Settings** and update the audio/video, presentation display, speaker notes, and file location
		tip: A shared file location must be specified for setup to continue
		• Click **OK**
		• If you want to invite participants, click **Invite Audience** to send e-mails
		tip: If you have Outlook, this will allow you to use the meeting request feature
		• Click **Start** to begin recording the broadcast
		• Click **Start** again to begin streaming audio and video
Schedule a Live Web Broadcast	PP 8.33	• Open the presentation to be broadcast on a computer with functioning audio and/or video equipment
		• On the **Slide Show** menu, point to **Online Broadcast** and select **Schedule a Live Broadcast**
		• Enter the information to create the lobby
		• Click **Settings** and update the audio/video, presentation display, speaker notes, and file location
		tip: A shared file location must be specified for setup to continue
		• Click **OK**
		• Click **Schedule** in the Schedule Presentation Broadcast dialog box
		tip: If you have Outlook, this will allow you to use the meeting request feature
Host an Online Meeting with PowerPoint	PP 8.34	• Open the presentation to be broadcast on a computer with functioning audio and/or video equipment
		• On the **Tools** menu, point to **Online Collaboration** and select either **Meet Now** or **Schedule Meeting**
		• Complete the NetMeeting dialog box and click **OK**
		• On the Online Meeting Toolbar, click **Call Participant** and use the Find Someone dialog box to invite attendees
		• Participate in the meeting
		• On the Online Meeting Toolbar, click **End Meeting**

REFERENCE

reference 4

Making the Grade Answers

making the grade

CHAPTER 1

SESSION 1.1

1. PowerPoint is a full-featured presentation graphics application that can be used to support speakers, guide the audience, or create stand-alone kiosks. Output can be printed, projected, or converted to overheads and slides.

2. Using the Slide Show view button on the View toolbar.

3. The Undo button can be used to reverse the last 20 actions. Selecting an item on the Undo list reverses that action and all actions above it on the list. The Redo button reinstates undone actions.

4. The Outline pane is used to add, edit, move, and delete slide text. The slides pane can also be used to add and edit text, but it is the only place to add and edit media elements of a presentation.

SESSION 1.2

1. A Design template contains backgrounds and colors that can be applied to an existing presentation or used to create a new presentation. Design templates are useful because they add interest to a presentation and provide a consistent look to all of the slides.

2. The AutoContent wizard is used to create a new presentation. The wizard applies a Design template and a Content template. The Content template provides suggested presentation content.

3. The indention level of a bulleted item can be changed using the Increase and Decrease indent buttons on the toolbar or using Tab and Shift+Tab.

4. There are several ways to get help on the topic of fonts, but the simplest is to type "font" in the Ask A Question text box and press Enter.

CHAPTER 2

SESSION 2.1

1. Print Preview is a visual environment that allows you to see the impact of changes you make. The limitation is that not all set-up options are available from Print Preview.

2. The header and footer contents set for notes pages use a different master and print at the top and bottom of each page regardless of how many slides are printed on a page. Slide header/footer settings are positioned by the Slide master and typically appear only on the bottom of each slide. Slide footer contents prints at the bottom of each slide, even when page headers/footers will also print.

3. Title slide is one of the PowerPoint layouts. Any slide in the presentation that has Title layout will not display the header/footer. Slides with any other layout will display the header/footer.

4. Remove a header or footer using the same dialog box that set the content. Uncheck the check boxes and delete any text. The placeholders are always present, but now have no content.

SESSION 2.2

1. Send To is an option of the File menu in Microsoft applications that will allow the user to send the current document as an e-mail or to another Microsoft application. PowerPoint can send outlines, notes, or handouts to Word for further formatting. Word can send a document to PowerPoint so that its content is added to the presentation.

2. When a bulleted item is promoted, it is moved to the left. Promoting a first level bulleted item would cause it to be a title on a new slide.

3. Expanding an outline that has been collapsed causes it to display all of the content on the slide. It has no impact on a slide that is already displaying all of its content.

REF 4.1

REFERENCE

making the grade

4. The default view controls how newly opened presentations will display. The default is customized from the Tools|Options menu, which displays a list of 10 possible default views.

CHAPTER 3
SESSION 3.1

1. Objects are anything that can be manipulated to create a PowerPoint slide. Each object can be positioned and formatted to create the look desired. Without objects, the user wouldn't have anything to look at.

2. Sizing handles allow the selected object to be resized by dragging the handle. Each object has multiple handles. When you pause over a handle, the pointer will indicate how the object can be resized using that handle. *Caution:* Resizing can distort images.

3. Text alignment controls how text is aligned within a placeholder, shape, or Text Box. For example, right aligned text will begin at the right side of the container object.

4. The Format Painter is used to retrieve formatting from text that is already formatted as you would like and then apply those formats to other text that you paint. To sue the feature, select the text with the desired format, click the Format Painter, and then select the text to be painted. Double-clicking the Format Painter will allow you to paint multiple selections with the same formatting.

SESSION 3.2

1. Summary Slides contain the titles of all the slides in the presentation. They can be used at the beginning of a presentation to introduce the topics and/or at the end of a presentation to review presented materials.

2. A template is a file that contains specifications that can be applied to any presentation including the background, text color, text font and size, placeholders, and bullet characters. Masters belong to a specific presentation and control the defaults for that presentation. When a Design Template is applied to a presentation, the Masters are created from the specifications on that template. The Masters can be customized to suit your needs and saved as another template for later use.

3. Nothing really. You can type text in the placeholder, but it will not display as a default value in slides. If you want to place default text on slides, use a Text Box or Shape control.

4. Assigning custom bullets in the Slide Master should do the trick, unless you have already customized a slide. If you have already customized a slide (which overrides the defaults set in the Slide Master), you will need to reapply the template (using the drop-down arrow) to cause such slides to conform to the new Master settings.

CHAPTER 4
SESSION 4.1

1. The format of an image file determines how readily it can be inserted into a PowerPoint slide and whether or not it can be edited once it is on the slide.

2. The green handle of a selected image allows you to rotate it so that it is no longer square.

3. The process of embedding places a copy of the original object into a slide. The copy can be modified independently of the original. Linked objects store the address of the image so that modifications in the original object are reflected in the linked object.

4. WordArt can be used to add dynamic style and impact to a few words of text. It is ideal for slide titles.

SESSION 4.2

1. Tables can be added to a slide using a content slide layout, the Insert Tables button, the Tables and Borders button, or by importing from another application. If the table exists in another application, it is easier to use it. If the table must be built from scratch, any of the methods to create a PowerPoint table is effective. Use the one that you are comfortable with and that provides the formatting options you need.

making the grade

2. The scores for each team would need to be organized with each team's data in their own row. The columns would represent the game number.

	Game1	Game2	Game3
Team1	score	score	score
Team2	score	score	score

3. Click the control box labeled 3.

4. Effectively any information that can be described using a hierarchy. For example, the playoff board of a sports tournament or the courses to be taken to obtain a specific degree.

CHAPTER 5
SESSION 5.1

1. Animation schemes are preset animations for slide text that can be applied from the Animation Schemes panel of the Task pane. Custom Animations are applied from the Custom Animation panel of the Task pane and will allow you to animate any slide object.

2. The rehearsal features will allow you to practice a presentation, but more significantly it will record timings that can be used during the presentation to automatically advance slides.

3. Kiosks are typically stand-alone presentations that are used to present information when support people are not present. Self-running kiosks can use the timings set while rehearsing so that users do not have to click through the presentation.

4. Slide objects such as images, text, and charts can be animated to add motion as they enter or leave the slide. Media clips are complete animations that can be added to a presentation from the Microsoft Media Gallery.

SESSION 5.2

1. Sound clips are inserted into a presentation and are represented by a sound icon. Inserted sounds can play automatically or based on a triggering event like a mouse click. Animation and transition sounds can only be added to animations and transitions. These sounds are very short like a chime. Sounds from external files can also be added to transitions and animations using the Other Sound selection.

2. If the track set to play exists on the CD, it will play. If the track does not exist, nothing will play.

3. Dragging the icon off the edge of a slide will leave the sound intact without displaying an icon.

4. Self-running presentations with narration on each slide are best recorded using the Slide Show menu to record the narration and set automatic slide timings. Narration for a single slide can be recorded from the Insert menu.

CHAPTER 6
SESSION 6.1

1. Intrinsic color schemes are the default color palettes assigned to each PowerPoint template. This is in contrast to custom color schemes that can be created by the user.

2. A wide variety of considerations are appropriate for this question. An overall color scheme could include bright primary colors since the presentation is for parents. Some students might feel that bright colors are inappropriate because the children are injured and choose calming pastels. The unique components of the presentation could each have a different color scheme to differentiate them. There is no absolute answer, but it is important to evaluate the impact of color on the topic and audience.

3. 8

4. The most important consideration for readable text is high contrast between the text and background. The size of the text can also have considerable impact on how easily it is read. Busy backgrounds should be matted either by formatting the slide placeholders or by adding a drawing object.

SESSION 6.2

1. Both rectangle shape objects are the same. The most commonly used

options are placed directly on the Drawing toolbar for faster access.

2. Use the Draw menu of the Drawing toolbar to access Flip options. Flip Horizontal creates a side-to-side mirror image. Flip Vertical creates a top-to-bottom mirror image.

3. Adjustment handles are visible when an adjustable object is selected. These handles allow you to alter the prominent features of the object. For example, the adjustment handles of block arrows will allow you to change the size of the arrowhead.

4. Select all three rectangles, activate the Draw button of the Drawing toolbar, pause the cursor over Align or Distribute, and click Align Left

CHAPTER 7
SESSION 7.1

1. Nonlinear navigation groups areas of the presentation by topic so the viewer can choose what to view. A presenter using a nonlinear presentation can choose how much to include on each topic as the presentation progresses.

2. Any clickable object such as text, graphics, charts, WordArt, and images can contain hyperlinks.

3. Select the object, click the Insert Hyperlink button, and then click the Remove Hyperlink button.

4. Hyperlinks can take you to another page in the current document, to another local document, or to Web resources.

SESSION 7.2

1. If you are familiar with PowerPoint, it is simple to create a presentation and save it in a Web format. Additionally, publishing to the Web is a good way to share the content of your presentation with a wider audience and Web pages are highly portable.

2. The intended audience determines where it is appropriate to publish. Intranets are typically for publications within an organization, while the Internet is for a broader audience.

3. Microsoft Internet Explorer 4.0 or higher provides the best browsing results.

4. PowerPoint does not have any facilities for directly editing the generated HTML. The only way to make changes from PowerPoint is to open the HTML file, edit it as a presentation, and then resave it to a Web format. You can also use a dedicated editor like FrontPage.

CHAPTER 8
SESSION 8.1

1. A backup copy of a presentation should be stored on a different media and, for critical files, in a different location. Backups are important to protect against accidental user errors like mistake updates to the file as well as mechanical failures like a bad disk drive.

2. The PowerPoint viewer is software that can be bundled with a presentation to allow it to run on any computer. PowerPoint does not have to be installed on the presentation computer when the viewer is used.

3. Packaging is the simplest way to ensure that all necessary files including fonts, graphics, and sounds are transported. It will also place files that are too large for a single disk on multiple disks and can be used to include the PowerPoint viewer in the package.

4. Macros store keystrokes and mouse operations to complete a task. Once these are stored, running the macro will repeat them, saving time and ensuring continuity. More interface steps are saved by attaching a macro to a toolbar button where it is activated in one mouse click rather than stepping through the Tools menu options.

5. The Customize dialog box is used to set options for toolbars and menus. The Options dialog box changes default settings of the application related to print, save, editing, and other common tasks.

SESSION 8.2

1. Simple e-mail attachments do not have any services to track or remind reviewers.

making the grade

2. False. Once the review has been terminated, no more revisions can be applied to the original file.

3. Reviewer suggestions appear as icons in the original file with the details in the Task pane.

4. The minimum requirements for Web broadcasting are PowerPoint 2002 and Internet Explorer 5.1 or later. If you want to broadcast live with audio, video, or both, you will need a video camera and microphone properly connected to your presentation computer.

glossary

Absolute links: Links that contain complete addresses to the resource.

Action buttons: Ready-made buttons used to provide navigation such as next, previous, first, and last. The action is controlled by adding a hyperlink.

Adjustment handles: The gold handles of a selected object that allow the prominent feature of the object to be adjusted. Not all objects can be adjusted.

Animation: Motion added to a presentation object.

Animation Schemes: Preset combinations of slide transitions and text animations.

AutoContent wizard: A wizard that will create a presentation with suggested content based on a series of questions answered by the user.

AutoCorrect: The facility that makes corrections to common mistakes as you type.

AutoFit: The facility that causes text to reduce its size to fit within a placeholder.

Backspace: The keyboard key used to move backwards through text deleting one character to the left of the cursor for each backspace.

Bitmap: A type of image composed of small dots of color. Also called a raster image.

Blank presentation: One method of creating a new presentation. When this option is used, the presentation has no background or color selections applied.

Bold: Text property that causes text to appear darker.

Bookmark: Used to mark a specific page or location within a file for linking.

Broken hyperlinks: Hyperlinks that do not work because the document is not at the indicated address.

Chat: Real-time Web-based communication that is typically accomplished by typing messages, but can include voice communication.

Clip art: Drawings that can be added to documents, including those in the Microsoft Media Gallery.

Clip Organizer: *See* Microsoft Clip Organizer

Collaborative meetings: Usually online meetings used to facilitate collaboration of groups who can't have face-to-face meetings due to time or geographic constraints.

Color scheme: The palette that controls default color values for the slide background, body text, lines, shadows, title text, fills, hyperlinks, and accents.

Control boxes: The gray boxes above and to the left of the cells in a datasheet that are used to select rows and columns.

Copyright law: The laws that give the person who owns a work the rights to control how the work is used.

Copy: Placing a duplicate of the selection on either the Windows Clipboard or the Office Clipboard so that it can be pasted in another location. This can be accomplished using the Standard toolbar's Copy button or from the Edit menu. See also Cut and Paste.

Custom animation: The pane of the Task panel that allows you to fully control object animation in a presentation.

Cycle diagram: One of the diagrams available in Microsoft PowerPoint that is used to show cyclical processes such as the water cycle.

Data series: The numbers of one group to be graphed in the same color or line. For example, the total sales values for each month of the year would be a data series.

Data value: The contents of one cell in a datasheet.

Datasheet: The rows and columns that hold the data for Microsoft Graph.

Default view: The view that will be used to open presentations. Set with the View tab of the Tools|Options menu.

Del: The keyboard key used to delete the character to the right of the cursor.

Design template: Templates that contain backgrounds and color selections that can be applied to a new or existing presentation.

Digital signatures: Information embedded in a file identifying the creator and the validity of the source. Digital signatures present as certificates to allow the user to decide whether or not to trust this source.

Dimming effect: The animation effect that causes an animated object to change color after the animation.

Dotted-line selection box: Selection border indicating that an object can be operated.

Drawing: Toolbar containing graphic objects that normally appear at the bottom of a screen.

Drawing toolbar: The toolbar with tools to draw lines, shapes, and other graphic objects. Typically displayed at the bottom of the screen.

Drawn pictures: A type of image created using calculated shapes so that they have small file sizes and resize well. Also called vector graphics.

Embedded: A method of placing a copy of an image or other objects into a document with no connection to the original file.

Embedded: When a file created in an external application is stored in PowerPoint, for example, an embedded voice narration file.

Expand All button: The toolbar button used to expand and collapse outlines.

Export: Sending data from the current application to another application. For example, using the Send To option of the File menu to send a PowerPoint outline to Word.

File converters: Programs that convert documents created in one application so that they are compatible with another. For example, converting a PowerPoint outline to Word format.

File transfer protocol (FTP): Software applications used to move files from a local computer to a Web server.

Font: The type face property of text.

Footer: Content to print in the bottom margin of a document.

Format Painter: Tool used to copy formats from text to be painted on other selections.

Formatting toolbar: The toolbar with options to format text, graphics, and slides.

Frames: A Web page that has multiple windows. Each window is a frame and displays a different HTML document.

Grayscale: A printing option that will print a color presentation in shades of gray.

Grids: Evenly spaced lines that display on the slide to help size and align objects. Grids are controlled from the Draw menu of the Drawing toolbar and do not display or print with the slide show.

Grouping: The ability to combine multiple objects into a single object. Grouped objects can be manipulated as one object, or each component can have individual properties set.

Guides: User positioned lines that display on the slide to help size and align objects.

Hanging indent: A style of paragraph indention where the first line is farther left than the rest of the paragraph.

Header: Content to print in the top margin of a document.

Home page: The opening page of a Web site that typically contains a list of available services, topics, and features.

HTML: See hypertext markup language.

HTML tags: HTML instructions enclosed in <> such as <b> or <i>.

Hypertext markup language: A tag based language used to describe to browsers how a Web page should be displayed. For example, <i>Hello</i> would display *Hello*.

Hyperlink: A clickable object that links to another point in the current document or to another document.

Hyperlink base: The common location used for all linked files of a project.

Importing: Moving content from another application into the current document.

Indent markers: Markers on the rule that control the placement of bullets and text.

Internet: A network of privately owned computers designed to share documents and services worldwide.

Internet search engine: Any of a group of Web products designed to search the Web based on the criteria that you enter, for example, Yahoo!, WebCrawler, AskJeeves, and so on.

Internet service providers (ISPs): Organizations that provide access to the Internet and Web services.

Intranets: Networks providing services within an organization similar to those provided by the Internet.

Intrinsic color schemes: Color schemes that are shipped with a particular PowerPoint template.

Intrinsic sounds: Sounds that ship as part of the Microsoft Office Media Gallery.

ISP: See Internet service providers.

Italic: Text property used for emphasis resulting in right-slanting text.

Keywords: Descriptive words used to locate clips in the media gallery.

Kiosk: A self-running slide show that can include custom animations, a recorded narration, and protects against presentation update.

License agreement: A legal agreement that outlines how copyrighted materials can be used.

Linked: When a link to an external file is used to display its contents in a PowerPoint presentation. For example, a linked voice narration file is separate from the presentation. A method of displaying images and other objects in a document using a link to the original file.

Local server: A computer providing services to an organization's local area network.

Macro: A facility used to store keystrokes and mouse operations so they can be replayed.

Macro security levels: Microsoft Office XP security features designed to verify the source of macros and reduce the risk of macro viruses.

Macro virus: A computer virus stored in a macro and spread by sharing the infected file.

Matting: Placing a solid background behind text to differentiate it more clearly from a busy background.

Media clip: Members of the Microsoft Media Gallery including sounds, animations, movies, pictures, and clip art.

Meeting Minder: Allows the presenter to take notes and track action items during a presentation.

Microsoft Clip Organizer: A collection of media clips (pictures, clip art, sounds, and animations) that installs with Office.

Navigation bar: Navigation controls such as next and previous added to a presentation saved as a Web page.

Normal view: The view most often used to develop presentations consisting of the Outline, Slide, and Notes panes.

Notes pane: The Normal view pane that allows you to add notes to a slide that will not be seen as part of the presentation. Typically these are printed as speaker's notes.

Object: Anything that can be manipulated on a slide.

Organization chart: One of the diagrams available in Microsoft PowerPoint that is used to show hierarchical relationships such as the management structure of an organization.

Outline pane: The Normal view pane that contains the Outline and Slides tabs. It is most often used to enter and edit text.

Outline view: A customization of PowerPoint's Normal view featuring the Outline pane.

Outlining toolbar: A special PowerPoint toolbar designed to work with outlines. Activate it from the View|Toolbars menu.

Pack and Go Wizard: The PowerPoint wizard used to prepare presentations for transport. The wizard ensures that all necessary files, including fonts and the viewer, are packaged. The wizard will also organize large presentations on multiple disks.

Page orientation: Setting that controls whether output is printed in landscape or portrait.

Page Setup: The dialog box used to select page orientation, slide number, and slide size when printing a presentation.

Palette: The selection of available colors that displays on color menus. Custom colors can be added to the palette.

Paste: The paste operation places the contents of the clipboard at the active cursor location. See also Copy and Paste.

Pen tool: Tool available during a presentation to annotate slides.

Playlists: The instructions followed by the PowerPoint viewer to play multiple presentations sequentially.

Point size: The height measurement of text size.

PowerPoint viewer: A software application used to display PowerPoint presentations on computers without PowerPoint loaded. The viewer is also capable of sequentially playing multiple presentations based on a playlist.

Print dialog box: The dialog box accessed from the File menu to select and customize printer options.

Print Preview: A "what you see is what you get" (wysiwyg) environment displaying documents exactly as they will print.

Print range: The page or pages to be printed as defined in the Print dialog box.

Properties: Settings that control how an object looks or behaves like font. The attributes that can be set to control object behavior, for example, the speed and type of transition.

Pyramid diagram: One of the diagrams available in Microsoft PowerPoint that is used to show foundational relationships like progressive levels of mathematics.

Radial diagram: One of the diagrams available in Microsoft PowerPoint that is used to show multiple relationships to a central element like multiple reports generated from the same data.

Raster image: A type of image composed of small dots of color. Also called a bitmap.

Redo: A button on the Standard toolbar that will reinstate actions that have been undone. *See also* Undo.

Regroup: Causing ungrouped objects to become a group or single object again.

Relative links: Links that use a default value for part of the resource address. For example, when only a filename is included, the drive, path, and folder of the current file is assumed to complete the address.

Rich text format: A file format commonly used in word processing applications capable of storing text, graphics, and their formats.

Rotation handle: The green handle above a selected image that will allow you to rotate the image.

Screen Tips: Text descriptions of screen elements that appear when the mouse pointer is paused over them.

Shadow: Property that places a shadow on a character.

Shapes tool: Tools on the Drawing toolbar used to place shapes like rectangles on a slide.

Sizing handles: White circles in a selection border that can be used to resize an object.

Slanted-line selection box: Selection border indicating that the contents of an object can be edited.

Slide Master: Sets the formats, placeholders, and backgrounds that will be used as the presentation default.

Slide layout: A pattern of text and media that control what can be entered on a slide. Slide layout is selected from the Slide Layout panel of the Task pane and can be updated at any time.

Slide pane: The pane of Normal view that displays a slide as it will appear during the presentation. Most often used to add and modify media elements of a presentation.

Slide Placeholders: The areas where text or media can be entered on a slide. Slide layout controls what placeholders are visible on a particular slide.

EOB 1.3

GLOSSARY

Slide show view: The view used to preview a presentation. Each slide fills the screen. No editing is possible in this view.

Slide sorter view: The view consisting of thumbnails of the presentation. Ideal for reorganizing the slides and adding transitions and animations.

Slide timings: The time that a slide will remain on the screen when the slide show is set to advance using timings. Timings can be set manually or while rehearsing the show.

Slide transition: The visual effect like dissolve or fade that ushers a slide onto the screen.

Slide transition: Controls how a slide enters and leaves the screen.

Slides tab: The tab that displays thumbnails of the presentation in the Outline pane of PowerPoint's Normal view.

Slide-title master pairs: The two slides that make up the slide master—the title slide and the body slide master.

Spelling Checker: Facility that places red wavy underlines under words that are not found in the dictionary.

Standard toolbar: The toolbar that is common to most Windows applications with options to save, print, cut, copy, and paste.

Style Checker: Facility that warns the developer of style rules violations.

Style rules: Style rules set the parameters for punctuation, fonts, number of bullets, and so on, that are used by the style checker to review the style of a presentation.

Target diagram: One of the diagrams available in Microsoft PowerPoint that is used to show steps toward a goal.

Task pane: A window used to access important tasks conveniently without leaving your document

Text animation: Effects that control how text enters and leaves a slide.

Text Box: The object that holds text and is added to a slide from the Drawing toolbar.

Title Master: The master that sets the default format for title slides.

Toggle button: Buttons that apply and remove properties. For example, the Bold button on the toolbar.

Toolbar: A horizontal or vertical ribbon of icons used to accomplish application tasks like save a file, change the font, and adjust paragraph identation.

Transparencies: Printing on transparent slides to be used with an overhead projector.

Underline: A format that applies an underline to the selected text.

Undo: A button on the Standard toolbar that will allow you to reverse up to 20 actions. See also Redo.

Ungroup: Returning a grouped object to its original state of individual objects.

Uniform resource locator: The address of a Web page or other Web resource.

URL: See uniform resource locator

Vector graphics: A type of image created using calculated shapes so that they have small file sizes and resize well. Also called drawn pictures.

Venn diagram: One of the diagrams available in Microsoft PowerPoint that is used to show overlapping relationships like two sets of data that share some values.

View: The current view controls what panes and operations can be accomplished. Normal, Slide Sorter, and Slide Show views are each designed to support a specific part of presentation development.

View toolbar: The toolbar used to move between PowerPoint views. Typically displayed at the bottom of the Outline pane in Normal view.

Web browser: Software application like Microsoft Internet Explorer and Netscape Navigator used to view Web pages.

Web discussions: A Web-based forum used to discuss Web pages viewed in Microsoft Internet Explorer 4.0 or later and set to allow discussion. Participants must have permission to join the discussion.

Web pages: Pages formatted with HTML for delivery through the World Wide Web or a local intranet.

Web server: A computer that provides access to and from the World Wide Web and Internet.

Web site: A group of Web pages published to be used together. A home page typically provides a starting point with a menu of available topics.

Whiteboard: A Web-based writing space used to present information to a group like a whiteboard in a classroom.

Workgroup software: A category of software designed to facilitate working in groups, for example, software to manage a review cycle or track edits to a shared document.

World Wide Web: A worldwide network of hyperlinked documents.

X-axis: The axis of a chart that identifies the data values of a series. For example, the days of the week. Usually the horizontal axis.

Y-axis: The axis of a chart that quantifies the values being charted.

Z-order: The order that objects are stacked as they are added to a slide. The first object added is closest to the slide.

Glossary for Common Microsoft Office XP Features

Access 2002: A relational database tool that can be used to collect, organize, and retrieve large amounts of data. With a database you can manipulate the data into useful information using tables, forms, queries, and reports.

Answer Wizard: Located in the Microsoft Help dialog box, it provides another means of requesting help through your application.

Application: A program that is designed to help you accomplish a particular task, such as creating a slide-show presentation or creating a budget.

Ask a Question: A text box located in the top-right corner of your window, it is perhaps the most convenient method for getting help.

Clipboard: A temporary storage location for up to 24 items of selected text that has been cut or copied.

Clippit: The paper clip office assistant.

Excel 2002: An electronic spreadsheet tool that can be used to input, organize, calculate, analyze, and display business data.

F1: The robot office assistant.

Formatting toolbar: Collection of buttons that allows you to change the appearance of text, such as bold, italicize, or underline.

FrontPage 2002: A powerful Web publishing tool that provides everything needed to create, edit, and manage a personal or corporate Web site, without having to learn HTML.

Integrated application suite: A collection of application programs bundled together and designed to allow the user to effortlessly share information from one application to the next.

Links: The Cat office assistant.

Menu bar: Displays a list of key menu options available to you for that particular program.

Office Assistant: Character that will appear ready to help you with your question.

Office XP: The newest version of the popular Microsoft integrated application suite series that has helped personal computer users around the world to be productive and creative.

Outlook 2002: A desktop information management tool that allows you to send and receive email, maintain a personal calendar of appointments, schedule meetings with co-workers, create to-do lists, and store address information about business/personal contacts.

Paste Options button: Button that appears when you paste into your document. When clicked it will prompt the user with additional features such as allowing you to paste with or without the original text formatting.

PowerPoint 2002: A popular presentation tool that allows users to create overhead transparencies and powerful multimedia slide shows.

Professional edition: Office XP version that includes Access, in addition to the Standard version of Word, Excel, PowerPoint, and Outlook.

Professional Special edition: Office XP version that includes Access, FrontPage, and Publisher, in addition to the Standard version of Word, Excel, PowerPoint, and Outlook.

Publisher 2002: A desktop publishing tool that provides individual users the capability to create professional-looking flyers, brochures, and newsletters.

Rocky: The dog office assistant.

Smart tag button: Buttons that appear as needed to provide options for completing a task quickly.

Standard edition: Office XP version that consists of Word, Excel, PowerPoint, and Outlook.

Standard toolbar: Collection of buttons that contains the popular icons such as Cut, Copy, and Paste.

Task pane: This window allows you to access important tasks from a single, convenient location, while still working on your document.

Title bar: Located at the top of each screen, it displays the application's icon, the title of the document you are working on, and the name of the application program you are using.

Toolbar: A collection of commonly used shortcut buttons.

Word 2002: A general-purpose word-processing tool that allows users to create primarily text-based documents, such as letters, résumés, research papers, and even Web pages.

index

a

Absolute links, PP 7.14, EOB 1.1
Access 2002, OFF 1.2, EOB 2.1
Accounting meeting presentation (project), PP 3.51
Action buttons, PP 7.11–7.14, 7.36, EOB 1.1
Add-ins, PP 8.17–8.19
Add Network Place, PP 8.35
Address book, PP 8.23
Adjustment handles, PP 6.20, 6.23–6.24, EOB 1.1
Administrators, PP 8.35
Advanced authors, PP 8.35
Advanced Timeline, PP 5.12
Alignment
 of objects, PP 6.24–6.26
 of text, PP 3.8–3.9
Anchored toolbars, PP 1.7
Animation Schemes, PP 3.40–3.42, EOB 1.1
Animations, PP 1.12, 1.13, 3.54, 5.3–5.19, EOB 1.1
 of chart objects, PP 5.13–5.14
 custom, PP 5.6–5.10, 5.13, EOB 1.1
 and dimming effects, PP 5.10–5.11
 of graphic objects, PP 5.11–5.12
 of slide objects, PP 5.3–5.16
 and slide timings, PP 5.5–5.6
 and slide transitions, PP 5.3–5.6
 of text, PP 5.6–5.11
 using media clips, PP 5.14–5.16
Annotating (slides), PP 3.44–3.45
Answer Wizard, OFF 1.8, PP 1.36, EOB 2.1
Application, OFF 1.2, EOB 2.1
Art, PP 4.3–4.22, 5.30–5.31
 clip art, PP 4.4–4.12
 custom, PP 6.18–6.39
 in files, PP 4.12–4.15
 picture types, PP 4.3
 saving art objects, PP 4.18–4.21
 WordArt, PP 4.15–4.18
Ask a Question, OFF 1.8, PP 1.36, 7.26, EOB 2.1
Atmospheric detection device presentation (project), PP 7.37
Attributes, object, PP 6.32, 6.39
Audio components, PP 5.19–5.27
 from CD's, PP 5.22–5.23
 equipment needed for, PP 5.19
 inserting, PP 5.19–5.27
 intrinsic sounds, PP 5.21–5.22
 narration, PP 5.24–5.27
 and order of multiple sounds, PP 5.25, 5.27
 sound files, PP 5.22–5.23
 sources for, PP 5.19
 and stop/delete sound objects, PP 5.24
Authors, PP 8.35
AutoContent wizard, PP 1.19, 1.25–1.29, 1.45, 1.47, 2.37, 7.19, EOB 1.1
AutoCorrect, PP 3.25–3.27, EOB 1.1
AutoFit, PP 3.25, EOB 1.1
AutoPreview, PP 5.4
AutoRecover, PP 1.18
AutoShape, PP 3.18–3.19, 6.19–6.22, 6.31–6.32
.avi files, PP 5.15–5.16

b

Background objects, PP 6.34–6.35
Backgrounds
 color of, PP 3.39–3.40
 customizing, PP 6.12–6.18
 gradient, PP 6.12–6.14
 hiding, PP 3.38–3.39
 matting, PP 6.16–6.17
 picture, PP 6.15–6.16
 printing, PP 6.7
 texture, PP 6.14–6.15
Backspace key, PP 1.32, EOB 1.1
Backup planning, PP 8.3–8.4
Balloon rides (projects), PP 4.50, 8.48
Bitmaps, PP 4.3, EOB 1.1
Blank presentations, PP 1.19–1.25, EOB 1.1
 indention of bullets in, PP 1.23–1.24
 opening, PP 1.19–1.20
 slide layout in, PP 1.20–1.21
 slide placeholders in, PP 1.21–1.23
 splitting list into two slides, PP 1.24–1.25
Bold, PP 3.11, EOB 1.1
Bookmark, PP 7.15, EOB 1.1
Bring Forward, PP 6.36
Bring to Front, PP 6.36
Broadcast Settings dialog box, PP 8.31
Broadcasts, Web, *see* **Web broadcasts**
Broken hyperlinks, PP 7.10, EOB 1.1
Browsers, Web, PP 8.35, EOB 1.4
Bullets, PP 3.9–3.11, 3.14–3.16
 cat web site (project), PP 3.53
 curbside recycling (project), PP 1.43
 in Design Masters, PP 3.35–3.37
 environmental alliance (project), PP 3.55
 exotic flora (project), PP 1.46
 games proposal (project), PP 2.37
 indention of, PP 1.14, 1.23–1.24, 1.32, 3.9–3.11
 meeting presentation (project), PP 1.44, 3.51
 Montgomery-Wellish Foods, Inc. (project), PP 2.38, 3.56
 picnic importers (project), PP 2.36
 pictures as, PP 6.17–6.18
 in Slide panes, PP 1.31
 splitting bulleted list into two slides, PP 1.24–1.25

c

Cameras, PP 5.30
Case, changing, PP 3.12
Cat web site (project), PP 3.53
Category, animation of, PP 5.13
CD's, audio from, PP 5.22–5.23, 5.26
Character formats, PP 3.11
Chart objects, animation of, PP 5.13–5.14
Charts and graphs, PP 4.27–4.40
 customizing of, PP 4.31–4.35
 diagrams, PP 4.38–4.40
 organization charts, PP 4.35–4.38, EOB 1.3
 radial charts, PP 4.38–4.40
 text in, PP 4.35
 titles and axis labels for, PP 4.32–4.34
 triathlon (project), PP 4.47
 types of, PP 4.29–4.30, 4.35
 updating data in, PP 4.30–4.31
Chat, PP 8.33, 8.34, EOB 1.1
Chat room, PP 8.31
Clip art, PP 4.4–4.12, EOB 1.1
 balloon rides (project), PP 4.50
 color changes for, PP 4.8–4.10
 formatting, PP 4.8–4.10
 inserting, PP 4.4–4.8
 keywords, PP 4.11–4.12
 placing images from, PP 4.10–4.11
 scaling, PP 4.8, 4.9
 stacking images, PP 4.11
 triathlon (project), PP 4.47
Clip Organizer, PP 5.14, 5.19, 5.30
Clipboard, OFF 1.5, EOB 2.1
Clippit, OFF 1.8, EOB 2.1
Collaboration, *see* **Online collaboration**
Collaborative meetings, PP 8.33, EOB 1.1
Collapsing outlines, PP 2.21
Color
 background, PP 3.39–3.40
 of clip art, PP 4.8–4.10
 customizing color menu, PP 6.11–6.12
 for printing, PP 2.13
Color schemes, PP 6.3–6.18, EOB 1.1
 applying, PP 6.6
 considerations for, PP 6.5
 copying, PP 6.9–6.10
 customizing, PP 6.7–6.9, 6.11–6.12
 deleting, PP 6.10–6.11
 for hyperlinks, PP 7.7, 7.10
 intrinsic, PP 6.3–6.7, EOB 1.2
 multiple, PP 6.5–6.6
 for notes pages/handouts, PP 6.7
 of slide backgrounds, PP 6.12–6.18
Compression of media, PP 5.28
Content manager, PP 8.35
Control boxes, PP 4.30, EOB 1.1
Cooking school (project), PP 4.49
Copy/copying, PP 2.23, EOB 1.1
 color schemes, PP 6.9–6.10
 files, PP 2.23
 WordArt, PP 4.17–4.18
Copyright law, PP 5.30, EOB 1.1
Ctrl key, PP 6.29–6.30
Culinary arts schools (project), PP 8.47
Curbside recycling (project), PP 1.43
Custom animation, PP 5.6–5.10, 5.13, EOB 1.1
Customizing
 backgrounds, PP 6.12–6.18
 color menu, PP 6.11–6.12
 color schemes, PP 6.7–6.9
 file properties, PP 8.16–8.17
 menus, PP 8.13
 objects, PP 6.20–6.24
 toolbars, PP 8.13–8.16, 8.45
 Web pages, PP 7.22, 7.24–7.25
Cycle diagrams, PP 4.39, EOB 1.1

d

Data labels, PP 4.33
Data series, PP 4.29, 5.13, EOB 1.1
Data value, PP 4.29, EOB 1.1
Datasheet, PP 4.29, 4.31, EOB 1.1
Date, in headers/footers, PP 2.7, 2.8
Decision-making seminar (project), PP 6.49
Default view, PP 2.19–2.21, EOB 1.1
Defaults, changing, PP 8.16–8.17
Del key, PP 1.32, EOB 1.1
Deleting
   color schemes, PP 6.10–6.11
   objects, PP 3.5–3.6
   slides, PP 1.14, 1.32
   sound objects, PP 5.24
Demoting (bullets), PP 1.24
Department meeting presentation (project), PP 3.51
Deselecting (objects), PP 3.3–3.5
Design considerations
   for action buttons, PP 7.13–7.14
   for hierarchical presentations, PP 7.4–7.5
   for hyperlink presentations, PP 7.7–7.8
Design Gallery Live, PP 5.29–5.30
Design Masters, PP 3.33–3.40
   customizing bullets in, PP 3.35–3.37
   formatting master text in, PP 3.33–3.34
   hiding master content in, PP 3.38–3.39
   repositioning indent markers in, PP 3.36
Design sales (project), PP 3.54
Design templates, PP 1.19, 1.29–1.34, EOB 1.1
   adding text in, PP 1.30–1.31
   cat web site (project), PP 3.53
   choosing, PP 1.29–1.30
   color schemes of, PP 6.3–6.4
   design sales (project), PP 3.54
   e-commerce florist (project), PP 1.46
   e-commerce importers (project), PP 2.36
   editing text in, PP 1.31–1.32
   environmental alliance (project), PP 3.55
   meeting presentation (project), PP 1.44, 3.51
   Montgomery-Wellish Foods, Inc. (project), PP 1.47, 3.56, 4.52
   reclamation services (project), PP 4.51
   travel (project), PP 2.35
Diagrams, PP 4.38–4.40
Digital cameras, PP 5.30
Digital signatures, PP 8.10–8.11, EOB 1.1
Digital video cameras, PP 5.30
Dimming effects, PP 5.10–5.11, EOB 1.1
Discussions, Web, PP 8.35, EOB 1.4
.doc files
   exporting from PowerPoint, PP 2.28
   importing into PowerPoint, PP 2.26–2.28
   opening in PowerPoint, PP 2.23–2.25
Donated vehicles presentation (project), PP 5.37
Dotted-line selection box, PP 3.3, EOB 1.1
Drawing, PP 3.17, EOB 1.1
   objects, PP 6.19–6.20, 6.30
   tables, PP 4.25–4.26
Drawing toolbar, PP 1.7, 6.19, EOB 1.1
   atmospheric detection device presentation project, PP 7.37
   rotate/flip from, PP 6.22, 6.31
Drawn pictures, PP 4.3, EOB 1.1
Duplicating of objects, PP 6.28–6.31

e

E-commerce florist (project), PP 1.46
E-commerce importers (project), PP 2.36
E-mail, PP 8.19–8.28
   and linked/embedded files, PP 8.19
   Microsoft Outlook for, PP 8.21–8.26
   routing, PP 8.26–8.28
Edit Hyperlink dialog box, PP 7.9–7.10
Editing
   in AutoContent Wizard, PP 1.27–1.28
   of objects, PP 6.28–6.29
   of slide text, PP 1.14
Embedded
   files, e-mail and, PP 8.19
   narration, PP 5.27
Embedded objects, PP 4.14, 4.26, EOB 1.2
Emphasis animations, PP 5.9
Entrance animations, PP 5.7–5.8
Entrance effects (projects), PP 5.37, 5.38, 5.41
Environmental alliance (project), PP 3.55
European Union currency (project), PP 5.39
Excel 2002, OFF 1.2, EOB 2.1
Excel files
   linking to, PP 7.15–7.16
   tables from, PP 4.26–4.27
Exit animations, PP 5.10
Exiting PowerPoint, PP 1.37
Expand All button, PP 2.17, EOB 1.2
Expanding outlines, PP 2.21
Export/exporting, PP 2.28–2.29, 3.51, EOB 1.2

f

F1 (function key), OFF 1.8, EOB 2.1
Favorites list, PP 7.26
File art, PP 4.12–4.15
File converters, PP 2.23, EOB 1.2
File management, PP 1.17–1.18
File properties, customizing, PP 8.16–8.17
File size, PP 5.28
File transfer protocol (FTP), PP 7.19, EOB 1.2
Fill effects, PP 6.32–6.33
Filters, graphic, PP 4.13
Find command, PP 3.24–3.25, 3.51
Flipping of objects, PP 6.22, 6.31
Floating toolbars, PP 1.7
Florist presentation (project), PP 5.40
Fonts, PP 3.11–3.13, EOB 1.2
   colors of, PP 6.11–6.12
   sizes of, PP 1.21–1.23
Food safety online form (project), PP 7.34
Footers, PP 2.4–2.11, EOB 1.2
   design sales (project), PP 3.54
   displaying, PP 2.8–2.9
   hiding, PP 2.8–2.9, 3.38–3.39
   Montgomery-Wellish Foods, Inc. (project), PP 3.56
   in Normal view, PP 2.6
   on Notes and Handouts, PP 2.5, 2.10–2.11
   in Print Preview, PP 2.7–2.8
   removing, PP 2.9
   in Slide Sorter view, PP 2.7
   and Title slide layout, PP 2.8–2.9
Format Painter, PP 3.11, 3.12, 6.9–6.10, 6.33, EOB 1.2
Formatting
   adjusting position of objects, PP 3.7–3.11
   AutoShape, PP 6.21–6.22
   of clip art, PP 4.8–4.10
   curbside recycling (project), PP 1.43
   of Design Master text, PP 3.33–3.34
   meeting presentation (project), PP 1.44
   Montgomery-Wellish Foods, Inc. (project), PP 1.47, 2.38
   neighborhood association (project), PP 2.34
   of numbers/bullets, PP 3.14–3.16
   of objects, PP 3.7–3.20
   of organization charts, PP 4.37–4.38
   in Outline view, PP 2.22
   of placeholders, PP 3.19–3.20
   setting character formats, PP 3.11–3.14
   of slides, PP 1.21
   status meeting presentation (project), PP 2.33
   of text objects, PP 3.18–3.19
   transfer of (object), PP 6.33
   of WordArt, PP 4.17, 4.18
Formatting toolbar, OFF 1.4–1.5, PP 1.7, EOB 1.2, 2.1
Frames, PP 7.22, EOB 1.2
FrontPage 2002, OFF 1.2, EOB 2.1
FTP, *see* File transfer protocol

g

Games proposal (project), PP 2.37
GIF files, animated, PP 5.14–5.16
Gold exploration presentation (project), PP 5.41
Gradient backgrounds, PP 6.12–6.14
Gradient fill (project), PP 7.33
Grandparent interviews (project), PP 7.35
Graph, Microsoft, PP 4.27–4.34
Graphic elements, PP 1.8, 4.22–4.40
   balloon rides (project), PP 4.50
   as bullet characters, PP 3.16
   charts/graphs as, PP 4.27–4.40
   cooking school (project), PP 4.49
   from files, PP 4.12–4.15
   hiding, PP 3.38–3.39
   picture types, PP 4.3
   reclamation services (project), PP 4.51
   tables as, PP 4.22–4.27
Graphic filters, PP 4.13
Graphic formats, PP 4.13, 4.21
Graphic objects, PP 5.11–5.12, 5.40
Graphs, *see* Charts and graphs
Grayscale, PP 2.13, EOB 1.2
Gridlines, PP 4.33
Grids, PP 6.25–6.26, EOB 1.2
Grouping, PP 5.13, 6.37–6.39, EOB 1.2
Guides, PP 6.25–6.26, EOB 1.2

h

Handouts, *see* Notes and handouts
Hanging indent, PP 3.36, EOB 1.2
Headers, PP 2.4–2.11, EOB 1.2
   displaying, PP 2.8–2.9
   hiding, PP 2.8–2.9, 3.38–3.39
   Montgomery-Wellish Foods, Inc. (project), PP 2.38

in Normal view, PP 2.6
on Notes and Handouts, PP 2.5, 2.10–2.11
in Print Preview, PP 2.7–2.8
removing, PP 2.9
in Slide Sorter view, PP 2.7
and Title slide layout, PP 2.8–2.9
Health products (project), PP 8.49
Health services (project), PP 4.48
Help, OFF 1.8–1.10, PP 1.36–1.37, 7.26–7.27
Hiding slides, PP 5.16–5.17
Hierarchical presentations, PP 7.4–7.5
History education (project), PP 6.47
Home object, PP 7.14
Home page, PP 7.19–7.22, EOB 1.2
Host, meeting, PP 8.33–8.34
.htm files, PP 7.21–7.22
HTML, *see Hyper text markup language*
HTML tags, PP 7.17, EOB 1.2
Hyper text markup language (HTML), PP 7.17, EOB 1.2
Hyperlink base, PP 7.14, EOB 1.2
Hyperlinks, PP 7.5–7.17, EOB 1.2
action buttons for, PP 7.11–7.14
broken, PP 7.10, EOB 1.1
color schemes for, PP 7.7, 7.10
creating, PP 7.5–7.8
design considerations for, PP 7.7–7.8
Edit Hyperlink dialog box, PP 7.9–7.10
to external sources, PP 7.14–7.17
Insert Hyperlink dialog box, PP 7.8–7.10
inserting, PP 7.6
second-level, PP 7.7–7.8
and underlining, PP 7.7–7.8

i

Images, PP 4.14, 4.15, 4.26
Importers (project), PP 2.36
Importing, PP 2.23–2.28, 2.34, EOB 1.2
Indent markers, PP 3.36–3.37, EOB 1.2
Indenting
bullets, PP 1.14, 1.23–1.24, 1.32, 3.9–3.10
hanging indents, PP 3.36, EOB 1.2
increasing/decreasing, PP 3.9
Insert Hyperlink dialog box, PP 7.8–7.10
Inserting
audio components, PP 5.19–5.27
clip art, PP 4.4–4.8
graphics (projects), PP 5.40
hyperlinks, PP 7.6
media clips, PP 5.15
notes, PP 1.34–1.35
objects, PP 3.5–3.6
slides, PP 1.15, 1.32–1.34
sound clips, PP 5.20
tables, PP 4.22–4.25
WordArt, PP 4.16
Integrated application suite, OFF 1.2, EOB 2.1
Interactive presentations, PP 7.3–7.17
adding navigation for, PP 7.3–7.10
linking, PP 7.11–7.17
Interactive quiz (project), PP 7.38
Internet, PP 5.29, 5.30, 7.17, 7.25–7.26, EOB 1.2
Internet search engine, PP 5.30, EOB 1.2
Internet service providers (ISPs), PP 7.18, EOB 1.2
Intranets, PP 7.17, EOB 1.2
Intrinsic color schemes, PP 6.3–6.7, EOB 1.2

Intrinsic sounds, PP 5.21–5.22, EOB 1.2
ISPs, *see Internet service providers*
Italic, PP 3.11, EOB 1.2

k

Keywords, PP 4.11–4.12, EOB 1.2
Kiosks, PP 5.17–5.19, EOB 1.2

l

Labels, data, PP 4.33
Layering, PP 6.35–6.36
Legends, PP 4.33
License agreement, PP 5.30, EOB 1.2
Line color, PP 6.33–6.34
Lines, PP 6.29–6.30
Linked files, e-mail and, PP 8.19
Linked objects, PP 4.14, 4.15, 4.26, EOB 1.2
Linking, PP 7.11–7.17
to another PowerPoint file, PP 7.14–7.15
to Excel files, PP 7.15–7.16
to external resources, PP 7.14–7.17
narration, PP 5.27
sound files, PP 5.21
using action buttons, PP 7.11–7.14
Links, OFF 1.8, EOB 2.1
absolute, PP 7.14, EOB 1.1
relative, PP 7.14, EOB 1.3
Live Web broadcasts, PP 8.32–8.33
Loading add-ins, PP 8.17–8.18
Local server, PP 7.18, EOB 1.2
Looping
media clips, PP 5.15–5.16
sounds, PP 5.21
.lst files, PP 8.7

m

Macro security levels, PP 8.10–8.11, EOB 1.2
Macro virus, PP 8.10–8.11, EOB 1.2
Macros, PP 8.9–8.11, 8.13–8.16, 8.45, EOB 1.2
Mall presentation (project), PP 5.38
MAPI (Messaging Application Programming Interface), PP 8.22
Masters, *see Slide masters*
Matting, PP 6.15–6.17, EOB 1.3
Media
compression of, PP 5.28
sources for, PP 5.14, 5.27, 5.29–5.31
Media clips, PP 5.14–5.16, EOB 1.3
Media elements, PP 1.8
Media Gallery, PP 4.11, EOB 1.3
clip art in, PP 4.4–4.5
retrieving art from, PP 4.19–4.20
saving art objects in, PP 4.19
Media Organizer, PP 5.27
Media placeholders, PP 4.5–4.7
Meeting host, PP 8.33–8.34
Meeting Minder, PP 3.42–3.43, 3.51, EOB 1.3
Meeting presentation (project), PP 1.44, 2.33, 3.51
Meetings
collaborative, PP 8.33, EOB 1.1
online, PP 8.33–8.34
Menu bar, OFF 1.4, EOB 2.1
Menus
color, PP 6.11–6.12

customizing, PP 8.13
personalizing, PP 8.12–8.13
standard, PP 8.11–8.13
Messaging Application Programming Interface (MAPI), PP 8.22
Microsoft Office XP, OFF 1.3. *See also specific programs, e.g.: Access 2002*
Microsoft Online Support, PP 7.26–7.27
Minutes, meeting, PP 3.42–3.43
Montgomery-Wellish Foods, Inc. (projects)
critical time lines and interactive quiz, PP 7.38
general financial and business training, PP 3.56
orienting new employees, PP 2.38
presentation skills, PP 4.52
presentation skills adaptations, PP 5.42
spice tracking presentation, PP 6.50
Web broadcast presentation skills, PP 8.50
welcoming new employees, PP 1.48
Movies, PP 5.14
controlling, PP 5.16
previews of (project), PP 6.46
Multiple objects, selecting, PP 6.30
Multiple shapes, changing, PP 6.32
Multiple slides
color schemes of, PP 6.9
and slide transitions, PP 5.4
Multiple sounds, PP 5.25, 5.27

n

Narration, PP 5.24–5.27
Navigation, PP 1.9–1.13, 7.3–7.10
of animation slides, PP 7.3
creating hyperlinks for, PP 7.5–7.10
and design of hierarchical presentations, PP 7.4–7.5
Navigation bar, PP 7.18, EOB 1.3
Neighborhood association (project), PP 2.34
NetMeeting, PP 8.33
New File Task Pane, PP 8.35
New presentations, PP 1.18–1.34
with AutoContent Wizard, PP 1.25–1.29
blank presentation, PP 1.19–1.25
considerations for, PP 1.19
with Design Template, PP 1.29–1.34
Normal view, PP 1.7–1.11, EOB 1.3
Notes and Handouts, PP 2.10–2.11
color schemes for, PP 6.7
curbside recycling (project), PP 1.43
headers/footers in, PP 2.5, 2.10–2.11
meeting presentation (project), PP 3.51
Montgomery-Wellish Foods, Inc. (project), PP 2.38
printing, PP 2.15–2.16
viewing masters, PP 3.30–3.31
in Web presentation, PP 7.22
Notes pane, PP 1.8, 1.34–1.35, EOB 1.3
Numbered lists, PP 3.14

o

Objects, EOB 1.3
adding shadows to, PP 6.33–6.34
adding text to, PP 6.20–6.21
adjusting, PP 6.23–6.24
animation of, PP 5.3–5.16
attributes of, PP 6.32
AutoShape, PP 6.19–6.22

changing shape of, PP 6.31–6.32
chart, PP 5.13–5.14
customizing, PP 6.20–6.24
drawing, PP 6.19–6.20
duplicating, PP 6.28–6.31
editing, PP 6.28–6.29
fill effects of, PP 6.32–6.33
formatting, PP 3.7–3.20
graphic, PP 5.11–5.12, 5.40
grouping, PP 6.37–6.39
inserting/deleting, PP 3.5–3.6
outside the slide area, PP 6.34–6.35
positioning, PP 6.24–6.26
rotating, PP 6.22–6.23
selecting/deselecting, PP 3.3–3.5
setting line color of, PP 6.33–6.34
stacking order of, PP 6.35–6.37
text added to, PP 6.20–6.21
text objects, PP 3.17–3.19
3-D options for, PP 6.26–6.28, 6.33–6.34
transferring format of, PP 6.33
Office Assistant, **OFF 1.8–1.10, PP 1.37, 7.26, EOB 2.1**
Office XP, **OFF 1.2–1.11, EOB 2.1**
  activating menu options in, OFF 1.5
  clipboard, OFF 1.5, 1.6
  Help with, OFF 1.8–1.10
  menu bar in, OFF 1.4
  opening multiple applications in, OFF 1.3–1.4
  Paste Options button, OFF 1.5, 1.6
  smart tag buttons, OFF 1.5
  switching between applications, OFF 1.4
  task panes in, OFF 1.5, 1.6
  title bar in, OFF 1.4
  toolbars in, OFF 1.4–1.5
Online collaboration, PP 8.19–8.28
  project, PP 8.47
  review via e-mail, PP 8.19–8.21
  reviewing with Microsoft Outlook, PP 8.22–8.26
  routing presentations, PP 8.26–8.28
Online form (project), PP 7.34
Online meetings, PP 8.33–8.34
Opening
  blank presentation, PP 1.19–1.20
  existing presentation, PP 1.5–1.6
  MSWord files in PowerPoint, PP 2.23–2.25
  new presentation, PP 1.18–1.34
  PowerPoint presentations, PP 1.5–1.6
Organization charts, **PP 4.35–4.38, EOB 1.3**
Orientation
  of objects, PP 6.21
  of slides, PP 2.14
Outline pane, **PP 1.7–1.8, 1.13–1.14, EOB 1.3**
  editing in, PP 1.31, 1.32
  Outline view *vs.*, PP 2.18–2.23
Outline tab, **PP 1.7–1.8**
Outline view, **PP 2.18–2.23, EOB 1.3**
Outlines
  of ideas, PP 2.18–2.29
  printing, PP 2.17
Outlining toolbar, **PP 2.25–2.26, EOB 1.3**
Outlook
  address book in, PP 8.23
  combining reviews with, PP 8.25–8.26
  and online collaboration, PP 8.21–8.26
  Return to Original Sender option, PP 8.24
  routing presentations with, PP 8.26–8.28
Outlook 2002, **OFF 1.2, EOB 2.1**

p

Pack and Go Wizard, **PP 8.4–8.7, 8.45, EOB 1.3**
Packaging presentation, **PP 8.4–8.7**
Page orientation, **PP 2.12, 2.14, EOB 1.3**
Page Setup, **PP 2.11–2.12, EOB 1.3**
Palette, **PP 6.3, EOB 1.3**
Panes, **PP 1.7–1.8**
Paste, **PP 2.23, EOB 1.3**
Paste Options button, **OFF 1.5, 1.6, EOB 2.1**
Pen tool, **PP 3.44–3.45, EOB 1.3**
Performance, improving, PP 5.28
Personalizing of menus/toolbars, PP 8.12–8.13
Photography interactive presentation (project), PP 7.36
Pictures
  as backgrounds, PP 6.15–6.16
  as bullets, PP 6.17–6.18
  drawn, PP 4.3, EOB 1.1. *See also* Graphic elements
Placeholders, PP 1.21–1.23
  formatting, PP 3.19–3.20
  media, PP 4.5–4.7
  moving, PP 3.7–3.8
  text, PP 3.4
Planning, backup, PP 8.3–8.4
Playlists, **PP 8.4, 8.7–8.9, EOB 1.3**
Point size, **PP 1.21–1.23, 3.11, EOB 1.3**
Positioning of objects, PP 6.24–6.26
PowerPoint 2002, **OFF 1.2, EOB 2.1.** *See also specific topics*
  creating new presentations in, PP 1.18–1.34
  exiting, PP 1.37
  integrating with MSWord, PP 2.23–2.29
  opening existing presentation in, PP 1.5–1.6
  starting, PP 1.3–1.4
PowerPoint viewer, **PP 8.4, EOB 1.3**
Presentation skills (project), PP 4.52
Previewing
  animations of charts and diagrams, PP 5.13–5.14
  Web pages, PP 7.22–7.23, 7.25–7.26
Print dialog box, **PP 2.12–2.18, EOB 1.3**
Print Preview, **PP 2.3–2.4, EOB 1.3**
  header/footers in, PP 2.7–2.8
  Notes and Handouts in, PP 2.10
Print range, **PP 2.13, EOB 1.3**
Printing, PP 2.3–2.18
  color options for, PP 2.13
  handouts, PP 2.15
  help for, PP 2.18
  notes, PP 2.16
  outlines, PP 2.17
  page setup, PP 2.11–2.12
  print dialog box, PP 2.12–2.18
  print preview, PP 2.3–2.4
  slides, PP 2.14
  text outlines, PP 2.17
Professional edition, **OFF 1.2, EOB 2.1**
Professional Special edition, **OFF 1.2, EOB 2.1**
Promoting (bullets), PP 1.24
Proofing tools, PP 3.20–3.27
Properties, **PP 3.3, 5.4–5.6, 8.16–8.17, EOB 1.3**
Publisher 2002, **OFF 1.2, EOB 2.1**
Pyramid diagrams, **PP 4.39, EOB 1.3**

r

Radial diagrams, **PP 4.38–4.40, EOB 1.3**
Raster images, **PP 4.3, EOB 1.3**
Reapply Layout (Slide Master), PP 3.33
Reclamation services (project), PP 4.51
Recorded Web broadcasts, PP 8.30–8.32
Redo, **PP 1.16–1.17, EOB 1.3**
Regroup, **PP 6.39, EOB 1.3**
Relative links, **PP 7.14, EOB 1.3**
Reorder buttons, PP 5.20
Reorganizing slides, PP 1.32
Replace **command, PP 3.24–3.25**
Resizing
  images, PP 4.8, 4.9
  linked objects, PP 4.27
  shapes, PP 6.21–6.22
  of slides, PP 1.21–1.23
Retrieving art (MSMedia Gallery), PP 4.19–4.20
Rich text format, **PP 2.28, EOB 1.3**
Rocky, **OFF 1.8, EOB 2.1**
Rotating
  images, PP 4.8, 4.9
  objects, PP 6.22–6.23
  text, PP 6.21–6.22
  Text Box, PP 3.19
Rotation handles, **PP 4.8, 6.22, 6.38, EOB 1.3**
Routing, PP 8.26–8.28
Royalty, **PP 5.30, EOB 1.3**

s

Saving
  art objects, PP 4.18–4.21
  presentations, PP 1.17
  Web pages, PP 7.21–7.25
Scheduled Web broadcasts, PP 8.32, 8.33
Screen Tips, **PP 1.6, EOB 1.3**
Search engine, **PP 5.30, EOB 1.2**
Security, customizing toolbars and, PP 8.14
Security levels, **macro, PP 8.10–8.11, EOB 1.2**
Selecting
  chart objects, PP 4.34
  multiple objects, PP 6.30
  objects, PP 3.3–3.5
Selection box, PP 6.37
Self-running slide shows, PP 5.17–5.19, 5.24–5.27
Send Backward, PP 6.36
Send to Back, PP 6.36
Send To option, PP 2.28
Series
  animation of, PP 5.13
  gold exploration presentation project, PP 5.41
Server, Web, **PP 7.18, EOB 1.4**
Settings, revising, PP 8.16–8.17
Shadows, **PP 3.11, EOB 1.3**
  adding, to objects, PP 6.33–6.34
  text, PP 6.17
Shapes, **PP 3.17–3.19, 6.31–6.32**
Shapes tools, **PP 3.17, EOB 1.3**
SharePoint Team Services, PP 8.35
Sharing presentations, PP 8.19–8.36
  collaborating on the Web, PP 8.35–8.36
  online collaboration, PP 8.19–8.28
  online meetings, PP 8.33–8.34
  Web broadcasting, PP 8.28–8.33

EOB 3.4

Shift key, PP 6.29–6.30
Show Formatting feature, PP 2.22
Signatures, digital, PP 8.10–8.11, EOB 1.1
Size, file, PP 5.28
Sizing, see Resizing
Sizing handles, PP 1.21–1.22, 3.4, 6.22, EOB 1.3
  on charts, PP 4.35, 4.40
  on clip art, PP 4.8
Slanted-line selection box, PP 3.3, EOB 1.3
Slide layout, PP 1.20–1.21, EOB 1.4
Slide Masters, PP 3.29, EOB 1.4
  saving, as template, PP 3.36–3.37
  viewing, PP 3.29–3.31
Slide pane, PP 1.8, 1.14–1.16, 1.31–1.32, EOB 1.4
Slide placeholders, PP 1.21–1.23, EOB 1.4
Slide show view, PP 1.9, 1.11–1.12, EOB 1.4
  for animations of charts and diagrams, PP 5.13–5.14
  annotating in, PP 3.44–3.45
  and hidden slides, PP 5.16
  navigating in, PP 3.43–3.44
Slide sorter view, PP 1.9, 1.32, EOB 1.4
Slide timings, PP 5.5–5.6, 5.12, EOB 1.4
  and animations, PP 5.5–5.6, 5.12
  and narrations, PP 5.26–5.27
  and playlists, PP 8.8–8.9
  in self-running presentations, PP 5.18–5.19
Slide-title master pairs, PP 3.29–3.31, EOB 1.4
Slide transitions, PP 1.12, 1.13, 3.40, 5.3–5.6, EOB 1.4. *See also* Entrance effects
Slides. *See also specific topics*
  annotating, PP 3.44–3.45
  footers, *see* Footers
  header, *see* Headers
  hiding, PP 5.16–5.17
  moving, PP 1.14, 1.32
  numbering, PP 2.7
  printing, PP 2.14
  summary slide, PP 3.27–3.28
Slides tab, PP 1.7–1.8, EOB 1.4
Smart tag buttons, OFF 1.5, EOB 2.1
Snap To Grid, PP 6.26
Sound, *see* Audio components
Sound card, PP 5.19
Sound files, PP 5.22–5.23
Speakers, PP 5.19
Spelling Checker, PP 1.23, 3.20–3.23, EOB 1.4
Spice tracking presentation (project), PP 6.50
Stacking
  clip art images, PP 4.11
  objects, PP 6.29, 6.35–6.37
Standard edition, OFF 1.2, EOB 2.1
Standard toolbar, OFF 1.4–1.5, PP 1.7, EOB 1.4, 2.1
Standardizing presentations, PP 3.27–3.45
Starting PowerPoint, PP 1.3–1.4
Status meeting presentation (project), PP 2.33
Stopping sound objects, PP 5.24
Storytellers presentation (project), PP 6.45
Style checker, PP 3.20–3.23, EOB 1.4

Style rules, PP 3.21, EOB 1.4
Summary slides, PP 3.27–3.28

t

Tables, PP 4.22–4.27
  cooking school (project), PP 4.49
  drawing, PP 4.25–4.26
  embedded, PP 4.26
  inserting, PP 4.22–4.25
  linked, PP 4.26–4.27
  slide layouts for, PP 4.24–4.25
  from Word or Excel files, PP 4.26–4.27
Tags, HTML, PP 7.17, EOB 1.2
Target diagrams, PP 4.39, EOB 1.4
Task Panels, PP 1.8–1.9
Task panes, OFF 1.5, 1.6, PP 1.4–1.5, 1.8–1.9, EOB 1.4, 2.2
Teachers' web site (project), PP 3.52
Team Web sites, PP 8.35–8.36
Templates, PP 3.29–3.33, 3.36–3.37. *See also* Design templates
Text
  adding, to objects, PP 6.20–6.21
  adding text objects, PP 3.17–3.18
  aligning of, PP 3.8–3.9
  animation of, PP 5.6–5.11
  and AutoShape objects, PP 6.20–6.21
  changing case of, PP 3.12
  in charts, PP 4.35
  considerations for, PP 1.21–1.25
  formatting in Outline view, PP 2.22
  formatting text objects, PP 3.18–3.19
  indention of, PP 3.9–3.10
  matting behind, PP 6.16–6.17
  in organization charts, PP 4.37
  outlines, PP 2.17
  in radial diagrams, PP 4.40
  rotating, PP 6.21–6.22
  size of, PP 1.21–1.23
  on slide placeholders, PP 1.22–1.25
Text animation, PP 3.40–3.41, EOB 1.4
Text AutoFit, PP 3.17
Text boxes, PP 3.17–3.19, 4.50, EOB 1.4
Text placeholders, PP 3.4
Texture backgrounds, PP 6.14–6.15
3-D effects, PP 6.26–6.28, 6.33–6.34
Thumbnail-sized images (thumbnails), PP 1.7, 1.8
Time, in headers/footers, PP 2.7
Timeline, PP 5.12
Timing, *see* Slide timings
Title bar, OFF 1.4, EOB 2.2
Title Master, PP 3.29, EOB 1.4
Toggle buttons, PP 3.12, EOB 1.4
Toolbars, OFF 1.4, PP 1.6–1.7, EOB 1.4, 2.2
  anchored, PP 1.7
  customizing, PP 8.13–8.16, 8.45
  drawing, PP 1.7, 3.17, EOB 1.1
  floating, PP 1.7
  formatting, PP 1.7, EOB 1.2
  outlining, PP 2.25–2.26, EOB 1.3
  personalizing, PP 8.12–8.13
  and security, PP 8.14
  standard, PP 1.7, 8.11–8.13, EOB 1.4
  view, PP 1.7, EOB 1.4
Trade consultants tracking (project), PP 1.47
Transitions, *see* Slide transitions
Transparencies, PP 2.14, EOB 1.4
Travel (project), PP 2.35

Trekking presentation (project), PP 6.48
Triathlon (projects), PP 4.47, 8.45, 8.46

u

Underline/underlining, PP 7.7–7.8, EOB 1.4
Undo, PP 1.16–1.17, 6.11, EOB 1.4
Ungroup, PP 6.39, EOB 1.4
Uniform resource locator (URL), PP 7.5, 7.14, EOB 1.4
Unloading add-ins, PP 8.18–8.19
Unpackaging presentation, PP 8.5–8.7, 8.45
Updating
  data in charts and graphs, PP 4.30–4.31
  presentations, PP 1.13–1.17
URL, *see* Uniform resource locator

v

Vector graphics, PP 4.3, EOB 1.4
Vehicles presentation (project), PP 5.37
Venn diagrams, PP 4.39, EOB 1.4
Video cameras, PP 5.30
Video files, PP 5.14
View toolbar, PP 1.7, EOB 1.4
Viewer, PowerPoint, PP 8.4, EOB 1.3
Viewing
  Handouts and Notes masters, PP 3.30–3.31
  objects outside slide area, PP 6.34
  PowerPoint viewer, PP 8.4
  slide masters, PP 3.29–3.31
  Web broadcasts, PP 8.28–8.29
Views, PP 1.7–1.12, EOB 1.4
  default, PP 2.19–2.21
  normal, PP 1.7–1.11
  outline, PP 2.18–2.23, 2.21, 2.22
  slide show, PP 1.9, 1.11–1.12, 3.43–3.45
  slide sorter, PP 1.9, 1.32, EOB 1.4
Virus, macro, PP 8.10–8.11, EOB 1.2
Visited hyperlinks, PP 7.7
Volunteer training (project), PP 1.45

w

Web broadcasts, PP 8.28–8.33
  balloon rides project, PP 8.48
  culinary arts schools project, PP 8.47
  health products projects, PP 8.49
  live, PP 8.32–8.33
  Montgomery-Wellish Foods, Inc. project, PP 8.50
  preparation for, PP 8.29
  recorded, setup for, PP 8.30–8.32
  scheduled, PP 8.32, 8.33
  viewing, PP 8.28–8.29
Web browser, PP 7.18, EOB 1.4
Web discussions, PP 8.35, EOB 1.4
Web pages, PP 7.17, EOB 1.4
Web publishing, PP 7.17–7.27
  access from PowerPoint for, PP 7.25–7.26
  background information on, PP 7.17–7.18
  building Home page for, PP 7.19–7.22
  creating Web site for, PP 7.18–7.21
  help with, PP 7.26–7.27
  saving existing presentations as Web pages, PP 7.22–7.25
  saving Home page as Web page, PP 7.21–7.22
  selecting Web browser for, PP 7.18

Web server, **PP 7.18, EOB 1.4**
Web site, **PP 7.18–7.22, 7.22, EOB 1.4**
Web toolbar, PP 7.25–7.26
Welcoming new employees (project), PP 1.48
What's This tool, PP 1.37
Whiteboard, **PP 8.33, 8.34, EOB 1.4**
Wildlife organization presentation (project), PP 7.33
Windows Media Encoder, PP 8.31
Windows Media Player, PP 5.16
Windows Media Services, PP 8.31
Word 2002, **OFF 1.2, 1.3, EOB 2.2**

Word files
  customizing content for PowerPoint, PP 2.25–2.26
  exporting from PowerPoint, PP 2.28–2.29
  integrating PowerPoint with, PP 2.23–2.29
  opening in PowerPoint, PP 2.23–2.25
  tables from, PP 4.26–4.27
WordArt, PP 4.15–4.18
  balloon rides (project), PP 4.50
  reclamation services (project), PP 4.51
Workgroup software, **PP 8.19, EOB 1.4**
World Wide Web (WWW), **PP 7.17, EOB 1.5.** *See also* **Web** entries

x

X-axis, **PP 4.29, EOB 1.5**

y

Y-axis, **PP 4.29, EOB 1.5**

z

Z-order, **PP 6.35–6.37, EOB 1.5**
Zooming, PP 2.14, 6.37

NOTES

www.mhhe.com/i-series

NOTES

NOTES

www.mhhe.com/i-series

NOTES